# HUMAN JUDGMENT *and* SOCIAL POLICY

# HUMAN JUDGMENT *and* SOCIAL POLICY

*Irreducible Uncertainty,*
*Inevitable Error,*
*Unavoidable Injustice*

KENNETH R. HAMMOND

New York    Oxford
Oxford University Press
1996

HM
73
.H314
1996

*For My Family*

Oxford University Press

Oxford    New York
Athens    Auckland    Bangkok    Bogota    Bombay
Buenos Aires    Calcutta    Cape Town    Dar es Salaam
Delhi    Florence    Hong Kong    Istanbul    Karachi
Kuala Lumpur    Madras    Madrid    Malbourne
Mexico City    Nairobi    Paris    Singapore
Taipei    Tokyo    Toronto

and associated companies in
Berlin    Ibadan

Library of Congress Cataloging-in-Publication Data
Hammond, Kenneth R.
Human judgment and social policy : irreducible uncertainty,
inevitable error, unavoidable injustice / Kenneth R. Hammond.
p.   cm.
Includes bibliographical references and index.
ISBN 0-19-509734-3
1. Social policy—Decision making.   2. Judgment.   3. Uncertainty.
I. Title.
HM73.H314   1996
302.3—dc20       95-35319

9 8 7 6 5 4 3 2 1

Printed in the United States of America
on acid-free paper

# Acknowledgments

First people first. And the first is Mary Luhring. Without her this book wouldn't have been written. Not only did she suffer through years of long hard drafts—indecipherable by any reasonable standard—which she worked up into a readable manuscript, but she was a pillar of support, of encouragement, of wisdom, ever providing—gently but firmly—the thoughtful criticism that every author craves. To her, my fullest gratitude.

Reid Hastie, director of the Center for Research on Judgment and Policy, gracefully gave me the staff support, office space, and computer access during my retirement that few retired academics ever receive. Abigail Seremet, an excellent librarian, tirelessly sought the documents I needed, often with only the slightest cues from me, as did Doreen Peterson during her years at the Center.

Thomas R. Stewart was a constant source of support, advice, and wisdom, as he has been ever since we began our collaboration in 1964. I owe a great deal to him, and I am sorry that I have never been able to balance the scale. Ray Cooksey commented on the manuscript and, in addition, has written a book titled *Judgment Analysis: Theory, Methods, and Applications* that provides the technical foundation for much if not all of what appears here. His book and this one, although not specifically geared to each other page by page, are intended to supplement each other. Robert Wheeler was particularly helpful with matters relating to clinical psychology. Joan Bossert, executive editor at Oxford University Press, earned my respect and gratitude.

The term "duality of error" is frequently used throughout the book, and it may be that I have unwittingly appropriated it from its originator without credit. It was offered to me (along with a lot of other good technical advice not directly related to this book) by Carol Nickerson, who is probably the originator of what is surely a felicitous term. Neither of us is sure that she invented it, but neither of us can recall seeing it elsewhere. I thank her for it—and hope I am not offending someone else.

Many people read and were kind enough to comment on parts of the manuscript during its preparation. These include Hal Arkes, Mats Björkman, Gary Bradshaw, Berndt Brehmer, David Buss, Edwin L. Crow, D. Wilson Crumpacker, Michael DeKay, Michael Doherty, Bo Earle, Timothy Earle, Paul Ehrmann, Seymour Epstein, Gerd Gigerenzer, Daniel Gigone, C. R. B. Joyce, Peter Juslin, Joshua Klayman, Lubomir Kostron, Frank Kreith, Anthony LaDuca, Franklin Lauffer, Lola Lopes, Lee Lusted, Andrew McClurg, John Payne, Leon Rappoport, Karen Siegel-Jacobs, David

Summers, Philip Tetlock, Kim Vicente, Torbjörn von Schantz, Judge Jack Weinstein, Lawrence G. Weiss, and Jack Werner. Critiques by the physicians Neil Dawson, Roy Poses, Thomas Tape, and Robert Wigton were especially helpful, as were the comments of Captain Kent Taylor, U.S. Naval Reserve.

I also thank Bernhard Wolf for his suggestions; Robert McKnown for his help regarding sources in economics; Thomas Grey for his comment on my treatment of Oliver Wendell Holmes; Ray Cooksey for pointing out the similarity between Richard Feynman's diagrams and those of Charles Darwin; Sandy Zabell for his suggestions about the duality of error in Judaic history and Rabbi Deborah Bronstein for her patient explanation of source material in that history; Tim Brennan and Gary McClelland for their thoughtful suggestions about sources I would otherwise have missed. All have my gratitude and are hereby absolved from the errors that are inevitable in an undertaking of this kind.

I have many teachers to thank. First and foremost is Egon Brunswik, professor of psychology at the University of California at Berkeley from 1937 until his death in 1955. I have described my relationship with him elsewhere;[1] the reader will find a biography in the book I edited in his honor[2] and in the *Encyclopedia of Social Sciences*.[3] Other persons who took the time and trouble to assist an often bewildered student and who became my unforgettable friends and inspirations were the psychologists David Krech and Robert C. Tryon, the anthropologist Alfred Kroeber—great men all.

Finally, I thank my wife, Virginia, for many years of patience with a not always cheerful but persistently egocentric husband; my daughter Pam afforded love and affection just when it was needed. Kathy and Bruce Armbruster, publishers of University Science Books, also provided advice and encouragement, as they should. After all, she is my daughter, and he is my son-in-law.

*Boulder, Colorado*                                                                          K. R. H.

Many thanks to the following for permission to use copyrighted works:

Excerpts from *The Index of Leading Cultural Indicators* (vol. 1) by William J. Bennett, published jointly by Empower America, the Heritage Foundation, and Free Congress Foundation, 1993. Copyright © by William J. Bennett. Reprinted with permission.

Excerpts from "Disraeli & Marx & the Search for Identity," from *Against the Current* by Isaiah Berlin. Copyright © 1955, 1959, 1968, 1969, 1970, 1971, 1972, 1973, 1974, 1979 by Isaiah Berlin. Used by permission of Viking Penguin, a division of Penguin Books USA Inc.

Excerpts from "The Hedgehog and the Fog," from *Russian Thinkers* by Isaiah Berlin. Copyright 1948, 1951, 1953, © 1955, 1956, 1960, 1961, 1972, 1978. Used by permission of Viking Penguin, a division of Penguin Books USA Inc.

Excerpts from *Personal Impressions* by Isaiah Berlin. Copyright 1949, 1951, 1955, © 19598, 1964, 1965, 1966, 1971, 1972, 1973, 1975, 1976, 1980 by Isaiah Berlin. Used by permission of Viking Penguin, a division of Penguin Books USA Inc.

Excerpt from "Controlling Variation in Health Care" by Donald M. Berwick, published in *Medical Care*, December 1991. Copyright © J. B. Lippincott Company, Philadelphia, Pa. Reprinted with permission.

Excerpt from "Nationwide Tests Set for Prostate Cancer, but Doubts Surface" by Jane E. Brody, published in the *New York Times*, September 20, 1992. Copyright © 1992 by the New York Times Company. Reprinted by permission.

Excerpts from *Perception and the Relative Design of Psychological Experiments* by Egon Brunswik, published by the University of California Press. Copyright © 1947, 1949, 1956 by The Regents of the University of California. Reprinted with permission.

Excerpt from "New Research on Expert Systems" by Bruce G. Buchanan in *Machine Intelligence 10,* edited by J. E. Hayes, D. Michie, and Y.-H. Pao. Copyright © 1982 by J. E. Hayes, D. Michie, Y.-H. Pao/Ellis Horwood Ltd. All rights reserved. Reprinted with permission.

Excerpts from *The Thinking Ape: Evolutionary Origins of Intelligence* by Richard Byrne. Copyright © Richard Byrne, 1995. Reprinted by permission of Oxford University Press.

Table from "The Poor Quality of Early Evaluations of Magnetic Resonance Imaging" by Lawton S. Cooper, Thomas C. Chalmers, Michael McCally, Jayne Berrier, and Henry S. Sacks, published in the *Journal of the American Medical Association,* June 10, 1988, p. 3278. Copyright © 1988, American Medical Association. Reprinted with permission.

Excerpt from "How 'Tactical Research' Muddied Diaper Debate" by Cynthia Crossen, published in the *Wall Street Journal,* May 17, 1994. Reprinted by permission of the *Wall Street Journal,* © 1994 Dow Jones & Comapny, Inc. All Rights Reserved Worldwide.

"Tree of Nature" by Charles Darwin. Reproduced by permission of the Syndics of Cambridge University Library.

Excerpts from "Will Clinton's Plan Be Fair?" by Ronald Dworkin, published in *The New York Review of Books,* January 13, 1994. Reprinted with permission from *The New York Review of Books.* Copyright © 1994 Nyrev, Inc.

Excerpt from "Individual Rights and Community Responsibilities" by Amitai Etzioni, published in *The Futurist,* November 1993. Reproduced with permission from *The Futurist,* published by the World Future Society, 7910 Woodmont Avenue, Suite 450, Bethesda, Md. 20814.

Excerpt from "The Art of Artificial Intelligence" by Edward A. Feigenbaum, published in *Proceedings of the International Joint Conference on Artificial Intelligence.* Reprinted with permission.

Sketch by Richard Feynman. Courtesy of Carl and Michelle Feynman and the Archives, California Institute of Technology.

Excerpts from *The Limits Of Social Policy* by Nathan Glazer. Copyright © 1988 by the President and Fellows of Harvard College. Reprinted by permission of the publishers.

Excerpt from *Genius: The Life and Science of Richard Feynman* by James Gleick, published by Pantheon Books. Copyright © 1992 by James Gleick. Reprinted with permission.

Excerpts from "A Quasi-Experiment Assessing the Effectiveness of TV Advertising Directed to Children" by Marvin Goldberg, published in the *Journal of Marketing Research,* November 1990. Copyright © 1990 by the American Marketing Association. Reprinted with permission.

Excerpts from *Social Experimentation,* edited by Jerry A. Hausman and David A. Wise, published by the University of Chicago Press. Copyright © by the National Bureau of Economic Research. Reprinted with permission.

Excerpts from "The End of the Modern Era" by Vaclav Havel published in the *New York Times,* March 1, 1992. Copyright © 1992 by the New York Times Company. Reprinted by permission.

Excerpts from *The Psychology of Interpersonal Relations* by Fritz Heider. Copyright © 1958 by John Wiley & Sons, Inc. Reprinted with permission.

Excerpts and table from *The Bell Curve: Intelligence and Class Structure in American Life* by Richard J. Herrnstein and Charles Murray. Copyright © 1994 by Richard J. Herrnstein and Charles Murray. Reprinted with the permission of the Free Press, a division of Simon & Schuster, Inc.

Excerpts from *The Death of Common Sense* by Philip K. Howard. Copyright © 1995 by Philip K. Howard. Reprinted by permission of Random House, Inc.

Excerpts and table from *Crucial Decisions: Leadership in Policymaking and Crisis Management* by Irving L. Janis. Copyright © 1989 by the Free Press. Reprinted with the permission of the Free Press, a division of Simon & Schuster.

Excerpts from *Memoirs: 1925–1950* by George Kennan. Copyright © 1967 by George F. Kennan. By permission of Little, Brown and Company.

Excerpt from "'Portfolio Management' Catches on for Bank Loans" by Steven Lipin, published in the *Wall Street Journal,* January 4, 1995. Reprinted by permission of the *Wall Street Journal,* © 1995 Dow Jones & Company, Inc. All Rights Reserved Worldwide.

Excerpts from "The Rationality of Intelligence" by Lola L. Lopes and Gregg C. Oden, published in *Probability and Rationality,* edited by Ellery Eells and Tomasz Maruszewski. Copyright © by Editions Rodopi B.V., Amsterdam and Atlanta, Ga., 1991. Reprinted with permission.

Figure from "Judgment and Decision Making in Dynamic Tasks: The Case of Forecasting the Microburst" by Cynthia M. Lusk, Thomas R. Stewart, Kenneth R. Hammond, and Rodney J. Potts," published in *Weather and Forecasting,* December 1990. Copyright © 1990 by the American Meteorological Society. Reprinted with permission.

Excerpts from "Feynman Issues His Own Shuttle Report, Attacking NASA's Risk Estimates" by Eliot Marshall, published in *Science,* June 27, 1986. Copyright © 1986 by the AAAS. Reprinted with permission.

Excerpts from "Logical Fallacies and the Supreme Court: A Critical Examination of Justice Rehnquist's Decisions in Criminal Procedure Cases" by Andrew J. McClurg, published in the *University of Colorado Law Review*, Fall 1988. Copyright © 1988 by the University of Colorado Law Review, Inc.

Excerpt from "GOP Takes Aim at FDA, Seeing to Ease Way for Approval of New Drugs, Medical Products" by Laurie McGinley, published in the *Wall Street Journal*, December 12, 1994. Reprinted by permission of the *Wall Street Journal*, © 1994 Dow Jones & Company, Inc. All Rights Reserved Worldwide.

Excerpt from "With Apologies to Havel, Let Reason Rule" [Letter to the Editor] by Herbert L. Meltzer, published in the *New York Times*, March 17, 1992. Copyright © 1992 by the New York Times Company. Reprinted with permission.

Excerpts from *Thoughtful Foragers: A Study of Prehistoric Decision Making* by Steven Mithen. Copyright © by Cambridge University Press 1990. Reprinted with the permission of Cambridge University Press.

Excerpt from "The Outlook: Economy May Benefit from Clinton's Woes" by Henry F. Myers, published in the *Wall Street Journal*, June 14, 1993. Reprinted by permission of the *Wall Street Journal*, © 1993 Dow Jones & Company, Inc. All Rights Reserved Worldwide.

Excerpts from "Equality Versus Discretion in Sentencing" by Irene H. Nagel, Stephen Breyer, and Terence MacCarthy, published in the *American Criminal Law Review*, Spring 1989. Copyright © 1989 by the American Criminal Law Review & Georgetown University. Reprinted with the permission of the publisher.

Excerpts from *Rules for Reasoning* by Richard E. Nisbett. Copyright © 1993 by Lawrence Erlbaum Associates, Inc. All rights reserved. Reprinted with permission.

Excerpts from *Potential Impacts of Sea Level Rise on South Florida Natural Areas* by Richard A. Park and Jae K. Lee. Reprinted with permission.

Excerpt from *World Hypothesis* by Stephen C. Pepper, published by The University of California Press. Copyright © 1942 by the Regents of the University of California and renewed in 1970 by Stephen Pepper. Reprinted with permission.

Excerpts from *Design Paradigms* by Henry Petroski. © Henry Petroski 1994. Reprinted with the permission of Cambridge University Press.

Excerpts from *Personal Knowledge* by Michael Polanyi, published by The University of Chicago Press. Copyright © 1958 by Michael Polanyi. Reprinted with permission.

Excerpt from "Bear market Isn't in Sight, Some Think, Noting Tempered Optimism of Investors" by Anita Raghavan, published in the *Wall Street Journal*, August 16, 1993. Reprinted by permission of the *Wall Street Journal*, © 1993 Dow Jones & Company, Inc. All Rights Reserved Worldwide.

Excerpts from *The Work of Nations* by Robert B. Reich. Copyright © 1991 by Robert B. Reich. Reprinted by permission of Alfred A. Knopf, Inc.

Excerpts from "Inference and Decision at the Bedside" by David L. Sackett, published in the *Journal of Clinical Epidemiology*, June 1989. Copyright © 1989 by Elsevier Science Ltd. Reprinted with kind permission from Elsevier Science Ltd., The Boulevard, Langford Lane, Kidlington OX5 1GB, UK.

Excerpts From "Prediction and Clinical Inference: Forty Years Later" by Theodore Sarbin, published in the *Journal of Personality Assessment*, Fall 1986. Copyright © 1986 by Lawrence Erlbaum Associates, Inc. Reprinted with permission.

Graphics from "What Could Go Wrong? Here Are Some Market 'Nightmares'" by Douglas R. Sease, published in the *Wall Street Journal*, June 1, 1992. Reprinted by permission of the *Wall Street Journal*, © 1992 Dow Jones & Company, Inc. All Rights Reserved Worldwide.

Excerpts from *Models of Man* by Herbert A. Simon. Copyright © 1957 by John Wiley & Sons, Inc. Reprinted with permission.

Excerpt from "EPA Analysis of Radon in Water Is Hard to Swallow" by Richard Stone, published in *Science*, September 17, 1993. Copyright © 1993 by the AAAS. Reprinted with permission.

Excerpts from *Psychology and Social Policy*, edited by Peter Suedfeld and Philip E. Tetlock, published by Hemisphere Publishing, New York. Reproduced with permission. All rights reserved.

Table from "Index of Leading Indicators Rises an Anemic p.1%" by Pearl Thevanayagam, published in the *Wall Street Journal*, June 3, 1993. Reprinted by permission of the *Wall Street Journal*, © 1993 Dow Jones & Company, Inc. All Rights Reserved Worldwide.

Excerpt from "The War on Drugs: A Judge Goes AWOL" by Jack Weinstein, published in *Harper's Magazine*, July 1993. Copyright © 1993 by *Harper's Magazine*. All rights reserved. Reproduced by special permission.

Excerpt from "The Outlook: Arguments Threaten to Divert Attention" by David Wessel, published in the *Wall Street Journal*, December 13, 1993. Reprinted by permission of the *Wall Street Journal*, © 1993 Dow Jones & Company, Inc. All Rights Reserved Worldwide.

# Contents

# HUMAN JUDGMENT *and* SOCIAL POLICY

# Introduction

Judgment as a topic of study gained the attention of scholars as soon as they began to wonder about how their minds worked, and it has occupied a central place in the history of thought ever since. Yet there were hardly any empirical attempts to study human judgment until the late nineteenth century, as psychologists were beginning to do laboratory experiments. Then it became one of the first topics on the research agenda. But all experiments require technology, and the limited technology of the nineteenth century restricted the researchers to asking their subjects to "judge," for example, whether they felt one skin prick or two—that is, to discriminate between stimuli, a pursuit that developed into a science known as psychophysics. Psychophysics may have been exciting to those early psychologists because at last they could see that they were doing real science. But by the middle of the twentieth century, psychophysics no longer attracted much enthusiasm; indeed it was deemed to be such a dull topic that it was believed to drive students—particularly the good ones—away from psychology rather than induce them to study it.

Around the middle of the twentieth century, however, several events occurred that made it possible to study empirically the kind of judgments scholars—and everyone else—really had in mind when they talked about "judgment," namely, judgments about events that take place in human society, the events that require direction and control—in a word, social policy. I was fortunate enough to be at the beginning of my graduate work at the time, and I have stayed with this topic ever since, so I am in a position to give my personal version of the significant events of the second half of the twentieth century. Of course, it will be "one man's view," presented by a man with a point of view and therefore biased, limited, and perhaps misleading. Be that as it may, the history of the field of judgment and decision making during this period has not, to the best of my knowledge, been recorded, so I will briefly mention a few major events, as I see them, and leave it to those who come after me to straighten matters out from their point of view. The reader may be one of these.

My version of the modern history of research on judgment and decision making begins with two articles, one published by Ward Edwards in 1954 ("The Theory of Decision Making")[1] and one published by myself in 1955 ("Probabilistic Functioning and the Clinical Method").[2] I like my version of this history, not merely because it risks overestimating my contribution but because it defines the beginning of the modern version of this field in terms of the two approaches to judgment and decision making that together form one of the foundations of this book.[3]

Edwards's emphasis was on the rationality of decision making. He made mathematics in general, and a particular form of mathematical probability known as Bayes' theorem in particular, the foundation of rationality. This was a momentous step, for he thus proposed the probability calculus as the standard of rationality by which a person's judgments under uncertainty—probabilistic conditions—were to be evaluated, criticized, and changed in order to achieve rationality. Of course, that idea was not entirely new: it reaches back to at least to the eighteenth century.[4] What was new was Edwards's ability to place it in the context of modern experimental psychology. He showed how various propositions about the rationality of human judgment under uncertainty could be empirically tested against a defensible standard, a mathematical probabilistic theory. This was a major step for the field of psychology in the 1950s.

And Edwards went further. He put forward the hypothesis that the *mind worked in the same way as the mathematical (Bayes') theorem*. This was indeed a significant next step because he was not simply advocating a criterion for rational decision making under uncertainty; he was proposing a specific *mathematical model* of how the decision process, using mathematics to lay out clearly his idea of how the process worked.

Of course, other researchers offered modifications of Edwards's ideas, as in fact did Edwards himself.[5] And it was from this beginning that the coherence theory of truth became the basis of a vigorous program for research that continues today and that I shall describe in some detail in this book.

The second strand of research in the field of judgment and decision making began with the article I wrote in 1955. I claim responsibility for the beginning of the use of the *correspondence* theory of truth in the field of judgment and decision making. The ideas in my article were based on a general theory of cognition under uncertainty that had been introduced by my teacher, Egon Brunswik, from the late 1930s until 1955. The correspondence theory of truth focuses on the correspondence of ideas with *facts*, rather than on the coherence of ideas with ideas. In the field of judgment and decision making, then, my work focused on the *accuracy* of judgments (regardless of their rationality), whereas Edwards's work focused on the *rationality* of judgments (regardless of their empirical accuracy). It could be fairly said that although my relationship with Edwards was always cordial, he went his way, and I went mine. And our divergent paths were clear in the separate conferences that we established.

Edwards established a conference on the Bayesian approach to judgment and decision making that marked its thirty-third consecutive year in 1995. I established the "Boulder Conference" in 1967. It was of a more general nature than Edwards's and included adherents of both points of view, each of which was described in a landmark article published in 1971 by P. Slovic and S. Lichtenstein.[6]

Although Edwards's conferences continue, the Boulder conferences led to the formation of the Judgment and Decision Making Society and were thus discontinued. The Judgment and Decision Making Society, founded by N. John Castellan (deceased), Charles Gettys, Lola Lopes, Gary McClelland, and James Shanteau, held its first meeting in 1980 and now has more than one thousand members. Two journals are devoted to the field of judgment and decision making, but, because of the multidisciplinary nature of the topic, related articles are published in more than five hundred different journals every year.

Much of the credit for the establishment of the field must go to Martin Tolcott, whose farsightedness as a program officer in the Office of Naval Research led to the funding in the 1970s of research projects on judgment and decision making. He saw the value in such research and showed his keen interest in it by closely review-ing proposals, visiting research sites, and not merely attending conferences but par-ticipating in them, thus contributing both science and wisdom.

Shortly after the Judgment and Decision Making Society was established in the United States, a parallel society was founded in Europe. In addition, in 1978 mem-bers of the medical profession founded the Medical Decision Making Society. This society publishes its own journal and has a membership of about the same size as that of the Judgment and Decision Making Society.

It is against this background of almost fifty years of research on judgment and decision making that I undertook to write a book that would bring at least a part of that work to bear on the process of policy formation.

Since the 1940s, hundreds of psychologists, among others, have taken a scien-tific approach to the study of human judgment that has direct significance for social policy formation. They have produced thousands of articles and numerous books on this topic. I intend to portray this activity in a manner that I trust will be interesting to academics, yet comprehensible to those laypersons who are curious about this topic.

This book describes current and some past academic efforts to understand human judgment and decision making under irreducible uncertainty—in other words, under the conditions that we encounter in the natural world and in the world of our mak-ing. This is not a textbook on judgment, decision making, human factors, cognitive psychology, or management science; indeed, it isn't a textbook in any field. It does, however, address problems related to all these disciplines (and possibly others) by virtue of the fact that it offers a description of human judgment under uncertainty and its role in human affairs, presents a comprehensive theory of human judgment, and demonstrates how the theory applies to policy formation. The importance of this undertaking lies in the fact that human judgment is the hidden, mysterious link in the process that forms the policies and plans that directly affect, if not control, the nature of our society, as well as its interaction with other societies. This approach to policy formation is, therefore, altogether different from the usual approach taken by policy analysts. Traditionally, students of policy formation focus on the *con-tent* of various policies. Here, however, the focus is on the *cognitive process*—the judgments—by which social policies are created. I examine that process in relation to the problems with which our judgment must cope and in the light of what research tells us about how competently humans can be expected to perform.

There are those who would oppose any effort to analyze human judgment. They argue that the very endeavor destroys the great gift of subjective judgment that, they say, has given us all that makes us human—the arts, literature, religion, romance, compassion, respect for the individual, the ability to separate the good from the bad, and, indeed, the intuitive wisdom we prize in our most respected citizens. To bring that gift under analysis, to subject it to puny experiments by psychologists, cognitive scientists, or perpetrators of artificial intelligence, to break it into parts or components in order to represent this marvelous process in terms of simpleminded algebraic equations, is in their eyes a travesty.

Are they right? I believe not. Although I sympathize with this view and, I hope, understand it, I cannot agree with it. There is too much evidence to support an opposing view—that subjective judgment can also be dangerous. Having lived through the bloodiest century of all (I was born during the carnage of World War I, participated in its bloody sequel, World War II, watched the wars in Korea and Vietnam and the fires and riots in cities, and witnessed the systematic slaughter, oppression, and suffering in what was the Soviet Union, Eastern Europe, the Balkans, and Africa (I leave it to readers to finish the list as they prefer), I can say with confidence that *something* ought to be done to improve the manner in which we human beings decide what to do.

I can think of nothing better than to try to understand the process by which we exercise our judgment, and I can think of no better means than a scientific approach. After all, this proposal suggests only that we do our cognitive best, exercise our most critical analytical reasoning, empirically test and compare our theories and ideas in order to determine which are false and which closely approximate the truth, and thus improve if possible the process which has surely proved, and continues to prove, to be so dismal and dangerous.

But there is something annoying about having someone peering into our thought processes with the aim of evaluating them that arguments won't entirely eliminate. Indeed, Sigmund Freud observed long ago that the human race had already suffered a number of blows to its sense of self-importance. His examples were compelling: Copernicus's discovery made us acknowledge that our world is not at the center of the universe, Darwin's discovery forced us to recognize that we are not the result of a special act of creation by a supernatural power, and Freud's own theories of the active role of the unconscious robbed us of our belief that we possessed full control over, and understanding of, our mental activity as well as our actions. As Mazlish noted, Freud believed that "the ego . . . is not even master in its own house, but must content itself with scanty information of what is going on unconsciously in the mind."[7] Although Freud's theory of the unconscious has not withstood the test of time, research in experimental psychology continues to offer solid evidence that not all aspects of our cognitive activity are under our conscious control. And that conclusion is not limited to experimental psychologists; even the self-confident John Kennedy noted that "*The essence of ultimate decision* remains impenetrable to the observer—often, indeed, to the decider himself. . . . There will always be the dark and tangled stretches in the decision-making process—mysterious even to those who may be most intimately involved."[8]

The question to what extent we know and control our cognitive processes is directly and tightly related to a second question: the competence of human judgment. If we don't *know* what we are thinking and can't *control* our mental activity, then how can we claim competence? When we hear phrases like "it is my judgment that . . ." or "in my judgment we must . . . ," should we draw back in fear of folly? Is this judgment the product of a process that remains "mysterious even to . . . the decider himself"? Or should we be prepared to acknowledge the "wisdom" that is about to be expressed? When heads of state offer their considered judgment about going to war, when commissions made up of our elders advise us about how to change economic and social policies, should we rest assured that we are on the right course, that they know best? When judges in courts of law express their judgments about how much time in prison a defendant should endure or how much society might suffer as a consequence of his or her being freed, or when they express their judgments about the competence of a young woman to apply the necessary wisdom—the good judgment—about whether to terminate a pregnancy without consulting her parents for *their* (good?) judgment about whether the action should be taken, should we be content? Or should we be mindful of the by now numerous studies that purport to demonstrate the flawed judgment processes of human beings and try to find a better way? What better way can there be? If not those judgments, flawed or not, then what? History is no guide; it offers us little but anecdotal evidence on both sides of the question, and folly appears to be at least as frequent as wisdom.

Then what does fifty years of research tell us? It tells us that there is little doubt that, at least in certain circumstances, (1) human cognition is not under our control, (2) we are not aware of our judgment and decision processes, and (3) our reports about those processes are not to be trusted. But exactly which internal or external factors produce flawed judgments remains seriously in doubt. And, unhappily, like so much of our unfinished scientific business, fifty years of research also tells us the opposite; at least in certain circumstances, human judgment is rational and our judgments *are* accurate. This is an unsatisfactory conclusion, of course, and regrettable for many reasons. But we are gaining ground; it is easy to see the difference between the situation in the 1950s and that in the 1990s. And, of course, empirical research in cognitive psychology and in judgment and decision making is a new endeavor (almost all of its originators are still alive). In this book I will offer an overview of the progress that has been made in understanding the uncertain competence of human judgment.

First, a caveat. It will occur to some readers that psychologists (the writer included) exhibit a certain arrogance in announcing that they have appointed themselves to examine the competence of human judgment. These readers will not deny the importance of investigating the topic, but, given the spotty, perhaps dubious, achievements of psychology, will wonder if it is a matter for which psychologists have established *their* competence. I won't deny the appearance of arrogance, or the basis for doubt about research accomplishments, or the need for caution no matter what conclusions are reached here. My purpose is to describe the manner in which this important subject has been approached, the general nature of the studies that have been conducted, and criticisms of them, as well as the general conclusions that have been drawn. And, of course, I want to advance our understanding of the topic.

The reader will be familiar with the perennial questions raised about the competence of human judgment. First, how good is human judgment in general? There is much to show that it is good, even astonishingly so, and much to show that it is often bad, even embarrassingly so. So we need to know: What helps, what hinders the achievement of good judgment? We are just beginning to learn about that. Second, how does one acquire competence in judgment? Can it be taught? Or must we depend on experience? We know little about this. Third, there is the question of differences among individuals. Which of us has good judgment? Who does not? And how do you find out? Who should be on that "blue-ribbon committee"? And who should not? And then we might ask why: Why does one person have it (if he or she does), and why does another not have it? Is it in the genes? Special environments? Is it all a matter of intelligence? Education? A certain worldliness? How do we find wisdom?

The reader will be keenly aware of the fact that these questions have been asked—and answered, one way or another—for as long as people have had the leisure to reflect on them. Such questions, and the answers to them, appear again and again, even in our earliest records of human thought. The Greeks, for one, loved to talk about these topics.

## Two Fundamental Distinctions

I make great use of the distinction between intuitive and analytical cognition. I also depend heavily on the distinction between the coherence theory of truth and the correspondence theory of truth. I do so because of the long-standing recognition of their relation to the way we think and to policy formation. Everyone is familiar with the first, almost no one with the second. Both are highly relevant to our topic, however, and therefore I now provide a brief explanation of each; detailed explanations appear in Parts I and II.

Intuition and analysis have been great rivals for our attention throughout history. R. W. Southern's classic, The *Making of the Middle Ages*, offers an impressive description of the struggle between rhetoric and logic to capture the intellectual energies of scholars a thousand years ago. He tells us that it was Gerbert in the tenth century who saw the practical importance of this distinction for politicians and statesmen: As Southern put it in paraphrasing Gerbert, "Rhetoric is static: logic dynamic. The one aims at making old truths palatable, the other at searching out new, even unpalatable truths."[9] Gerbert was on to something here. When logic drives us to "unpalatable truths," it appears that we are often inclined to reject them in our reasoning; we prefer palatable rhetoric that appeals to our intuition—not always, of course, but the danger lurks constantly. As I will show, even those of us most trusted to depend on logic have denied its value and turned instead to intuition to guide our judgments.

Southern also shows us how Gerbert compared rhetoric—induced intuition—and logic in social policy formation: "Rhetoric is persuasive, logic compulsive. The former smoothes away divisions, the latter brings them into the open. The one is a healing art, an art of government; the other is surgical, and challenges the foundations of conduct and belief."[10] We find, a thousand years later, the same distinctions, the same struggles between intuition and analysis.

Of course, this old wine comes in new bottles. Although there has been little change in rhetoric—the maneuvers of the modern politician offer little that is new—there has indeed been a change in "logic." We are no longer restricted to Aristotelian logic as our standard of reason, our only means for the production of unpalatable truths. Useful as that logic may be even now (and I give an example of it in the text), we are now not only capable of using an expanded and more differentiated logic but capable of coping analytically with irreducible uncertainty and its consequence, inevitable error, although we have yet to come to grips with a further consequence—the *injustice* that follows unavoidably from imperfect decisions. Just how we cope with these consequences and how we should cope with them, and the necessary limits on our achievement of success—all these are primary topics of this book.

That is why Part I is titled "Rivalry." It describes the age-old struggle between intuitive and analytical cognition to form the basis for coping with the irreducible uncertainty in our environments, natural and artificial. In particular, Part I describes how two disciplines—law and medicine—recognized irreducible uncertainty and its consequences, inevitable error and inevitable injustice, and what they did—and do—about it. Rivalry between intuition and analysis is very much alive in science, medicine, law, and other fields.

The second major distinction—between the coherence and the correspondence theories of truth—is equally deserving of our attention but unlike intuition and analysis has rarely captured it. Part II describes the tension—the uneasy and contentious relationship—between these two grand theories. Lofty as they may sound, these theories (or metatheories as they are sometimes called) have direct, concrete, and simple referents. Coherence theories demand that the facts "hang together," that they tell a good story, one that is plausible and compelling because there are no discordant elements. Thus, coherence is often used as a criterion for whether we choose to believe a story or a theory. Indeed, it is *the* criterion for whether we accept a theory. Logic and mathematical formulas are generally the testing grounds for coherence theories of truth. And we shall find that coherence is often used as a criterion for the *competence* of our judgments—but not always; sometimes we ignore coherence and demand accuracy, especially from our weather forecasters and our financial advisers.

Far different is the correspondence theory. This theory asks not for logic or consistency but only for *accuracy*—the correspondence of judgments with the facts. A person's competence is judged entirely by the accuracy of his or her judgments. There are direct practical consequences of deciding which theory should prevail, and I provide in the text examples from engineering, law, medicine, and economics. Tension arises from the fact that right from the beginning, researchers have chosen one of these two very different paths in their search for understanding the nature of human judgment, and that difference—and the accompanying tension—persists today. Therefore, in Part II, I trace that story and its current consequences and show the reader why he or she should attend to this difference.

While Parts I and II describe contention—rivalry and tension—Part III focuses on reconciliation. It does so in order to further our comprehension and our constructive use of both the rivalry between intuition and analysis and the tension between coherence and correspondence theories. Too often these differences have gone unrecognized for what they are and have been translated into nonproductive and personal disputes.

Part IV describes the limits to learning by policymakers, through the use of social experimentation, computer models, and other analytical procedures. It also describes our search for possible wisdom in our leaders and anticipates the possible—and differential—rewards of cognitive competence in the future. It offers a more differentiated and somewhat more optimistic view of how both more and less fortunate members of society might make use of their cognitive competence.

While I have indicated what topics readers might encounter in these pages, I haven't said why they should pick up this book in the first place. What purposes will be served?

There are two purposes. One is to offer academics an opportunity to look at this topic in a new light, one that may add to the unification of their efforts. A second is to offer laypersons an opportunity to learn what researchers have discovered about how human beings try to make use of the enormous fund of knowledge they have acquired and stored in books, libraries, computer files, and other depositories in order to guide social policies. Why? Because these tremendous resources are applied to society's problems only through human judgment—human, that is, because only human beings have access to that stored fund of knowledge. The most timeless question of all is, How best can human judgment be employed to create social policy?

I have not included work from the fields of artificial intelligence, expert systems, linguistics, logic, or philosophy. There is too large a gap between these fields and the field of judgment and decision making. For the sake of achieving a broad approach, I have also omitted references to mathematical treatments of this topic; there are no equations in this book. Nor have I developed here the scientific research basis for the general propositions I put forward. My goal has been to demonstrate their implications for the formation of social policy. The reader who wishes to learn about that research base is in luck, however, for it has been laid out in highly readable fashion by Ray Cooksey in his book *Judgment Analysis: Theory, Methods, and Applications*, in which he presents the experimental and statistical foundations of the general theory described in Part III.

I acknowledge that I have not developed or described all the aspects of this topic with the depth that a comprehensive treatment would require; there is much more to say. Fortunately, there are many who are prepared to say it.

# I   RIVALRY

Uncertainty, doubt, and fear are common experiences we would prefer not to have, or at least not to have very often. But we do have these experiences, and the policymaker has them often, frequently all three at once. That is because policymakers must act in the face of irreducible uncertainty—uncertainty that won't go away before a judgment has to be made about what to do, what can be done, what will be done, what ought to be done. Part I describes the nature of irreducible uncertainty, why it is accompanied by inevitable error and results unavoidably in injustice. Part I also comes to grips with the question of which cognitive processes policymakers can and must bring to bear on this situation. The role of intuition and analysis and, most important, what we now know about the rivalry between them are also described.

# 1 Irreducible Uncertainty and the Need for Judgment

> There is no such thing as absolute certainty, but there is assurance
> sufficient for the purposes of life.
>
> —*John Stuart Mill*

Irreducible uncertainty refers to uncertainty that cannot be reduced by *any* activity at the moment action is required. The idea of irreducible uncertainty is as old as recorded history. Thucydides, one of the great historians of antiquity, writing in the fifth century B.C., tells us that the Spartan king Archidamus, in the course of an address to his fellow Spartans on the eve of war with Athens, noted with approval that Spartans were taught "that it is impossible to calculate accurately events that are determined by chance."[1] But, he added, they were not afraid of that fact. So the king said nothing further about "chance" events and the impossibility of calculating them accurately, and the Spartans voted confidently and enthusiastically to go to war. As the king suggested, irreducible uncertainty would not deter them, any more than it deters today's generals and admirals, investors in stocks and bonds, industrial entre-preneurs, government planners—anyone who must predict the course of future events.

That idea, the impossibility of calculating "accurately events that are determined by chance," persists. Seldom, however, are its consequences for social policy put to us in such harsh, down-to-earth terms as those used by David Brooks, a deputy editorial page editor for *The Wall Street Journal Europe*. Expressing his disdain for those internationalists who wish "to plan ahead and work out rational, coordinated strategies," he argued that "ultimately, what . . . [the internationalist] lacks is . . . a sense that life is a bunch of knuckleballs thrown at your head. Instead . . . [the internationalist] thinks it's a place where it is possible to see and understand the field, to plan ahead and work out rational, coordinated strategies."[2] Brooks notes with approval the view of the former prime minister of Czechoslovakia: "Mr. Klaus's world is . . . a crazy place where chaos is normal." Nevertheless, neither Brooks nor Klaus nor anyone else simply throws up his hands and says, "Since it's chaos out there, let's

13

just roll the dice." Instead, they do just what we all do: They exercise their judgment, sometimes carefully, sometimes impulsively, and they plan. That truth was evident the very next day in Brooks's newspaper, which prominently displayed and described in detail the economic plans of the three candidates for president in 1992. No candidate said, "Look, it's a crazy place out there where chaos is normal; why plan?"

There are two important points here. One is the persistence and the centrality of the idea of irreducible uncertainty; approximately twenty-five hundred years separate the Spartan king's reminder to his fellow citizens about the importance of irreducible uncertainty and a modern newspaper editor's expression of a similar, if somewhat overwrought, admonition. The second point is that even those who remind and admonish us act as if their words were not true; they plan—and an apology for inconsistency rarely appears. Why? Because they—and we—can do nothing else; planning in the face of irreducible uncertainty is inescapable. Planning under uncertainty demands—and gets—human judgment; policies and plans spring from the minds of persons. Social policy can be produced in no other way.

Of course, there are classes of events about which we can be certain. All living things die, there will be ill health, there will be crime and violence, the laws of physics and chemistry will continue to apply in the future as they have in the past. How do we know this? For the same reason that we know that the sun will appear tomorrow; it always has, we reason, so it always will. Thus policymakers must plan for deaths, for ill health, for crime and violence, and for similar classes of events and be prepared to implement policies within the limits of physical restraints. It is the formation of plans to cope with the uncertainty *within* these classes that brings us to the question of human judgment.

The term "irreducible uncertainty" is certainly not mysterious. It takes two principal forms: subjective uncertainty and objective uncertainty. Think of subjective and objective time; your estimate of time is subjective, but the clock provides an objective assessment of time. Subjective uncertainty refers to the state of mind of the person making a judgment (about time, for example), regardless of the state of the objective system (the clock) about which the judgment (telling time) is to be made. Of course, subjective and objective uncertainty may vary independently. For example, a person betting on a horse race may be highly (subjectively) uncertain about whether the horse on whom the bet is riding will win, but in fact the race may be fixed— determined in advance—so that a certain horse *will* win; thus, subjective uncertainty may be high although objective uncertainty is almost zero. The opposite conditions may also occur; the bettor may be highly confident about which horse will win (low subjective uncertainty) even under conditions of high objective uncertainty (all horses of equal handicap, running an honest race).

Once we separate subjective and objective uncertainty, large questions arise. Among those who have noticed them are many who try to forecast the behavior of the economy. John Maynard Keynes, an economist whose ideas greatly influenced the politicians trying to find a way out of the Great Depression of the 1930s, had a great interest in uncertainty and probability and had much to say about it.

Robert Heilbroner offers a good description of Keynes's thoughts on uncertainty in the economy:

At the core of Keynes's rejection of existing theory was an emphasis on an aspect of the economy . . .—its inherent and pervasive uncertainty. The rational judgments that underpinned conventional theory could not be formed in the marketplaces of the real, as opposed to textbook, world. Instead, what Keynes called "animal spirits"—moods of optimism and pessimism, often based on little more than rumor, follow-the-leader impulses, or sheer desperation—dictated the investment decisions on which the level of employment depended.[3]

## Determinism in the Objective World

It can be argued—and is argued in some textbooks—that in nature *all* uncertainty is in the mind of the person and that there is no uncertainty in the objective world. If one had all the necessary information and knew how to use it, so the argument goes, one would know the outcome in advance. Under this view, all uncertainty is ultimately reducible; because all systems are fully determined, once all the information about any one system is available, uncertainty disappears—an argument made famous by the scholar Pierre Simon de Laplace (1749–1827) regarding the fall of a snowflake. Laplace argued that if all the physical facts were known, the exact location of the fall of each snowflake could be predicted correctly. In one of the most memorable sentences in the history of science, Laplace stated the deterministic principle:

> Given for one instant an intelligence which could comprehend all the forces by which nature is animated and the respective positions of the beings which compose it, if moreover this intelligence were vast enough to submit these data to analysis, it would embrace in the same formula both the movements of the largest bodies in the universe and those of the lightest atom; to it *nothing would be uncertain*, [italics added] and the future as the past would be present to its eyes.[4]

This view, which has generally been called "determinism,"[5] is held by some today. For example, in an influential textbook on judgment and decision making, R. M. Hogarth argues that

> *it is necessary to recognize that we live in a probabilistic environment.* However, the environment is not probabilistic because of its inherent properties; it is probabilistic because our representation of it is necessarily imperfect. *That is, the source of the uncertainty lies in us rather than in the environment.*[6]

Hogarth wants students to recognize—that is, to accept—Laplace's deterministic proposition. Uncertainty there may be, but the uncertainty is in us, not the environment. The reason this is important is that it implies that the *reduction* of uncertainty will require changes in human beings, not in the environment, for it is already—in principle—perfectly predictable.

Hogarth is not alone in the perpetuation of Laplace's two-hundred-year-old doctrine. L. Lusted, a distinguished researcher in the field of medical decision making, agrees: "I believe that uncertainty is a property of my knowledge about an event, and not of the event itself."[7]

I will return to this doctrine later in this chapter, but first we need to consider an opposing view.

## Indeterminism in the Objective World

Those supporting the point of view known as probabilism argue, in strong opposition to determinism, that aside from the hard, practical matters associated with acquiring sufficient information and the knowledge necessary to know how to use it, uncertainty is an inherent aspect of the objective world. The uncertainty of events is reducible only in part; fully accurate, precise predictions of about future events will never be possible, and only a stubborn Laplacean would argue otherwise. The source of uncertainty does lie in the environment, as well as in us. Indeed, many will argue that there is more inherent uncertainty in the environment than there is in us.

The history of the indeterministic view reaches back to antiquity, but as G. Gigerenzer has pointed out, the indeterminate character of nature became a legitimate viewpoint when concepts such as chance and probability became fundamental theoretical concepts in various scientific disciplines: "The work of Mendel in genetics, that of Maxwell and Boltzmann on statistical mechanics, and the quantum mechanics of Schrödinger and Heisenberg that built indeterminism into its very model of nature are key examples of that revolution in thought."[8] All these arguments have been strengthened by the recent introduction of the idea of "chaos" in physical systems. J. Gleick's popularizations of these ideas not only make the concept of irreducible uncertainty plausible, he offers numerous physical examples that are taken seriously by modern physicists. Gleick's description of the fate of a snowflake, for example, is very different from that offered by Laplace.

> As a growing snowflake falls to earth, typically floating in the wind for an hour or more, the choices made by the branching tips at any instant depend sensitively on such things as the temperature, the humidity, and the presence of impurities in the atmosphere. The six tips of a single snowflake, spreading within a millimeter space, feel the same temperatures, and because the laws of growth are purely deterministic, they maintain a near-perfect symmetry. But the nature of turbulent air is such that any pair of snowflakes will experience very different paths. The final flake records the history of all the changing weather conditions it has experienced, and the combinations may as well be infinite.[9]

The final word "infinite" defines the theory. Were the combinations "finite," a solution would be possible, at least in principle, but not if they are "infinite."

This dispute about absolute uncertainty in the objective world was epitomized perhaps for all time in a letter written by Albert Einstein to the physicist Max Born: "You believe in a God who plays dice, and I in complete law and order." For our purposes, however, the dispute can remain unsettled. My main purpose in describing it is to set the groundwork for the view to be adopted here—conditional indeterminism.

### Conditional Indeterminism

Conditional indeterminism is simply a shorthand way of indicating that judgments are made under conditions of irreducible uncertainty *at the time the judgment is made.* Thus, the degree of indeterminism, or irreducible uncertainty, is conditional and dependent on the time the judgment must be made. Later we may discover that the circumstances to which we applied our judgment were, in fact, fully determined (just as Laplace, Hogarth, and Lusted insisted they were). Such a discovery, while perhaps fatal to Peirce's "absolute chance" or other forms of enthusiastic indeterminism, would not be fatal to conditional indeterminism. But accepting the premise of conditional indeterminism does bring a responsibility—accepting the need to inquire into the kind and the amount of uncertainty that exist in the environment at the time a judgment is being made. Accepting that responsibility brings us to the systems view of how an organism interacts with its environment.

A Systems View

In the systems view there are two independent uncertain systems—the objective ("outside") system and the subjective ("inside") system. Uncertainty in the world outside the observer generates uncertainty in the observer's cognitive system—the judgments and predictions—of laypersons and experts alike. Discovering the relation between these two uncertain systems constitutes the research task for students of human judgment.

Discussions about uncertainty almost invariably become increasingly complex and generally drive one either to abandon the idea of uncertainty or to pursue the arcane works on the subject—a rare activity. In an effort to avoid these unattractive alternatives yet convey the essential idea of how irreducible uncertainty affects policy formation, I have chosen two excerpts from the *New York Times* that focus on uncertainty and thus are written in a manner designed to maximize comprehension at a level appropriate for our discussion. The articles appeared on the same day (January 3, 1993) and address two topics of interest to everyone: the prediction of events in physical systems (earthquakes) and the prediction of events in social systems (politics). Here are the warnings of Allan Lindh, chief seismologist of the United States Geological Survey, regarding future earthquakes in California: "It's time to act as if the damn thing will happen tomorrow." The author of the article explains that "Dr. Lindh uses mathematical probabilities, a staple of earthquake science in the United States for nearly a decade, to educate public officials." Lindh explains the situation to them in this way: "Society is always playing a high-stakes poker game when there's only so much money to spend . . . you move some problems to the foreground and others to the background." And how to decide how to do that? Probabilistically, that is, "quantify hazards in terms of the likelihood they will occur." He then says that "the chance of a major earthquake within the lifetime of a California is between 1 in 2 and 1 in 10."[10] Here is irreducible uncertainty writ large; these chances are different indeed. Lindh, of course, hopes that his uncertainty will in time be reduced, but no one thinks that it will be reduced to zero soon, and it is reasonable to doubt that it ever will be. Be that as it may, there is *now* irreducible uncertainty in the physical world as far as judgments about the future occurrence of earthquakes are concerned. That is what is meant by conditional indeterminism.

Those concerned with political events also face irreducible uncertainty at the time a judgment must be made. As the *New York Times* writer Leslie Gelb indicates in a column headed "Surprise, Surprise, Surprise": "Almost yearly since World War I, profound surprises have knocked us out of comfortable orbits. They came as bolts from the blue beyond human capacity to predict [like earthquakes?]. They surprise us in whole (the events themselves) or in crucial part (the precise when, where and how)."[11] There is little doubt that Gelb sees judgments about social events as based on conditional indeterminism. And in a column in the *New York Times*, the noted historian Arthur Schlesinger Jr. laughed at *The Wall Street Journal* for asking ten American winners of the Nobel Prize in economics to assess President Bill Clinton's plan for improving the economy. "The result," Schlesinger said, "was cacophony. Economists are about as useful as astrologers for predicting the future (and, like astrologers, they never let failure on one occasion diminish certitude on the next)."[12] Some readers will add that in this respect they closely resemble historians, or psychologists, or physicians—and all the rest of us.

It's also true that social policy is always future oriented; that's another reason why social policy is always made under uncertainty. Although it is conventional among political scientists to explain that social policy is directed toward who gets what, it is becoming increasingly obvious that more is now at stake: Policy also is directed toward what ought to be, what can be, and what will be.

Consider this paragraph from R. J. Herrnstein's and C. Murray's controversial book *The Bell Curve*, which places so much emphasis on intelligence:

> Predicting the course of Society is chancy, but certain tendencies seem strong enough to worry about:
>
> • An increasingly isolated cognitive elite.
> • A merging of the cognitive elite with the affluent.
> • A deteriorating quality of life for people at the bottom end of the cognitive ability distribution.
>
> Unchecked, these trends will lead the U.S. toward something resembling a caste society, with the underclass mired ever more firmly at the bottom and the cognitive elite ever more firmly anchored at the top, restructuring the rules of society so that it becomes harder and harder for them to lose. Among the other casualties of this process would be American civil society as we have known it. Like other apocalyptic visions, this one is pessimistic, perhaps too much so. On the other hand, there is much to be pessimistic about.[13]

If we take this view of society seriously, then the question is: How to cope? Generally, we put our faith in consensus. Faced with uncertainty about the course of the U.S. economy, *The Wall Street Journal* regularly asks forty-four economists to predict future events, such as the future path of interest rates and the rate of growth of the economy in the coming year. Why forty-four? Why not one? Or two? Because *The Wall Street Journal* knows that such predictions are made under conditions of irreducible uncertainty and that therefore there will be wide variations in the predictions. Which is the correct one? The newspaper reduces *its* uncertainty by averaging them; apparently, there is safety in numbers. By this procedure the newspaper hopes that errors in the forecast will be canceled and that a close approximation to a correct prediction will be achieved. Of course, as Schlesinger indicated, economists are notorious for their widely varying judgments and predictions. But is averaging really a good idea? In the 1992 presidential elections, five hundred economists endorsed one candidate's economic plan, while two hundred others were marshaled to oppose it. Should we have assumed that if we split the difference between the forecasts, truth would be unveiled? Averaging of judgments and predictions deserves more thought than it usually gets, and I will address this topic in later chapters.

Subjective uncertainty also varies from nation to nation, depending on its laws concerning freedom of speech. It's quite possible that the framers of the U.S. Constitution did not imagine when they wrote the words of the First Amendment—"Congress shall make no law . . . abridging the freedom of speech or of the press"—that they were thereby increasing for all foreseeable time the level of uncertainty in U.S. citizens' minds. For as Anthony Lewis makes clear in his book *Make No Law: The Sullivan Case and the First Amendment,*[14] the volume and the variety of protected opinions, judgments, and beliefs, ranging from the doubtful to the looney, that are broadcast in the United States are hard to comprehend. Nevertheless, citizens are hard pressed to distinguish one from the other, and one's uncertainty becomes ever more difficult to reduce as a result.

Perhaps the best example of irreducible uncertainty can be found in deeper questions: Why are we here? Who, or what, put us here? How did it all happen? And what of the future? Do human beings actually have a soul? Is there life after death? If there is, what will it (and we) look like? Answers to such questions from religious enthusiasts get us as close to positive certainty as one gets, except perhaps for firm atheists, who are equally certain of their answers. In between is represented every possible degree of certitude. Averaging of positions here would gain us little indeed.

Although judgments about God and existential issues are often made with high confidence in the face of irreducible uncertainty, it has long been recognized that such questions may not be wholly academic; there may be risk in expressing the wrong answer. More than three hundred years ago the great French philosopher, mathematician, and pioneer in probability theory Blaise Pascal (1623–1662) recognized this risk and put the problem in terms of the *duality of error*, no small feat at a time when very few persons even recognized the concept of probability. Which would be worse, he wondered—making the error of believing in God when in fact no God exists or making the error of not believing when God does exist? (This question may have occasionally entered the reader's mind.) We will return to Pascal's conception of these errors—and his answer—in our discussion of social policy.

In short, irreducible uncertainty is an acknowledged fact in the subjective forecasts of the future behavior of physical systems in the natural environment, as well as the future behavior of political, social, and economic systems. For many, if not most, systems there is no means of prediction other than subjective judgment.

In addition to eliminating the need to wrestle with the question of the truth of the Laplacean view—that all uncertainty lies within us rather than in the objective world—the conditional indeterminism view, a systems view, offers an additional advantage. It looks at the environments in which we make decisions (earthquakes, social systems) as part of a continuum, moving from those that are completely determined—that offer no uncertainty—at one end to those that contain completely uncertain, random events at the opposite end. Environments that are fully determined are usually those created by technologists who seek to rationalize decision making in the workplace. Irreducibly uncertain tasks, on the other hand, usually occur in those natural environments that have yet to be rationalized by humans. The systems view also takes as a premise that cognitive systems can be ordered in the same way. The two continuums parallel each other. I will offer much more detail on these continuums and the relationship between them in Chapter 6, which provides the theoretical foundation upon which this book is based.

Now, however, it will suffice if the reader has learned why I argue that virtually all policy formation is carried out in circumstances in which there is irreducible uncertainty—sometimes more, sometimes less. The consequences, I suggest, are judgments that result in both inevitable error and unavoidable injustice, with a frequency that varies with the amount of uncertainty in these systems. First, however, I turn to the reasons *why* irreducible uncertainty evokes human judgment and conflict.

## Human Judgment and Uncertainty

If one is faced with a set of circumstances that demand action, it may be possible to turn to a rule. Rules are of various types—some are better than others—and generally constitute the core of a professional person's activity.[15] But circumstances that require a social policy—developing a transportation system, a health care system, a method for reviving a neighborhood or a city—are not dealt with so easily; there are no proven if-then rules for these circumstances. It is these conditions that involve irreducible uncertainty; it is these conditions that make judgment necessary.

What does irreducible uncertainty demand of judgment? If judgment is defined as the process whereby persons apply their knowledge (as I defined it earlier), persons can either apply whatever personal knowledge they have or seek knowledge from other sources. But if irreducible uncertainty exists in the environment, then all our knowledge will not completely eliminate all errors from our actions. Moreover, there is always the likelihood that others will reach different judgments. At that point one must resort to "It is my judgment that. . . ." This stage is usually reached when there is tacit agreement that no fully defensible solution is available and, it is to be hoped, the parties recognize that the proposed solution is "reasonable." Of course, this stage may be reached only after long disputes and after charges of bad faith. Or agreement on what is reasonable may never be reached; conflict may then be reduced by other means.

Fortunately, policymakers are not without some assistance in matters involving uncertainty. Application of analytical, mathematical techniques to the problem of uncertainty began in the seventeenth century and is vital today. The story of the development of probability theory and statistical methods, and of their use in society, has been told in interesting fashion in I. Hacking's classic *The Emergence of Probability*[16] and in his recent *The Taming of Chance*,[17] as well as in *The Empire of Chance: How Probability Changed Science and Everyday Life* by G. Gigerenzer and his colleagues.[18] Statistical methods have indeed "changed science and everyday life," and everyday policymaking as well. I will, in the next section, focus on the relationship between human judgment and that aspect of chance or uncertainty that bears directly on social policy—that is, the differential allocation of the consequences of the inevitable errors that follow from actions based on judgments under uncertainty.

## Different Consequences of Different Errors

We are all familiar with the mistakes that follow from the adoption of a wrong policy. What is not so familiar to us is the fact that any policy—even a good one—formed under irreducible uncertainty can lead to error. There are, in fact, two types of error, each with its own consequences. And these different consequences very likely affect different people. The two kinds of error are taking an action when one shouldn't have and not taking an action when one should have. These erroneous actions result from information that comes to us in the form of *false positives* and *false negatives*.

### *False Positives, False Negatives*

The false positive, although usually associated with medicine, in fact has general applicability; it refers to accepting a warning sign or signal as true when in fact it is (or will be shown to be) false. Thus, when the smoke detector, burglar alarm, laboratory report, or expert witness sends an alarm when in `act there is no fire, burglary, disease, or malfunction present, or when no disaster ensues despite the expert's warning, we have a *false positive*. Had we acted as if the alarm were true, an error would have been made, and, ordinarily, a cost would be attached. If an alarm system is not absolutely perfect (almost none is), action in response to the signal is risky; the costs for acting unnecessarily, which may invoke risks of its own, will have to be paid by someone. And those costs and risks may be considerable—for example, evacuating thousands of persons from coastal areas or mountain canyons when the warning turns out to be false and the threatened fire, hurricane, or flood does not occur.

On the other hand, there is the *false negative*—the alarm that does not sound when it should. This may be a costly error, also; the fire burns down the building and lives are lost. Thus any action or nonaction in the face of irreducibly uncertain information always faces two risks—the consequences of a false positive or a false negative.

It is usually possible and often necessary to tinker with the alarm system. For example, it may be desirable to set it so that it is very sensitive, thus catching (almost) every event we want to catch. Unhappily, a very sensitive system will produce many false positives and may thus prove to be a very undesirable, costly system. (Automobile theft alarm systems and most home burglar alarm systems suffer from being overly sensitive.) The reverse error occurs when we set the system so that it is not sensitive enough; dangers fail to be detected and the consequences must be endured. *But the consequences may be different for different people.* For example, some segments of the population may have a greater interest in *avoiding* false alarms (and thus unhappily inviting the occurrence of undetected danger); those who must cope with the threat are usually in this category. (The police hate car alarms.) Others may have the reverse interest: those for whom a false alarm is of little consequence, such as the owner of the car with the overly sensitive alarm. The one who is adjusting the sensitivity of the system thus allocates greater risk to different segments of the population. In broader terms, *policymakers, not the person who suffers the risks, allocate the risks*, a matter to which I will return. The chief of police in Boulder, Colorado, has recently taken an action that illustrates this point nicely. He decided that because 99 percent of all burglar alarms are false the police will no longer respond to alarms: it is "not a good use of the department's officers"[19] This policy statement brought sharp criticism from business establishments and home owners, illustrating the point that each error develops its own constituency.

A second critical point to be observed is that, for any given level of accuracy, the link between the two types of errors is *rigid*. Decreasing false positives increases false negatives, and vice versa; decreasing one risk inevitably increases the other. It is that fact that makes policy formation under irreducible uncertainty so difficult, so subject to criticism, and so likely to produce injustice.

I will discuss this general problem in more detail in later sections of this chapter. At this point, however, I want to show the reader that although the concept of irreducible uncertainty and subsequent error has been with us for millennia, and the concept of false positives and false negatives for perhaps two thousand years, these ideas have yet to be fully recognized in the formation of social policy. Most important, the failure to do so is costly. Rather than attempt to persuade the reader of the truth of this assertion through abstract arguments, I present a brief history and current examples of formal attempts in two professional fields that reveal how we cope with the problem of false positives and false negatives in the modern world.

## Duality of Error in Law and Medicine

Irreducible uncertainty is tolerated under many circumstances, but it presents severe difficulties when there are large consequences of error, for an admission of irreducible uncertainty is an admission that the possibility of error—and its consequences— cannot be eliminated at the time the decision is to be made. As a result, doubt always remains. It may be large or infinitely small, but doubt there will be, and doubt brings fear, hesitancy, dispute, and even guilt over having taken an action that could be called a gamble. Much of this book will explore the consequences of doubt that refuses to disappear. We shall see its effects on the rationality of judgments and decisions and on the cyclical course of social policy, as well as how it induces guilt over errors.

Nowhere does this recognition of doubt occur more explicitly or with more human consequences than in courts of law. It is therefore not surprising that it was legal scholars who first wrote about the difficulties of "judging" in the face of irreducible uncertainty and recognized its consequences, inevitable error and unavoidable injustice. It was legal scholars who first recognized the *duality* of error.

### A Brief History of Doubt: False Positives and False Negatives in Law

B. J. Shapiro, in a remarkable history of doubt from 1600 to 1850, quotes from an 1850 Massachusetts court decision (*Commonwealth v. Webster*) as follows:

> It is not merely possible doubt; because every thing relating to human affairs, and depending on moral evidence, is open to some possible or imaginary doubt. [Note the clear expression of irreducible uncertainty in 1850; "every thing relating to human affairs

. . . is open to . . . doubt."] It is that state of the case, which, after the entire comparison and consideration of all the evidence, leaves the minds of jurors in that condition that they cannot say they feel an abiding conviction, to a moral certainty, of the truth of the charge. . . . The evidence must establish the truth of the fact to a reasonable and moral certainty; a certainty that convinces and directs the understanding, and satisfies the reason and judgment. . . . This we take to be proof beyond a reasonable doubt.[20]

Note that it is "reasonable judgment" that must be satisfied despite "reasonable doubt," a phrase still used. Here is the court's recognition of the uncertainty that cannot be reduced further when all that can be said and done has been. As we shall see, irreducible uncertainty is still a problem for judges and juries 150 years after *Commonwealth v. Webster.*

Allowing the Guilty to Escape in Order to Avoid
Punishing the Innocent

*The British Tradition.*   The first quantification of the ratio of false positives to false negatives is often attributed to Sir John Fortescue (c. 1394–1476). His suggested rule regarding false positives and false negatives is quoted in an 1895 U.S. Supreme Court ruling (*Coffin v. United States*): "One would rather that twenty guilty persons should escape punishment of death than that one innocent person should be condemned and suffer capitally."[21] Fortescue's fifteenth-century recommended ratio of false positives to false negatives was therefore 1 to 20. However, Fortescue's rule was not the only one to be remembered, for *Coffin v. United States* also cites Lord Hale (1678), who asserted, some 250 years after Fortescue's pronouncement, that "It is better five guilty persons should escape unpunished than one innocent person should die."[22]

So far as I can ascertain, Lord Hale did not explain why he chose a harsher rule than Sir John Fortescue, nor does *Coffin v. United States* pursue the question. Evidently, these citations were used by the court only to justify the tradition of the general principle of presumption of innocence. In fact, the Court could have cited a better known source, Sir William Blackstone (1723–1780), who offered still another ratio roughly one hundred years after Lord Hale: "It is better that ten guilty persons escape than one innocent suffer."[23] Blackstone not only was closer to Fortescue's more benevolent (to the accused) ratio of 20 to 1 than to Hale's 5 to 1; he also broadened his rule to include noncapital offenses. By 1972 the Supreme Court, in *Furman v. Georgia,* had discovered Blackstone's ratio; it quoted Justice William Douglas's paraphrase of it: "We believe that it is better for ten guilty people to be set free than for one innocent man to be unjustly imprisoned."[24]

My own informal survey of acquaintances in which I ask: "How many guilty persons should escape in order to prevent an innocent person from being unjustly punished?" has brought ratios ranging from "even" to "1,000 to 1," which I cite to indicate that wide disagreement remains regarding this most fundamental aspect of social policy. How different it would be to live in a society that followed Lord Hale's ratio of 5 to 1 than to live in a society in which that ratio was 1,000 to 1! And such variations may actually exist. In Japan 99 percent of all criminal defendants are found guilty; in Colombia only 3 percent of all murders result in convictions.[25]

Steps were taken later to clarify matters for judges and juries. Instead of appealing to a ratio, jurors are now instructed to adhere to three different "standards of proof," ranging from the least rigorous ("preponderance of the evidence") through the intermediate level ("clear and convincing evidence") to the most rigorous ("beyond a reasonable doubt"). Such differentiation is, of course, simply a way of attempting to apply different ratios of false negatives to false positives in different situations. The explicit use of different standards allows judges to indicate to juries that the acceptable ratio of false positives to false negatives—whatever it may be—is different for different types of offenses. Thus, the "preponderance of evidence" standard that is used in civil cases indicates to the jury that only slightly more often will the guilty go unpunished in order to prevent the innocent from being wrongly punished, whereas the ratio is somehow to be increased in the case of criminal justice; more—how many more, we don't know—guilty persons shall go unpunished in order to prevent punishment of the innocent.

D. K. Kagehiro has recently demonstrated what most psychologists—and others— would suspect: These verbal distinctions are of dubious value. On the basis of empirical work, Kagehiro concluded: "Quantified definitions, (in which the standard of proof was expressed in probability terms), and combined quantified and legal definitions had their intended effect; verdicts favoring the plaintiffs decreased in number as the standard of proof became stricter. *Nonquantified definitions did not achieve their intended effect on verdicts* [italics added]."[26]

Few members of the legal profession are likely to dispute or to be surprised by Kagehiro's conclusions. Although the legal language of doubt may be agreed upon, its consequences for the behavior of juries are far from clear.

*The Judaic Tradition.*   If we look at the Judaic tradition, we find the individual is favored over society to a greater degree than in the British tradition, as may be seen in this quotation from the twelfth century: *"It is better and more desirable to free a thousand sinners, than ever to kill one innocent."* Most interesting is the fact that this commandment from Maimonides (1135–1206), a famous Talmudic scholar, was quoted by an American judge in *U.S. vs. Fatico* in 1978.[27] The Judaic tradition has not been as closely studied as the British tradition, perhaps because it is older, but we do know that as early as the twelfth century Maimonides demonstrated that he clearly understood the idea of false positives and false negatives, for in his Negative Commandment 290 he put the matter very plainly and very differently from the British. Fortunately, a remarkable book by N. L. Rabinovitch titled *Probability and Statistical Inference in Ancient and Medieval Jewish Literature* provides many examples of statistical reasoning among rabbis and others during these periods. Rabinovitch observes that shortly after Maimonides, Rabbi Levi ben Gershon (1288–1344?) "went so far as to limit God's knowledge to the probable [by] arguing that 'perfect knowledge of a thing is to know it as it is' . . . that is to know that aspect that is determined and bounded and to know also that indeterminacy which is in it."[28] (That statement could be made today to refer to the distinction between true and error variance in modern statistical measures.) But so far as I know, ben Gershon did not link the meaning of indeterminancy to errors of different types, as did Maimonides.

Rabinovitch also cites Rabbi Joseph di Trani the elder as urging in the sixteenth century that decisions make use of what are now called "base rates":

> If the law is lenient for some alternatives but stringent for others, this gives two sets of possibilities, and the decision follows the larger set. In other words, follow the majority of possibilities.[29]

In the Memorandum dealing with *U.S. v. Fatico*, Judge Jack Weinstein thoroughly explores the problem of false positives and false negatives in the face of irreducible uncertainty. He not only reminds us that the concept of the duality of error has existed for at least a thousand years in the Hebraic tradition; he also calls our attention to Justinian's civil code. Judge Weinstein says that according to Sandy Zabell, a professor of mathematical statistics, the earliest reference to the abhorrence of punishment based on suspicion in nonreligious legal literature is found in the Digest: "The Divine Trajan stated in a Rescript to Assiduus Severus: 'It is better to permit the crime of a guilty person to go unpunished than to condemn one who is innocent'"[30]

Trajan's (A.D. 52–117) principle of compassion for individuals was not a mere pious expression devoid of application: Gibbon in his classic, *The Decline and Fall of the Roman Empire,* tells us that this principle was directly applied to the treatment of both Christians and Jews, who were assumed to constitute an equally serious threat to his rule. Without "general laws or decrees of the senate in force against the Christians,"[31] Trajan had little to support him in efforts to suppress either group. Gibbon's description of Trajan's "answer" to this problem is that "Trajan . . . discovers as much regard for justice and humanity as could be reconciled with his mistaken notions of religious policy. Instead of displaying the implacable zeal of an Inquisitor . . . the emperor expresses much more solicitude to protect the security of the innocent than to prevent the escape of the guilty."[32] It is interesting that Gibbon wrote this in England about two hundred years after Fortescue had proposed his "twenty to one" rule.

Had Gibbon been more interested in the appearance of the duality of error in human history, he could have pursued it beyond the Romans. For it appears early in the Bible, in Genesis in fact, under what must be considered very strange circumstances—in a book renowned for its strange circumstances.

The strange circumstances are these: Genesis tells the story of Abraham pleading with God to temper His demand for strict justice, specifically, the death penalty for the sinners of Sodom and Gomorrah (Genesis 18: 20–23). Abraham's plea interests us because in it God is confronted with irreducible uncertainty, inevitable error, and unavoidable injustice—*and* in quantitative form! For here we find Abraham asking God: "Wilt thou also destroy the righteous with the wicked?" That is, is God prepared to commit injustice? "Peradventure [what if] there be fifty righteous within the city: Wilt thou also destroy . . . the fifty righteous that are therein [as well as the sinners]?" Astonishingly, God accepts Abraham's plea; instead of destroying everyone, he will spare fifty innocent persons in order to avoid injustice to them. But now the parallel with contemporary circumstances increases, for Abraham now bargains with God over exactly how much injustice God will accept: What if "there shall lack five of the fifty righteous: Wilt thou destroy all of the city for lack of five?" God ignores Abraham's reference to five but accepts the relaxation of the criterion from fifty to forty-five: "If I find forty and five, I will not destroy it."

Abraham now apparently believes he has hit on a moral principle that God finds appropriate, for he then takes his argument one step further: What if "there shall be forty found there?" And God relaxes the criterion yet again: "I will not do it for forty's sake." And so on down to ten, which God also accepts, thus ending the dialogue.

Note that Abraham was careful to focus God's attention on one error only, the error of punishing the innocent in the attempt to punish the guilty. Sacrilegious as it might appear, a contemporary judgment researcher might well ask: Why didn't God remind Abraham about the *other* error—How many guilty persons will escape punishment if I do *not* destroy the city in order to save the lives of ten innocent persons? Of course, Abraham's God is considered to be omniscient; therefore, He knew about the duality of error; He just didn't bother to bring it up. Did this omission of a reference to the duality of error mark the beginning of a tradition? One might readily think so in view of the long history of policy discussions that focus only on the error that best serves the policy maker's constituents and ignores the other error and its consequences. Apparently this was Abraham's tactic, and apparently he was successful. So far as I can ascertain, there is no mention in this episode of the duality of error.[33]

Nevertheless, the Judaic-Christian tradition emphasizes mercy and compassion as well as strict justice, and, indeed, compassion seems to outweigh strict justice. Preference for the error that leads to "compassion" rather than the error that follows from "strict justice" may have its roots in Exodus, if not Genesis. There we find God's compassion directed toward the Jews who escaped from the Egyptians through the miraculous parting of the waters of the Red Sea and who then participated in a disgraceful orgy. For it is on this occasion, as told in Exodus, that God will be "keeping mercy for thousands, forgiving iniquity and transgression and sin [but] that will not clear the guilty" (Exodus 34:7). Indeed, it may well be that this celebrated occasion on which compassion is combined with an acknowledgment of "not clearing the guilty" that is the source of Fortescue's fifteenth-century dictum that it is better that twenty guilty be allowed to escape punishment than that one innocent person be wrongly punished.

Whether *Homo sapiens* understood the concept of the duality of error—either explained by an omniscient God or somehow part of the natural cognitive competence of the very first members of this species—is debatable. We are thus left uncertain as to whether *Homo sapiens* were, at an early date, endowed with this concept, either by the supernatural or by natural selection. If, however, we accept the "solicitude" attributed to Trajan, then we should conclude that the concept of the duality of error was recognized at least by some people roughly 2,000 years ago. Nevertheless, it did not become formalized by mathematicians until 1933 (as I describe in Chapter 2).

Modern Acknowledgments of the Duality of Error

Irreducible uncertainty is acknowledged frequently by judges but never more clearly than by Justice William Brennan in *In re Winship* when, quoting from an earlier case, he declared, "There is *always* [italics added] in litigation a margin of error in fact-finding."[34] Significantly, Brennan linked irreducible uncertainty to due process: "Due process commands that no man shall lose his liberty unless the government has borne the burden of . . . convincing the factfinder of his guilt."[35] In the same case, Justice John Harlan, also a Supreme Court justice of considerable reputation, agreed with Brennan's views about irreducible uncertainty: "In a judicial proceeding in which there is a dispute about the facts of some earlier event, the factfinder cannot acquire unassailably accurate knowledge of what happened. Instead all the factfinder can acquire is a belief of what *probably* happened."[36]

Justice Harlan went beyond the acknowledgment of irreducible uncertainty; he showed his awareness of two types of error:

> A second proposition . . . is that the trier of fact will sometimes, despite his best efforts, be wrong in his factual conclusions. In a lawsuit between two parties, a factual error can make a difference in one of two ways. First, it can result in a judgment in favor of the plaintiff when the true facts warrant a judgment for the defendant. The analogue in a criminal case would be the conviction of an innocent man. On the other hand, an erroneous factual determination can result in a judgment for the defendant when the true facts justify a judgment in plaintiff's favor. The criminal analogue would be the acquittal of a guilty man.
>
> The standard of proof influences the relative frequency of these two types of erroneous outcomes. If, for example, the standard of proof for a criminal trial were a preponderance of the evidence rather than proof beyond a reasonable doubt, there would be a smaller risk of factual errors that result in freeing guilty persons, but a far greater risk of factual errors that result in convicting the innocent. Because the standard of proof affects the comparative frequency of these two types of erroneous outcomes, the choice of the standard to be applied in a particular kind of litigation should, in a rational world, reflect an assessment of the comparative social disutility of each.[37]

Although Harlan did not indicate what the ratio of errors should be, he did state his preference regarding which error should prevail:

> I view the requirement of proof beyond a reasonable doubt in a criminal case as bottomed on a fundamental value determination of our society that it is far worse to convict an innocent man than to let a guilty man go free.[38]

Those ringing words might well seem to have settled the matter by 1970: "Proof beyond a reasonable doubt" seems to lead directly to a value judgment that the error of letting the guilty go free is preferable to the error of convicting an innocent person. But Justice Hugo Black dissented. After admitting that he had joined in some opinions that stated that "proof of a criminal charge beyond a reasonable doubt is constitutionally required," he then stated his revised views:

> The Court has never clearly held, however, that proof beyond a reasonable doubt is either expressly or impliedly commanded by any provision of the Constitution. . . . Nowhere in that document [is] there any statement that conviction of crime requires proof of guilt beyond a reasonable doubt. . . . I shall not at any time surrender my belief that that document itself should be our guide, not our own concept of what is fair, decent, and right. . . . I prefer to put my faith in the words of the written Constitution itself rather than to rely on the shifting day-to-day standards of fairness of individual judges.[39]

Although we do not learn from Justice Black exactly what his personal error preference is, time has favored Justices Brennan and Harlan; their views of what the Constitution implies have prevailed over Justice Black's, and as a result their concept of reasonable doubt and their error preference prevails today. If Justice Black were to return to the Court after a quarter century's absence, however, he might feel that time had stood still. For he would find that "the shifting day-to-day standards of fairness of individual judges" remain as much an issue in the 1990s as they ever were. Not only is this issue reflected in today's mandatory sentencing rules (about which more later), but concern over error continues to evoke disputes at the U.S. Supreme Court.

In 1994 Justice Harry Blackmun, in a highly publicized decision, announced that "from this day forward I no longer shall tinker with the machinery of death"[40] and thus proclaimed the death penalty to be unconstitutional. But he was also forthright in his acknowledgment of potential, indeed, inevitable, error: "The problem is that the *inevitability* [italics added] of factual, legal, and moral error gives us a system that we know must wrongly kill some defendants."[41] He was directly challenged by Justice Antonin Scalia, whose stand would have cheered Justice Black. For Justice Antonin Scalia, opposed Justice Blackmun's dissent by referring to the "text and tradition of the Constitution" and asserted that it "ought to control,"[42] much as Justice Black preferred to put his "faith in the words of the written Constitution,"[43] thus implying that strict adherence to the text of the Constitution would somehow prevent the occurrence of the opposite error, a topic to which I now turn.

Punishing the Innocent to Prevent the Escape of the Guilty

Justice for individuals has not always been given priority, however. Throughout history Blackstone's ratio has been reversed; punishing the innocent to avoid the escape of the guilty has frequently been the error of choice. Despite the long Anglo-Saxon and Judaic history of favoring justice for the individual, Blackstone's ratio was reversed in clear, well publicized, and often boastful fashion by the Germans in World War II. Frequently members of entire communities were executed as punishment for the act of a single person (e.g., shooting a German soldier). American soldiers in Vietnam were accused of similar actions. Wu Ningkun[44] describes the willingness of a government to punish the innocent in an effort to prevent the escape of the guilty in his story of his return to China. Although a dedicated communist, he suffered long imprisonment by the Chinese government after his return. He notes that his treatment was "ordinary" because, in order "to catch a half a dozen 'genuine rightists' the great, glorious and correct party had not scrupled to net half a million innocent intellectuals and their families for a devastating ordeal of 22 years."[45] Less dramatic examples can be found in ordinary circumstances; many of us can remember instances of an entire classroom of children being punished for the act of a single child.

It seems clear that when a government, or some element of it, believes that it is under siege and that its rule is threatened, ruthless pursuit of the guilty becomes standard practice and punishment of the innocent an error that is readily tolerated. One of the prime examples of a government long committed to Blackstone's ratio reversing itself under threat is the action of the United States when it imprisoned Japanese-American citizens shortly after the Japanese bombing of Pearl Harbor in 1941. Tens of thousands of undoubtedly loyal citizens, many of whom actually served in combat in the U.S. Army *after* being imprisoned, were thus punished in order to prevent the escape of those who *might* in the future be guilty of sabotage. The nation's collective guilt over this action became evident when the U.S. government, approximately fifty years later, offered payments to survivors. Allowing the guilty to escape in order to protect the innocent appears to be a luxury of peace and security. In short, both types of error remain acceptable today; choice of error is conditional upon the security of the policymaker.

*Values Determine Error Preference.*    Terry Connolly's analysis of the consequences of irreducible uncertainty takes us one step beyond the recognition of the duality of error.[46] Although his analysis increases the complexity of the issues, I present his main ideas because he advances the discussion in an important way.

Until this point I have discussed only the probabilities associated with the two errors. But Connolly points out that uncertainty results in *four* probabilities: (1) the probability of conviction when guilty ($P_{cg}$); (2) the probability of conviction when innocent ($P_{ci}$); (3) the probability of acquittal when innocent ($P_{ai}$); and (4) the probability of acquittal when guilty ($P_{ag}$). These probabilities are illustrated in Table 1-1.

All four actions are possible; two are correct, two are in error. But since irreducible uncertainty prevails, there is a probability associated with all four—the two correct actions and the two erroneous ones.

The first observation made by Connolly following the presentation of the four cells is that presenting only two cells—Blackstone's ratio (ten innocent to be freed rather than convict one innocent, thus 10:1)—can be quite misleading. For the ratio in fact depends on the mix of cases brought before the court as well as the rule adopted: "Other things being equal, a doubling of the ratio of [truly] guilty to [truly] innocent defendants brought before the court will double Blackstone's ratio."[47] That is, under these conditions Blackstone's ratio will change from 10 to 1 to 20 to 1. One must consider all four cells—those in which correct actions are taken as well as those in which incorrect actions are taken.[48]

Although Connolly makes no claim to be first to show the need for considering all four cells of judicial decision making under uncertainty, his demonstration of the effect of the ratio of the truly innocent to the truly guilty on Blackstone's ratio is important, for it shows that one might believe the ratio to apply when it doesn't.

Table 1-1    Four probabilities associated with two actions by a jury and two states of truth.

|  |  | Truth | |
| --- | --- | --- | --- |
|  |  | Innocent | Guilty |
| Jury | Acquittal | $P_{ai}$ (correct) | $P_{ag}$ (error) |
|  | Conviction | $P_{ci}$ (error) | $P_{cg}$ (correct) |

Second, and most important, Connolly calls our attention to the fact that different values will be placed on each of the four cells and that brings us to a new topic—the relative values associated with each correct decision and each error. That is to say, not only may the same person assign different values to the different cells; different persons may assign different values to each of the four actions. If, for example, one's values are such that one weights acquitting the innocent more highly than convicting the guilty, the cell containing $P_{ai}$ will receive greater weight than the cell containing $P_{cg}$. And, of course, persons will differ in their differential assignment of weights to these cells. But if one is not aware of the possibilities inherent in such decisions, confusion and poorly informed disputes are inevitable.

In short, any analysis of judicial philosophy regarding error preference should contain the social *values* as well as the *probabilities* associated with each (as in Table 1-2). This structure of the problem should be made clear to the persons taking the action if the decision is to be an informed one, but, of course, it never is. Nor is it obvious that the Supreme Court justices who discussed these error preferences were aware of the two points emphasized by Connolly: the application of Blackstone's (or any other policy) ratio is dependent on the mix of cases brought before the court, and the verdict is based implicitly on a four-cell table that includes the relative weights placed on all four outcomes indicated in the table. The Greeks didn't know this; neither did the scholars of the Middle Ages. It is doubtful that modern justices do. Is the situation different in the field of medicine?

## Medicine

Physicians have always lived with irreducible uncertainty in diagnosis, prognosis, therapy, and, indeed, virtually all phases of their professional activities—and, of course, they still do. Error has long been acknowledged to be a significant element of their work, which physicians and their researchers have energetically and successfully aimed at reducing—to a degree. But recognition of the duality of error—the false positive and false negative—and its formal introduction into the education of medical students and practitioners has occurred only within the last fifty years or so, centuries after their appearance in the practice of law.

### False Positives and False Negatives in Medical Research

In response to a query from me, Professor Harry Marks of the Institute of the History of Medicine at Johns Hopkins University looked into the history of the concepts

Table 1-2   Four probabilities (*P*) and values (*V*) associated with two actions by a jury and two states of truth.

|  |  | Truth | |
| --- | --- | --- | --- |
|  |  | Innocent | Guilty |
| Jury | Acquittal | $P_{ai}(V_1)$ | $P_{ag}(V_2)$ |
|  | Conviction | $P_{ci}(V_3)$ | $P_{cg}(V_4)$ |

of error in medicine. Although Professor Marks would not wish his reply to me to be considered definitive, the results of his efforts are highly informative. For example, he found the first evidence of the use of the terms "false positive" and "false negative" in a report of a study by the U.S. Public Health Service titled *The Evaluation of Serodiagnostic Tests for Syphilis in the United States*, published by several authors, that was read at a Conference of the American Society of Clinical Pathologists in 1935.[49] In addition to those terms, the terms "sensitivity" and "specificity," which are analogous and now in frequent use in medicine, also appear. These concepts were employed then exactly as they are today, with the exception that the customary fourfold table was not used. Nor did the report make any reference to any other articles; there is no bibliography. Nevertheless, it is clear that the authors were well aware of what they were doing. We may assume, therefore, that at least some epidemiologists were aware of these concepts at least fifty years ago.

An article by Jacob Yerushalmy that appeared in 1947 apparently was responsible for bringing the false positive/negative concept to the attention of the medical community.[50] According to Marks, Yerushalmy's article "seems to have started something," for three important articles followed shortly thereafter: J. Berkson on cost utility;[51] S. Greenhouse and N. Mantel on the evaluation of diagnostic tests;[52] and W. J. Youden on an index for rating diagnostic tests.[53] The question remains, however, whether these ideas had in fact made their way into medicine before 1947, for the article by J. Neyman and E. S. Pearson that introduced the idea of Type I and Type II errors (analogous to false positives and false negatives) was published in 1933.[54] Because researchers, if not practitioners, in medicine, are generally quite sophisticated in statistical matters and read statistical journals, one would not expect a decade to intervene between the introduction of these ideas and their use. Moreover, the fact that the report on diagnostic tests for syphilis appeared in 1935 suggests that some epidemiologists were aware of Neyman's and Pearson's 1933 article. The epidemiological research was carried out within what is generally called the "frequentist" theory of probability; that is, the researchers count the relative frequency of cases that occur in one category or another and thus calculate the probability of the two types of errors under discussion.

A different approach to probability focuses largely on subjective "probability judgments" made by persons who observe the numbers (or other information) in various categories (or displays). The emphasis on subjective probabilities was introduced into medicine by R. S. Ledley and L. B. Lusted[55] and later by Lusted[56] in a landmark book, *Introduction to Medical Decision Making*. Lusted later described his point of departure

> We [Ledley and Lusted] observed that medical knowledge was usually presented as symptoms associated with a disease, rather than the reverse, that is, the diseases associated with a symptom. In probability terms we said medical knowledge should be expressed as the probability of a disease given the patient's symptoms. This information is what the physician needs to know for the diagnosis of a particular patient's condition.[57]

But when Ledley and Lusted wrote up these ideas and offered them to medical journals, every one refused to publish their manuscript. It was published in *Science*, however, and was an instant hit; there were hundreds of requests for reprints, and it was promptly translated into Russian. (So much for the wisdom of peer review!)

The authors' suggestion in the paragraph just quoted amounts to this: Medical students are taught about diseases—that is, what diseases do, how they disrupt the normal functions of various physiological systems, and how they manifest themselves in various signs and symptoms. In frequentist terms, the student must learn that given a disease X, the probability (relative frequency) of occurrence of symptom Y is large or small. But the practicing physician is faced only with the signs and symptoms (Y) and must infer or deduce the disease, X. Thus, the practicing physician is faced with the opposite of the problem given to the student—that is, given Y (the symptom), what is the probability of X (the disease)? (Or, more to the point, what is the probability of each of several possible diseases $X_1, X_2, \ldots, X_n$?) Ledley and Lusted were pointing out that students were being provided with one type of probability knowledge (given X, the probability of Y is . . . ) in their textbooks, when in practice they need to learn, somehow, the opposite—given Y, what is the probability of X?[58]

These questions lead directly to the calculation of false positives and false negatives. Lusted offers the following example from an earlier study in which he asked physicians to decide on the basis of an x-ray

> whether there was evidence of tuberculosis or no evidence of tuberculosis. The opinion of eight expert radiologists was used as the "gold standard" [a criterion of truth] for comparison. A performance score of each physician was computed as the percentage of positive tuberculosis cases that he called negative (percent false-negative cases) and the percentage of negative cases that he called positive for tuberculosis (false-positive cases).[59]

This may well have been the first time that the false-positive, false-negative concept was employed in research on subjective probabilities in medical decision making, although, as we have seen, the duality of error had been introduced at least by 1947 in epidemiological (frequentist) research.

## Current Application of the Duality of Error Concept in Medicine

Medical researchers, if not clinicians, thus apparently became aware of the duality of error approximately fifty years ago in frequentist terms and some thirty-five years ago in subjectivist terms. There seems little doubt that there is widespread awareness of this concept in medical research today and that many medical schools routinely teach their students about it. Nevertheless, there is also reason to doubt that this concept is currently used as widely as might be hoped or expected. For example, in a widely known textbook edited by two well-known authors, J. C. Bailar III and F. Mosteller,[60] J. A. Freiman and his coauthors present a chapter in which they survey two sets of "negative" trials—that is, clinical trials in which negative results were reported regarding patient improvement in response to treatment. Specifically, in 1978 they examined seventy-one controlled trials that produced negative results and found that "sixty-seven of the trials had a greater than 10 percent risk of missing a true 25 percent therapeutic improvement, and with the same [10%] risk, 50 of the trials could have missed a 50 percent improvement."[61] They observe that "a follow-up of this study 10 years later, this time including 65 'negative' randomized controlled trials from 1988, revealed no essential improvement in recognition of the importance of beta [false negatives]."[62] They summarize by saying that "the conclusion is inescapable that many of the therapies discarded as ineffective after inconclusive negative trials may still have a clinically important effect."[63] This is a startling conclusion indeed in an age when clinical trials are very costly and when it is unlikely that, after a failure, a therapy will be tried a second time. (In a later chapter I will describe the current intense dispute over whether the Food and Drug Administration favors false negatives over false positives.)

Further evidence that current research does not take account of the duality of error is shown in an article in the *Journal of the American Medical Association*. The paper reviewed fifty-four evaluations of the "clinical efficacy of diagnostic imaging with magnetic resonance [MRI procedure]." The authors found that "the terms sensitivity, *specificity, false-positive* or *false-negative, accuracy*, and *predictive values* were used infrequently [see Table 1-3]. . . . Not one evaluation contained an appropriate statistical analysis of the distributions of quantitative readings."[64] Again, a startling conclusion—fifty-four evaluations with infrequent reference to false positives or false negatives as recently as 1988!

Thus it seems fair to conclude that although some medical researchers are aware of the problems raised by irreducible uncertainty and the statistical methods developed to cope with the duality of error that follows from it, it is not yet standard practice for medical researchers to employ these ideas. This state of affairs becomes all the more puzzling when one realizes that false positives and false negatives are frequently discussed in the press, as the next examples show.

### Implications for Social Policy of Irreducible Uncertainty and the Duality of Error in Medicine

Recognition of errors of both kinds now appears with increasing frequency in the daily press in reports on decisions by the Food and Drug Administration (FDA) to permit or not to permit the sale of drugs for use in treating life-threatening diseases such as AIDS, Alzheimer's disease, and prostate and breast cancer. The desperate situations of patients suffering from these diseases puts extreme pressure on the FDA to license unproven drugs. The argument is often reduced to "What have these patients got to lose by taking an unproven drug?" The medical profession and the

Table I-3   Fourfold Table of Diagnosis Applied to Magnetic Resonance Imaging.*

| Magnetic Resonance Image | Disease or Disorder | |
|---|---|---|
| | Present | Absent |
| Abnormal | True positive (a) | False positive (b) |
| Normal | False negative (c) | True negative (d) |

*Sensitivity is calculated as a/(a + c); specificity, d/(b + d); positive predictive value, a/(a + b); and negative predictive value, d/(c + d).
Source: Cooper, Chalmers, McCally, Berrier, & Sacks, 1988, p. 3278.

FDA often reply, in effect, "A great deal—possibly," thus presenting the patient and family with irreducible uncertainty.

Current examples are easy to find—I offer one later in this chapter—but the persistence of the social policy problems created by irreducible uncertainty is the most important lesson here. This persistence is apparent when one considers that the same issues exist today in connection with the introduction of AIDS-related drugs that were apparent when sulfonamides were first introduced in the mid-1930s. It is perhaps shocking that although enormous scientific and technical progress has been made in the production of therapeutic medicine, little progress has been made in the intervening half century with respect to improving the manner in which human judgment is brought to bear on their *use*. Are we any better at making effective use of scientific information in medicine than we are in law?

B. H. Lerner's history of the development of the use of sulfonamides in the 1930s draws strong parallels with the current FDA dilemma. He notes that in the "largely unfettered [by federal control] sulfonamide era":

> When faced with life-threatening infections and no other therapeutic modalities, clinical researchers generally prescribed sulfonamides for all patients rather than conduct controlled trials. They justified this practice on the basis of animal data and isolated clinical reports. This strategy often proved unwise. Patients sometimes suffered toxic and even fatal reactions to drugs they should not have received.[65]

But, Lerner noticed:

> Occasionally, researchers investigating severe infections, such as Evans and Gaisford, included an untreated control group. The fact that 19 more deaths occurred among their 100 untreated patients with pneumonia, however, helps to explain why Evans and Gaisford's contemporaries usually treated all their subjects: Withholding therapy—even unproven therapy—meant that patients might die unnecessarily. The current willingness to prescribe zidovudine and FK-506 to all patients, then, represents the continuation of a long clinical tradition. When confronted with life-threatening disease and no alternative treatments, physicians sacrifice design in order to attempt to save lives.[66]

That is, physicians prefer to make the error of using the drug when they shouldn't, rather than not use it when they should. It is very easy to see from these circumstances how error can readily translate into injustice. Doctors with humanitarian motives recognize this and seek to avoid injustice to specific patients whose lives have been entrusted to them. As Lerner observes in discussing the FDA's policies in the 1990s:

> By releasing medications before completion of definitive studies, the new, less stringent FDA regulations place the interests of current patients ahead of the long-term concerns of science and future patients. As a result, decision making by doctors and patients is becoming more autonomous, but it is also . . . becoming less informed. . . . In this sense, modern practitioners will be operating in an atmosphere similar to that experienced by their counterparts 60 years ago.[67]

The print media take this issue out of the arena of arcane medical journals and make plain the relationship between irreducible uncertainty, inevitable error, and unavoidable injustice. The following excerpt, from an article in the *New York Times,* describes a massive effort to screen men for prostate cancer; it makes explicit the anxiety created by irreducible uncertainty and its consequences. The *New York Times* reported:

> A drug company is sponsoring a nationwide effort to screen more than half a million middle-aged and elderly men for prostate cancer amid heated disagreement over whether the testing will do more harm than good.
>
> The debate is fueled by the imprecision of the detection tools. They may suggest cancer in up to a third of men who are screened but who are actually cancer-free. Or they may fail to pick up a smaller but significant number of potentially deadly cancers. Also being weighed are the costs of follow-up tests for the many men with suspicious findings on the initial exams. Another concern is that test results that suggest or establish the presence of cancer may generate unnecessary anxiety even when patients are assured that the tumor is tiny, localized and either curable or not in need of treatment. . . .
>
> But Dr. Curtis Mettlin, who has been directing a national study of prostate cancer screening for the American Cancer Society, offered a different view. "For myself," he said, "I'd rather be unnecessarily cured of a disease than to fail to be cured of a disease that could be the cause of my death."[68]

It didn't end there. The next stage of testing indicated not only that the test was of dubious predictive value but that its advocacy was tainted by the fact the drug companies urging the tests were among several that "picked up the entire $80,649 hotel tab" for the four-day conference of urologists from which a "crucial step toward the screening recommendation" was made.[69] Of course, information of this sort increases the uncertainty about the value of the screening procedure over and beyond its false positives and false negatives.

In short, uncertainty in medicine is treated roughly the same today as it was a half century ago. There is little evidence that we are any more proficient today at making use of the hard-won medical knowledge that is available to us than we were a half century ago, and much evidence that we are not. Irreducible uncertainty and its inevitable consequences remain formidable barriers to an effective distribution of that knowledge.

Judgment under uncertainty is one of the most pervasive and difficult aspects of life. Uncertainty in the creation of social policy makes error inevitable, and error makes injustice unavoidable. These conclusions were recognized in antiquity; yet it is only within the past five hundred years that they were formalized in jurisprudence; today they remain somewhat cloudy in the administration of justice. Medicine has only recently begun to take steps to cope with the consequences of uncertainty, despite the introduction of useful statistical methods more than fifty years ago.

Coping with irreducible uncertainty is one of the most formidable tasks facing us. Chapter 2 shows how the duality of error in social policy-making has been neglected, and with what consequences.

# 2 Duality of Error and Policy Formation

The distinctive character of practical activity, one which is so inherent that it cannot be eliminated, is the uncertainty which attends it.

—*John Dewey*

Grave errors of judgment are brought to our attention as a result of catastrophes immediately linked to wrong decisions. The explosion of the space shuttle *Challenger* in January 1986 is such a catastrophe; it will stand out for generations not because of a large loss of life but because of its dramatic character—a flaming explosion high in the sky—captured on television and replayed countless times. In addition, it is a clear and compelling example of how a wrong decision—"launch" instead of "don't launch"—produced a catastrophe. The *Challenger* disaster clearly was the result of a decision made under uncertainty and thus increased the visibility of this topic.

In order to understand the situation confronting the launch managers, and its implications for judgment and policy, we need to approach the subject of probability, a highly technical, perhaps arcane, topic involving philosophy and mathematics. But this is not a technical book and there are thousands of books on statistics and probability, so we need not approach it very closely. All we need to do is to grasp the distinction between the two major views of probability so that we can see how they affect human judgment and social policy.

Despite their fundamental differences, the two views—frequentist and subjectivist—have survived in peaceful coexistence for centuries. The *frequentist* view defines and explains probability in terms of the relative frequency of repeatable events. For example, the frequency of specific repeatable events (i.e., heads on tosses of a coin) relative to the total number of trials (tosses) defines the probability (i.e., heads relative to tosses) of the event (heads). It is this theory that led to the development of the "normal probability distribution" of events, the "bell curve" recently given prominence by a controversial book of that title by Richard J. Herrnstein and Charles Murray.[1] The normal probability curve has the distinction of being one of the great

36

achievements of mathematics and statistics, prized because it brings together the coherence afforded by mathematics and a host of empirical realities; the mathematical explication of the bell curve fits many, many empirical phenomena. Indeed, the theoretical and empirical match plays such a large role in modern society that it is hard to imagine how we could function without it.

A second view of probability—the *subjectivist* view—relies not on relative frequencies but on subjective judgments of single, unrepeatable events. What is the probability that *this* bridge will fall down next year? That *this* child will succeed in school this term? That *this* person is guilty of the crime in question? Thus, the probability of interest lies within the cognitive system of the person making the judgment of probability rather than in the behavior of numerous objective events.

There is a large system of mathematics supporting and explicating both the subjectivist and the frequentist, or objectivist, views. Expert statisticians are familiar with both views; students, on the other hand, rarely learn about the subjectivist view.[2] Arcane as its roots may be, this distinction can be of considerable significance, even a matter of life and death, as suggested in the following section.

## Misconceiving Probabilities and Its Consequences

Richard Feynman's comments on the *Challenger* disaster and the way they were treated by other experts deserve our close attention because almost everyone is now familiar with the idea that Feynman was not only a Nobel Prize winner but a genius.[3] The following excerpt is from an article in *Science* published in 1986:

> "When playing Russian roulette, the fact that the first shot got off safely is little comfort for the next," writes Richard Feynman in a scathing commentary he released on the space shuttle disaster. . . .
>
> Feynman objects most strongly to NASA's way of calculating risks. Data collected since the early days of the space program, including records used by NASA's range safety officer, Louis Ullian, show that about one in every 25 solid rocket boosters has failed. About 2900 have been launched, with 121 losses. Feynman says it is reasonable to adjust the anticipated crash rate a bit lower (to 1 in 50) to take account of today's better technology. He would even permit a little more tinkering with the numbers (to 1 in 100), to take credit for exceptionally high standards of part selection and inspection. In this way, the *Challenger* accident, the first solid rocket failure in 25 shuttle launches (with two boosters each), fits perfectly into Feynman's adjusted rate of one crash per 50 to 100 rocket firings.[4]

Here we can see Feynman taking the frequency view of probability. But then he learned that NASA was taking a subjectivist view.

> But Feynman was stunned to learn that NASA rejects the historical data and claims the actual risk of a crash is only 1 in 100,000. This is the official figure as published in "Space Shuttle Data for Planetary Mission RTG Safety Analysis" on 15 February 1985. It means NASA thinks it could launch the shuttle, as is, every day for the next 280 years and expect not one equipment-based disaster. Feynman searched for the origin of this optimism and found that it was "engineering judgment," pure and simple. Feynman concluded that NASA, "for whatever purpose . . . exaggerates the reliability of its product to the point of fantasy."[5]

That is, without doubt, severe criticism. But that remark tells us more; it shows that Feynman is apparently committed to a frequentist (objectivist) point of view, whereas NASA explicitly ignores it, as may be seen in these remarks by NASA's chief engineer:

> It is not really as bad as that, according to Milton Silveira, NASA's chief engineer in Washington. "We don't use that number as a management tool," he said in a telephone interview. "We know that the probability of failure is always sitting there, and we are always looking for it and trying to prevent it." The 1 in 100,000 figure was hatched for the Department of Energy (DOE), he says, for use in a risk analysis DOE puts together on radioactive hazards on some devices carried aboard the shuttle. . . .
>
> To speak in DOE's language, NASA translates its "engineering judgment" into numbers. How does it do this? One NASA official said, "They get all the top engineers together down at Marshall Space Flight Center and ask them to give their best judgment of the reliability of all the components involved." The engineers' *adjectival* [italics added] descriptions are then converted to numbers. For example, Silveira says, "frequent" equals 1 in 100; "reasonably probable" equals 1 in 1000; "occasional" equals 1 in 10,000; and "remote" equals 1 in 100,000.
>
> When all the judgments [i.e., subjective judgments] were summed up and *averaged,* [italics added] the risk of a shuttle booster explosion was found to be 1 in 100,000. That number was then handed over to DOE for further processing.[6]

This startling figure (1 in 100,000) was thus a product of "engineering judgment," a probability derived not from a historical record of relative frequencies but a judgment (actually an indefensible *average* of a number of persons' subjective judgments—just as *The Wall Street Journal* averages 44 economists' predictions) of *current* circumstances that includes improvements mentioned by Feynman (which he assessed by means of *his* subjective judgment). Thus, if there is a difference between Feynman and the NASA officials, it must be that Feynman used subjective methods only when he had to, whereas NASA failed to use frequentist methods when it could have and, perhaps, *should* have. In his press conference of June 10, 1986, Feynman went to considerable lengths to justify his use of the frequentist approach but did not acknowledge that, on occasion, the subjective approach *must* be used, as his own behavior indicated.

The strong differences between those who (apparently implicitly) hold different views on probability are evident in the remark of a "consultant":

> "The process," [meaning the process of collecting and averaging subjective judgments] says one consultant who clashed with NASA, "is positively medieval." He thinks Feynman hit the nail exactly on the head. There are ways of taking experience into account while totting up the statistics, he added, but "once you divorce it from a scientific process, you make it susceptible to the whims of political necessity." Unless the risk estimates are based on some actual performance data, he says, "it's all tomfoolery."[7]

But this comment also has its share of ambiguity. What does the consultant mean by "scientific process"? By referring to "actual performance data" he makes it sound as if "scientific process" means counting relative frequencies. But many scientists would call that "blind empiricism," lacking coherence (about which more later) and hardly worthy of the term "scientific process." And, they would argue, it is precisely the engineers' judgments that *do* take the "scientific process" into consideration, whereas "blind empiricism" doesn't.

There is no doubt about the disagreement among experts about the probability of a particular disaster. In the *Challenger* case, what was discouraging was that confusion remained rampant among the scientists, engineers, and administrators *long after the event*. One should not be surprised, then, to find that there was confusion among the managers *during* the pressures of the night-long assessment of the risks associated with the launch.[8]

## *Only One Type of Error?*

Left out of all the discussion of the risk of one error (allowing the launch to be made when it shouldn't have been) was a discussion or even a recognition of the other possible error—*not* allowing the launch to be made when it should have been. Yet that error surely was in everyone's mind: "What if it is discovered that we held back *unnecessarily* or failed to launch when we should have?" There was no calculation of that probability comparable to Feynman's calculations of the probabilities of the error of a disaster. How should the unmentioned probability have been calculated? And what would the consequences of that error have been? Of course, we know that the consequences of wrongly launching were of enormous proportions, but what would have been the consequences of failing to launch when the launch was in fact safe? We can only guess. A congressional uproar? Some managers might have lost their jobs? Although there is no indication that this kind of error and its consequences were explicitly considered, there can be little doubt that fear of this error was on everyone's mind. Thus, there are two aspects of the tragedy of the *Challenger* that are related to the theme of this book: The distinction between objective and subjective uncertainty was ignored, and the duality of error was ignored.

I pause for a moment to ask the reader to contrast the competence—the enormous amount of engineering ingenuity, knowledge, and skill that went into the ability to construct the spacecraft *Challenger*, and all those spacecrafts and rockets that preceded it, as well as the launching and communication systems that made it possible—with the ineptitude in the exercise of human judgment that led to the ill-fated launch. Rarely do we have an opportunity to see so plainly the contrast between our coherent knowledge of the physical world and our skill in applying that knowledge under conditions of uncertainty. Yet, in all likelihood, few experts would have performed differently or will perform differently in the next situation of deep uncertainty.

## *The Statisticians' Review*

Some years after the *Challenger's* explosion, a team of professional statisticians revisited the disaster to try to sort out the many probability assessments that surrounded the event at the time. What, they asked, was the correct probability estimate of an O-ring failure on the day of the *Challenger* launch? S. R. Dalal and his coauthors used the "data from the 23 preaccident launches . . . to predict O-ring performance under the *Challenger* launch conditions."[9] They concluded that "there is strong sta-

tistical evidence of a temperature effect on incidents of O-ring thermal distress."
Indeed, "at 31 degrees F., the temperature at which *Challenger* was launched" there
was "at least a 13% probability of catastrophic field-joint O-ring failure."[10] This probability is higher than Feynman's estimate of 1 in 50, or 2 percent. Was this probability too high to risk the launch had it been known to the managers? We don't know,
because we don't know what the threshold probability was—what probability was
too high to risk a launch. In fact, we don't know today if NASA has such a figure in
mind for launches. Was a probability threshold specified before the *Challenger*
launch? No one ever mentioned one. But if one was specified, how was it calculated?
Was it calculated by a subjectivist? By a frequentist? What if they differed? Who
would decide which threshold to use? Who would decide which approach—subjectivist or frequentist—to use? No one can authoritatively answer those questions today.

## The Slow Formal Recognition of the Duality of Error

The eighteenth-century French probability theorists the Marquis de Condorcet (1743–
1794) and Laplace long ago saw that probability theory carried implications for social policy formation. But it was not until Neyman and Pearson wrote their famous
article in 1933 that the duality of error (they referred to Type I and Type II errors)
was formally introduced and treated mathematically.[11] In their landmark article, they
recalled that Laplace had demonstrated the social implication of false positives and
false negatives when he asked: "Is it more serious to convict an innocent man or to
acquit a guilty?"[12] Neyman and Pearson indicated that the answer depended on social
value judgments, and they quickly eschewed a role in forming such judgments: "From
the point of view of mathematical theory all we can do is show how the risk of errors
may be controlled and minimized. The use of these statistical tools in any given case,
in determining just how the balance should be struck, must be left to the investigator."[13] They were thinking of the researcher as "investigator," but their intention was
clear: The statistician was not to set the criterion by which the relative frequency of
either error was to be made; that was to be done by policymakers. It was not until
well into the twentieth century that scholarship produced a formal, mathematical treatment of the duality of error.

Following the Neyman and Pearson article, H. C. Taylor and J. T. Russell introduced the idea of the inevitable linkage between uncertainty and false positives and
false negatives into psychology. But they did so using a diagram and without men-
tioning these concepts by name.[14]

Type I and Type II errors were introduced to psychologists by Q. McNemar in
his 1949 statistics textbook, but he gave no indication of their source (one might have
supposed he thought of them himself), nor did he use the term false positive or false
negative.[15] These terms initially appear in psychological research in W. B. Tanner
Jr. and J. A. Swets,[16] but it was the introduction of signal detection theory in the early
1950s that brought the importance of the matter home to psychologists.[17]

### Signal Detection Theory

Signal detection theory (SDT) provides one of the best and most sophisticated
approaches to the problem of judgment and decision making in the face of irreduc-

ible uncertainty and duality of error. Moreover, it makes plain the inevitable consequences of uncertainty—injustice to some. SDT offers an excellent clarification of the fact-versus-value problem in addition to its other advantages.

Origins of SDT

SDT apparently was first developed in the early 1950s by John Swets, Wilson Tanner, David Green, Theodor Birdsall, and their colleagues. The theory was brought to the attention of psychologists in 1954 by an article in the *Psychological Review* by Tanner and Swets.[18] Because the theory originated in the study of psychophysics (the psychology of discriminating among stimuli) and because psychophysics prizes simple cases, SDT began with the simple case of one stimulus (a signal) to be discriminated from another (noise)—obviously a very important discrimination and one highly relevant to electronic communication.

The basic theory is that

> For any criterion, there will be four kinds of decision outcome: two types of errors, false positive and false negative, and two types of correct decisions, true positive and true negative. A fundamental point is that a compensatory relationship exists among the proportions, or probabilities, of the four outcomes. Exactly where the positivity criterion is set determines the balance among those proportions. If a low or lenient criterion is set, the proportions of both true-positive and false-positive outcomes will be relatively high and the proportions of both true-negative and false-negative outcomes will be relatively low. The converse is the case when a high or strict criterion is set.[19]

Once the numbers become available, all these calculations can be made and the consequences of any specific setting of the decision criterion can be determined. That is, we can determine just how many, or what proportions of, false positives and false negatives will (or would be) produced, as well as the proportion of true positives and true negatives. And when it is possible to calculate the *costs* of the errors and the *benefits* of identifying the true positives and true negatives, we can determine the cost/benefit ratio that follows from a specific action—that is, the decision criterion at a point that produced these propositions. But as Swets points out: "The concept of adjusting the threshold to the situation is [still] not appreciated in many important practical arenas."[20]

Generality and Applicability of SDT

Once it was recognized that it was not necessary for a "signal" to be a "stimulus" (in the sense of a pinprick) but that it might be an *event*—for example, a symptom reported to a doctor or a sign or warning of any kind—the generality of SDT loomed large. For example, students of medical decision making R. S. Ledley and L. B. Lusted took note of SDT and made direct use of it.[21] They also included the duality of error formalized by Neyman and Pearson, a concept that is part of the foundation of SDT.

In 1979 B. D. Underwood, a professor of law, noticed the relevance of SDT to the problem of the duality of error in legal decisions; she wrote that "the literature of signal detection theory provides a helpful framework for considering the general problem of a fallible observer who attempts to detect signals sometimes giving false alarms and sometimes missing true signals," thus placing the matter of observation in a modern scientific context.[22]

Swets illustrated the generality and applicability of SDT by showing how it applies to such diverse problems as the diagnosis of AIDS, the detection of dangerous flaws in aircraft structure, and the detection of breast cancer:

> The best balance of TP [true positive] and FP [false positive] will vary from one diagnostic situation to another. For instance, mammograms taken to detect breast cancer are currently interpreted with a lenient criterion (say, at 2 on the scale of 10, referred to earlier); any suspicion of malignancy is followed up in some way, in order to achieve a high TP even at the expense of a high FP. In contrast, a strict criterion (say, at 9 on the scale) will be appropriate in those instances in which one will accept a smaller TP in order to keep FP down; for example, following on the notoriety given Willie Horton in the 1988 presidential campaign, governors held responsible for prison furloughs are reported to be tending toward such conservatism.[23]

SDT has been widely used since its inception in the 1950s. By 1988, according to Swets, more than one thousand articles on SDT in perceptual and cognitive psychology alone had been published.[24] And the use of SDT has been extended from psychophysics to a variety of fields, including weather forecasting,[25] and medicine,[26] particularly X-ray diagnosis, and quality control.

### Duality of Error and the Taylor-Russell Diagram

The Taylor-Russell diagram in Figure 2-1 offers a pictorial means of appreciating the duality of error in relation to policy formation. The diagram adds two important features not made apparent by the four-cell table we viewed in Chapter 1. First, it shows the *degree of accuracy* of the predictive system, which is indicated by the *size of the ellipse*—the larger the ellipse, the less the accuracy of the predictive system. If the ellipse is very large (as in Figure 2-1), the size of the error areas is very large, thus indicating that the predictive system is poor. If the ellipse is narrow (as in Figure 2-2A), the error areas shrink, thus indicating that the predictive system is good. If it is very narrow (as in Figure 2-2B), prediction is very good indeed. It goes without saying that it is the role of the scientist, or technologist, to make the predictive system as accurate as possible.

A good example of an actual plot of the data points that are the basis of an ellipse, such as that presented in Figures 2-1 to 2.6, is provided in the well-known and controversial book *The Bell Curve* by Herrnstein and Murray. Their table (Table 2-1) demonstrates the lack of *individual* predictability in high-ellipse (low-correlation) situations.[27] To see this point, the reader need only select a point on the horizontal axis of the graph and then notice the large range of data points on the vertical axis of the graph. Note, for example, that there are nine individuals who have thirteen years of education; their annual incomes in 1990 ranged roughly from $12,000 to $45,000. The column with the most data points, and thus the most reliable column, shows that the annual incomes in 1990 of the individuals with twelve years of education ranged from zero (!) to $75,000. In short, conditions such as those indicated in Herrnstein's and Murray's table offer very little individual predictability, a point the authors emphasize.

Correlations of the magnitude of the one for the data in Table 2-1 are fairly represented by the ellipse in Figure 2-1. The reader might test this assertion by attempting to draw an ellipse around the data points in the Herrnstein and Murray diagram shown

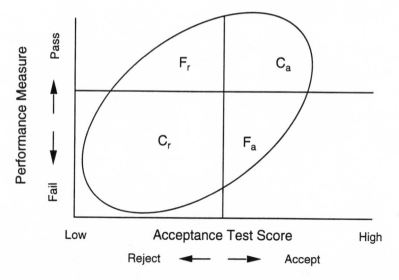

Figure 2-1   The Taylor-Russell diagram for university admissions. The four areas under the ellipse indicate correct acceptances ($C_a$), correct rejections ($C_r$), false or incorrect acceptances ($F_a$), and incorrect or false rejections ($F_r$). The vertical line marks the cutoff score on the admissions test; all those applicants who score above this point are admitted. The horizontal line indicates the level of acceptable performance; all those who perform above this level (e.g., a grade point average of 2.5) are deemed successful; all those below this point are deemed failures. The size of the ellipse indicates the degree of accuracy of the predictive system, often reported in terms of a correlation coefficient; the larger the ellipse the lower the coefficient. Smaller ellipses (higher correlation coefficients) reflect greater accuracy in prediction. (*Adapted from Taylor and Russell, 1939.*)

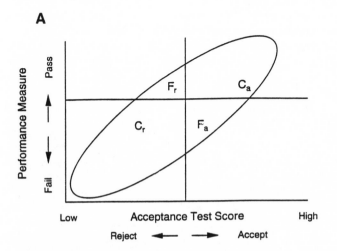

Figure 2-2a   A moderately good predictive system indicated by the size of the ellipse; error regions are smaller than regions of correct decisions.

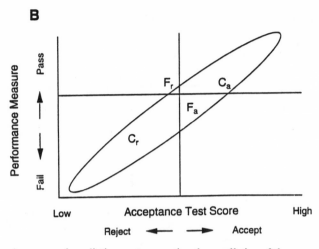

Figure 2-2b   A very good predictive system; notice the small size of the error regions relative to the size of the regions of correct admissions and rejections.

in Table 2-1. For a correlation of .33 the ellipse is large indeed, hardly different from a circle.

The Taylor-Russell diagram also makes explicit the *role of the policymaker* and makes it possible to see how that role differs from the *role of the scientist or technician.* That is, this diagram shows how facts can be separated from values in policy-making. As one moves the vertical line that determines the size of the four regions to the left or right, all four regions change in size *simultaneously*; the size of the four

Table 2.1   Variation among individuals that lies behind a significant correlation coefficient.

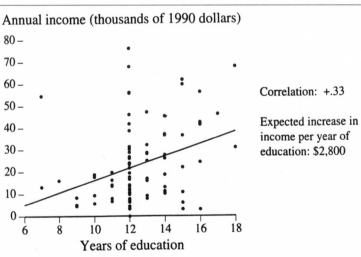

Source: R. J. Herrnstein & C. Murray, 1994, p. 68.

regions is rigidly linked. That is significant, for it illustrates what was pointed out earlier—namely, decreasing one error (region) *automatically* increases the other error (region). Shifting the decision criterion to the right or left does not affect the total amount of injustice; it simply changes its allocation from one region to the other. Policymakers, however, generally focus on one error and make changes in the belief that only *one* error is being affected. Only by increasing the accuracy of prediction—decreasing the size of the ellipse—can both kinds of error be reduced simultaneously. When the degree of accuracy (which will be modest in most cases) has reached its maximum, then the policymaker must choose which error to tolerate—seldom a pleasant situation, for errors mean that some constituents will suffer injustice (about which more later) and will blame the policymaker for it.

The scientist or technologist plays a different role from that of the policymaker in the decision process. I've already mentioned that it is the responsibility of the scientist or technologist to increase the accuracy of the predictive system (to reduce the size of the ellipse) as much as possible. It is the task of the policymaker to decide which error to minimize—that is, which constituency is to suffer the most (or the least) from the fact of irreducible uncertainty. Unfortunately, most, if not all, predictive efforts related to social issues are very imprecise; increasing accuracy invariably costs a great deal of time and money, and efforts to do so are likely to increase only slightly the poor predictive accuracy that already exists. Thus, the Taylor-Russell diagram provides a direct pictorial means for separating the task of the scientist and technician—better science will lead to the increased accuracy of prediction—and the task of the policymaker—deciding which constituency will suffer least (and most) from implementation of a policy. That decision will rest with the judgment regarding differential injustice—injustice to individuals versus injustice to society.

## Injustice to Individuals Versus Injustice to Society

Herrnstein and Murray provide a good example of these two forms of injustice in their discussion of the use of IQ tests for purposes of personnel selection. They admit the existence of a weak relationship between the test scores and performance but maintain that IQ tests are economically valuable nonetheless. Putting this assertion in the context of the Taylor-Russell diagram illustrates how the use of low-validity tests differentially affects both employer and employee and thus injustice to both society and individuals.

> Even a marginally predictive test can be economically important if only a small fraction of applicants is to be selected. Even a marginally predictive test may have a telling economic impact if the variation in productivity is wide. And for most occupations, the test is more than marginally predictive. In the average case, a test with a .4 validity, the employer who uses a cognitive test captures 40 percent of the profit that would be realized from a perfectly predictive test—no small advantage. In an era when a reliable intelligence test can be administered in twelve minutes, the costs of testing can be low—lower in terms of labor than, for example, conducting an interview or checking references.[28]

Herrnstein and Murray explain this situation perfectly correctly and should be complimented for their candor. The reader should note, however, that there is nothing in this paragraph about the duality of error; only one error is considered, that of hiring someone who should not have been hired. Nothing is said about the error of not hiring someone who should have been hired. Clearly, only the employer's interest in not hiring those who will not perform on the job is being considered here. By limiting their concern to that error, they focus on eliminating injustice to the employer. But there is another error to be considered—that of not hiring those who should have been hired because they would have succeeded had they been allowed to perform on the job. That error results in injustice to those individuals, just as hiring those who will fail constitutes an injustice to the employer. Under conditions of uncertainty (and the correlation of .33 in Table 2-1 shows what that uncertainty looks like), duality of error is inevitable, and injustice is thus unavoidable.

Herrnstein and Murray make it clear that employers can easily reduce the injustice done to them by reducing the selection ratio, that is, by moving the vertical line farther to the right, thus selecting fewer from the applicant pool. Employees do not control the selection ratio, however, and therefore cannot reduce their injustice. Employers can ignore the injustice to those who are falsely deprived of admission to the workplace because they can claim that this injustice is not their responsibility. A government that claims to represent all the people cannot be so cavalier, however. That is why tests that afford such weak relations cannot be the basis of a social policy. Both of the injustices that are incurred have constituents, and these constituents will protest—with justification.

The example from Herrnstein and Murray illustrates the costs of ignoring the duality of error in the private sector. But the duality of error is also ignored in the public sector. Suppose, for example, that the diagram in Figure 2-1 represents the situation for admissions to a university. The ellipse in Figure 2-1 represents reasonably well the actual empirical accuracy of systems for predicting success at a university. The horizontal line represents the pass-fail situation. Figure 2-1 represents a hypothetical university with fairly high standards for performance (most students do not succeed) and fairly high admission standards (most applicants are not accepted). Figures 2-3A and 2-3B illustrate the effects of two different policies. Figure 2-3A shows the results of lowering admissions standards over those shown in Figure 2-1 while maintaining the same performance standards. This change increases the number of incorrect acceptances—that is, the number of accepted students who will fail. (This can be seen in the increased size of the $F_a$ area.) A change of this sort actually reflects the experience of the open admissions policy of several universities in the 1970s. Figure 2-3B shows the results of *raising* admissions standards over those shown in Figure 2-1 while maintaining performance standards. This policy increases the number of correct rejections—indeed, makes it possible to accept only those students who will succeed (the $F_a$ region has disappeared despite a very weak predictive system) at the cost of increasing the number of students wrongly rejected, those who would have succeeded if given the opportunity to try. If one is indifferent to the injustice to these students, raising admission requirements is a very effective way of overcoming a weak predictive system and thus decreasing injustice to society.

There is no way to know in advance which of all the students with the same test score will fail and which will succeed; therein lies the irreducible uncertainty and

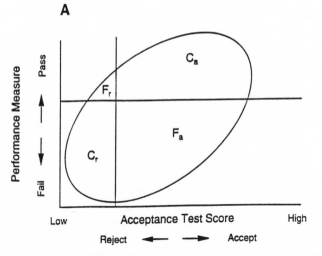

Figure 2-3a    Lowering the cutoff score for admissions increases the number of false acceptances ($F_a$) while reducing the number of false rejections ($F_r$).

subsequent injustice. As long as irreducible uncertainty prevails, unfairness will remain a part of the admissions policy. Because of the rigid link between changes in errors, decreasing the $F_a$ region automatically increases the $F_r$ region, and vice versa.

If the university is a public university, then the admission of students who will fail represents a cost to the public that provides support to the university. The money that is spent on students who fail represents an injustice to society, for society does

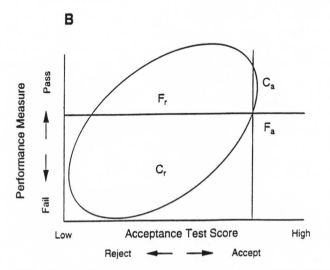

Figure 2-3b    Raising the cut off score reduces incorrect acceptances ($F_a$) but increases false rejections ($F_r$).

not get what it paid for. The greater the size of the cell $F_a$, the greater the injustice to society. Now consider cell $F_r$, false rejections. This region represents the number of students who would have succeeded had they been admitted; they were falsely rejected because of the lack of predictive accuracy of the selection system, and it is these students who pay the price for that. The size of the $F_r$ cell represents the injustice to individuals, specifically, those students who would have succeeded had they been admitted, had it not been for the error in prediction. The rigid trade-off between injustice to society and injustice to individuals is unavoidable because of the imprecision of the admission system, which itself results from our ignorance of how to make it more accurate. Thus, if both types of injustice are to be reduced, scientists will be the ones that have to do it.

Policymakers rarely understand that this tradeoff is inevitable, and seldom do they see that the resulting injustice is unavoidable. Without a clear grasp of this inevitability, policymakers do not recognize—or wish to ignore the fact—that it is their responsibility to decide, and to justify, where the decision criterion in the Taylor-Russell diagram should be placed. And that is *all* that they can do. But policymakers rarely recognize or acknowledge that error is inevitable; they try to produce policies in which there will be none (just as employers in the private sector try to do). Some major universities have tried to avoid this problem by removing admission requirements altogether. Others have reduced performance requirements to the vanishing point. Neither step, of course, has solved the problem of reducing error; the errors and the accompanying injustices have merely been shifted from one set of constituents to another. Prediction during this period has not improved; yet it is only through improvement in predictive accuracy that both errors can be reduced.

## Civil Liberty Versus Law and Order

Initially, it was the goal of reducing injustice to individuals that led to mandatory sentencing. The disparities in sentencing between members of minority groups and members of other groups became so apparent in the 1950s, when sentencing was left entirely to the discretion of individual judges, that Congress introduced mandatory sentences for specific federal offenses. Although these laws were repealed in the 1970s, they were reinstituted by Congress in the 1980s, and many states followed suit for crimes under their jurisdiction. But this time it was the drive to reduce the perceived injustice to society (as against injustice to individuals in the 1950s) that led to mandatory sentencing. The bombing of the Federal building in Oklahoma City in 1995 led to widespread discussion at all levels of society—from President Clinton to callers on talk radio—of the extent to which speech should be curtailed in order to prevent future tragedies of this sort. Thus the pendulum swings from an emphasis on one form of inevitable error—and unavoidable injustice—to the other.[29]

A particularly compelling example of unavoidable injustice has taken place in the state of Washington, which in 1990 passed a law called the Community Protection Act that called for the preventive detention of sexual predators. Because these persons have committed heinous sexual crimes, there is reason to fear that they may commit similar crimes after their release. Therefore, upon completion of their sentences, they are tried once more in front of a jury. If, after hearing testimony from mental health experts and others, the jury decides that the person on trial is indeed likely to commit similar crimes, the law permits that person to be imprisoned indefinitely, thus protecting society from (predicted) future criminal behavior. Thus, the preventive detention law, upheld by the Washington State Supreme Court, seeks to provide justice for society at the risk of injustice to individuals.

There is, without doubt, irreducible uncertainty in this situation; all concerned acknowledge that the predictive system is far from perfect. Therefore, there will be errors of both kinds; some of the innocent (those who will never commit another crime) will be imprisoned (indefinitely), and some of those guilty (those who will commit further crimes) will be freed. The preventive detention law reflects society's interest in gaining protection at the cost of punishing those who might be innocent. But those being tried under this law claim that their rights are being violated in a most fundamental way; they are being incarcerated for crimes they have yet to commit, and more specifically, for crimes someone *predicts* (with an admittedly imprecise predictive system) they will commit. Surely this is injustice to these individuals; releasing them, however, places society at risk.

But at least one of those sexual predators who had already spent ten years in prison and who was to be detained indefinitely was able to see the ambiguity and the uncertainty in this situation. He said that he understood why communities feared people like him. "'There may be some people here [in prison] who need to be here,' he said. 'Honestly I am not one of them. But the scary thing is that most of us feel the same way'."[30]

The constant struggle between civil libertarians and those who call for more "law and order" comes down to the same question: Which value system will prevail? Because there is no general resolution of the problem and no precise expression of the values to be assigned to each of the cells in the Taylor-Russell diagram, the pendulum swings between the two; the decision criterion in the Taylor-Russell diagram moves from left to right and back again as social conditions change. When crime increases, or is believed to increase, the decision criterion moves to the left in Figure 2-4; few of the guilty escape, but more of the innocent are penalized. (I will say much more about the cyclical nature of this activity later in this chapter and throughout the book.)

Many psychologists will, of course, be involved in developing and improving predictive systems, as in the university admissions case described earlier. And many psychologists will be involved in providing other forms of science-based information—for example, in relation to mental health, child care and development, and education and learning. The question of when, or if, a person diagnosed as mentally ill or as possibly mentally ill should be released from an institution—a jail or a mental hospital—fits exactly into the university admissions problem diagrammed in Figure 2-1. There is a very large and well-known degree of uncertainty in psychologists' and psychiatrists' predictions of the future behavior of such persons. The duality of error—false positives and false negatives—looms large in such decisions. Each type of error has had a large constituency ever since the closing of state-run mental hospitals in the 1970s. Civil libertarians who were largely responsible for this step argued that individuals were being institutionalized against their will without evidence that they were a danger to themselves or others, thus coming out strongly for

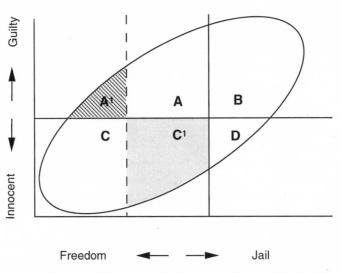

Figure 2-4   The Taylor-Russell diagram applied to criminal justice. The dashed vertical line indicates the effect of lowering the criteria for imprisonment from that indicated by the solid line. Fewer of the guilty will go free (the shaded area indicated by $A^1$ is smaller than A plus $A^1$), and far more of the innocent will go to jail (the area shaded $C^1$ will be added to D).

preferring injustice to society over injustice to individuals. Taking the opposite point of view, those responsible for protecting the nonmentally ill members of society from harm and from other aspects of the behavior of the mentally ill provided a constituency for reducing the *other* error—releasing patients who shouldn't have been let go. *Their* constituents—members of society who suffer the consequences of the error—are quick to express their outrage at what they believe to be an indifference to their safety and the safety of their families. As long as we must accept imperfect predictions, those who must form a social policy regarding this matter will be faced with a dilemma that is a result of inevitable error that produces unavoidable injustice.

The Taylor-Russell diagram not only explicates this situation but shows how the role of the scientist must be disentangled from the role of the policymaker.[31]

## Differential Injustice in a Health Plan

Ronald Dworkin, a professor of law at Harvard, has written extensively about matters involving social justice.[32] In the *New York Review of Books,* he addressed the question of the fairness of the health care plan proposed by President Clinton in 1993. He went on to ask how one should decide *whether* the plan was fair.[33] First, he declared that "health care is unjustly distributed in America" because "forty million Americans have grossly inadequate medical coverage, or none at all." He then addressed a question of values: "But how much health care *should* a decent society make available for everyone? . . . How do we decide what lesser level of care justice demands even the poorest should have?"[34]

Dworkin's statements are interesting because they face head on the matter of justice *and* the question of how we decide such matters. Dworkin directly confronts both in his evaluation of the complex plan put forward by the Clinton administration: "I shall concentrate on the issues of justice. . . . Though the [Clinton] administration is careful not to mention the word, the act plainly rations health care."[35] That means that the fairness of the rationing system (who gets what) must be examined. Dworkin points out that rationing will be done by a National Health Board that has been assigned "the responsibility of determining what kinds of treatment are necessary and appropriate and in what circumstances."[36]

As always, it is fair to wonder about the wisdom attributed to such committees. And Dworkin does indeed question it: "Does the act—or would the board—ration health care fairly?" As examples of the difficult questions the board would face, he asks: "Should women have routine mammograms before age fifty? When should expensive magnetic resonance imaging be covered?"[37]

Although Dworkin approaches the problem of the duality of error in the answers to such questions, he fails to come to grips with it. He continues, "[T]here is an emerging consensus among doctors that routine mammograms for women under fifty, which are expensive, do not save many women's lives. But they do save some."[38] He then moves to the costs of these "expensive" procedures, addressing the question of justice in monetary terms when he says: "We cannot avoid the question of justice: what is 'appropriate' medical care depends on what it would be unfair to withhold on the grounds that it costs too much. That question has been missing from the public debate [actually it hasn't]. . . . But it is time the public began to take the question seriously."[39] Cost, then, is the essence of the matter of justice for Dworkin; he does not pursue the question of the distribution of injustice that arises from the duality of error.

Dworkin does, however, describe two types of value systems that result in the preference for one type of error over another. One such value system is what he calls the "rescue principle." To quote him again:

> For millennia doctors have paid lip service, at least, to an ideal of justice in medicine which I shall call the rescue principle. It has two connected parts. The first holds that life and health are, as René Descartes put it, chief among all goods: everything else is of lesser importance and must be sacrificed for them. The second insists that health care must be distributed on grounds of equality: that even in a society in which wealth is very unequal and equality is otherwise scorned, no one must be denied the medical care he needs just because he is too poor to afford it. These are understandable, even noble ideals. They are grounded in a shared human understanding of the horror of pain, and, beyond that, of the indispensability of life and health to everything else we do. The rescue principle is so ancient, so intuitively attractive, and so widely supported in political rhetoric, that it might easily be thought to supply the right standard to answering questions about rationing.[40]

Dworkin, however, denies that the "rescue principle" is useful for determining how health care should be rationed: "No sane society would try to meet that standard."[41] (In terms of the duality of error paradigm used here, the "rescue principle" would simply reduce to zero the error of injustice to individuals; no sane society would go that far because of the injustice it would impose on society.) Finding this "rescue principle" useless for purposes of rationing health care, Dworkin proposes a different analysis that "points to a more satisfactory ideal of justice in health care—the 'prudent insurance' ideal."[42] This ideal requires the removal of the deficiencies of the rescue principle and the addition of three features—one of which dooms Dworkin's proposal. The fatal feature is this: "All the information that might be called state-of-the-art knowledge about the value and cost and side effects of particular medical procedures—everything . . . that good doctors know—is generally known by the public at large as well."[43]

This feature mars Dworkin's proposal; we cannot assign everything that "good doctors" know to every member of society, for such knowledge cannot be applied without duality of error. In some cases the error will be great, in some small, but it will always be there in some degree, and usually in a significant degree, no matter how "good" the doctrine is. Thus, the question of whether injustice to society will prevail over injustice to individuals must be faced. Dworkin's analysis does not face it. How much should society bear? How much should individuals bear? The fundamental question is: How should unavoidable injustice be distributed between individuals and society?

I treat Dworkin's analysis at length because it illustrates how a thoughtful professor of law, deeply concerned about matters of social justice, overlooks the matter of irreducible uncertainty and its consequences for unavoidable injustice in the rationing of health care.

The same kind of dilemma is faced by policymakers at the Food and Drug Administration (FDA) in its efforts to decide which drugs or procedures will be placed at the disposal of physicians and patients. If regulations are too stringent, good drugs will be withheld from the public and lives that could have been saved will be lost. If regulations are too lax, unsafe drugs will be approved and the public will be exposed to their harmful, perhaps fatal, side effects. In an effort to reduce *that* error, useful drugs will be withheld from use in hospitals and clinics.

The FDA staff tries to reduce both kinds of error by increasing the accuracy of its predictive system, turning to panels of medical and pharmacological experts and asking for their judgment with regard to each drug that comes before the agency. Each drug is accompanied by evidence from numerous clinical trials, some of which provide a positive result (of which some are false) and some of which provide a negative result (of which some are false). Irreducible uncertainty prevails at the time the decision is made. And because of irreducible uncertainty, on some occasions useful drugs will be prohibited and on some occasions drugs causing adverse reactions will be accepted. The same problems arise with the diagnostic tests themselves. And each error develops a constituency with high visability.

Consider Dworkin's mention of the issue of whether women under age fifty should receive routine mammograms and whether mammograms for these women should be subsidized. On December 27, 1993, the *New York Times* ran a long article regarding the current debate beginning on the front page. The question was: "Should insurance companies continue to pay for the tests in younger women, and should President Clinton's health plan hold fast to its proposal to refuse payments for routine mammograms in women under age fifty?"[44] At this point the reader should be able to anticipate the nature of the problem, for it is the same problem we have met before in many forms. There will be those whose value system will cause them to emphasize the importance of correct diagnoses of individual patients; these translate into precious lives saved. That will be reason enough for those who place a high value on lives saved to argue that routine mammograms should be continued for women under age 50. Others will point out the large number of false positives that occur and the costs of useless biopsies. In short, each cell of the Taylor-Russell diagram will attract attention and will attract a constituency.

The specter of injustice to women under age fifty was raised by Dr. Sarah Fox, an associate professor of family medicine at the University of California at Los Angeles, who "said that not paying for the tests would, in particular, penalize poor women, who are already underserved. . . . 'Shouldn't we rather be safe than sorry?' asked Dr. Fox, who believes that younger women should be screened. . . . [Otherwise] 'we will be enforcing a two-tier medical system,' she said. 'That's the direction we wanted to get away from.' "[45] But Dr. Ann Flood, a health policy analyst, said "that now more than ever, was a time for health policy planners to hold firm,"[46] meaning that we should rely on the studies that show that women under age fifty should *not* be routinely screened.

Thus we can readily see how a constituency for one type of error over another develops. The doctor who teaches about family medicine has developed a high value and concern for individual patients; we should expect no less. Therefore we are not surprised to find that she places considerable emphasis on avoiding injustice to individuals ("not paying for the test would . . . penalize poor women"). The health policy analyst, however, invests her knowledge and skill in analyzing the question of costs and benefits of routine tests from the point of view of society; we should expect no less from her, either. Therefore we are not surprised when we find that she has developed a high value and concern for injustice to society ("now more than ever, was a time for health policy planners to hold firm"; "if we cannot show that something is beneficial, we should not pay for it.")[47] There is a clear statement of values in both points of view; poor women *ought* not to be penalized; we—meaning society—*ought* not to pay for it. There is a preference for injustice to individuals on the one hand, and a preference for injustice to society on the other. Those who become part of these constituencies rarely acknowledge—perhaps because they do not recognize it themselves—that decreasing injustice to their constituency inevitably and unavoidably means increasing injustice to the other constituency.

One of the pioneers and outstanding exponents of recognizing this inevitability is Dr. David Eddy, who is also quoted in the same article. What should we expect from him? His judgment is a very important one, indeed, for we can be sure that no one understands this problem better than he. It turns out that Eddy was a member of the Clinton health care team and views "the mammogram question as a highly visible test case for the Clinton health plan."[48] The fact that Eddy was a member of the Clinton health care team, which we might reasonably believe was concerned about health policy from the point of view of the nation as a whole, leads us to anticipate that he would place a higher value on reducing injustice to society than to individuals, for he cannot escape that choice either. What did he say?

Even for women over age 50, Dr. Eddy said, where routine mammograms can cut the death rate from breast cancer by as much as a third, there is no way to justify them on a cost basis. He said that health planners rightfully endorsed insurance coverage for the tests in older women not because they saved money but because they saved lives. But, he emphasized, the life-saving benefits themselves are not established for younger women.

The conclusion that mammography screening of women over age 50 does not save money "might seem paradoxical," Dr. Eddy said. He explained that the problem is that thousands of older women "who don't have and never will have breast cancer" must be screened to find one woman who does. "By the time you take into account all the exams for all the women and all the biopsies for all the false positives, you overcome the potential savings by a factor of 10," he said.[49]

Thus, even the expert on medical decision making is faced with the same unavoidable difficulty as everyone else—choosing between injustice to society and injustice to individuals. He makes his value system explicit, however, even though he is serving as a technical expert. And his value system moves him to choose injustice to individuals, even though the American College of Radiology and the National Cancer Society argue that "the studies so far have not conclusively ruled out a potential benefit, and so it is not correct to say that mammograms are useless in younger women."[50] But Dr. Eddy was unmoved: "If we yield every time there's a constituency that can make an emotional argument for coverage of something that is not supported by actual evidence, . . . then we [society] will have a chaotic, expensive and inefficient health care system in this country."[51] He doesn't want that.

Do it Yourself!

In a curious move, the National Cancer Institute said that "rather than recommend that women in their 40s either have or not have the test it would lay out the data and let each woman decide for herself."[52] Is such a step reasonable? That is tantamount to saying: "Here are the data—which, of course, even experts find difficult to interpret—which we are 'laying out' for you. Interpret them and decide for yourself, even though we will acknowledge that you in all likelihood cannot reasonably be expected to do in a dependable way." This step is, of course, disingenuous; it may relieve the cancer institute of its responsibilities, but it certainly places the women who must decide in an impossible situation. If the professionals and the expert staff of the cancer institute do not know how to decide, then untrained persons will not know how to decide; the members of the cancer institute should surely know that. Or do they?

Situations involving such vacillation, uncertainty, unnecessary mutilation, expense, and the risk of death are bound to fester. So, soon after the December article, the *New York Times* carried an editorial under the heading "The Mammogram Controversy: It Confuses Women, Raises Unfounded Fears."[53] The editorial cited the earlier story and presented some additional information. It noted, for example, that "[s]ome scientists angrily question the trials; they say the tests included too few women and didn't follow them long enough. That argument rages on, with no resolution in sight," a conclusion that will not inspire confidence in the medical profession. But this editorial raises the question of the value to be attached to the rate of false positives. It asks, for example, "Why shouldn't younger women have mammograms anyway? Younger women have breast tissue of a kind that [produces more false positives]. . . . That's costly and frightening, but is it dangerous? In most cases, no, but in rare instances, the scar tissue could make it harder to detect malignant cells should they develop later on, unrelated to biopsy." The editorial further admonishes women that they "have an obligation to themselves to avoid misinformation that could cost them their lives"; indeed, don't we all? Thus, we come face to face with the fact that these admonitions are unclear; in situations of irreducible uncertainty—and this is certainly one—error is inevitable, injustice is unavoidable. What can be done?

We can continue to support scientific research that will reduce both the injustices to society and the injustices to the individual by increasing the accuracy of prediction devices. We can increase our understanding of the inevitability of the duality of error and of its consequence—injustice. Policymakers can make explicit the values that lead them to choose which injustices they support or reject. And last, we can anticipate that *cycles* of differential injustice to individuals and society will occur.

## Are Cycles of Differential Injustice to Individuals and Society Inevitable?

The idea that there are regular oscillations in the dominance of political parties and their associated philosophies has long claimed the attention of historians and political scientists. This idea, although not accepted by everyone, is not merely for dusty history books; it deserves the attention of nearly everyone. For if such oscillations can be shown to exist, and if they can be shown to have a definite period—and certain historians and political scientists argue that both propositions are true—then we have at hand not only a means for predicting our future political climate far in advance but an important phenomenon that strongly invites, indeed, demands, analysis and interpretation. Are such cycles related to irreducible uncertainty, duality of error, and unavoidable injustice?

The most notable advocate of the theory of political cycles is Arthur Schlesinger Jr., who claims not only that political cycles exist but that he has discovered their period; they last, he says, about thirty years from peak to peak—at least in American history.[54] His theory has become widely known and has achieved a certain respectability because of his status as a historian and because he was a member and chronicler of the Kennedy administration.[55]

The theory is worthy of our attention, not only because of its intrinsic significance but because the demand for the analysis and interpretation of the (putative) phenomenon of cycles has yet to be satisfied. In the remainder of this chapter I offer an explanation of Schlesinger's cycle theory based on the two types of injustices we have defined in the Taylor-Russell diagram (see Figure 2-5) and show how these injustices are related to Schlesinger's thirty-year cycles.

Schlesinger defines a cycle as "a continuing shift in national involvement, between public purpose and private interest."[56] Within this framework, the "polarity between public action and private interest"[57] can be seen to have a long history of oscillation that deserves analysis, irrespective of hypotheses regarding specific periods of the swing of the pendulum.

Recall that the Taylor-Russell diagram asserts that false positives and false negatives are rigidly linked. It also shows that moving the decision criterion to the right decreases the amount of injustice to society but increases the amount of injustice to individuals; moving it to the left accomplishes the opposite. I make the bold assumption here that this tradeoff constitutes an iron law of social policy. The effect of this iron law is apparent in the age-old argument about who is deserving of welfare benefits, and, therefore, Figure 2-5 illustrates these arguments in terms of this debate.

Injustice to *society*? Yes, one constituency will assert. Too large a number of the "undeserving" are given the rewards that society offers; "too many are on welfare, too many are receiving too many undeserved benefits." This situation will give rise to pressure to move the decision criterion (the vertical line) to the right, thus reducing the injustice to society. Unfortunately, because of the iron law of duality of error, this move will also result in increasing the number of the deserving (those who work hard, establish their credentials) who will now be deprived of what *they* deserve. This situation—increased injustice to individuals—will create pressure to move the decision criterion back to the left (I chose politically appropriate directions), thus continuing a cycle that does not end. It does not end because there is no consensual optimal point; each form of injustice will always have its constituents who, not unreasonably, will demand change that will reduce the inequity they suffer, or believe they suffer. Although policymakers will set, or try to set, the decision criterion at a point that satisfies *their* sense of justice, that point will provide only an uneasy truce between each form of injustice; each constituency will remain convinced that it is being unjustly treated.

An example of how deeply rooted such a sense of injustice can be and how it can move ordinarily peaceful citizens to violence could be seen when Dan Rostenkowski, then chair of the House Ways and Means Committee, participated in a move to change the health benefits of the elderly in a manner they judged to be unfair. A large group

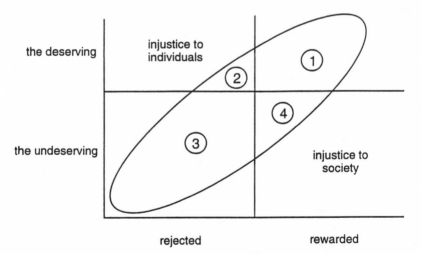

**Figure 2-5** The Taylor-Russell diagram applied to the welfare problem. The root cause of cycles of injustice lies in the imprecision with which the deserving are separated from the undeserving. The size of the ellipse in this figure is merely a hypothetical example. 1 = the deserving who are correctly rewarded; 2 = the deserving who are wrongly rejected; 3 = the undeserving who are correctly rejected; 4 = the undeserving who are wrongly rewarded.

of elderly citizens personally attacked him, screamed epithets at him, and pelted his car with stones. He thought he was acting to restore justice to society (too many of the elderly were receiving undeserved benefits), whereas they thought he was making the opposite error, creating injustice for individuals, in particular, elderly citizens, and they attacked him for it.

This iron law has existed as long as welfare has existed, and it can be seen today. Because the determination of who deserves and who does not deserve support from society has never been made with any degree of precision and cannot be made precisely, errors will be made and will become apparent, and action will be taken.

The diagram in Figure 2-6 depicts a society that has approached stability, one in which most of the deserving get what they deserve and most of the undeserving get what *they* deserve or, more precisely, do *not* get what they do *not* deserve. Under this circumstance, in which there is high accuracy and thus little injustice in the application of a policy, there will be less pressure to move the decision criterion; cycling, therefore, will be minimal, compared to a situation in which there is large inaccuracy in the policy (a large ellipse and large numbers of errors) and therefore considerable injustice of both kinds. The precision indicated in Figure 2.6 may represent utopia.

It may well be that this theory of cycles has generality beyond politics. Henry Petroski, well known for his histories of engineering, apparently wants us to consider seriously the possibility that thirty-year cycles also occur in the failures of large bridges. He notes:

> The relationship between success and failure in design constitutes one of the fundamental paradoxes of engineering. The accumulation of successful experience tends to embolden designers to attempt ever more daring and ambitious projects, which seem almost invariably to culminate in a colossal failure that takes everyone by surprise. In the wake of failure, on the other hand, there is generally a renewed conservatism that leads to new and untried design concepts that prove ironically to be eminently successful precisely because the design process proceeds cautiously from fundamentals and takes little for granted. As the new design form evolves and matures, however, the cautions attendant upon its introduction tend to be forgotten, and a new period of optimism and hubris ensues. This cyclic nature of the engineering design climate has been elaborated upon here and elsewhere and is supported by numerous case studies.[58]

Petroski then turns to case histories reported by P. G. Sibly and A. C. Walker,[59] who observed four major catastrophes and noted the existence of a thirty-year time lapse between the occurrence of each disaster. Petroski states that

> Whether coincidence or not, the striking pattern noted by Sibly and Walker seems inevitably to call attention to the years around the turn of the millennium as a period during which a major bridge failure of a new kind might be expected to occur.[60]

It should be interesting, important, and useful to attempt to apply the cycle theory developed here not only to bridge failures but to a wide variety of other situations involving uncertainty and cycles in the duality or error—for example, banking. A column in *The Wall Street Journal* published in 1995 asserted that "the investing record of the nation's big banks during the past decade is less than enviable. First they loaded up on loans to developing countries. Then they loaded up on loans to

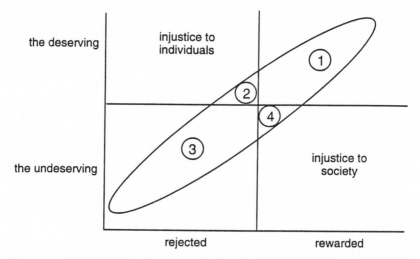

Figure 2-6    The root cause of cycles of injustice lies in the imprecision with which the deserving are separated from the undeserving. The size of the ellipse in this figure is merely a hypothetical example. 1 = the deserving who are correctly rewarded; 2 = the deserving who are wrongly rejected; 3 = the undeserving who are correctly rejected; 4 = the undeserving who are wrongly rewarded.

real estate-developers and highly leveraged companies. Tens of billions of dollars in losses later, they may be learning their lesson."[61] What is the lesson that is supposed to be learned? Unsurprisingly, the lesson is that it's better to use a more cautious, more analytical approach—in short, to make the error of being too conservative rather than the error of taking too many risks. How long did it take the managers to learn this lesson? The article suggests that the academics showed the bankers how to do this—about thirty years ago![62]

Whether thirty-year cycles are generally to be expected when uncertainty and duality of error are apparent is, of course, little more—well, a little more—than speculation. That speculation can be put to use, however, in seeking to specify the conditions that lead to a movement of the decision criterion from left to right and back again. The conditions may turn out to be specific to the area of interest—politics, bridges, banks—but the generality may simply be that the tradeoff between the types of risk of error is, for some reason(s) we have yet to understand, unavoidably cyclical.

Because the duality of error is highly visible in the activities of the Food and Drug Administration, we should expect to find similar periodic cycling in its decision making. There should have been a point in history at which there was very little risk of keeping efficacious drugs off the market but a large risk that drugs that produced harmful side effects would readily come to the market. And there was indeed such a time—about thirty years ago (prior to 1962). An act of Congress in 1938 authorized the FDA to regulate the relevant industries but gave the agency power only to demand safety. Pharmaceutical companies were not required to prove that a drug actually offered therapeutic benefits; indeed, physicians had hardly learned how to do this. In 1962, however, the law was amended to keep unfit drugs off the market, and "unfit" was redefined as "ineffective as well as unsafe."[63] Since that time the decision criterion has moved steadily to the right, bringing a steady decrease in the error of permitting a drug to appear on the market when it shouldn't have and a concomitant increase in the error of not permitting a drug to appear on the market when it should have—until the mid-1990s. After the Republican electoral sweep in 1994, conservative politicians expressed outrage at the FDA's policies, and the speaker of the House of Representatives, Newt Gingrich, called the FDA commissioner "a thug and a bully"; he called the agency the country's "No. 1 job killer" and "repeatedly criticized it for discouraging innovation and not approving medical products quickly enough." The effort to reduce the objectionable error is not limited to politicians, of course. "'Every major conservative think tank in Washington from the Washington Legal Foundation to the Cato Institute to the American Enterprise Institute' is working on FDA overhaul plans, says Stephen Conafay, executive vice president of the Pharmaceutical Research and Manufacturers of America, which represents drug companies," reported *The Wall Street Journal*.[64]

Given the ambiguities and confusions about probability and its measurement that beset even the best informed among us, it is not surprising that misconceptions about probability should lead to tragedies such as the *Challenger* disaster. Our policymaking world is rife with such misconceptions. Furthermore, I suggest that these circumstances will always be with us, because imprecision in prediction will always be with us and will account for the periodic swings between demands for one type of error and demands for the other.

In this chapter I have tried to substantiate my thesis that irreducible uncertainty inevitably results in error and that injustice is thus unavoidable. It is our "quest for certainty," as John Dewey put it in 1929,[65] that leads us to rely on our judgment for policies and the actions that implement them. In Chapter 3 I take up the question of how we make our judgments under uncertainty.

# 3 Coping with Uncertainty

## The Rivalry Between Intuition and Analysis

There are two modes of . . . thought, each providing distinctive ways of ordering experience, of constructing reality.

—*Jerome Bruner*

Traditionally, two forms of cognition—analysis and intuition—have been distinguished. This sharp dichotomy was made early; indeed, it is as old as the history of thought. Plato, Aristotle, Hume, and Kant all recognized that the difference between the two forms of cognition is fundamental. Even today, almost every study of human judgment employs these concepts, implicitly or explicitly. As I will show, they are an integral part of our daily lives.

First, let me define these terms. The meaning of analysis or analytical thought in ordinary language is clear; it signifies a step-by-step, conscious, logically defensible process. The ordinary meaning of intuition signifies the opposite—a cognitive process that somehow produces an answer, solution, or idea without the use of a conscious, logically defensible, step-by-step process. Analysis has always had the advantage over intuition with respect to the clarity of its definition for two reasons: (1) Its meaning could be explicated by the overt reference to a logical and/or mathematical argument, and (2) analytical thought forms the basis of rationality, because rational argument calls for an overt, step-by-step, defensible process. Thus, analytical thought and explicit, overt definition are part of the same system of thought. Not so with intuition; throughout its history it has acquired powerful claims to efficacy despite its ineffable, undefinable character.

### Intuition and Analysis in the History of Thought

Isaiah Berlin provides an impressive account of the role of the dichotomy between intuition and analysis in the history of modern thought from the seventeenth century on. He describes intuition and analysis as "rival forms of knowing"—the idea

60

of rivalry being an important characterization of the relationship between these two forms of cognition, and one that I pursue throughout this book. Berlin states:

> The quarrel between these rival types of knowledge—that which results from methodical inquiry, and the more impalpable kind that consists in the "sense of reality", in "wisdom"—is very old. And the claims of both have generally been recognised to have some validity: the bitterest clashes have been concerned with the precise line which marks the frontier between their territories. Those who made large claims for non-scientific knowledge have been accused by their adversaries of irrationalism and obscurantism, of the deliberate rejection, in favour of the emotions of blind prejudice, of reliable public standards of ascertainable truth; and have, in their turn, charged their opponents, the ambitious champions of science, with making absurd claims, promising the impossible, issuing false prospectuses, of undertaking to explain history or the arts or the states of the individual soul (and to change them too) when quite plainly they do not begin to understand what they are; when the results of their labours, even when they are not nugatory, tend to take unpredicted, often catastrophic directions—and all this because they will not, being vain and headstrong, admit that too many factors in too many situations are always unknown, and not discoverable by the methods of natural science. . . . This is the distinction that permeates the thought of Pascal and Blake, Rousseau and Schelling, Goethe and Coleridge, Chateaubriand and Carlyle; of all those who speak of the reasons of the heart, or of men's moral or spiritual nature, of sublimity and depth, of the "profounder" insight of poets and prophets, of special kinds of understanding, of inwardly comprehending, or being at one with, the world.[1]

The great mathematician Pascal (1623–1662), while he uses plainer language than does Berlin, was concerned with the same distinction:

*Difference between the mathematical and the intuitive mind.*

> In the one [i.e., analytical cognition] principles are obvious, but remote from ordinary usage, so that from want of practice we have difficulty turning our heads that way. . . .
>
> But, with the intuitive mind, the principles are in ordinary usage and there for all to see. There is no need to turn our heads, or strain ourselves: it is only a question of good sight, but it must be good; for the principles are so intricate and numerous that it is almost impossible not to miss some. . . .
>
> Thus it is rare for mathematicians to be intuitive or the intuitive to be mathematicians, because mathematicians try to treat these intuitive matters mathematically, and make themselves ridiculous, by trying to begin with definitions followed by principles, which is not the way to proceed in this kind of reasoning. . . . Intuitive minds, on the contrary, being thus accustomed to judge at a glance, are taken aback when presented with propositions of which they understand nothing (and of which the necessary preliminaries are definitions and principles so barren that they are not used to looking at them in such detail), and consequently feel repelled and disgusted.[2]

Although many have followed in Pascal's footsteps in asserting the incompatibility of the "mathematical and intuitive mind," it is a dubious proposition. Darwin, for example, was clearly capable of the effective use of both modes of cognition; they appear together in his diagram of the "tree of nature." (See Figure 3-1, retrieved from one of Darwin's notebooks by H. Gruber during his study of Darwin's creation of the theory of evolution.[3])

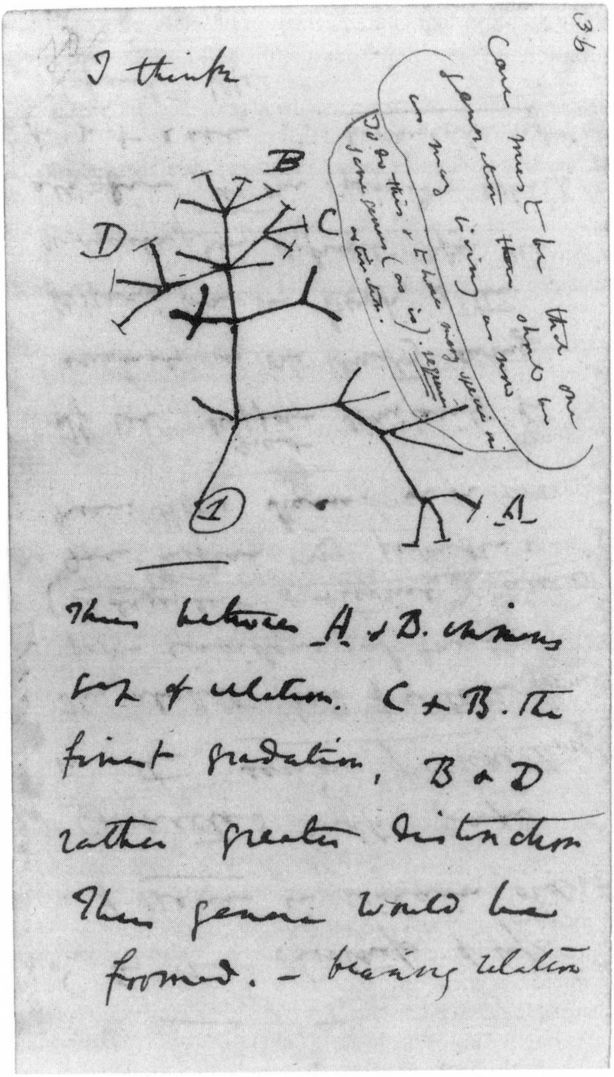

Figure 3-1    Darwin's third tree diagram, on page 36 of the First Notebook. (*Source: Cambridge University Library.*)

Darwin presented his intuitive idea of the "tree of nature" in the form of a pictorial image. Contrast that effort with his analytical-verbal deduction (indicated by the underlining of "requires" in the upper right). We are thus provided with a marvel of cognition: Intuition and analysis are joined by Darwin on the very same page as he labors to provide us with one of the greatest cognitive achievements known to us. Darwin clearly was a man who could employ both modes of cognition with considerable skill, thus defying Pascal's either-or view.

I trust that these examples clarify the distinction and serve to show that scholars have taken it very seriously. Now let me show that the distinction is in current use and is ubiquitous by quoting from C. M. Abernathy and R. M. Hamm, who present the most complete and up-to-date-survey of the use of the term "intuition" in their book *Surgical Intuition*. They classify the use of the concept in medicine and other fields (e.g., education, psychology) as follows:

> Intuition is different from other thinking.
>> Intuition is thought without analysis.
>> Intuition produces different results than analytic thinking.
>> Intuition is different from everyday thinking.
>> Intuition is infallible.
>> Intuition is a sense of a solution not yet fully developed.
>> Intuition has a feeling of certainty.

Additional categories are:

> Intuition uses special information.
>> Intuition is visual insight.
>> Intuition requires attention to one's own internal feelings.
> Intuition is characteristic of people's performance of familiar tasks.
>> Intuition is fast and easy.
>> Intuition is pattern recognition.
>> Intuition is expert pattern recognition.
>> Intuition is habit or automated thought.
>> Intuition arises from complex systems of symbolic rules.
>> Intuition is nonsymbolic thought, as in a neural network.
>> Intuition involves functional reasoning.
> Intuition is an option: If one can choose to do it, one can choose *not* to do it.
>> Intuition is just lazy thinking.
>> Intuition is an unavoidable necessity.
>> Intuitive cognition can outperform analysis.
>> Intuition is the prudent choice in some situations.
>> Intuition is the use of fallible heuristic strategies.
> Intuition involves judgment of importance.[4]

As we can see from this survey, intuition is generally identified with the mysteries of creativity, imagination, and the pictorial representation of ideas, whereas analysis is identified with logic, mathematics, and rigorous, retraceable thought.

These rival forms of knowing will surely continue to appear throughout all forms of cognitive endeavors, including science, medicine, law, politics, and literature. In the next sections of this chapter I present current examples of this rivalry in all these fields, because I want the reader to see how pervasively, how deeply these conceptions of human cognitive activity run through our lives. I cannot provide examples in depth for all of these fields—each field would demand a book in itself. I therefore present an example within each field in the hope that the reader will come to agree with me—and with Isaiah Berlin—that this rivalry is of great significance, not only to students of judgment and decision making, but to all members of society who wish to understand human judgment and social policy. The examples show that each form of cognition competes for our attention and demands highest status.

## Science

There is a tradition among scientists interested in their own behavior that began in 1938 with Hans Reichenbach, a famous philosopher of science. Reichenbach drew a distinction between "the context of discovery" and "the context of verification,"[5] which served very well to mark off different types of cognitive activity in the work of a scientist. He wanted to serve notice that whatever went on in the scientist's mind in the context of discovery was beyond our power of understanding (at least for the present) and therefore of little professional interest to the scientist. For our purposes, we can assign those cognitive processes to intuition. Reichenbach thought the context of verification was another matter, however; that *is* the scientist's business. Verification of an idea, a hypothesis, a theory demands rigorous empirical proof, of course, but it also demands retraceable (analytical) cognitive activity, open to all for criticism.

So far, Reichenbach's distinction seems right; the mysterious properties of intuition are associated with the context of creativity, whereas analysis is associated with verification. But physicists have either forgotten or have chosen to ignore his distinction. On May 1, 1989, at a special session of the annual meeting of the American Physical Society devoted to the "miracle" of "cold fusion," a physicist named Steven Koonin stood up before two thousand physicists and declared: "Based on my experience, my knowledge of nuclear physics, and my *intuition* [italics added] . . . the experiments are just wrong."[6] Thus, contemporary physicists apparently find intuition to be acceptable in the context of verification. Reichenbach surely would have shuddered. But the physicists gave Koonin an ovation.

In this section I will be reporting on how several prominent scientists described their cognitive activity, and we shall see that Reichenbach's distinction remains useful. We begin with the role of visualization versus equations in the creation of theory in physics.

J. Wechsler asserts that "aesthetic judgments played a major role" in the development of quantum theory; his point is that the division between the visualizers (Bohr, Born, and Schrödinger) and the nonvisualizer Heisenberg was "strong" and made a real difference in their work:

> Whereas Heisenberg's mode of thinking committed him to continue to work with a corpuscular-based theory lacking visualization, Bohr, Born, and Schrödinger believed otherwise; their need for the customary intuition linked with visualization was strong. Heisenberg's reply was that a new definition of intuition was necessary, linking it with the mathematical formalism of his new quantum mechanics. Visualization was regained through Bohr's personal aesthetic choice of the complementarity of wave and particle pictures, thereby linking physical theory with our experiences of the world of sensations.[7]

Among contemporary scientists, the contrast between pictorial intuition and mathematical analysis is vividly illustrated by Freeman Dyson in his description of his dialogues with his famous colleague, the Nobel Prize winner Richard Feynman:

> The reason Dick's physics was so hard for ordinary people to grasp was that he did not use equations. The usual way theoretical physics was done since the time of Newton was to begin by writing down some equations and then to work hard calculating solu-

tions of the equations. This was the way Hans and Oppy and Julian Schwinger did physics. Dick just wrote down the solutions out of his head without ever writing down the equations. He had a physical picture of the way things happen, and the picture gave him the solutions directly, with a minimum of calculation. It was no wonder that people who had spent their lives solving equations were baffled by him.[8]

Dyson sums it up exactly as Pascal would have: "Their minds were analytical; his was pictorial."[9]

J. Gleick in his biography of Feynman, titled *Genius*, emphasized the same distinction:

> In the long run most physicists could not eschew visualization. They found that they needed imagery. A certain kind of pragmatic, working theorist valued a style of thinking based on a kind of seeing and feeling. That was what *physical intuition* meant. Feynman said to Dyson, and Dyson agreed, that Einstein's great work had sprung from physical intuition and that when Einstein stopped creating it was because "he stopped thinking in concrete physical images and became a manipulator of equations."[10]

Note how the distinction between intuition and analysis is cast into "rival" forms of knowing by Berlin and into a "struggle" by Wechsler, and how Dyson deepens the distinction by asserting that Feynman's mind, being "pictorial," was incomprehensible to "people who had spent their lives solving equations," thus repeating an observation similar to Pascal's. But Pascal, Gleick, Dyson, and others who want to catagorize people as *either* intuitive or analytical types are wrong. Darwin showed us that by his ability to engage in both in the same diagram—and so does Feynman. Gleick's biography provides an extraordinary example of Feynman's uses of both the pictorial and the analytical modes of cognition in the same diagram, exactly as in the case of Darwin. Figure 3-2 shows Feynman's representation of the path a particle would take under certain conditions, both in purely schematic terms and in mathematical as well as deductive, analytical terms. Feynman, like Darwin, could shift from one to the other.

Is such shifting between modes restricted to geniuses? Of course not. Quite the reverse. It would be hard to find anyone, other than the neurologically damaged (autistic children, for example), whose cognitive activity is restricted to one form of cognition or the other. All of us shift—oscillate is a better term—back and forth from intuition to analysis as we form our judgments when time permits. Such oscillation was no stranger to Feynman. Gleick reports that, when queried as to whether he literally saw the answer, Feynman replied:

> The character of the answer, absolutely. An inspired method of picturing, I guess. Ordinarily I try to get the pictures clearer, but in the end the mathematics can take over and be more efficient in communicating the idea of the picture.
>
> In certain particular problems that I have done it was necessary to continue the development of the picture as the method before the mathematics could be really done.[11]

Yet, according to Gleick:

> He could not retreat into the mathematics alone. . . . [Nor did] visualization . . . have to mean diagrams. A complex, half-conscious, kinesthetic intuition about physics did not necessarily lend itself to translation into the form of a stick-figure drawing. Nor did a

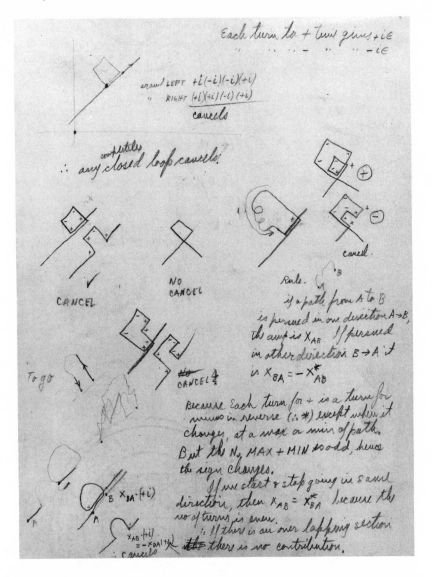

Figure 3-2  Feynman's diagram of the path of a particle in both schematic and analytical forms. (*Source: California Institute of Technology.*)

diagram necessarily express a physical picture. It could merely be a chart of a memory aid. At any rate diagrams had been rare in the literature of quantum physics.[12]

I will have more to say about oscillation between intuition and analysis in my theory of judgment in Chapter 7.

Social scientists are not as likely to reflect on the modes of cognition, but it is natural to find Herbert Simon doing so, for he is one of the great innovators within the field of cognitive psychology. Simon, a Nobel laureate, said that "mathematics is my language of *discovery* [italics added]. . . . It is the tool I use to arrive at new ideas."[13] This would be in the tradition of Heisenberg except that Simon claims his mathematics is "relatively unrigorous, loose, heuristic." He also noted that "even if we do think in images, neither Hadamard nor Einstein have had much success in describing just what these images are or how they are represented in a biological structure like the brain. Nor have I."[14] Nor has anyone else, although work is on the way.[15]

## Engineering

The rivalry between intuition and analysis has also been discovered by engineers. E. S. Ferguson has made a strong case for the value of intuition and the pictorial mode of cognition in the education and training of engineers. He did so because he thinks that the analytical aspect of engineering—that most practical of professions—has been overemphasized at the expense of the intuitive aspect; he also thinks the imbalance has had serious consequences.

Ferguson pleads for a move away from the scientific approach to engineering and urges that engineers develop "intimate, firsthand internalized knowledge"[16] and thus "an intuitive sense"[17] of the technology. He complains that the current curriculum emphasizes "analytical approaches;"[18] as a result, "sound judgment and an intuitive sense of fitness and adequacy"[19] have been lost. Moreover, Ferguson blames recent engineering catastrophes, such as the collapse of large buildings and the failure of the Hubble telescope, on the commitment of engineers to the scientific aspects of engineering and the neglect of the "art of engineering."[20] These suggestions by an engineer will be surprising, as well as interesting, important, and relevant to those who hold positive views of intuition.

One might ask, however: Exactly how does one teach engineers (and others) to develop intuitive cognition that does what those with a positive view claim it will do—provide "sound judgment and an intuitive sense of fitness and adequacy"? It is one thing to *urge* that engineers develop "intimate, firsthand internalized knowledge" but quite another to show how this is to be accomplished, other than by experience or by tutelage by someone who is alleged to possess the appropriate intuitions.

To his credit, Ferguson can answer such critics; he does not restrict himself to issuing pronouncements. In his book he provides example after example of the importance of "visualization" and "non-verbal knowledge" throughout the history of technology from Leonardo forward. In the introduction to his chapter "The Mind's Eye," Ferguson shows his enthusiasm for these aspects of cognition by quoting from Richard Feynman's autobiography:

> One time, we [Feynman and his boyhood companion, Bennie] were discussing something—we must have been eleven or twelve at the time—and I said, "But thinking is nothing but talking to yourself."
> "Oh yeah?" Bennie said. "Do you know the crazy shape of the crankshaft in a car?"
> "Yeah, what of it?"
> "Good. Now tell me: how did you describe it when you were talking to yourself?"
> So I learned from Bennie that thoughts can be visual as well as verbal.[21]

Ferguson is not the only engineer to hold a positive view of intuition; his persuasive text was followed by an equally compelling one by another engineer, H. Petroski, who also warned against overreliance on analysis in school of engineering. His historical treatment of design failures reaches back to the days of Greek architecture. Petroski points out that "for all of its use of sophisticated mathematics and computational models, design today involves the human mind in fundamentally the same way it did for the first builders,"[22] and he notes that "this is implicit in Ferguson's (1977) classic description of the nonverbal aspect of conceptual design (namely, that it relies more on pictures than on words or numbers), and it is evident in all current attempts to model the design process."[23] Petroski also wants us to know that "*current* [italics added] attempts to model the design process and its methodology in artificial intelligence and expert systems"[24] attempt to mimic human cognitive processes. And he supports Ferguson's view that much of the important work in design occurs when "neither words nor logic is necessarily available for rationalization. However, once the flash, inspiration, leap of imagination, or whatever it might be called, occurs, then the designer's verbal or logical faculties are certainly available for communicating with other[s],"[25] an observation that conforms with the view to be developed here, that oscillation between these two modes of cognition is common to all of us.

Berlin's brief history of the rivalry between intuitive and analytical cognition was not a reference to days gone by. The rivalry he spoke of was clearly present in the upheavals of physics during the 1930s, and it is present in the physics and social science of today as well as in the field of engineering. We also find it in the field of jurisprudence.

## Law

The rivalry between intuition and analysis appears in a sharp form in the legal thought of Oliver Wendell Holmes (1841–1935). Although Holmes's views on intuition and analysis were expressed nearly a century ago, they still deserve our attention, for M. J. Horwitz, a noted historian of law, refers to Holmes as "the most important and influential legal thinker America has had."[26] Benjamin Cardozo, also an esteemed Supreme Court justice, called him "the greatest of our age in the domain of jurisprudence, and one of the greatest of the ages."[27]

The best point of departure for understanding the development of Holmes's thought within the context of analysis and intuition is to consider the following sentence on the first page of Holmes's highly influential—and only—book, *The Common Law*. The sentence reads, "The life of the law has not been logic: it has been experience."[28] Although this sentence may be well known to students of law and legal theory, it must come as a shock to outsiders. Do we not believe that logic guides our judges? If we cannot depend on our judges to think in a logical fashion, to dispense justice by means of logic, who shall we depend on? If we cannot find analytical cognition—logic—at the base of our system of justice, then where? What can it mean for us to depend on "experience," that vague alternative to logic? Here is Holmes's explanation:

> The life of the law has not been logic: it has been experience. The felt necessities of the time, the prevalent moral and political theories, intuitions of public policy, avowed or unconscious, even the prejudices which judges share with their fellow-men, have had a good deal more to do than the syllogism in determining the rules by which men

should be governed. The law embodies the story of a nation's development through many centuries, and it cannot be dealt with as if it contained only the axioms and corollaries of a book of mathematics.[29]

When we find exactly what Holmes meant by "experience," our puzzlement increases, for he defines it as "the felt necessities of the time" and tells us that it includes "the prevalent moral and political theories." Those who expect legal theorists to be analytical, to pore over the meaning(s) of every word, will be critical of this explanation. When Holmes says that experience includes the "felt necessities" of the time, they will ask: "'Felt'?" What can "felt" possibly mean? And *whose* "prevalent moral" theories will be our guide? *Whose* "political theories"? Are we to believe that Supreme Court justices should somehow arrive at "intuitions of public policy"? If Holmes meant to say that logic, as represented in the syllogism, was to be tempered, modified, relaxed, made more flexible, or simply ignored in favor of the "felt necessities of the time," or even "the prejudices which judges share with their fellow men," he was certainly encouraging his readers to accept an intuitive mode of cognition. In short, it is clear where Holmes wanted to go—away from logic, away from analytical cognition.

It is also clear that Holmes was not merely describing the "life of the law" as it had been, but explaining that it should be so. Not only have those "intuitions of public policy" affected judicial cognition, not only have they "had a good deal more to do than the syllogism in determining the rules by which men should be governed"; they represent the necessary and desirable form our cognitive processes *should* take.

Thus, Holmes was forthright in his declaration of the role of intuitive cognition in "determining the rules by which men should be governed." And whatever else Holmes may have meant by intuition, he certainly understood that it referred to a *covert* cognitive process, one that could not be fully explicated, for he added that these "intuitions" might be "avowed *or* [ italics added] unconscious."

Max Lerner, the editor of *The Mind and Faith of Justice Holmes*, offers some historical context for Holmes's emphasis on "experience." He notes that Holmes's book "was written at a time when legal scholars in Germany and England were beginning to view law as anthropologists might view it—as an organic part of the culture within which it grew up."[30] This may explain why Holmes said that "the law embodies the story of a nation's development through many centuries, and it cannot be dealt with as if it contained only the axioms and corollaries of a book of mathematics."

Is our friend from the Middle Ages, Gerbert, listening? Gerbert, you may recall, said that "rhetoric . . . aims at making old truths palatable." Are "old truths" not the "prejudices which judges share with their fellow men"? Gerbert would have thought so and would have reminded us that one of the benefits of logic is that it "search[es] out new, even unpalatable truths." Are we not dependent on our judges to search out those unpalatable truths by logical means? Apparently not, from Holmes's view.

Of course, I am not the first to note Holmes's abandonment of logic as "the life of the law" and his endorsement of intuitive cognition as the expression of experience. Virtually every student of Holmes's life and thought focuses on this aspect of his legal theorizing. For example, Lerner, in his introduction to *The Mind and Faith of Justice Holmes*, showed his uneasiness with Holmes's famous sentence when he tried to explain away Holmes's central point, saying that "logic was not excluded [by Holmes]: it could not be. But experience was the starting point where logic began; and where different logics clashed, experience was used a touchstone for the selection of the relevant logic."[31] These are charming words indeed (Gerbert would assign them to rhetoric), but how does one explain to a person convicted in a court of law that "different logics clashed," that "experience was used as a touchstone for the selection of the relevant logic," and that therefore justice was served? Holmes's famous paragraph can hardly be treated so casually.

If one were to charge that Holmes's abandonment of logic casts us adrift into a sea of irreducible uncertainty, Holmes would not be intimidated in the slightest; he would urge us to acknowledge that "such is life." For Holmes was forthright in linking certainty with logic and uncertainty with experience. He surely understood the concept of irreducible uncertainty and its everpresent place in law. Holmes's famous lectures on "The Path of the Law" contain the following acknowledgment of the place of logic in the education of lawyers:

> The training of lawyers is a training in logic. The processes of analogy, discrimination, and deduction are those in which they are most at home. The language of judicial decision is mainly the language of logic. And the logical method and form flatter that longing for certainty and for repose which is in every human mind.[32]

Although Holmes could sympathize with the human longing for certainty, it is clear from the following extract that he found the power of logic to be mere facade:

> Certainty generally is illusion, and repose is not the destiny of man. Behind the logical form lies a *judgment* [italics added] as to the relative worth and importance of competing legislative grounds, often an inarticulate and unconscious judgment, it is true, and yet the very root and nerve of the whole proceeding.[33]

Lerner saw that Holmes's philosophy of life, his frank acknowledgment of the ubiquitous nature of irreducible uncertainty, was central to his philosophy of law. He reminds us that in *The Common Law* "Holmes was concerned to show that life was a perilous matter, and that law could not be less perilous and more secure than the intrinsic nature of life itself. . . . He is skeptical of the possibility of finding absolute and secure answers to the problems life poses for law."[34]

At this point I offer some examples of how some legal theorists reacted to Holmes's famous sentence. S. J. Burton, in his book, *An Introduction to Law and Legal Reasoning*, provides a recent example. He makes plain the difficulties created by Holmes's bold grasp of irreducible uncertainty, acknowledging that

> [t]he absence of certainty in predictions, persuasions, and decisions might lead some to question whether such legal interpretation is possible. It might be thought that anything less than certainty in legal reasoning leaves the judge free to classify cases as a function of their personal value preferences, rather "than law."[35]

Is it dangerous for judges to be "free to classify cases as a function of their personal value preferences"? Not to Burton. He dismisses the dangers resulting from uncertainty by relying on Roscoe Pound, the author of the influential *Spirit of the Common Law*[36] and a friend and supporter of Holmes, who, in a burst of legal arrogance, stated: "It is an everyday experience of those who study judicial decisions that the results are usually sound, whether the reasoning from which the results purport to flow is sound or not."[37] Pound did not say what he meant by "usually," nor did he say by which criteria the soundness of the reasoning was to be judged. But lest the reader fail to understand Pound's self-serving defense of covert (and admittedly incorrect) reasoning, Pound offered this defense: "The trained intuition of the judge continually leads him to right results for which he is puzzled to give unimpeachable legal reasons."[38] Pound apparently was driven to this—surely indefensible—conclusion by his antipathy toward analytical cognition, which he termed "mechanical jurisprudence."[39]

Pound and Burton thus join Holmes in departing from a full commitment to analytical cognition, endorsing and advocating the use of a judge's "intuitions of public policy, avowed or unconscious" to be "the life of the law" and acknowledging irreducible uncertainty in the formation, as Holmes put it, of "the rules by which men should be governed."

Burton describes these rules in terms of "soft formalism," a felicitous concept. But, of course, soft formalism—analysis tempered by intuition—opens the door to multiple interpretations of circumstances; once there is a departure from a standard, be it a metric system or a prescriptive, a defensible rule for making a judgment, or a logical deduction from a legal rule or principle, a defense of that departure will have to be constructed. What should—or can—the defense of that departure be? If appeals to mysticism or religion are ruled out, the defense will be an appeal to "experience," as it was with Holmes, no matter what area of life we consider. Thus, for example, during the eighteenth-century debates over the framing of the U.S. Constitution, Robert Livingstone (1746–1813) asserted in his argument against "rotation" (term limits) for legislators that "[w]e all know that experience is indispensably necessary to good government."[40]

As we will see, however, although Justice Holmes and his colleagues may have admired "trained intuition" on the bench, by the middle of the twentieth century many of the people's representatives in Congress and state legislatures demanded an end to it; they wanted sentencing to be taken out of the hands of judges. This introduced the concept of mandatory sentencing.

### Mandatory Sentencing

Because the rivalry between intuition and analysis in the law has been discussed here in terms of Oliver Wendell Holmes's philosophy, some readers may consider the matter to be anachronistic, academic, and perhaps even whimsical. If so, remember that I chose to describe Holmes's philosophy because of his place as a highly respected justice in U.S. history. Moreover, the relevance of his remarks can be seen in thousands of cases heard every day in the U.S. halls of justice, where the rivalry between intuitive and rule-bound cognition is played out in the application of the rules of mandatory sentencing. This procedure explicitly limits judges' intuitive ("discretionary") judgments regarding the sentencing of those pronounced guilty of a legal offense in favor of "guidelines" that specify the period of time the offender must spend in prison for each type of crime committed. Thus, specific sentences are mandated for various classes of felonies, and judges must apply them whether they like it or not. When judges wish to depart from the "guidelines"—in either direction—they must justify their departure from them; they must declare in writing their reasons for doing so. They cannot merely state that their "trained intuition" is sufficient justification for departure from the rule; "soft formalism" will not suffice. And that tends to annoy judges; their intuitions must somehow stand up to analysis.

Here is an example of how Jack Weinstein, a well-known, scholarly, senior federal judge from whose Memorandum I quoted in Chapter 1, departed from the guidelines and how he justified his departure. The *New York Times* on March 11, 1992, reported:

> Nearly six months after his arrest on a rainswept street in Queens, a young Colombian who authorities in South America say is a vicious drug-cartel assassin was sentenced today to six years in prison for giving a false name to Federal officers as they surrounded him, guns drawn, at a corner pay phone.
>
> The sentence imposed on the young man, Dandeny Muñoz-Mosquera, by Judge Jack B. Weinstein in Federal District Court in Brooklyn was far more severe than the maximum of six months suggested in sentencing guidelines.[41]

Judge Weinstein justified his departure from the sentencing guidelines by referring to the defendant's "criminal history in Colombia." As explained in the *New York Times* article,

> Officials there have linked Mr. Muñoz-Mosquera, 26 years old, to the killings of more than 50 police officers, judges and other officials; of helping plan the assassination of a presidential candidate, and of setting off a car bomb that destroyed the headquarters of the Colombian equivalent of the F.B.I. . . .
>
> Judge Weinstein also took the unusual step of fining Mr. Muñoz-Mosquera $35,000 and ordering him to pay the expenses of maintaining him in a maximum-security prison, which are estimated at $1,500 a month. After serving the term, Judge Weinstein said, Mr. Muñoz-Mosquera is to be deported to Colombia.[42]

In view of Mr. Muñoz-Mosquera's history, Judge Weinstein's "trained intuitions" weren't greatly taxed in this case. Clearly, it was easy for him to justify his departure from the guidelines. Of course, the defendant's lawyers disagreed, arguing that the sentence was "totally unjustified." But there was no public outcry; the defendant lacked a constituency.

It is easy to find an example of an override of sentencing guidelines in the direction of leniency as well. Indeed, the same edition of the *New York Times* that carried the story of Judge Weinstein's sentencing of the Colombian to six years in prison for giving a false name, the columnist Anna Quindlen sharply criticized the justice system for continuing to incarcerate Jean Harris, a convicted murderer, because of *her* background.[43] As it happens, Ms. Harris not only has a history that is exactly the opposite of that of the Colombian; she has a constituency. The former head mistress of the prestigious Madeira School, She is simply put, a member of the intellectual establishment. In her argument for disregarding the sentencing guidelines, Quindlen describes Ms. Harris as spending her time in prison reading "during the course of a single year . . . many periodicals as well as biographies of Queen Victoria, Tolstoy and Lyndon Johnson, and some Dostoyevsky, Gogol and Eudora Welty," adding that Ms. Harris writes as well as reads. Why, then, Quindlen wants to know, does "our society still bother to allocate scarce resources . . . keeping someone like Mrs. Harris in prison"? Put otherwise, Ms. Harris's background and character are sufficient cause for overriding the rule. Quindlen may have been persuasive; shortly after her column appeared, Ms. Harris was granted clemency by then Governor Mario Cuomo.

Thus, even in a discipline committed to the impersonal analysis of the facts and of the law brought to bear on them, analysis does not suffice. Judges and legal scholars find that they are not merely servants of analysis, driven inexorably to conclusions. Indeed, they do not want to be, for they believe there is something more important that is neither apparent nor predictable; the derivatives of "experience," of "trained intuition," of "soft formalism," of, in short, cognitive processes no one— including the judge—quite understands. Often enough, however, intuitive cognition will not be tolerated by those affected by it or by their constituents, who will demand the consistency and coherence provided by analytical cognition. Rules will then be imposed on the judges; when that happens, the judges will fight them in the name of "good judgment" and "wisdom."

Judge Weinstein, for example, was so outraged by the mandatory minimum sentences for drug offenders set by Congress that he announced that he would no longer preside over trials of those charged with drug offenses. He is not alone; apparently about 50 of the 680 federal judges have taken the same step. In a speech announcing this policy, Judge Weinstein stated:

> The sentencing guidelines which Congress requires judges to follow result, in the main, in the cruel imposition of excessive sentences, overfilling our jails and causing unnecessary havoc to families, society, and prisons. Most judges today take it for granted, as I do, that the applicable guideline for the defendant before them will represent an excessive sentence. . . .
>
> I am now so depressed by the drug situation that this week I sent a memorandum to all the judges and magistrate judges in my district stating:
>
>> One day last week I had to sentence a peasant woman from West Africa to forty-six months in a drug case. The result for her young children will undoubtedly be, as she suggested, devastating. On the same day I sentenced a man to thirty years as a second drug offender—a heavy sentence mandated by the Guidelines and statute. These two cases confirm my sense of frustration about much of the cruelty I have been party to in connection with the "war on drugs" that is being fought by the military, police, and courts rather than by our medical and social institutions.
>>
>> I myself am unsure how this drug problem should be handled, but I need a rest from the oppressive sense of futility that these drug cases leave. Accordingly, I have taken my name out of the wheel for drug cases. . . .
>
> Until we can address and deal with the rotten aspects of our society that lead to drug dependence, we will not deal effectively with the drug problem.[44]

Judge Weinstein's intuitions about proper sentencing clearly came into conflict with the relentless analytical interpretation of laws anticipated by society's elected representatives.

## Medicine

The large role of intuitive cognition in legal decision making may have come as a surprise to the reader, but it will come as no surprise to find that intuition has long been recognized in the "art" of medicine. As patients we have learned that doctors do not rely fully on science. Many seem to be proud of their "art," their intuitive prowess. Every medical school has its folklore about the wondrous intuitive diagnostic powers attributed to certain physicians and surgeons. I cite one example from my own experience.

In the early 1950s when I was conducting research on medical education, I was told that a serious danger to patients on the operating table was a sudden, inexplicable loss of blood pressure that often resulted in death. I was also told that surgeons in preoperation discussions with patients often attempted to predict whether this undesirable event would occur so that they could alert the anesthesiologist to the danger. I raised this question with a genial and accommodating surgeon, who was quick to say, "Of course, I can predict which patient will do this. How do I do it? I make a point to shake hands with the patient before the operation, and I can always tell from the handshake whether this will happen." He couldn't, or wouldn't, say exactly what it was about the handshake that revealed this predisposition. I found this remark to be incredible, but I didn't pursue the matter. He seemed to think that his intuition was based on a handshake, he had tested it, he knew it worked, and that was that.

But not all physicians, particularly today, are comfortable with such intuitive judgments. They have received considerable education in science and the scientific method, and they are keenly aware of the dangers of judgments that cannot be defended. Their dilemma lies in the rivalry between intuition and analysis. Intuition offers an immediate if risky judgment; analysis, though safer, takes longer—if it can be done at all.

Medical folklore is full of such instances, and for good reason. Of all the disciplines of applied science, medicine can claim to have the most difficult task of separating or integrating intuition and analysis. The prestige and the authority of physicians rest in good measure on doctor's scientific, analytically derived knowledge base, that part of their knowledge that is proven and demonstrable. But that knowledge must be somehow applied to a specific patient here and now; physicians must exercise their intuitive judgment in the face of uncertainty because the uncertainty is frequently stubbornly irreducible.

Those intuitive judgments must combine information based on multiple fallible signs and symptoms in a fashion that is only in part justifiable. But as the penalty for judgments (diagnoses, prognoses) that lead to erroneous actions becomes ever more threatening, physicians will—as is currently happening—rely more and more on hard information (laboratory data) that they can organize into a retraceable, justifiable judgment and, as a result, suppress judgments that are intuitively derived. Thus, just as judges have been driven by legislatures to accept processes designed to eliminate their intuition-based discretion in sentencing, physicians are being driven by fear of malpractice suits to avoid their intuition-based judgments and to rely increasingly on retraceable and analytically justifiable processes in diagnosis and prognosis.

Fifty years ago a physician may well have been able to fend off a lawsuit by referring to his or her twenty-five years of clinical experience as a primary defense of a diagnosis later proven to be wrong. But in today's courtroom the surgeon who told me that he made his predictions about cardiac collapse on the operating table by shaking hands with his patients and justified that practice on the basis of long experience would be humiliated. Failure to have made an analytically derived judgment can no longer be justified by an appeal to (presumed) intuitive wisdom gained through long experience. Rule-based knowledge has become ever more present in the physicians' cognitive activity (a matter I will discuss in more detail in connection with competence in clinical judgment in Chapter 5). One of the major consequences of that change is the increasing development of "expert systems" in medicine, for such systems are nothing more than rule-based systems.

In short, physicians in practice are now induced ever more strongly to rely on analytical cognition as a means of practicing "defensive medicine"; the rivalry with intuition is being sharply reduced in favor of analysis.

Now I turn to a story of how one physician confronted this rivalry and what his response was.

### Acquisition versus Application of Knowledge

For the past thirty to forty years there has been a standard method for generating therapeutic knowledge: controlled clinical trials of a drug. Such trials employ experimental and control groups. That is, (1) a proposed new medication is given to a sample of patients with the disease the drug is supposed to alleviate or cure; (2) a placebo (an innocuous medication, such as a "sugar pill") is given to a second sample of similar patients; and (3) the number of patients who respond positively to the medication in each group is compared.

Now suppose that this has been done, and suppose that the drug has been found to be effective in 80 percent of the cases, with only 15 percent of the patients given the placebo responding positively and fewer than 5 percent of the cases showing side effects. Assuming adequate sample size, this drug will surely be approved. Now suppose you are a physician and you have diagnosed your patient to have the disease for which this drug is indicated to be useful on the basis of the results of the controlled experiment. Should you administer it to your patient? The question you must ask yourself is: Will the drug help *this* patient? After all, it was not tested on her. And neither she nor I is interested in the long run. At the moment, it is her health that is my responsibility. I must remember that. And there were many patients it did not help. And although not many patients showed side effects, some did. In short, by what cognitive means am I to bridge the gap between results derived from *some* patients (unknown to me) and *this* patient in front of me who trusts me to do no harm? Who can tell me what that cognitive process, that analytical method, should be? This is a topic seldom addressed, but there is one physician who not only faced these difficulties but wrote about them and how he sought—and found—a solution; his story is a fascinating one.

David Sackett, a well-known and highly respected clinical epidemiologist, decided to become a "bedside physician" after approimately twenty years of studying the methods and results of clinical trials of various medical interventions. Sackett's prob-

lem was created by his change from being a *producer* of knowledge as an epidemiologist—an expert in clinical trials—to being a *user* of knowledge as a practicing
physician. The problem for the bedside physician is this: Thousands of clinical trials
have been conducted, and an enormous amount of information has been derived from
them. But these results never reduce all uncertainty; each trial produces its own rate
of false positives and false negatives (see Chapter 1). How is this vast store of uncertain information to be used? How is it to be applied to a specific patient? Are there
rules for this? What is the role of analysis? Of intuition? Sackett put his problem this
way:

> It should be possible for me to take a set of epidemiologic and biostatistical strategies
> developed to study the "distribution and determinants of disease" in groups and popu-
> lations, recast them in a clinical perspective, and use them to improve my clinical per-
> formance. I therefore set about trying to do so.
>
> As I spent more and more time in attempts to apply, in the frontlines of clinical
> medicine, the results of the randomized trials I and others had been executing, I iden-
> tified three issues in inference and decision making at the bedside: first, how should
> clinicians decide whether the results of a randomized trial, performed at another time
> in another town by other clinicians among other patients, apply to their own particular
> patient, today, in their own town? That is, how ought we consider the generalizability
> or external validity of internally valid randomized trials? Second, faced with an ever-
> expanding array of validated, efficacious preventive and therapeutic maneuvers, how
> should clinicians decide which ones deserve the highest priorities, especially when they
> may not have the time or other resources to pursue them all? That is, can we develop
> a clinically useful and easily understood yardstick for comparing the payoffs, for our
> patients, of pursuing and treating different disorders? And, finally, how are we to select
> the best therapy when there are no randomized trials to guide us? Is there any way to
> try to bring the powerful inferential methods of the randomized trial to bear on the
> assessment of the efficacy of treatment in the individual patient?[45]

Sackett uses the word "speculation," but readers who have by now become used
to the words "intuition" and "analysis" will realize what has happened. Sackett is
describing a situation in which the physician realizes that a fully analytical deduction is *not* going to take place; rather, cognitive activity that "more closely resembles
speculation than deduction" will occur. In short, the physician is moving toward the
use of intuitive (and, therefore, not fully recoverable) cognition in the act of applying his or her analytically derived, scientific knowledge.

All the problems mentioned by Sackett are fundamental, have rarely been addressed, follow from the uncertainty offered by the clinical trial, lead to the risks
posed by the duality of error (see Chapter 1), and therefore risk possible injustice to
patients. Sackett, however, was both determined and creative; he did not stop with
the identification and explication of this problem. He tried to find a solution—an
analytical solution. He begins this way:

> The incorporation of formal statistical analysis into the randomized trial has provided
> the essential ingredient for both specifying and avoiding drawing incorrect conclusions
> about the efficacy of the experimental therapy—namely, the false-positive conclusion
> that it works when, in truth, it doesn't, and the false-negative conclusion that it doesn't
> work when, in fact, it does.[46]

That is his point of departure; his solution will have to keep these essential elements—the risk of duality of error—in his procedure. He laments their absence in therapeutic efforts:

> It is the absence of these essential elements of science from the uncontrolled trial of therapy in the individual patient that has condemned this aspect of clinical practice to an "art." However, ... in responding to a challenge issued to me as a discussant in a Medical Grand Rounds 3 years ago, it dawned on me that this need not be so. The challenge was to present a rational approach for deciding how to treat a case of chronic active hepatitis of a form in which no randomized trials could provide any guidance. I had to provide a rationale for making a decision about whether a treatment was helpful to an individual patient.[47]

Sackett comes back again and again to the need for rational analytical cognition:

> In pondering this challenge, it dawned on me that we regularly make the alternative decision about whether a treatment was harmful to an individual patient every time we decide if an adverse drug reaction has occurred, and it was in reviewing attempts to bring science into this latter area that some interesting ideas occurred to me.[48]

He asks the question "Why not systematically—indeed, why not randomly—dechallenge and re-challenge the individual patient with a drug thought to help, rather than harm him?"[49] What Sackett really is asking is, Why not employ the fruits of analysis, the scientific method of the randomized clinical trial? And this is exactly what he did.

I cannot present the details of this approach here, but the method worked; the physicians learned what they needed to know for *this* patient. Their cognitive activity was analytical—that is, public, retraceable, and defensible, with respect to both form and content. How different from intuition or speculation "at the bedside"!

Sackett's remarks are highly significant to us because they illustrate the rivalry between intuition and analysis within one person. "Speculation" made Sackett uneasy; he clearly did not like departing from the analytical mode of cognition. He regretted the "absence of [the] essential elements of science from the uncontrolled trial of therapy in the individual patient"; he saw therapy as an "uncontrolled trial"—anathema to one who has spent his professional life improving controlled clinical trials. It is "uncontrolled" cognitive activity that has "*condemned* [italics added] this aspect of clinical practice to an art"—not a science. Not only did Sackett frankly and explicitly identify and analyze the problem of inference and decision at the bedside; he worked out a solution that met the criterion of containing the "essential elements of science."

Sackett's report on his struggle with the rivalry between intuition and analysis allows us to see that rivalry being worked out in a new context—the clinical practice of medicine. The scientific education of the physician, the acquisition of knowledge, is an education demanding analytical cognition, but the application of knowledge often takes place in the context of irreducible uncertainty that induces intuitive cognition. Different physicians work out the rivalry between the two in different ways. Some accept intuition as part of the art of medicine; some, like Sackett, condemn it, seeking analytical solutions instead. All find that the rivalry between intuition and analysis must be resolved somehow.

## Politics

I return again to Isaiah Berlin, who describes for us the cognitive activity of two giants of history, Benjamin Disraeli and Karl Marx. Berlin uses the intuitive-analytical distinction to contrast and compare the manner in which these two political theorists approached their work. Here is part of what Berlin has to say about Disraeli (1804–1881), who earned a place in history for greatly extending the power and scope of the British Empire during the nineteenth century:

> Disraeli was always drawn to the non-rational sides of life. He was a genuine romantic not merely in the extravagance and flamboyance of his works, the poses that he struck, and the many vanities of his private and political life—these could be regarded as relatively superficial. He was a romantic in a deeper sense, in that he believed that the true forces that governed the lives of individuals and societies were not intelligible to analytical reason, not codifiable by an kind of systematic, scientific investigation, but were unique, mysterious, dark and impalpable, beyond the reach of reason. He believed deeply in the vast influence of superior individuals—men of genius lifted high over the head of the mob—masters of the destinies of nations. He believed in heroes no less than his detractor Carlyle. He despised equality, mediocrity, and the common man. He saw history as the story of conspiracies by means of hidden power everywhere, and delighted in the thought. Utilitarianism, sober observation, experiment, mathematical reasoning, rationalism, common sense, the astonishing achievements and constructions of scientific reason—the true glory of humanity since the seventeenth century—these were almost nothing to him. . . . He was passionately convinced that intuition and imagination were vastly superior to reason and method. He believed in temperament, blood, race, the unaccountable leaps of genius. He was an antirationalist through and through. Art, love, passion, the mystical elements of religion, meant more to him than railways or the transforming discoveries of the natural sciences, or the industrial might of England, or social improvement, or any truth obtained by measurement, statistics, deduction.[50]

Berlin's elegant prose leaves no doubt in our minds about Disraeli's reliance on intuitive cognition. Karl Marx's enthusiasm for and commitment to analysis, on the other hand, is so well known that Berlin does not pursue his examination of Marx in similar detail. What he does tell us, however, is sufficient to make clear the difference between Disraeli and Marx in the preferred modes of cognition:

> I shall not dwell at length on Disraeli's diametrical opposite, Karl Marx, whose case is better known. Karl Marx, as we all know, took a path directly contrary to that of Disraeli. So far from spurning reason, he wished to apply it to human affairs. He believed himself to be a scientist, Engels saw him as the Darwin of the social sciences. He wished to perform a rational analysis of what caused social development to occur as it did, why human beings had hitherto largely failed, and why they could and would in the future succeed in attaining peace, harmony, cooperation and, above all, the self-understanding which is a prerequisite of rational self-direction.
>
> This was remote from Disraeli's mode of thought; indeed it was what he most deeply abhorred.[51]

Berlin draws a similar distinction between two twentieth-century politicians of great stature—Woodrow Wilson and Franklin Roosevelt, asserting that they represent contrasting types of statesmen. First, Wilson:

The first kind of statesman is essentially a man of single principle and fanatical vision. Possessed by his own bright, coherent dream, he usually understands neither people nor events. He has no doubts or hesitations and by concentration of will-power, directness and strength he is able to ignore a great deal of what goes on outside him. This very blindness and stubborn self-absorption occasionally, in certain situations, enable him to bend events and men to his own fixed pattern. His strength lies in the fact that weak and vacillating human beings, themselves too insecure or incapable of deciding between alternatives, find relief and peace and strength in submitting to the leadership of a single leader of super-human size, to whom all issues are clear, whose universe consists entirely of primary colours, mostly black and white, and who marches towards his goal looking neither to right nor to left, buoyed up by the violent vision within him. Such men differ widely in moral and intellectual quality, like forces of nature, and do both good and harm in the world.[52]

Berlin then offered this description of a second type, unmistakably Roosevelt:

The second type of politician possesses antennae of the greatest possible delicacy, which convey to him, in ways difficult or impossible to analyse, the perpetually changing contours of events and feelings and human activities round them—they are gifted with a peculiar, political sense fed on a capacity to take in minute impressions, to integrate a vast multitude of small evanescent unseizable detail, such as artists possess in relation to their material. Statesmen of this type know what to do and when to do it, if they are to achieve their ends, which themselves are usually not born within some private world of inner thought, or introverted feeling, but are the crystallisation, the raising to great intensity and clarity, of what a large number of their fellow citizens are thinking and feeling in some dim, inarticulate, but nevertheless persistent fashion. In virtue of this capacity to judge their material, very much as a sculptor knows what can be moulded out of wood and what out of marble, and how and when, they resemble doctors who have a natural gift for curing, which does not directly depend upon that knowledge of scientific anatomy which can only be learned by obsenation or experiment, or from the experiences of others, though it could not exist without it. This instinctive, or at any rate incommunicable, knowledge of where to look for what one needs, the power of divining where the treasure lies, is something common to many types of genius, to scientists and mathematicians no less than to businessmen and administrators and politicians. . . . Roosevelt was a magnificent virtuoso of this type, and he was the most benevolent as well as the greatest master of his craft in modern times. He really did desire a better life for mankind.[53]

One modern politician who has reason to understand the nature and implications of Marx's theory is Vaclav Havel. A leader of dissent against communism and imprisoned for many years, Havel became the first president of Czechoslovakia in 1989, after the overthrow of communism. I include here part of a speech he gave at the World Economic Forum on February 8, 1992, because in it he articulates his preference with regard to the kind of cognitive processes to be employed in the political process—surely a new event in the history of politics and surely a matter of interest not only to cognitive psychologists but to anyone interested in governance.

The modern era has been dominated by the culminating belief, expressed in different forms, that the world—and Being as such—is a wholly knowable system governed by a finite number of universal laws that man can grasp and rationally direct for his own benefit. This era, beginning in the Renaissance and developing from the Enlightenment to socialism, from positivism to scientism, from the Industrial Revolution to the information revolution, was characterized by rapid advances in rational, cognitive thinking.

This, in turn, gave rise to the proud belief that man, as the pinnacle of everything that exists, was capable of objectively describing, explaining and controlling everything that exists, and of possessing the one and only truth about the world. It was an era in which there was a cult of depersonalized objectivity, an era in which objective knowledge was amassed and technologically exploited, an era of belief in automatic progress brokered by the scientific method. It was an era of systems, institutions, mechanisms and statistical averages. It was an era of ideologies, doctrines, interpretations of reality, an era in which the goal was to find a universal theory of the world, and thus a universal key to unlock its prosperity.

Communism was the perverse extreme of this trend. It was an attempt, on the basis of a few propositions masquerading as the only scientific truth, to organize all of life according to a single model, and to subject it to central planning and control regardless of whether or not that was what life wanted.

The fall of Communism can be regarded as a sign that modern thought—based on the premise that the world is objectively knowable, and that the knowledge so obtained can be absolutely generalized—has come to a final crisis. This era has created the first global, or planetary, technical civilization, but it has reached the limit of its potential, the point beyond which the abyss begins. The end of Communism is a serious warning to all mankind. It is a signal that the era of arrogant, absolutist reason is drawing to a close and that it is high time to draw conclusions from that fact.[54]

Havel thus makes a strong appeal to the softer, intuitive cognitive processes. In further remarks he asks for "a politician [who] must become a person again" and who will put his trust not in "a scientific representation and analysis of the world" but in the "world itself," trusting not mere "sociological statistics" but "real people." All this, no doubt, was in response to having to bear the consequences of Marx's analytical, scientific socialism.

As might be expected, however, replies from those whose lives have been devoted to the pursuit of problems in hard, analytical terms were not long in coming. Havel's speech was printed in the March 1, 1992, edition of the *New York Times*, and the replies appeared two weeks later, in the March, 17 edition. Here is one scientist's reply:

The theme of distrust of scientific reasoning, which pervades Mr. Havel's remarks, appears to me to represent misperceptions of science common to all too many nonscientists. From the first day to the last day of my 45–year career as a research scientist, I never had either the reason or the inclination to believe that scientists were capable of "objectively describing, explaining and controlling everything that exists" or that "the world is a wholly knowable system."

Nor did most of my scientific colleagues, except, perhaps, for those who were the politicians of the scientific establishment. Science, for me, was always an adventure of the human intellect, a search for partial understanding, which was occasionally rewarded by the emergence of theories that had the potential to improve the human condition.

The problem is not too much trust in objectivity, too much rationality, but rather that in more than 5,000 years of human civilization, not just the last 200, human irrationality has been the common denominator of human behavior. In this country, in our time, we are paralyzed by successful appeals to irrationality. Talk to someone about how an expanding population will someday outgrow the food supply, and the response is likely to be that such a problem will not occur for 500 years! Mention the need to make guns completely unavailable to unauthorized civilians, and you are told that we cannot infringe on the rights of hunters!

It is not some undefined journey to "the heart of reality through personal experience" or some even less definable, mystical trust in "the world itself" that will be our salvation, but rather a determined effort, guided by scientists in many disciplines and supported without reservation by politicians, to begin loosening the grip of human irrationality.[55]

Thus, the rivalry between intuition and analysis has had a definite place in politics; as Havel's speech indicates, it is likely to continue to do so.

Because of its elusiveness, an appeal ot intuition can bring a political interrogation to a halt, as the following interchange between reporters and the Speaker of the House Newt Gingrich illustrates:

At a breakfast with reporters . . . Speaker Newt Gingrich was asked why seven years was so important (for balancing the budget). He replied. "Seven is the longest period in which you can maintain the discipline to insist on it happening."
And what is the basis for that view?
"Intuition," Mr. Gingrich answered.[56]

And that apparently was that.

### Literature

In literature meaning is constructed in a manner that is never completely retraceable, logically perfect, or coherent. Literature is thus always partly a product of intuition on the part of the writer, its meaning always partly a product of intuition on the part of the reader. When the intuitions of writer and reader join, meaning emerges, revealing what seems to be the true nature of certain aspects of existence, which at other times seem cloaked in ambiguity.

I cannot pretend to be a critical reviewer of such literature; therefore, my examples of the role of intuition and analysis will be highly personal. For example, *Zorba the Greek* dramatizes for me the virtual impossibility of communication between a cool, analytical Englishman and a passionate, intuitive Greek. When the Englishman patiently and carefully lectures Zorba on all the reasons why his recent behavior has been outrageously wrong (spending all the money entrusted to him by the Englishman on wine, women, and song), Zorba, after listening intently, replies, "Ah, Boss, if you could only dance that for me!" Surely the author, Nikos Kazantzakis, was intent on demonstrating the incompatibility between the language of logic and the language of pictorial imagery.

Kazantzakis wanted to show the incompatibility, yet the legitimacy, of both analysis and intuition. George Steiner, one of our great literary critics, wanted to show that the writer Simone Weil had only one goal in mind:

At every possible point and beyond, Simone Weil chose thought against life, logic against the pragmatic, the laser of analysis and enforced deduction against the fitful half-light, the compromise, and the muddle that allow the rest of us to carry on our existence.[57]

Steiner thus shows us an author's clear preference for analytical cognition. Mark Twain, however, in the practical context of describing how he became a riverboat pilot in the era before the Civil War, demonstrates that this choice has a price. In his autobiography, *Life on the Mississippi* (1896), Twain describes the emotional aspects of the rivalry between intuition and analysis; he shows why people are often loath to give up intuitive approaches to tasks in favor of analytical ones, even on those occasions when they know that the latter works far better than the former.

When Twain began his tour as a student pilot there were no navigational aids on the river; the novice had to learn to "read" the river, to recognize intuitively various cues on the surface of the water so as to avoid all the hazards—sand bars, tree trunks, and other dangers lying hidden beneath the surface—and to pilot the boat accordingly. Mistakes could be costly, if not fatal. Twain reports on one session with his teacher, an experienced pilot, who tried to explain to him how to detect the difference between a dangerous "bluff reef" and a harmless "wind reef":

> "Now don't you see the difference? It wasn't anything but a *wind* reef. The wind does that."
>
> "So I see. But it is exactly like a bluff reef. How am I ever going to tell them apart?"
>
> "I can't tell you. It is an instinct. By and by you will just naturally *know* one from the other, but you never will be able to explain why or how you know them apart."[58]

This statement by Mark Twain's pilot-teacher is an excellent one for our purposes; here is rivalry between intuition and analysis personified by student and teacher. The student wants rules ("How am I ever going to tell them apart?"). Twain wants his teacher to explain; that is, provide him with clear, retraceable if-then rules ("If you see this, then do that"). Twain, like all students, wants rules that are defensible (that will stand up to the question "why?"). With such rules, Twain would have an analytically derived knowledge base.

Instead, the teacher tells Twain that although *he*—the teacher—can tell the difference between a "wind reef" (harmless) and a "bluff reef" (dangerous), unfortunately he can't tell Twain how he does it. (How many experts have made similar remarks to their apprentices?) The addition of "by and by you will just naturally know one from the other" means that because his teacher can't tell him what he needs to know, Twain will have to rely on his intuition. Nevertheless, he *will* learn. How? Through experience. And when Twain does learn, he "never will be able to explain [to *his* students] why or how"; his knowledge will also be applied intuitively.

The relationship between good intuitive judgment and experience is widely accepted today. Airplane pilots carefully log their hours of flight time to prove that they have acquired the requisite good judgment, physicians who are "experienced" are valued more highly than those who are not—all on the assumption that "by and by" they have come "just naturally to know" what to do. Many teachers of professional skills, especially those involving different modes of perception (visual—nurses, physicians, livestock judges; auditory— musicians; tactile—soil experts; taste— culinary experts, oenologists) have expressed similar opinions to their students, who, although perhaps frustrated, were also perhaps thrilled to know they would somehow learn a highly valued skill, the basis of which would remain inexpressible. The idea that "experience" will teach us what our teacher can't is an old one and an important one, and I will examine it in detail in later chapters.

It is within the framework of the narrative itself, however, that literature makes use of the rivalry between intuition and analysis. For the narrative reveals information to us over the course of the story, appealing on one occasion to our intuitions and on another to our analytical capacity and often pitting these against one another in suble and enchanting ways.

No one has made importance of the narrative more evident than the eminent psychologist Jerome Bruner.[59] His work is particularly relevant to the matter of rivalry between intuition and analysis: He states:

> There are two modes of cognitive functioning, two modes of thought, each providing distinctive ways of ordering experience, of constructing reality. The two (though complementary) are irreducible to one another. Efforts to reduce one mode to the other or to ignore one at the expense of the other inevitably fail to capture the rich diversity of thought.[60]

Not only are these two modes of thought "irreducible to one another, . . . each of the ways of knowing, moreover, has operating principles of its own and its own criteria of well-formedness . . . the structure of a well-formed logical argument differs radically from that of a well-wrought story."[61]

Bruner elucidates the manner in which these two modes of thought differ by considering the narrative. But I want to turn to the place of the narrative in the criminal justice system, for this is where psychologists have shown that it plays a crucial role. Both prosecutors and defense attorneys generally try to construct a story regarding the plaintiff's behavior, the plausibility of which will be determined largely by its coherence. And studies of jurors' decision-making behavior show that jurors are persuaded either by the plausibility—the coherence—of the story offered by either side or by the story they construct for themselves. N. Pennington and R. Hastie "propose four certainty principles—coverage, coherence, uniqueness, and goodness-of-fit—that govern which story will be accepted, which decision will be selected, and the confidence or level of certainty with which a particular decision will be made."[62] Evolutionary psychology lends credence to their theory. Stories must have been the vital source of communication as soon as *Homo sapiens* constructed language. Who did what, when, and where, communicated in narrative form, would have been the vital stuff of social life. Sending and receiving information via stories and the ability to appraise accurately the truthfulness of a story would have been positive assets in a society where storytelling was the primary, if not the only, source of information.

In modern society virtually every child develops a familiarity with stories and, to some extent, develops the ability to appraise their truthfulness. Thus, every juror is familiar with storytelling and with ways of testing truthfulness. If Pennington and Hastie are right, jurors test the stories offered to them in terms of "coverage, coherence, uniqueness, and goodness-of-fit." More specifically, the researchers say that "the juror organizes the evidence into a story that emphasizes the causal and intentional relation among evidence items."[63] It will be difficult indeed to persuade any juror to give up a story that meets these criteria in favor of one that is based on analytical reasoning from facts, unless the facts are few, simple, and readily understandable. In short, a coherent story will carry the day unless the evidence is so unmistakably clear that no story, no matter how plausible, can stand against it. Otherwise, stories will have to compete on the grounds supported by Pennington and Hastie.

## Rivalry Between Intuition and Analysis in the Psychology of Judgment and Decision Making

I have discussed the ubiquity of irreducible uncertainty and the need to use human judgment in a variety of fields. I have also described the rivalry between two sharply different modes of cognition—intuition and analysis—that are employed to cope with uncertainty. Have psychologists taken account of this rivalry? Do they take account of it in their research on judgment and decision making? Do they favor one over the other? Can they justify their choice? In this chapter I describe how psychologists have addressed this topic; in Chapter 6 I will describe how researchers studying judgment and decision making have addressed it.

S. Epstein has reviewed psychologists' approach to this rivalry. He notes first that "the most influential division of the mind has been Freud's distinction between the primary process and the secondary process."[64] Epstein then adopts an evolutionary point of view from which he criticizes Freud's description of the (unconscious) primary process:

> A critical weakness in Freud's conceptualization of the unconscious is that it makes little sense from an evolutionary perspective. It is essentially a maladaptive system, capable, perhaps, of generating dreams and psychotic aberrations but not up to the task, for either human or nonhuman animals, of promoting adaptive behavior in the real world. Operating under the direction of the primary process alone, individuals would starve to death amidst wish-fulfillment hallucinations of unlimited gratification. That they do not, Freud attributed to the secondary process. This ad hoc solution leaves unexplained the questions of how the maladaptive system evolved in the first place and how nonhuman animals are able to adapt to their environments at all without a secondary process (which is intimately tied to language).[65]

Epstein notes that Pavlov also "proposed a distinction between a first and second signaling system, the former including nonverbal conditioning and the latter verbally mediated processes" and adds that several other experimental-cognitive psychologists—Anderson, Johnson-Laird, Rosch, and Winograd[66] among others—have done so as well. Several developmental psychologists, including Piaget,[67] make a similar distinction. Epstein emphasizes the distinction drawn by researchers, particularly A. Tversky and D. Kahneman,[68] between judgment and decision making. He explains that "they concluded that there are two common forms of reasoning—a *natural,* intuitive mode and an *extensional,* logical mode." He asserts that "an extensive body of research on heuristic processing has supported this view"[69]—that is, that there are two separate cognitive systems. Social psychologists (including Brewer[70]) have made use of the distinction in their studies of stereotyping, and the eminent cognitive psychologist Jerome Bruner "has proposed two modes of mental representation, *propositional* and *narrative.*"[71]

Epstein also presents his own view, endorsing the notion of a rational system in contrast to an "experiential" system, which I will describe later in more detail.

In their important review in the *Annual Review of Psychology,* P. Slovic, B. Fischhoff, and S. Lichtenstein emphasize a trend in research that focuses on the inadequacies of intuitive cognition in relation to the logical or mathematical requirements of models of analytical cognition.[72] Subsequent reviews through 1993 make it clear, however, that different researchers hold different views of the value of intuition and that these differences motivate and guide current research.

## Positive Views of Intuitive Cognition

Some psychologists hold a generally positive view of intuition, seeing it as an unmitigated cognitive asset that allows the enormous benefit of unconscious "leaps" to new discoveries. And indeed, such benefits have often been cited in the history of mathematics, science, the arts, and the humanities. Seldom, if ever, does the positive view of intuition admit that there might be flaws in this process or mention the possible costs of error; seldom does the positive view acknowledge that intuition might also have intrinsic *negative* aspects.

The positive view of intuition has a long history. The intuitive mode of cognition was generally favored by the supporters of the "counter-Enlightenment" of the eighteenth century, which denigrated the scientific, rational approach to human affairs as inappropriate, false, and misleading. Even modern definitions of intuition are positive. Webster's *Third International Dictionary* defines intuition as "Coming to direct knowledge or certainty without reasoning or inferring; immediate cognizance or conviction without reasoning."

It is not surprising, therefore, that Jerome Bruner, who initiated much of what is now called cognitive psychology, found it necessary to define the concept of intuitive cognition. His definition is positive: "the intellectual technique of arriving at plausible but tentative formulations without going through the analytic steps by which such formulations would be found to be valid or invalid conclusions."[73] Surely it is desirable to achieve plausible answers by "leaping over" the analytical steps necessary to produce and thus to justify them. That is exactly what startled Freeman Dyson and many others when they found that Richard Feynman "just wrote down the solutions out of his head without ever writing down the equations." And it was a similar ability that called the mathematician Godfrey Hardy's attention to the work of the untutored genius Ramanujan, who wrote proofs in a manner that left mathematicians bewildered.

The shortcuts offered by intuition are compelling and indeed often compel hardheaded scientists to embrace in themselves what they might find dubious in others. Here is H. A. Simon on the ability to determine a person's character by looking at his or her eyes:

> In the early 1950s, when I was on a faculty recruiting trip from Pittsburgh, I had dinner with Marschak [a famous economist] one evening in the Quadrangle Club at the University of Chicago. The conversation turned to the selection of faculty. As he had assembled a spectacular group of stars in the Cowles Commission, I asked him what qualities he looked for in selecting staff. "Oh," said he, "I pick people with good eyes." I stared at him. Good eyes—what could he mean? I told him he was joking [Simon's scientific background asserts itself], but he insisted: He looked at their eyes. And then I began thinking of the clear dark Armenian eyes of Arrow, the cool blue Frisian eyes of Koopmans, and the sharp black Roman eyes of Modigliani. It was certainly true that they all had remarkable eyes. Ever since, I think I have included that among my own selection criteria; intelligence shines through the eyes.[74]

Astounding as that remark may be, Simon is not alone; here is Bruner's praise of "uncanny" abilities: "I am struck," he says, "by the uncanny sense with which a gifted New York magazine editor can circulate cannily among the aspiring and promising at a cocktail party, while bypassing the disgruntled and rejected."[75] Such intuitive visual appraisals, usually expressed with great confidence, go on throughout the day—and night—and have affected the lives of all of us throughout history. The importance of the topic can hardly be overestimated, and, of course, it falls within the same general area of judgment as the quotations from Simon and Bruner. Such judgments are an integral part of the appraisal of persons in all areas of life everywhere, from one's appraisals of one's safety on an elevator to one's assessment of the enemy in war. Indeed, a correct appraisal of a person's character can be a matter of life and death, as the following anecdote from Thomas Powers's book, *Heisenberg's War,* shows: Powers says that the instructions for a U.S. intelligence agent were to "size up" the German scientist Heisenberg, whom the U.S. intelligence agency suspected of developing an atomic bomb for the Germans, while Heisenberg was at a meeting of physicists in Switzerland. If Heisenberg were to somehow indicate that he was indeed working on the development of an atomic weapon for the Germans, the agent was to kill him. The agent, a former baseball player, fully prepared to follow his orders, listened and looked. He, like Marschak, Simon, and Bruner, made judgments about Heisenberg's eyes and concluded that they indeed had a "sinister" look. Perhaps he was looking for what Socrates had already noticed: "Did you never observe the narrow intelligence flashing from the keen eye of a clever rogue?"[76] But other aspects of Heisenberg's behavior suggested that he was not working on an atomic weapon. The agent did nothing, and Heisenberg survived.[77]

Heisenberg was lucky; put at the mercy of the unexplained power of intuition, he escaped. It took Powers fourteen years of research to reach the same conclusion that the agent reached in the brief period of the lecture. This was indeed a case of "arriving at plausible [but final] . . . formulations without going through the analytic steps by which [the] . . . formulations would be found to be valid or invalid," as Bruner put it.[78] If ever there was a case of a positive view of intuition and a heavy reliance on its accuracy, it was this decision of the high command of the wartime intelligence agency, the Office of Strategic Services, to entrust a life-or-death judgment to a single agent's intuition.

The psychologist Egon Brunswik first presented a model of intuitive cognition, developed from his theory of visual perception. The principal idea behind the model was that perception of the physical (and social) world was derived from multiple fallible (i.e., probabilistic) sources of information. Perception psychologists call these fallible sources of information "cues." Because I extend the model to include social and political judgments, I replace "cues" with "indicators," a term in more general use outside psychology. Where Brunswik and perception psychologists talk about how the organism responds to "multiple fallible cues," I will refer to "multiple fallible indicators." The word "fallible" is of critical importance; this term brings us face to face with uncertainty in the natural world around us. Brunswik's model of this situation is called the "lens model" because it represents the organism in an environment that offers a variety of fallible indicators and focuses that information in a cognitive system that reaches inferences about external objects. As may be seen from

Figure 3-3, the lens model tells the researcher what to look for. What *tangible* indicators are present and available to the organism in its effort to reach an inference about an *intangible* object or event of interest? That is, what information that can be "seen" is available to make inferences about the "unseen"? How is the information that can be "seen" used by the organism to make inferences about the "unseen"?

This model transfers nicely from visual perception to social judgment. We can ask what tangible indicators are available to us when we want to infer an intangible state residing within another person—intelligence, for example. And we can ask what observable tangible indicators a person uses when inferring the intangible, the unobservable, in another person. In the case of intelligence, we know that there are many indicators of another's intelligence, but none are trustworthy (unless we include records of accomplishments, and even these may fool us). That's why the statements by Marschak, Simon, and Bruner about their reliance on eyes as indicators of a person's worth or ability seem peculiar. We know they are wrong; we know that there is no single reliable indicator for these intangible states, states that are not directly observable. The spy who found Heisenberg's eyes to have a sinister look also knew that was wrong; he took other factors into consideration and decided not to kill him. We can forgive Socrates for his mistake in relying on a single indicator; after all, he did not have decades of research to which to refer. But can we forgive Simon and Bruner? Were they carried away by a lapse in judgment?

The lens model thus represents an uncertain world represented by many fallible indicators and an organism that has the capacity to integrate them—without awareness—into a judgment that displays remarkable accuracy in visual perception and various degrees of accuracy in other circumstances. It is our lack of awareness of how we integrate information that makes it an intuitive process.[79]

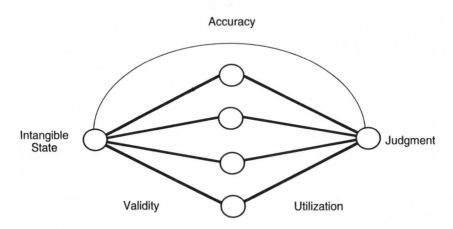

**Figure 3-3**    Schematic depiction of Brunswik's lens model that illustrates how a person's judgment of an intangible object, event, or state is made on the basis of multiple fallible indicators (left side of the lens). The right side of the lens shows the utilization of the several indicators.

I will have much more to say about the lens model and its representation of intuitive cognition in later chapters.[80]

## Negative Views of Intuitive Cognition

According to the negative view of intuition, the cognitive process that "arrives at plausible but tentative formulations without going through the analytical steps" (in Bruner's words) is usually (if not always) not only wrong but misleadingly convincing, both to those who provide the "formulations" as well as to those who hear them. No one can read through the literature of social psychology from the 1960s through the 1980s without drawing the conclusion that intuition is a hazard, a process not to be trusted, not only because it is inherently flawed by "biases" but because the person who resorts to it is innocently and sometimes arrogantly overconfident when employing it.[81] According to this point of view, human beings are blissfully ignorant of their cognitive "biases," "shortcomings," "distortions," and generally "crippled"[82] cognitive ability.

The negative views of intuition, generated over the past three decades, have widespread implications; they speak directly to scientific work, legal philosophy, judgments from the bench, the education of medical students and clinical psychologists, the diagnostic and therapeutic efforts of physicians at the bedside, and policy formation, among many other professional endeavors. The implications of the negative view of intuition for policy formation are brought together in a coherent, organized form by the psychologist Robyn Dawes in a book titled *Rational Choice in an Uncertain World*. In the introduction Dawes states that "the basic point of this book is that we often think in automatic ways about choice situations, that these automatic thinking processes can be described by certain psychological rules ('heuristics') and that they systematically lead us to make poorer choices than by thinking in a more controlled manner about our decisions."[83] Although Dawes contrasts automatic and controlled thinking, rather than intuitive cognition and analytical cognition, his characterization of these processes makes them equivalent. Indeed, his entire effort is to demonstrate that automatic (intuitive) cognition does lead to poorer choices than does analytical cognition. His analysis of choice processes and his examples leave no doubt that he wishes to persuade his readers to turn away from the use of automatic, unexamined choices in favor of rational analytical methods of choice.[84]

In short, the positive view of intuition observes and celebrates successes, while its failures are ignored or forgotten; the negative view observes and, one suspects, also celebrates, as psychologists are inclined to do, failures; accounts of successful intuition are conspicuously absent from the research that endorses the negative view. Among psychologists, the negative view currently remains predominant.

Their sharp differences notwithstanding, holders of both positive and negative views share a common point of departure, namely, analytical cognition. The positive view praises, the negative view denigrates, the ability of intuitive cognition to reach useful conclusions that no analytical model can provide. If opinions are divided with respect to the value of intuitive cognition, however, they are also divided with regard to analytical cognition.

## Positive and Negative Views of Analytical Cognition

It is unnecessary to detail and explicate the positive views of analytical cognition; its successes have been with us since the earliest philosophers, the earliest scientists, and the earliest technologists. Indeed, analytical cognition has come to define the best of thought—the crowning achievement of humankind—and thus it provides the standard by which all but creative cognitive activity is judged (as Gerbert noted, analytical cognition can make a contribution even here). As a result, analytical cognition—logic—is frequently *taught*, but intuitive cognition never is; no one knows how to do it, although, as we have seen, the engineering professors Ferguson and Petroski wish it could be done.

Few psychologists have dared to question the positive value of analytical cognition. One, however, did so in rather dramatic fashion. Striking foresight regarding the dangers of analytical cognition, written before the widespread use of computers, is contained in the following sentence written by Egon Brunswik in 1956: "The constantly looming catastrophes of the intellect would be found more often to develop into catastrophes of action were it not for the mellowing effect of the darker, more feeling-like and thus more dramatically convincing primordial layers of cognitive adjustment [i.e., intuition]."[85] J. March confirms these "catastrophes" of the intellect by referring to the "tales of horror [that] have become contemporary clichés of studies of rational analysis."[86] Indeed, it is the catastrophes of the intellect produced by analytical, scientific engineering that Ferguson describes as the source of the catastrophes of failed structures (he cites the Hubble telescope; Petroski cites bridge failures) produced by engineers who were not taught that engineering is an art.[87]

Examples of "catastrophes of the intellect" are becoming easy to find, as March notes, as the analytical methods of science and management technology are increasingly applied to solve problems inherent in large industrial societies. A failure in a small part of a network of relationships (e.g., highways, communications) can result in disasters of staggering proportions. As a result, the presumed benefits of analytical cognition are frequently challenged.

In later chapters I will describe how contemporary researchers in the field of judgment and decision making have pointed to the dangers of analytical cognition. L. L. Lopes and G. C. Oden, for example, refer to the "fragility" of analytical cognition.[88] In the area of social policy, a prominent book by P. K. Howard titled *The Death of Common Sense* is directed entirely to the absurdities that arise from the rigorous application of rules and regulation;[89] policymakers have been eager to accept Howard's conclusions (matters I will discuss in Chapter 11). For the present, however, we need to ask: Which view is correct?

## Which View Is Correct?

My view is that human cognition is clearly capable of both intuition and analysis and that each has value. Modern existence would hardly be possible without both; there have been positive contributions from both, and modern existence has suffered from the imperfections of both. The rivalry, the competition between them, can be ended by recognizing the properties and merits of each in the various contexts in which they are applied. Reichenbach's distinction between the context of discovery and the context of verification may not be sufficiently general, but it is certainly a step in the right direction.

Egon Brunswik made clear the relative value of each mode of cognition. In describing analytical cognition, for example, he indicated its assets (e.g., precision) and its liabilities (e.g., catastrophic error):

> The entire pattern of . . . [analytical] reasoning [in contrast to intuitive perception] . . . resembles the switching of trains at a multiple junction, with each of the possible courses being well organized and of machine-like precision yet leading to drastically different destinations only one of which is acceptable in the light of the cognitive goal. This pattern is illustrative of the dangers inherent in explicit logical operations. The relative ease of switching off at any one of a series of choice points in a basically linear, unidimensional, all-or-none series of relays is at least in part the result of the precise formulation, yet *relatively* small number of basic cues, involved in most typical reasoning tasks.[90]

This analogy points to weaknesses and dangers of analytical cognition that are never mentioned by those who praise it while denouncing intuition. Never mentioned is the fragility of analysis that can lead to striking, costly errors within the carefully thought out analytical systems designed to remove intuitive cognition.[91]

In the following paragraphs we see Brunswik's views of the advantages and the disadvantages of intuition:

> On the other hand . . ., intuitive perception must simultaneously integrate many different avenues of approach, or cues. . . . [It] must remain based on insufficient evidence, that is, on criteria none of which is foolproof or fully "ecologically valid."[92]

He then points out the advantages of intuition:

> A further . . . distinction between intuitive perception and thinking, is the flash-like speed of perceptual responses. It is a biologically very valuable feature, especially where life is constantly threatened by sudden danger or where chances of success depend on quick action. [But] the almost instantaneous promptness of perception could hardly be achieved without the stereotypy and superficiality in the utilization of cues which we have noted and which makes for a certain intrinsic "stupidity" of the perceptual apparatus (see Brunswik, 1934, pp. 119 f., 128, 223 ff.).
>
> The various rivalries [cf. Berlin] and compromises that characterize these dynamics of check and balance in perception must be seen as chiefly responsible for the above noted relative infrequency of precision. On the other hand, the organic multiplicity of factors entering the process constitutes an effective safeguard against drastic error. . . . the "stupidity" of perception thus is by no means to be construed to mean maladaptiveness; as we all know, life has survived on relative stupidity from time immemorial.[93]

And then he offers a startling conclusion:

> If threatened in its existence it is so by malfunctioning of the intellect rather than by malfunctioning of perception.[94]

That conclusion is startling because it flies in the face of conclusions taken for granted by virtually all contemporary students of judgment and decision making, economists, and nearly all students of policy-making; it restores intuition to a place at the table of reason, as I earlier showed that Havel wishes to do. And it does so because it points to the risk of "malfunction of the intellect," a topic rarely, if ever, considered by the proponents of analysis and the denigrators of intuition. These remarks by Brunswik constitute a principal part of the theme of this book.

Seymour Epstein and his colleagues have emphasized the evolutionary nature of intuitive cognitive processes in contrast to rational, analytical cognition.[95] Epstein states that the "reason why I believe the experiential-nonexperiential [intuitive-analytical] divide is the most fundamental of all is that it is eminently reasonable from an evolutionary perspective."[96] He goes on to observe that an experiential system that learns from past experience "operates in a very different manner from a system developed much later that solves abstract problems by the use of symbols and logical inference."[97] And he finds it "inconceivable" that the "hard-won gains of millions of years of evolution"[98] were simply somehow abandoned or lost once our capacity for analytical cognition was developed, and that only recently.

Epstein becomes very specific about the role of evolution:

> The experiential system is assumed to have a very long evolutionary history and to operate in nonhuman as well as in human animals. Because of their more highly developed brains, it is assumed to operate in far more complex ways in humans. At its lower levels of operation, it is a crude system that automatically, rapidly, effortlessly, and efficiently processes information. At its higher reaches, and particularly in interaction with the rational system, it is a source of intuitive wisdom and creativity. Although it represents events primarily concretely and imagistically, it is capable of generalization and abstraction through the use of prototypes, metaphors, scripts, and narratives.[99]

Epstein's contrast with analytical cognition is persuasive:

> The rational system, in contrast, is a deliberative, effortful, abstract system that operates primarily in the medium of language and has a very brief evolutionary history. It is capable of very high levels of abstraction and long-term delay of gratification. However, it is a very inefficient system for responding to everyday events, and its long term adaptability remains to be tested. (It may yet lead to the destruction of all life on our planet.)[100]

Epstein's approach is independent of the one developed here. It is based on the literature of personality and social psychology; there is virtually no overlap with the judgment and decision-making literature.

The strengths and weaknesses of these two modes of cognition are best summed up by Brunswik:

> Considering all the pros and cons of achievement, the balance sheet of perception [intuition] versus thinking may thus seem seriously upset against thinking, unquestioned favorite of a culture of rational enlightenment as the latter has been. From the point of view of strategy, perception would likewise appear to have gained in stature by our realization of its inherent "vicarious functioning" [i.e., ability to shift reliance from one piece of redundant information—cue—to another]. [Thus] perception must appear as the more truly behavior-like function when compared with deductive reasoning with its machine-like, precariously one-tracked, tight-rope modes of procedure.[101]

By calling our attention to the risk of error in the use of analysis and intuition and by pointing out the pros and cons of each mode of cognition, Brunswik puts us in a position to ask: In which set of conditions is a particular mode of cognition more appropriate? What social or ecological context is likely to induce more of the advantages and fewer of the disadvantages of each cognitive mode?

## Implications for Policy Formation

We have seen that intuition and analyses are modes of cognition that are prominent, not only in the history of thought, but in science, law, medicine, literature, and, of course, psychology. The prominence of these concepts has led scholars to take them for granted; as a result, their properties remain largely implicit rather than explicit. And because the rivalry between them is embedded in almost every discussion of cognition, and certainly in every discussion of judgment and decision making, it remains fundamental and unresolved.

Why are these two forms of cognition rivals? What are they competing for? They are rivals for the right to claim the virtue of superior cognitive competence. Those competing claims carry great significance for policy formation, for, as Isaiah Berlin tells us:

> Those who made large claims for non-scientific knowledge have been accused by their adversaries of irrationalism and obscurantism . . . and have, in their turn, charged their opponents, the ambitious champions of science, with making absurd claims, promising the impossible, issuing false prospectuses . . . and all this because they will not, being vain and headstrong, admit that too many factors in too many situations are always unknown, and not discoverable by the methods of natural science.[102]

Berlin's all too familiar description of the rivalry is based on his examination of centuries in the history of thought. Is it outdated? Hardly.

B. Berger and her colleagues, in their stirring description of "The Idea of the University," argue that antirationalism continues to thrive where one least expects it, in universities:

> While the storm troopers of the counterculture have long since disappeared and the more extreme of their radical claims no longer attract the blanket endorsement they once did, the antirational cognitive style of the culture has managed to survive in many ways. . . . More than any place else, the antirationalist tenets of the counterculture managed to survive in the academy. Here left to flourish unchecked by the harsh realities of the ordinary world, they continue to flourish and expand. There are virtually no intellectuals in the academy today who are not in their heart of hearts antistructuralists and infected by the bug of antirationalism in one way or another.[103]

Gerald Holton, perhaps today's most prominent historian of science, has similar worries about the role of antiscience today: "It was not on the better calculation of planetary orbits or cannon ball trajectories that scientists in the seventeenth century based their chief claim to attention, but on their role in replacing the whole prescientific belief system."[104] But "today there exist a number of different groups which from their various perspectives oppose what they conceive of as the hegemony of science-as-done-today in our culture. . . . Each, in its own way, advocates nothing less than the end of science as we know it."[105] Holton also refers to "a new wing of sociologists of science who wish, in Bruno Latour's words, to 'abolish the distinction between science and fiction.'"[106]

Yet we must remember Vaclav Havel's remarks in which he finds the demand for rational analytical cognition to have been drastically wrong and claims that it produced one of the most oppressive social systems of all time:

> Communism was the perverse extreme of this trend. It was an attempt, on the basis of a few propositions masquerading as the only scientific truth, to organize all of life according to a single model, and to subject it to central planning and control regardless of whether or not that was what life wanted.
>
> The fall of Communism can be regarded as a sign that modern thought—based on the premise that the world is objectively knowable, and that the knowledge so obtained can be absolutely generalized—has come to a final crisis. This era has created the first global, or planetary, technical civilization, but it has reached the limit of its potential, the point beyond which the abyss begins. The end of Communism is a serious warning to all mankind. It is a signal that the era of arrogant, absolutist reason is drawing to a close and that it is high time to draw conclusions from that fact.[107]

I will pursue in detail the implications of this rivalry for social policy in later chapters. I end this chapter with the conclusion that, as matters stand, no one can claim superiority for his or her favorite mode of cognition, nor should one; the evidence won't permit it. The rivalry will continue, as it should. Nevertheless, as long as the rivalry does continue, the study of human judgment must attempt to cope with the question of the competence of human judgment, whether analytically or intuitively based. In order to do so, I turn next to the second part of the foundation of this book— the distinction between the coherence and the correspondence theories of truth.

# II TENSION

The pervasive and persistent rivalry between intuition and analysis that can be seen in so many of our academic and intellectual pursuits is paralleled by another rivalry. Two grand metatheories have been persistent rivals in the history of science in general and in the history of research in judgment and decision making in particular. Research programs in judgment and decision making can easily and usefully be classified into one of these two well-established types of scientific endeavor, namely, the correspondence metatheory of judgment and decision making and the coherence metatheory of judgment and decision making. Because the reader is likely to be unfamiliar with these terms, I offer here a brief explanation.

The goal of a correspondence metatheory is to describe and explain the process by which a person's judgments achieve *empirical accuracy*. The goal of a coherence metatheory of judgment, in contrast, is to describe and explain the process by which a person's judgments achieve logical, or mathematical, or statistical *rationality*. Thus, the word "correspondence" can be roughly translated into *accuracy*: Did the interest rates go up, as the banker predicted? Did it rain, as the weather forecaster predicted? The word "coherence" can be roughly translated into *rationality*: Did the argument for that conclusion meet the test of logical or mathematical consistency?

It may come as a surprise to the reader that rationality does not directly imply accuracy and vice versa, but brief reflection shows that this is not the case. Rationality always operates in a closed system; given the premises, certain conclusions always follow *if* a rational reasoning process is followed. When the reasoning process satisfies a logical test, the system is termed coherent, and that is all it is and all it claims to be. Many people, for example, believe that every word in the Bible is true. It would be rational for these people to believe that the world is flat, for the Bible indicates that that is the case. Historically, however, the empirical question of whether the earth is flat has been largely ignored; medieval scholars spent their time arguing about the *rationality*, the logical coherence, of various theological propositions. The correspondence of any theological statement with empirical observations was beside the point. It was Galileo, with his stubborn insistence on empirical facts, who created the tension between truth based on coherent dogma and truth based on the correspondence of ideas with facts. The church resolved this tension by arresting and imprisoning Galileo and then denying his conclusions for more than three hundred years. It takes very, very strong empirical contradictions to overturn a highly coherent theory in which a great deal has been invested on the assumption that it is true. Religion is not unique in its stubbornness. Coherence, in and of itself, is a very powerful organizing principle. It is seldom given up easily.

Scientific research seeks both coherence and correspondence but gets both only in advanced, successful work. Most scientific disciplines are forced to tolerate contradictory facts and competitive theories. Researchers must, therefore, live with the tension created by those who wish to pursue the reconciliation of facts and those who wish to resolve the contradictions of theories. But policymakers find it much harder than researchers to live with this tension because they are expected to *act* on the basis of information. Here is an example of how the implicit use of a coherence theory led to one policy recommendation and the implicit use of a correspondence theory led to another.

At the Science and Public Policy Seminar sponsored by the Federation of Behavioral, Psychological, and Cognitive Sciences in July 1994, Nancy Adler addressed congressional staff members on the question of the cognitive competence of adolescents to decide whether to engage in sexual behavior. Her criterion for competence is rationality, and her criterion for rationality is coherence: "Insofar as people are consistent in their reasoning, insofar as they are making the choice that maximizes their perceived benefits and minimizes their perceived costs, we can consider them rational."[1]

The same sort of argument that is applied to the judgment that the earth is flat—if you believe that every word in the Bible is true and if the Bible indicates that the earth is flat, then it is rational to believe the earth is flat—is thus also used to defend adolescents' judgment that "if you think that you can't get pregnant it may be perfectly rational not to use a contraceptive."[2] If you believe that adolescents are capable of rational cognition, therefore, then it is the adolescents' perceptions of reality that should be changed and it should be the goal of social policy to provide better, more accurate information that would change those perceptions. For on the assumption that rationality will prevail—that is, accurate information will be used in a rational, coherent manner—then rational behavior will follow ("you can affect . . . [the] behavior if you can correct the information"[3]).

Adler's conclusion flies in the face of the results obtained by coherence researchers over the past twenty years, which have emphasized exactly the opposite conclusion (as I will show in Chapter 8). Irrespective of the tenuous basis of Adler's conclusion, it is implicitly based on the coherence theory of truth.

But it is not difficult to find exactly the opposite conclusions drawn from researchers who employ a correspondence theory. G. Loewenstein and F. Furstenberg indicate that merely offering correct information is insufficient to affect behavior: "Imparting knowledge . . . [is] unlikely to be successful in affecting either sexual activity or contraception. Once we controlled for other variables, the effect of knowledge virtually disappeared."[4]

The implications of these two sets of conclusions for public policy could hardly be more pronounced. One researcher tells us that adolescents are rational information processores who simply need better information in order for their decisions to become rational ones; the other researchers tell us the opposite. The fact that these conclusions rest on the use of different methods derived from different theories of truth (and thus different methodologies) was not acknowledged, however. Therefore, the policies they advocate will be based on an implicit choice of methodology as well as explicit choice of result.[5]

# 4 Tension Between Coherence and Correspondence Theories of Competence

Don't you understand the principles of probability?

Richard Feynman to the official who
approved the launch of the Challenger

The use of the terms "coherence" and "correspondence" in the history of judgment and decision making will be unfamiliar to most readers, and although I offered a description of each in the introduction to Part II, the reader will want to see some examples of the difference between these metatheories. I therefore begin this chapter with examples from three different fields in order to demonstrate the cogency and the practical value of making the distinction.

## Engineering

Consider the launch of the space shuttle Challenger. We know from Chapter 2 that considerable confusion and uncertainty existed regarding the probability of a launch failure; the probabilities mentioned in press reports ranged from 1 in 100,000 to 1 in 25. And we know that Richard Feynman was appointed to the presidential commission that investigated the Challenger disaster and that as a result of his inquiries, he judged the probability of a failure to be 1 in 50, much higher than the official estimate. Feynman was so much at odds with the final report on the disaster issued by the presidential commission that he wrote a separate report. In addition, he wrote an eleven-page memoir highly critical of the work of the commission that was published in *Physics Today* in February 1988.[6] This memoir is fascinating because in it Feynman reports, with his usual frankness, on his encounters with various officials of NASA and other agencies regarding the probability of a launch failure. He interviewed an official of the engineering company that had manufactured the Challenger equipment that had failed (the O-rings), the very engineer who, as the critical moment for the launch approached, changed his decision from "no-go" to "go." When Feynman challenged him with the question "Don't you understand the principles of probability?"[7] it is clear that he was challenging the official's competence with regard to his knowledge of how to assess the probability of an event.

Consider the replies the official might have made to Feynman:

- "Of course, I do. Here are the calculations I've made (based on the principles of probability); they show that the probability of a failure is less than 1 in 100,000."
- "I did the calculation in my head (based on my knowledge of the principles of probability), and I could see the probability of failure was minuscule."

Or he might have relied on someone else's knowledge and said:

- "That is a statistician's job; she/he knows the principles of probability; I don't but I don't have to."

Or he might have decided that the principles of probability were irrelevant and said:

- "No, I don't, but I am an engineer, and engineering judgment was simply that the risk of failure was such that it was safe to launch."

In fact, we know how four officials of the company answered this question because Feynman sat down with them and inquired about their estimates of the likelihood of a failure of a launch in this fashion:

> I gave each person a piece of paper. I said, "Now, each of you please write down what you think the probability of failure for a flight is, due to a failure in the engines."
>
> I got four answers—three from the engineers and one from Mr. Lovingood, the manager. The answers from the engineers all said, in one form or another (the usual way engineers write—"reliability limit," or "confidence sub so-on"), almost exactly the same thing: 1 in about 200. Mr. Lovingood's answer said, "Cannot quantify. Reliability is determined by studies of this, checks on that, experience here"—blah, blah, blah, blah, blah.
>
> "Well," I said, "I've got four answers. One of them weaseled." I turned to Mr. Lovingood and said, "I think you weaseled."
>
> He says, "I don't think I weaseled."
>
> "Well, look," I said. "You didn't tell me *what* your confidence was; you told me *how* you determined it. What I want to know is: After you determined it, what *was* it?"
>
> He says, "100 percent." The engineers' jaws drop. My jaw drops. I look at him, everybody looks at him—and he says, "Uh . . . uh, minus epsilon?"
>
> "OK. Now the only problem left is, what is epsilon?"
>
> He says, "1 in 100 000."[8]

But, as we learned earlier, Feynman found the probability of a failed launch to be 1 in 50, a probability far different from 1 in 100,000. Notice the difference in approach between Feynman and the engineers and the manager. For his part, Feynman relies on a single indicator—the relative frequency of failure in recent launches. He hasn't the slightest interest in the engineering judgments based on the coherence of the physical system; he dismisses these merely as "the usual way engineers write—'reliability limit,' or 'confidence sub so-on'." And Feynman scorns the answer given by the manager's efforts to rely on engineering knowledge: "'Cannot quantify. Reliability is determined by studies of this, checks on that, experience here'—blah, blah, blah, blah, blah."

In short, Feynman is contemptuous of the attempts by those responsible for the launch to justify their decision by an appeal to the coherence afforded by engineering knowledge. His judgments of the safety of the launch rest entirely on correspondence—how often did a launch fail? Indeed, his judgment was based on a *single* empirical indicator—relative frequency of failure. Because the officials apparently ignore this indicator, he is led to ask them: "Don't you understand the principles of probability?" And he expresses no interest whatever in the *reasons why* the launch failed. The officials, however, took the reverse course; they expressed little interest in the relative frequencies of empirical failure—even expressed their contempt for these—and placed confidence in their judgment to launch in the coherence of the system. Feynman dismissed that justification as so much nonsense ("blah, blah, blah, blah, blah").

The *Challenger* catastrophe illustrates fundamental differences in judgment and decision making in the face of irreducible uncertainty that should have been resolved before the occasion demanded a judgment. But in this case each side showed contempt for the metatheory employed by the other.

As we have seen, some statisticians later gathered sufficient data to enable them to take a correspondence approach to the decision to launch. They focused on the probability of failure of the O-rings used to seal the rocket and, as would be expected from a correspondence approach, used multiple fallible indicators to establish that probability. They concluded that there was "at least a 13% probability of catastrophic field-joint O-ring failure"[9] at the temperature at which the *Challenger* was launched, a notably higher risk than Feynman offered (1 in 50, or 2 percent) and far different than the one-thousandth of 1 percent chance of failure offered by the officials. These statisticians, then, focused their attention on a specific feature of the system (the O-ring seals) and calculated the risk of the failure of these at a specific temperature, rather than the frequency of failure of any launch as did Feynman.

In the final analysis, however, someone had to say whether the risk—however calculated—was too high to hazard a launch. We (and the astronauts) deserve to know exactly how the decision makers arrived at *that judgment.* Was coherence reconciled with correspondence? We now know that it wasn't. Were subjective probabilities reconciled with relative frequencies? They weren't. How was the threshold—the choice of a specific probability for a "safe" launch—justified? It wasn't. Finally, was the catastrophe due entirely to scientific and technical matters, or were some people simply unwilling to speak up about their doubts? Feynman apparently thought it was both. In any event, no one asked the questions related to the cognitive activity of the decision makers—nor would they today. Would asking them have made a difference? Would all concerned have been better off had they been asked? My answer, of course, is yes.

## Medicine

A physician, David Eddy, who later became known as a consultant to the Clinton administration in its efforts to introduce health care reform, offered an example more than a decade ago of the importance of coherence in medical judgments that retains its relevance today.[10]

He addressed the question of what recommendation a physician would give to a patient whom he has just examined and who has "a breast mass that the physician thinks is probably benign."[11] As a result of his experience the physician thinks that the probability that the patient has breast cancer is 1 percent. Now, Eddy suggests, let us assume that the physician orders a mammogram and receives a report that the lesion is malignant. In a telling paragraph Eddy describes a (weak) correspondence approach:

> A physician who turns to the literature can find innumerable helpful statements, such as the following: "The accuracy of mammography is approximately 90 percent" (Wolfe, 1966, p. 214); "In [a patient with a breast mass] a positive [mammogram] report of carcinoma is highly accurate" (Rosato, Thomas, & Rosato, 1973, p. 491); and "The accuracy of mammography in correctly diagnosing malignant lesions of the breast averages 80 to 85 percent" (Cohn, 1972, p. 98). If more detail is desired, the physician can find many statements like "The results showed 79.2 per cent of 475 malignant lesions were correctly diagnosed and 90.4 per cent of 1,105 benign lesions were correctly diagnosed, for an overall accuracy of 87 per cent" (Snyder, 1966, p. 217).
>
> At this point you can increase your appreciation of the physician's problem by estimating for yourself the new probability that this patient has cancer: The physician thinks the lump is probably (99 percent) *benign*, but the radiologist has produced a *positive* X-ray report with the accuracy just given.[12]

Eddy then illustrates the power of the coherence approach by offering two opposing probabilities. He reports that when given this situation physicians generally estimate the probability that the patient has breast cancer to be about 75 percent. But the correct answer (calculated by probability theory—a coherence theory) is far different: 7 percent.[13] That difference is, of course, a difference that matters; each probability, based on very different forms of reasoning, will lead to an action of great importance. Eddy offered his example in 1982; numerous examples have been offered since.[14]

But action—to perform surgery or not to perform surgery—should be taken only when the action can be justified to the best of our knowledge. And the "best of our knowledge" includes the best of our knowledge about the appropriate decision process. That knowledge comes from the mathematics of probability theory—that is, the coherence of the logic of the process. If you deny that, you must be prepared to offer an alternative form of justification. What will that be? You may find a variety of forms of coherence (different mathematical statistical methods), but they will all depend on coherence and thus claim your allegiance. Unless, of course, you adhere to a correspondence approach. In this case, as the reader will anticipate, you will employ multiple fallible indicators—diagnostic signs and symptoms—in addition to the results of the mammogram. And some evidence from correspondence studies may overwhelm the mammogram evidence, if the X-rays are not as definitive as one hopes. Correspondence theory would then offer results that would contest, perhaps, the conclusions from the mammogram, and if that were so, there would indeed be tension between these approaches. Would all physicians resolve that tension in the same way? Would they be aware of the cognitive problem they were facing?

The correspondence approach does, of course, have its supporters in medicine; the tension persists. For example, in a 1994 issue of the *Archives of Internal Medi-*

cine, Marvin Moser, a physician at the Yale University School of Medicine, argues that "we should judge where we are going in the management of hypertension by the results of treatment rather than by theories suggesting that we may be doing something wrong. We should judge by outcome rather than by process."[15]

## Economics

The use of economic models—a coherence approach to forecasting the future states of the economy—can be contrasted with a correspondence approach to economic forecasting—namely, the use of the Index of Leading Economic Indicators. The tension between the advocates of these two different approaches is quite evident. P. Newbold and T. Bos state:

> The econometric approach attempts the construction of formal models, firmly grounded in often quite sophisticated economic theory. The leading indicators approach is far more informal and *ad hoc* . . . [in which] no attempt is made to build a formal model reflecting the analysts' theoretical understanding of the way the economy behaves. To many economists, this casual attitude to theory has been a source of considerable irritation.[16]

That "irritation" can be seen in the way textbook writers treat these two approaches. The correspondence approach as exemplified by the "leading economic indicators" is ordinarily given little consideration; the coherence approach, on the other hand, is given a great deal. The nine hundred-page textbook by W. A. McEachern allots just one-half page to an explanation of "leading economic indicators." The author does, however, tell the student that "the economic profession thrives because its models [italics added] usually do a better job of making economic sense out of a confusing world than do alternative approaches."[17] He also urges students to "keep in mind that forecasts are nothing more than educated guesses."[18]

There is a second form of tension between the coherence and the correspondence approaches in economics—the tension between expert judgment and the use of "simple models." Curiously, this form of tension parallels that in clinical psychology. In the case of clinical psychology tension exists between those who advocate (expert) clinical judgment and those who advocate simple "actuarial" or statistical prediction. In economics the tension is between (expert) economic judgment and simple statistical extrapolations of "time series," or trends. As the reader might be willing to guess, the results are similar in the two cases. Newbold and Bos state: "Depending on one's perspective [coherence versus correspondence], one might be surprised to learn that forecasts by experts are often inferior to those generated from very simple time series extrapolation methods."[19] Why would we be surprised? Because "after all, these simple quantitative approaches cannot incorporate the wealth of knowledge, experience, and insight of the human expert."[20] By now, however, the reader should have developed a healthy skepticism about the "wealth of knowledge" among experts (exactly how good from a correspondence point of view is that wealth of knowledge?) and "experience" (experience of what? how effective was the empirical feedback from all that experience in enabling the expert to correct his or her mistakes?). Was the "experience" simply feedback from another expert—for example, a teacher perhaps equally misguided by his or her teacher? As for "insight," well, we all have insights at one time or another; we need "box scores" for experts' "insights," as well as for those of palm readers, astrologists, and others whose coherence theories are rubbish, as well as for those whose coherence theories are *not* rubbish but remain to be justified empirically.

Now consider the "wealth of knowledge" that Newbold and Bos say "cannot be incorporated" by the "very simple time series extrapolation methods." In fact, the time series does incorporate a wealth of knowledge, much of which may well have been forgotten by the expert. Many useless predictors will have been tried and found wanting, and that "wealth of knowledge" will be documented. As for "experience," the simple time series method knows nothing but experience. That experience, however, is based on the results of testing predictions against empirical facts, not on tests of coherence (argumentation with other "human experts"). Of course, the simple time series method never has any insights, but then who keeps the score regarding the good and the bad insights of the "human expert"?

The tension between "wealth of knowledge" and experience has been with us for ages. It was made plain by John Dickinson, Delaware's representative at the writing of the Constitution of the United States in 1787, when, speaking against what would now be called "term limits," he said, "*Experience* must be our only guide. . . . *Reason* may mislead us."[21] Surely that comment was not greeted with enthusiasm by *all* the representatives; Madison, among others, must have objected, if only to himself. The tension between these two theories of truth is ubiquitous, even today.

## Science

According to L. Laudan, a historian of science, the differentiation between correspondence and coherence theories reflects a broad, persistent "tension" in the history of science.

> Running through much of the history of the philosophy of science is a tension between coherentist and correspondentist accounts of scientific knowledge. Coherentists stress the need for appropriate types of conceptual linkages between our beliefs, while correspondentists emphasize the grounding of beliefs in the world. Each account typically makes only minimal concessions to the other. . . . Neither side, however, has been willing to grant that a *broad range* of both empirical and conceptual checks are of equal importance in theory testing.[22]

But this distinction is more than a matter for philosophers and historians of science. When the prestigious Oak Ridge Associated Universities panel wanted to indicate that it did not accept the conclusions of certain Swedish researchers who claimed to have found a link between proximity to power lines and rates of occurrence for certain forms of cancer, the panel did so by asserting that "the evidence for such an association is empirically weak [lacks correspondence with the facts] and biologically implausible [does not cohere with current beliefs about biological systems]."[23] In short, the conclusions were rejected on both grounds.

K. J. Vicente, a design engineer, has stressed the practical importance of this distinction in connection with the design of systems. He observed that "the correspondence/coherence taxonomy provides a powerful conceptual tool for addressing fundamental issues in human-computer interaction."[24] Vicente was interested in the question of which type of interface would be most likely to be supportive when the unexpected occurs, that is, when stress is induced. His recognition of the distinction between coherence and correspondence is therefore important for the future of stress research in the workplace. The broad "tension" Laudan finds in the history of science maintains its place under the most practical of contemporary applications.

## Coherence and Correspondence Theories Introduced into Judgment and Decision Making

The coherence approach was introduced to psychologists interested in judgment and decision making by Ward Edwards in 1954 in an article entitled, "The Theory of Decision Making."[25] The next year, I introduced a correspondence approach to judgment in an article titled "Probabilistic Functionalism and the Clinical Method."[26] Fifteen years later there was a sufficient accumulation of research to allow P. Slovic and S. Lichtenstein to publish a review article describing the research conducted within both approaches.[27]

W. Edwards and his colleague Detlof von Winterfeldt have emphasized that the goal of decision analysis is the achievement of *rationality*.[28] This is evidenced in a subhead on the first page of their book: "What this book is about: rationality." On page two they state: "Explicitly, this book is intended to help people be rational in making inferences and decisions. . . . The notion of rationality is prescriptive: In any version it explicitly says that some thoughts and actions are appropriate and others are not." Von Winterfeldt and Edwards do not claim that readers of their book will become more *empirically* accurate in their inferences and decisions. Accuracy is not under discussion; it isn't even indexed. In parallel fashion, correspondence theorists, such as myself, ignore the question of coherence to focus on empirical accuracy; the rationality of the process is hardly addressed.

Until the present little has been said in the field of judgment and decision making about the distinction between coherence and correspondence metatheories. And what little has been said has largely been ignored. Although R. Hastie and K. A. Rasinski treat the matter in some detail,[29] their article has seldom been cited. J. F. Yates's textbook on judgment and decision making does, however, make use of the correspondence-coherence distinction.[30] (He uses the term "accuracy" rather than "correspondence," but the distinction is the same.) His chapter on accuracy begins with a treatment of the empirical accuracy of weather forecasting, and his chapter on coherence begins with "coherence and probability theory," thus demonstrating the different reference points for each topic. Yates makes a further contribution by raising the question of the "practical significance of coherence,"[31] a matter I will discuss later in this chapter.

In 1990 I contrasted what I called "functionalism" and "illusionism" in judgment and decision making research as a way of introducing the distinction between correspondence (functionalism) and coherence (illusionism). I suggested that those researchers who focused on errors and cognitive illusions in judgment and decision making were working within the context of the coherence theory, whereas those who focused on accuracy (functionalism) were working within the correspondence theory of truth. In an effort to show the complementarity of the two approaches, I stated:

> In sum, the theories derived from functionalism and illusionism are not competing theories about judgment and decision making; rather, they are complementary theories about cognition that takes place under different conditions, conditions that induce subjects to employ different theories of truth. Because both types of inducement frequently occur in human ecologies, it is costly for *persons* to deny truth to either theory; it is, however, highly beneficial to be able to employ either, particularly when one knows which theory to apply under which conditions. Additionally it is costly for *researchers* to deny that subjects can employ either or both forms of cognition, but it is beneficial to learn the consequences of their application in various circumstances. It is this argument that leads me to believe that integration [of these approaches] could strengthen the research effort to understand human judgment and decision making.[32]

D. Frisch and R. T. Clemen have presented a similar point of view. In the course of their argument they note that L. J. Savage, one of the prominent early students of the topic, saw that the standard Subjective Expected Utility theory was based on coherence: "To use the preference [utility] theory is to search for incoherence among potential decisions. . . . The theory itself does not say which way back to coherence is to be chosen."[33] And Frisch and Clemen add: "Thus, violations of S[ubjective] E[xpected] U[tility] imply internal inconsistency. . . . This is known as the *coherence argument*."[34] They conclude that utility theory not only fails as a descriptive theory; it "does not provide an adequate standard for this [the decision] process."[35]

Frisch and Clemen thus find coherence to be the basic criterion for this bedrock theory and then dismiss the theory as *neither* descriptively nor normatively useful. Their "alternative framework" offers three features to be included as "part of good decision making": (1) consequences, (2) thorough structuring, and (3) trade-offs. Thus, these authors come close to the correspondence metatheory but do not embrace it. Their dismissal of (coherent) *utility theory* may well be justified on grounds of irrelevance. But that dismissal should not cause one to overlook the value of coherence as a criterion for rationality—where rationality may be demanded. Coherence remains an essential feature of certain mathematically oriented theories, which then have to meet the additional test emphasized by Frisch and Clemen— namely, relevance to the process of interest. Correspondence theory does not, of course, propose to meet the test of coherence, but it does propose to describe the process by which empirical accuracy is achieved.

The three features of good decision making offered by Frisch and Clemen may well be related to correspondence theory. As they note, "In our view the ultimate justification of a standard of decision making is empirical. This is in contrast to the SEU approach, which is based on the premise that the justification of a normative model is logical or mathematical,"[36] that is, coherence.

Herbert Simon's remarks about SEU theory make the distinction between coherence and correspondence clear:

> Conceptually, the SEU model is a beautiful object deserving a prominent place in Plato's heaven of ideas. But vast difficulties make it impossible to employ it in any literal way in making actual human decisions. . . .

The SEU model assumes that the decision maker contemplates, in one comprehensive view, everything that lies before him. He understands the range of alternative choices open to him, not only at the moment but over the whole panorama of the future. He understands the consequences of each of the available choice strategies, at least up to the point of being able to assign a joint probability distribution to future states of the world. He has reconciled or balanced all his conflicting partial values and synthesized them into a single utility function that orders, by his preference for them, all these future states of the world. . . .

When these assumptions are stated explicitly, it becomes obvious that SEU theory has never been applied, and never can be applied—with or without the largest computers—in the real world.[37]

Striking the final blow, he says: "I hope I have persuaded you that, in typical real-world situations, decision makers, no matter how badly they want to do so, simply cannot apply the SEU model."[38]

Having indicated how the coherence and correspondence theories provide a context for understanding judgment and decision making research, I now use them as a framework for discussing *competence*.

Finally, there is new evidence from the field of neuroscience that the coherence/correspondence distinction may well have a counterpart in the architecture and function of the brain. Vilayanur Ramachandran, a neurologist, has studied brain function in stroke victims, paying particular attention to the different forms of cognitive activity carried out by the left and right hemispheres of the brain. His studies—some of which are quite remarkable—lead him to conclude: "The left [hemisphere's] job is to create a model and maintain it at all costs"[39]; that is, the left hemisphere seeks coherence ("create[s] a model") from the information it has been -provided and "maintains" the coherence of that model "at all costs." Although the latter phrase may be an exaggeration, we have all observed persons who hold firmly to a model (theory, ideology), and continue to maintain its truth despite all the evidence against it. Ramachandran goes on to say that "the right [hemisphere's] job is to detect anomalies," to discover instances in which the model is empirically erroneous. And "when anomalous information reaches a certain threshold, its job is to force the left hemisphere to revise the entire model and start from scratch."[40] A difficult task as we all know only too well. Without the left hemisphere to organize all the information in a coherent form, we would be hopelessly confused by all the information we receive from the world around us. As Ramachandran puts it: "At any given moment in our waking lives, . . . our brains are flooded with a bewildering variety of sensory inputs, all of which must be incorporated into a coherent perspective. . . . To act, the brain must have some way of selecting [and organizing detail into] . . . a story that makes sense."[41]

No wonder students of the history of science have found a persistent tension between coherence and correspondence. That tension appears to be built into our brains.

## A Framework for Evaluation of the Competence of Human Judgment

The principal components of the framework for our investigation of the competence of human judgment are the correspondence metatheory and the coherence metatheory; both have persisted in the history of science, and both persist today in the field of judgment and decision making. Although largely unrecognized by researchers, the great majority of studies in the field take place within one or other of these metatheories, and research results are obtained by virtue of their different methodologies. Once this is recognized, it becomes possible to understand—and to reconcile—conflicting and contradictory conclusions.

Correspondence theory focuses on the *empirical* accuracy of judgments, irrespective of whether the cognitive activity of the judge can be justified or even described. Although correspondence researchers may be interested in describing the processes that produce the judgment, they rarely inquire into the question of whether these processes are *rational,* that is, conform to some normative, or prescribed, model of how a judgment ought to be reached. They are interested, however, in the extent to which the experiments represent the conditions to which the results are generalized.

Coherence theorists have opposite interests; they examine the question of whether an individual's judgment processes meet the test of rationality—internal consistency—irrespective of whether the judgment is empirically accurate. Indeed, no test of empirical accuracy may be available in principle or fact. Thus, for example, if a problem is offered to a subject that is susceptible to a solution by a standard statistical model, the coherence theorist first compares the subject's answer with that produced by the statistical model, declares the answer to be correct or incorrect, tests (if possible) the process by which the answer is produced, and then evaluates the rationality of the cognitive process(es) involved. In addition, if the answer is incorrect, the research tradition has been to offer a description of the incorrect cognitive process, thus not only demonstrating irrationality but offering a description of the irrational "heuristic" that produced the "bias" that led to the wrong answer.

In short, correspondence theorists are interested in the way the mind works in relation to the way the world works, while coherence theorists are interested in the way the mind works in relation to the way it ought to work. That description is useful because it suggests immediately that each approach to the evaluation of competence in judgment has its own criteria. Correspondence researchers are interested in the empirical accuracy of judgments; coherence researchers are interested in the intentional rationality of judgments. What conclusions has each set of researchers drawn?

## Current Conclusions About the Competence of Human Judgment

Although the question of competence was present in the 1950s, it gained prominence in 1974 when A. Tversky and D. Kahneman[42] published research results and conclusions that led to what are now widely accepted negative views about the competence of human judgment. It may come as a surprise to some readers, but most students of judgment and decision making now regard the situation as "bleak"; human judgment, they believe, has been clearly demonstrated to be irrational, badly flawed, and generally not only wrong but overconfident; in a word, untrustworthy.[43]

## Coherence Theorists' Conclusions

The gestalt psychologists, prominent during the 1930s and 1940s, provide a natural background for the coherence theorists of today. The gestaltists' emphasis on "good figure," "completeness," "wholes," and pattern illustrates their interest in coherence rather than correspondence. In addition, their interest in perceptual illusions was a forerunner of modern judgment and decision-making coherence theorists' interest in "cognitive illusions."[44] Today's coherence theorists generally have little to say about the empirical accuracy of judgments; they also have little to say about adaptation, or functionalism, and, surprisingly, nothing to say about the relation of their work to that of the earlier coherence theorists, the gestalt psychologists. Current coherentists are more concerned with the rationality, that is, the prescriptive, logical, mathematical coherence of a person's cognitive activity and the description of the "cognitive illusions," labeled "heuristics." Heuristics are precisely those cognitive activities that deceive us (thus "illusions") and prevent the achievement of coherence, and thus rationality. This work extends the gestalt psychologists' interest in perception to higher-level cognitive functions (albeit from a perspective different from that of the gestaltists).

Beginning in the 1970s Daniel Kahneman and Amos Tversky initiated a series of studies that described in detail the lack of coherence and therefore rationality in human judgment. Their anthology brings together an impressive body of evidence that supports their generally negative views of the competence of human judgment and the "cognitive illusions" or "biases" that, they argued, decrease it. Their work has resulted in the widespread use of these terms in the judgment and decision-making literature and beyond, a usage that reflects the authors' emphasis on error. Although these authors deny the charge that they have denigrated the rationality and competence of human judgment (e.g., "the focus on bias and illusion . . . neither assumes nor entails that people are perceptually or cognitively inept"[45]), the charge remains, for the denial seems disingenuous in view of the persistent demonstration—and celebration—of ineptness.[46]

The negative demonstrations of errors in probabilistic judgment by Kahneman and Tversky have become so widely accepted that by 1994 R. L. Klatzky, J. Geiwitz, and S. C. Fischer, writing in a book titled *Human Error in Medicine*, used them almost exclusively to illustrate physicians' errors in statistical reasoning.[47] Physicians and researchers reading this chapter on "using statistics" therefore learn only that a failure to achieve coherence in their judgments will lead to error and that achievement of coherence is enough to achieve competence. Avoiding "cognitive illusions" and achieving coherence came to exhaust the meaning of competence.

The negative conclusions regarding competence have been cited and quoted thousands of times by researchers and textbooks in a variety of disciplines, as well as in the popular literature, not only because of their significance but because of the simple and compelling nature of the demonstrations that produced them. For example, D. N. Kleinmuntz and D. A. Schkade state: "Two decades of research have emphasized the shortcomings of human judgment and decision-making processes,"[48] an emphasis that has rarely been disputed by psychologists (but frequently disputed by economists who believe that it contradicts fundamental premises of the "rational expectations" school in economics). The generally accepted pessimistic view of the quality of human judgment by researchers in this field should be given very serious consideration by those who must rely on it—and that means most of us most of the time. Because this conclusion is now accepted outside the narrow circle of judgment and decision making researchers, it may well turn out that research on judgment and decision making will provide the empirical support for Freud's third blow to our self-esteem that neither he nor his followers were able to offer.

Specifically, human judgments under uncertainty—probability judgments—are claimed to be subject to numerous "biases"; when we are asked to make probability judgments, our answers are biased and thus wrong. Here is an example that has been cited on numerous occasions:

Problem 1 ($N = 152$): Imagine that the U.S. is preparing for the outbreak of an unusual Asian disease, which is expected to kill 600 people. Two alternative programs to combat the disease have been proposed. Assume that the exact scientific estimates of the consequences of the programs are as follows:

If Program A is adopted, 200 people will be saved. (72%)

If Program B is adopted, there is a one-third probability that 600 people will be saved and a two-thirds probability that no people will be saved. (28%)

Which of the two programs would you favor?[49]

Kahneman and Tversky report the responses to this question but first explain why the question is formulated as it is:

The formulation of Problem 1 implicitly adopts as a reference point a state of affairs in which the disease is allowed to take its toll of 600 lives. The outcomes of the programs include the reference state and two possible gains, measured by the number of lives saved. As expected, preferences are risk averse: A clear majority of respondents prefer saving 200 lives for sure over a gamble that offers a one-third chance of saving 600 lives. Now consider another problem in which the same cover story is followed by a different description of the prospects associated with the two programs:

Problem 2 ($N = 155$): If Program C is adopted, 400 people will die. (22%)

If Program D is adopted, there is a one-third probability that nobody will die and a two-thirds probability that 600 people will die. (78%)[50]

Kahneman and Tversky explain the nature of this problem as follows:

It is easy to verify that options C and D in Problem 2 are undistinguishable in real terms from options A and B in Problem 1, respectively. The second version, however, assumes a reference state in which no one dies of the disease. The best outcome is the maintenance of this state and the alternatives are losses measured by the number of people that will die of the disease. People who evaluate options in these terms are expected to show a risk seeking preference for the gamble (option D) over the sure loss of 400 lives. Indeed, there is more risk seeking in the second version of the problem than there is risk aversion in the first.[51]

When people are given the problem they do not see the numerical equivalence of the options; they do not see that options C and D are, as the authors put it, "indistinguishable in real terms" from options A and B. (Did the reader see this? If not, take another look at the problem and do the arithmetic.)

Similar errors have been demonstrated many times over a wide variety of problems. As a result, most students of judgment and decision making have attributed these errors to a fundamental flaw in the reasoning capacity of human beings.[52]

Thus, in the short space of twenty years Kahneman and Tversky and their colleagues have turned the field of judgment and decision making in a new direction. Moreover, they have given it a degree of visibility and prestige it never before enjoyed. Both authors received the Distinguished Scientist Award from the American Psychological Association and other prizes for their work. The publication of the anthology in 1982, barely ten years after their initial contributions were made, constituted a landmark in the field. The entire theme of this anthology is that human judgment under uncertainty is error-ridden and resistant to improvement and that a new approach to the study of human judgment is on its way. The anthology contains convincing evidence for all three points. Subsequent research has driven home the argument time and again. The recent textbook by S. Plous is an example of the enthusiasm with which the negative views of competence are presented; the text offers 252 pages of undiluted reports of studies that discover incompetence in virtually all aspects of judgment and decision making. (The alternative view gets five pages.)

But there has been serious dissent from these negative conclusions (which I will describe later in this chapter). Not every researcher in this field has accepted them, and some have bitterly resented them.[53]

### Correspondence Theorists' Conclusions

Correspondence theorists commit themselves, implicitly if not explicitly, to a Darwinian approach. They use either the term "adaptive"[54] or "functional,"[55] terms used in psychology since the early twentieth century to signify a Darwinian approach. The common research aim among these theorists is to examine the correspondence between a person's judgments and a specific state of the world to which those judgments are supposed to correspond (how often does it rain when the weather forecaster says it will?). They also share a common presumption, derived from their Darwinian commitment, namely, that a high degree of correspondence will in fact be found, for competence in the form of correspondence is fundamental to survival. It is natural to ask: How could human beings have been so successful in their survival if they did not make accurate judgments of the world around them?

The modern origin of the correspondence view of competence in judgment and decision making can be found in the classical treatment of perception by Egon Brunswik.[56] Brunswik challenged the gestalt psychologists' emphasis on perceptual illusions (which after all are perceptual inaccuracies) by presenting evidence for the high degree of accuracy of perception regarding events in the natural world outside the psychologists' artificial laboratory conditions. Brunswik's general theory of perception was introduced into the topic of judgment in 1955 by the present author[57] and has been further developed by many researchers (e.g., Björkman, Brehmer, Cooksey, Doherty, Einhorn, Funder, Gigerenzer, Gillis, Holzworth, Joyce, Klayman, and Stewart[58]).

Correspondence theorists found competence to be largely determined by task conditions that I shall describe in detail later in this book. In general, however, judgments mediated by perception (e.g., the visual perception of objects and events) have been found to be remarkably good but to become less so as judgment moves from *perceptual* to *conceptual* tasks and materials. That is, perceptual judgments of physical attributes such as size and color under a wide variety of conditions in the natural environment are excellent, but judgments and predictions about the behavior of objects and events (people, weather, economic conditions) that are complicated by considerable irreducible uncertainty, as well as by conceptual confusion, are often far from accurate. The central feature of the correspondence theory of judgment is its emphasis—inherited from Darwin—on the flexibility of the organism in its adaptive efforts, its multiple strategies, its ability to rely on various intersubstitutable features—what are called *multiple fallible indicators*—in the environment.

Thus, it is not surprising that the differences in viewpoint between those pursuing the question of competence within the frameworks of correspondence and coherence theories has produced tension between them. I will take up the matter of this tension again in Chapter 8, but first I will introduce the reader to the evolutionary character of correspondence competence.

# 5 The Evolutionary Roots of Correspondence Competence

> Males display with the most elaborate case, and show off in the best manner, . . . [and] perform strange antics before the females.
>
> —*Charles Darwin*

We cannot recreate our earliest ancestors and examine their cognitive activity: thoughts do not "fossilize." We can only extract highly presumptive evidence about their judgments from archeological and anthropological research and look at the way in which other species make judgments, particularly in regard to their choice of mates. Darwin's 1871 observations are the starting point for the latter research strategy (although he also devoted a few pages of his 1859 *Origin of Species* to this matter).

## Mating Judgments

Darwin's evidence for the use of multiple fallible indicators in sexual selection may have been anecdotal and anthropomorphic, but recent quantitative evidence from field studies shows that he was essentially correct. In an extraordinarily detailed research effort, the behavioral ecologist T. von Schantz and his colleagues studied mate selection by female pheasants and showed, for the first time, that female pheasants are accurate in their judgments of which males are most likely to be reproductively successful. This is a finding of major significance for evolutionary biologists and correspondence theorists.

One hundred years after Darwin prepared his thesis, von Schantz and his colleagues pursued the topic of sexual selection from the female point of view, one might say, in those species in which the female has the opportunity to observe and select the male who will father her progeny. As they described the situation:

> Recent theory on sexual selection suggests that females in species without paternal care choose mates by their secondary sexual characters because these indicate genotypic quality which will be transmitted to the offspring.[1]

But they noted that this idea had yet to be empirically supported, because

> data quantifying the relationship between female mate choice and female reproductive success are lacking. Only in one case, in *Colias* butterflies, has it been demonstrated unequivocally that females choose "good genotypes" as mates and there is only one study, on *Drosophila*, demonstrating that mate choice increases one component of offspring fitness.[2]

They then reported that they had found that

> Spur length of male pheasants (*Phasianus colchicus*) correlates with various fitness-related properties. We here present the first experimental field data showing that female pheasants select mates on the basis of male spur length and that female mate choice correlates with female reproductive success.[3]

The claim of von Schantz and his colleagues is strong because their research program meets certain criteria: They did observe choice, copulation, and did measure the viability of eggs produced for choice-versus-nonchoice pairing—all under naturalistic conditions. By 1990 they could report on "male characteristics, viability, and harem size in the pheasant":

> A population of pheasants was studied for 4 years in southern Sweden to determine how sexual selection operates among males. Morphological characters, viability, dominance, territory quality, date of territorial establishment, harem size and reproductive success of males were measured; 81 males and 101 females were radio-tracked. The spur length of males was the most important predictor of harem size. Phenotypic condition and viability were significantly related to spur length, the best single predictor of the reproductive success of males. These are the first data to show that a sexually selected male character correlates significantly with male viability. The results support models suggesting that viability-based processes can contribute to the evolution of mate choice and secondary sexual characters.[4]

The significance of this (and subsequent) research for the correspondence view of social perception is great indeed, for the foundation of a correspondence theory of judgment (particularly as set forth by Brunswik)[5] is that (1) the natural environment offers *multiple fallible indicators* (in this case, spur length and other indicators such as body weight and wing span) of an *intangible attribute* of the male (here, potential for reproductive success) and that (2) organisms perceive these indicators and use them in such a manner as to (3) make *correct (corresponding) judgments* regarding the intangible aspects of members of the same species so that the likelihood of survival (fitness) of the gene pool is enhanced. And it is exactly those points to which the work of von Schantz and his colleagues is directed and for which their results provide support. They take pains to state that these are the "first experimental field data" that show not only which of the multiple fallible cues the female responds to but that "female mate choice correlates with female reproductive success."[6] In sum, von Schantz and his colleagues have provided empirical, naturalistic support not only for the Darwinian theory of sexual selection introduced over a century earlier but also for the evolutionary, biological roots of the concept of multiple fallible indicators and the correspondence theory.

In Figure 5-1 the lens model illustrates the use of multiple fallible indicators by the female pheasant.

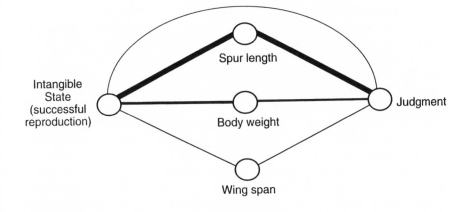

Indicators

Figure 5-1   Lens model depiction of female pheasants' judgment policy for selection of male pheasant most likely to produce largest number of viable eggs. Indicators are weighted proportionately to their predictive validity (heavier lines indicate greater weight).

The female pheasants are, of course, unaware of their cognitive activity nor can they learn how to make these judgments. As is the case with virtually all intuitive judgments based on multiple fallible indicators, the feedback necessary for learning is missing. Natural selection provides the learning process for the pheasant.

But these conditions are different in *Homo sapiens*. Darwin believed that the idea of sexual selection "was applicable to man."[7] Is it? That is the question addressed by David Buss in a field experiment.[8]

Buss began with human female preferences: What should we expect females to be interested in? The von Schantz study of pheasants is predicated on the assumption that females are interested in reproductive success, defined as the number of viable eggs that result from mating. The pheasants therefore use the multiple fallible indicators (cues) to reproductive success provided by males. Buss, however, made the important observation that "humans often mate at ages before a man's potential resources are fully known. Therefore, females are often in the position of relying on cues that are only probabilistically associated with future resources."[9] In short, human females' search for reproductive success depends on the same cognitive process that von Schantz and his colleagues observed in female pheasants—the use of—that is, the perception and utilization of—multiple fallible indicators to intangible states or situations, those that are not yet observable.

Buss also examined sexual selection by human males and pointed out that "for males more than females, reproductive success is limited by sexual access to reproductively valuable or fertile mates."[10] The Darwinian assumption would be that the reproductive success of males depends on their ability to judge which females are "reproductively valuable or fertile mates." Again, however, "reproductive value and fertility are not attributes that can be observed directly."[11] How then are males to know with whom to mate? They must infer the state of these intangible but critical attributes in females by observing and judging those tangible cues that are available—that is, by observing multiple fallible indicators such as "(a) physical features (e.g., smooth, clear, and unblemished skin . . . ), (b) behavioral features (e.g., sprightly and graceful gait . . . ), and (c) reputation (i.e., knowledge gleaned from others regarding the age, health, condition . . . )."[12] And "because . . . [female reproductive capacities] are not directly observable, selection has favored preferential attention to the cues that afford reliable information about them."[13]

J. S. Gillis and F. J. Bernieri have studied another, more subtle aspect of mating judgments: Can one person make accurate judgments about the rapport that exists between two other persons? After conducting a series of studies,[14] they concluded that persons can accurately infer rapport from observable behavior but that the accuracy of those judgments was well below the level that could have been achieved if observers had used the correct information, that is, the most valid fallible indicators. If the observers had known which behavioral cues to attend to, they would have been much more accurate. That is important because it shows that there was in fact useful information regarding rapport in the behavior of those observed; the observers just didn't know what it was. Indeed, the observers would have been more accurate had they given less weight to animation cues (expressivity and smiling, neither of which is a valid indicator of rapport) and more weight to expressivity cues (e.g., leaning toward one another).

On the basis of their review of related studies, the authors began to suspect that members of different cultures would rely on different cues. They pursued this question by studying differences in Greek and American students seen conversing on videotape. (The Greek students knew little or no English.) They found that the accuracy of the American and Greek students in judging rapport was "remarkably similar," as was their use of different cues to infer rapport. Again, the failure to achieve the highest level of accuracy made possible by the information offered was a result of both groups' giving insufficient weight to valid indicators of rapport (leaning toward one another, mutual silence), while "placing their principal reliance on two apparently compelling but invalid cues, smiling and expressivity."[15]

Thus, two findings interest us: (1) There were no cultural differences in Greeks' and Americans' ability to judge rapport; in fact, the two groups were remarkably similar in the information they used and the accuracy with which they used it (irrespective of language comprehension); (2) both groups used the information offered less effectively than they could have—they erred in the same way. In short, the same universality Buss observed in his mate preferences may appear in the more subtle but important area of the use of multiple fallible indicators to judge rapport between others.

## Navigation

Is the use of multiple fallible indicators limited to sexual selection, to judgments regarding the mate most likely to perpetuate one's genes? Not at all; in all likelihood, this is a phenomenon of great generality. For example, scientists investigating the mysterious abilities of various birds and marine species to navigate, to find mating grounds, feeding grounds, or their way home over long distances, have learned that these species also depend on multiple fallible indicators. Biologists try to find out exactly what these are and how they are used by various species. Pigeons, turtles, land crabs, lobsters, and other marine species have been found to use olfactory cues, the location of the sun, magnetic lines of force, direction of light, or waves for guidance.[16] Moreover, the use of these fallible indicators often seems to be hierarchical; that is, if the most favored cue is not available, a second, less often depended on, cue is sought; if this is unavailable, a third is sought, and so on.

This is exactly the process that correspondence theorists have found to be used by human beings. The word that has been used for this process is "vicarious functioning"; it was introduced in 1943 by Brunswik. Vicarious functioning refers to circumstances in which, if cue A is absent, cue B may function "vicariously" for it. A "warm smile" may function vicariously for a "warm handshake" if the persons involved are not in close proximity. When pigeons are unable to locate the sun because of a cloud cover, magnetic lines of force function vicariously for the sun. Thus, "under complete overcast, if the sun compass fails to operate, the second step seems to be achieved by a magnetic compass."[17] Similarly with the loggerhead sea turtles, which also "carry a remarkably sophisticated magnetic compass in their heads" that "enables them to sense how far north or south they've come"[18] in their search for their feeding grounds. And sea turtles, like pigeons and humans, are prepared to resort to secondary cues if and when the primary cue is not available. Obviously, the ability to shift dependence from one cue to another is a great advantage in a shifting uncertain ecology that offers redundant information.

## Combat

Multiple fallible indicators are, of course, commonly used by insects and by virtually all birds and animals, often as warning signals when they are preparing to engage in combat. This is certainly true of human beings, who signal aggressive intent not only in various direct ways (facial expression, posture) but also symbolically. Certain words and phrases have a long history of ritual use in diplomatic exchanges and serve as well recognized indicators of current intentions and states of mind. Efforts to hide indicators or to use them to deceive the other are commonplace. For example, an article in the *New York Times* stated, with regard to tensions between North Korea and the United States, that "[b]oth sides . . . treasure ambiguity, Mr. Kim about what he has built, Mr. Clinton about what he would do. The important question is this: Which side will prove more adroit at sending, and reading, signals that are so deliberately mixed?"[19]

## Use of Multiple Falliable Indicators by Apes

The chimpanzee, gorilla, gibbon, and orangutan are all adept in their use of multiple fallible indicators. They use them to find appropriate mates, to find friends and avoid enemies, to find food and resting places. Indeed, most of their daily activity could be described simply as the search for and the use of multiple fallible indicators in both the physical and the social domains.

This aspect of the cognitive life of apes is detailed in an excellent book by R. Byrne, who shows the use of signs, signals, and cues —all fallible indicators—in all essential aspects of the lives of the apes. We learn not only that apes make effective use of the most inconspicuous cues to find edible, nonpoisonous food but that cue use varies widely among apes according to the demands of their different diets. Those apes whose diets are readily satisfied by easily accessible food sources need use only a few cues to determine what is edible and what isn't. Those apes who must forage far and wide to satisfy their diets use a wide range of different cues.[20] Byrne points out that "theories about the environmental problems that most challenged and shaped monkey and ape intelligence have centered on efficiency in food acquisition"[21] and that he "was continually amazed at the subtle cues that they must use to identify some of their plant foods."[22] In fact, in recent years there has been increased recognition of signaling among apes with regard to directions for foraging:

> Chimpanzees also communicate about spatial directions, in different ways in the two species. Sometimes when a pygmy chimpanzee group is resting, some males will break off small trees and drag the branches through the forest for around 10 metres; the group will subsequently set off in just this direction. . . . It seems the chimpanzees are using the branches as a tool to convey symbolic information. In common chimpanzees, Boesch . . . has found that drumming on tree root buttresses signals movement direction. If a particular male drums on two different trees in quick succession, the group generally begins moving, in the direction indicated by the two trees' relative locations; if he drums on the same tree, they generally rest, and if he combines these displays, then the group will first rest, then move off in the indicated direction.
>
> These scattered revelations of the remarkable navigational skills of some monkeys and apes give credence to the "cognitive-map hypothesis" of primate intellectual origins.[23]

Social signaling among apes is remarkable for its sophistication. Byrne notes that among baboons the top-ranking male is "only able to monopolize about 50 percent of matings with potentially fertile females."[24]

> For the other 50 per cent, he is outwitted by pairs of other males, acting in coalition. . . . One male will solicit another's help by characteristic head and face movements; one of the pair then threatens the consorting top-rank male; when he retaliates in defence, the other male is often able to obtain a mating with the fertile female. The decoying action seems altruistic, but this is reciprocal altruism—because on a future occasion, the other helps him in turn.[25]

Nor is the ability of primates limited to direct observations of objects and events; they apparently are successful users of multiple fallible indicators to infer social relations among others. Byrne reports, for example, that vervet monkeys "take into account the rank of the caller in interpreting the calls' meaning. For instance, if X is heard to give a 'grunt to dominant,' and X is below the hearer in rank, there is no reaction; . . . but if X is higher in rank than the hearer, there is significant reaction from the hearer. . . . Getting this difference in reaction means that vervet monkeys have some understanding of the relative ranks of third parties, not just their own position relative to others as researchers had always assumed."[26] Indeed, Byrne also reports additional research that shows that macaques who are beaten by others often go after *relatives* of the monkeys who beat them. And "vervets prefer to threaten the relative of monkeys who have recently attacked *their* relatives. This monkey 'vendetta' suggests that they know very well who everyone else's allies are, and remember grievances."[27]

I mention this because studies of *Homo sapiens* have only recently begun to use naturalistic circumstances in their efforts to evaluate the extent to which we ascertain correctly the degree of rapport between other persons.[28]

Byrne makes it clear that both physical and social correspondence competence based on the use of multiple fallible indicators has long existed among *Homo sapien*'s predecessors. He also documents the appearance of "insight," that is, the intellective grasp of causal relations among the "orangutan/human ancestor."[29] It is this ancestor that showed us that, "for the first time, an animal could mentally represent and conjure with other 'possible worlds': what other animals might be thinking, and what other animals might think of it. . . . For the first time, animals could be said to be capable of 'thought' in the sense of anticipatory planning."[30]

The "chimpanzee/human ancestor" of 6 million years ago seems to represent the next advance because

> one of the two chimpanzee species always seems to be represented in the most impressive demonstrations of cognitive skill: intentional teaching, intentional deception, grammatical comprehension, distinguishing between malice and accident, and so on. In particular, the more extensive evidence of tool-making and mechanical comprehension in the chimpanzee line cannot be ignored. Nevertheless, the chimpanzee/human's behavioural expression of insight would most likely not have been very conspicuous, any more than it is in modern chimpanzees. Why these animals, which give evidence of the insight that we humans consider so crucial to behavioural intelligence, show so few signs of its use in everyday life, remains a mystery.[31]

But Bryne's most important conclusion is drawn in his final sentence: "What this book has shown is that, from the chimpanzee/human's array of cognitive capacities, the gulf to 'the thinking primate' is a bridgeable one: human cognition has a long history, extending back in time to well before the inscrutable era of the hominids."[32] That is to say, correspondence competence based on multiple fallible indicators is a cognitive activity with a history extending far back in time and over a large variety of species. It should therefore come as no surprise that this form of cognitive activity is widespread among species living today.

## Use of Multiple Fallible Indicators by Early *Homo Sapiens*

I am not prepared to make a catalog of those existing species that possess the remarkable ability to use multiple fallible indicators in this intersubstitutable fashion to select mates, to signal (and read) aggressive intent, to find feeding grounds or breeding grounds, or more generally, to navigate. Nor am I prepared to catalog those species (many insects) that do not have this ability.[33] So far as I know, not even biologists have made such catalogs. The important point is that biologists have found that the use of multiple fallible indicators is widespread. Anthropologists believe that signs were used by both hominids and early *Homo sapiens* (prior to the use of language). I am encouraged in this belief when I reflect upon the environmental conditions our earliest ancestors faced—namely, the savanna, flat meadows, or grasslands in tropical or subtropical regions. Evidently, they were hunters and gatherers, the earliest lacking tools even after they began to walk erect. Since they lacked language, their cognitive activity must have consisted largely of intuitive reliance on multiple fallible indicators of what to eat, with whom to mate, and where to find what they wanted. Most important, they must have also relied on multiple fallible indicators regarding the attitudes of other people. Analytical cognition would not have appeared until there was something to be analytical about, as tool use and language developed; which occurred first, I'm not prepared to say.[34] Darwin, of course, was well aware of the conscious and involuntary use of facial expressions as multiple fallible indicators of emotions that were clearly used and understood by primitive peoples;[35] it has long been known that apes also respond to indicators of emotion.

Anthropologists interested in our ancestors have too often ignored our use of multiple fallible indicators; in particular, they have ignored the organizing principles of cognition that made early survival possible, despite the fact that this form of cognition continues to occupy a large part of our cognition today and probably will continue to do so. This bias appears in a recent work by two prominent anthropologists, K. D. Schick and N. Toth. In a chapter titled "Dawn Breaks: The First Stone Tool Makers," the authors offer a hypothetical scenario that describes the first use of a stone tool:

> The stream meanders sluggishly through the grassland plain, lined on either side by a gallery of huge fig and acacia trees as well as scrubby underbrush. . . . A group of bipeds is foraging along the river. One of the females notices the gravel bar.
>
> She goes down the grassy slope to the edge of the stream, where half buried lava cobbles are exposed in large numbers, their dull, gray and brown surfaces highlighted in patches from the sunlight streaming through the canopy. *She looks around to be sure that there are no crocodiles in or near the water, nor any terrestrial predators nearby.* Crouching down, she selects a cobble that has a *smooth, uncracked surface* and turns it to examine the *one relatively thin edge* [italics added throughout].
>
> Selecting an egg-shaped hammer stone with her right hand, she directs a hard, glancing blow against the thinner edge of the cobble held in her left hand.[36]

What the authors overlook here are the words I have put in italics. If that female does not possess the ability "to be sure that there are no crocodiles in or near the water, nor any terrestrial predators nearby," tool making won't happen. In order to survive, she must have an effective cognitive mechanism that employs multiple fallible indicators and a powerful, effective principle for organizing the information thus acquired; otherwise she won't have a chance to make that tool or engage in further cognitive development.

This observation might be considered obvious or banal if it were not for two facts: (1) Cognitive activity itself should not be taken for granted (as the authors and other anthropologists generally seem to do), and (2) the same cognitive activity persists today in same form that it had on the side of that stream, existing today in parallel with the remarkable advances in our analytical comprehension of causality that resulted in the technology now surrounding us.

One archeologist did see the connection between the early use of multiple fallible indicators and modern humankind, however. Steven Mithen in a remarkable book titled *Thoughtful Foragers* first reviews the contemporary judgment and decision-making literature and then applies the knowledge they contain in a particularly skillful manner. He calls attention to the role of multiple fallible indicators and the narrative and offers informed hypotheses about learning among early *Homo sapiens*. He begins his text by noting the absence of interest among archeologists in this topic:

> One of the unique characteristics of the human species is the possession of highly developed capacities for learning, decision making and problem solving, as T. S. Eliot reminds us. These result in a behavioural flexibility unparalleled in any other species. Although such capacities often require a social context for their use, they reside in the individual. Quite simply, it is these that constitute the source of cultural behaviour. It is remarkable, therefore, that archaeology, a discipline with the human species as its centre and which claims a pre-eminent role for under standing cultural behaviour, has paid scant attention to the processes of learning and decision making by individuals.[37]

Mithen devotes several pages to the use of "cues" (i.e., fallible indicators) among hunter-gatherers. He divides these cues into eight classes—"tracks, excretions, terrain, vegetation, sounds, smells, animals/plants, and weather"[38]—and cites numerous instances in which the use of such cues was necessary for survival. Mithen also describes various types of learning that involve the exchange of information; the hunter-gatherers identify useful cues for one another but never instruct one another about adding or averaging "cue values"; by this time evolution had selected an organism that was, somehow, endowed with this robust organizing principle.

Remarkably, Mithen also calls attention to what judgment researchers refer to as the "ecological reliability" of a cue—that is, its truthfulness, a matter distinct from its validity:

> While the ethnographic record is rich with examples of information exchange within and between groups there has been no detailed study of the type of information that is passed on in terms of whether or not it is "true". Studies of modern fishermen (e.g. Anderson 1972) demonstrate that the type of information passed between foragers may be highly variable from "true" to absolutely false. Passing on information to another may act as a social strategy to manipulate the receiver's behaviour. Consequently information may be required as to the worth of the information received, creating a hierarchy of information about information levels. Kurland and Beckerman (1985) focus on this problem in relation to the evolution of human cognition. There is little comment in the ethnographic literature as to the type of information passed on. Gubser (1965: 227), however, remarks that the Nunamiut are very concerned with the truth of a person's statement implying that both "true" and "untrue" information may be flowing within the communication network. Blurton-Jones and Konner (1976: 318) describe how the !Kung are careful to discriminate data from theory, interpretation and hearsay. Moreover the !Kung are very ready to disbelieve each other and to express scepticism over some piece of information (Blurton-Jones and Konner 1976: 331).[39]

These were astute observations regarding the conscious attention that people pay to the trustworthiness of fallible indicators. Such levels of attention would be important to people entirely dependent on correspondence competence. Buss makes similar observations about the conscious attention contemporary men and women pay to the risk that misleading information will be presented by members of the opposite sex. The *ecological reliability* of indicators is an important concept, particularly in a society that can create multiple fallible indicators for so many purposes.

In short, there is reason to believe that the use of multiple fallible indicators to achieve correspondence with the world of objects and events is broad (existing across numerous species) as well as deep (having a long history among *Homo sapiens* and their forerunners) and that reliance on multiple fallible indicators persists today. In addition to observing the use of multiple fallible indicators in nature, researchers have demonstrated their appearance in numerous laboratory studies.[40] Their present use in social perception has recently been demonstrated by D. Buss, and also by F. Bernieri and J. Gillis and by D. Funder.[41]

## The Construction of Multiple Fallible Indicators for Policymaking

Our natural dependence on multiple fallible indicators, central in our evolutionary history, is so pervasive and enduring that we constructed indicators for ourselves at virtually every opportunity. Navigation, traffic control, and library catalogs provide only a hint of the thousands of indicators we have created for ourselves in order to reduce the uncertainty of our environment. And this effort to construct indicators extends from the physical environment to our social situation. Countless tables of data appear in our newspapers and journals, all purporting to indicate the state of our health, our economy, and even our moral circumstances. Indeed, so many studies on multiple fallible indicators are being done that a journal now exists (*Social Indicators Research*) for reporting new research in the field.

The idea of using statistical indexes as indicators of the state of society apparently originated with Quetelet (1796–1874), an astronomer, meteorologist, mathematician, statistician, and, especially, genius. It is Quetelet who gets credit for introducing the idea of "the average man." And it was Quetelet who promulgated methods for collecting various social statistics to provide a profile of the state of society.[42] Such indicators are employed for purposes of social policy in two ways, either as *predictors* of future states, or as *descriptors* of current states.

### Indicators as Predictors

To reach as far as possible from the primitive circumstances of our ancestors, I now consider the most relied-on forecast of the future state of the U.S. economy, what *The Wall Street Journal* calls the "government's chief gauge for the forecasting of the future of the economy"[43]—which is nothing more or less than a set of multiple fallible indicators.

In 1922 no less a figure than John Maynard Keynes considered the possibility of using "leading indicators" to forecast business conditions. As his biographer R. J. A. Skidelsky wrote, "An 'important and novel feature' of [Keynes's columns for the *Manchester Guardian*] . . . was the business 'barometer,' based on an 'index' of business conditions . . . [and] these barometers claimed to be able to forecast change in the economic weather."[44] Skidelsky went on to say that despite Keynes's personal skepticism, "Keynes helped start the London and Cambridge Economic Service—a regular survey of business conditions—in 1923."[45]

In the United States in 1960 the Bureau of the Census began assembling what it called the leading economic indicators as a way to both assess the state of the economy and predict its future; among the statistics included were such fallible indicators as consumer expectations and stock prices (the complete list of indicators appears in Table 5-1). These are fallible indicators in the sense that each one has some validity but none is a perfect, or infallible, predictor, a fact indicated by the numbers in Table 5-1.

The fallibility of these numbers is hardly a secret. A writer on economic matters in *The Wall Street Journal* pointed out in 1993 that although *consumer confidence* (another indicator of the future state of the economy) happened to be down, "consumer surveys have historically proved only modestly useful as a forecasting tool. . . . A [recent] sharp drop in all three major surveys of consumer expectations didn't stop people from buying 13.7% more cars and trucks than in May 1992. In April, new home sales surged 22.7%, the biggest gain since September 1986."[46]

Here is further evidence of the centrality of multiple fallible indicators in our personal economic life: The Internal Revenue Service constructs such indicators in order to find likely tax evaders. Tax advisers warn their clients that a return that includes such (fallible) indicators as complex tax shelters, home office deductions, high deductions for losses from theft or damaged property, high travel deductions, and

Table 5-1   Leading Economic Indicators.

|  | April 1993 | March 1993 |
|---|---|---|
| Workweek | .22 | −.22 |
| Unemployment claims | .01 | −.26 |
| Orders for consumer goods | .02 | −.10 |
| Slower deliveries | .06 | −.04 |
| Plant and equipment orders | −.14 | −.12 |
| Building permits | .18 | −.28 |
| Durable order backing | −.11 | −.01 |
| Materials prices | −.11 | −.03 |
| Stock prices | −.09 | .10 |
| Money supply | −.13 | −.07 |
| Consumer expectations | .02 | −.18 |

The seasonally adjusted index numbers (1982=100) for April, and the change from March, are:

| | | |
|---|---|---|
| Index of leading indicators | 152.0 | 0.1 |
| Index of coincident indicators | 125.3 | −0.4 |
| Index of lagging indicators | 104.2 | 0.1 |

The ratio of coincident to lagging indicators was 1.20, down from 1.21 in March.

Source: P. Thevanayagam (1993, p. A2).

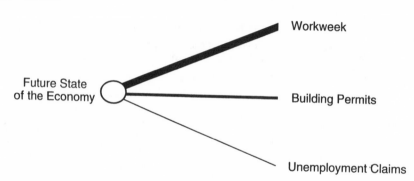

Figure 5-2   Differences in predictive validity of three leading economic indicators.

business losses is likely to call forth an audit. In principle, this procedure is exactly like any other use of multiple fallible indicators. It is based not on theory but on simple historical associations.

Nor are such indicators restricted to hard numbers. Even professional money managers and investment counselors are prepared to make use of "soft" indicators such as "sentiment." According to one analyst, for example, "Sentiment is one of those anecdotal indicators you can't look for in a database or quantify. . . . [The analyst] gets his sense of sentiment by noting the prevalence of such things as articles [in the business press] about the dangers currently confronting the stock market. Lots of cautionary stories in the press, he says, are a sure [!] sign that investors are far from reaching the comfort stage that could trigger a bear market."[47]

Moreover, indicators are rarely fixed in number; some are added, some dropped as their statistical relevance increases or diminishes. Nature also operates in this fashion but has done so, for the most part, very slowly. And nature is severe; when the ecological relevance of an indicator changes, the individuals who are "fixed" on that no longer valid indicator become unfit and are eventually eliminated.

But we human beings can be adept—and abrupt—in changing the indicators by which we live. In 1994, for example, the Commerce Department took steps toward including in the leading indicators a measure of the impact of economic growth on the environment.[48] The new measure would indicate the extent to which economic growth results in the increase or the depletion of natural resources. At present, removing trees from a forest through logging, thus producing timber for housing, adds to the measures of economic growth but is not reflected in any measure of the depletion of the resources supplied by the forest. The new measure changed that and thus produced a new indicator.

The effort to reduce uncertainty often takes the form of seeking a single infallible indicator such as those we construct so that we can avoid the perils of navigating in a world of naturally fallible indicators. The chairman of the Federal Reserve, Alan Greenspan, made his preference for such a single infallible indicator plain in his testimony before Congress in February 1994 when he said that he considered the price of gold "to be a very good indicator" of future inflation. Resurrecting the navigation metaphor, *The Wall Street Journal* added, "and thus a useful star by which to guide monetary policy."[49]

Greenspan's reliance on gold as "a very good indicator" led the newspaper's editorial writers to offer some history about previous chairmen who had relied on indicators that proved—after hard experience—to be *too* fallible for use and to suggest caution about overreliance on gold. "We'll be watching," they announced. In a world of multiple fallible indicators, there are also multiple fallible watchdogs. But Greenspan is not alone in seeking a single indicator. In Bob Woodward's recent book on the operation of the Clinton White House, the author indicates that the president is "obsessed" with the bond market.[50] Just how frequently policymakers develop a fascination for a single fallible indicator is not known, but it is clearly a dangerous practice in an uncertain, unstable environment.

### Indicators as Evidence of a Current State

Questions about the current state of society are not limited to economics. One does not have to be a member of the intelligentsia to have an opinion about the "progress" of our society, our "cultural" status. And, of course, everyone has an opinion about whether matters are getting better or worse. Three politically prominent organizations (Empower America, the American Heritage Foundation, and the Free Congress Foundation) addressed that question in a joint publication, *The Index of Leading Cultural Indicators*. The author, William Bennett, a well-known spokesman for conservative causes, states in the "Introduction" that the *Index* "is an assessment of the moral, social, and behavioral condition of modern American society"[51] but also observes that this is not a new idea: "In the 19th century . . . historian Thomas Carlyle spoke about the 'condition of England question.' For Carlyle the answer to the 'condition of England question' lay not in 'figures of arithmetic,' but in the realm of behavior, habits, beliefs, and mores—matters which in our time often travel under the banner of 'values.'"[52] Carlyle, however, offered no index of behavior, whereas Bennett does. His index consists of nineteen (fallible) social indicators offering the "most comprehensive statistical portrait available of behavioral trends over the last 30 years."[53] Bennett concludes: "According to this Index, in many ways the condition of America is not good."[54] He further concludes:

> Since 1960, population has increased 41 percent; the Gross Domestic Product has nearly tripled; and total social spending by all levels of government (measured in constant 1990 dollars) has risen from $143.73 billion to $787.0 billion—more than a five-fold increase. Inflation-adjusted spending on welfare has increased 630 percent and inflation-adjusted spending on education has increased 225 percent. The United States has the strongest economy in the world, a healthy entrepreneurial spirit, a still-healthy work ethic, and a generous attitude—good signs all.
>
> But during the same 30-year period there has been a 560 percent increase in violent crime; more than a 400 percent increase in illegitimate births; a quadrupling in divorce rates; a tripling of the percentage of children living in single-parent homes; more than a 200 percent increase in the teenage suicide rate; and a drop of almost 80 points in the S.A.T. scores. Modern-day social pathologies, at least great parts of them, have gotten worse. They seem impervious to government spending on their alleviation, even very large amounts of spending.[55]

The following list contains the nineteen cultural indicators used by Bennett:

Crime

> Number of crimes committed
> Median prison sentence for all serious crimes
> Juvenile violent crime arrest rates

Poverty

> Children relying on aid to families with dependent children
> Child poverty

Natality

> Infant mortality
> Teenage pregnancy, birth, and abortion rates
> Births to unmarried women
> Total abortions

Family

> Child abuse
> Teen suicide rate
> Marriage and divorce
> Children affected by divorce
> Single-parent families
> Living arrangements of children

Education

> SAT scores
> High school dropout rates

Drugs

> Drug use

Television viewing

> Daily television viewing[56]

But Bennett is not the only commentator on life in the United States; indeed, virtually everyone who comments on the status of society—any society—makes use of multiple fallible indicators, although not always in the documented form employed by Bennett. Here, for example, is the well-known sociologist Amitai Etzioni's description of the current situation and forecast for the future. I use this example from Etzioni because his evaluations and forecasts are presented in the more frequently used casual, textual (rather than graphical) form and thus offer the reader some practice in recognizing the appearance of multiple fallible indicators in written material.

> Historians will look back on the 1990s, I believe, and see them as a period in which the reconstruction of American society took place. The United States is beginning to experience a movement from "Me-ism" to a commitment to the "We." From a preoccupation with rights, American society is moving to demand that people shoulder their responsibilities and pay greater attention to the needs of their families and communities.
> A few examples make the point. More and more U.S. states demand that those who receive welfare seek work, and if they cannot find work, they must perform some kind

of public service. Americans are increasingly expected to drink in moderation and avoid smoking in order to reduce the burden on health care. Deadbeat fathers are being persuaded with new vigor to support their children. There is a new willingness to face the deficit in the national budget, and there is also an increase in the number of people who vote.

Standards in schools are beginning to rise. Many schools have dropped the notion of automatic advancement from grade to grade. The concept of minimum competence as a requirement for graduation is catching on. By the end of the decade, I believe, fairly stringent national standards for education will be in place. Such standards will encourage schools to aim higher and spotlight those that do not.

The grand debate about the future of the family will lead to new efforts to enable parents to attend to their children. The 1993 Family and Medical Leave Act, which now covers only those who work for larger companies and grants 90 days of unpaid leave will be extended, I predict, to cover all Americans and grant them six months of paid leave—as is the case in most of Europe—by the year 2000.

Nonetheless, I believe that the United States will face more urban crises, such as the one in Los Angeles, and that the nation will not be immune to the worldwide drift toward tribal conflicts, already affecting 23 countries. Americans need to rebuild not just their communities, but also the ties that bind communities into one overarching society.[57]

It is apparent that Bennett, the conservative, and Etzioni, the liberal, have in common a commitment to the use of multiple fallible indicators as a method for drawing their sharply different conclusions about the state of U.S. society. But they differ in the fallible indicators upon which they prefer to base their conclusions. Bennett chose crime, poverty, natality (infant mortality), teenage pregnancy, births to unmarried women—all areas of increasing concern, whereas Etzioni focused on areas in which society's health could be said to be improving—drinking, smoking, child support payments, voting. These differences in the choice—and the use—of multiple fallible indicators provide a very important clue to sources of conflict in policy formation. They also demonstrate how different value systems drive one's choice of social indicators. We should expect such *cognitive* differences to lead to sharp disputes between Bennett and Etzioni; moreover, we should anticipate that such disputes will not be easy to resolve.

Despite its highly coherent theories, physical science also seeks indicators when trying to measure physical events outside the laboratory, events not under the scientists' control, such as weather phenomena and earthquakes. For example, in an article in *Science* titled "Detecting Climatic Change Signals: Are There any 'Fingerprints'?" Stephen Schneider, a well-known atmospheric scientist, criticizes what he calls "univariate measures"—that is, single measures of climatic change. He points out that "a number of researchers have suggested that such [univariate] measures . . . be replaced with multivariate methods, which they call fingerprints."[58] He is, in short, suggesting the use of *multiple* fallible indicators in detecting climatic change (and thus warning against the single indicator procedure favored in other arenas by Greenspan and Clinton). Earthquake researchers employ essentially the same methodology.[59]

Medicine offers numerous examples of the use of multiple fallible indicators are used in making diagnoses, as J. A. Del Regato makes clear in the following passage:

Chronic cystic disease is often confused with carcinoma of the breast. It *usually* occurs in parous women with small breasts. It is present *most commonly* in the upper quadrant but *may* occur in other parts and eventually involve the entire breast. It is *often* painful, particularly in the premenstrual period, and accompanying menstrual disturbances are *common*. Nipple discharge, *usually* serous, occurs in *approximately* 15% of the cases, but there are no changes in the nipple itself. The lesion *is* diffuse without sharp demarcation and without fixation to the overlying skin. Multiple cysts are firm, round, and fluctuant and *may* transilluminate *if* they contain clear fluid. A large cyst in an area of chronic cystic disease *feels* like a tumor, but it is *usually* smoother and well delimited. The axillary lymph nodes are *usually* not enlarged. Chronic cystic disease *infrequently* shows large bluish cysts. *More often*, the cysts are multiple and small [italics added throughout].[60]

The description illustrates how a textbook on cancer explains to medical students and physicians "how non-malignant diseases [e.g., chronic cystic disease] can be differentiated from cancer."[61] Just how the student translates the probabilistic terms is unknown.

Farmers and ranchers are so close to nature that we should expect to find frequent use of multiple fallible indicators—and that is what D. G. Burnside and E. Faithfull did find.[62] In Australia, as in many other countries with a large agricultural base, the question of the proper use of rangeland for sheep and cattle is a prominent and contentious one. Burnside, a member of the Australian range extension service, used the general correspondence theory described here, including the lens model, to discover the judgment policies of the two main interested parties regarding grazing practices. The two parties include the pastoralists (as ranchers are called in Australia) and members of the extension service (called advisers), who oversee the grazing practices of the pastoralists. As elsewhere, problems arise in range management because, as Burnside and Faithfull put it:

Although objective monitoring of range trend is underway in most states in Australia, there has been inadequate attention paid to the interpretation and application of this information to management. Given the absence of rules for the assessment of monitoring data in Australia, subjective interpretation is the current option for pastoralists and other land management decision makers in applying the data to management.[63]

Burnside's approach to the reconciliation of disputed judgments over grazing practices was to make direct use of the lens model together with modern computer technology. He presented pastoralists with information (including photographs of various rangeland situations) and asked for judgments about the range of conditions, which were entered directly into a computer and analyzed (see Figure 5-3). As a result, Burnside was able to determine the consistency with which such judgments were made, the weighting policies used by pastoralists and advisers, and therefore the sources of agreement and disagreement between them. What had been an entirely covert set of judgments thus became overt and subject to discussion in terms of rangeland practices and regulations.

L. I. Dalgleish has similarly studied the use of indicators by judges and social workers in their decisions about whether abused or neglected children should be separated from their parents.[64]

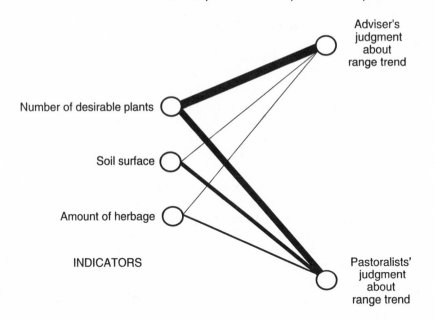

Figure 5-3    Use of the lens model to show how conflicting judgments can arise from differential weighting of fallible indicators. The adviser places considerable weight on the *number of desirable plants* (68%) but ignores other indicators of range condition. The pastoralist gives greatest weight (46%) to *number of desirable plants* but also takes into account *soil surface* (24%) and *amount of herbage* (18%).

## What Do Indicators Indicate?

Too often the mere fact of the creation, publication, and media presentation of indicators serves to justify their use. But justification may be an illusion, for at least three reasons: (1) The indicators may be *unreliable*, providing highly imprecise data; (2) they may be *invalid*, providing data that are not related to the situation as claimed; and (3) most important, the situation or outcome described *or* predicted may itself be unexamined, taken for granted. For example, how can the indicators used by Bennett or Etzioni be justified? the authors' would probably answer that these indicators stand on their own as "descriptors," they are not "predictors," that is, they are value-driven. They were chosen because the authors' values led them to believe that they describe what is important to them—and ought to be important to everyone; the indicators need no other justification.

But indicators that claim to predict are different. The economics-relevant "leading indicators" are clearly intended to be predictors of the future state of the economy. Therefore we can ask: How well do they do that? How is the state of the economy to be measured? And how is that measure justified? We shall find that justification takes the same form that Bennett and Etzioni use for their *descriptive* indicators—a set of values that inform the authors about what is important to them. Very often, however, we do not learn what these values are because the authors of the index never tell us; they have taken their values for granted. And that is what happened in the case of the widely used, widely reported, and critically important, Gross Domestic Product (GDP)—the accepted measure of the state of U.S. economy.

Recently Cobb, Halstead, and Rowe[65] made a detailed critique of the current composition of the GDP. Why, they asked, was this measure included and not that one? The answers made it clear that the GDP is composed of value-driven measures. They provide information that favors special industrial interests and ignore the more general interests of society. Yet this peculiarity is overlooked: "Somehow the GDP manages to induce a kind of collective stupor in which such basic questions rarely get asked."[66]

The composition of the GDP index is indeed startling, particularly for a measure that is intended to advise U.S. citizens about changes in something as central as the state of the economy. For example, according to Cobb and his colleagues: "It does not distinguish between costs and benefits, between productive and destructive activities, or between sustainable and unsustainable ones. . . . It treats everything that happens in the market as a gain for humanity."[67] Interestingly, the authors contrast William Bennett's "Index of Leading Cultural Indicators" with the indicators in the GDP and find that many of the indices that Bennett deplores (crime, divorce, and so on) actually *add* to the GDP! That is because increased crime leads to increases of sales in the crime prevention and security industry; divorce leads to "a small fortune in lawyers' bills." Cobb and his colleagues note that "while social conservatives like Bennett are rightly deploring the nation's social decline, their free-marketeer counterparts are . . . breaking out the champagne."[68] Similarly with the natural environment: "The more the nation depletes its natural resources, the more the GDP increases. . . . Depletion of capital [is thus counted] as current income."[69] In short, the critical measure of the U.S. economy that the Leading Economic Indicators is intended to predict doesn't make sense, it lacks coherence.

### Predictors vs. Descriptors

Earlier I pointed out the distinction between correspondence and coherence theories and showed how these theories encompass different approaches to the study of judgment and decision making. That distinction will also serve us well here, for the inclusion of indicators in a descriptive index such as Bennett's or Etzioni's will depend on their coherence with one another and with the value system that directs their choice. But when indicators are used as predictors, they stand or fall in terms in their correspondence, their contribution to the accuracy of the index. Nothing else matters. The predictors may be theoretically incompatible, or be associated with different value systems; it doesn't matter, for prediction simply demands accuracy. Thus, we can anticipate cool-headed, pragmatic discussions about the inclusion of one *predictor* over another—the data will cast the ballots. But there will be heated discussions over the inclusion of one *descriptor over* another because values will clash. And indeed that is apparent in the attack by Cobb and his colleagues on the present composition of the GDP. They find that it is so at odds with so many social values— interest in reducing crime and divorce, interest in sustaining the nation's natural resources—that it has become worse than useless; it misleads.

Indeed, even the composition of the critically important "Index of Leading Economic Indicators" is itself a hodge podge of predictors, those justified by historical confidence, and those "justified" by resorting to unexamined human judgment. As stated in a textbook in economic forecasting, in a section titled "The Search for Indicators," "the scores [on the indices] . . . are based more on opinion than on any sophisticated analysis."[70] Thus, the nation's policy makers are forced to depend on a set of predictors in which the data are based "*more* (italics added) on opinion than on any sophisticated analysis," as well as a measure of the economy's performance that is composed of an incoherent set of descriptors.

Careful scrutiny of the role of human judgment in the composition of both predictors and descriptors remains an important task. Both predictors and descriptors remains an important task. Both predictors and descriptors must be examined carefully—and continually—in terms of their correspondence and coherence. The value systems that drive both should be made explicit.

Value-driven Predictors in Academia

Economics is not the only area in which values affect the selection of predictors and descriptors. A dramatic, yet seldom remarked upon, change in the predictors used to select students for admission to universities occurred during World War II.

Prior to World War I the indicators used by Ivy League colleges and universities were "legacy" indicators: If your parents or grandparents were graduates of Harvard or Princeton, for example, you were likely to be an ethnically appropriate white Protestant and your chances of being admitted to these universities were very good; indicators of intellective abilities other than graduation from a (usually, private) high school, were not serious at issue. But the scores on tests that purport to be predictors of academic success began to displace "legacy" indicators shortly after World War II, and ethnic indicators began to be *reversed* after the 1960s. How did this happen?

Lemann[71] has recently described how this shift in predictive indicators was produced during the 1930s and 1940s by the efforts of two men—Henry Chauncey, director of admissions, and James Bryant, president of Harvard University. Their main goals were to introduce an orderly and defensible method of selecting students for admission, thus improving the quality of students, as well as higher education, in the United States. Their efforts, combined with others, and spurred by the advent of World War II, resulted in the establishment of the Scholastic Aptitude Test (SAT) as a standard method for selecting students. That shift in value-driven indicators— legacy indicators to indicators of academic competence—reflected a remarkable shift from aristocracy to meritocracy, at least in the Ivy League schools, and a shift toward fairness as well.

This remarkable change in social poilicy was accompanied by a shift in theory. The aristocratic legacy approach to the selection of predictors depended on certain attributes—white, Protestant, old family, graduate of a prestigious high school—to correspondence between predictor and student performance. When the value of the SAT is examined, it is examined in terms of the accuracy of its prediction not coherence among the predictors. There are, of course, some assumptions about what intellective capacities a student must have to succeed. But the inclusion of a predictor stands or falls on its accuracy in prediction, not what one's value system dictates.

In sum, multiple fallible indicators have no doubt always been an important part of the lives of numerous species. The next question, then, must be: How good are we at making effective use of these indicators? What is our correspondence competence?

### Competent Use of Indicators by Homo Sapiens

Empirical research by psychologists on the accuracy of people's judgments in relation to objects and events began very late in the nineteenth century with the study of psychophysics by the German researcher Gustav Fechner.[72] The research problems were related to "on-the-skin" judgments—for example, is this weight heavier than that one? Is the distance between these pin pricks greater than the distance between those? Similar studies were conducted for vision, audition, and the other senses.

By the 1930s research on the accuracy of perception of physical objects (size, shape, color) "beyond the skin" had begun. Psychologists, however, also turned their attention to the study of error; from roughly 1910 to 1950 the gestalt psychologists produced and studied a wide variety of perceptual illusions, and it was not until the 1940s that psychologists replaced the study of illusions with systematic studies of the accuracy of perception.[73]

The new studies grew out of two sources. One was James Gibson's participation in efforts by the Army Air Force during World War II to understand better the accuracy of airplane pilots' perception of size, distance, and other physical dimensions. Gibson, given the chance to work in natural conditions, made the most of his opportunity. By 1947 Gibson was reporting that subjects in his studies could judge size accurately from distances up to eight hundred yards under naturalistic circumstances. The idea that psychologists would have to prove—in 1947—that human beings possessed accuracy of that sort can be comprehended only if one realizes that psychologists had been immersed in the study of perceptual illusions for decades. But Gibson showed what he thought of the matter when he asked this question in 1950: "Why are the optical illusions . . . [shown in] the textbooks actually the exception rather than the rule?"[74]

The second source for the new kind of study was Egon Brunswik's work during the 1930s. Brunswik too thought that the efforts of the gestalt psychologists were badly misguided. To demonstrate that the study of illusions was beside the point, Brunswik carried out a field study in which he followed a person during the day in her natural habitat (Berkeley, California) and asked her to estimate the sizes of various objects upon which her eyes happened to be focused. He found that she made highly accurate estimates for a wide range of objects and conditions.[75] Similar studies of perception under natural conditions have also found perception of the physical properties of objects to be highly accurate. Even Brunswik found these results "astonishing,"[76] an indication of the extent to which the study of optical illusions had influenced perception researchers.

Because Brunswik and Gibson insisted that the study of illusions was a misguided, nonproductive endeavor based on laboratory research environments that were unrepresentative of the natural ecology, and because they wanted to study behavior in a natural environment, they became known as ecological psychologists. A similar debate between those who emphasize error and illusion, on the one hand, and those who emphasize the accuracy of human perceptions, on the other, as well as a dispute about the relative value of laboratory research and naturalistic or field research, is currently taking place in the field of judgment and decision making, with no recognition that history is repeating itself.[77] The more positive views about the accuracy of human judgment derive from the anchoring point of correspondence theory— visual perception.

There can be little doubt that visual perception is extraordinarily competent. Look about you; your environment rarely fools you. You do not see a pencil diminish in size when it moves away from you; you can accurately gauge the speed and direction of the path of a frisbee (and so can a dog and a bird); you do not think a plate changes its shape despite its changing orientation in space. With a little instruction you can easily fly an airplane and move about in three-dimensional space. The same is true for sound; you can determine that a loud explosion has occurred far away even though the sound is barely audible. And so on. This most impressive ability is summed up by the phenomenon known as *constancy*—perhaps psychology's most important discovery.

The fact of constancy proves that our physical perception judgments are excellent, although not perfect, on most occasions. We can be fooled occasionally, but it takes considerable time, effort, and knowledge for experimental psychologists to create conditions that produce perceptual illusions, and such conditions appear only infrequently outside the psychologists' laboratory. But our judgments begin to deteriorate in accuracy as the conditions under which they are made become increasingly ambiguous. Ambiguity increases as matters become remote in *time* (next week's weather rather than today's) and *space* (farther away rather than close up) and as they become *conceptually* abstract (rather than concrete)—in short, as irreducible uncertainty increases. And as these conditions increase in importance in the judgment task, and as the importance of the more direct perceptual conditions diminishes, the greater becomes the role of *thought* in relation to perception and thus the likelihood of error.

The danger of thinking in circumstances that are wholly perceptual (and motor) is well known to football fans. When the outcome of a game depends on the success or failure of a field goal attempt, the team that is defending against the kick will, if circumstances permit, invariably call for a time-out just as the kicker is about to kick. This is done, as the TV announcers never fail to mention, "to give him time to think about it," thus, the defending team hopes, inducing an error.

Perception occurs without awareness. When reaching for the pencil on your desk, you do not make note of the fact that your perceptual judgment tells you how far to reach; you cannot explain how you know how far to reach because, in fact, you do *not* know, in the intellectual sense of knowing. But when you are reaching for a response to criticism from your wife, mother, brother, friend, you are often aware that responding is not easy and that your judgment is, or should be, guiding your response. Visual perception may have a place in this process; you may be watching the facial expression and the posture of the other person, but you probably will be *thinking* about the consequences of your response. And when you are asked your opinion about the most recent step taken by the city council, the school board, or the president, visual perception plays little or no role in the judgment you express; thinking does. When assessing correspondence competence, we need to consider carefully the differences in task conditions.

The nature of ambiguity in the tasks we confront can be differentiated further according to the *number* of cues or indicators offered. Some tasks offer us one, two, three, or more cues or indicators about the state or event about which we are making a judgment. Indicators can also be differentiated in terms of their *fallibility*: Some indicators are very nearly infallible, while some are highly fallible. The study of the competence of human judgment allows us to comprehend the reasons for the accuracy, or correspondence, of judgment about objects and events, near and far, here and now, abstract and concrete. We turn now, however, to a consideration of a more difficult topic—how psychologists study perception and judgment of people.

### Clinical Judgment

The judgment of psychiatrists, psychologists, and other mental health professionals came under research scrutiny about half a century ago with the publication in 1941 of three articles by Theodore Sarbin in which he reported that predictions by clinical psychologists were less accurate than predictions made from a statistics-based formula.[78] These articles caught the attention of Paul Meehl, who in 1954 took the first hard, critical look at the competence of clinical judgment in psychology; the scrutiny has continued (and has spread to clinical judgment in medicine[79]). The 1947 meeting of the American Psychological Association included a symposium on clinical and statistical methods, but Meehl noted that it was "poorly attended";[80] psychologists did not yet see the issue as interesting or important, but Meehl's book changed that. He did not claim that clinical judgment was inherently flawed, but, following up on Sarbin's work, he did call for objective, scientific appraisal of it. Meehl not only sanctioned Sarbin's comparison between actuarial and clinical inference but drew out the theoretical, methodological, and procedural consequences in a compelling and sophisticated manner. Meehl put his request for the analytical treatment of clinical judgment this way:

> Is any clinician infallible? No one claims to be. Hence, sometimes he is wrong. If he is sometimes wrong, why should we pay any attention to him? There is only one possible reply to this "silly" question. It is simply that he tends (read: "is likely") to be right. "Tending" to be right means just one thing—"being right in the long run." Can we take the clinician's word for this? Certainly not.[81]

This sort of skepticism may seem somewhat tame in light of what has happened since, but clinicians were automatically awarded a certain authoritative mystique in the 1950s that they do not enjoy today. Indeed, research inspired by Meehl's work has largely been responsible for eroding that mystique.

In fact, however, Meehl's demands were modest. All he asked was that clinicians keep track of their work; he claimed that "statistics are unavoidable."[82] He wanted clinicians to justify themselves by showing that their judgments and predictions could do something that simple statistical equations couldn't do; if record keeping was necessary for that, so be it.

One reason that Meehl's book had such impact is that it demonstrated that there was *no* evidence for the superiority of the clinician over the equation and presented considerable evidence in support of its argument. Meehl's conclusion was not only hard to believe, it was hard to take—and still is. Meehl's hypothesis that clinical expertise was no more accurate than a very simple equation was clearly a plausible hypothesis worthy of investigation.

Although Meehl was not the first to make this assertion, his book had great impact because of his evenhanded and sophisticated treatment of the issues. Few of those inclined to dispute his argument had philosophical erudition and technical skills to match his. One could not lightly turn aside his thesis. Moreover, Meehl was a practicing clinician and thus knew whereof he spoke on both sides of the question.

There is a second aspect to Meehl's work that struck at clinicians' professional pride—his doubts about clinicians' ability to discern "patterns." But if wisdom, clinical or otherwise, is anything, it is the ability to see a pattern in the evidence that the novice, or the "unwise," does not see and that a simple equation cannot see. Yet simple equations of the sort Meehl was advocating as competitors for clinical wisdom were anything but pattern seekers or pattern recognizers. This was more than ego-deflating; it was insulting. Meehl drove his point home with this remark: "It is sometimes said that the differential weights of the regression equation . . . were devised specifically to take account of pattern relationships. It is obvious that the kind of patterning which we are considering here is *not* adequately dealt with by such procedures."[83] He emphasized that the equations or formulas that were to compete with clinical wisdom were *very* simple, straightforward, and linear in form.

Meehl examined several aspects of the "dynamics of this [intuitive] process" but came to no conclusion about that process. He certainly made his views clear to clinicians and researchers alike: The process of clinical inference (1) *ought* to be studied, (2) *can* be studied, and (3) can be usefully *compared* to simple actuarial processes. The last point proved to be a bombshell.

Meehl's analysis of the contrast between statistical and clinical prediction was based on the need to examine the *accuracy* of clinical judgment and statistical prediction in terms of the empirical comparison of predictions and outcomes. Clinical judgment was found wanting. Meehl was largely disinterested in the coherence of such judgments, a point to which I will return.

My contribution to this topic was made at a conference on unified science at Berkeley in 1953—a most rarefied atmosphere. My article, entitled "Probabilistic Functionalism and the Clinical Method,"[84] had a different purpose from the publications of Sarbin and Meehl. Those authors focused on the differential accuracy between clinical and statistical predictions; I wanted to show that clinical judgment could be studied in terms of a specific psychological theory of judgment taken from Brunswik's lens model of visual perception. My purpose was to apply a theoretical model to the clinical psychologists' process of clinical judgment. The test of the model would be its ability to predict the *clinician's judgments* of patients' attributes from the clinician's reading of patients' Rorschach test protocols. The test of the model was successful.

The model was a simple one; indeed, it was based on the same regression equation as the actuarial process that Sarbin and Meehl and others had found to be more accurate than clinicians' judgments. This led me to the hypothesis that the clinician's judgments were the product of the same process as the actuarial process; this in turn led me to the conclusion that the actuarial process—an equation—was likely to be more accurate only because it was perfectly consistent and not subject to the errors that the clinician is likely to make because of a lack of perfect cognitive control. (I was not the first to reach this conclusion. Henry Wallace, later a vice president of the United States, made similar observations in 1923 about corn judges who appraised the quality of farmers' crop exhibits.[85])

After the publication of Meehl's book, so much research was undertaken on the topic of clinical judgment that the American Psychological Association held a second symposium on clinical and statistical prediction in 1984. There Sarbin offered his conclusions, forty years later:

> The earlier controversy between clinical and statistical prediction has faded into the shadows. Few people today challenge the necessity for both approaches in seeking to develop and apply knowledge. In more contemporary terms, the issue of which prediction method should be preferred involves choosing between a quest for *historical* truth (i.e., correspondence demonstrated by statistical methods) and a quest for *narrative* truth (i.e., coherence achieved by clinical formulations).[86]

Sarbin's article is important. For although his statement that "the earlier controversy . . . has faded into the shadows" turned out to be wrong (within a few years R. M. Dawes, D. Faust, and Meehl[87] would publish a major article on this topic in *Science*, about which more later), his review was very useful. He acknowledged that Meehl was right in criticizing him for confusing the context of discovery with the context of verification. He also brought the topics of irreducible uncertainty, inevitable error, and unavoidable injustice into the discussion. As he put it, "Hardly anyone would today challenge the use of statistical predictions in those circumstances where the personal and societal costs of the inevitable false positives and false negatives are morally defensible."[88] Sarbin apparently intended this sentence to mean that no one would any longer argue against the replacement of a clinical psychologist or psychiatrist by statistical simple actuarial predictions merely because he or she found such replacement to be personally repugnant; the unavoidable injustice (i.e., the "personal and societal costs of the inevitable false positives and false negatives") produced by use of the less accurate method would be deemed morally *in*defensible (thus anticipating the general theme of this book). But although Sarbin was correct about what *ought* to be the case, he was wrong in his prediction about what *would* be the case. Otherwise, there would have been no need for Dawes and his colleagues to write their article in 1989 pointing out how little had changed.

Sarbin anticipated the framework of this book when he placed the debate between clinical and statistical approaches to prediction in the context of coherence-versus-correspondence theories of truth. He quoted John Dewey to illustrate his point:

> [T]he novelist and the dramatist are so much more illuminating as well as more interesting commentators on conduct than the schematizing psychologist. The artist makes perceptible individual responses and thus displays a new phase of human nature evoked

in new situations. In putting the case visibly and dramatically he reveals vital actualities. The scientific systematizer treats each act as merely another sample of some old principle, or as a mechanical combination of elements drawn from a ready-made inventory.[89]

Sarbin then drove home his point by stating: "The test of the truth value of the therapist's story [diagnosis] is coherence, rather than correspondence. The appropriate question to ask is: Does the story hang together?" On the other hand, "the ultimate test of the truth value of the [predictive] equation is the degree of correspondence between the expressed predictions and the observed outcomes."[90] In these remarks Sarbin differentiates between the goals of therapy and behavior prediction.

Finally, in further anticipation of the conclusions offered here, Sarbin raised the matter of differential application:

Before the dust is settled, some wise man or woman will ask: Under what conditions and for what purposes should we choose the test of correspondence or the test of coherence? To frame useful answers, that same wise person might then direct us to seek out appropriate moral guidelines. And a voice from the back of the room may exclaim: Moral guidelines? Is there no way of calling upon the scientific method for answers, tell me, I implore?

Quoth the raven: Nevermore.[91]

Sarbin was as prescient as former Vice President Wallace; the field of judgment and decision making has yet to find the answer to his question "Under what conditions and for what purposes should we choose the test of correspondence or the test of coherence?" Indeed, the question has barely been recognized, let alone answered. *Can* it be answered by scientific investigations? Sarbin's quote from Poe indicates that he is doubtful. For my part, I believe that the question can be settled in this way; the theory developed in Part III of this book is directed to this goal.

In the same year that Sarbin offered his reflections "forty years later," Meehl reentered the debate thirty years after the publication of *his* book with a brief article titled "Causes and Effects of My Disturbing Little Book."[92] He remained enthusiastic about what he had done, writing: "Review and reflection indicate that no more than 5% of what was written in the 1954 book . . . needs to be retracted 30 years later."[93] Strangers to the field of academic psychology may perhaps not realize the significance of that remark, but others will realize that this is surely a rare event; psychology is not known for the longevity of its general conclusions.

Meehl then asks: "Why should people have been so surprised by the empirical results in my summary chapter?"[94] There Meehl

emphasize[d] the brute fact that we have here . . . from 16 to 20 studies involving a comparison of clinical and actuarial methods [by 1989 nearly 100], in all but one of which the predictions made actuarially were either approximately equal or superior to those made by a clinician.[95]

He then asserted that "surely we all know that the human brain is poor at weighting and computing."[96]

Here I begin to part company with Meehl. I do not believe that in 1954 we all knew that "the human brain is poor at weighting and computing," nor do we know that now. I believe that the evidence indicates that the human brain is good—not perfect, but good—at weighting and computing in conditions where (1) "weighting and computing" are good things to do and (2) feedback conditions are such that the person can learn. I do not mean to say that the human brain is *as* good at weighting and computing on an intuitive basis as an analytical, straightforward mathematical procedure is, for the latter defines the ceiling; nothing that we know of can be better. But we shouldn't be surprised at this; many studies demonstrate this point.[97]

I also disagree with Meehl when he says that "there are no strong arguments, from the armchair or from empirical studies of cognitive psychology, for believing that human beings can assign *optimal* [italics added] weights in equations subjectively."[98] In fact, there are numerous studies that show that human beings can learn to apply weights that closely match those in the task.[99]

The problem with clinical judgment, in my view, is that clinicians do not know that they can *learn to be almost as good* as certain (simple) equations. Rather, their problem is that they have been led to believe that they are *superior* to simple procedures by virtue of their putative capacity for pattern recognition. They have been, in short, seduced by the coherence theory of truth and the conceit that not only do they know how to implement it but that when they do, their predictions are in greater correspondence with empirical truth than those derived from an equation developed directly from a correspondence methodology. Unfortunately, Meehl misleads clinicians by supporting them in that conceit. He points out, for example, that there are some things that "even the modern super computer cannot as yet do very well"; "the first is pattern recognition, where the computer still cannot recognize a slightly battered typeface as well as the human eye and brain."[100] That example misleads because it is beside the point. The visual examination of a test score cannot be equated with the visual recognition of a battered typeface. Those are two different visual phenomena; we are not asking the clinician to determine whether the badly printed "5" on the sheet of paper is really a "5." Rather, we ask clinicians to understand exactly what the "5" (uniformly agreed to as a "5") *signifies*. So the kind of visual pattern recognizing skill Meehl describes—which is surely there—is irrelevant to clinical pattern recognition, particularly that which he described in 1954.

The clinicians' problem with pattern recognition is not a failure to recognize patterns; it is that clinicians do not have an accepted icon to recognize. The clinician has only badly formulated and never validated theories or models of behavior to recognize; indeed, the clinician often must invent a new model for a new patient. What deceives clinicians is their confidence in their ability to *understand* such models (they are not fully understandable), to *apply* them (they lack rules for application), or to *invent* models that hang together (inventions need validation, too). It is this conceit that leads clinicians away from what they *can* do, and often do do, *almost* as well as the best correspondence method (the equation). In short, it is a misplaced conception of competence that is at the root of the matter. The reader will note that once more we are encountering the competition between correspondence and coherence in the forms of indices (test scores) versus models, or patterns, of behavior.

Clinical rules ordinarily perform better than clinicians because clinicians almost never perform entirely consistently and the empirically derived rules do.[101] The only way clinicians can do better is to (1) make use of variables or information not included in the clerical rules (a situation that occasionally occurs) and (2) make use of a coherence model—if there is one—that also has correspondence truth value greater than the clerical rule. So far, there does not seem to be one. But there is no a priori reason why such competence cannot be developed; coherence theories with correspondence truth value exist elsewhere in science. Physiological diseases, for example, exhibit patterns—that is, necessary functionalities among variables that are empirically demonstrable. To deny this possibility is to posit an untested theory of behavior—namely, that behavior never occurs in a patterned form. Is anyone prepared to do that? Be that as it may, patterned behavior remains elusive.

The most recent overall review of the contest between clinical (human judgment) and actuarial predictions of behavior was conducted by Dawes, Faust, and Meehl in 1989. This informative review not only confirms but adds confidence to the previous conclusion that actuarial methods are almost invariably more accurate than clinical methods; the authors also explain the reasons for this, in much the same terms as I have used. Then why beat what is apparently a dead horse? Because the horse isn't dead; it lives, despite all the previous beatings; that is, "research on clinical versus statistical judgment has had little impact on everyday decision making, particularly within its field of origin, clinical psychology."[102] Dawes and his colleagues explain the lack of impact in rather harsh terms; clinicians are unfamiliar with the scientific evidence, don't read the literature, don't believe what they read, misconceive the problem, or find that the work threatens their status as professionals or that the use of predictive equations "dehumanizes their clients."[103]

Whether one more review will change any of this is doubtful, as the authors are likely to agree. D. McCauley is rather sure it won't. He examined the manner in which the National Science Foundation selects its graduate fellowships, which are "among the most prestigious awards for college students seeking a Ph.D. in science or engineering,"[104] considering this to be a unique opportunity to study whether psychologists would make use of the research reviewed by Dawes, Faust, and Meehl. He reports that "for the 1990 psychology panel, there were 374 applicants to be judged by 18 psychologists."[105] The question McCauley asked was: Will the assembled psychologists act like everyone else in this situation, that is, will they assume that we have learned nothing about how such judgments should be made, or will the psychologists apply what judgment and decision researchers have discovered over the past fifty years? Dawes, Faust, and Meehl probably would predict the former, and it turns out they would be right. None of the knowledge was applied; indeed, when offered the opportunity to make use of a "derived score" (the validity of which was known to be high), fifteen of the eighteen psychologists voted against receiving the information. This prompted McCauley to ask: "If a select panel of psychologists chooses to ignore the results of substantial research, results that are as compelling as any in psychology, what should nonpsychologists conclude about the value of psychological research?"[106]

One might ask why clinical psychologists are offended by the discovery that their intuitive judgments and predictions are (almost) as good as, but (almost) never better than, a rule. That achievement is no small feat, particularly since the rules involve different content and different occasions. We do not feel offended at learning that our excellent visual perception can often be improved in certain circumstances by the use of a tool (e.g., rangefinders, telescopes, microscopes). The answer seems to be that rules are used by clerks (i.e., someone without professional training); if psychologists are no different, then that demeans the status of the psychologist. ("If that's all it comes down to, why is the psychologist paid more than the clerk?") But it is the psychologist who discovers what information should go into the rule; the clerk could not discover that. It is therefore the psychologist who should control the prediction system since she or he understands it; the clerk doesn't. This viewpoint places the psychologist largely in the role of researcher, rather than of clinician.

## Social Perception

The first study of social perception (or social judgment) was carried out by the learning psychologist E. L. Thorndike in 1918.[107] His task was to help the U.S. Army in World War I rate enlisted men for their potential as officers.[108] A number of studies of the accuracy of social perception were undertaken in the early 1920s.[109] The interesting point about these studies carried out some three-quarters of a century ago is that they are methodologically superior to many contemporary studies, not in any sophisticated, statistical sense but in a fundamental sense. The early studies frequently used a (barely) sufficient number of persons for the judges to rate, but many current studies ignore this matter and use the minimum number—namely, *one* person as a target person! In 1956 Brunswik criticized these early studies for failing to present a sufficient number of social objects, or targets, to be judged. For example, R. Pintner[110] presented twelve; P. C. Gaskill, N. Fenton, and J. P. Porter[111] also presented twelve; S. G. Estes[112] presented fifteen; and M. S. Viteles and K. R. Smith[113] presented ten. Although the size of these samples is not satisfactory, they compare favorably to the numbers of social objects used today. In one recent study, P. Ekman and M. O'Sullivan[114] used ten social objects, five of whom were lying and five were not, to test whether specialists in such activities (e.g., Secret Service agents) could detect which persons were lying. Few subjects could do so beyond chance levels. With so few test objects, however, the specialists would have had to get nine of ten correct in order to be performing above chance levels; the *power* of the test was far too low because of these small numbers.

L. D. Anderson, however, understood the point as early as 1921;[115] he presented 670 persons to be judged. That size sample would be rare in any study today, not merely because of logistics but because many contemporary researchers do not grasp the point that generalization about persons always requires consideration of sampling theory, whether the people are being judged or doing the judging.

A little-known study carried out by G. U. Cleeton and F. B. Knight in 1924 is worthy of our attention because the authors' work (1) was inspired by the gullibility of "industry" (meaning businessmen), (2) employed a research methodology that has yet to be grasped by many if not most contemporary researchers, and (3) produced results that would attract interest today.

The authors' first sentence expresses a viewpoint as applicable today as in 1924: "Industry, fully aware of the advantage of an accurate and dependable means of estimating men and women, gives ear to any method of judging character which is at all plausible and which is earnestly presented."[116] Cleeton and Knight, then professors at the Carnegie Institute of Technology and the University of Iowa, respectively, observed and made note of the practical importance of accuracy in the judgment of others in the business world. And just as Nancy Reagan in the 1980s regularly planned the schedule for the President of the United States according to the implausible but, we can suppose, "earnestly presented" advice of an astrologer, businessmen in the 1920s were "aided" in their judgments of character by phrenologists (those who judged character by the size, shape, and location of protuberances of the skull). Cleeton and Knight thought this was a ridiculous procedure but noted that, since "business uses phrenological methods of character judgment rather freely and with some satisfaction,"[117] it would be their purpose to provide "statistical refutation" of "phrenological methods" and thus remove this ridiculous practice from the expenses of industry. They indicated that they would make empirical measurements, analyze their results in terms of statistical methods, and refute the methods of the phrenologists, thereby saving businessmen money (as well as prevent them from making fools of themselves and inflicting injustice on the people being judged). They concluded, with good reason, that their study "furnishes such statistical refutation."[118]

Their methods attract our attention because they used a fairly good sample of "person-objects" or "targets" for evaluating the accuracy of the phrenologists' judgments—thirty persons (ten in each of three groups) whose skull protuberances were measured. The "character traits" of these thirty person-objects were also measured—that is, rated—by the judgments of sixty "close associates" and seventy "casual observers." Cleeton and Knight offer interesting reasons for choosing both close associates and casual observers: "There is a possibility that character may be judged by external signs and then the wrong signs reported. That is, by intuition true judgments may be made but the judges are unaware of how judgments are made; and so very naturally report some method."[119] That statement shows an astute recognition of the fact that (1) judgments of intangible variables or states, such as "intelligence" or "sound judgment," are made on the basis of tangible *cues*, such as height of forehead, width between the eyes, and attractiveness of appearance, and (2) persons use such cues *intuitively*, that is, without awareness, and (3) persons are apt to report some—*any*—plausible method to the investigator simply because they are asked to do so. Not every investigator today is as conscious of these three aspects of research in social perception as Cleeton and Knight were in 1924.

Their decision to use thirty target persons compares favorably to much contemporary research. It is easy to find studies of judgments of persons' character that include only one or two or three target persons.[120] It is as ludicrous to draw a conclusion about a person's judgment about a trait when the judge is tested with only one, two, or three target persons as it would be to test a person's ability in other respects by including only one, two, or three questions on a test. The painfully slow recognition of this methodological flaw, so prevalent today but avoided without the need for explanation three quarters of a century ago by Cleeton and Knight, is something students of psychology should ponder.

Both recent and current work by social psychologists on the topic of social perception has been in the opposite direction from the correspondence approach; accuracy of social perception has been steadfastly ignored in favor of *inaccuracy*; error has once more captured the attention of psychologists. For example, E. E. Jones in his book-length review, *Interpersonal Perception*, gives "accuracy" in interpersonal perception a mere two out of 259 pages of text. But "biases" (e.g., correspondence bias, confirmation bias, egocentrism bias, self-reference bias, self-serving bias, and false consensus bias) are given the remainder of the book; indeed, Jones offers a virtual catalog of the types of errors to be found in social perception.[121] After citing L. J. Cronbach,[122] who carefully delineated the several components of accuracy, Jones observes that "an important consequence of [Cronbach's] papers was to make researchers very skittish about asking *any* questions that involved assessing judgmental accuracy."[123] In other words, as recently as 1990 the important topic of accuracy was avoided because it was too complicated.

But Jones pointed to a second reason, one that has traditional roots: the psychologists' bias toward looking for explanations of person-environment interaction *within* the person.[124] He observes that "as the field of person perception developed in the 1960s, the concern with judgmental accuracy was increasingly seen as a diversion from the more important and theoretically significant study of the *processes* of personal perception,"[125] another form of the search for coherence. This turn toward coherence in intrapersonal processes, together with a concomitant indifference to correspondence with environmental or task conditions, is one of the more regrettable aspects of the history of psychology (reflected in part by the emphasis on error in studies of coherence).

D. C. Funder's work on social perception[126] is in direct opposition to the work reported by Jones; it is directly aimed at studying accuracy. Funder also notes the peculiar abandonment of the topic of accuracy in social perception and the current concentration on the incompetence of social judgment:

> The accuracy of human social judgment is a topic of obvious interest and importance. It is only natural to wonder to what degree the judgments we make of the personalities of ourselves and others might be right or wrong, and to desire to improve our accuracy. Nonpsychologists are often surprised and disappointed, therefore, when they begin to take psychology courses and discover that the field has largely forsworn interest in the accuracy issue. The discipline's early, direct interest in accuracy (e.g., Estes, 1938; Taft, 1955; Vernon, 1933) was all but completely stifled some years ago by the publication of a series of methodological critiques by Cronbach (1955), Hastorf and Bender (1952), and others. As a result, according to one authoritative textbook:
>
> > The accuracy issue has all but faded from view in recent years, at least for personality judgments. There is not much present interest in questions about whether people are accurate. . . . There is, in short, almost no concern with normative questions of accuracy. On the other hand, in recent years there has been a renewed interest in how, why, and in what circumstances people are inaccurate. (Schneider, Hastorf, & Ellsworth, 1979, p. 224; see also Cook, 1984)
>
> Specifically, the psychology of social judgment has been dominated in recent years by a flood of research on the subject of "error." Studies of error appear in the literature at a prodigious rate, are disproportionately likely to be cited (Christensen-Szalanski & Beach, 1984), and fill whole books (Kahneman, Slovic, & Tversky, 1982; Nisbett & Ross, 1980). Psychology instructors have found that the various experimental demonstrations of error, like other counterintuitive phenomena, provide a sure way to spice up an undergraduate lecture in introductory or social psychology.[127]

Funder notes that "psychology's widespread fascination with error research continues to stem primarily from its apparently dramatic implications for accuracy in daily life (e.g., Crandall, 1984; Evans, 1984), *not* from its value for understanding the mechanisms of judgment."[128] Curiously, this is precisely the opposite of what Jones claimed, for he asserted that the move away from the study of accuracy was a "*diversion* [italics added] from the more important and theoretically significant studies of the *processes* of interpersonal perception."[129] Jones does not cite any of Funder's articles, which may partly explain the curious contradictions regarding which is the better path to understanding.

But Jones's treatment of the topic is misleading in other ways as well. He muddles the facts of (visual) perceptual constancy and incorrectly describes Heider's views. For example, he offers a nice illustration of the phenomena of perceptual constancy:

> I see the person at the end of the hall as roughly the same size as the person walking three yards from me, even though the sizes of the two on my retina are vastly different. I see a red blouse as about equally red whether the person wearing it is in the light or in the shade.[130]

And he notes that it is "very functional to do so; it promotes one's own survival."[131] But his claim that Heider somehow blended the gestalt view with this sort of functionalism is wrong. And he forgets Heider's "functionalism" as soon as he puts the topic of accuracy behind him and concentrates on error in perception and causal attributions. Brunswik and Heider see eye-to-eye on these matters with one exception; Heider rejects Brunswik's probabilism, although Heider accepts the idea of the intersubstitutability of cues.

Funder draws a distinction between "errors and mistakes" that parallels (and could substitute for) the distinction drawn here between coherence competence and correspondence competence. He defines an "error" as "a judgment of a laboratory stimulus that deviates from a model of how that judgment *should* [italics added] be made."[132] That is, an error is the discrepancy between a prediction, probability number, or other form of answer produced by a normative model; an "error" is *not* the difference between a prediction of an empirical event (e.g., rain) and the actual occurrence of the event. A "mistake," on the other hand, is just that: "an incorrect judgment in the real world, such as a misjudgment of a real person."[133] I regard Funder's distinction between errors and mistakes as highly appropriate and useful but find his terminology less so. I believe this distinction would serve us better if made in terms of coherence and correspondence. Thus, an "error" is based on the use of a coherence theory (Funder's "normative and rational" model), whereas a "mistake" is simply failure of correspondence between a judgment and an empirical event. That distinction has rarely been made because of the general tendency to overlook the correspondence/coherence distinction. Funder's 1987 views are in direct opposition to those of Jones (and current social psychology) on almost every point.

Funder makes his affinity with the Brunswikian correspondence point of view clear in his criticism of generalizations from laboratory research:

> Interestingly, when the great perceptual psychologist Egon Brunswik (1944) decided that arbitrary stimuli in the lab were inadequate tools for assessing the adaptive mecha-

nisms of vision, he moved his own research into the real world. Rather than exclusively study visual illusions, he followed a subject around in the environment and asked her to estimate the distances [sizes] of various objects. Brunswik found that her judgments of . . . [size] correlated with actual . . . [size] (after logarithmic transformation) with an r = .99 [i.e., the subject was almost perfectly accurate].[134]

In a recent study Funder and Sneed found support for Funder's general supposition that social judgment has been studied incorrectly and that such judgments are more accurate than recent studies have indicated. In a study of 140 "undergraduate Ss [who] were videotaped in 2 social interactions, and 62 behaviors were coded for each tape,"[135] the authors conclude "subjects seem to rank order available behavioral cues as to their trait diagnosticity in a way that corresponds remarkably closely with the actual, relative validity."[136]

It is the colleagues of Tversky and Kahneman who have carried the implications of their general conclusions very far and have damaged their case. For example, L. Ross and R. E. Nisbett[137] have been the most enthusiastic in emphasizing the putative incompetence of human judgment, and in his review of their book Funder castigates them for it. For example, he notes that their "method is an all-out frontal assault on the validity of everyday human judgment."[138] Funder then indicates the conclusion one would draw from this book:

Laypeople are guilty of being naive (p. 119), oblivious (p. 124), and insensitive (p. 139). They also suffer from ignorance (p. 69), lack of awareness (p. 82), dramatic overconfidence, general misconceptions, and a whole range of other shortcomings and biases (p. 86), so it is no wonder that lay judgment is seriously deficient (p. 168). The only question left is "How could people be so wrong?" (p. 139).[139]

Funder challenges the research bases of all these conclusions put forward by Ross and Nisbett and chides them for their one-sided narrative; he claims that their readers will never learn that there is another side to their story (a similar criticism can be made of Plous).

In conclusion: Correspondence accuracy in judgments is very high in physical perception and in any circumstance in which the information environment offers cues of high reliability and an environmental target system of high predictability. The best overall descriptive model of human judgment engaged in correspondence judgments is what is known as a linear model, which simply means that the indicator is linked to the target in a straight-line fashion and that the information from the indicators is combined by simply adding or averaging it. Most clinicians still resist this conclusion. Indeed, McCauley's results suggest that most psychologists resist it despite its solid research base; strangely, Congress, uninformed by research, insists that judges adhere to it. (I provide an example of a judge's use of an additive rule in an important court case in Chapter 12.)

But correspondence accuracy diminishes as uncertainty in the information environment increases or as the task system takes on coherence or assumes any organization for which the person is neither phylogenetically nor ontogenetically prepared. As we would expect from an evolutionary point of view, correspondence competence diminishes as the task becomes less perceptual and more conceptual, as it does in clinical psychology.

Thus we see that multiple fallible indicators remain almost as ubiquitous in our lives as they were in the lives of our primitive ancestors and as they are in the lives of many subhuman species. The centrality of our need for and dependence on multiple fallible indicators can be seen in the fact that *we construct them for ourselves.* As a result, multiple fallible indicators pervade virtually every aspect of life. They are apparent in the forecasting of weather, avalanches, the relative dangerousness of people, the future performance of stock and bond markets, the proper allocation of livestock over rangeland; in clinical judgment of a person's mental state; in decisions on the amount of bail to be required; in sentencing of convicted criminals; in personnel selection, in deciding on friendship; and, indeed, in almost all aspects of our lives. I say "almost" because we have constructed—have "engineered"— *infallible* indicators for those aspects of our lives that *can* be engineered, and we continue to do so where and when we can at an ever increasing rate. Thus. for example, we build, or try to build, infallible indicators for the safety of air, sea, and rail travel, and billions of dollars are spent in the health care field in the effort to remove the fallibility of cues, or indicators, in medical diagnosis. The journal *Social Indicators Research* published 1,027 articles on social indicators between 1974 and 1990; 1,016 "quality of life" articles based on multiple fallible indicators were published in the same period.

Interest in evolution, biology, and the correspondence approach to judgment go hand in hand. When economists forecast the future state of the economy or evaluate its present state, when sociologists and others appraise the present status of our society, or when evolutionary biologists or psychologists study judgment, virtually all of them refer to multiple fallible indicators and the correspondence theory of truth. Not only did as our most remote ancestors (and many other species) rely on multiple fallible indicators, they are in use (almost) everywhere today.

# III COMPROMISE AND RECONCILIATION

In Part III I try to meet Karl Popper's requirements for a general, unifying theory: "The new theory should proceed from some *simple, new, and powerful unifying idea* about some connection or relation (such as gravitational attraction) between hitherto unconnected things (such as planets and apples) or facts (such as inertial or gravitational mass) or new 'theoretical entities' (such as field and particles)."[1] In his endorsement of these requirements J. Bronowski suggested why unifying ideas are attractive: "We want to feel that the world can be understood as a unity, and that the rational mind can find ways of looking at it that are simple, new and powerful exactly because they unify it."[2] My goal in what follows is to present a "simple, new, and powerful unifying idea" in the manner suggested by Popper.

To meet this goal I must take into account the two major ideas I have presented in Part I: the unresolved rivalry between intuition and analysis and the unresolved tension between the correspondence theory of truth and the coherence theory of truth. In my view, these are the two major cognitive mechanisms of human judgment we employ in our effort to cope with irreducible uncertainty, inevitable error, and unavoidable injustice.

My theory is based on the idea of a *cognitive continuum* that is paralleled by a *task continuum*. The cognitive continuum is anchored at one end by the concept of analysis and at the other by the concept of intuition; the task continuum is anchored by analysis-inducing tasks and intuition-inducing tasks. Replacing the age-old dichotomy between analysis and intuition with a continuum makes possible the reduction of the rivalry between them through compromise. Five premises constitute the foundation of the theory. Because task structure, or structure of the information environment, is of such importance to judgment and decision making, I devote a separate chapter to the topic.

In Chapter 8 I address the tension between coherence and correspondence theories and offer a reconciliation by means of "constructive complementarity."

# 6 Reducing Rivalry Through Compromise

There is no sudden leap from uncriticized to criticized fact.

*—Stephen Pepper*

I begin with a rejection of the traditional view of the dichotomous, either-or relationship between intuition and analysis. I replace it with the concept of a continuum marked by pure intuition at one pole and pure analysis at the other. The concept of a cognitive continuum leads to a reduction in rivalry through compromise.

## Premise 1: A Cognitive Continuum

*Various modes, or forms, of cognition can be ordered in relation to one another on a* continuum *that is identified by intuitive cognition at one pole and analytical cognition at the other.*

So far as I know, this premise constitutes the first published rejection of the dichotomous view of analysis and intuition and the explicit replacement of it by the concept of a cognitive continuum.[1] I take this step because the dichotomous view of analysis and intuition has served us badly. When seen as either-or modes of cognition, intuition and analysis become rivals, with the usual results; enthusiasts for each exaggerate strengths, minimize weaknesses, and fail to acknowledge the virtues of the rival, as I demonstrate in the following pages. The dichotomous view has also diminished the scientific value of both concepts: It has mystified intuitive cognition, both in praise and in criticism, and led us to take the superiority of analytical cognition for granted by failing both to explore the limits of that modality and to understand the successes of intuitive cognition. Furthermore, as I shall explain later in this chapter, ignoring the range of cognition that lies between these two idealized concepts has led psychologists to overlook much of our ordinary cognitive activity known as common sense.

Numerous invidious comparisons have been made between these cognitive modes when conceived of in terms of a dichotomy. I cite only two. David Hume's well-known admonition expresses disdain for intuition: "If we take in our hand any volume ... let us ask, Does it contain any abstract reasoning concerning number or volume? No. Does it contain any experimental reasoning concerning matter of fact and existence? No. Commit it then to the flames, for it can contain nothing but sophistry and illusion." William Blake, on the other hand, boldly attacks rational analysis: "I come in the grandeur of inspiration to abolish ratiocination." But Pascal's comprehensive viewpoint, "Two extravagances: To exclude Reason, to include only Reason," urges us to exclude neither analytical cognition nor intuition. Pascal's view is adapted here because it rejects the either-or dogma and is compatible with the concept of a cognitive continuum.

Most important, the dichotomous view not only provides two "extravagances"; it exerts a powerful negative influence by excluding from our research agenda perhaps the most important topic of all—*common sense.* Thus it excludes from our theory and research our most frequently employed cognitive activity, and it does so by reducing cognition to extreme forms rarely employed or encountered in our normal existence.

If, for example, we hold the dichotomous view, each of our judgments must be assigned to one or the other category. But in general, our judgments are more likely to be largely intuitive or largely analytical depending on the circumstances. If we are untrained in weather forecasting but must decide whether to carry an umbrella, we may take a quick look at the sky, see that it is mostly clear, but remember that the weather forecaster called for rain later, then decide to be rational and rely on the forecaster, just as we notice that our neighbor is not carrying an umbrella and recall that he is an airline pilot and therefore decide to follow his example. That decision would be hard to defend as a completely analytical effort; yet it is not without its analytical components—relying to some extent on the forecaster, noticing that the airline pilot is weather-conscious, taking account of the current clear sky.

Now consider a continuous, rather than an either-or, response situation—for example, deciding how much money to invest in securities. This can be done by following an investment program on one's personal computer. One enters the information about one's finances, and the program indicates that one's wealth should be distributed among various securities, with a certain proportion going to each type. Should one proceed in a completely analytical manner—each step will be *retraceable* (in the program), each step will be *defendable* (by the program's developer), each step will be individually analyzable (by studying the program), and one will have to invest *considerable time* to execute these (and other) steps. Few investors will actually do this, however. They may access the program and read its conclusions but say to themselves, "I feel like that's too much in the foreign sector, and somehow I feel as if I should be doing more in the health sector (I think I read somewhere that these businesses will boom), ... " and so modify the response, not by rejecting entirely the advice provided by an analytical procedure or relying entirely on one's intuitions about where to invest but by reaching a compromise between the two.

When challenged, we like to defend our judgments on analytical grounds as long as possible, whenever circumstances call for rationality. But many circumstances call for us to work from the other pole of the continuum, from intuition. When we are in an art museum and our companion asks us whether we like the picture we are looking at, we hesitate only briefly and render our judgment in terms of "well, a little," or "yes, a lot," and so on. If an amateur is pressed with a "why" question, the amateur can reply only in general terms—for example, "It appeals to me; it reminds me of someone (or someplace) I like." The art critic or historian can do better, indeed, may be prepared to write an article on the picture, and in doing so his or her cognitive activity will move closer to the analytical pole of the continuum; the judgment will contain both analytical and intuitive components ("the design somewhat appealed to me") on the assumption that judgments of works of art can never be completely analytical.

Earlier we learned from Epstein's valuable review how continuous and pervasive the dichotomous—"two modes of thought"—view is in psychology. Further evidence of its hold on psychological theorizing can be seen in the rich and complex half century of work by Jerome Bruner.[2] I quote from Bruner not only because he was one of the innovators of the cognitive revolution but because he represents the broadest, most comprehensive view of cognition available today. Indeed, he has been—and remains—the most thoughtful defender of the positive view of intuitive cognition from the beginning.[3]

Despite his broad view of cognition, however, Bruner's theorizing is restricted by the dichotomous view. Chapter 2 of *Actual Minds, Possible Worlds* is titled "Two Modes of Thought," which he describes in this way:

> There are two modes of cognitive functioning, two modes of thought, each providing distinctive ways of ordering experience, of constructing reality. The two (though complementary) are irreducible to one another. Efforts to reduce one mode to the other or to ignore one at the expense of the other inevitably fail to capture the rich diversity of thought.[4]

What does Bruner see as the essential differences between these two modes of thought?

> Each of the [two] ways of knowing . . . has operating principles of its own and its own criteria of well-formedness. They differ radically in their procedures for verification. A good story and a well-formed argument are different natural kinds. Both can be used for consuming another . . . one verifies by eventual appeal to procedures for establishing formal and empirical truth. The other establishes not truth but verisimilitude [i.e., the appearance of truth]. . . . They function differently.[5]

Bruner says nothing about the blending of the two or about the relative contribution of each to a judgment or an argument. Thus Bruner's stance does not differ in this regard from that of cognitive psychologists in general; Epstein's review finds that there is a "convergence" among psychologists regarding the dichotomous view of "two modes of thought." He does not mention the continuous view advocated in this book.

The idea of a cognitive continuum thus challenges the age-old tradition of a dichotomy between intuition and analysis; in fact, it denies the validity of that dichotomy, endorsed and explicated by Bruner and many others. An important advantage of the concept of a continuum over a dichotomy is that it makes it possible to recognize and thus study all the combinations of intuition and analysis that cognition may employ. Acknowledgment of this range of possibilities for cognition allows us to come to grips with the most frequently used—but never explained or defined—form of cognition, and that is "common sense," the very form of cognitive activity the reader is bringing to bear on the material she or he is now reading.

As used here, "common sense" refers to cognition that is as analytical as it can be and as intuitive as it must be, or the converse, depending on the inducement from task conditions. That is, one is as rational (or intuitive) as one can be, needs to be, or is induced to be in each task situation. When the limit of one's rationality is encountered, one begins to draw upon intuitive cognition, and vice versa.

Consider the cognitive activity of airline pilots. Under normal flight conditions, their performance is rule-bound; they are engaging in fully rational analytical cognitive activity in which every action is—must be—fully justifiable. If asked why something is being done at any moment in the flight, the same definite explanation would be given by all pilots—under normal flight conditions. Each is operating at the analytical pole of the cognitive continuum, that is, using the same set of if-then rules.

But if circumstances change to unforeseen conditions and a rapid response is required, departure from the rules will occur and may even be necessary; such departures are generally based on "my best guess at the time," a move in the direction of the intuitive pole; how far depends on circumstances.

Similarly, persons making a wholly intuitive, unexplainable judgment about a preference for a work of art may well modify that judgment when called upon to defend it. Art or literary critics call upon analytical cognition, cite reasons for valuing the work, and thus move as far as possible toward the analytical pole in order to justify their judgment. A mix of inexplicable intuitions and analytically based reasons can be observed in any but the most technical or least technical conversations, and that is what is meant here by common sense, a topic to which I now turn.

## Premise 2: Common Sense

*The forms of cognition that lie on the continnum between intuition and analysis include elements of* both *intuition and analysis and are included under the term* quasirationality. *This form of cognition is known to the layperson as "common sense."*

Discussions and elaborations of the idea of common sense are to be found in antiquity, and lengthy discussions persist throughout the history of philosophy.[6] It can hardly be our purpose to trace the history of this concept, but it will be instructive to observe how the philosopher Bertrand Russell makes use of it in his *A History of Western Philosophy*. When discussing Aristotle's contributions. Russell says, "The Orphic elements in Plato are watered down in Aristotle, and mixed with a strong dose of common sense";[7] "Aristotle's metaphysics, roughly speaking, may be described as Plato diluted by common sense. He [Aristotle] is difficult because Plato and common sense do not mix easily";[8] and "Here again there is a common sense basis for Aristotle's theory."[9] Finally, according to Russell, "All that is said [by Aristotle] about friendship is sensible, but there is not a word that rises above common sense."[10]

My purpose in quoting from Russell's free and casual use of this term is to show that he assumes that his readers will readily understand what is meant when, for example, he tells us that "Plato and common sense do not mix easily." In this and other statements, Russell counts on us to believe that Plato's expositions are strange, unsatisfactory, puzzling, contrary to our understanding of the topic, if not the world. Thus, Russell is using "common sense" as shorthand, as a "code word," to appeal to us to engage in and rely on a form of cognitive activity we are completely comfortable with, yet do not understand completely and, if asked, could not define. It is that lack of understanding, that lack of defensibility, that has deprived "common sense" of its standing among intellectuals—but not all the time, and not among all intellectuals.

An excellent example of a scientist's criticism of common sense can be seen in the attack on a creationist argument made by the well-known evolutionary biologist E. O. Wilson in his recent book *The Diversity of Life*. Wilson says that the creationist W. Paley used the watchmaker analogy: "The existence of a watch implies a watchmaker. In other words, great effects imply great causes. Common sense would seem to dictate the truth of [Paley's] deduction." But Wilson challenges Paley by putting forward a definition of common sense for the reader: "But common sense is merely unaided intuition, and unaided intuition is reasoning performed in the absence of instruments and the tested knowledge of science."[11] Wilson then ridicules common sense: "Common sense tells us that massive satellites cannot hang suspended 36,000 kilometers above one point on the earth's surface, but they do, in synchronous equatorial orbits."[12]

Like most writers who offer off-the-cuff definitions of common sense or intuition, Wilson does not find it necessary to provide his readers with an authority or any source whatever for his definitions; evidently he believes, as do most writers, that his word should be enough. But he is wrong; even simple dictionary definitions[13] do not deny the place of "instruments" or the "tested knowledge of science" in the use of common sense.

It is also instructive to learn that one of the most serious charges against the development of (symbolic) artificial intelligence (AI) is that AI software has never been developed that will match the "common sense" exhibited by four- and five-year old children. Every AI program fails this test no matter how successful it may be in the domain for which it was developed. The reason, of course, is that the rules contained in the software are highly specific to the problem; AI programs are "deep" but narrow; children are broad but shallow, as is "common sense."

Most surprising, however, is the reliance of the Supreme Court on "common sense" to justify a ruling. Justice Antonin Scalia, who enjoys a reputation for incisive, clear opinions, wrote the majority (6–3) opinion in a 1993 case on the right of antiabortion protesters to prevent women from entering abortion clinics and summarized the two principal objections to the abortion clinics' case as follows: "Neither common sense nor precedents support" the claim of the respondents. Common sense appears in lower courts also. Reporting on the trial of four Los Angeles police officers accused of beating a black man, Rodney King, the *New York Times* for April 9, 1993 recorded that the prosecutor "urged the jury to use its common sense."[14]

Throughout his impressive biography of Harry Truman, David McCullough emphasizes the "common sense" attributed to Truman.[15] Other presidents have used this concept to mock their opponents. In President Bill Clinton's first major address to the nation after his inauguration, he said:

> During those twelve years, as Governor of Arkansas I followed a very different course, more like what you've done at home and at work. I invested in the future of our people and balanced the state budget with honesty and fairness and without gimmicks. It's just common sense.
>
> But in the twenty-six days I've been your president, I've already learned that here in Washington common sense isn't too common and you've paid a lot for that loss of common sense.[16]

Mysterious as the meaning of the term may be, even the most thoughtful citizens use it in the effort to convey serious and important ideas. George Kennan, described by the *Atlantic Monthly* (April 1989) as "the last wise man," says that "one of the unique features of American government is, in comparison with other modern systems, its neglect of intelligent and discriminating administration. . . . Nowhere does it provide for the use of flexible judgment and common sense [italics added] in [the] administration of its laws."[17] That's an important criticism from an important person, but what exactly does he mean when he indicates that there is no provision for common sense? Readers might test Kennan's assertion by looking for common sense in the "Common Sense Legal Reform Act" proposed by the 104th Congress in 1995.

Vague and undefined as this concept may be, one can be certain that it is always on the side of the author; one may acknowledge that a conclusion is counterintuitive or not completely rigorous without apology, but no one *ever* claims with pride that his or her argument defies common sense.

Of course, it is the layperson who most frequently resorts to the use of this concept. In reply to those who employ complex terms or arguments, "it simply isn't common sense" is often the last stand against the expert's advice or advice given by someone relying wholly on intuition. The use of common sense in an invidious manner is frequent; the implication is always the same: "I have it; you don't." Exactly what it is that one has, however, remains a mystery.

The admiration of common sense reached a new level of newsworthiness with the publication of P. K. Howard's *The Death of Common Sense: How Law is Suffocating America*,[18] which was greeted with enthusiasm by the public (it made immediate and protracted appearances high on the *New York Times* best-seller list) and by politicians of both parties eager to claim that Howard's thoughts were their thoughts. Whatever else this book by a lawyer teaches us, it teaches that interest remains high in the possibility that the application of common sense, whatever that might be, might save us from circumstances that displease us. I will have more to say about Howard's book in Chapter 11.

In short, researchers and theorists who seek to understand human judgment and decision making can hardly avoid examining this frequently referenced and idiosyncratically used concept. What steps have they taken to do this? Almost none; the "middle ground" of "common sense" has been largely overlooked. Nevertheless, some have tried, and to these I now turn.

## Contemporary Defenders of the Value of "Common Sense"

Among late-twentieth-century psychologists, F. Heider, perhaps more than any other psychologist, has challenged the scientists' and intellectuals' disdain for common sense and forthrightly expressed his admiration for it:

> The study of common-sense psychology may be of value because of the truths it contains, notwithstanding the fact that many psychologists have mistrusted and even looked down on such unschooled understanding of human behavior. For these psychologists, what one knows intuitively, what one understands through untrained reflection, offers little—at best a superficial and chaotic view of things, at worst a distortion of psychological events [cf. Kahneman, Slovic, & Tversky, 1982; Nisbett & Ross, 1980, who are disdainful of intuition]. They point, for example, to the many contradictions that are to be found in this body of material, such as antithetical proverbs or contradictions in a person's interpretation of even simple events. But can a scientist accept such contradictions as proof of the worthlessness of common-sense psychology? If we were to do so, then we would also have to reject the scientific approach, for its history is fraught with contradictions among theories, and even among experimental findings.[19]

Heider, in short, does not demand that all cognitive activity meet the standards of analytical cognition before it may be considered worthy. He then makes an active, positive defense of common sense:

> Scientific psychology has a good deal to learn from common-sense psychology. In interpersonal relations, perhaps more than in any other field of knowledge, fruitful concepts and hunches for hypothesis lie dormant and unformulated in what we know intuitively. . . . Whitehead, writing as a philosopher, mathematician, and educator, has still further elevated the status of common-sense ideas by according to them an essential place in *all* sciences. . . . Actually, all psychologists use common-sense ideas in their scientific thinking; but they usually do so without analyzing them and making them explicit.[20]

Heider thus only goes so far as to offer common sense as a source of "fruitful concepts and hunches." But Whitehead went further: "Science is rooted in what I have just called the whole apparatus of common sense thought. That is the *datum* from which it starts, and to which it must recur. . . . You may polish up common sense, you may contradict it in detail, you may surprise it. But ultimately your whole task is to satisfy it."[21] Whitehead was prepared to accept common sense as justification for accepting a conclusion.

In his autobiography, H. A. Simon's defense of his concept of bounded rationality shows that the general theme of Heider's common-sense psychology has persisted for nearly forty years, despite the negative view of it taken by mainstream psychology: "The creature of bounded rationality that I am has no illusions of attaining a wholly correct and objective understanding of my world. But I cannot ignore that world. I must understand it as best I can."[22] Further, "I am an adaptive system, whose survival and success, whatever my goals, depends on maintaining a reasonably veridical picture of my environment of things and people. Since my world picture approximates reality only crudely, I cannot aspire to optimize anything. . . . Searching for the best can only dissipate scarce cognitive resources; the best is the enemy of the good."[23]

This strongly positive view of common sense by Heider and Simon is in sharp contrast to the negative view expressed by the great majority of researchers in judgment and decision making, as well as by many scientists in other fields. R. E. Nisbett and L. Ross,[24] for example, emphasized the "distortions" and "shortcomings" of common sense in line with the general trend noted by P. Slovic, B. Fischhoff, and S. Lichtenstein in their 1977 review,[25] which was confirmed by H. J. Einhorn and R. M. Hogarth in their 1981 review,[26] celebrated by A. Tversky and D. Kahneman in numerous publications,[27] and reiterated in virtually every *Annual Review of Psychology*, every textbook in judgment and decision making, and every textbook in psychology that mentions judgment and decision making. But there is a recent turn toward the older view favored by Heider and Simon. It is to be found in the newer work on "practical intelligence" by R. Sternberg and his colleagues, a topic I will discuss in later chapters.

### Beyond Common Sense

Why is common sense so frequently invoked by virtually everyone except, perhaps, cognitive psychologists? Why do so many people call upon it so often? Why not go beyond common sense? Why not *always* be fully analytical? Analytical cognition has many valuable properties: Thought processes can be made explicit, can be retraced, can be criticized; if contradictions or inconsistencies appear, they can perhaps be removed. The clarity thus achieved surely leads us to the discovery of truth and enlightenment and promotes the reduction of disputes that arise from unexplained, or unexplainable, thought processes. On the other hand, why not turn in the other direction, away from the middle ground, and become fully intuitive? It's easy, it's quick, and it often simply makes one feel good.

There are several reasons—several obstacles—to moving to the polar extremes of the cognitive continuum. In the next section I indicate what these obstacles are.

### Obstacles to Analytical Cognition

Analytical cognition generally follows a *model*—that is, a *prescription*—for how one should think about the problem at hand. Three examples of obstacles to the use of a prescriptive model follow.

1. *The use of a single specific model cannot be justifiably employed on analytical grounds by either researcher or subject.* Circumstances in which analytical models are available but cannot be justifiably employed include those in which there is no single, consensus-based criterion that permits the investigator to choose among competing analytical models. This topic receives the following comment from Einhorn and Hogarth in their chapter in the *Annual Review of Psychology*:

> *Task vs Optimal Model of Task*
> We begin by offering a definition of optimality; namely, decisions or judgments that maximize or minimize some explicit and measurable criterion (e.g., profits, errors,

time) *conditional on certain environmental assumptions and a specified time horizon.*
The importance of this definition is that it stresses the conditional nature of optimality.
For example, Simon (1979) points out that because of the complexity of the environment, one has but two alternatives: either to build optimal models by making simplify-
ing environmental assumptions, or to build heuristic models that maintain greater environmental realism (also see Wimsatt, 1980). Unfortunately, the conditional nature
of optimal models has not been appreciated and too few researchers have considered
their limitations. For instance, it has been found that people are insufficiently regressive in their predictions (Kahneman & Tversky, 1973). While this is no doubt true in
stable situations, extreme predictions are not suboptimal in nonstationary processes.
In fact, given a changing process, regressive predictions are suboptimal. The problem
is that extreme responses can occur at random or they can signal changes in the underlying process. For example, if you think that Chrysler's recent large losses are being
generated by a stable process, you should predict that profits will regress up to their
mean level. However, if you take the large losses as indicating a deteriorating quality
of management and worsening market conditions, you should be predicting even more
extreme losses. Therefore, the optimal prediction is conditional on which hypothesis
you hold.[28]

In short, the user of analytical models as evaluative devices must very carefully
delineate the conditions in which such models are employed, a delineation that has
seldom occurred, as Einhorn and Hogarth noted. Most important, on those occasions
in which the researcher identifies or employs a task that is not fully susceptible to
analytical cognition, the behavior of the subject should be evaluated in light of that
information. In this way, economists who prefer (analytical) optimizing theories but
exercise quasirational cognitive activity in their choices among such theories, are
simply coping with a less than fully analytical task (for which no singular analytical
model is available) in a less than fully analytical manner. In Whitehead's words, they
are attempting to "satisfy" common sense; in Simon's words, they "satisfice"; in
Brunswik's terms, they are "quasirational." In any case, they are behaving appro-
priately; when analytical models are not unconditionally employable, they move from
the analytical pole to a point on the cognitive continuum at which intuitive components contribute to "satisfaction." Just how far such movement will go depends on
what the circumstances, including supervisors and colleagues, will allow. At what
point will your colleagues allow you to say, "That's as far as logic will take me; it's
my gut feeling that we should . . ."?

*2. A model is available but there is a poor data-model fit.* This circumstance is
obvious but deserves mention because of its relevance to three important cases. Lack
of current data demanded by a forecasting model frequently frustrates the use of
forecasting (e.g., meteorological, economic) models and encourages the use of quasirational cognitive activity; the forecast *must* be made somehow. In such cases forecasters often rely on *documented* experience; that is, meteorologists rely on "persistence" (tomorrow's weather will be the same as today's) or climatology, the sheer
empirical, statistical probability (relative frequency) of the occurrence of the event
of interest; economists rely on statistical trends in their data sources.

A second case in which the lack of data prevents the use of an analytical model
is one that has been cited often by Simon and that forms the basis for his notion of

"satisficing" and bounded rationality; that is, persons simply do not have the resources in time, skills, tools, or processes to explore fully the entire problem space and thus acquire the data that fully rational optimization would require.

There is a third case (dramatically illustrated by the *Challenger* tragedy) in which the use of an analytical model is frustrated by the appearance of unanticipated data for which the model is unprepared; as a result, quasi-rational cognition ("a judgment call") must be substituted for the model.

*3. Analytical models are not available at all.* Analytical models cannot be employed in many circumstances in which they might otherwise be useful because no relevant model exists; in other circumstances, only partially analytical models are available. There is a continuum from "hard" to "soft" along which models of environmental tasks can be ordered At one end, physical dynamics of the terrestrial macrophysical environment (or at least large segments of it) can be modeled by a "hard," singular (e.g., Newtonian) model. Such analytical models are "hard" because they are fully explicable by reliably measured parameters, long theoretically and empirically justified. At the other end of the continuum are those personal-social environments for which only partially defensible models exist.

There are also environments that are only partially understood, often called unstructured or "ill structured" (Simon's phrase) tasks. These environments contain some "hard" parameters that are measurable and for which some empirical relations are verifiable. They also include some "soft" parameters for which nonretraceable human judgments must be substituted for physical measurements. P. Newbold and T. Bos indicate that "there are particular areas where it is easy to behave on a priori grounds that informal expert judgment is likely to be the best in predicting the future." In their discussion of attempts to forecast political events they point out that "what seems to be the most relevant available information simply cannot be incorporated into any formal model, so that any model built would be a crude, unsophisticated approximation of the world, and therefore of little value."[29] Regrettably, expert judgment also seems to be of little value in this area. These authors note that J. Mumpower, S. Livingston, and T. J. Lee[30] have shown that forecasts by experts "differed little from those of a group of undergraduate students."[31]

Of course, some personal-social environmental models are completely "soft," with all the data coming from human judgment. The competition between the two types of data provides judgment and decision-making researchers with a rich field to investigate.

A comprehensive view of judgment and decision making must take into account not only those tasks for which analytical models may be employed to evaluate the rationality or logical defensibility of cognition but also those tasks in which analytical models cannot be employed, either because (1) analytical models cannot be unconditionally employed, (2) data for such models are not available, or (3) no analytical model is available. The fragility of analytical systems constitutes a risk, well known to all users of them but seldom considered by judgment and decision-making researchers.

In any case, analytical models are available only for those persons who have been educated or trained sufficiently to be aware of them and, possibly, to use them. One cannot be expected to make use of statistical models to solve problems involving uncertainty if one has not had the opportunity to learn how to do so. A comprehensive view of judgment and decision making must also account for the cognitive activity that occurs when persons do not know about such models or procedures and thus cannot employ them. It is these circumstances that have been studied so thoroughly by the coherence theorists in the field of judgment and decision making.[32]

There is a further obstacle to the use of analytical cognition; it might be called emotion, or the use of a "moral sense,"[33] an occasion when one refuses to violate an intuition of what justice demands. For example, Judge Jack Weinstein (whom I mentioned in Chapters 1 and 3) had to rule on the claims of veterans who believed that they had been harmed by a defoliating herbicide used in the Vietnam War. In a class action suit, more than 2.4 million veterans and others claimed that they suffered from a variety of illnesses caused by exposure to the herbicide. "On the eve of the trial, under intense pressure from trial Judge Jack Weinstein, the parties agreed to settle the action for $180 million, at that time the largest such settlement on record. . . . [Weinstein decided that] since no plaintiff could possibly trace his individual injury to Agent Orange with any certainty [another instance of irreducible uncertainty] . . . that 'compassion—not scientific proof' [would] be the basis for at least some of the awards."[34] Thus, Judge Weinstein overcame the legal, analytically based obstacle to what he saw as justice by declaring that compassion would prevail over analysis, namely, scientific proof of cause.

But intuition will encounter obstacles, as well.

## Obstacles to Intuition

In contrast to analysis, or the use of analytical models, intuition is always available. It is readily induced by irreducible uncertainty produced by time pressure, confusing circumstances, or information overload—in short, when analytical models cannot be readily applied. Indeed, intuition thrives on these circumstances. Moreover, intuition requires no special preparation, although, of course, experts as well as novices employ intuition, usually under the circumstances just described. But intuition can be, and usually is, driven out by critical analysis, either by oneself or by others. Such criticism takes time; therefore, the pressure of a deadline always encourages the use of intuition. But *if* time permits, and *if* the resources for analysis are sought, found, and used, analysis will drive out intuition. It is the inexplicable character of intuition that makes it vulnerable to analytical attack.

Criticism of intuitively derived judgments is easily recognized; it begins with "Why?" or "How do you know?" or "What makes you say that?" Answers designed to deflect demands for analysis are also familiar to all of us; they move from the brain to the heart to the intestines—for example, "I don't know *why*, I just *know* what's in my heart" or, a great favorite, "my *gut* tells me" These anatomical references can withstand the drive for analysis only if the decisionmaker holds sufficient power over those demanding analytical accountability to deny their demands with impunity. As a result, those lower in the organizational hierarchy must show greater cognitive responsibility than those higher up. Those on the lower rungs cannot defend decisions by saying, "That was my gut reaction" and expect to get away with it, but those at the top can; indeed, it is precisely because they are supposed to possess good "gut reactions" that those at the top are given the top positions. Analytical models are rarely available to them for the kind of decisions they must make; they have nowhere else to turn but to intuition. And success brings praise.

But when intuitive judgments err, then analysis begins; "gut reactions" or other descriptions of intuitive cognition draw sneers, and the leader is dismissed for his or her poor judgment. The reason that intuition cannot stand up to analysis is that analysis defines the terms of the dispute. If the upper-level person's intuitions are challenged by "why" or "how do you know," she or he must either refuse to engage in the dispute or engage in an argument in which logic, not rhetoric, is in control. At that point analysis drives out intuition, and the voice of authority is diminished. Smart teenagers occasionally ruin their parents' day in this fashion.

But if intuition fails to carry the argument, it does not follow that analysis will. Conditions for the use of a model, a theory, or a plan may not *fully* justify its use; all the necessary data may not be available, or no analytical model may be available. As a result the critic will not be able to make a complete argument; analysis may be able to drive out intuition up to a point, but only up to a point. In short, although the intuitive argument may come under analytical attack, the critic's argument may not be fully justifiable, either. When that happens, we return to the middle ground, quasirational cognition, or what the layperson calls "common sense."

There are two other properties of cognition that require our attention. These are the *precision* and the *robustness* of the process, two attributes that are often in opposition. I describe these attributes and their consequences briefly.

### Precision Versus Robustness

Analysis provides precision in specific circumstances, and intuition provides robustness—that is, accuracy within limits over a wide range of conditions.

### The Fragility of Precision

Champions of analytical cognition are also champions of planning, of arranging systems that not only "get it right" but allow one to know why it is right. Analytical cognition focuses on process. Moreover, analytical cognition and its products offer precision. Much of the machinery that holds the modern world together is testimony to the success of this form of cognition. But the champions of analysis, planning, and tight control seldom mention an important aspect of that approach—its fragility. The fragility of analytical systems is well illustrated by the following quotation from a thoughtful physician concerned about "the control of unintended variation" in medical care. Note his striking illustration of how a single mistake in a carefully worked-out system can result in catastrophe:

> Kim, aged 3 years, lies asleep, waiting for a miracle. Outside her room, the nurses on the night shift pad softly through the half-lighted corridors, stopping to count breaths, take pulses, or check the intravenous pumps. In the morning, Kim will have her heart

fixed. She will be medicated and wheeled into the operating suite. Machines will take on the functions of her body: breathing and circulating blood. The surgeons will place a small patch over a hole within her heart, closing off a shunt between her ventricles that would, if left open, slowly kill her.

Kim will be fine if the decision to operate on her was correct; if the surgeon is competent; if that competent surgeon happens to be trained to deal with the particular anatomic wrinkle that is hidden inside Kim's heart; if the blood bank cross-matched her blood accurately and delivered it to the right place; if the blood gas analysis machine works properly and on time; if the suture does not snap; if the plastic tubing of the heart-lung machine does not suddenly spring loose; if the recovery room nurses know that she is allergic to penicillin; if the "oxygen" and "nitrogen" lines in the anesthesia machine have not been reversed by mistake; if the sterilizer temperature gauge is calibrated so that the instruments are in fact sterile; if the pharmacy does not mix up two labels; and if when the surgeon says urgently, "Clamp, right now," there is a clamp on the tray.

If all goes well, if ten thousand "ifs" go well, then Kim may sing her grandchildren to sleep some day. If not, she will be dead by noon tomorrow.[35]

It is not merely the fragility of analytically derived systems that is worrisome, but the escalating consequences of errors, mistakes, and accidents that occur when matters go awry. And in the heyday of nuclear energy, of vast systems of dams, of electric power, of large aircraft, examples of catastrophe —real or imagined—come readily to mind. Mishaps occur infrequently, but when they do occur they are likely to have catastrophic consequences. In D. M. Berwick's example, Kim would be the only casualty. But far more frequently, the casualties are numerous. The release of radioactive material at the Chernobyl nuclear power plant near Kiev in 1986 offers an example, as does the 1984 disaster at the Union Carbide chemical plant near New Delhi. Similarly, modern oil tankers provide examples of analytically driven vehicles that, when accidents occur, create disasters. Although the *Challenger* accident resulted in the death of only seven persons, its other costs were considerable.

Nor is this feature restricted to contemporary life. In his study of the development of railroads, W. Schivelbusch offers a principle regarding technology and catastrophe: "The more civilized the schedule and the more efficient the technology, the more catastrophic its destruction when it collapses."[36] He goes further: "There is an exact ratio between the level of technology with which nature is controlled, and the degree of severity of its accidents. . . . The breaking of a coach axle in the eighteenth century merely interrupted a slow and exceedingly bumpy trip on the highway; the breaking of a locomotive axle between Paris and Versailles in 1842 leads to the first railroad catastrophe that causes a panic in Europe."[37] Terrorists, of course, are well aware of the fragility of analytical systems, and these constitute their principal targets.

The fragility of analysis is often seen in the work of lawyers who produce the rules and regulations that increasingly control all aspects of society. Indeed, the results of their analytical work are so often ridiculous, frustrating, and counterproductive that they can incite Congress to pass laws prohibiting any new regulation. It is these circumstances that motivated Philip Howard to write a book on this topic, which, because of the anger it directs at the work of lawyers, became a best-seller. Howard, a lawyer himself, attacks the manner in which "law is suffocating America," as he put it. He believes lawyers have relied excessively on rational analysis and rational

responses to problems, producing overly specific, bureaucratic processes; "rationalism, the bright dream of figuring out everything in advance and setting it forth precisely in a regulatory system, has made us blind. Obsessed with [seeking] certainty,
we see almost nothing."[38] Howard wants us to reinstate "judgment" (although he
never considers exactly what that term entails): "Law itself, not the goals to be advanced by law, is now our focus. Indeed, the main lesson of law without judgment
is that law's original goal is lost."[39]

He praises the "common law" because "the most important standard is what a
reasonable person would have done."[40] "More than anything else," he says, "the common law glorifies the particular situation and invites common sense."[41] Of course,
as the reader might now expect, Howard is no more explicit about what common
sense is than anyone else. He knows that he has it, however, and that his opponents
don't. And he wants the return to judgment in place of rules because "judgment is
foreclosed by the belief that judgment has no place in the application of the law."[42]
Thus, for example, we have mandatory sentencing.

### The Coarseness of Robustness

The precision of analysis encompasses both virtue and vulnerability; as might be
expected, the robustness of intuition has its virtues and vulnerability as well. The
principal virtue of the robustness of intuition lies in its ease of application, its lack
of demand on cognition. As I noted earlier, Jerome Bruner wanted to define intuition as "the intellectual technique of arriving at plausible but tentative formulations
without going through the analytic steps by which such formulations would be found
to be valid or invalid conclusions."[43] Bruner's concept of intuition (which fits the
one offered here) thus indicates a great virtue—low cognitive effort with, possibly,
a great reward, the right answer. This answer is seldom precisely correct, but it is
within range of the right answer most of the time.

Long ago the psychologist Egon Brunswik carried out a nice, simple demonstration of this distinction and of the trade-offs involved. He asked subjects to estimate
the height of a bar intuitively (by eye, that is) and then examined the distribution of
errors. The error distribution followed the normal (bell-shaped) curve, with the mean
judgment at approximately the right answer. He then asked a second group to *calculate* the height of the bar by means of trigonometry. Most of the calculated answers were *exactly* correct, but those that weren't were far off the mark. Intuitive
perception is robust but imprecise; analytical cognition is precise but subject to large
error—when errors are made. (I found similar results when studying the judgment
of highway engineers.[44])

Our enthusiasm for common sense arises from the many obstacles to both analysis and to intuition, as well as from the need for a compromise between the advantages and the dangers of analytical cognition and those of its rival, intuition. Do we
wish to sacrifice the precision, the justifiability, the scientific and technological arguments derived from analytical cognition for the advantages of robust, rapid, and easily
produced intuitive judgments? Of course we do—*some of the time.* And vice versa;
some of the time we reject "feel right" intuition for analysis. The question is: When
do we choose which? And what are the consequences of such choices? And when
do we choose to compromise, to employ some of each?

## Quasirationality: A Cognitive Compromise Between Intuition and Analysis

Brunswik was unique among psychologists in going beyond the general remarks of Heider and Simon; he developed a theory and a model that allow us to have a new understanding of common sense. Brunswik was intent upon incorporating the elements of both intuition and analysis within common sense, and he chose the concept of quasirationality. What was the source of this idea?

### Origins of the Concept of Quasirationality

The concept of quasirationality arose from Brunswik's description of the perception of the size of an object as a "compromise" between its size as projected on the retina and its physical size in the environment, the specific degree of the compromise depending on local conditions.[45] Brunswik then extended the notion of compromise to refer to cognitive activity in general and judgment in particular. That is, just as perceptual conditions of illumination, say, may pull the perception of an object *toward* the pole of retinal size and thus *away from* object size (or the reverse), so may general ecological conditions pull general cognitive activity *toward* intuition and *away from* analysis (or vice versa). In between these poles, cognition can include elements or properties of *both* intuition and analysis. Thus, the traditional either-or position with regard to intuition and analysis is avoided. It is the idea of perceptual "compromise," grounded in empirical fact, that led to the idea of quasirationality and of a cognitive continuum set forth in Premise 1.

Brunswik made the concept of quasirationality subject to quantification in his 1952 monograph:

> In an attempt at rational reconstruction of the ways of the quasi-rational, with its reliance on vicarious cues each of which is of limited validity, one may best refer to a remark of Thorndike [1918] comparing the impressionistic or intuitive judge of men to a device capable of performing what is known to statisticians as multiple correlation.[46]

Thus Brunswik introduces the theoretical basis for the use of multiple regression statistics as a mathematical model for quasirational cognition. Furthermore, in order to emphasize the dependence of quasirationality on multiple fallible cues or indicators, as early as 1956 he drew a sharp contrast between quasirationality and "thinking machines": "Man-made gun or tank-stabilizers and the related 'thinking machines' may . . . perform in a practically foolproof manner. This is due to the fact that they can usually be built with a concentration on a few cues of maximal trustworthiness and thus dispense with the services of cues of limited validity." As Brunswik put it, "In this light perception and the different varieties of thinking begin to reveal themselves as but different forms of imperfect reasoning." Thus, rather than merely restating the conventional view of imperfect intuition and perfect analytical cognition, Brunswik introduced the idea of "different forms of imperfect reasoning." By applying the modifier "imperfect" to both perception (intuition) and thinking (analysis), he implies that each has assets and liabilities ("each with its own particular brands of virtues and of 'stupidity')."[47]

By acknowledging that each form of "imperfect reasoning" has assets and liabilities, Brunswik opened the door to studying various forms of cognition other than the traditional, pure forms of analysis and intuition. He thus anchored the (theoretically neglected) intuitive pole of cognition in theory and task conditions as strongly as the (mathematically well-treated) analytical pole of cognition. As a result, the full range of task conditions and the cognitive activities that lie between the poles of the cognitive continuum could be addressed, theoretically and mathematically, and made subject to research. That proposition is fundamental to the ideas and purposes of this book. But we need to be more specific. What are the properties of the cognitive activities that lie between the poles of the continuum?

### Properties of Quasirationality

As a result of evolution, we *Homo sapiens* are able to rely "on vicarious cues each of which is of limited validity." Cues can serve "vicariously" for one another because they covary; they are *redundant* and thus intersubstitutable. A warm smile can substitute for a warm handshake as a signal for intended friendship; a scowl can reach across a room and substitute for a harsh word to signal the opposite. Part of a physician's skill, the *art* of medicine, is knowing and recognizing the intersubstitutability, the redundancy of various signs and symptoms that mediate information about that which is not directly observable. And, because of our evolutionary history, human beings can respond to the *vicarious mediation* of information; we can do so because of our cognitive capacity for *vicarious functioning*—that is, our ability to make use of this cue *or* that one in order to make inferences about objects or events. *Vicarious mediation of information* about the environment from cues of limited validity, and *vicarious functioning by the human cognitive system* in the use of that information are parallel, critical features of quasi-rational cognition.

Darwin recognized the parallels between vicarious mediation (of information in the environment) and vicarious functioning (in the organism).[48] He saw that reproductive ability in the male was signaled to the female by a variety of intersubstitutable cues (e.g., size, weight, activity, color) within species, and he saw that the female responded to not one but different cues on different occasions. Von Schantz and his colleagues documented this in their study of pheasants.[49] Buss sees this same process in sexual selection among *Homo sapiens* of both sexes.[50] It is the necessity of making inferences about the "unseen" from the "seen," of coping with vicarious mediation of information by means of vicarious functioning, that leads to and defines quasirational cognition.

In general, natural conditions offer information in terms of multiple fallible indicators. But in our efforts to increase the accuracy and thus the competence of our judgments, we human beings regularly construct *infallible* indicators. So we have lighthouses, road signs, cash registers; indeed, much of our environment has been engineered to provide infallible indicators. This is certainly true of the workplace.

Human beings encounter task conditions that offer both fallible (in the natural world) and infallible (in the engineered world) indicators of the circumstances they wish to infer. And some tasks offer more of one than the other. The physician who reads lab reports has analytically based material to rely on but still must visually appraise her patient's overall condition. The physician who cannot completely reduce her uncertainty with those lab reports or other information is forced to rely on her intuition. It is this differential in information that moves cognition toward a greater use of intuition or analysis.

To the extent that persons are induced to employ quasirational, rather than analytical, cognition, their behavior will exhibit inconsistency of both a temporal and logical variety. They will show less awareness of their judgment processes and have less ability to retrace them; will exhibit brief response times; and will exhibit event memory rather than memory for principles than would be the case if they were fully analytical.

## Inducing Cognition to Become Intuitive

Characteristics of the judgment task—that is, of the information environment—that induce cognition to move away from its analytical form *toward* the intuitive pole of the continuum include: (1) the presence of a large number of cues of limited validity that present themselves simultaneously rather than sequentially; (2) the need to define, label, and measure the cue values oneself, and, most important, (3) the absence of a familiar, readily applied, explicit principle for organizing information into a judgment (other properties of intuition-inducing tasks are listed and discussed in detail later in this chapter), and (4) a short time in which to make a judgment.

Learning to make correct judgments in uncertainty-based tasks is not easy. This is the type of task that made Mark Twain's efforts to learn to be a riverboat pilot so difficult, why it was so difficult to "read the face of the river." Recall that his instructor said to him, "I can't tell you. It is an instinct. By and by you will just naturally *know* one [reef] from the other, but you never will be able to explain why or how you know them apart."[51] Indeed, in almost any profession that requires one to cope with similar circumstances—and they are more common than any others—similar words will be uttered by the teacher; clinical medicine is the classic example. But it is not the only example.

Earlier I noted that a newspaper columnist had called for the relaxation of mandatory sentencing rules for Jean Harris, who had been convicted of the murder of her estranged lover, because of her poor health, among other reasons. Jean Harris was in fact given clemency. Prior to her release she underwent coronary bypass surgery. But on her return to prison she was shackled in leg irons, which her doctors said may have caused a blood clot in her leg to form. In an editorial, the *New York Times* criticized the use of leg irons in the situation: "Rigid adherence to conventional procedure [putting all prisoners in transport in leg irons] may easily defy decency, not to mention common sense."[52] (One can generally count on common sense to be pitted against rules.)

What did the *New York Times* editorial writer have in mind? She or he almost certainly meant: "It is stupid to shackle people who can't run; because they can't run *without* the shackles, the shackles serve no purpose, and, moreover, the shackles may hurt the prisoner, as perhaps they did in the case of Jean Harris." In other words, the *New York Times* writer wants officials to use their own judgment about which prisoners should have to wear leg irons and which should not.

Custodial officers would thus be driven away from a *rule* (all prisoners must wear leg irons) toward a situation in which they must, in the short time available, consider multiple fallible indicators (cues of limited validity), take the responsibility for defining, labeling, and measuring the cue values (e.g., strength, ability to run, likelihood of trying to escape), as well as develop a principle for organizing the information so derived into a *defensible* judgment despite the inevitablility of mistakes. Extreme cases would be easy (e.g., elderly ladies recuperating from surgery don't need shackles, athletic-looking young men do), but what of those people who are not quite that old, not quite that young, those who may or may not be psychotic? These cases would require that guards rely on multiple fallible indicators and thus introduce elements of intuitive cognition, with the inevitable errors (of both kinds) and outraged charges of discrimination (why me? and not him or her?).

Demands for common sense are often simply demands for the greater use of intuitive cognition in place of an analytically derived rule when the analytical rule produces clear injustice or is simply stupid. Indeed, demands for common sense often imply no more than that, although authors of such demands would never say so, because they do not understand, as the reader does, what they are demanding—more intuition. On other occasions, however, demands for the use of common sense imply an increased use of *analytical* cognition.

## Inducing Cognition to Become More Analytical

Failure, of course, is one of the most significant factors leading to change of any sort. When intuitive judgments turn out to be wrong, demands for retracing the reasons for the judgments that led to the failed policy inevitably arise. If there were no analytically justifiable reasons in the first place (as is the case in intuitive judgments), then the reasons offered a posteriori will be ad hoc and thus easy to criticize.

Consider the case of the shackled prisoners in transport. If the guards are required to make a judgment in the face of irreducible uncertainty (as they will be once deprived of a rule that requires no judgment on their part), they will inevitably make the two types of errors I have described in Part I of this book. As soon as a number of errors occur that result in prisoners being left unshackled who should have been (i.e., escapes occur), there will be a demand for reasons why the escapees were not shackled. At this point, it will be argued that "common sense" tells us that guards should *not* be given the responsibility of deciding who should and who should not be shackled; egregious errors will become the subject of editorials. It will be pointed out that the way to eliminate saddling guards with a task they cannot carry out without error is to have a simple rule: *Shackle everybody.* And indeed, that is precisely why Jean Harris *was* shackled and why virtually everyone who is put in a police patrol car is handcuffed. The analytical rule—shackle (or handcuff) all prisoners—will make sense to administrators and security personnel; they will not have to exercise their judgment. The inevitable errors and the obvious injustice exemplified by Jean Harris's unfortunate experience will have to be tolerated in order to avoid the more costly error of escapes and their consequences. In the language of the Taylor-Russell diagram described in Chapter 2, false negatives will not be tolerated, but false positives will.

The reader should also note in passing the differential burden of different errors. The consequences of the error of shackling those who shouldn't be shackled—the pain and humiliation—fall on the individual shackled. The consequences of the error of not shackling those who should have been shackled—the costs of recapturing the escapees—fall on society.

The demand for common sense ordinarily means that erroneous judgments based on intuition will be driven—or pulled—toward analysis, and erroneous judgments based on analysis will be driven—or pulled—toward intuition. Common sense occupies that middle ground that attempts to satisfy *both* polar forms of cognition but never does when closely examined. And that, of course, is the reason that the term never is closely examined and is used only to justify one's own point of view *at a particular time*. Common sense will always be available to pull the cognition of one's opponent in the direction of one's own cognition of the moment.

## Comparison of Simon's Bounded Rationality and Brunswik's Quasirationality

The concept of "bounded rationality" is surely an important one; it is generally thought to be one of Simon's most important contributions to the study of judgment and decision making, and, indeed, bounded rationality has a large role in many of his articles dealing with economic theory. In his speech accepting the 1978 Nobel Prize in economic science, he noted that bounded rationality is largely brought about by the "limits of man's ability to comprehend and compute in the face of complexity and uncertainty."[53] But Simon's use of the concept is uneven; it is not mentioned in the opening chapter of his large volume *Foundations of Cognitive Science* or in his *The Sciences of the Artificial*, or in his article, written with J. Larkin and others, on "physical intuition."[54] Indeed, physical intuition appears to be anything but "bounded"; rather, its rational character is emphasized. The concept of bounded rationality was also omitted from Simon's summary of progress in the social sciences.[55]

J. March has usefully elaborated Simon's conception of limited rationality:

> Ideas of *limited rationality* emphasize the extent to which individuals and groups simplify a decision problem because of the difficulties of anticipating or considering all alternatives and all information.[56]

Moreover, March explains, bounded rationality is likely to be found in connection with "limitations of memory organization and retrieval and of information capacity."[57] Indeed, in this article March begins to look askance at the normally unquestioned superiority of rationality. After describing various types of rationality other than "calculated rationality" (using mathematical models), for example, March observes that "if behavior that apparently deviates from standard procedures of calculated rationality can be shown to be intelligent, then it can plausibly be argued that models of calculated rationality are deficient not only as descriptors of human behavior but also as guides to intelligent choice."[58] This comment elevates the concept of bounded rationality to something better than "calculated rationality," one of the very few occasions in the literature of judgment and decision making in which this suggestion has been made. Furthermore,

> One of Simon's contributions to the theory of choice was his challenge of the self-evident proposition that choice behavior necessarily would be improved if it were made

more like the normative model of rational choice. By asserting that certain limits on rationality stemmed from properties of the human organism, he emphasized the possibility that actual human choice behavior was more intelligent than it appeared.[59]

These ideas are important indeed. They are similar to those offered by Brunswik and Heider and suggest that elements other than "calculated rationality" may serve to enhance "intelligent"—that is, adaptive or successful—behavior; they are consistent with the positive view of the forms of cognition that are not rigorously analytical or "calculated" (an argument also put forward in 1990 by John Anderson). Is it possible that March and Simon are suggesting that bounded rationality is a superior form of cognition and of judgment and decision making compared to that afforded by mathematical models of rationality?

But if bounded rationality needs to be marked off from calculated rationality, it must also be separated from irrationality. And in his earliest discussions of bounded rationality, Simon took pains to do just that:

> *Bounded Rationality Contrasted with "Irrationality."* It is important to distinguish between the principle of bounded rationality . . . and the contemporary emphasis in social psychology upon the affective, nonrational factors in human behavior. Fashion in the scientific explanation of man's behavior oscillates between theories that assign supremacy to his reason and those that give predominance to his passions. The synchronized push that Freud and Pareto gave to this pendulum has, for the past generation, kept it far over on the side of passion. . . .
>
>   One of the difficulties—perhaps the most serious—in incorporating cognitive processes in the theory of social behavior is that we have not had a good description of those processes. . . . The received theory of rational choice is a theory that almost completely ignores the limits of humans as mechanisms for computation and choice—what we have called the principle of bounded rationality.[60]

The parallel between Simon's views and those of Brunswik regarding the "rational reconstruction of the ways of the quasirational" can be seen in the following paragraph from Simon:

> The central task of these essays, then, is not to substitute the irrational for the rational in the explanation of human behavior but to reconstruct the theory of the rational, making of it a theory that can, with some pretense of realism, be applied to the behavior of human beings. When we have made some progress with this reconstruction, I believe that the return swing of the pendulum will begin, that we will begin to interpret as rational and reasonable many facets of human behavior that we now explain in terms of affect. It is this belief that leads me to characterize behavior in organizations as "intendedly rational."[61]

Thus, Simon hints that we may someday change our views about what is "rational," and that the change may be toward demanding a less analytical form of rationality.

The apparent similarity that existed some forty years ago between Simon's bounded rationality and Brunswik's quasirationality has now disappeared. Simon's recent blunt statements about the absence of the need for the concept of intuition makes it clear that he does not believe that intuition (however defined) supplements rational processes if and when necessary. Instead, "bounded rationality" means that cognitive activity has neither the time nor the resources to explore, examine, or contemplate fully and completely the "problem space" of the task. The problem space that *is* explored, however, is explored in a rational or analytical fashion. Thus, rationality continues to be employed; it is simply "bounded," or limited by task conditions. As conditions permit, rationality is extended to more aspects of the "problem space." The apparent similarity between bounded rationality and quasirationality is therefore misleading; the terms are in fact incompatible. Although both terms imply that there is a middle ground between intuition and analysis, Simon has explicitly eliminated that middle ground, whereas my Premise 1 insists on it and Premise 2 explicates it.

Simon has recently become definite about the absence of any need for the concept of intuition: "Intuition is nothing more and nothing less than recognition."[62] That is, "the situation has provided a cue; this cue has given the expert access to information stored in memory, and the information provides the answer."[63] But if intuition is to be reduced to "nothing more and nothing less than recognition" of information that the expert (or anyone else) already has, then Simon robs this concept of almost everything that has attracted all students of intuition. When, according to Freeman Dyson, Richard Feynman "just wrote down the solutions out of his head without ever writing down the equations," was he merely recognizing information already stored in his memory? If so, where did he get the information? Not from anyone else. Did he write out the equations earlier and simply fool Dyson into thinking he was writing out those diagrams "without ever writing down the equations"? Did Darwin merely "recognize" the "entangled bank" in *his* diagram from previous diagrams stored in memory? If so, where did the first diagram that he "recognized" come from? How did it enter his memory in the first place?

Simon's treatment of intuition leaves no room for creativity, for the innovations that have been identified for so long as being characteristic of intuitive cognitive activity.[64]

There is, in short, a great difference between Simon's concept of bounded rationality and the idea of quasirationality as formulated by Brunswik (and myself). These concepts are not mutually exclusive, nor do they compete—at least within the theory put forward here; each has its own legitimate area of application. I draw the distinction because of the apparent similarity in meaning, a similarity brought about by a similarity in terminology.

## A Model of Quasirationality

Once one has accepted the idea that multiple, interrelated sources of information about the environment are available and that organisms have evolved that can use multiple sources, it is natural to ask how it all works. The lens model offers a description of the process.

### The Lens Model

Inspection of the diagrammatic model presented in Figure 6-1 makes it obvious why it is called the "lens model." An organism is depicted as a lens; that is, it "collects" the information from the many cues that emanate from an object and refocuses them within the cognitive system of the organism in the form of a judgment about the

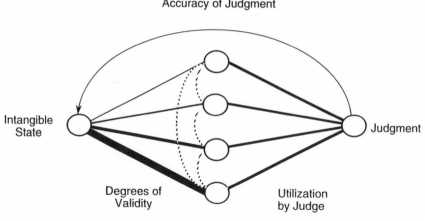

Multiple Fallible Indicators

Figure 6-1    The lens model: the pictorial representation of the presence of (1) multiple fallible indicators (center), (2) their differential degrees of validity (thickness of lines indicates degree of validity), (3) their interrelationships (dashed lines), (4) degree of utilization (or weight by judge), and (5) accuracy of judgment.

object. There are several functional, procedural reasons for this depiction of quasi-rational cognition, the most important of which is that these are the circumstances that evoke quasirationality.

When describing the environmental side, the left side of the model represents (1) multiple fallible indicators (cues), usually simultaneously displayed, (2) the degree of limited validity—and thus fallibility—of each, (3) interrelationships—redundancy—among indicators, and (4) the extent to which cues or indicators are weighted by the person making a judgment about some intangible event. Although not shown in the diagram, the form (linear or nonlinear) of the relationship between the cue or indicator and the inferred event is also considered, among the other lens model parameters (described by Cooksey[65]). The lens model thus offers a diagrammatic definition of quasi-rationality that is quantifiable. It can also be applied to the concept of common sense.

Progress has been made in the effort to put the idea of quasirationality in researchable terms. A mathematical interpretation was suggested as early as 1952 by Brunswik, enlarged upon by the present author and colleagues,[66] and improved upon by L. R. Tucker.[67] Both the conceptual suggestions that follow from the diagrammatic model and its mathematical/statistical implications have led to numerous experimental and field studies, summarized under the rubric of Social Judgment Theory.[68]

Some Examples of the Lens Model and Multiple Fallible Indicators

Consider the judgment that must be applied by practical men and women who invest money—theirs and others'—in the stock market. Do they employ quasirational cognition based on multiple fallible indicators? Yes, unless they rely fully on a substitute for human judgment such as an algorithm or computer program that models, mimics, or simulates the quasirational cognition of common sense in a precise and reliable manner and which itself is usually based on multiple fallible indicators. For an example, see Figure 6-2, taken from the June 1, 1992, issue of *The Wall Street Journal*,[69] in which four fallible indicators (interest rates, inflation rates, earnings, and the state of economies abroad) are presented to the investor. There is no single infallible (i.e., perfectly valid) indicator available to the investor, nor is there any combination of indicators that will reduce uncertainty, and thus unpredictability, to zero (as numerous investors have learned the hard way—slowly and painfully through experiences with outcomes).

The lens model, its quantification in terms of the Lens Model Equation, and its associated theory have enjoyed a remarkably long life, particularly for the field of psychology; they have existed from Brunswik's original writings in the 1930s up to the present—more than sixty years. This longevity is due in large part to their sim-

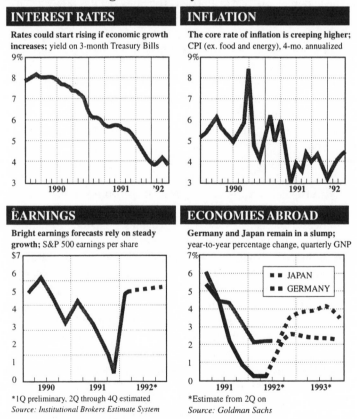

Figure 6-2    Information about four fallible indicators of the future of the U.S. economy offered by the principal financial newspaper published in the United States. The reader should place these in the context of the lens model in Figure 6-1. ( *Source: Sease, 1992, p.C1.*)

plicity (the diagram makes the theory obvious), to their abstractness (there are few circumstances involving correspondence judgments to which they cannot be applied), and to their generality (most of our judgments are based on multiple fallible indicators, represented in the lens model as cues). In addition, the lens model has a further compelling quality: It is compatible with Darwinian theory, it can be readily applied to other organisms besides people; and it can be readily applied to hominids (early *Homo sapiens* as well as modern *Homo sapiens*), and to the wide variety of judgment tasks encountered today.

The lens model and its associated quantification can be used to decompose the meaning of the term "fallible" as used in the phrase "multiple fallible indicators." The lens model allows us to see that indicators are fallible in two different ways: Accuracy of *information* can be described in terms of its *ecological reliability;* the accuracy of a *cue* or *indicator* is described as its *ecological validity*.[70] Thus, for example, wetting one's finger and holding it up to the wind does not provide as much *ecological reliability* with regard to wind direction as does a modern wind gauge built for that purpose, but wind direction may have a high *ecological validity* for predicting rain. The importance of that distinction is obvious, but it is rarely given any attention. Buss's examples of deception by males and females in sexual selection,[71] however, give the distinction the importance it deserves, because they show that the exhibitor of a signal who knows (or who has been taught by sexual selection, whether or not she or he "knows" it) that the perceiver of the signal will be depending on it may provide false data in order to deceive the perceiver; a male who is weak or poor may send a signal indicating that he is strong or rich. In short, a cue itself may have validity, but the data may be unreliable.

But there is one important caution. Some signals can be changed by the sender, and some cannot. For example, persons can send false signals regarding wealth status, even physical features, but the male pheasant cannot deceive the female by changing the length of his spur, on which female pheasants largely depend for their inferences about a male's reproductive potential. Reliability of the data for the indicator of the state to be inferred—its ecological reliability—is a critical aspect of the inference process, and that is why it is so jealously guarded in market-oriented economics; providing false information to purchasers of securities can result in imprisonment. Indeed, ecological reliability of indicators is a critical feature of any system that is providing information to those who must use that information to make inferences about the state of the system.

The *time available* for making the judgment about investments varies for different investors and different circumstances. Ordinarily, the time to make a judgment is not as brief as occurs in ordinary visual perception (virtually instantaneous); it may vary from a few minutes to several days of musing, searching for other, putatively less fallible indicators, such as the judgments of others (who are also considering multiple fallible indicators). The longer the time period, the more analytical the judgment is likely to be (although long periods of musing occasionally end in frustration, followed by a snap judgment of the sort that might have been made immediately upon seeing the indicators). In any case, it is criticism, provided by oneself or others, or punishment from the environment that induces movement from intuition to analysis. Criticism takes time; when more time is taken for analysis, cognition will move along the cognitive continuum in the direction of higher awareness and greater defensibility.

The necessity for defining, labeling, and measuring the cues or indicators has been eliminated in the example from *The Wall Street Journal* (the newspaper having provided clear numerical data in the form of charts). Here, then, is a second feature of the judgment task that will induce the investor to be more analytical than intuitive. When questioned about the information she or he used, it is easy to point to the charts. Contrast this situation with one demanding a social judgment regarding, say, the danger lurking in the bush, the dependability of a person to be hired, or the aesthetic value of a painting to be purchased. A person's characteristics may be presented numerically as a result of a psychological test, but no one treats these as precise measurements (although their ecological reliability and validity are usually available). And no painting has ever been assessed in this way. I have used these examples, first, to show the descriptive generality (domain independence) of the lens model; that generality is due to the ubiquitousness of information environments that require us—and many other organisms—to depend on multiple fallible indicators to develop stable relations with the natural world, and now, with the socially constructed world.

### The Robustness of the Linear Model and Its Relation to Evolutionary Psychology

One feature of the lens model is its explicit representation of the cues used in the judgment process. Although such diagrams are useful, they do not show one of the most important aspects of the judgment process—the *organizing principle,* the cognitive mechanism by which the information from multiple fallible indicators is organized into a judgment. One such principle is simply "add the information." Thus, if the task is selecting a mate, and, on a scale from 1 to 10 cue No. 1 (wealth) is a 5, cue No. 2 (physique), is a 7, and cue No. 3 (chastity) is a 2, the organism simply adds these cue values and reaches a judgment of 14 (where the maximum score is 30). Another principle involves *averaging* the cue values; another principle requires weighting each cue according to its importance before averaging them. An interesting and highly important discovery, first introduced to judgment and decision-making researchers by R. M. Dawes and B. Corrigan,[72] is that organizing principles of this type will be *extremely robust* in irreducibly uncertain environments. That is, if (1) the environmental task or situation is not perfectly predictable (uncertain), (2) there are several fallible cues, and (3) the cues are redundant (even slightly), then (4) these organizing principles (it doesn't matter which one) will provide the subject with a close approximation of the correct inference about the intangible state of the environment, *no matter which organizing principle may actually exist therein*—that is, even if the organism organizes the information incorrectly relative to the task conditions!

I cannot overemphasize the importance of the robustness of what the professionals call the linear model. "Robustness" means that this method of organizing information into a judgment is powerful indeed. *Any* organism that possesses a robust cognitive organizing principle has a very valuable asset in the natural world, or in any information system involving multiple fallible indicators and irreducible uncertainty. Its value is twofold:

1. It allows one to be right for the wrong reason—that is, one can make correct inferences even if the principle used to organize the information is not the correct one (one may exhibit correspondence competence without correct knowledge of the environmental system and without coherence competence).

2. One does not have to learn what the correct principle is in order to make almost correct, useful inferences. This conclusion suggests that learning was *not* an important cognitive activity in the early days of *Homo sapiens*. Whether early *Homo sapiens* learned this robust organizing principle or were endowed with it—that is, their biological make-up included it from the very beginning—I cannot say, of course, nor can anyone else. I can say, however, that any organism possessing such a robust principle would have—and I will insist, *did* have—an evolutionary advantage over any organism that relied on a more analytical—and thus less robust and more fragile—organizational principle.

Evolutionary theory leads us to anticipate that one of the most successful organisms, *Homo sapiens,* will be found to employ an advantageous cognitive organizing principle. Early *Homo sapiens* may well have been stupid, in the sense of lacking analytical skills, but they could hardly have been ineffectual in the use of multiple fallible indicators. If they were, however, a robust organizing principle such as has been observed in modern human beings on countless occasions would have compensated for a lack of skill. And although we cannot recover early hominids or early *Homo sapiens*, that is exactly what has been found in lower organisms (e.g., the pheasants studied by von Schantz and his colleagues), as well as by judgment and decision-making researchers studying current *Homo sapiens*.

In his autobiography, the great evolutionary biologist E. O. Wilson describes his "biophilia hypothesis" this way:

> In a pioneering study of the subject, Gordon Orians, a zoologist at the University of Washington, diagnosed the "ideal" habitat most people choose if given a free choice: they wish their home to perch atop a prominence, placed close to a lake, ocean, or other body of water, and surrounded by a parklike terrain. The trees they most want to see from their homes have spreading crowns, with numerous branches projecting from the trunk close to and horizontal with the ground, and furnished profusely with small or finely divided leaves. It happens that this archetype fits a tropical savanna of the kind prevailing in Africa, where humanity evolved for several millions of years. Primitive people living there are thought to have been most secure in open terrain, where the wide vista allowed them to search for food while watching for enemies. Possessing relatively frail bodies, early humans also needed cover for retreat, with trees to climb if pursued.
>
> Is it just a coincidence, this similarity between the ancient home of human beings and their modern habitat preference?[73]

Clearly Wilson doesn't think all this is just a coincidence; nor do I. Wilson doesn't specifically mention multiple fallible indicators and the robustness of the linear model—and the evolutionary advantage they offer; nevertheless, that form of cognitive activity is implicit in his description of life in the savanna.

There is one additional aspect of the lens model that should be mentioned because of its importance, and that concerns the various forms that the relationship between a (tangible) indicator and the (intangible) variable, object, or event indicated can take. One form of the relationship is a simple one—the more of this, the more of that, indicating a positive linear relationship between the (tangible) indicator and the (intangible) event. For example, the greater the cloudiness, the heavier the rain is likely to be; the stronger the wind, the greater the damage it is likely to cause. Most relationships between indicators and events in our ecology take a positive linear form. That must have been true in the savanna Wilson describes, and it must be the reason people making judgments based on multiple fallible indicators base those judgments *first* on the hypothesis that the relationship between an indicator and event is a positive linear one.

But there are other forms as well. Obviously, there is the possibility of a *negative* linear relationship—the more of this, the *less* of that. For example, the larger the number of people who attend a public event, the fewer the available parking spaces; the greater the preventive steps taken, the fewer the illnesses. It is only when the first (positive linear) form of the relationship between indicator and event is tried and is found to fail (to lead to incorrect judgments) that the second (negative linear) will be tried.

This knowledge can be put to use in the study of how age affects our cognitive processes. Groups of young and elderly persons in Tours, France, were studied by G. Chasseigne in an effort to discover whether elderly persons could make use of negative linear relationships between indicators and indicated.[74] He set up a task in which one indicator was negatively related to the criterion variable. He found that his control group of young persons did indeed test the positive linear relationship first but quickly learned that it did not work; for a second hypothesis, they tried a negative linear relationship, which did work. The elderly patients performed about as well as the young persons in a task that consisted only of positive linear relationships, but when they tried to !earn the task with a negative linear relationship between indicator and indicated, they performed very poorly. These results led Chasseigne to believe that as we age we do not lose our skill in *using* positive linear relationships but that we do lose the ability to *detect* negative linear relationships and make use of them. Chasseigne took one more step, however. He *instructed* the elderly people; he told them that a negative linear relationship existed between indicator and the criterion, identified the indicator, and then observed their performance. This time the group did almost as well as the young persons. He concluded that although the elderly persons could not *find* negative relationships they could *use* them if they knew they were there. Chasseigne continues to pursue these findings. I describe them here to show a feature of the lens model not otherwise apparent and to show another evolutionary aspect of correspondence competence, namely, the hierarchical nature of our hypotheses derived from the early experience of *Homo sapiens.*[75]

In the comprehensive view advocated here *all* forms of cognition make special contributions to achievement, and every form of cognition carries its own risks and benefits in relation to the task to which it is applied. None is to be seen as the prototype, or normative model, for *all* others, for *all* tasks on *all* occasions. A comprehensive view is a pluralistic view. Zeal for the benefits of analytical cognition is to be avoided both by those who must exercise their judgment and by researchers as well, just as the romantic vision of an all-powerful intuition is also to be treated with skepticism. A good part of the skill with which one applies his or her judgment lies in recognizing those task conditions that are appropriate for the use of analysis, those for which one's intuition is appropriate, and those which require quasirationality—that is, some of each. The frequently occurring cognitive tasks of the middle range for which analytical models are useful and appropriate only *in* part need more study than they are getting. Our research should not be confined to those tasks for which an appropriate analytical model can be readily found. Indeed, the tasks of the middle range, those that offer multiple fallible indicators, should have the highest research priority, because they pose the frequently occurring cognitive problems of everyday life, those that the layperson recognizes as demanding "common sense."

### Quasirationality in Economics

Curiously, the term "quasirational" is now beginning to be applied to cognition in articles written by economists, although they fail to realize that the term has been in use by Brunswikian theorists, particularly social judgment theorists, for decades. R. G. Nelson and D. A. Bessler, for example, use it in the title of their article "Quasi-Rational Expectations: Experimental Evidence," in the *Journal of Forecasting*.[76] They attribute the introduction of this term in economics to M. Nerlove, D. M. Grether, and J. L. Carvalho.[77] Nelson and Bessler contrast "quasirational expectations" with the "rational expectations" model in economics, yet "emphasize its close correspondence" with that theory "in certain conditions."[78] Although they oversimplify an environment to which quasirational expectations might apply, they nevertheless offer very sophisticated analyses that show the plausibility of their analysis. Because the psychological or cognitive aspects of quasirationality are severely restricted in Nelson and Bessler's article, it is difficult to determine how much overlap exists between them in the use of this concept.

R. H. Thaler, an economist, employs the term quasirationality in a very broad fashion in his book *Quasi Rational Economics*,[79] which contains a collection of his articles. Curiously, the term does not appear until page 191, where Thaler describes behavior as "systematically different from the axioms of economic theory" and then states that "I like the term 'quasi rational' to describe such behavior. Someone who systematically overreacts to new information in violation of Bayes's rule is predictable yet only quasi rational." Just how the person "overreacts" is not explained, however.

This term appears a second time in a chapter by T. Russell and Thaler titled "The Relevance of Quasi Rationality in Competitive Markets."[80] Here the authors refer to findings reported by Kahneman and Tversky that suggest that when the formal properties of a problem are framed in different ways the subjects' responses change, although they should not according to economic theory. (In other psychological studies this phenomenon is referred to as "context" effects.) Russell and Thaler then state: "We propose calling any such regular yet nonrational behavior *quasi rational*. Quasi rational behavior will include some actions that can be considered mistakes in the classification scheme described above."[81] But "nonrational" behavior cannot, of course, be quasirational behavior.

Thaler makes no reference to the use of this term by Nerlove, a fellow economist, or to the decades of usage in the judgment and decision-making literature. One might not expect Nelson and Bessler or Nerlove to have encountered the term quasirationality in the judgment and decision-making literature, but it is somewhat surprising that Thaler apparently has never encountered it, inasmuch as he rests his case for the fallibility of economic theory on the results of research in judgment and decision making. Failure to acknowledge prior usage that includes both theoretical and empirical work indicates limited comprehension of the topic, as well as of the literature. Nevertheless, the use of the term quasirationality by coherence theorists is a step forward; it implies a recognition that any heuristic, any "rule of thumb," used implicitly or explicitly, is a compromise between analysis and intuition.

To summarize: Quasirationality is a concept that depends on the premise of a cognitive continuum that permits a variety of forms of "imperfect reasoning." This means that there is a place for intuitive processes as well as analytical ones. Most important, however, is the claim that such "imperfect reasoning" is robust, adaptive, and useful. Quasirationality has many advantages, which may be one of the reasons that the notion of common sense has persisted and been valued by the layperson for so long, despite the fact that virtually no one has convincingly described it.

The main advantage of quasirationality is its potential for compromise; it does not demand adherence to specific criteria as the polar types of cognition do. It admits elements of intuition or analysis as deemed necessary or as available. And compromise does seem the dominant mode of cognition in policy formation, at least in governments that are not slaves of ideology. It is far easier to reach a compromise on a policy or plan within a framework of quasirationality than if either polar form of cognition is controlling the process. Strict adherence to intuition demands that the mysteries of judgment be left untouched by criticism; strict adherence to analysis is intolerant of deviations from any step in the process.

Compromise also offers the advantage of avoidance of catastrophe. All rigorous, analytically derived systems, including systems of thought, work well, that is, work as intended, within the controlled circumstances for which they were constructed. When errors occur, however, they tend to be catastrophic. Trains run very well on the complicated switching systems designed for them, but when a switch fails, the result can be catastrophic. The same is true for rigorous, analytical systems of thought, planning, and policy formation. A single mistake in the decision tree or other form of logic applied to a problem may result in disaster. Analysis tempered by intuition, in contrast, is seldom free of error, but its errors tend to be less than catastrophic. Railroad systems may not have this choice available to them, but many, if not most, social systems do.

In analogous fashion, policies based on intuitive judgments often provide their proponents with emotional satisfaction. They are, however, so imprecise and irresponsible in their formulation and execution that they are unsatisfactory; because of their lack of rigor, no one can know how or why the policy succeeds, or fails.

In short, the traditional dichotomy between intuition and analysis collapses in the face of a theory that makes room for cognitive activity over a continuum. The comprehensive theory not only acknowledges common sense but defines it and offers a model of it that has withstood the test of reasonable time and research. The theory places a great demand on researchers, however. It requires them to describe the variety of conditions that evoke judgment, to discover the varieties of quasirational cognition that different conditions induce, and to discover the outcomes of the relation between varieties of task conditions and the various forms of cognitive activity. Does such a theory speak to the judgments that control social policy?

### Quasirationality in the Courtroom: Compromise Between Discretion and Equality in Mandatory Sentencing

One of the clearest examples of the role of quasirationality in policy formation can be seen in the effort to find a compromise between the discretionary powers of judges and the provision of sentencing guidelines, or, as it is sometimes described, between "discretion and equality."

Although a federal sentencing law was passed without opposition by Congress in 1984, conflict between those on opposite sides of the issue was not unexpected by Congress, the American Bar Association, or the Sentencing Commission that wrote the report establishing the sentencing guidelines.[82] Only four years later, Frank Easterbrook, a judge on the United States Court of Appeals for the Seventh Circuit, would say: "There was a national consensus in 1984 that reducing discretion [for judges] is a great idea, [but] this consensus has evaporated."[83] But Ilene Nagel, a member of the Sentencing Commission, pointed out why sentencing guidelines were so badly needed:

> Despite conviction for serious felonies, under past federal sentencing practices, over 50 percent of the federal offender population was sentenced to serve zero time. For tax violations, where the government and the taxpaying public are the victims, fifty-seven percent of those convicted were sentenced to zero time, and for property offenses, the percentage reaches sixty percent. Is it no wonder that the absolute rate of crimes committed continues to soar? Under past sentencing practice, for many offenses, there is little doubt that crime pays.[84]

She also noted: "The question of equality versus discretion lies at the heart of each of these problems, and at the heart of the controversial proposed remedies."[85] And Stephen Breyer (now a Supreme Court Justice) added:

> People were fed up with a system in which a judge would order a twelve year sentence, but the Parole Commission would make the offender serve only four years. If a judge, believing that an offender sentenced to twelve years would serve only four years and wanting him to serve twelve, gave him thirty-six years, he might find the Parole Commission requiring the offender to serve thirty of the thirty-six years.
>
> This back-and-forth benefited nobody. Most of all, it confused the public, who could not understand what the judges were doing and how the system worked. Therefore, Congress passed the law to ensure "honesty in sentencing." Honesty in sentencing means that the sentence given is the sentence served. . . .
>
> Under prior law, judges in Massachusetts would carefully "individualize" sentences. Judges in Texas would also carefully "individualize" sentences. Unfortunately, these sentences would be very different for cases that seemed identical. Although each judge believes that what he does is correct, when you look at the results of such sentencing

across the country, you find a great deal of disparity. Indeed the federal district court in New York introduced a lottery, so that defendants would understand that the choice of judge is random. This fact suggests that the defense bar believed that sentencing depended less on the crime and the offender than on the judge.[86]

Breyer describes the struggle to find a remedy as a struggle to find a compromise between intuition and analysis:

> The United States Congress, in crafting the enabling legislation for the United States Sentencing Commission, opted not to choose between: (A) a system calling for the continuation of unfettered discretion [i.e., judge's intuitions]; and B) one with excessive rigidity [analytical rigor], giving only the appearance of equality; but, rather, to *compromise* [italics added]. The vehicle was to be mandatory sentencing guidelines, binding on the court, but from which the court could depart for unusual, atypical, extraordinary cases.[87]

That is, judges retained the power to move their cognitive activity along the cognitive continuum, staying with analytically based rules when they wished but moving toward an intuitive decision when they believed they should and could defend doing so. Breyer anticipated attacks from left and right and defended the mandatory sentencing rule by arguing that quasirationality was appropriate:

> Contrary to the characterization by some, often repeated in the press, that the new federal Sentencing Guidelines eliminate judicial discretion, substituting in its place a mechanistic computer program where judges have no role, the Guidelines, in fact, *strike a balance* [italics added] between the prior system of unfettered discretion, on the one hand, and rigid presumptive sentences tied to the offense of conviction without regard to variation in the offense or the offender's criminal history, on the other. To be sure, judicial discretion [intuition] in federal sentencing has been curtailed greatly, but we believe that it has been done so on the basis of *logic and rationality* [italics added], pursuant to the statutory purposes as specified, clearly by Congress.[88]

The Sentencing Commission thus attempted to strike a balance, that is, a *compromise* between a judge's discretion—the product of intuitive cognition—and a rule developed on the "basis of logic and rationality." At this point, the reader may well have anticipated this compromise between intuition and analysis and perhaps also anticipated that the compromise would draw fire from both sides, from those who demand a greater role for their preferred mode of cognition. Philip Howard, for example, in his sharp attack on the law, argues that the guidelines have resulted in an overly rational process that is an inherent obstruction of justice: "The point of the criminal sentencing grid was to eliminate unevenness in the sentences meted out by judges . . . [but] there could be no worse result."[89]

Howard was firm and effective in presenting this view; he believed that the rational, analytic process involved in the use of guidelines is a corrupting influence. His remedy, to give the process back to the judge ("Judges, at least, are impartial"), ignores the problem that he acknowledges motivated the search for impartiality— "unfairness in the sentences meted out by judges." Howard's book became a persistent best-seller, and his views were endorsed by prominent politicians.[90]

Howard's complaint is not unsubstantiated. As we saw in Chapter 3, Judge Jack Weinstein and other judges refused to accept certain cases involving the sale of drugs because they believed the mandatory sentences were far too harsh, especially for first offenders. (Despite the acclaim for his book, Howard's case was weak, as I will show in Chapter 11.)

It can be expected that mandatory sentencing will be used when public sentiment favors "truth in sentencing" and harsh sentences, but we can also anticipate an eventual return to discretionary sentencing. The first mandatory sentencing act was passed in 1958 and the second in 1984; the cycle thus approaches the thirty-year cycle we have encountered in relation to other phenomena. Irrespective of speculations about time periods, the primary point to be observed is that the compromises achieved are unstable; we should anticipate movement on the cognitive continuum.

Defense attorneys prefer discretion for judges. For example, Terence MacCarthy, chair of the American Bar Association's Criminal Justice Section, has also spoken for discretion over equality in sentencing. But his argument goes beyond Howard's simple plea for the elimination of analytical processes; it rests largely on his belief that "it is impossible to quantify . . . the matters surrounding a particular offense; nor can you 'quantify' the individual characteristics of a particular defendant."[91] The remainder of his argument provides specifics regarding the flaws in the attempt at quantification and rule building. That, too, is an argument we shall meet again and again.

Nagel has rebutted MacCarthy's argument against quantification; she has said that MacCarthy "makes the point that it is very difficult to quantify offense characteristics and offender characteristics; I think that is true. . . . [But] this quantification process is precisely what judges have been doing for 200 years. What we did was really no different, except to make those quantified judgments uniform."[92] Nagel's point is precisely the one that researchers on judgment and decision making have been urging for decades.

Because defense attorneys appear to favor greater discretion on the part of judges, it appears that discretion is always on the side of leniency. Not so. There is an entire literature devoted to describing the manner in which judges, bureaucrats, and other agents of government and the private sector use their discretionary powers to oppress the poor and the weak. J. Handler, for example, describes a variety of uses of discretion for this purpose, as do others.[93]

Mandatory sentencing rules that embody analytical cognition may on one occasion favor society (i.e., produce injustices against individuals rather than society) and on others favor individuals (produce injustices against society rather than individuals). The same can be said for the intuitive cognition that is at the root of discretion; sometimes it is on one side, sometimes on the other. Both policies have in common the fact that they are subject to error and the injustices that are the result of irreducible uncertainty. All of this is a result of the compromise between intuition and analysis that results in the common sense of everyday life, the search for the quasirationality we find at once so irritating that we condemn it and so satisfactory that we cannot proceed without it.

The seminar on equality and discretion in sentencing provides an excellent example of the manner in which the rivalry between intuition and analysis is realized in policy formation. The remarks by the participants in that seminar also illustrate the critical role of compromise, the value of which the participants explicitly recognize but the weaknesses of which will be attacked from either side.

If it were possible we would like to ask Justice Holmes if the discussion in this high-level seminar might not reflect exactly what he had in mind when he said that "the life of the law has not been logic: it has been experience."[94] Was he not thinking of the compromise exemplified here when he went on to explain that "the felt necessities of the time, the prevalent moral and political theories, intuitions [note!] of public policy, avowed or unconscious, even the prejudices which judges share with their fellow-men have had a good deal more to do than the syllogism in determining the rules by which men should be governed"?[95] This is, of course, a beautiful expression of what Holmes evidently believed to be a hard fact of human judgment, one that he welcomed. Does it not express the principle of compromise?

# 7 Task Structure and Cognitive Structure

In this chapter I further develop the idea that cognitive activity is influenced by the structure of the task, by the nature of the information environment. Here I describe the effect of differences in task structure on cognition, and show how the structure of cognition is induced to change as the information environment changes. I also address the correspondence-coherence distinction in terms of functional relations and pattern recognition.

## Premise 3: Theory of Task Structures

*Cognitive tasks can be ordered on a continuum with regard to their capacity to induce intuition, quasirationality, or analytical cognition.*

Premise 3 asserts that tasks—information environments—can be ordered on a continuum in terms of the cognitive activity they are predicted to induce. That is, a set of objective task properties can be described, independent of the subject's behavior, from which a single quantitative measure can be derived that defines the location of a task on a Task Continuum Index (TCI). Once a set of task properties is described, a number can be assigned to any task such that it locates the task on the task continuum. Cognitive activity can also be described by a set of properties that allows the assignment of a number that specifies the activity's location on the Cognitive Continuum Index (CCI). Taken together, these numbers make it possible to test the hypothesis offered earlier—that task properties induce matching cognitive properties; for example, a task with a TCI number that places it near the intuition-inducing pole of the task continuum will induce cognitive behavior that will be characterized by an (independently derived) CCI number that places it near the intuition pole of the cognitive continuum. The same holds for tasks with a TCI location at or near the analytical pole of the task continuum. In short, a positive correlation is predicted between TCI values and CCI values. This is an important principle underlying the theory.

An easy way to see the nature of the (matching) correlates is to recall the advantages of each mode of cognition. Analysis provides precision; intuition provides robustness; quasirationality offers something of both. Thus, an information environment that offers multiple fallible indicators, many if not all of which should be considered but none of which is a sure guide to accurate prediction, is an environment in which robustness (approximating accuracy most of the time) but not precision can be achieved. No one expects the Leading Economic Indicators Index to be a precise indication of the future state of the economy, but the Index number itself is taken as a fallible indicator of the future of the economy that cannot be ignored; it is given some weight, a sure indicator of the inducement of at least some degree of intuitive cognition. When a task is represented by multiple fallible indicators, it receives a TCI number that places it near the intuition-inducing pole of the task continuum; it will be a *robust* predictor.

If a person uses a mathematical model to predict the future state of the economy, the economy will be represented not by multiple fallible indicators but by a series of interlocking equations that provide the user with a prediction that is retraceable and logically or theoretically defensible—in a word, *coherent*. The prediction will therefore be *precise* and because of these properties will induce the user to become analytical.

No one regards analytically derived predictions as robust. Changes (or errors) in inputs to the model are likely to make the prediction quite wrong indeed. The less than perfect coherence in our understanding of how the economy works, together with the unpredictability of shocks to the system—unpredictable natural disasters, unpredicted political upheavals, unpredictable behavioral or cognitive changes in the minds of policymakers—renders few, if any, predictions of such models infallible, despite (or perhaps because of) the precision of their output.

We can expect our user of information to make use of forecasts from the robust Leading Economic Indicators or some other, more precise source such as those provided by any number of mathematical models. If so, the forecaster will be left with task information somewhere in the midrange of the Task Continuum Index, thus inducing midrange cognitive activity, or, in other words, *quasirationality*; elements from both intuition *and* analysis will enter the forecasts. (Examples can be found daily in the financial pages of newspapers as well as in the columns and articles of political analysts.)

A truncated listing of the properties of intuition and analysis can be seen in Table 7-1, where I have listed the differences in six of the more important characteristics that differentiate these two major forms of cognition. And because a theory should be coherent these properties should "hang together," they should appeal to the reader's sense that the properties in each column belong together. A high degree of cognitive control, for example, implies a tight command over cognitive activity, and that requires a high degree of awareness of that activity (knowing what you are thinking) which in turn implies that there will be a fixation on just a few indicators rather than a wide and interchangeable use of indicators (consistent with low cognitive control). Additionally, the rate at which cognitive activity takes place in analytical work is slow (it usually involves checking for mistakes), in contrast to rapid intuitive judgments that occur in seconds. Judgments often depend on memory, but analytically-based judgment depends on recalling principles related to the task (e.g., the inertial principle in physical circumstances), in contrast to the recollection of specific events, often vivid ones, in intuitive cognition. Both forms of cognition rely

Table 7-1    Properties of intuition and analysis.

|  | *Intuition* | *Analysis* |
|---|---|---|
| Cognitive control | Low | High |
| Awareness of cognitive activity | Low | High |
| Amount of shift across indicators | High | Low |
| Speed of cognitive activity | High | Low |
| Memory | Raw data or events stored | Complex principles stored |
| Metaphors used | Pictorial | Verbal, quantitative |

on metaphors: Analytical cognition tends to rely on verbal or quantitative ones, whereas intuition will rely on pictorial, easy-to-use metaphors.[1]

Once the properties (and location) of the tasks are known, prediction of cognitive activity is straightforward; cognition will have the properties of a matched location on the cognitive continuum. All that is necessary is a method for locating tasks and cognitive activity on their respective continuums. The method for doing that has been worked out and applied.[2]

Now I want to lend some meaning to Premise 3 beyond what I have already said. I do so because Premise 3 may, perhaps, appear excessively abstract, divorced from our subject matter and, therefore, possibly of no use to our efforts to understand human judgment and social policy. If the reader is tempted to reach that conclusion, consider the words of Vaclav Havel, the first president of Czechoslovakia after the fall of communism in that country and later the president of the Czech Republic. In his address to the World Economic Forum in Switzerland in 1992, he made an impassioned plea for those who shaped the presentation of information to him each morning to give him an opportunity to move away from what he believed were the limits of analytical cognition. Havel wanted the properties of the cognitive tasks presented to him to induce not only analysis but intuition. As he put it:

> Sooner or later politics will be faced with the task of finding a new, postmodern face. A politician must become a person again, someone who trusts not only a scientific representation and analysis of the world, but also the world itself. He must believe not only in sociological statistics, but also in real people. He must trust not only an objective interpretation of reality, but also his own soul; not only an adopted ideology, but also his own thoughts; not only the summary reports he receives each morning but his own feeling.[3]

Readers more devoted to rigorous, analytical approaches to judgment and decision making than the former playwright Havel will wonder what it means to demand information about the "world itself" and will want to know how information about "real people" rather than "sociological statistics" is to be provided. But readers who have examined Premise 3 will see that Havel is pleading for an intuition-inducing presentation of information. He does not want to be limited to an "objective interpretation of reality"; he does want the properties of the task—his information environment—to encourage him to interrogate his "own soul" and his "own thoughts." He certainly does not want to be forced to consult an "adopted ideology" (the analytical framework of Marxism) as he was once forced to submit to the rigors of the Marxist code. Deviations from code meant prison; Havel's years in prison taught him that. He wants to be free to trust "not only the summary reports he receives each morning but his own feeling." Thus Premises 1, 2, and 3 of the comprehensive theory offered in this book make it possible to see what it is that Havel wants from the structure of the morning's information upon which he is to act. He wants an opportunity, even an inducement, to be free of the demands of analysis; he wants an opportunity for the information environment to induce his intuitions. This is a new conception of freedom of thought; freedom to organize information, or require that it be organized for you, so that you are able to move your cognitive activity to different points on the cognitive continuum. And that may be why the most analytical of recent U.S. presidents, John F. Kennedy and Bill Clinton, chose to have poets recite original work at their inaugurations; they wanted, perhaps, to demonstrate that they appreciated the power of intuitive as well as analytical cognition. But it was Havel who showed that he understood what Premise 3 asserts—namely, that the properties of cognitive tasks induce a matching form of cognition.

It is my view, derived from the pathfinders Brunswik and Simon, that theories of cognitive tasks cannot be avoided. Simon made his commitment to the importance of the task as a determiner of cognitive activity in this remark, often quoted but seldom observed in practice: "A man, viewed as a behaving system, is quite simple. The apparent complexity of his behavior over time is largely a reflection of the environment in which he finds himself—provided that we include in what we call man's environment the cocoon of information, stored in books and long-term memory, that man spins about himself."[4] Indeed, when researchers carry out their work, a theory of task structures is implicit in their description of tasks as well as in their generalizations from them. Every experiment brings some representation of the environment, acknowledged or not, into the laboratory along with the subject. A description of that representation may be reduced to nothing more than a description of a "stimulus"—still a favorite, brought forward from psychophysics—that carries an aura of objectivity and real science. But, in fact, the objectivity offered by such descriptions has exacted a great price—uncritical, unjustified generalizations of results to conditions not represented in the task. As might be expected, few such generalizations have lasted. It was the gradual abandonment of the concept of a "stimulus" as a useful representation of the environment that allowed cognitive psychology to develop and that has led to the gradual disappearance of the stimulus-organism-response paradigm.

Premise 3, therefore, has direct implications for the manner in which human judgment is brought to bear on social policy. For Premise 3 asserts that presenting information in different ways, representing the world in different ways, will have predictable effects on the cognitive activity of the policymaker. Specifically, representations can be ordered a priori in terms of their capacity to induce cognition at various points on the cognitive continuum, from intuition to analysis; and specific representations located on the Task Continuum can be expected a priori to induce intuition, quasirationality, or analysis. If information is presented in terms of numerous multiple fallible indicators with implications of considerable uncertainty and in largely pictorial form, intuitive judgments will be induced, and we can anticipate the consequences of intuitions of various policymakers being pitted against one another, not a circumstance offering optimism for a rational resolution of differences. Opposite conditions induce analysis with its own consequences. And here I can do no better than to quote again Vaclav Havel, who saw at first hand what Premise 3 implies: "A politician must become a person again, someone who trusts not only a scientific representation and analysis of the world, but also the world itself." Havel thus protests against the inducement of analysis and asks for representation of the social and ecological world that will induce his intuition.

But in fact few representations of policy-related problems will be located at either pole of the Task Continuum; the great majority will induce quasirationality, because elements of both intuition and analysis will be included. There will usually be some data, some representation of causal relations, but there will also be some references to fallible indicators, appeals to what "common sense tell us," and references to a "comfort level," "feelings," and indications of what "my sense is." The reader will find examples of such language even in the minutes of the Federal Open Marketing Committee in Chapter 11. Quasirationality will make its appearance; to what degree more intuitive elements or more analytical elements will be induced will depend largely on the appearance of these elements in the representation of the problem situation. The important point is that Premise 3 asserts that these cognitive consequences are predictable from the knowledge of the properties of the information environment.[5]

## Representation of the World

The natural world and its representation have undergone persistent change, but it is modern men and women who, as tool makers and users, began to design the world itself, as well as its representation, to suit their purposes. Designing the world is the business of politicians, government officials, businesspeople, and engineers, but it is not the business of judgment and decision-making researchers. Representation of the world, however, can be and should be within the purview of students of cognition such as judgment and decision-making researchers. To pursue the navigation metaphor one further step, notice that, in addition to learning how to ascertain longitude, the navigators change not the world itself, unlike the interveners, the experimenters, but the physical *representation* of the world. The navigators did not use control groups; they created indicators, markers, for themselves.

That change didn't take place overnight. Mark Twain noticed it long ago when he returned to the Mississippi thirty years after learning to "read the face of the water" (i.e., how to use information from multiple fallible indicators, "cues on the faces of the river"). He found that the new pilots made direct observations of manmade landmarks (e.g., buoys, lighthouses) that were *infallible* indicators of shoals and other hazards. All the excitement and challenge of exercising intuitive judgments was now gone as far as Twain was concerned, possibly because the thrill of danger, of mistaken judgments, was largely gone. Today the infallible physical indicators have been replaced by infallible electronic indicators (lighthouses are coming down all over the world), and infallible electronic navigation has been extended from the Mississippi to the entire world; uncertainty in navigation has been virtually eliminated from major transportation systems.

That strategy, changing the representation of the world so as to induce analytical cognition, is congruent with Premise 3 ("cognitive tasks can be ordered on a continuum with regard to their ability to induce intuition, quasirationality, and analytical cognition"). The natural world—Mark Twain's unmarked river—induced intuitive cognition; that worked well but was not without error, and the error could not be tolerated. That led to the representation of that river by marks—lighthouses, buoys—in a way that induced analytical cognition; the pilot was instructed to travel from this marked point to that marked point, and errors were virtually eliminated.

### How Far to Go?

Although we knew we wanted to eliminate intuition from navigation, and many want to eliminate it from medical diagnosis and engineering,[6] the critical question is: To what extent do we want to eliminate intuition from our judgments about social policy? Creating infallible social indicators requires that we create a rigidly ordered society. How far we should go in that direction in social navigation? George Kennan has warned us against it emphatically: "Nothing," he said "is more greatly to be feared ... than the effort to create government systems that are logical, uncomplicated, efficient, and vast in scope. . . . A governmental system that strived too hard for these apparent advantages would be bound to do violence to people's deepest needs."[7]

Despite this warning, the representation of the social world continues in the direction of inducing analytical cognition, and it continues despite the lack of a dependable social science, where and when it can; many steps toward that reorganization have been taken in the past one hundred years, all in the same direction. Just as the seafarers of the eighteenth century found that "in the long run it would be easier to provide cheap clocks than to turn out mathematically educated sailors"[8] (contrary to the urging of Sir Isaac Newton), we have been finding that it is easier to provide various forms of "navigational aids" for social circumstances, such as economic indicators, social indicators, and the like, than to create skilled policymakers. But the indicators we must rely on are so fallible, so error-ridden, and our basic theoretical understanding is so frail, that progress remains slow, and we remain largely dependent upon our intuitions, a situation that those who admire our intuitive powers will applaud but a regrettable fact to those who admire our analytical capacities.

The present theory offers a means for answering the question of how the world should be represented in order to improve the competence of human judgment. As the reader will recall, the theory is based on five premises: Premise 1 asserts that cognition runs from intuition to analysis on a continuum; the distinction is not a dichotomous one. Premise 2 defines and explains "common sense," or quasirationality, and explains why it is so "common." But it is Premise 3 that speaks directly to the question of how the world *should* be made to work so that proper judgment will be induced. For Premise 3 states that "cognitive tasks [information environments] can be ordered on a continuum with regard to their ability to *induce* intuition, quasirationality, and analytical cognition." That means that we have it in our power to induce the type of cognitive activity we deem to be appropriate for the task at hand. And that means that we can improve competence. For if we believe policy should be created by intuition, the theory described in Part II tells us how to represent the world so that intuition (probably) will be induced and applied to the policy problem. Similarly with quasi-rational cognition or analytical cognition. Vaclav Havel recognized this situation when he pleaded for information to be presented to him in a manner that would allow him to exercise his intuitive judgment, rather than require him to think in analytical terms. Havel was asking his aides to represent the world for him in a manner that would enable him to make his judgments in a manner he believed to be appropriate to the policy-making situation. He has continued to do so.

But judgment and decision-making researchers in the main believe Havel is wrong, because they think that analytical cognition is what we should strive for in the formation of policy or in any serious work. The researchers' position is that if we want to improve competence and thus social policy-making, we must structure the policymaker's information environment so that it will permit, induce, and encourage the use of analytical cognition—up to a point. The present theory tells us how to achieve this goal. Our success can be seen most vividly in navigation. Let me again use this metaphor as a means for demonstrating the putative value of analytical cognition.

Our urge to explore the world and to travel led to the development of technology that reduced navigational uncertainty to near the vanishing point. That was accomplished by representing the world so that judgment was virtually eliminated from navigation. Notice that no changes were made in the pilots of airplanes or ships. That is, the advances in navigational accuracy were not brought about by selecting (somehow) navigators who were born with the ability to navigate. Nor was this problem solved by selecting a "council of elder navigators." Rather, changes were made in the environment in which navigation takes place, and the changes were always the same; the *representation* of conditions were made to induce the desired cognitive condition, namely analytical cognition, leaving as little as possible to intuition.

In contrast with physical navigation, our attempts to navigate through our *social and ecological* worlds still leave much to be desired. Here people get lost regularly; meetings wander and fail; misunderstandings abound, some never to be corrected; false agreements and false disagreements are common. In these worlds we remain dependent on multiple fallible indicators, and irreducible uncertainty induces intuitive cognition, exactly the circumstances the early navigators found themselves in. The dissatisfaction with these circumstances has led many people in many professions to do their best to erect infallible, or at least less fallible, indicators, just as the eighteenth-century students of navigation tried to do. Our physicians, for example, and their associates (often engineers) try, with apparent success—too slowly to suit us—to develop *infallible* indicators of health and specific physiological dysfunctions. Again it is the surroundings, the representation of circumstances, that has improved, the fallibility of indicators that has been reduced (e.g., the physicians' five senses have been largely replaced by the x-ray, the MRI, the numerous lab tests). It is these changes, not changes in the physician, that have led to a reduction in uncertainty and greater competence, although, of course, physicians have learned to make use of these changes. (Recall also the efforts by Bennett and Etzioni to make use of social indicators in an organized fashion.)

Pleas for Greater Use of Analysis

One who has been forthright as well as energetic in his demands for an analytical approach to social problems is Robyn Dawes. He explains why "technical calculation" may be superior to the "mysteries of the human mind":

> The philosophy presented . . . [here] is based on the premise that "mere numbers" are in fact *mere* neither good nor bad. Just as numbers can be used to achieve either constructive or destructive goals in other contexts, they can be used for good or ill in decision making. *Research* indicates that numbers in a linear model can be well used in making predictions. The implication that they can serve well also in choice and preference contexts is immediate. Using them, however, requires us to overcome a view (*not* supported by the research) that the "mysteries of the human mind" allow us to reach superior conclusions without their aid. The mysteries are there, but not in this context. To do well by ourselves and to treat other persons fairly, we must overcome the hubris that leads us to reject adding numbers to evaluate them, and to experience no more shame when we do so than when we use numbers in determining how to construct a bridge that will not collapse.[9]

Dawes is not unmindful of the need to "treat other persons fairly" (as well as doing "well by ourselves"). He rejects the supposition that those impressed with "the mysteries of the human mind" (he means intuition) are somehow more sensitive to injustice, to the plight of others, or are somehow more "humane" than those who "use numbers." His argument is simply that it is the *rationality* of our policy judgments that matter and that research shows that judgments based on analytical reasoning "allow us to reach superior conclusions." (Dawes might have added that no one would now think of getting on a plane or ship whose navigational system was no better than that afforded by the fallible economic or social indicators in use today.)

The principal advantages of the quantitative approach advocated by Dawes and many others in the judgment and decision-making field are obvious: It is explicit and specific, and it enables researchers to decompose the topic into manageable, researchable pieces. As a result, not only does it offer theoreticians and researchers specific, concrete problems; it provides the basis for "rationality" in policy formation.

But there have been objections to following the path of analytical cognition in the search for competence and thus successful policy formation.

Resistance to Analysis

The resistance to the analytical approach within the field of judgment and decision making is restricted to those who are prepared to argue for the efficacy of intuitive cognition—at least under certain conditions. These researchers have challenged the negative view of the competence of human judgment expressed by the coherence researchers. Although acknowledging that errors in judgments can be made and are made, they emphasize the fact (acknowledged by the coherence researchers) that such errors are likely to be inconsequential.

Neil Postman, a well-respected student of human affairs, makes an angry denunciation of modern technology and its effect on society:

Because the computer "thinks" rather than works, its power to energize mechanistic metaphors is unparalleled and is of enormous value to Technopoly which depends on our believing that we are at our best when acting like machines, and that in significant ways machines may be trusted to act as our surrogates. Among the implications of these beliefs is a loss of confidence in human judgment and subjectivity. We have devalued the singular human capacity to see things whole in all their psychic, emotional and moral dimensions, and we have replaced this with faith in the powers of technical calculation.[10]

Postman reaches back to Frederick Taylor's *The Principles of Scientific Management*[11] to find

the first explicit and formal outline of the assumptions of the thought-world of Technopoly. These include the belief . . . that technical calculation is in all respects superior to human judgment; that in fact human judgment cannot be trusted, because it is plagued by laxity, ambiguity, and unnecessary complexity; that subjectivity is an obstacle to clear thinking; that what cannot be measured either does not exist or is of no value; and that the affairs of citizens are best guided by experts.[12]

Postman's critique can readily be applied not only to Taylor in 1911 but to virtually every researcher and theorist in the field of judgment and decision making *today*—though Postman takes no notice of them. Vaclav Havel is one man who, because of his years under totalitarian government, has good reason to resist the trend toward analytical, rule-bound cognition:

We all know civilization is in danger. . . . Man's attitude to the world must be radically changed. We have to abandon the arrogant belief that the world is merely a puzzle to be solved, a machine with instructions for use waiting to be discovered, a body of information to be fed into a computer in the hope that, sooner or later, it will spit out a universal solution.[13]

Kennan, too, points out that restructuring society in a rigid, analytical fashion that removes uncertainty (much as military organizations must do), thus making it easier to understand, carries intolerable dangers. All these critics seem to be saying that if we continue to restructure the world and its representation in order to reduce uncertainty for policymakers, then we risk the loss of our humanity, placing ourselves on a sure road to totalitarianism.

By the 1970s the limits of analytical competence and its inevitable supplement— if not replacement—by intuitive cognition was clearly identified in its modern context. Analytical competence diminishes as the network of probabilistic interdependencies among multiple fallible indicators grows, as the network becomes resistant to empirical manipulation, and as its objective uncertainty increases and thus makes the problem subject to the vicissitudes of multiple alternative plausible explanations. Because analysis begins to fail precisely at the point where the policy process needs it most, the demand for broad conclusions induces, even compels, legislators, jurists, scientists, and engineers to offer their intuitive judgments, singly or as members of a committee of experts. Since these judgments are based on cognitive processes that are largely covert, conflict is inevitable, and polarization between opposing perspectives becomes acute. It is also at this point that despair leads us to turn to a commission, for once we do that, we no longer have to think; it's their problem.

The proper representation of the policymakers' information environment is not a simple matter. Although the theory presented here tells how to change the representation of the world, it is not yet clear exactly how far the move toward analytical representation of the world should go. As we have seen, Havel thinks that it has already gone too far. He is prepared to argue that if we value freedom and wish to exercise it, policymakers will have to "abandon the arrogant belief that the world is merely a puzzle to be solved, a machine with instructions for use waiting to be discovered."[14]

Senator Patrick Moynihan, in lectures given at Oxford University in 1991, supported that view. He argued that it was an overreliance on analysis that caused social scientists to fail to anticipate the collapse of the Soviet Union, that the analytical, rational aspects of social organization gained more attention from social scientists than they deserved. Moynihan referred to "a fine essay" published in the *American Scholar*, "Why Were We Surprised?" by W. R. Connor, who "suggested that . . . we were surprised because . . . we confined our analysis to 'hard,' quantifiable (or so we thought) measures that made no provision for the passions—the appeal of ethnic loyalty and nationalism, the demands for freedom of religious practice and cultural expression, and the feeling that the regime had lost its moral legitimacy."[15]

Although Dawes could claim that most, if not all, arguments against hard, quantitative analysis of both decision processes and decision problems are not supported by research, his claim for the superiority of analytical cognition is challenged by other judgment and decision-making researchers and by serious students of political behavior such as Havel, Connor, and Moynihan. Thus, we meet again the topic of Chapter 3—the persistent rivalry between intuition and analysis. Should the representation of the world induce intuitive cognition? Analysis? Or quasirationality?

### The Persistent Rivalry Between Intuition and Analysis As Applied to Policy Formation

The importance of the rivalry between intuitive and analytical cognition can be seen in the context of policy formation and the theory of judgment (described in Part II). We can see that although increasing the analytical structure of policy tasks may well be desirable, progress in reducing the fallibility of our social and economic indicators is very slow and in all likelihood will remain so. It is clear that we cannot now, and perhaps never will be able to, construct infallible indicators for the future behavior of social institutions or of human beings.[16] Nor is it always obvious to us exactly which indicators we should be using in the effort to find where we are. Too much irreducible uncertainty at the time of decision remains in the unstable social world. It is therefore no surprise to find that the rivalry between intuition and analysis persists in the process of policy formation.

Let us once more compare our situation in regard to policy formation with that of the early navigators. Even by the 1400s seafarers had a sufficient number of (nearly) infallible indicators to guide them, except for longitude. By 1700, however, it had become clear that determination of longitude would have to come through analytical methods. Enough was known about astronomy that it soon became a matter of developing good technology—a workable sextant, an accurate chronometer, and celestial tables—for gathering and using the necessary information.[17] In our social navigation, however, all that coherent, useful, celestial theory so necessary to physical navigation is sadly lacking. Indeed, the grand, coherent, and highly analytical Marxist economic and social theory recently crashed on the rock of correspondence.

The dubious value of the expert judgment of economists is substantiated by Moynihan, who points out the significant errors in economists' estimation of the economic health of the Soviet Union shortly before its collapse:

> The economics profession egregiously overestimated the size and growth of, and was calamitously mistaken about, the Soviet economy. Thus, in the mid-1970s the C.I.A. had Soviet G.N.P. at 62 percent of U.S. G.N.P.; later, East Germany ahead of West Germany in per capita output. . . . These were consensus estimates among the allies and within the profession. Dale Jorgenson at Harvard has suggested that "this has to be one of the great failures of economics—right up there with the inability of economists . . . to find a remedy for the Great Depression of the 1930's."[18]

Those who make claims for the advantages of increasing our analytical approach to policy problems[19] must face up to the fact that our insufficient grasp of the structure of the tasks confronting policymakers, and our lack of theoretical knowledge, will defeat that effort. Indeed, students of social policy have found that to be the case.

Nathan Glazer, a prolific writer, a highly respected sociologist, and a long-time student of government policy, has recently come to the conclusion that the analytical, rational organization of society can lead to disappointing surprises among those who have placed their hopes in rationality of thought and action. His remarks—and experience—deserve close attention. He examines in detail the role of social science in policy formation and notes the emphasis on order.

> A new discipline of policy sciences or policy studies expanded [in the 1960s], and new schools were founded to teach it [in] . . . a new age in which we would rationally and pragmatically attack our domestic social problems. We could relegate the ideological conflicts between conservatives and liberals and radicals to the past because we now knew more and because we had the tools, or were developing them, to do better.
>
> By the end of the 1960s I was not alone in thinking that something had gone wrong. . . . We seemed to be creating as many problems as we were solving.[20]

Note Glazer's emphasis on the price to be paid for bureaucratic, that is, rational, analytical organization:

> It remains true, in Britain as well as America, that the optimistic vision of social science guiding policy by the use of its knowledge of the fine structure of society, of how policy impinges on family, neighborhood, community, has faded considerably. One hears more and more voices raised against the impersonal administrator, the blind effects of large policies. The startling thing is that these policies were designed *precisely* to respond to human needs, to shore up families, to strengthen neighborhoods, ensure better care for damaged children, better rehabilitation for juvenile delinquents. The work of the modern state is increasingly a work for social ends: for better housing, health, education, treatment of the handicapped; for the overcoming of poverty and distress. Yet the modern state reminds one, in the descriptions of its critics, of a friendly but clumsy giant, who, in his efforts to help, tramples delicate and sensitive growths.
>
> In the United States housing and neighborhood policies are revised, sometimes radically, every few years, and with considerable input from social scientists. And yet the cry goes up ever louder that neighborhoods are ignored, are made incapable of

maintaining their distinctive values and integrity, very often just because of govern-ment policies, which make it difficult to maintain old buildings or to keep out undesir-able individuals and uses. Our welfare system also undergoes continual expansion and correction, again with input from social scientists. Despite all these changes, almost everyone agrees that welfare, or some feature of it, is damaging the family, encourag-ing family breakup, encouraging fathers to abandon children, even though many of the changes welfare has undergone in the past twenty years were designed to over-come just these untoward efforts.[21]

What produced these disappointments, recognized by all except those most en-trapped in ideology? Glazer offers a startling conclusion that will be an anathema to the advocates of analytical cognition. Because of their strong commitment to ratio-nality, the intelligentsia of the time failed to recognize the important *constructive role of the irrational* in society. Glazer returns to the work of Peter Berger and Richard Neuhaus,[22] as well as of Claude Levi-Strauss, in blaming "excessive rationality,"[23] and he quotes Berger and Neuhaus:

Liberalism's blindness can be traced to its Enlightenment roots. Enlightenment thought is abstract, universalistic, addicted to what Burke called "geometry" in social policy. The concrete particularities of mediating structures find an inhospitable soil in the lib-eral garden. There the great concern is for the individual ("the rights of man") and for a just public order, but anything "in between" is viewed as irrelevant, as even an obstacle, to the rational ordering of society. What lies in between is dismissed, to the extent it can be, as superstition, bigotry, or (more recently) cultural lag.[24]

Glazer then turns to the rivalry between intuition ("custom, tradition, irrational allegiance") and analytical cognition ("the rational ordering of society") discussed in Chapter 3:

[These authors] give a grand role to superstition—custom, tradition, irrational alle-giances—in the defense of liberty, one to which Tocqueville and Burke also pointed, as well as Démeunier, Renan, and Maine. I would emphasize too another role: custom, tradition, irrational allegiance give people a footing, an identity, a sense of modest security, all of which are private and public, dominate and spread a sense of helpless-ness among ordinary people. And yet it is just this—custom, tradition, irrational alle-giance, superstition—that modern social policy cannot accommodate itself to, despite all the shouting and advice from the sidelines by journalists and sociologists, anthro-pologists and architectural critics, socialists and free enterprisers. Despite every effort to adapt social policy to the needs of the fine structure of society, one senses, with some gloom, that it is not an easy task. It is easier to recognize these needs symboli-cally than to do something about them in concrete policy.[25]

Sobering as Glazer's remarks may be, no one will believe, or assert, that all efforts toward developing a rational, organized society should cease. That leaves us with this question: How far from either pole of the cognitive continuum should we move? If we don't go far enough from the intuitive pole, if we don't reduce intuition, if we don't do enough to order society so as to reduce the fallibility of our indicators, then we shall continue to suffer the consequences: inevitable error, unavoidable injustice. But if we go too far, try to remove the error in our indicators by insisting on large increases in social order, thus reducing individual opportunity to act irrationally, then we risk the dangers of the catastrophic errors associated with analytical cognition, that is, the likelihood of developing a totalitarian state, and more errors and more injustice. Havel would claim that we have already seen this happen in the Soviet Union and eastern Europe during the twentieth century. What he is seeking is an optimal point for policy formation on the cognitive continuum. Under these circumstances we should not be surprised to see the persistence of the cycling phenomenon described in Chapter 2.

## Premise 4: Dynamic Cognition

*Cognitive activities may move along the intuitive-analytic continuum over time; as they do so, the relative contributions of intuitive and analytical components to quasi-rationality will change. Successful cognition that maintains constancy with the environment inhibits movement; failure and loss of constancy stimulate it.*

In his essay devoted entirely to the analysis of Darwin's imagery in relation to the "tree of nature," H. E. Gruber notes that "it took about fifteen months from . . . [the drawing of the diagram] until Darwin grasped the principle of natural selection as a key operator giving the tree of life its form."[26]

Gruber's approach to the study of cognition is certainly atypical.[27] Virtually all researchers in experimental psychology have chosen to use cognitive tasks that require no more than the college sophomore's fifty-minute hour at most, and it is not unusual for tasks to require only minutes—even seconds—of cognitive activity. Indeed, because the problems are so limited in time and scope, researchers seldom bother to record the time that their subjects take to solve them, unless the problem is so reduced that it becomes necessary to record time in milliseconds. If we simply observe the length of time (years, in many cases) that many significant problems have required (and received) from their subjects, we will see that the tasks used in current judgment and decision research are unrepresentative of normal circumstances of everyday life with respect to the dimension of time.[28]

On the other hand, many judgments and decisions even very important ones are made in brief periods of time, perhaps in a few minutes at the end of several weeks' or months' discussion. Often there is virtually no time for thought; therefore, much of the work that involves tasks requiring only moments is in fact representative of at least some tasks outside the laboratory, particularly those considered "stressful." Nevertheless, the restriction of research to those situations that *permit* very little time points to one obvious limitation to current generalizations about the cognitive competence of human beings. Time limitation should be kept in mind.

A more subtle restriction of generalization occurs in connection with the use of tasks that *require* little time from subjects, primarily because the subjects would not know how to use additional time if it were available to them. Much of the question-answering methodology used in the coherence research program uses problems of this type. In these tasks, the problem is stated in a few brief sentences and appears to be simple, but the proper solution requires that the subject have considerable statistical knowledge. Unless the subject has learned the necessary principles and has a fairly sophisticated understanding of probabilities, there is little the subject *could* do with an extended time period, even if it were available; unless the subject has the intellective means to *invent* the proper principle, more time would be of little use. Still, one must be cautious, as the following anecdote suggests.

A research assistant in our laboratory was presenting a group of subjects with many judgment and decision-making tasks that required knowledge of Bayes' Theorem for their solution. One subject stubbornly ignored the fifty-minute time limit, and the research assistant allowed him to continue. After roughly one hour and twenty minutes this subject (with little or no training in statistics or mathematics) discovered for himself Bayes' Theorem and thus produced the correct analytical solution to all the problems. How often such solutions might occur if it were possible to arrange for subjects to take hours, days, or weeks to work on such problems we don't know. Most of the current results regarding competence in judgment are contingent on the use of tasks in which people *require* only brief time periods because they lack the training in statistics or the logic of probability that would have given them the skills to solve the problem. In short, the manner in which time is treated is a critical dimension of a research program; it determines the results achieved and conclusions drawn.

Although judgment and decision-making researchers typically have been indifferent to the matter of time and generally employ tasks that require or allow only brief periods of time, students of problem-solving behavior often permit or require long periods. What difference does that make? The difference is that problem-solving research allows *movement* of cognition—from one pole to the other—on the cognitive continuum, a topic to which we now turn.

## Movement on the Cognitive Continuum

Consider the behavior of persons attempting to cope with a highly structured task, a problem in physics, say, or mathematics, that they expect to solve by analytical means. It is common to observe that problem-solvers proceed by trying an analytically derived solution, discovering failure, and, at that point, making a new attempt. When all analytically derived efforts fail, the subject's cognitive activity moves away from analysis to quasirationality; that is, the subject's cognitive activity begins to acquire elements of intuitive cognition. "Hunches" begin to guide behavior; undefended, perhaps indefensible, ideas spontaneously appear and affect decisions about what to do. If the problem is so difficult that "hunches" refined by analysis fail to provide a solution, then the subject's cognitive activity will move far enough along the cognitive continuum to become predominantly intuitive; cognition may consist almost entirely of pictorial imagery, as in the case of Darwin's "tree of nature." (A well-known example of the role of pictorial imagery is F. Kekule's reported discovery of the six-carbon benzine ring.)

But if the problem-solver finds that intuition provides an idea to be tested and is therefore sufficient to move him or her to an analytical mode (as, according to Dyson, it was in Feynman's case and as Gruber showed in Darwin's case), the subject may be said to move, not necessarily continuously or smoothly, from analysis through quasi-rationality to intuition and then back again to analysis. The path from the context of discovery to the context of verification is a cyclical one.

The concept of a cyclical, or better, oscillatory movement from intuition to analysis was described by the scientist and philosopher M. Polanyi:

To start working on a mathematical problem, we reach for pencil and paper, and throughout the stage of Preparation we keep trying out ideas on paper in terms of symbolic operations. If this does not lead straight to success, we may have to think the whole matter over again, and may perhaps see the solution revealed unexpectedly much later in a moment of Illumination. Actually, however, such a flash of triumph usually offers no final solution, but only the envisagement of a solution which has yet to be tested. In the verification or working out of the solution we must again rely therefore on explicit symbolic operations. Thus both the first active steps undertaken to solve a problem and the final garnering of the solution rely effectively on computations and other symbolic operations, while the more informal act by which the logical gap is crossed lies between these two formal procedures. However, the intuitive powers of the investigator are always dominant and decisive. Good mathematicians are usually found capable of carrying out computations quickly and reliably, for unless they command this technique they may fail to make their ingenuity effective—but their ingenuity itself lies in producing ideas. Hadamard says that he used to make more mistakes in calculation than his own pupils, but that he more quickly discovered them because the result did not *look* right; it is almost as if by his computations he had been *merely drawing a portrait* [italics added] of his conceptually prefigured conclusions. Gauss is widely quoted as having said: "I have had my solutions for a long time but I do not yet know how I am to arrive at them." Though the quotation may be doubtful it remains well said. A situation of this kind certainly prevails every time we discover what we believe to be the solution to a problem. At that moment we have the vision of a solution which *looks* right and which we are therefore confident to *prove* right.[29]

Here is Polanyi's description of the movement of cognition from intuition to analysis and the return:

The manner in which the mathematician works his way towards discovery, by shifting his confidence from intuition to computation and back again from computation to intuition, while never releasing his hold on either of the two, represents in miniature the whole range of operations by which articulation disciplines and expands the reasoning powers of man. This alternation is asymmetrical, for a formal step can be valid only by virtue of our tacit confirmation of it. Moreover, a symbolic formalism is itself but an embodiment of our antecedent unformalized powers—an instrument skillfully contrived by our inarticulate selves for the purpose of relying on it as our external guide. The interpretation of primitive terms and axioms is therefore predominantly inarticulate, and so is the process of their expansion and re-interpretation which underlies the progress of mathematics. The alternation between the intuitive and the formal depends on tacit affirmations both at the beginning and at the end of each chain of formal reasoning.[30]

Polanyi uses the word "alternation" to describe the movement from "intuition to computation and back again from computation to intuition," presumably because he has assumed the dichotomous view of the distinction between intuition and analysis.

Another student of scientific thought, N. R. Hanson, also emphasized the movement of cognition but, in addition, emphasized *continuity*, rather than "alternation," between the "intuitive and the formal": "[T]he *steps between* [italics added] visual pictures and statements of what is seen are many and intricate. Our visual consciousness is dominated by pictures; scientific knowledge is primarily linguistic. . . . Only by showing how picturing and speaking are different can one suggest how [they] may [be brought] together; and brought together they must be,"[31] as, for example, Darwin's diagram of the "tree of life" shows how they were indeed brought together in the construction of the theory of evolution. Thus, Hanson's remarks are consistent with the content of Premises 1 and 2.

These remarks are intended to raise the question of whether judgment and decision-making researchers have done justice to the role of time in relation to cognitive activity, whether they have given due consideration to the extent to which time is required for the relative contributions of intuition and analysis to cognition to become apparent. Gruber, Polanyi, Hanson, and others might well dismiss the negative view of intuition drawn by current researchers because it is based on a peculiar and misleading view of cognition derived from current research practices that provide only "snapshots" of cognitive activity that are unrepresentative of what human beings can and do accomplish when they are allowed to have the time to employ all the characteristics of cognition available to them. Gruber would argue that, if time were permitted, subjects would be able to make far better use of their pictorial imagery, as well as of the verbal and computational abilities demanded of them and the interchange or oscillation between them; that is, increased time would permit the analytical testing of the results of pictorial imagery for inconsistencies, contradictions, and fallacies, the return to imagery to envision the coherence of a result, the return to further analytical testing, and so on. Time would thus permit the cognizer to "work his way towards discovery, by shifting his confidence from intuition to computation and back again from computation to intuition, while never releasing his hold on either of the two," as Polanyi put it. These students of the history of science and scientists' thought may be wrong, of course, but it is clear that they do not ignore the full range of the continuum of cognitive activity of which human beings are capable.

What form does this movement on the cognitive continuum take? That is the topic I address next.

## Oscillation

If time permits a person to employ the full range of cognition, then cognition will *oscillate* over the cognitive continuum. For purposes of simplification I suggest that such oscillation takes the form of a sine wave.

I know of no other theoretician or researcher in the field of judgment and decision making who has put forward the hypothesis of oscillation, and I know of no definitive test of it. I was, however, able to begin a study of the occurrence of oscillation in the cognitive activity of medical students and their clinical teachers, and the results were generally encouraging—as preliminary results always are.[32]

Oscillation can, of course, occur at different rates, take different forms (e.g., sine or rectangular), and result in different degrees of efficiency and accuracy, as well as different types of error. Indeed, there may well be an optimal type and amount of oscillation that should take place in any task. If one accepts the concept of oscillation, then several interesting and important research questions occur. What is the relationship between different rates of oscillation on accuracy? On coherence? Does stress induce greater or lesser amounts of oscillation? Steeper or flatter curves?

In short, once the dimension of time is added to the theory of judgment and decision making, and once the dimension is placed in the context of the cognitive continuum, the observations of historians of science lead us to the concept of oscillation on the cognitive continuum. This in turn leads to a number of important hypotheses for policymakers' judgments. Although the empirical basis for oscillation is almost nonexistent, the rationale for its presence is intuitively compelling.

## Premise 5: Pattern Recognition and Functional Relations

*Human cognition is capable of pattern recognition and the use of functional relations.*

Recently H. Margolis reintroduced pattern recognition to the field of judgment and decision making by making it the centerpiece of a treatise.[33] Margolis's book is important if only because it points to a conceptual gap in judgment and decision-making theory and research. None of the research programs in the field of judgment and decision making explicitly acknowledge the possibility that pattern recognition might have a role in judgment and decision making. And pattern recognition was largely ignored in the judgment and decision-making literature (other than to deny empirical support for its presence) until Kahneman and Tversky introduced the concept of "representativeness" in the 1970s. Even these authors never employed the term "pattern," although "representativeness" could hardly have meant anything else. Neither does the term "pattern" appear in the indexes of the anthologies by H. R. Arkes and K. R. Hammond, B. Brehmer and C. R. B. Joyce, R. M. Hogarth, D. Kahneman, P. Slovic, and A. Tversky, or M. F. Kaplan and S. Schwartz,[34] or in the indexes of contemporary textbooks by J. Baron, R. Dawes, R. H. Hogarth, or S. R. Watson and D. M. Buede.[35] Neither is it present in reviews by K. R. Hammond, G. H. McClelland, and J. Mumpower, or P. Slovic and S. Lichtenstein,[36] in the judgment and decision-making glossary *Concepts in Judgment and Decision Research*,[37] in D. von Winterfeldt and W. Edwards's treatise.[38] Indeed, it is not to be found in any treatise on subjective expected utility theory that the author has seen.

D. E. Broadbent's treatment of the pattern recognition concept parallels that produced by the researchers in the judgment and decision-making tradition who searched for configurality in human judgment, particularly among clinical psychologists: "Throughout this book, we are leaving aside most of the problems of pattern perception as such; . . . our concern lies elsewhere." He concludes, "We have simply taken it for granted that somehow this process [of pattern perception] is achieved."[39] This conclusion is, however, exactly opposite from that reported by other judgment and decision-making researchers of the same period.

### Origins of Pattern Recognition

It was the gestalt psychologists of the first half of the twentieth century who made the concept of pattern so persuasive, as a descriptor of both environmental objects and events and cognitive activity. Patterns, or "gestalts," were set in sharp opposition to the reductive "elements" that constituted the units of cognition in nineteenth- and early-twentieth-century psychophysics, and countless demonstrations of the role of "good figure" and "wholeness" have been provided and remain a staple feature of introductory textbooks in psychology today. Gestalts, however, retain the ephemeral character that led to their demise as explanatory constructs. As W. R. Garner described it: "A gestalt is a form, a figure, a configuration, or a pattern. But gestalt is also the quality that forms, figures, and patterns have. . . . The school of psychology was given this name because of its emphasis on studying the form and pattern characteristics of stimuli, rather than on studying the elements which make a stimulus but which do not in and of themselves constitute the pattern."[40] Nevertheless, Garner noted, "It is not always clear just what we do mean by saying a pattern or figure is good or has goodness, but we certainly can agree that circles are good patterns, sequences almost as good. . . . The research seemed to produce as many explanations of pattern goodness as there were patterns to have goodness or to be good."[41] Garner offered a remedy (information theory) that has yet to be accepted as a general solution for the problem he described.

Gestalt psychology is a coherence theory, and all coherence theories seem to have the same advantages and disadvantages. The main advantage is that coherence induces a strong intuitive sense of validity bolstered by the perceiver's ability to point to clear examples, such as the circle or the square (which is why textbooks writers invariably offer them to students; the reader sees the importance of the idea immediately). The disadvantage, as Garner noted, lies in its difficulty of definition and measurement, which frustrates research and prevents it from getting beyond the demonstration stage of "see what I mean." (That problem is avoided by the coherence theorists in judgment and decision-making research because they have mathematical explications of rationality to support their claims of coherence.)

Although pattern recognition has largely been absent from the judgment and decision-making literature in the past quarter century, engineers interested in human performance in complex information-processing circumstances make a point of emphasizing the importance of pattern recognition. W. B. Rouse, an engineer with long experience in research on cognition, states flatly that "humans, if given a choice, would prefer to act as context-specific pattern recognizers than attempting to calculate or optimize."[42] N. Moray, an industrial psychologist expert in ergonomics and the design of systems displays, agrees with Rouse but claims that preference for patterns is a source of error, thus once more contributing to the uncertain value of pattern recognition. He states, for example, that "people tend to *avoid reasoning* [italics added] their way to solutions, and prefer to pattern match. When pattern matching, people decide that a present situation is identical to one that has occurred before and that it is more or less resembles."[43] Moray calls this "similarity matching," as do others.[44] Thus, Moray pits similarity matching against reasoning.

Computer scientists have also given pattern recognition a prominent place in their work.[45] Nonetheless, judgment and decision-making researchers tend to see pattern recognition only as a source of error. R. M. Hogarth, for example, uses this concept in an important way in his textbook: "In particular, since people are motivated to order and make sense of their world, they have tendencies to seek patterns where none exist and to make unjustified causal attributions."[46] He does not index the word "pattern," perhaps thus showing his disdain for this concept. This is an orientation long established in judgment and decision-making research. Hogarth's point of view is also taken by A. R. Feinstein in his classic work *Clinical Judgment*, in which he states: "Gestalt observations [those which do not distinguish between description, designation, and diagnosis] are a major source of error in physical examinations and help perpetuate the errors in the clinicians who perform and teach the process."[47] Feinstein then gives us more detail; he makes the psychological observation that gestalts "close the observer's mind to the possibility that the observed entity may represent something other than the conclusion assumed in the gestalt,"[48] thus putting his finger on a danger peculiar to pattern recognition—namely, the emotional satisfaction of recognizing a pattern and therefore not seeking further information or testing other hypotheses. Feinstein notes that gestalts "prevent the physician from recording the evidence that can help him distinguish why he was wrong if his conclusions are later found to be erroneous."[49]

But it can no longer be taken for granted that pattern seeking leads only, or inevitably, to errors of judgment. Pattern seeking and pattern recognition are useful cognitive activities when employed in appropriate circumstances—that is, on tasks that offer coherence that we can recognize, either through our natural capacities to do so or through our trained capacities to do so. The reintroduction of the concept of pattern recognition to the psychology of judgment and decision making requires, however, the refinement of concepts concerning representation of the environment, now offered in terms of mental models, images, prototypes, or templates. Because pattern recognition implies that the person holds some prior idea of what is subsequently "recognized," the researcher is therefore required to say a priori exactly what is "held" in a cognitive system. One should, for example, distinguish between those cognitive templates that are organized on the basis of natural capacities and those that depend on trained capacities.

## Alternation Between the Use of Indicators and Patterns

The argument between gestalt psychologists and stimulus response psychologists that so sharply divided the field in the first half of the twentieth century is surely an anachronism as far as modern researchers are concerned. Both "element" and "pattern" seem to be irrelevant to current topics. Although the term "element" means nothing to modern researchers, the persistent use of the term "stimulus" in the judgment and decision-making literature indicates a failure to bring theoretical and experimental language in line with practice. The term "stimulus" has long outlived its usefulness; it has no meaning in the context of a field that considers "information processing" or "information integration" to be a fundamental feature of cognitive activity.

But if the concepts of "element" and "stimulus" have become outmoded, does that mean that the gestalt psychologists' "pattern" has become dominant? Hardly. We have seen that "pattern" is nowhere to be found in judgment and decision-making research aside from Margolis's book.[50] The argument now lies between those who consider only the coherence point of view and those who consider only the correspondence point of view. Research based on mathematical, "normative" theories[51] ignores multiple fallible indicators and focuses on rationality; research based on the lens model, on the other hand, focuses on nothing but indicators and functional relations.

Perhaps the most important reason for the absence of the concept of pattern in current judgment and decision-making research is the failure of the early judgment and decision-making researchers to find any evidence for it in the judgments and predictions of clinical psychologists who were among their first subjects. Indeed, the failure to find anything but the simplest form of cognitive activity involving functional relations led to the dismissal of the idea that information was organized in terms of patterns or configurations by human beings, even by those who claimed that pattern seeking was their primary mode of cognition and the mode of cognition that made their services indispensable. Functional relations—and only the simplest ones— appeared to be all that mattered.

It is nonetheless impossible to ignore the role of pattern and coherence in visual and other forms of perception as demonstrated by the gestalt psychologists. And it is also impossible to ignore the role of coherence in other forms of cognitive activity, such as the narrative. Although the concept of pattern still contains conceptual difficulties, therefore I believe that it deserves a place in judgment and decision-making theory. It does so in Premise 5, which asserts that over time—an *alternation*, a complete shift from one to the other, takes place between reliance on correspondence and reliance on coherence. Thus, by introducing the dimension of time into judgment and decision-making theory, we can identify two new concepts— oscillation (Premise 4) and alternation (Premise 5). Oscillation (a continuous change) takes place between intuition and analysis; alternation (a dichotomous change) takes place between the reliance on coherence and the reliance on correspondence.

Indeed, it is precisely oscillation between intuition and analysis that permits cognition to become quasirational as it approximates one pole or the other. That is, oscillation permits a compromise-quasirationality—as cognitive activity moves along the cognitive continuum (as Pepper and others have explained). That is not the case when cognition changes from seeking functional relations (operating in the correspondence mode) to seeking or recognizing patterns (operating on the coherence model). There is no compromise here; this change is all or none; one cannot engage in some of one and some of the other, as one can with intuition and analysis. A good example of an information environment that offers both a correspondence (functional relations) approach and a coherence (pattern-seeking) approach is that provided for meteorologists. Modern meteorologists have a "menu" of more than a thousand ways of representing the weather available in their work stations. Some of these offer *patterns* of information (fronts, entire weather "pictures," such as are offered in the newspaper but, of course, with far more detail), some offer *indicators* (e.g., barometric readings, temperature gradients), and some offer both on the same display. Meteorologists can (and do) alternate between presentations, first calling for pattern (coherence) information, then calling for indicator (correspondence) information or, when both types of information are offered on the same display, alternating between them. Which is the most effective way to present and use this information is unknown. It has never been considered.

### The Narrative

One of the most frequently used forms for reaching a judgment—either for oneself or to persuade another—is by means of a narrative, which is another form of achieving coherence, making sense of a series of events. But this is a topic that lies almost untouched by judgment and decision researchers, although there is a substantial literature now available. My primary reason for including this topic is to encourage other to pursue the matter of the narrative as a judgment process on equal footing with that of the more familiar kinds. Reid Hastie and Nancy Pennington are prominent among the judgment and decision-making researchers who have begun the pursuit of this topic.[52] They are persuaded by studies of jury decision making that the predominant decision-making process involves the creation of a coherent story. Hastie indicates that "a 'narrative' structure is imposed on evidence as it is comprehended by a juror who is making a decision."[53] He believes that "empirical research supports the 'psychological validity' of story structures as descriptions of jurors' representations of evidence and demonstrates that the juror's story structure predicts his or her decision."[54] Hastie offers a detailed description of how the narrative functions as a determiner of the juror's decisions. In his view, the coherence of a story plays a key role in the acceptability of the story and its use in decision making. (The strain toward coherence is evident in Judge John Davies's effort to construct a narrative that would lead to a mitigation of the mandatory sentence he was required to reach for the two white Los Angeles police officers convicted of the beating of Rodney King, a black motorist, described in Chapter 12.)

One cognitive psychologist who has taken the process of narration very seriously is Jerome Bruner.[55] His books on the subject should eventually bring the topic closer to mainstream judgment and decision-making research. Curiously, however, pressure to do this may well come from a very different source—engineering. Henry Petroski, a well-known professor of engineering, explains the virtues of storytelling for engineers, if not for others, in his prize-winning book *Design Paradigms*. He does so in the context of reminding engineers of the "scale effect," a term he uses to point to the fact that one cannot always solve problems by simply making an effective tool bigger. (Current designers of airplanes, office buildings, and trucks, for example, face this problem.) Petroski wants not only to make his point about the scale effect—he thinks it is too often ignored even today—but to direct the attention of engineers to the value of storytelling in relation to teaching. After providing a fascinating discussion of the recognition of the scale effect in the first century B.C., which he contrasts to the modern failure to detect it and the disasters that have occurred because of that failure, he says this about the importance of the narrative for engineers:

> The story of Diognetus . . . has its greatest value for modern design in pointing out the limitations of size in a memorable way. The very details of the story, the names of the designers and the commonness of the materials used to . . . serve to make it real and thereby more effective. This paradigm is not an anonymous and dry rule such as "models

cannot be scaled up indefinitely," but rather a human drama full of sights and smells. Such associations with design problems should not be seen as distracting so much as making the lessons more effective.[56]

Petroski then reveals his theory of "similarity matching" by expressing his hopes for educating engineers:

> If paradigms such as this can become more regularly a part of the lore and language of engineering, so that the mere mention of Callias or Diognetus, for example, brings to mind the cautions that must go with scaling up designs, then perhaps the ageless caveats about scale will be more heeded and large-scale errors in design can be averted. If vivid case studies of failure attributable to scale effects do nothing else than cause designers to treat with more suspicion their scaled up versions of successful designs, there is reason to believe that the mistakes of the past will not be thoughtlessly repeated.[57]

Petroski's own work offers excellent examples of narrations that may well serve the goals he hopes they will.

## Summary

I began Part II with the goal of presenting a simple, new, and powerful unifying idea that provides a general theory of judgment and decision making. That idea is the existence of a cognitive continuum, paralleled by a task continuum. The theory is elucidated in terms of five premises that are intended to be sufficiently general and comprehensive to accommodate the major conceptual frameworks that are currently present in the field. These are:

1. The traditional dichotomy between intuition and analysis is a conceptual barrier to research as well as being demonstrably false. The dichotomy should be replaced by a continuum.
2. The cognitive continuum that replaces the dichotomy allows for the analysis of common sense and the specification of the properties of quasirationality, the most common form of cognitive activity in judgment and decision making.
3. The properties of the task—the information environment—induce a matching form of cognitive activity; if the policymaker's information environment consists of analysis- (or intuition-) inducing properties, then judgments and decisions will be made accordingly.
4. Cognition applied to policy problems is rarely static; cognitive activity will move along the cognitive continuum over time, and thus the relative contribution of intuition and analysis will change. Psychologists have only recently begun to study this phenomenon; little is known about the conditions that lead to specific changes. The theory asserts, however, that successful cognition inhibits movement; failure stimulates it. The theory also asserts that when movement occurs, cognition oscillates between analysis and intuition.
5. Human cognition is capable of recognizing patterns as well as making use of functional relations. Pattern recognition has barely been touched by judgment and decision-making researchers. The present theory, however, asserts that cognition alternates between coherence-seeking (pattern-seeking) and correspondence-seeking explanations—that is, seeking functional relations between indicators and targets.

Oscillation between intuition and analysis allows for the appearance of quasi-rationality, the compromise between them; alternation between pattern recognition and functional relations does not allow for compromise.

This is not the place for spelling out the manner in which this can be accomplished. My principal goal has been to present a theory that allows some major ideas about human judgment to be applied to the topic of social policy formation. That is the subject of Part IV.

# 8 Reducing Tension Through Complementarity

Tension exists between the coherence and the correspondence approaches to judgment and decision making largely because of differences in conclusions regarding the cognitive competence of *Homo sapiens*. Coherence theorists have encouraged the conclusion that human beings suffer from cognitive illusions and are thus incompetent in their judgments under uncertainty. But many researchers have disputed that conclusion. S. Epstein, for example, conducted a review that led him to emphasize the positive contributions of intuitive cognition, which the coherence theorists denigrate. He asserted that "the experiential system [as opposed to the intellectual, analytical system] is generally adaptive in concretive, natural situations, and *therefore* [italics added] people are unlikely to make CEs [cognitive errors] in situations that arise in everyday living"[1]—exactly opposite from the conclusions drawn by coherence theorists. Epstein is not alone. I therefore present four critiques that are illustrative of, but do not exhaust, the negative reactions to the conclusions offered by coherence theorists. One follows from the research by R. E. Nisbett;[2] others are offered by G. Gigerenzer,[3] L. L. Lopes and G. C. Oden,[4] and P. Suedfeld and P. E. Tetlock.[5] An overview and summary of these critiques is provided by J. M. Fraser, P. J. Smith, and J. W. Smith Jr.[6] Following these critiques, I suggest that the coherence and the correspondence views should coexist, despite their opposing conclusions, because their differences are complementary rather than contradictory.

## Critiques of Negative Views of Coherence Competence

### Nisbett: Education Matters

If we accept the pessimistic conclusion that people are deficient in their judgments made under uncertainty, then it is only natural to ask: Why not teach, or train, people to overcome their deficiencies? A few serious, systematic efforts were made to train people to overcome or avoid errors of judgment during the 1980s. These were usually carried out in terms of what was called "debiasing," that is, removing the "biases" that D. Kahneman and P. Tversky and their colleagues claim to be widespread. But efforts to "debias" have largely been deemed to be unsuccessful.[7] These studies generally lead to the conclusion that "things are even worse than we thought"; not only is judgment incompetent, it resists remedial efforts. That conclusion is startling; it suggests that *Homo sapiens* are not only "fundamentally irrational" as indeed the coherence view emphasizes,[8] but that we cannot be taught to be otherwise, a strange conclusion in view of the fact that thousands, if not tens of thousands, of people are taught the principles of probability each year and that problems in probability are included in college admissions tests and apparently solved correctly by some applicants.

By 1987, however, R. E. Nisbett and his colleagues, who had believed the pessimistic conclusions so strongly advocated by the heuristics and biases researchers, began to reach different conclusions:

> Research suggests a much more optimistic view: even brief formal training in inferential rules may enhance their use for reasoning about everyday life events. Previous theorists may have been mistaken about trainability, in part because they misidentified the kind of rules that people use *naturally* [italics added].[9]

D. R. Lehman, R. O. Lempert, and R. E. Nisbett[10] reiterated this argument, as did Lehman and Nisbett, in a later article, drawing similar conclusions:

> The effects of undergraduate training in the natural sciences, humanities, and social sciences on inductive reasoning requiring the use of statistical and methodological principles and on reasoning about problems in conditional logic were examined. Social science training produced large effects on statistical and methodological reasoning, whereas natural science and humanities training produced smaller, but still marginally significant, effects. Natural science and humanities training produced large effects on ability to reason about problems in conditional logic, whereas social science training did not.[11]

In the book in which he summarizes his change in views, Nisbett states:

> Ten years ago, I held a version of the received views about reasoning. I was dubious that people had any abstract rules for reasoning and confident that even if they did, such rules could not be taught. Indeed, I had just completed 10 years of work that seemed to me to give substantial support to these views. I had worked on questions of reasoning about human social behavior, finding that people often violated the requirements of statistical, causal, and even logical rules of inference. This work was very much in the tradition of Kahneman and Tversky's research showing that people substitute simple judgmental heuristics for the more formal inferential rules that are necessary to solve the problems they gave their subjects. I believed not only that my subjects did not possess the necessary statistical rules, I believed that instruction in statistics resulted only in inserting a sterile set of formal rules that could make contact only with scientific problems or problems for which there existed some massive and probably ecologically uncommon cue triggering their use.[12]

Nisbett had previously believed that his subjects did not "possess the necessary statistical rules" and that they had not learned such rules as part of their ordinary experience in the world. Worse still, he believed, even if his subjects were taught such rules, they would not be likely to use them. But then he reconsidered.

The event that prompted Nisbett's reconsideration of the accepted "pessimistic" views occurred during what was to be a demonstration of one of Kahneman and Tversky's standard examples of the failure of probabilistic reasoning.

To my surprise, most of the students got the problem right. I then asked students to indicate how much statistics they had had. . . . The results were clear-cut. The students who had had no statistics duplicated the pattern of the Kahneman and Tversky subjects, those who had had at least one course in statistics were unlikely to get the problem wrong. Subsequent work showed that there was no anomaly here. Problems that Kahneman and Tversky had looked at [i.e., that is, had used to test their subjects], . . . turned out to be *highly influenced* [italics added] by statistical training.[13]

The implications of this systematic series of studies are clear: Whatever the validity of the negative views of coherence competence, training in statistical reasoning can prevent (or reverse) the putative failures in judgments and predictions under uncertainty so often cited. This is a significant result because Kahneman and Tversky had, in the course of a twenty-year research program, carried out studies that demonstrated that people apparently are *inherently* unable to reason under uncertainty correctly. But they had never systematically pursued the possibility that this putative flaw was due simply to a lack of statistical education. Once this was done, the results showed that education mattered. Nisbett and his colleagues showed that people are capable of proper statistical reasoning once they are taught how to do it.

Nisbett's solution to the puzzle of "cognitive illusions" was direct and simple: Teach people what they need to know. And it worked; his students did not exhibit the "cognitive illusions" previously taken to be ubiquitous and impervious to instruction. The view prior to Nisbett's work was that cognitive illusions—errors in judgment—were due to some inherent persistent flaw in cognitive functioning—inherent and persistent because of their invulnerability to education and training. That proved to be wrong. Learning to make proper statistical inferences turned out to be much like learning similar quasi-mathematical material—difficult but not impossible to acquire.

The serious implications of the conclusions regarding our cognitive incompetence in the use of the probability calculus were picked up by a mathematician who regularly writes about our mathematical incompetence, particularly in relation to probability. John Paulos included several examples from the work of Kahneman and Tversky among his hundreds of examples of regularly recurring mathematical incompetence. After noting that "probability enters our lives in a number of different ways," he asserts that "any sufficiently complex phenomenon, even if it's completely deterministic, will often be amenable only to probabilistic simulation."[14] He goes so far as to say that "giving due weight to the fortuitous nature of the world is, I think, a mark of maturity and balance" (see the remarks by David Brooks cited in Chapter 1). What should the remedy be for all this immaturity, for all those who do not accept the indubitable fact of irreducible uncertainty in our lives? His answer is clear (if unusual): "May they all burn in hell for 10 years (just kidding) *or* (italics added) take a course in probability theory."[15] (It is not obvious whether Paulos intended to indicate that these alternatives are equally painful!)

At this point, readers may find the question of our competence with regard to problems in probability theory bordering on the trivial, if not the absurd. Had researchers declared that they had discovered that persons *untrained* in the differential calculus (which focuses on physical problems of time and motion) make errors when asked to solve calculus problems, whereas those *trained* in calculus do not, the announcement would hardly have attracted attention. And it certainly would be considered an absurd topic for research. What is the problem that needs to be studied? Why did psychologists think the parallel situation regarding persons untrained in the probability calculus was not absurd?

There were several reasons. First, psychologists have always been enthusiastic about discovering human error and are increasingly so; the discovery of accuracy and competence does not make news, whereas the discovery of error and incompetence does. Admittedly, that professional bias hardly excuses the absurdity, but it is so pervasive that it deserves comment. The second reason is more defensible. The results of these studies were broadly generalized as discoveries of fundamental flaws in the most esteemed aspects of human nature—our ability to think. *That's* news! Third, the errors were described as due to "cognitive illusions" analogous to those perceptual illusions that are also dear to psychologists' hearts as compelling examples of human error, so easily demonstrated in the pages of introductory textbooks that they have appeared in them for over half a century. From perceptual illusions—now well known—to "cognitive illusions"—a new idea—was a powerful generalization indeed; this too deserved attention, and got it. Fourth, the basis of the research was startlingly simple; one could ask a person (what appeared to be) very simple questions (e.g., which is more likely in a sequence of coin tosses: HTHTHT or HHHTTT?), get the wrong answer from the subject (does the reader know the right answer?), and thus pronounce an "illusion." No mysterious statistical calculations, no hard-to-follow experiments, no complicated theory, just simple, obvious demonstrations in which (most) people provide the wrong answer. (The right answer is that the sequences are equally likely.) Fifth, there were some indications that even "experts" were susceptible to these illusions. Sixth, efforts to teach people how to overcome them, as noted earlier, seemed ineffectual. All of this began to acquire the aura of "discovery," the discovery of something very fundamental—and very disturbing—indeed.

But perhaps the most important reason that these results were accepted with enthusiasm is that they are not irrelevant to our daily pursuits; irreducible uncertainty is not only highly prevalent but highly salient in our experience, whereas calculus problems are not. Paulos's quote from Pascal catches the idea: "We sail within a vast sphere, ever drifting in uncertainty."[16] The words "probable," "maybe," "unlikely," and "uncertain" occur so frequently in our conversations—especially important conversations—that we hardly notice them. Therefore, when we are told that we suffer from "illusions," that we are incompetent in our reasoning under uncertainty, virtually anyone will agree that we *should* pay attention. As Kahneman and Tversky observed:

> The emphasis on the study of errors is characteristic of [our] research in human judgment, but it is not unique to this domain. We use illusions to understand the principles of normal perception [the perception researchers Brunswik and Gibson and many others deny this] and we learn about memory by studying forgetting [but A. Baddeley[17] and others criticize this approach]. Errors of reasoning, however, are unique among cognitive failures in two significant respects: They are somewhat embarrassing and they appear avoidable.[18]

Thus, despite some debatable declarations, they make the undeniable point that these "errors of reasoning . . . are somewhat embarrassing"; somewhat less convincing is the statement that "they appear avoidable."

There can be no doubt that errors in judgment are taken seriously because we are jealous of our reputation for good judgment. As La Rochefoucauld said, "Everyone complains about their memory; no one complains about their judgment." The quality of our judgment is an important criterion for defining our place among our peers; it determines our respectability among intellectuals, politicians, or gang members. Therefore, when the announcements that fundamental deficiencies in human judgment had been discovered were made, they were rapidly accepted, first, by the judgment and decision-making research community, then by psychologists, and eventually by others in business schools, medicine, engineering, and even international relations. In short, these results were seen as cogent by a wide variety of disciplines and will continue to be seen as such, despite criticisms to which I now turn.

## Gigerenzer: Theory Matters

While Nisbett and his colleagues were discovering that education mattered, others were criticizing the research that produced the negative conclusions; G. Gigerenzer was the most vigorous and most empirically oriented. He carried out experiments intended to show that conclusions drawn by Tversky and Kahneman were wrong.[19] His criticisms are well informed and thorough and represent a formidable attack on the conclusion that human judgment is an irrational, incompetent process.

Gigerenzer took the correspondence point of view, developed a theory of probabilistic mental models based on Brunswikian theory and method, and attacked the coherentist view in several articles. The abstract for an article written in 1991 is instructive:

Most so-called "errors" in probabilistic reasoning are in fact *not* violations of probability theory. Examples of such "errors" include overconfidence bias, conjunction fallacy, and base-rate neglect. Researchers have relied on a very narrow normative [i.e., "coherence"] view, and have ignored conceptual distinctions—e.g. single case versus relative frequency—fundamental to probability theory. By recognizing and using these distinctions, however, we can make apparently stable "errors" disappear, reappear, or even invert. I suggest what a reformed understanding of judgments under uncertainty might look like.[20]

In the same vein Gigerenzer, G. Hoffrage, and H. Kleinbölting state:

Research on people's confidence in their general knowledge has to date produced two fairly stable effects, many inconsistent results, and no comprehensive theory. . . . [Our] theory (a) explains both the overconfidence effect (mean confidence is higher than percentage of answers correct) and the hard-easy effect (overconfidence increases with item difficulty) reported in the literature, and (b) predicts conditions under which both effects appear, disappear, or invert. In addition, (c) it predicts a new phenomenon, the confidence-frequency effect, a systematic difference between a judgment of confidence in a single event (i.e., that any given answer is correct) and a judgment of the frequency of correct answers in the long run. Two experiments are reported that support PMM theory by confirming these predictions, and several apparent anomalies reported in the literature are explained and integrated into the present framework.[21]

In short, Gigerenzer explains away the numerous findings of incompetence in judgment that are produced by those who pursue the coherence point of view. He does so by criticizing the research and by using a correspondence theory to predict when such errors will and will not occur.

Gigerenzer thus pits the relative frequency approach to probability—a correspondence view—against the subjectivist approach (in the extract he refers to the "single case")—a coherence view. This is one of the few occasions in which this controversy has erupted in the field of judgment and decision making. Gigerenzer makes clear that his arguments are based on Brunswikian theory and method.

Gigerenzer also challenges the assumption that there exists a single norm for evaluating rationality ("Uncontroversial norms: A single yardstick for rationality?") and argues that we cannot defend the use of a single normative (i.e., coherence) theory by which to judge competence, for there are many coherence theories.[22] He challenges the interpretation of each of the standard problems used by Tversky and Kahneman. He further objects that in these problems context and content are ignored but should not be. He argues that "by choosing a proper content and context, you then will be able to produce reasoning that either does or does not follow a given formal rule, or any point in-between."[23] To support his case, Gigerenzer shows that, if the content of the problem used by Tversky and Kahneman is changed from engineers and lawyers to soccer games, the results are reversed.[24] In general, then, Gigerenzer rejects the entire set of conclusions put forward by Kahneman and Tversky on both theoretical and empirical grounds. His arguments have not been directly answered as yet.

### Lopes and Oden: Method Matters

Lopes and Oden also present a detailed analysis of the question of the competence of human judgment and provide a critical review of the experiments that have been conducted by Kahneman and Tversky and their supporters: They conclude, as does Gigerenzer, that faulty research has led to false conclusions.

They begin their analysis of the question of competence by pointing out the anomaly that has arisen within the fields of cognitive psychology and cognitive science, including artificial intelligence. They describe the anomaly—and it is indeed an anomaly—as follows:

> On the one hand, there is a large body of research that documents striking failures of naive humans when confronting relatively simple tasks in probability theory, decision making, and elementary logic. [Here they are referring to the research by Kahneman and Tversky and colleagues.] On the other hand, there is the continuing belief of psychologists and computer scientists that by understanding human problem solving performance we will be better able to build machines that are truly intelligent. One can only wonder at the puzzlement of lay readers who come across articles like one published recently in *Newsweek* that spent several columns describing people's failures at decision making in scathing terms ("sap", "sucker", "woefully muddled") only to conclude that researchers hope to "model human decision makers' rules of thumb so that they can be reduced to computer software" and so speed the progress of artificial intelligence, the aim of which is "not to replace humans but to give them an important tool."[25]

Lopes and Oden were slightly ahead of their time in pointing out this anomaly. The "puzzlement" of lay persons is only now reaching the researchers. That AI researchers, on the one hand, should be desperately trying to capture what they consider the most powerful aspect of human cognition—its "intuition," or "common sense"—while judgment and decision researchers, on the other hand, are proclaiming that process to be fundamentally flawed is surely an anomaly. D. Crevier's recent book, *The Tumultuous History of the Search for Artificial Intelligence*, makes it clear enough that AI's failure to cope with problems that require even a minimum of "common sense" has been its greatest embarrassment.[26] At present the successes of AI lie in the development of "small" expert systems, those computer programs that carry out stepwise, analytically based procedures that mimic the clearly understood and clearly defensible rule-based problem-solving procedures readily explainable by experts but that have little relation to the power of human cognition. What AI has striven for—and has failed so far to achieve—is to reproduce the intuitive powers of human cognition, exactly those that, Lopes and Oden point out, Tversky and Kahneman and their colleagues[27] are telling us we should avoid using.

Having pointed to this puzzle—one field of research denigrating what another hopes to achieve—Lopes and Oden suggest that there is a different kind of cognitive activity than that employed in the laboratory tasks that demonstrate incompetence namely, that competence which is applied in the world outside the laboratory. The point of departure for Lopes and Oden is

> to suggest that the apparent failures people manifest in many laboratory tasks actually signal the operation of a quite different kind of intelligence than is implied by conventional notions of rationality, an intelligence reflecting the properties of the massively parallel computational system that has evolved to meet the requirements of existence in a noisy, uncertain, and unstable world.[28]

Thus Lopes and Oden distinguish between two different sorts of intelligence; moreover, one of these "evolved." This distinction between "intelligence" and "rationality" parallels the distinction between correspondence and coherence that is the essence of the framework used in this book.

Following a description of the heuristics that Kahneman and Tversky believe are responsible for incorrect decisions—that is, decisions that fail to conform to probability theory—Lopes and Oden offer a critique of the "assumptions underlying heuristics and biases research."[29] In a nutshell, they argue:

> The first assumption is that elementary probability theory provides a good first-order approximation to understanding the uncertainty in natural situations. Almost certainly this is false, as can be verified by perusing some of the serious attempts by statistical experts to apply probability models to real-world problems.[30]

This is a strong assertion, for Lopes and Oden are arguing that the coherence of probability theory should not be used as an argument for its correspondence value, a clear example of *tension*. Moreover, they go on:

> [R]esearch on heuristics tends to hide this assumption by carefully selecting word-problem domains in which some simple statistical idea does hold and then subtly switching the emphasis when the question is posed to subjects.[31]

Can this be true? They provide an example in connection with the following problem used by Kahneman and Tversky:

> All families of six children in a city were surveyed. In 72 families the exact order of births of boys and girls was GBGBBG. What is your estimate of the number of families surveyed in which the exact order of births was BGBBBB?[32]

(Note: Readers should try to answer this question and then ask themselves how confident they are in their answer.) Lopes and Oden argue:

> Almost everyone has reasonably sound qualitative intuitions about likely *ratios* [italics added] of boys to girls in families of various sizes. But the experimental problem concerns *sequences* [italics added] of births. Here people appear either not to know that all birth sequences with a given N are equally likely or not even to recognize that the problem is asking about sequences (it is impossible to tell which) suggesting that birth sequence in human families is unimportant enough that intuitions about sequences are undeveloped in this particular area.[33]

Further assumptions are described and criticized in a similar fashion; these authors intend to leave their readers doubting the negative conclusions, doubts that should be raised because of faulty research.

It is easy to sympathize with their criticism. One might ask why a person should be asked to solve problems found at the end of a chapter in a textbook on statistics before taking the class or reading the book. Lopes and Oden could also have pointed to the problem frequently employed by Kahneman and Tversky to show the incompetence of the layperson:

> There are two programs in a high school. Boys are a majority (65%) in program A, and a minority (45%) in program B. There is an equal number of classes in each of the two programs. You enter a class at random, and observe that 55% of the students are boys. What is your best guess—does the class belong to program A or to program B?[34]

Lopes and Oden would ask: Why should anyone untutored in the statistical method be expected to provide the exactly correct answer to this question *before* taking the course? Does the reader know the answer?

In addition to the objections to the experimental methods used and the problems chosen, Lopes and Oden take pains to explain the difference between intelligence and rationality—a matter to which I will return in later chapters. Their goal is to point out the general robustness of intelligence in contrast to the fragility of rationality, as well as the narrowness and specificity of its application; intelligence, they might have said, is "robust," whereas rationality offers "precision." They believe that Kahneman and Tversky and their followers have greatly overemphasized rationality as a standard for the competence of human judgment and essentially ignored the importance and robustness of intelligence. This brings them back to their earlier observation of two forms of cognitive activity, one of which has "evolved," the other of which has been created by ourselves.[35] And they ask, "Why *didn't* extensional reasoning [e.g., the probability calculus] arise as a fundamental feature of biological intelligence?"[36] Their final paragraph is instructive in this regard:

> Rationality . . . is so much a human artifact that one never even speaks of artificial rationality. Like all things human this rationality is limited in its scope and usefulness

in a complex world. Intelligence is bigger, murkier, and more serious stuff. It has had to keep us alive, as a species and as individuals even at the cost of error. Robustness, generality, and practicability are the demands of life itself. They reside in intelligence because they must.[37]

The reader will encounter this distinction between rationality (coherence) and intelligence (correspondence) in many forms throughout this book; it is worth bearing in mind. Coherence is the name for systems that begin with premises and work their way according to logical and/or mathematical rules to conclusions. Correspondence is the name for systems that attempt to achieve empirically accurate relationships with the world of independently real objects and events. Also worth bearing in mind is that the distinction opens the way to establishing the complementarity of research programs that focus on coherence and those that deal with correspondence, a matter discussed later.

Finally, there is a simple criticism that can be—and often is—directed toward all studies that depend on coherence as the standard of truth. It is one that is stated with clarity by well-known students of medical decision making:

> If intuitive clinical decisions do not conform to the recommendations of a formal analysis . . . how can we decide whether human judgment is suboptimal in that instance or whether the model has been inadequately formulated [for that situation]? The standard view for some time has been that human judgment is easily susceptible to errors. . . . It may well be argued, however, that human judgment is influenced by aspects of the task that are excluded by the . . . model but ought to be included.[38]

These questions, A. S. Elstein and his colleagues assert, "will continue to occupy and perplex researchers in the field of clinical decision-making for some time."[39]

## Lopes: Details Matter

It is Lopes who has made the sharpest and most detailed criticism of the research conducted by Tversky and Kahneman. It is clear that she not only has decided that almost all conclusions reached by these coherence theorists are wrong, but that she resents the manner in which the conclusions regarding cognitive defects have been publicized by the authors as well as the press.[40] Lopes reaches conclusions about the research by examining very carefully the logic of the research and the details of the experiments upon which Tversky and Kahneman's conclusions depend.

She notes, for example, that the logic of the research follows what has been called "strong inference."[41] Strong inference is the experimental method that guarantees that one or the other of two hypotheses will be supported by the data. This is in contrast to the method of testing one hypothesis against the null hypothesis (or chance). But Lopes believes that strong inference in these studies is more apparent than real because examination of the details of the experiment show that in fact alternative plausible hypotheses explaining the results remain. For example, consider this problem used by Tversky and Kahneman: "Consider the letter R. Is R more likely to appear in the first position of a word or the third position of a word?"[42] This problem was used to demonstrate the "availability" heuristic. Tversky and Kahneman predict that most people will—incorrectly—say that the letter R is more likely to appear in the first position because it is easier to think of words beginning with R than words which have R in the third position. Because one answer supports the "people have correct knowledge" hypothesis whereas the other answer supports the "people use the availability heuristic," the method illustrates the "strong inference" method. In all cases, error is pitted against correctness. And in virtually all the research reported by Tversky and Kahneman, error prevails. But in examining the details of the letter R study, Lopes asks: "Why was the letter R chosen for study and not, say, B? Was it simply an arbitrary choice. The answer is no. Of the 20 possible consonants, 12 are more common in the first position and 8 are more common in the third position. All of the consonants that Kahneman and Tversky studied were taken from the third-position group even though there are more consonants in the first position group."[43]

This selection of *R* rather than, say, B appears to stack the deck in favor of the results Tversky and Kahneman wish to show. But Lopes says this is not so: "This selection of consonants was not malicious. Their use is dictated by the strong inference logic since only they yield unambiguous answers to the processing question."[44] But Lopes shows that the strong inference logic "constrains the interpretation of the data" in several problem situations used by these researchers. Her conclusion: "We can conclude that people use heuristics instead of probability theory but we cannot conclude that their judgments are generally poor. . . . [Yet] it is the latter, unwarranted conclusion that is most often conveyed by this literature, particularly in settings outside psychology"[45] And it is the "unwarranted conclusion" that bothers Lopes—and certainly bothers many others.

Her article proceeds in detailed fashion to attack the nature of the studies and the conclusions reached. After pointing to the "negative focus" in their papers, she shows that Tversky and Kahneman mislead when they draw an analogy between perceptual errors and cognitive biases. In my view, Lopes is certainly correct in this criticism.

Finally, the extravagant language used by these authors has drawn her resentment: "If Tversky and Kahneman call people's intuitions a 'multitude of sins'[46] and label their judgments with words like 'ludicrous,'[47] indefensible,'[48] and 'self defeating,'[49] why should we expect popular authors to display greater meekness in their choice of words?"[50]

### Suedfeld and Tetlock: Circumstances Matter

In their recent book, *Psychology and Social Policy*, P. Suedfeld and P. E. Tetlock examine the research by Tversky and Kahneman (as well as by I. Janis and others) and consider its implications for policymakers in a chapter entitled, "Psychological Advice About Political Decision Making: Heuristics, Biases, and Cognitive Defects."[51] They criticize the research on several grounds and conclude:

> In our judgment, the psychological literature (experimental and extrapolated) does not justify any serious belief that decision making is generally poor, nor that complex decisions (i.e., those not using shortcuts) are necessarily better than simple ones. This is true even for complicated situations and critical issues. We reject the view that human beings are cognitive misers, preferring to think of them (that is, us) as *cognitive managers.*[52]

Suedfeld and Tetlock base their conclusions on an examination of both the literal and the external validity of the research. They do not find the research conclusions compelling, largely because of the specificity of the research materials, the specific form of the problem, the specific phrasing of the questions, and the fact that when these are changed, the results change markedly (again, the problem of generalization of results).[53]

Their criticisms of the external validity of the research are equally severe. They take the position that "findings in laboratory situations—and even in the most convincing field experiments—can best be thought of as hypothesis generating, not hypothesis testing, in the study of high level decision making."[54] In other words, the research on heuristics and biases at best can only provide ideas that might prove interesting to test—somehow—in the context of true political decision making. It appears, however, that after examining the details of the research, Suedfeld and Tetlock do not find the conclusions regarding "cognitive defects" sufficiently well established even for that purpose. Their verdict: "not proved."[55]

### Views of a Mathematical Statistician

What does an expert in probability theory think about this? Fortunately, we have the views of a mathematical statistician, S. Zabell, on the question of people's competence in achieving coherence in their probability judgments. Zabell's views are important; he is a person with indubitable credentials with regard to the application of probability theory, but he has not participated in the debate so far.

Zabell issued a disclaimer—"I do not want to argue that probability theory can be employed as a serious tool in too many natural contexts"[56]—by which he presumably means "very many natural contexts." In this statement he seems to agree with a similar observation by Lopes and Oden quoted earlier. He points out that we should not think that because the statistical problems that are used by coherence theorists to demonstrate incoherence *look* easy (because they are stated in such a simple fashion), they are, *in fact*, easy. As he puts it,

> I find it helpful, when I get confused trying to think through some of the paradoxes . . . to have the theory [probability calculus] at my disposal and be able to use representations such as sample spaces and probabilities to analyze what is going on and to remove some of the confusions and obscurities that arise.[57]

Because he is a trained mathematical statistician, Zabell can turn to his knowledge to "analyze what is going on and to remove some of the confusions and obscurities that arise" in the problems that coherence theorists use to show the incompetence of their subjects. The untrained subjects who have not studied mathematics, probability, and statistics for the many years that Zabell has cannot of course, do that. As a result, their judgment and decision-making processes have been described as "irrational."

### Does Incoherence Matter?

J. W. Payne and his colleagues were influenced primarily by the work of Herbert Simon and of Kahneman and Tversky (particularly their ideas about the heuristics people employ to make judgments, decisions, and choices). As indicated earlier, the dominant idea among researchers between 1975 and 1990 was that people's judgment processes are seriously flawed; they do not meet the criteria of rationality.

Payne and his colleagues developed a broader view. Although they accepted Simon's suggestions regarding bounded rationality, they developed the hypothesis that the various heuristics that Kahneman and Tversky had suggested (along with others) as mechanisms by which judgments are made could be profitably thought of as cognitive *strategies*. In the preface to their book, *The Adaptive Decision Maker,* they observe that "over the past 20 years a number of different strategies used by people to solve decision problems have been identified."[58] They note that "as a consequence of using such selective heuristics, people sometimes make substantial decision errors"[59] and, most important, that "human decision behavior is highly sensitive to a wide variety of task and context factors." More specifically, they remark that "strategy selection . . . is highly contingent on the properties of the decision problem."[60]

The reader will recall that the correspondence view emphasizes the survival value of flexibility in the use of various sources of information (as did Darwin). Payne and his colleagues also refer to some contemporary researchers who emphasize "flexibility of response."[61] Although they do not reference Brunswik's 1952 introduction of flexibility in the use of information, one can anticipate that Payne and his colleagues will emphasize the adaptive value of that flexibility in response to a "wide variety of task and context factors." And they do: "Our hypothesis is that the [task] contingent use of strategies (heuristics) represents an intelligent response to decision problems." Indeed, they suggest that such *intelligent* [italics added; recall Lopes and Oden] decision makers will engage in a compromise between accuracy and effort. Finally, they write, "In short, we believe that individuals are adaptive decision makers."[62]

This is clearly an advance. Until this point the coherence view consisted largely of a collection of interesting results, an unremitting attack on human judgment but one lacking any organizing principle and in particular, a theory of judgment processes. Payne and his coauthors, however, pursued their hypothesis by engaging in a series of systematic studies. Because their experimental work is set forth in considerable detail in their book, I will not describe the experiments here. But it is important for us to contrast their approach with the usual steps taken and to consider the major concepts these researchers employ, particularly the concepts of accuracy and adaptation. What is it that their subjects are to be accurate about? And to what circumstances do they adapt? First, however, what did these researchers learn? And why do they refer to their subjects' behavior as *intelligent* (as do Lopes and Oden)?

Payne and his colleagues discovered what will surely be a surprise to many: "There is clear evidence that people often use decision strategies adaptively: They exhibit intelligent, if not optimal, responses to changes in such task and context variables."[63] And although "failures in adaptivity do occur," they "can be traced to such factors as difficulties in assessing task and context factors, deficits in knowledge of appropriate strategies, . . . difficulties in assessing effort and accuracy, and lack of ability to execute appropriate strategies."[64] In short, they provide us with a far different picture of judgment and decision making than the coherence theorists have been presenting. Their results show that judgment is not badly flawed; it is intelligent and adaptive. (These conclusions are in flat contradiction to those in Plous's 1993 textbook on judgment and decision making.)

These findings, among others, are very important; no doubt, they will influence the direction of theory and research concerning the competence of human judgment for some time. We must be cautious, however. Because the authors emphasize the "accuracy" and "adaptiveness" of their subjects, their readers will believe that this work furthers our knowledge about the accuracy of human judgment in general, including empirical accuracy related to real objects and events. But that is decidedly not the case. The work by Payne and his colleagues tells us nothing about *correspondence competence*. Rather, it tells us a great deal about *coherence competence*. That is, the research conducted by Payne and his colleagues changes the concept of adaptiveness from correspondence competence—empirical accuracy—to coherence— *conformance to a rule*. The authors thus define "accuracy" in the context of a normative theory; people are "accurate," and thus achieve coherence, if they make judgments in accordance with the calculations included in this rule.

Payne and his coauthors did not choose this type of accuracy naively or without considering its implications. They indicate that "use of information by rules like E[xpected] U[tility], represents a 'process' view of rationality: A good decision is seen as one that follows a good decision process." That is different from arguing that a good decision is one that provides the right answer. The authors appreciate this difference, for they note that "[a]lternatively one could define a good decision solely in terms of correspondence, that is, on the basis of the outcome that is experienced; a good decision is one that yields a good outcome."[65] It is clear that Payne and his colleagues are well aware of the fact that these are two very different ways of evaluating behavior, for they say that, "in the case of decisions involving risk or uncertainty, process and outcome measures of decision quality can differ." They make the nature of their choice clear by asking, "Is normative accuracy the only criteria [*sic*] for a good decision?"[66] The answer is no.[67]

Finally they state:

> We generally have emphasized a measure of accuracy that compares the performance of heuristic strategies (or an individual's choice) *relative* both to the upper limit on performance expected if one followed a strict expected value rule and to the lower baseline of performance in terms of E[xpected] V[alue], represented by a random choice rule.[68]

Payne and his colleagues thus not only recognize the difference between the coherence and correspondence approaches to judgment and decision making: they deliberately choose coherence as their measure of performance. In their study, the correct answer is an answer provided by the Subjective Expected Utility rule, not by real objects or events. (Earlier we saw Herbert Simon's sharp rejection of this rule as wholly irrelevant to human judgment.)

Think for a moment how Darwin might have reacted to this research program as the authors describe it. Surely he would have admired, as I do, the authors' efforts to carry out a systematic, broad-scale attack on the understanding of the use of multiple cognitive strategies in terms of an (empirical) trade-off between accuracy and effort. But just as surely he would have wondered why the authors chose to study adaptation to a rule devised by mathematicians, rather than adaptation to the behavior of objects and events.

Nevertheless, Payne and his colleagues demonstrated that people are generally competent in achieving coherent judgments over different task conditions and that they achieve competence through the use of different—that is, multiple—cognitive strategies, thus demonstrating the potential flexibility of cognition. In doing so, they demonstrate an "intelligent" compromise between effort and the achievement of coherence. That is a great step forward. And they established generality over conditions. (Their results do not, however, afford information about the "accuracy" of human judgment in the sense of correspondence accuracy.)

In order to further the distinction between a coherence-focused study, such as that by Payne and his coauthors, and a correspondence-focused study, I now describe a correspondence-focused study carried out by several of my colleagues and myself.[69] These studies have many similar characteristics, and therefore this second study should provide a useful contrast.

We studied the judgments of twenty experienced highway engineers in relation to the aesthetics, safety, and capacity of highways. To analyze correspondence judgments, the *empirical accuracy* of each engineer with regard to these three tasks (aesthetics, safety, and capacity) was examined. Because the *empirical accuracy* of these judgments was under scrutiny, it was necessary to establish an empirical criterion with which the judgments could be compared. Therefore, the aesthetic judgments of a panel of citizens who saw pictures of numerous highways was used as the measure of the aesthetic value of each highway. If the engineers' judgments agreed with the judgments of the citizens' panel, the engineers were right; if not, they were wrong. A citizens' panel was used because there is no objective measure of the aesthetic value of highways and it is citizens who use highways and decide whether they are beautiful or ugly. For a measure of safety, the accident record of each highway was used. The capacity of each highway was defined by a formula—a rule—that is in standard use for this purpose. In this case agreement with a rule determined accuracy, as in the study by Payne and his colleagues; there was a numerical criterion for each of these three tasks with which a numerical judgment, or rating, by each judge could be compared.

Payne and his colleagues carefully read this article and made several useful comparisons between this work and theirs; they noted the several points of agreement and correctly pointed out one important feature of their work that is entirely absent from our study of engineers—namely, their emphasis on, and measurement of, cognitive *effort*.

It is possible that results from correspondence-focused studies may be applicable to coherence-focused studies, or vice versa, but we cannot take that generalization for granted. It would, however, be of great importance to test that generalization, to discover that descriptions of one type of competence are—or are not—generalizable to the other. It may well be that seeking the answer to this question should be a primary item on the judgment and decision-making research agenda. We would learn that the multiple strategies about which Payne and his coauthors have done so much to enlighten us are or are not to be found in correspondence judgments, such as those made by highway engineers, weather forecasters, and all those who make judgments about empirical events. It would be a considerable step forward if such generalizations were to be found; textbooks would be thinner, much as textbooks in physics became thinner as general laws were discovered. If the generalization were disproved, that advantage might not be achieved, but our theory and research would become more justifiably differentiated, better integrated, and thus more coherent. At a minimum, an implicit, unjustified generalization would be eliminated.

### Summary

Coherence competence theories start with principles and axioms, deduce mathematically coherent processes (equations) and correct answers (when specific numbers are inserted into the equations), then compare processes used by people to produce answers, as well as their answers, with those of the logically impeccable process chosen by the researcher. Human competence is thus compared with a mathematical "standard" (of which there may be more than one). (Ward Edwards[70] was one of the first contemporary psychologists to undertake this form of research.) Current researchers who study coherence competence have concluded that human judgment and decision making are deeply flawed; coherence, or rationality, is seldom achieved. As I have indicated, it is a view that has been stated vigorously and often. The general acceptance of this conclusion and the research that produced it can best be seen in the publication of Plous's prize-winning textbook, *The Psychology of Judgment and Decision Making*, that contains only reports of research leading to and supporting this conclusion. No student who reads this textbook will ever suspect that this conclusion may not be universally held.

It is *not* universally held, however, as I have indicated by citing critiques of it. As Nisbett and his colleagues have shown, education matters; if one is taught the principles that include coherence, one can achieve coherent judgments. Gigerenzer showed that theory matters when he found that studies that followed from the application of correspondence theory produced diametrically opposed results. Lopes and Oden showed that method matters when they showed the consequences of failing to distinguish between intelligence (correspondence) and rationality (coherence). Perhaps most important is the work of Payne and his colleagues, who showed that the employment of heuristics does *not* automatically lead to a failure to achieve close approximations to judgments produced by adherence to mathematical rationality. That is, failures of rationality do not matter much, a conclusion hinted at but never demonstrated by Kahneman and Tversky. Moreover, the results from Payne and his colleagues support Lopes and Oden's emphasis on the intelligent, flexible character of human judgment.

Thus, considerable doubt remains concerning the claims of the "fundamental" irrationality of human judgment—despite their widespread acceptance.

## Resolving the Tension Between Coherence and Correspondence Through Complementarity

Can this tension be resolved? Should it be? The rivalry between intuition and analysis can be and should be resolved through *compromise*—that is, through common sense, as I have described it. The tension between coherence and correspondence, however, cannot be resolved by compromise; one replaces the other in entirety. But these two metatheories can enjoy peaceful coexistence, and that coexistence can be, and should be, constructive. Each may compete for our attention and our energy, even our treasure (as they have), but given the successful history of each, there is no need for researchers or policymakers to deny the value of one or the other. And although compromise cannot be achieved, there is always the grand goal of *complementarity*. But that would require that the researcher and policymaker alike be able to comprehend which metatheory is being proposed on which occasion.

Increased predictability (correspondence) is surely a worthwhile goal, even if a completely coherent model is not yet available, and in the social sciences, there seldom is. But no one will dispute that increased understanding (coherence) is desirable even when high predictability has been achieved. Achieving both is, of course, possible, although rare. Social science has not yet made the progress hoped for with regard to establishing truth based on coherence, although it has certainly tried; and, indeed, it is fair to ask whether it ever will. Greater correspondence in more and more areas of society is slowly but surely being achieved, but it surely has its limits as well. Efforts by scientific disciplines aside, it will always be valuable to understand that although one person may be expressing a judgment that strives for coherence (e.g., using the probability calculus, or modern science), another may be expressing a judgment based on multiple fallible indicators.

It is also important to recognize that judgments based on coherence have an all-or-none character. That is, irrespective of whether such a system was arrived at intuitively or analytically, coherence-based systems demand wholehearted acceptance or rejection; tinkering destroys coherence. Correspondence judgments, on the other hand, can be tinkered with—adding a predictor here, omitting one there, adding weight to this one, subtracting weight from that one. Coherence-based judgments are therefore much more likely to evoke unresolvable interpersonal conflict than are correspondence-based judgments. In the well-known PBS Civil War television documentary, the historian Shelby Foote indicates that the war was inevitable because there was no possibility of a workable compromise between slavery and freedom.

One politician who discovered that is Senator Patrick Moynihan. In an interview with the *New York Times,* he said:

> If you're outside a paradigm [a coherence-based model], people will think you're crazy. It is by that kind of pattern in the sciences, and what is *wanly* called social sciences, in which no argument ever gets settled in one generation. A *huge* argument breaks out, and it just goes on until another generation comes along and it has accepted one or the other views. No one will say: "*Gosh,* oh golly-gee, I got that *wrong!* My courses for the last 25 years have been *wrong,* but I have now changed my ways."[71]

That is Moynihan's way of indicating that one coherence-based theory, or model, or worldview, is always exchanged for another; they are not tinkered with. Nor is there enthusiasm for change, in his view. And those committed to a coherence model are seldom interested in correspondence-based challenges. Indeed, persons who defend coherence-based judgments are prepared to scorn correspondence-based judgments and vice versa (think of the *Challenger* disaster). Is this of importance to policymakers? Yes. Grasping the distinction between these two metatheories and being able to identify their use enables the policymaker to anticipate where and when difficult, perhaps irreconcilable, dispute will occur and, possibly, to find complementarity, irrespective of the content of the policy.

## Complementarity of Theory and Research

No one doubts that good judgment is an important aspect of human behavior; indeed, it is hard to think of anything more important, more valued, more admired, more necessary in human affairs. It is hard, therefore, to imagine a topic more deserving of hard empirical research; fortunately, that is precisely what the researchers in this field have been engaged in over the past half century, and what they continue to be engaged in. But it is clear that we still lack unambiguous conclusions regarding the competence of human judgment. Numerous studies demonstrate irrationality, and current textbooks emphasize these findings. On the other hand, there has been much criticism of this research, and there are numerous demonstrations of accurate judgments. For better or worse, the world remains guided by human judgment. In short, although considerable progress has been made, the present situation is disturbing because of the claims and demonstrations of irrationality, and confusing because of the more ambiguous claims and demonstrations of accuracy.

The conceptual framework provided in this book, however, is intended to reduce that confusion. It shows that there are two theory-independent and two research-independent domains of human judgment, each with its own set of problems. Both have been researched rather thoroughly, and much has been learned, although, as always, much remains to be done. Indeed, this organization of the field of judgment and decision making might well clarify its future, for it shows that these two approaches to judgment and decision making complement, rather than contradict, each other. In the next section I show how complementarity can be achieved and the positive consequences that can, and should, follow. I propose that we place these two approaches in the context of Karl Popper's "three worlds."

## Correspondence and Coherence in Popper's "Three Worlds"

M. Björkman provided the first application of Popper's three-world framework to questions about the competence of human judgment when he noted that "World 1 is the world of physical objects and states, World 2 is the subjective world (perception, thinking, dispositions to act), and World 3 is the world of scientific concepts, problems and theories."[72] We are accustomed to thinking about World 1 (the world of objects, the ecology that is "out there") and World 2 (the subjective world, our cognitive systems) and the stability of the relationship between them. It is in the latter context that the question of *correspondence* arises: How accurately does a person's cognitive system (World 2) perceive, judge, appraise, in short, *correspond* to, the observable properties of the objects in World 1? That is one of the major topics of interest to judgment and decision-making researchers. Thus, correspondence judgments often take the form of "how often will an event of that kind happen?" (as in "will it rain today?"). Everyone is familiar with the idea of a World 1 and a World 2, but not the idea of an independent world of concepts and ideas.

Popper's conception of an independent *third* world helps to clarify matters, for we can now think of ideas as having an objective status of their own, in books and libraries, for example, outside the cognitive systems of persons. These are "the objective contents of thought,"[73] as Popper would have it. That concept is helpful because it permits us to see that World 3 contains not only, for example, scientific knowledge, history, and geography, but also all those concepts described by statisticians, such as randomness, averages, and probability—the very ones we are using to cope with uncertainty, the very ones Nisbett and his colleagues[74] taught to their students and that, as we will see, enabled them to escape from the errors made by their untutored peers. It is World 3 that contains the concepts of rationality, the probability calculus, all those propositions by which the rationality—not the accuracy—of the cognitive activity of a person's World 2 are evaluated; it is World 3 that contains the knowledge and the criteria by which the coherence of a person's judgment and decision making activity is evaluated.

In short, whereas the *correspondence* of a person's judgments (World 2) is evaluated in terms of its accuracy in relation to World 1, the *coherence* of those judgments is judged in relation to the relevant knowledge in World 3. The relationship between World 3 and World 2 informs us about the coherence of a person's judgment process, but it does not directly inform us about its correspondence with World 1. One's judgments may be coherent but inaccurate, or the reverse. (Recall the rationality but also the inaccuracy of a pre-Galileo priest's belief in a flat earth.) It is possible to employ completely coherent arithmetic or a coherent probability judgment incorrectly, as, for example, those who are learning statistical methods often do, and as professionals occasionally do. On the other hand, judgments may be incoherent but accurate, either by chance or because the target is so broad that it can't be missed no matter how irrational the judgment process may be.

It is easy to gloss over the important differences between these criteria for evaluating competence; indeed, these differences have rarely been given any attention.[75] Kahneman and Tversky, for example, correctly note the distinction: "The presence of an error of judgment is demonstrated by comparing people's responses *either* [italics added] with an established fact (e.g., that the two lines are equal in length) or with an accepted rule of arithmetic, logic, or statistics";[76] but they do not pursue the implication of this distinction. They simply go on to add that:

> not every response that appears to contradict an established fact or an accepted rule is a judgmental error. The contradiction could also arise from the subject's misunderstanding of the question or from the investigator's misinterpretation of the answer. The description of a particular response as an error of judgment therefore involves assumptions about the communication between the experimenter and the subject.[77]

Thus Kahneman and Tversky do not make a distinction in the nature of the criteria for evaluating the error. For in the case of the correct judgment of the line (an "established fact" of World 1), they were discussing a judgment error relating to correspondence, whereas in the case of the judgment that does not agree with an answer produced by an "accepted rule of arithmetic, logic, or statistics," they were discussing coherence. Nor did they note the implication of the distinction—namely, that these are two types of theory and research that need to be distinguished because they refer to different cognitive processes.

In short, the type of judgment and decision making studied by correspondence theorists evaluates a person's relations between World 2 and World 1 with little regard to World 3, whereas the type of judgment and decision making studied by coherence theorists evaluates a person's relation between World 2 and World 3 with little regard to World 1. Popper's distinctions, brought to bear on judgment and decision-making research by Björkman, provide us with a more differentiated view of competence. Moreover, we can now see how one type of theory and research complements the other.

## Two Types of Theory and Research

If I have correctly identified and described two views about the competence of human judgment and their independent development, we can now turn to how this distinction has developed in modern science and in social policy. Psychological research on physical perception has shown us that evolution provided us with correspondence competence in which World 2 relates to World 1; education and training provide access to knowledge in World 3. Popper's three worlds offer us a more differentiated view of competence than we possessed earlier, for we can now ask: Competence? With respect to which tasks? Competence in bringing our personal (World 2) knowledge to bear on our environment (World 1)? Or competence in bringing knowledge from World 3 to World 1?

Björkman points out that researchers have failed to consider these distinctions introduced by Popper—an omission with considerable consequences. He notes, for example, that M. Bar-Hillel, a coherence theorist, states that "in the typical Bayesian reasoning contexts which people encounter in daily life, there is every reason to expect the fallacy to operate."[78] And he points to a similar comment by D. Lyon and P. Slovic, who state: "Since the world operates according to Bayes' Theorem, experience should confirm the importance of base rates."[79] But Björkman points out: "World 1 is not in itself Bayesian, it is the Bayesians' representation of it that is Bayesian. What 'people encounter in daily life' are not 'Bayesian reasoning contexts'. They encounter objects, events, other people, all entities of World 1."[80] Björkman further criticizes the coherence theorists for their failure to make this distinction. He notes that Tversky and Kahneman ignore the distinction in their comments on learning when they say:

> What is perhaps surprising is the failure of people to infer from lifelong experience such fundamental statistical rules as regression toward the mean, or the effect of sample size on sampling variability . . . [and] very few people discover the principles of sampling and regression on their own. Statistical principles are not learned from everyday experience because the relevant instances are not coded appropriately.[81]

Björkman points out that this is an inappropriate generalization, for "appropriate coding would require some knowledge of what to observe. . . . Discovery of statistical and other principles of World 3, e.g. the Pythagorean theorem, the law of the inclined plane, regression toward the mean, by pure induction is quite *impossible* [italics added]. Had everybody's induction been sufficient it would not have required a Pythagoras, a Galileo, a Galton to make the discoveries."[82] Statistical principles are acquired from World 3, not from experience with World 1.[83]

Thus Björkman makes it plain that the coherence theorists, particularly Kahneman and Tversky and their colleagues, however valuable their work might be on other grounds, greatly overgeneralized their results through a failure to consider the distinctions between Popper's three worlds. They learned through a prolific research program that extended over twenty years that many, if not most, of their subjects had not acquired the statistical knowledge necessary to solve the problems put to them, subjects who had not been informed about, or grasped, the statistical knowledge that exists in World 3. The coherence researchers thus learned that their subjects do not exhibit the coherence in their statistical reasoning that World 3 offers to—and demands from—them until they are taught.[84] By failing to recognize the distinction drawn by Popper and advanced by Björkman, however, these researchers have described their results as if they applied to the relationship between World 2 and World 1 instead of that between World 3 and World 2.

For example, the coherence researchers give their subjects the following problem:

1. A certain town is served by two hospitals. In the larger hospital about 45 babies are born each day, and in the smaller hospital about 15 babies are born each day. As you know, about 50% of all babies are boys. The exact percentage of baby boys, however, varies from day to day. Sometimes it may be higher than 50%, sometimes lower.

   For a period of 1 year, each hospital recorded the days on which (more/less) than 60% of the babies born were boys. Which hospital do you think recorded more such days?

|  | More than 60% | Less than 60% |
|---|---|---|
| The larger hospital | 2 | 9* |
| The smaller hospital | 10* | 11 |
| About the same (i.e., within 5% of each other | 28 | 25[85] |

The correct answers are starred. More people in the study gave incorrect answers than gave correct answers. How could one arrive at a correct answer? Only by chance (a lucky guess) or by virtue of training in statistics, that is, through participation in World 3. But the coherence researchers went far beyond that conclusion to suggest that our judgment and decision-making activity is fundamentally flawed (as I will show in the next chapter).

Correspondence theorists such as Björkman, B. Brehmer, M. Doherty, Gigerenzer, T. Stewart, and others,[86] on the other hand, have focused on the correspondence between the judgments produced in World 2 and the properties of objects, events, and people in World 1. They have inquired into how people learn about the less tangible aspects of World 1 from its multiple fallible indicators and have given special attention to the consequences of the interdependency of such indicators, as well as the effects of various forms of feedback from World 1, which, after all, provide the essential features of learning. They have found that their subjects do in fact learn— albeit slowly and often with a lack of awareness of what they are learning—from the experience of outcomes, when outcomes are available. Thus, researchers emphasizing the correspondence point of view continue to demonstrate that human judgment is generally competent with respect to World 1, *insofar as the properties of the task allow it to be,* a matter I discussed in detail in earlier chapters.

Current theorists in cognitive development are implicitly incorporating Popper's distinctions and explicitly including evolutionary theory in their research. D. C. Geary, for example, uses instances from animal and insect navigation to suggest that

> many species of animal, including humans, have an implicit, although imprecise, understanding of some fundamental features of Euclidian geometry (e.g., that a line from one point to another is straight). . . . However, this implicit knowledge appears to reflect the evolution of sensory and cognitive systems that are sensitive to basic geometric relationships among objects in the physical universe and does not mean that individuals have an explicit understanding of the formal principles of Euclidian geometry.[87]

This idea corresponds to our view of the distinction between the correspondence and coherence approaches to judgment under uncertainty. *Homo sapiens* have implicit competence with regard to multiple fallible indicators offered by World 1, but that "does not mean that they have an explicit understanding of the formal principles" of the probability calculus. Researchers studying correspondence competence seek out the determinants and limits of our competence with regard to the objects and events of World 1; coherence theorists seek out the determinants and limits of our competence with regard to our untutored understanding stored in World 2 of the probability calculus stored in World 3. All these efforts are of equal importance; taken together they add to our knowledge of our ability to cope with uncertainty.[88]

Thus, we *need* both approaches if we are to understand the way in which human judgment guides our actions and creates social policy. Without the coherence approach all our knowledge of formal systems of probability that reaches back for centuries would be lost; we would not know how to study the *rationality* of judgments and decisions that should achieve coherence; we would have no standard with which to compare our uneducated, intuitive quasirational efforts to calculate probabilities of future events. And not only do we engage in that activity frequently in our ordinary lives; our policymakers do little else. Without the correspondence approach we would not understand our use of multiple fallible indicators, the robustness of the organizing principles associated with them, and the enormous advantages that have followed and still follow even as our information environment changes from a natural to an artificial one. The tension between these approaches can be, and should be, transformed to *constructive complementarity.*

It may well be that complementarity can be achieved, but if it is, it will most likely be achieved within the next generation of researchers. Current researchers, like the priests who imprisoned Galileo, are heavily committed to the coherence of their ideas and are not likely to be convinced of the need for change. And change will be required in the methodological dogma of each approach.

The tension that has persisted for so long is so widespread and evokes such emotional responses from respected scientists that it is not likely to be reduced easily or rapidly. It has appeared only recently in the field of judgment and decision making, however. It may well be that even if the first generation of researchers fails to see the enormous advantages of achieving complementarity, the current (second) generation of researchers will. In Part IV I apply the theory described in Part III to the limitations and possibilities of making use of information in the process. But first I want to show that there is methodological dogma as well as theoretical dogma.

Research Dogma and Its Consequences

Not only do the two metatheories—correspondence and coherence—have different goals and different concepts; the researchers associated with them employ different methods. Although this is not the place to examine this matter in detail, it should be mentioned, because this topic is seldom addressed even though the different methods employed often make results and conclusions incommensurable. The differences in method are best subsumed under the concepts of *systematic* and *representative* design, terms introduced by the correspondence theorist E. Brunswik.[89]

A systematic design is one that (generally) arranges conditions of the experiment so that the effect of one variable or condition can be ascertained. This goal led to the development of the well-known experimental-control group method familiar to most high school students. The experimental group consists of subjects (persons, animals, plants), who receive a treatment (e.g., a drug, reward, punishment), and a control group that does not receive the treatment (receives the placebo). *All other conditions are held constant.* The goal is to evaluate the effect of a variable in as pure a set of circumstances as possible; all competing causal explications are thus ruled out. This method, and its elaboration, is the method all students of behavioral science learn because, they are told, it is the method of basic research. The hope of the researchers is that the results of such studies can somehow be extended to broader circumstances outside the laboratory. But after almost a century of use, that hope has rarely been critically examined—or realized—in the behavioral sciences.

Coherence theorists prefer systematic design because their research strategy is to discover whether a certain condition upsets what is traditionally, and typically, believed to be a rational process. Thus, for example, if a problem in the probability calculus is "framed" (i.e., described) in two different forms and the framing is found to produce different answers in the two groups, then it will be asserted that the framing condition had an effect on rationality and that the laws of the probability calculus have therefore been "violated"; rationality has been affected by framing, although it should not have been. If, for example, we present a problem for which the probability calculus tells us we must multiply, not add, two probabilities, and if the experimenter "frames"—phrases—the problem in such a way that the person trying to solve the problem adds (rather than multiplies), then we have found a "violation" of "rationality."

Will rationality be affected in other framing conditions? There are two answers to this: One is that "once is enough"; if the result can be demonstrated in clear and convincing conditions, that settles it; the other is to demand that we pursue the question by conjuring alternative plausible hypotheses by which the result might have been obtained, conducting further tests always by the same method ad infinitum until a consensus has been reached. The fundamental problem with the systematic design of experiments is whether the results apply to conditions not present in the experiment. Tests of that question must be undertaken one condition at a time because the method examines the effect of *one variable* at a time. As a result, the issue rarely gets a final answer. In Chapter 9, I will show how the failure to eliminate uncertainty makes this research method—systematic design—virtually useless for policy formation.

The problem of generalization from systematic research designs, long ignored by "basic researchers," is now beginning to be acknowledged. For example, William Estes, a renowned classical basic researcher, states in a recent and important book: "I share the hope of many investigators that the kind of theory described here will prove useful in dealing with problems that arise outside the laboratory—in areas of education, health, business, and the like."[90] That statement is a surprising reversal from the point of view of "basic" researchers in the past, who denied any interest whatever in such extrapolations. Pure basic research was constructed for its own sake; basic research tested basic theories under rigorous ("rule of one variable") conditions. Whether the results were of any use was of little interest, and basic researchers said as much, often with a certain pride. Even Estes acknowledges that the realization of his hope is not likely to be easy:

> The degree to which the experimental simulations capture the essentials of the applied problems need verification, which is not easy to obtain. . . . A time-tested strategy is to draw on those areas [education, health, business, and the like] for interesting and important practical problems that can be simulated to some degree in the laboratory, but to rely on experimental analyses in the controlled laboratory environment to guide the development and testing of theories.[91]

Just a moment! "Simulations" and "a time-tested strategy"? Psychologists of one generation ago did not think in terms of simulations. Basic researchers did not, and still do not, aim at "simulating"—another term for "representing"—"education, health, business, and the like." Instead they aim at testing a theory under conditions *best suited to testing a theory.* Estes correctly describes this goal: "to rely on experimental analyses in the controlled laboratory environment [i.e., systematic design] to guide the development and testing of theories."[92]

Absolutely! It is indeed "experimental analyses in the controlled laboratory environment" that is relied upon to "guide the development and testing of theories"—not the chaos of the world of "education, health, business." Those circumstances could *not* be used because they are not susceptible to systematic design of experiments.

Advocates of the conventional systematic design cannot cope with the problem of generalizing their results from the laboratory to the world outside. At least, they never have. At best, as Estes frankly indicates, they can only "hope."

Nevertheless, Estes's remarks—particularly his repeated use of the idea of simulation—suggest that he and other basic researchers are beginning to recognize the value of *representative* design, for, after all, simulation is just another way of representing any information environment. Thus, airline pilots now learn to fly, and are tested, in simulators, as many other professionals are tested in simulations of their work environments. The computer has made simulation and thus representative design possible, and, as a result, the way has been opened for psychologists (and others) to design experiments in a manner that permits generalization—extension of results from the (simulation) laboratory to the situation of interest, provided they can free themselves from the iron grip of current research dogma. Simulation justifies generalization from the laboratory because the simulation includes (represents) the conditions toward which the generalization is intended.[93] Correspondence researchers have been carrying out simulations of greater or lesser fidelity for more than forty years, despite the discouragement from journal editors who are interested in "control of all extraneous variables" rather than in representations, a dogma that often precluded publication as late as the 1980s.[94] As a result, it is the applied psychologists (e.g., human factors researchers) who now carry out the research that realizes the hope expressed by Estes—that research results will in fact carry meaning for circumstances outside the laboratory. Simulation (representation) by correspondence researchers in judgment and decision making has usually taken the form of representing a judgment task—an information environment—in terms of the various fallible indicators that a person in an information environment will face. For example, to learn how highway engineers judge the safety of roads, a study was carried out by representing roads under three different conditions: (1) direct representation (motion pictures of highways taken from a driver's viewpoint), (2) statistical descriptions of roads in terms of bar graphs representing different safety-related variables, and (3) mathematical safety formulas.[95]

What is at issue in the representative design of experiments is the fidelity (accurate representation) of the laboratory simulation of the actual circumstances of interest, rather than the *control* of all variables other than a single independent variable. (Pilots do not learn to fly in a simulator that presents one variable at a time.) Current state-of-the-art computer graphics makes such simulation highly representative of a wide variety of circumstances, including social circumstances.

The power of computer science to generate representations is probably what led two pioneers of cognitive science, Alan Newell and Herbert Simon, to depart from conventional group comparisons to the analysis of the cognitive activity of each individual separately (urged by those who employ representative designs). As they put it in 1972:

> [Our] procedure leads naturally to constructing information processing systems that model the behavior of a single individual in a single task situation. Full particularity is the rule, not the exception. . . .
>
> The situation is just the reverse of the one faced in earlier psychological theorizing. Indeed, a terminological line is usually drawn just to distinguish clinical efforts that deal with the individual in all his uniqueness (*idiographic*) from efforts of experimental psychology to deal with an individual only as an intersection of statistically defined populations (*nomothetic*). . . .
>
> We never use grouped data to test the theory if we can help it.[96]

Newell and Simon credit Brunswik (and his colleague Edward Tolman) as their "forerunners."[97]

This distinction in methodology runs throughout science, as L. Laudan noted, creating tension between adherents of each approach. Indeed, that tension often reaches a point where researchers despise those who hold to the opposite approach. Jared Diamond, a well-known biologist, in his review of E. O. Wilson's autobiography, draws this distinction in terms of the tension that exists between "reductionist experimentation" carried out by molecular biologists and the field work carried out by ecologists. "Reductionist experimentation" refers to tightly controlled laboratory research that follows from coherence theory; ecologists, of course, do not generally have recourse to laboratory experiments and therefore often operate under the same loose conditions as judgment and decision making psychologists who are correspondence theorists and who eschew laboratory experiments in favor of field experiments. Here is Wilson's reactions to James Watson, whose laboratory work (with Francis Crick) won a Nobel prize for discovering the molecular structure of DNA:

> I found him the most unpleasant human being I had ever met. . . . He arrived with a conviction that biology must be transformed into a science directed at molecules and cells and re-written in the language of physics and chemistry. What had gone before, "traditional" biology—*my* biology—was infested by stamp collectors who lacked the wit to transform their subject into a modern science. . . . At department meetings Watson radiated contempt in all directions. He shunned ordinary courtesy and polite conversation, evidently in the belief that they would only encourage the traditionalists to stay around. . . . Watson, having risen to historic fame at an early age, became the Caligula of biology.[98]

Diamond describes this antagonism as "the latest in a long history of frequent and deep-seated disagreement among scientists, pitting so-called reductionists . . . against scientists interested in higher levels of organization."[99] He shows that this disagreement is not limited to personal hostility but affects how a department's resources are allocated: "Wilson quotes Watson's response to this proposal that Harvard appoint even just one ecologist: 'Anyone who would hire an ecologist is out of his mind.'"[100]

But, as Diamond reminds us: "The dispute is not a mere academic cat fight, but a tragedy with heavy consequences for all of us. Now that the risk of nuclear holocaust appear to have receded, the chief risk to the world in which my sons will reach maturity has become the risk of an ecological holocaust."[101]

It is clear that if we need both the coherence and correspondence approaches, then we need the research methods of both approaches. Methodological dogma is the worst enemy of all concerned—the researchers, their students, and the research consumer. Different methods are appropriate for different problems. It's a good thing that Watson and Crick were so committed to their reductionism; as a result, now we understand the structure of the DNA molecule. It's a good thing that Wilson is such a committed ecologist; we understand far more of the importance of biodiversity than would have otherwise been the case. It's a good thing that Kahneman and Tversky became interested in extending Ward Edwards's work on coherence theory of judgment and decision making; we now understand the departures from rationality better than we otherwise would have. And it's a good thing that the correspondence theorists such as Brehmer and his colleagues pursued their interest in multiple fallible indicators; we now understand their role in the history of *Homo sapiens* better than otherwise would have been the case.

But it isn't easy to reach beyond the laboratory. I close this section with the example of three physicians—R. M. Poses, R. D. Cebul, and R. S. Wigton—who wanted first to discover whether improving physicians' judgments of the probability (relative frequency of appearance) of streptococcal sore throats would affect their use of—prescriptions for—antibiotics. There are many sources of uncertainty in the diagnosis of this disease, which is reflected in the frequency with which prescriptions for antibiotics are issued, all of which made this an interesting research problem.

The investigators found prior to any attempts to change prescribing habits that "the physicians [under study] often overestimated the probability of streptococcal infection . . . and they frequently prescribed . . . antibiotics for patients who turned out not to have streptococcal pharyngitis."[102] Their method of improving the physicians' judgments was effective, however, and the physicians' frequency of prescriptions of antibiotics declined. Roughly two years later the same physicians' diagnoses and prescriptions for antibiotics were examined in their practice. The researchers concluded that "an intervention that caused a marked decrease in physicians' numerical judgments of the probability of streptococcal infection did not decrease (and perhaps increased) their use of . . . antibiotics."[103] Poses, Cebul, and Wigton were not the first to be disappointed when conclusions are extended from laboratory to practice. Indeed, it is my impression that such disappointments occur far more frequently than do successful generalizations. The problem of generalizing results from any form of research to circumstances that demand judgments about policy formation is a problem that bedevils all of us.

## Part III Summary

In Part III I put forward a theory that attempts to meet Karl Popper's requirements for a general, unifying theory. I have developed a theory that reduces the rivalry between intuition and analysis and the tension between the coherence and the correspondence theories of truth. That step allows the major approaches to the topic of judgment and decision making to complement, rather than to attempt to displace, each other.

Reconciliation of the rivalry between intuition and analysis can be found in the concept of a cognitive continuum that replaces the age-old dichotomy between these two well-recognized modes of cognition. The concept of a continuum, anchored at one pole by pure intuition and at the other pole by pure analysis, permits us to recognize a middle ground, quasirational cognition, known since antiquity as "common sense." Quasirationality is not a panacea; the positive and the negative features of quasirationality will be with us forever. Its virtues lie in its robustness and its flexibility; its vices are its imprecision and its inconsistency. The former allows it to cope with changing information conditions (as described in Chapter 6); the latter plagues us with inaccuracy, interpersonal conflict, and irrationality.

The principal conclusion to be drawn from Part III regarding this long-standing rivalry is that our cognitive endowment directs and forms the nature of human judgment as it is applied to the construction of social policy, an endowment that enables us to cope with a wide range of information conditions. Confining these activities to either pole of the continuum is appropriate for certain situations, but not for policy formation. We function best at the middle range of cognition where compromise between extremes exists. Yes, mistaken judgments will be made as a result of quasirationality; there will be overreliance on intuition or analysis, and, yes, injustice will unavoidably result.

The wide range of information conditions with which we can cope includes information organized in a coherent form, and our pattern recognition ability serves us well. We do not, however, make compromises between these two forms of cognition in our judgments; we alternate between them. Nor do we compromise between coherence and correspondence theories of judgment and decision making. When each is applied to the circumstances to which it is appropriate, each informs us in a manner in which the other could not. Thus, the tension between the correspondence and the coherence theories of truth is reconciled by acknowledging the complementarity of the two approaches. Compromise can be achieved in the rivalry between intuition and analysis by virtue of the concept of a cognitive continuum, but the tension between coherence and correspondence theories cannot be reduced in that way. Complementarity has its own virtues, however, for each theory, together with its associated methodology, affords the researcher an opportunity to explore the nature of human judgment in ways that supplement one another. And when both are applied, they help us overcome the limitations of each alone and thus afford us knowledge we would not obtain otherwise.

In the field of judgment and decision making the correspondence and coherence approaches have stood side by side for some twenty-five years, each pursuing its own goals by its own methods. Independently, they appear to reach different conclusions and thus leave the newcomer without loyalties to defend, puzzled as to where the truth lies. This puzzlement is particularly acute in relation to the question of cognitive competence. For the coherence theorists have been steadfast in their confidence that we lack cognitive competence, whereas the correspondence theorists, although less comprehensive in their claims, have found competence where anticipated. Once we recognize the empirical fact of complementarity, that is, that *Homo sapiens* are capable of making use of multiple fallible indicators, on the one hand, and of stored knowledge on the other, we can recognize the value of both in appropriate circumstances. And that creates a challenge. What are the limitations imposed on us by virtue of our cognitive endowment? What are the possibilities that this endowment offers us? These are the topics addressed in Part IV.

# IV POSSIBILITIES

Treatises on social policy typically focus on the content of various policies: Will they do what the authors want them to do in the way they want it done? This book has a very different focus. Here the question has been: How does social policy—any social policy—grow out of the policymaker's judgment about what to do, what can be, what will be, what ought to be? All the answers to these questions emerge from human judgment, and nowhere else. Yet we have never before been in a position to examine the cognitive processes that produce them. Now, however, we are in a good position to do so. And that brings us to Part IV, which takes us to the possibilities offered by human judgment.

In Part IV I raise this question: Is it possible for us to learn about whether our policies do what we want them to do, either as a result of intervention or representation? I then address the possibilities of wisdom now, and of cognitive competence in the future.

During the 1990s the role of human judgment in all these matters became more and more apparent. Whereas it had been taken for granted that we could and should learn—somehow—from our actions, doubts began to appear. Is it really possible for us to *learn* whether our policies do what we want them to do? Is it possible to achieve the wisdom necessary to develop and maintain the civilized societies we yearn for?

In Part IV I take up the questions of the possibility of learning, and of developing wisdom.

# 9 Is It Possible to Learn by Intervening?

Exhaust the limits of the possible

—Pindar

In this chapter I describe various modes of inquiry used by policymakers to reduce uncertainty. "Modes of inquiry" is a term introduced by C. W. Churchman.[1] This is a useful idea, because it allows us to examine *all* manner of efforts to understand the world around us, not only purely scientific ones. We can examine all modes of inquiry in terms of how well they serve specific purposes; the critical examination of different modes of inquiry allows us to evaluate their characteristics in relation to how well they fit the needs of policymakers. In addition, examining modes of inquiry is critical to our purposes because different modes of inquiry make different demands on human judgment. We may find that some, indeed, *all,* are found wanting because they were designed for needs other than policy formation. As Churchman put it:

> The current tendency in designing inquiring systems is to bolster science and its research as it is conceived today. But in every age when men have struggled to learn more about themselves and the universe they inhabit, there have always been a few reflective thinkers who have tried to learn how men learn, and by what right they can claim that what they profess to learn is truly knowledge. This is reflective thinking in the literal sense: it is the thinking about thinking, doubting about doubting, learning about learning, and (hopefully) knowing about knowing. If we accept the thesis that these reflective minds did indeed learn about learning, then their contribution to knowledge is quite important for the designer of inquiring systems. . . .
>
> We can regard the history of epistemology (theory of knowledge) not as a description of how men learn and justify their learning, but as a description of how learning can be designed and how the design can be justified.[2]

I follow Churchman; my goal is to examine several modes of inquiry in terms of how well they help us to learn about our efforts to learn to improve society and the lives of persons within it.

233

In pursuit of this goal I borrow from a another well-known historian and philosopher of science, Ian Hacking, who categorized various methods into two principal modes of inquiry that he called "representing and intervening."[3] I make use of Hacking's distinction, first, by describing three main types of "intervening," that is, the three main types of *experimentation* that are employed to inform policymakers about the effects of social programs or other actions taken by them. Second, I use Hacking's term "representing" to refer to efforts to provide information about the social and ecological world, as it is or as it might be, to policymakers; that is, I describe three ways of representing—without intervention—social and ecological circumstances to policymakers for their judgments about what the situation is, what it will be, what it can be, and what it ought to be. It is my purpose to describe these six current modes of inquiry for both intervening and representing in terms of how well they serve the needs of the policymaker and of the demands they make on human judgment. I do so by making use of a "modes of inquiry matrix."

The theory presented in Part II provides a set of predictions in relation to each mode of inquiry. These predictions are made explicit in the form of a diagram (see Figure 9-1). Six modes of inquiry are described in terms of six continuous dimensions:

1. *Modes of cognition,* running on the continuum from analysis to intuition
2. *Degrees of manipulation* or control over conditions by policymakers (or scientists)
3. *Feasibility* of the use of each mode of inquiry in forming social policy
4. The extent to which each mode of inquiry is *conflict-reducing* or *conflict-producing*
5. The *covertness* of the degree of cognitive activity of the user of the information generated in each mode
6. The extent to which each mode of inquiry is based on *correspondence* theory or on *coherence* theory.

The shaded area in each box in Figure 9-1 indicates the covertness of the judgment process that is involved in each mode of inquiry. "Covertness" is used in its nonpejorative sense; it merely indicates that the cognitive process underlying the judgments of the user is not apparent to the user or the observer of the results. An important cognitive boundary is crossed (as indicated by the dashed horizontal line in Figure 9-1) once the active manipulation of variables is reduced to the point where covert judgmental cognitive activity becomes more important than the manipulation of variables.

The general conclusions that follow from the predictions encompassed in Figure 9-1 are these:

- The information to be derived from even the most powerful modes of inquiry (Modes 1, 2, and 3) suffers from irreducible uncertainty.
- Newer methods (Modes 3 and 4) offer the best combination of feasibility, uncertainty reduction, and analytical justification for the policymaker.
- Conventional methods that involve the use of expert judgment and the use of opinion, Modes 5 and 6, are least desirable.
- Use of this matrix should lead to a recognition of the inherent limitations of all modes of inquiry and should, in turn, lead to more modest expectations of what can be learned.
- Acknowledgment of such limitations could—and should—inspire the creation of new methods presently unimagined.

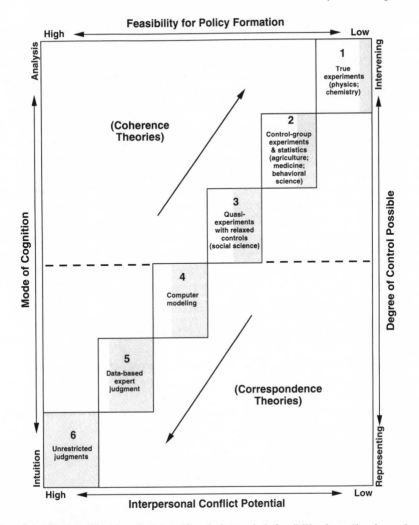

Figure 9-1   Modes of inquiry are located in relation to their feasibility for policy formation, the extent to which they involve intervention or representation of circumstances, the extent to which they induce interpersonal conflict, and the extent to which they induce degrees of intuition and analysis. The shaded area in each box indicates the degree to which the cognitive activity induced is covert. The closer a mode of inquiry lies to the upper right-hand corner the more likely it is to be associated with a correspondence theory; the closer a mode of inquiry lies to the lower left-hand corner the more likely it is to be associated with a coherence theory.

*Mode 1* (*strong analytical experimentation*) refers to the form of inquiry typified by the traditional laboratory experiment carried out by physical scientists. Although the most powerful mode of inquiry known to us, it is completely infeasible for policy formation (except in the case of certain risk analyses) because of its strong demand for control and precise measurement.

*Mode 2 (moderately strong analytical experimentation)* refers to the control-group experiments that are carried out in agriculture, medicine, and the behavioral sciences, as well as in related fields. This random-assignment experimental-control-group method is based on the logic of statistical inference and thus invariably leaves us with irreducible uncertainty—sometimes more, sometimes less. As a result, it requires a degree of covert judgment not present in the traditional experiments in the physics laboratory and is a less powerful mode of inquiry than Mode 1. Consequently, there is far more dispute in agriculture, medicine, and behavioral science than in physical science regarding the substantive facts of their disciplines.

*Mode 3 (weak analytical experimentation)* refers to the quasi-experiments (and surveys) carried out by social scientists (and others) when strict random assignment, double-blind, pre- and post-test experiments are not feasible. Such quasi-experiments thus fail to meet the criteria demanded by Mode 2 for the application of statistical logic and require more judgment on the part of the policymaker (as indicated by the increase in the shaded area in Figure 9-1). Mode 3, therefore, provides the weakest of the three active, manipulative, analytical modes of inquiry. But it is also the most feasible.

I turn now to three types of representation of social and ecological circumstances of interest to policymakers.

*Mode 4 (strong quasirational judgment)* refers to imagined experimentation, or "thought" experiments. This mode is frequently employed among experts when the necessary experiment has not been, or cannot be, carried out. Mode 4 does not have the analytical power of Mode 3 because it does not provide for separating relations among variables by physical, experimental manipulation. Inability to hold certain variables constant while manipulating other variables in order to ascertain their independent effects leaves ambiguous the question of causal relations. As a result, the differential effects of interdependent variables must be disentangled by a person's cognitive efforts; the knowledge that certain variables are found to operate independently in the laboratory will not help. Under field conditions they may well be entangled.

Therein lies the reason why Mode 4 is, in principle, a weaker mode of inquiry than Mode 3: The disentanglement of (possibly) causal relations by (passive) cognition instead of (active) experimentation is subject to a variety of ecological as well as psychological factors, such as memory loss, information overload, and recency and primacy effects, to mention only a few. Indeed, it is precisely at this point that the question of the competence of human judgment becomes important.

But something new happened in the latter half of the twentieth century—computer simulation was discovered. It was found that *computer* models of the system under analysis (and of the policymakers' cognition) could be employed to represent the dynamics of sociological, economic, and ecological circumstances. Thus, Mode 4 became the *strongest* of the quasirational modes of cognition and a strong competitor to the long-established Modes 5 and 6.

Policy making may be supported in three ways in Mode 4.

1. By conventional post hoc statistical analysis (e.g., computation of averages, variation, and correlation) of the data available to the policymaker.

2. By computer simulation of *changing* environmental circumstances (e.g., computer models of the future *activity* of river basins, of the economy, of institutions, and of the ecology, as, for example, in weather simulations), thus offering a set of predictions whose basis is analytically retraceable. This was clearly an advance over conventional statistical analysis of static conditions.[4]

3. By analysis of the judgment and decision making processes of the policymaker.[5]

(Because the last two features of Mode 4 are new, I will elaborate on their use in the next section.)

Computer models of social policy problems are now being developed for the users of personal computers. For example, as this is being written, one can purchase a computer program for home use that will allow the private citizen to act "as an administrator in control of the United States health care system . . . it's visually interesting to watch the choices you make be put into effect." For example, "anybody who uses it can get a much more concrete feeling for the trade-offs that must be made and whether they can be made successfully and whether they get at the values you are trying to maximize. If you institute universal health care, for example, you believe that equality is important. But universal health care may diminish freedom of choice and liberty. There are lots of trade-offs like that in the game."[6]

An important element is missing from that description of the computer model of how the health care system works, however, and that is that someone has to write the computer program that simulates the environment in which the user activates his or her plan. And it is that program that will determine the trade-offs mentioned in the description. But who knows how the socioeconomic system will make those trade-offs work? One can make educated guesses—quasirational judgments about the relation between "universal health" care and "freedom of choice and liberty"—but there is wide variation among experts' judgments about such matters, and the irreducible uncertainty is high. Most important, however, is the fact that the nature of the choice made by the computer programmer will not be apparent to the user, nor will the justification of that choice be apparent. Thus, what appears to be a fully analytical undertaking is only partially so; it is diluted by the intrusion of Mode 5, covert expert judgment about how the socioeconomic system works, or should work. (Note, however, that Figure 9-1 indicates that covert judgment enters all modes to some degree.)

*Mode 5* (moderately strong quasirational thought) refers to the cognitive activity of persons who base their decisions on a known, delimited set of data but who must act on those data largely in a passive and intuitive fashion; physicians practicing clinical medicine provide an example, as do weather forecasters. Expert judgment is one form of Mode 5 that policymakers must depend on, as they have, in countless congressional hearings. Moreover, as indicated in Figure 9-1, the greater covertness of the cognitive activity of the expert (compared to a computer model) means greater potential for interpersonal conflict among experts; different judgments will be assigned to different (selfish) motives rather than to different cognitive activity. As a result, suspicion will grow, and a dispute about facts may become a dispute over claims to superior morality.

*Mode 6* (*weak quasirational thought*) represents the kind of thought most of us engage in most of the time. It involves a dubious, often mythical data base, no manipulation of variables, no statistical controls, the inconsistent use of information in a manner never made explicit, and the substitution of rhetoric for logic. Because it depends wholly on a covert cognitive process, this common mode of quasirational, largely intuitive thought is methodologically extremely weak. Under these conditions, no one (not even the person making the judgment) can be sure of what the judgment process is. It carries therefore the greatest potential for conflict, a potential frequently realized. In short, Mode 6 is not only the weakest means for solving problems; because of its strong appeal to intuition it is also the most wasteful and the most dangerous one.

Mode 6 is also oriented toward *objects* rather than *variables*; thus it is Aristotelian rather than Galilean. That is why classical Greek philosophers would be perfectly at home in a discussion with almost any policymaker regarding almost any public policy problem. Both would focus on *this* plan for desegregation versus *that* one, the choice of *this* form of energy use versus *that* one. In short, Modes 5 and 6 represent the same modes of inquiry that have been applied to problems of social policy over the past two thousand years.

Greek scientists, however, would not find themselves equally at home with modern scientists, not merely because modern scientists know so much more but because they employ a wholly different, variable-oriented mode of cognition that was given great prominence by Galileo. Galileo did not ask which *objects* behaved in which ways; instead, he asked how *variables* (such as time and distance) affected the behavior of all objects. The critical task for scientists, then, is to move policymakers from the object-focused mode of cognition they currently use to the more powerful one that is oriented toward variables. The weaker the mode of inquiry, the more the policymaker will depend on coherence rather than correspondence. Impassioned pleas in Mode 6 will urge the listener to note how the "facts" directly "fit together" (cohere), because the correspondence of each "fact" to reality is weak.

I now provide an example of how a social problem moves through the matrix of modes of inquiry.

## An Example

Consider the question of permitting a new drug to be used by physicians. First, Mode 1 (strong analytical experimentation) is employed to discover the molecular structure of the chemical agent in question as well as its behavior in the presence of other chemical agents. Mode 2 (moderately strong analytical experimentation) is then employed in animal experiments and clinical trials involving random assignment of subjects to experimental and control groups with appropriate pre- and posttest (and perhaps continuous) measurements. This stage often includes epidemiological studies, some of which meet Mode 2 requirements, but many of which do not. Mode 3 (weak analytical experimentation) is employed when subsequent data regarding the actual use of the drug takes place—that is, when practicing physicians test it on their patients. Random assignment of subjects and pre- and posttesting cannot be achieved. Despite these difficulties, the knowledge of strengths and weaknesses of various types of quasi-experiments, laid out in great detail by Cook and Campbell,[7] lies virtually untouched. And although the data from physicians' reports, hospital records, and data from government agencies are by no means useless, they must be interpreted—that is, judgment must be employed in order to reach a conclusion; therefore, dispute over the meaning of the data is not only frequent but vigorous. To further dilute the analytical process, the final scientific conclusion is often reached by a jury of laypersons.

Mode 4, in which aids to judgment make a strong form of quasi-rational thought possible, has not yet been employed in the process of deciding whether a drug is efficacious and safe to use, although studies of physicians' judgments indicate that much can be done to improve matters.[8] Mode 5 (moderately strong quasirational thought) is used during clinical trials with patients; its function there is to appraise—that is, judge—the progress of patients and thus the efficacy of the drug. In this case, the data upon which the judgment is based may be known, but the manner in which the data are used by physicians as they exercise their clinical judgment is not.[9] Who knows how each clinician reaches his or her judgment? Because both of these modes of thought involve considerable covert cognitive activity, disagreement is frequent and disputes arise as to the safety or efficacy of the drug. A public hearing will then be held, and Mode 6 (weak quasirational thought) will be applied. At this point, all varieties of data and judgment will be applied, and the chaos of dispute will follow.

## The Modes of Inquiry Matrix as a Predictor

The diagram in Figure 9-1 is more than a didactic device; it offers a set of predictions that follow from the general theory described in Chapters 6 and 7. It applies the concepts and principles of that theory to the cognitive activity of policy formation. Its predictions are clear: Given the mode of inquiry permitted or chosen, the diagram predicts the nature of cognition—that is, the judgment and decision process as well as interpersonal behavior, conflict, and dispute—related to policy formation. Intuitive judgments and interpersonal disputes that reach the level of name calling and references to personal self-seeking behavior are a function of the departure from Mode 1; they reach a maximum when circumstances permit only Mode 6. When circumstances encourage or permit the use of the more analytical methods, such as those approaching Mode 1, these undesirable behaviors diminish. I turn now to some examples of attempts to use these modes of inquiry in policy formation.

Human judgment and the making of social policy take place in a political context. That means that experiments will not always be welcomed by politicians or administrators. As Campbell put it, some administrators are "trapped"[10]—they cannot move from preannounced positions—whereas some can move, can "experiment" with new policies. Experiments are sometimes undertaken because administrators are *desperate*; events have worked them into a corner where they are ready to try anything. Let's consider some examples.

## "Trapped" Administrators

The term "trapped" was introduced by Campbell in order to make clear that he understood that some administrators and politicians were often trapped by their preelection promises and postelection rhetoric; in his words, those administrators "whose political predicament would not allow the risk of failure" and therefore could not afford to become an "experimenting administrator" were "trapped." Let me give an example of a "trapped administrator" from my own experience.

The governor of my state had made a pre-election promise that he would decentralize the state government. He pledged to move the major state agencies (e.g., Department of Agriculture, Department of Natural Resources) out of the major city where all the state agencies were concentrated and into the less-populated rural areas of the state where they would be a boon to the economy. Once elected, he tried to implement this policy but was frustrated by the resistance of various department heads and employees, who argued that such a move was not a reasonable action, although it was strongly suspected that they simply did not want to relocate in rural areas. Since the governor had no empirical evidence that such a move would prove to be either beneficial or detrimental, he found that he could merely argue his point. Furthermore, because it was impossible to treat this issue as an experiment, the resolution would rest largely on human judgment. The governor's office turned to my research group and asked for a nonpartisan research project that would study, and possibly settle, the matter. We agreed, after receiving assurance that the project would indeed be nonpartisan and that the results would be taken seriously.

The project was completed in about six months' time, and a report was sent to the governor's office and to the various department heads (whose cooperation had been acquired on the premise that they would receive a copy of the report). The results clearly showed that, by the governor's own criteria, decentralization of state government was a poor idea. We knew that this would be bad news for the governor and that it would test his courage. Because we realized the serious implications of these results, we carefully checked our work (e.g., carried out sensitivity analyses). We became convinced of the validity of the conclusion.

Two days after the governor received the report, an appointment was made for us to discuss our report with him. To our astonishment, we were met not by the governor but by an aide who, closing the door to the governor's office firmly behind him, stated flatly: "Good or bad, right or wrong, we are going ahead with decentralization."

In short, the governor was trapped by his unfounded pre-election promises and postelection declarations about the value of decentralization. He took the risk of failure and failed, but he was trapped; he could not acknowledge his error, and he never did. He could not go ahead with his plans for decentralization, however, because our report, now in the hands of several of his department heads, was an insurmountable obstacle. The report itself lay buried, but it was not forgotten.

### The Disappearance of Trust

This incident provides us with a further distinction in addition to the distinction between "trapped" and "experimenting" administrators, and that is the one between "naive" and "skeptical" researchers. I was certainly a naive researcher in the case just described. But naiveté of this sort is apparently rapidly disappearing. Just as skepticism has become the norm in the media, it has become part of the general practice in relations between researchers on the one hand and government officials and others on the other—in both directions. Nonresearchers are as skeptical of researchers as the latter are of everyone else. In short, trust between researchers and their sponsors and the consumers of research has largely disappeared.

One of the most publicized efforts to bring science to bear on a social issue was carried out by the Public Health Service in 1992. The head of the Alcohol, Drug Abuse, and Mental Health Administration, Dr. Frederick Goodwin, described research on violence as "our number one initiative" and implied that there was some link between primate and human violent behavior, remarks that apparently led to his resignation (although he later became head of the National Institute of Mental Health). These remarks and others by Goodwin were taken by members of the African-American community to be racist in tone and intent. A Committee to Oppose the PHS Violence Initiative was formed with the intent of blocking what the committee believed to be a racially oriented research program on violence. The committee was particularly opposed to the funding by NIH of a conference entitled "Genetic Factors in Crime," and NIH canceled the funding for the conference.

The APA's executive director for science, William Howell, took a firm stand on the side of a neutral science, however, stating:

> Because violence has been the leading cause of death for Black men and Black women ages 15–24, there must be a strong response from the Public Health Service in the form of funded research. And a spectrum of research, from basic primate research to applied intervention research, should be involved. Unfortunately, until there is a resolution, scientists will find it difficult to conduct research in this area because of the atmosphere of suspicion in which these projects may be viewed.[11]

Whether the disappearance of trust is good or bad, trust has gone for the foreseeable future. Trapped administrators will be reluctant to participate in nonpartisan, scientific empirical studies of their policies, and highly qualified but encumbered scientists will avoid participation in research likely to bring criticisms of their motives.

## Desperate Administrators

Events—often unanticipated—may push administrators into situations in which they become desperate in their search for solutions. Trusted colleagues are found wanting, intellectually, ethically, or morally, past indiscretions surface, programs turn out to be embarrassing failures, opponents work themselves and the administrator into zero-sum situations in which there is no room for compromise, and the administrator may assume that desperate situations require desperate measures. It is when this point is reached that caution may be discarded in favor of action—*any* action—or calls for help go out to old friends, old enemies, and experts from the business or academic worlds. These remedies may move the desperate administrator to a calmer atmosphere (think of John Kennedy's assembly of experts at the time of the Cuban missile crisis) and a more analytical treatment of the problem.

## Experimenting Administrators

Experimenting administrators appear to be our best hope. These are the administrators who are trapped neither by ideology nor campaign promises or other forms of prior commitment; they are willing to acknowledge that they do not know the most effective amelioration of a problem and are prepared to learn, if they can, from the actual manipulation of conditions. They are prepared to be as thoughtful, as rational, as analytical, as circumstances will allow them to be. The question we now address is: What modes of inquiry are available to the "experimenting" administrator? What research methods are available to the policymaker who is committed to an honest empirical pursuit of a good solution to a problem? And, most important, how useful are our current "modes of inquiry" to policymakers?

## Mode 1: Methods of Physical Science

Physical science research is generally so carefully controlled and employs variables that are so precisely measured that statistical sampling methods are unnecessary. But these methods cannot be brought to bear on such policy questions as the value of Head Start programs, the effects of various welfare reforms, the best form of rehabilitation in prison, or the best drug therapy.

There are, however, points at which physical science can be brought to bear on issues, primarily risk. The journal *Risk Analysis* was created in 1980 for the purpose of bringing the expertise of physical scientists (mainly engineers) into the policy-making process. Engineers and experts from physics and chemistry conduct numerous laboratory studies in order to produce factual information regarding risky substances, risky processes, and risky storage practices, as well as other problems, in response to the large demand for scientific information from policymakers. The Environmental Protection Agency, the National Conference of State Legislators, and the Department of Energy all serve as communication channels that bring expertise and scientific information to policymakers.

Information produced by physical scientists in the laboratory often is unequivocal, but social policy must always apply scientific information outside the laboratory; it is at this point that trouble begins. The effective use of scientific information is not one of our great skills. For centuries, scientists have tried to introduce scientific information into policy formation, with only modest success.[12]

## Mode 2: Randomized, Experimental-Control Group Experiments

If the most powerful form of inquiry, the strong analytical thought and controlled procedures associated with Mode 1, could be brought to bear on policy questions, it would be most desirable to do so. Scientific information can be produced most effectively in the laboratory, where our analytical abilities and control of circumstances reach a maximum, as does civilized behavior. But policy questions can seldom be answered there. And it is seldom that they can be answered by the moderately strong analytical procedures of Mode 2. Random assignment of people to various conditions and manipulation of restricted conditions without exception can rarely be achieved in a democratic society. Even when they are achieved, the inherent uncertainty that remains as a result of the statistical analysis frustrates those who—

understandably but fruitlessly—demand that policymakers take the action that supports their view. Some experiments by economists are illustrative.

### Experiments by Economists

The National Bureau of Economic Research, a research organization that includes numerous prestigious economists among its officers and board of directors, sponsored a conference in 1981 that "addressed the question of the success of the experiments in achieving" the goal of evaluating "the potential effect of a policy option"[13] by trying it out within the framework of Mode 2. The editors of the conference proceedings, J. A. Hausman and D. A. Wise, begin by observing that "during the past decade the United States government has spent over 500 million dollars on social experiments"[14] to indicate to the reader that a great deal of social experimentation has already taken place. They explain that "this approach is an alternative to making *judgments* [italics added] about the effect of the proposed policy from inferences based on observational (survey) data, but without the advantages of randomization."[15] The editors thus describe one of the prime advantages of Mode 2 (randomization) over Mode 5, in which judgments are based on some set of agreed-upon data, such as those produced by a survey. They also note that, as of 1981, "this development [experimentation] is a relatively new approach to the evaluation of the effect of proposed government policies."[16] By "relatively new" they meant dating back only to about 1950. "But," they point out, "the most important question is whether the experiments have been successful in their primary goal of providing precise estimates of the effects of a proposed government policy."[17] Being economists, they also address the question of whether "the experiments were worth the cost." Most interesting, by 1981 they could ask: "Could similar information have been provided by the use of econometric models?"[18] thereby referring to the greater feasibility of the use of Mode 4.

The editors show their awareness of the place of Mode 2 experimentation in social experimentation by observing that "the methodology of randomized experiments was formalized and achieved wide acceptance due to the fundamental research of R. A. Fisher.... Yet most of ... [this] research dealt with agricultural experiments. Complex statistical questions arise when this methodology is applied to social experiments."[19] This is an astute observation that, odd as it may seem, was seldom made by social scientists or psychologists prior to Campbell's work.[20] Although they indicate only one such question—biased sampling that occurs through a refusal to participate or through attrition—many other problems are described throughout the text. Thus, they review the efforts of economists to move the level of inquiry as far in the direction of Mode 1 as possible. The feasibility of Mode 2 inquiry for the purpose of aiding the policymaker is directly addressed. What did the editors and the authors conclude?

The conclusions are mixed. Most of the authors concluded that it was better to have done the experiments than not to have done them, but they were uncertain about whether the benefits were worth the costs (the experiments were very expensive), and considerable doubt was expressed over whether the results were of real use to the policymakers, largely because of the length of time between the initiation of the research and the appearance of results, which are not always definitive.

For example:

- L. D. Taylor comments on D. J. Aigner's "The Residential Electricity Time-of-Use Pricing Experiments: What Have We Learned?"[21]: "I had hoped that Aigner would conclude that enough information now exists to provide at least a preliminary assessment of the costs and benefits of implementing TOU [time-of-use] pricing, but those hopes are clearly dashed."[22]
- G. K. Ingram: "Social experiments clearly have a place in the social scientists' tool kit."[23]
- S. Rosen: "It has been said that one of the main things economists have learned from social experiments is how to run experiments. To my mind that is surely a second-rate benefit because it is an awfully expensive way to learn."[24]
- Z. Griliches: "As I see it, we need experiments for two related reasons: (1) randomization of treatment allows us to ignore a whole slew of otherwise complicating variables and considerations [cf. Goldberg, p. 248, this chapter]; (2) application of treatment makes the relevant variable 'exogenous'."[25]
- L. L. Orr: "I heartily endorse . . . the suggestion of random selection of treatment and comparison sites from matched pairs. . . . My office has just completed a survey of about a dozen experiments. . . . While we did not attempt any rigorous pooling of data or results, it quickly became clear that the diversity of treatment design, data collection, outcome definition, and sample selection . . . almost defied description."[26]
- D. L. McFadden: "Balking and attrition are potential sources of severe bias in social experiments and require careful treatment. . . . I believe the focus of further research on social experimental methodology should be on robust methods for correcting self-selection biases."[27]
- H. Aaron comments on all of the chapters and offers general observations that are important:

  Inspired by genuine uncertainty about how to deal with a problem or by the belief that research evidence will persuade opponents, supporters of a policy initiate a social experiment. . . . Economists and other social scientists step in and design a test to estimate the key parameter. On the basis of the experiments, the parameter is found. It resolves doubts about which line of policy to pursue, and policymakers act on it.

  Such is the Platonic image of the social experiment, and indeed of research in general, that many of us hold. . . .

  But as we sharpen our instruments, we should recognize that the process is quite unlike the naïve model I have sketched. . . . The social experiment or the research paper with policy implications is part of an adversary process. . . . The fact [is] that the adversaries are contending for power, not truth. And deep down, that is what many of us are contending for too, how else can one explain the appalling lapses from analytical evenhandedness that Stromsdorfer mentions and documents.[28]
- F. Mosteller and M. C. Weinstein provide a detailed examination of the costs and benefits of clinical trials that should be read by every student of social experimentation. The arguments rest on some understanding of the mathematics of probability theory, so I will not include all of them here. The following paragraphs, however, afford the reader some insight into the complexities of a Mode 2 experiment intended to test the efficacy of an antihypertensive drug:

  A calculation of the potential benefits and costs of such a trial was made at that time by one of the authors and his colleagues (Laird, Weinstein, and Stason

1979). First, the cost of the trial was estimated at $135 million, assuming 28,000 subjects followed for five years. Next, the size of the population at risk was estimated to be 20 million, of which 10 percent were already being treated. Now, to simplify considerably, there were three possible results of the trial: not efficacious, efficacious, and inconclusive. . . .

We would also have to consider the false-negative case (treatment is efficacious, but the study says it is not), and the false-positive case (treatment is not efficacious, but the study says it is). We would then plug all this into the cost-effectiveness model and assess the value of the study. . . .

[The study showed that] there was a significant and important treatment effect, especially in the mildly hypertensive group. Now the controversy continues around whether this community-based study was really measuring the effects of antihypertensive medication or whether other differences between the treatments could have accounted for the difference in mortality. *The value of the HDFP [drug]—and of the placebo trial that was never conducted—is still not known* [italics added].[29]

I think these comments speak for themselves; social experiments in Mode 2 are certainly expensive, but their value is limited; the required conditions are seldom met, and the large residual uncertainty leaves the policymaker vulnerable to criticism no matter which course she or he takes. The clinical trials carried out by physicians, however, offer examples of Mode 2 experimentation at its best.

## Mode 2 at Its Best: Clinical Trials

The controversy over the question of whether routine mammograms should be given to women under age 50 offers a further example of how even high-level research in Mode 2 fails to resolve issues for policymakers.

As we observed earlier, under conditions of irreducible uncertainty, there will always be a constituency for each type of error—one that prefers injustice to society over injustice to the individual and one that prefers the opposite. Because Mode 2 always leaves us with some irreducible uncertainty, each error always carries the potential for its constituency to claim that action should be taken to support its view and, often, its rights. We should not be surprised, therefore, that the mammogram controversy brings this differential orientation toward injustice to the surface and evokes passionate responses from both sides, even from professionals who might be expected to eschew emotion. For example, Bernadine Healy, formerly the director of the National Institutes of Health (perhaps the most prestigious position in the health profession), surprisingly argued for risking the error that would increase injustice to society. Healy wanted to encourage women under age 50 to have mammograms taken despite the research results (developed by Mode 2 methods) that showed that there was no benefit in doing so. Her argument was well publicized; it appeared in *The Wall Street Journal*[30] and drew sharp reactions from members of the medical profession, on both sides.[31]

Divergent views illustrate the point that Mode 2 (the randomized, experimental control-group method of experimentation), which is the strongest form of intervention, has its weakness for policy formation. In the cases just described, painstaking studies did what they were supposed to do; data were collected under the procedures sanctioned by trained researchers and were analyzed under the scrutiny of expert statisticians. None of this prevented passionate dispute over the injustice to individuals or to society that would unavoidably occur because of the errors produced by irreducible uncertainty.

There have been and will continue to be occasions when it is possible to learn from interventions, but these occur infrequently and are rarely the results of careful experimentation. Conclusions are more often drawn by acclamation than by results from carefully controlled, statistically impeccable experiments. J. E. Innes summarizes the situation well when she says: "Social experiments are time-consuming, expensive and difficult to set up and conduct without [involving] so many intervening influences that they cannot be interpreted as experiments."[32]

## Mode 3: Quasiexperimentation

Campbell and others have long advocated—and justified—the next best mode of inquiry, the weak analytical Mode 3, which employs quasiexperiments. Although quasiexperiments lack rigor (i.e., do not require random assignment of subjects to conditions) and thus produce information of less certain validity than Mode 2 experiments, they are far more feasible, and many quasiexperiments have been carried out.[33] But the weakness of the information produced requires that policymakers exercise their judgment to a large degree; as a result, disagreement and interpersonal conflict and many of the other difficulties described earlier reappear. Quasiexperiments have serious liabilities as well as assets as aids to decisionmakers.

What motivated the inventors of quasiexperimental designs to urge the use of a *weaker* form of experimentation than those already at hand? What could possibly have persuaded Campbell and J. C. Stanley in 1966[34] to advocate the use of a mode of inquiry that produces results more susceptible to varying interpretations than the very sophisticated, mathematically tested, known-to-be-effective methods introduced by R. A. Fisher[35] and J. Neyman and E. S. Pearson?[36] What was it that induced Campbell and Stanley to write strange sentences such as: "We must instill in our students the expectation of tedium and disappointment and the duty of thorough persistence, by now so well achieved in the biological and physical sciences"?[37] Needless to say, their plea to "instill . . . the expectation of tedium and disappointment" in students was not implemented or even acknowledged by their peers; the reverse was (and will always be) the case; every discipline attempts to recruit new students by instilling expectations of the opposite, the excitement and thrills of success. Disappointment? Never!

But worse was yet to come, for in the next sentence Campbell and Stanley announce: "We must expand our students' vow of poverty to include not only the willingness to accept poverty of finances, but also a *poverty of experimental results* [italics added]."[38]

These were extraordinary exhortations: Instill boredom and disappointment? Instill a prior expectation that the most powerful form of inquiry recently installed in psychology would yield a "poverty" of results? How could they say such things at the time when powerful statistical methods had elevated psychology to a point when it could at last with some justice claim the status of a science? Why would two outstanding social scientists make such remarks? The answer is worth pursuing, for our pursuit will lead us to a better understanding of the role of human judgment in social policy formation.

Campbell and Stanley began their monograph by expressing the general disillusionment with conventional experimentation in educational research. They noted the pain and frustration that followed from the "nonconfirmation of a cherished hypothesis"[39] and observed that "if, as seems likely, the ecology of our science is one in which there are available many more wrong [i.e., disconfirming] responses [from the experiment] than correct ones, we may anticipate that most experiments will be disappointing."[40]

They went on to list "12 factors jeopardizing the validity of various experimental designs,"[41] all of which apply to the use of conventional experimental methods (Mode 2 in Figure 9-1). Among these are such matters as:

> "*History,* the specific events occurring between the first and second measurement in addition to the experimental variable."
>
> "*Maturation,* processes within the respondents operating as a function of the passage of time. . . ."
>
> "*Testing,* the effects of taking a test upon the scores of a second testing. . . ."
>
> "*Experimental mortality,* or differential loss of respondents from the comparison groups. . . ."
>
> "*Reactive effects of experimental arrangements,* which would preclude generalization about the effect of the experimental variable upon persons being exposed to it in nonexperimental settings."[42]

These and similar "threats" to the validity of conclusions drawn from Mode 2, documented by Campbell and Stanley, are what produce divergent and disappointing results. They also lead to the frustration of policymakers—"experimenting" administrators—who honestly try to discover the better, if not best, method for coping with problems such as crime and health care reform.

It took courage for Campbell and Stanley to point out the weaknesses of the conventional experimental (Mode 2) methodology and the implications of these weaknesses for students, researchers, and policymakers. It also took intellect to see that the disappointment was not solely due to weak theory or poorly designed experiments and that the difficulties could not possibly be alleviated by working harder in the *same way.* It took even greater courage and intellect to urge change, to be frank about the small likelihood of finding success and about the weaknesses inherent in each and every conventional experimental design that might be employed in the service of policy formation. That is a message no one wants to hear, and it has not been heard by many.

One of Campbell and Stanley's strongest arguments concerning experimental designs remains one of the least discussed and most avoided in social science research. They point to the problem of *induction*—inferring or generalizing from the observed to the as yet unobserved (a problem for which we often employ our judgment). The logic of statistical sampling theory justifies our inductions from samples of people (or animals or plants) observed to those unobserved (as in surveys or agricultural experiments). But induction to *conditions* beyond the specific ones used in the experiment (or survey) cannot be so readily justified; sampling theory cannot be as readily applied to conditions as to people (or plants or animals). But Campbell's teacher, Egon Brunswik, made it clear that psychology must address the problem of generalizing over conditions.

As Campbell and Stanley strongly put it: "*Logically,* we cannot generalize beyond . . . [the] limits [of those conditions]. . . . But we do attempt generalization by guessing at laws and checking out some of these generalizations in other . . . conditions."[43] This rather simple statement cuts at the heart of the problems facing the policymaker who attempts to make use of high-level, social-science generalizations. It means that generalizations from people observed to people unobserved can be defended analytically by referring to sampling theory, but generalizing from the conditions employed in the experiment to those in which the results will be applied cannot be analytically (logically) defended by recourse to sampling theory, because sampling (generally) has not occurred. As a result, "guessing"—that is, quasirational cognition—has to be employed. That almost inevitably results in dispute, which has two sources: (1) the covert nature of the cognitive processes employed (no one knows exactly what anyone else is thinking), and (2) the different political philosophies or ideologies that underlie "natural laws" guessed at or depended on. It is in this fashion that even the most powerful mode of inquiry (Mode 2) generates dispute among policymakers; generalization from experimental conditions to conditions of application must rely on quasirational cognition. But Mode 2 is rarely available in any event, because of its demand for random assignment of people to circumstances, a condition almost impossible to meet. Therefore, Mode 2's strongest attribute—generalization over people—is difficult to achieve; generalization over conditions is generally impossible to achieve.

I have provided only the broadest outline of a very complex matter—experimental design—that Campbell and Stanley's classic monograph treats in great detail and that is treated further in subsequent publications.[44] Before leaving Campbell and Stanley, the reader should recognize that, although they addressed their remarks to their peers, these remarks hold equally well for policymakers. They, too, must expect "disappointment" and the "duty of persistence," as well as "poverty of experimental results," and be resigned to the weaker modes of inquiry—quasiexperimentation and hypothetical experimentation—and all they imply for interpersonal conflict and the likelihood of successful policies. For it is this situation that leads to irreducible uncertainty and thus to the inevitability of the duality of error and unavoidable injustice.

### An Example

Although there have been several applications of quasi-experimental design, one of the more recent is the study of the effect of TV advertising on children by Marvin Goldberg. This study is important for several reasons: (1) It illustrates the role of quasiexperimentation in policy formation; (2) it is directed toward a substantive question of considerable social concern—namely, the extent to which TV advertising affects children's economic behavior (e.g., purchases of goods such as cereals and toys); and (3) it is indirectly related to the question of whether TV affects children's acceptance of violence.

Goldberg took advantage of a policy-produced event to conduct his study. A law put into effect in Quebec in 1980 eliminated advertising to children on Quebec-based media. That action resulted in the elimination of "commercials directed at children throughout most of the TV schedule."[45] There was a complication, however, that served Goldberg's purposes:

> Though the law eliminated advertising to children on Quebec TV stations, American border TV channels reaching Quebec (the three commercial networks) still carry heavy levels of TV commercials directed at children. Consequently, it was reasoned that the law ought to have maximal effects on children watching little if any American children's commercial TV (ACTV) and minimal effects on those watching considerable amounts of ACTV. This study design provided for a comparison of those exposed to higher and lower levels of ACTV and, by extension, the commercials inserted therein.
>
> Two subgroups highly likely to have had different levels of exposure to ACTV were French-speaking and English-speaking children in Quebec. Bureau of Broadcast Measurement (BBM) data indicate that English- and French-speaking children aged 2 through 11 in Montreal watch identical amounts of TV: an average of 22 hours per week (or just over 3 hours per day, as reported by Caron, Letendre, and Van Every 1988). However, because their mother tongue facilitates access to American TV, it was reasoned that English-speaking children ought to watch considerably more ACTV programs than French-speaking children, and ought to be exposed to a commensurately higher level of children's TV commercials. Consequently, one central aspect of this study was a comparison of similar groups of English- and French-speaking children.[46]

In short, policymakers in Quebec acted on a theory that was essentially without empirical foundation (that is, without backing from a correspondence theory) because the commercials directed at children offended a social belief that depended on coherence with other beliefs (children shouldn't be subjected to this sort of thing). Goldberg then proceeded as follows:

### Hypotheses

The following hypotheses are based on two premises: (1) given the law outlawing advertising to children in Quebec, children were not exposed to advertising for children's products on Quebec TV stations and (2) English-speaking children watch considerably more ACTV and the commercials therein than do French-speaking children (data pertaining to this assumption are reported subsequently).[47]

Goldberg found the following:

- English-speaking children did indeed watch more commercial TV on American stations than did French-speaking children, and, "hence, a quasi-experimental design could be structured to compare the two groups of children."[48]
- English-speaking children recognized more toys and reported having more children's cereals in their houses than did French-speaking children.

These results, together with those produced by sophisticated statistical analyses, indicate that advertising directed at children did have its intended effect. As Goldberg put it: "This study demonstrates that the causal effect for exposure to children's TV commercials, as previously noted in laboratory experiments, is also observed in a natural setting without the artificial disentangling of other causal agents."[49] From this he drew the obvious policy-related conclusions:

Though this study does not address whether the effect of exposure to children's TV commercials is larger or smaller than that of other potential causal agents, the issue is one that can be addressed legislatively. The Quebec law served to reduce children's exposure to commercials for sugared cereals and hence appears to have reduced consumption of those cereals. There is no reason to believe that comparable legislation in the U.S. would not have comparable results. For toys, the expectation was that reduced exposure to commercials would leave children unaware of the toys and thus less able to pressure their parents to buy them. The law seems to have been effective in this context. Here, too, one might anticipate that comparable legislation in the U.S. would be equally effective.[50]

Thus, despite the lack of control or, rather, *because* of the lack of control of related variables, Goldberg was able to provide results that carried direct policy implications. Goldberg could, and did, argue that his results were "observed in a natural setting without the artificial disentangling of the causal agents."[51] Of course, those who do not like these results will be quick to argue that *because* "other causal agents" were not controlled, the results were due to these agents rather than the TV advertisements. Thus we see why Mode 3 is generally weaker, although more feasible, than Mode 2.

These remarks about Modes 1, 2, and 3 are placed in the context of the theory described in Chapters 6 and 7. They are based on the premises that (1) cognition takes place on a continuum that runs from intuition to analysis, and (2) as cognitive activity moves from highly analytical activity as demanded by Mode 1 to circumstances such as those implicit in Mode 3, which encourage more intuitive activity, certain consequences of importance to policymakers will follow. Mode 3 is less demanding and thus more feasible than Mode 1, but cognition becomes more covert, and thus the potential for interpersonal conflict increases. Mode 2 offers the potential for greater analytical cognition through the use of rigorous statistical analysis, but its demands for random assignment, double-blind conditions, and control over attrition add to its cost and decrease its feasibility, as the economists and the statisticians point out.

As already mentioned, a problem that is particularly difficult for psychologists is the problem of generalizing from the *conditions* of an experiment. It is a problem raised over half a century ago by Brunswik,[52] and emphasized again by Campbell and Stanley and by me on several occasions,[53] yet addressed by few others and, indeed, ignored by the vast majority of psychologists. This problem is particularly acute for policymakers. They accept the idea of generalizing over *people*—that is, applying the results of a social experiment—to people not in the experiment, because we are all accustomed to the idea of sampling people from the widespread use of public opinion surveys. The question of generalizing from the *specific conditions* of the experiment is another matter. On the one hand, the researcher must be specific if she or he is to claim the rigor of an experiment—that is, claim that the conditions were carefully delimited and controlled—and claim that the results can be depended on. On the other hand, the more specific the conditions, the more restrictive the application of the results to other conditions and, therefore, the less confidence we can have that the results apply outside the narrow, highly specific conditions of the experiment.

Two well-known social psychologists, P. Suedfeld and P. E. Tetlock, directly attack the foundations of scientific psychology and laboratory research in this way: "Findings in laboratory situations—and even in the most convincing field experiments—can best be thought of as hypothesis generating, not hypothesis *testing* [italics added]."[54] This is exactly the opposite of the current role assigned to laboratory research by a well-known experimental psychologist, W. K. Estes, when he asserts that "a time-tested strategy is to . . . rely on experimental analyses in the controlled laboratory environment to guide the development and *testing* [italics added] of theories."[55] It is more than passing strange that a psychologist (Estes) who has devoted most of his research career to the laboratory rather than life and Suedfeld and Tetlock, who have devoted their research careers to life rather than the laboratory, would assign exactly opposite roles to laboratory and life, each emphasizing his career area as the proper site for the testing of hypotheses and theories—in short, the proper place for the final say.

One might paraphrase this dispute in this way: Want the *fundamental* truth? "Find it in the laboratory," say the laboratory researchers. "No," say the "real world" researchers. "Find it out here where *we* work."

These contradictory opinions held by prominent psychologists regarding the contributions of laboratory and life are important. They show that psychologists have yet to resolve their dispute over the generalizability of results from laboratory research and the utility of field research. The reader should, therefore, treat with great caution the pronouncements of psychologists—prominent or otherwise—about the proper roles of laboratory and life.

The solution to this problem offered by Brunswik and elaborated on by me,[56] and by others[57] is straightforward: Generalization over people or conditions involves the same reasoning. That is, generalization is justified by representative sampling, whether one is sampling people or conditions. Therefore, when designing experiments, researchers should include those *conditions,* as well as people, toward which their generalization is intended.[58] This idea is central to the question of the utility of experimental research to policymakers.

### An Example from Health Care Reform

Some of the most important ongoing research currently being conducted, the effect of various treatments for certain medical conditions, is being examined by quasi-experimentation. Figure 9-1 predicts the results of the mode of inquiry in terms of the location of the judgment process on the intuition-analysis continuum, the implications for interpersonal conflict, and its appeal to both metatheories of both correspondence and coherence. A recent article in *Science* describes these circumstances and provides anecdotal evidence that tests the predictability of the theory.

Titled "Measuring What Works in Health Care," the article examines the steps being taken by a newly formed governmental agency to discover "which medical interventions work best."[59] The author notes that "physicians themselves, let alone government bureaucrats, often don't know which medical interventions work best" and that "even a relatively straightforward comparison—between a 10-cent aspirin and a $1,000 shot of a genetically engineered anticlotting drug, for example—requires a clinical trial [Mode 2 experimentation] costing tens of millions of dollars and lasting upward of a decade."[60] This comment reflects those of the economists; Mode 2 experiments in society—outside the laboratory or the agricultural experiment station—are very expensive indeed, and although the aspirin versus genetically engineered comparison was successfully resolved, many aren't. But as the need for a better health care policy became more visible in the 1990s, the need for examination of "what works" led epidemiologists and others to argue "that some clues might be found relatively cheaply and early in the records that have been accumulated by hospitals"[61] and by health care professionals. It was the introduction of electronic databases that made such searches feasible. "Comb through these vast databases, they argued, and you might get a good idea of which medical interventions produced the best outcomes."[62] Note the change in language here. Elsewhere in *Science* one does not find reports that claim only that their results "might" provide the reader with "a good idea" of the outcome of an experiment. But the cost of carrying out many Mode 2 experiments (several billion dollars) makes them impossible; the policymakers and scientists knew that and were willing to settle for "getting a good idea" of the results by a less analytical, more feasible means. Indeed, the charm of more for less led Congress to create the Agency for Health Care Policy and Research to expedite "outcomes research."

The article quotes Dr. David Eddy as saying that "the premise of outcomes research . . . is based on . . . 'natural experiments.'"[63] That is, he is quoted as saying, "'just observe the experiment—mine the data—and you can get pretty good information' about what works and what doesn't."[64]

That, of course, is raw optimism. The theory in Figure 9-1 makes a different prediction: Intuitive judgments and disputes will follow. And that is what has occurred. The sharpest critic has been Richard Peto, a well-known epidemiologist who made exactly the comment Figure 9-1 predicts he would make from the location of Mode 3 quasiexperiments on the cognitive continuum in Figure 9-1: "A lot of money has been spent on nonrandomized [note!] outcomes research because the claim was made that it was going to give us reliable comparisons between the main effects of different treatments. . . . [But] it has utterly, totally, and predictably failed to do so."[65] Even worse, he said, "Investing in a lot of outcomes research 'is worse than just destroying the money . . . because it gives the illusion of information.'"[66] Figure 9-1 predicts conflict as a result of Mode 3; Peto's remarks provide it, for proponents of Mode 3 (outcomes research) won't give up easily. "Outcomes researchers argue that, whatever the limitations of their methodology, it is better than nothing [but compare this with Peto's claim that it 'is worse than just destroying the money']. And nothing, they say, is what they would get in many cases if they relied on [Mode 2] clinical trials."[67] The article then quotes the outcomes researcher Barbara McNeil: "The real aim is to ask: Can we identify variations of practice for further study?"[68]

From the point of view of Figure 9-1, the real issue is: Why are these researchers discovering this dispute five years *after* the agency has been created, the research carried out, and $200 million spent? The answer is that this episode involving human judgment and social policy represents a classic case of irreducible uncertainty (as all the researchers would agree), inevitable error (as one study reported in the article has already demonstrated), and unavoidable injustice; some people who would have benefited from a treatment won't get it, and some who won't benefit from that treatment will get it.

## Summary

Of the two major approaches to learning, intervening and representing, intervening is generally considered the more powerful and the most productive. Experiments offer a better chance of informing us about causal relations because of the active manipulation of conditions and because of the standards of control we impose along with our interventions, such as random assignment and the use of control groups. These rigorous methods have been tremendously useful in producing the knowledge we now possess and that makes up the content of World 3. As these methods diminish in their rigor and we are required to move from active physical manipulation of conditions to representing conditions (as indicated in Figure 9-1), however, analytical cognition is reduced and intuitive cognition is increased. That is, the advantages of rigor are reduced as cognition moves along the cognitive continuum, as described in Chapter 6, from the analytical pole to the intuitive pole. The consequences are that cognitive activity becomes less accessible and interpersonal conflict becomes more prevalent, more acute, and far more difficult to resolve. As these methods become less rigorous, they become more feasible for policymakers to employ—or ask to be employed—and therefore become more frequently employed. As the experimental methods lose rigor—move from Mode 1 to Mode 3—and as representational methods lose their rigor—move from Mode 4 to Mode 6—policymakers must rely increasingly on their intuitive judgment, with the resultant increase in dispute so often observed.

Without knowledge of the weakness of our experimental methods for purposes of policy formation there is a danger, easily observable, of blaming persons for not accomplishing what their tools will not allow them to accomplish, accusations that waste time, resources, and good will. Recognition of these weaknesses should reduce our tendency to blame others for what cannot be helped and should lead to a greater emphasis on developing—indeed, inventing—experimental methods more appropriate for policymakers.

There is no reason to believe that we cannot or will not invent new modes of inquiry that will be more useful to the policymaker than those we now possess; after all, we have been inventing new modes of inquiry ever since the Enlightenment, and even before. But our main efforts have been directed toward developing better research methods for scientists. As Figure 9-2 indicates, during the last decade far more articles cited in the Social Science Index are devoted to experimental design—primarily variation upon variation of standard design for scientists—than to any other aspect of methodology. Computer simulation is next. But the least amount of effort has been given over to the general topic of scientific method and to quasi-experimental design. Figure 9-2 indicates that the vast preponderance of our efforts to develop analytical means for learning have not been directed toward the needs of policymakers; instead, our intellectual energies have gone into modes of inquiry that were developed to enable scientists to learn. Unfortunately for policymakers, these

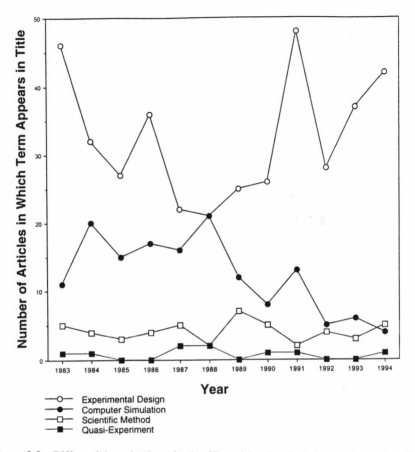

Figure 9-2    Differential production of scientific articles that include experimental design, computer simulation, scientific method, or quasi-experiment in the title for each year from 1983 to 1994. (*Source: Social Sciences Index.*)

methods are largely infeasible for helping policymakers to learn. As a result, they learn slowly, if at all.

One social scientist has acknowledged that there are limits to learning either by intervening or representing. James Q. Wilson, one of the nation's outstanding social scientists, wrote that, despite the many reasons to consider the present a great improvement over the recent past, "we feel that there is something profoundly wrong with our society. Not with our own lives . . . but with the conditions and prospects of our communal life."[69] Yet he stated that "I do not know what ought to be done and assert that I do not think anyone else knows either."[70] Many believe that Wilson has made an announcement equivalent to "the King is naked."

We are slow, ineffective learners about the effects of our social policies (and other sociological and political events), not because we are stupid animals (we are not), not because we are "fundamentally irrational" (we are not), not because we are controlled by villains (we are not, although there are villains among us), but because our means for learning from even the best forms of intervention—experimentation—are not efficacious. Why should they be? They were invented for different purposes. The "experimental designs" described in Mode 2 do indeed represent great achievements, but they were intended for circumstances in which a researcher would have great control over the objects of study (plants, animals, people in the laboratory) and conditions (fertilizing, food, rewards and punishment, information and responses). The much more feasible quasiexperiments of Mode 3 leave so much room for dispute that they do not serve us well. The hypothetical experiments carried out by computer models hold great promise but remain subject to doubts and criticism. The use of expert judgment, town meetings, and "blue ribbon" commissions are of very dubious value.

Nor am I the first to raise this question. Gigerenzer and his colleagues asked: "Are the experimental designs developed by statisticians in agriculture and biology really a good model for all experimentation in the social sciences?"[71] It is the uncertainty, doubt, and dispute that so often remains after the most painstaking experiments that cause policymakers to groan when social scientists tell them "more research is needed" to answer their questions. They have learned—painfully and slowly—that although more research may indeed be needed, more research of the kind already done will not reduce their uncertainty to the degree needed to reduce dispute engendered by different intuitions about what to do. In short, methods with better combinations of feasibility and uncertainty-reduction need to be invented and developed.

The reader—especially if a social scientist—will find this view iconoclastic, for it appears to strike at the heart of social science, at the very methods that allow it to claim scientific status. That is not my intention; the logic of "experimental design" is one of our great achievements and has not had the acclaim it deserves. But this methodology, however useful for scientific purposes, serves neither the policymakers nor their constituents well.

# 10 Is It Possible to Learn from Representing?

Is it possible we might learn to do better in the future? Are such things ever "learned"? I do not know.

—*Senator Daniel Patrick Moynihan*

Several academic disciplines—ecology, geology, geography, history, and paleontology, among others—are based on representing what has been observed. Indeed, that was Darwin's method. Some of the most significant additions to our knowledge come from representing social, ecological, and physical phenomena.

Sometimes representation is easy; for example, we have discovered that the population of the world is growing rapidly. But sometimes it is hard. The ongoing debate about the health care system in the United States provides an example. Speeches are regularly given in which we are told that "U.S. citizens have the best health care in the world," but with equal regularity we are told that the "system is broken and needs to be fixed." Worse still, the representation of the true situation— whatever it is—is of doubtful validity because its representation is closely linked to the political affiliation of the speaker. In short, as is the case with intervening, some modes of representation are more trustworthy than others. I begin with the best—Mode 4.

Our ability to represent the world around us took an enormous step forward with the invention of the electronic computer; the term "computer model" is now a household word. As the reader will anticipate, there are two major types of computer models of interest to the policymaker—those that model interventions (experiments) and their effects and those that model representations. In the next section I describe Mode 4A, computer modeling of interventions; Mode 4B describes computer modeling of representations.

## Mode 4A: Hypothetical Intervention and Manipulation of Variables and Conditions: The Coherence Approach

Strong modes of experimentation have been with us for centuries, certainly since Galileo, and arguably since Archimedes and his contemporaries. Weaker, yet still powerful, modes of experimentation involving modern statistical analyses are mainly the product of the first half of the twentieth century.[1] The second half of this century saw the introduction of quasiexperiments as well as of an entirely new way for human beings to investigate their world—computer modeling. Some social scientists, mainly economists, were quick to see the opportunities offered by this mode of inquiry. Until the advent of the computer, modeling the environment (of any kind) was simply too difficult to be carried out to any significant degree. But the computer's ability to store and manipulate rapidly large amounts of data made modeling possible.

One great advantage offered by computer modeling is that it allows the use of "what if" procedures ("sensitivity analysis") to test the dependence of a set of results on the theory. For example, if minor changes in the theory underlying the model result in large changes in results, the theory or model is considered weak because of its restricted range of application. But if the results are little affected by changes, the theory (and thus the model) are deemed "robust"—insensitive to small changes— and generally reliable. Similarly with regard to data used by the computer model; "what if" procedures can be used here as well. For example, "what if" our data are in error by as much as 1 percent? 5 percent? 10 percent? 20 percent? How large an effect will that have on the results and thus our conclusions? In short, how sensitive is our model to errors or imprecision in our data? Low sensitivity to imprecision gives reason for confidence in the model. (Those who use the now common "spreadsheets" will be familiar with "what if" procedures.)

Computer modeling thus offered an entirely new and valuable mode of inquiry for policy formation. If a reasonable model of the circumstances about to be affected by an intervention (natural, artificial, or socioeconomic) could be produced, the policymaker would be able to manipulate the circumstances in symbolic form without suffering the expense and consequences of changing the actual physical or economic or social conditions. Computer models allow us to manipulate conditions *hypothetically*; that extraordinary advantage has led to the widespread use of computer modeling, particularly in economics, in the effort to predict what will happen. Computer simulation of economic ("what if we should spend more—or less—on this program") and environmental ("what if we should build a smaller dam") systems can provide an invaluable aid to decisionmakers because it allows them to manipulate variables in a hypothetical world and to observe the outcomes of such manipulations without suffering the consequences of mistaken policies undertaken in a real world.

It is for these reasons Mode 4A is labeled the strong quasirational mode. It offers the best basis for policy formation when actual, physical manipulation and control of variables and empirical observation of results cannot be achieved in a timely fashion, as is ordinarily the case. These new aids to cognition provide the first radically new mode of inquiry since the introduction of the mathematics of statistical inference in the eighteenth century and the development of "experimental designs" in the twentieth century. As the reader will anticipate, computer modeling depends to a large extent on coherence for its justification.[2]

## An Example of Computer Modeling in Mode 4A: Global Warming and Its Potential Effects on the Florida Flora

During the 1980s it was widely reported that atmospheric scientists were beginning to believe that the temperature of the Earth might rise significantly; were that to occur, several dramatic events would follow. The sea level would rise, rainfall and temperature patterns would change, and vegetation over the Earth would change markedly. That raised the question of what steps might be taken now to minimize the negative consequences of global warming, should it occur. In addressing this question, policymakers encounter all the problems discussed earlier in this book. These include the problems of irreducible uncertainty, duality of error, and unavoidable injustice.

1. *Irreducible uncertainty.* No one can say with certainty whether global warming will occur, when it will occur (if it does), to what extent it will occur (if it does), or how long it will last (if it does occur). Nor is there agreement on the degree of uncertainty involved.

2. *Duality of error.* This error concerns the risks and costs of taking precautionary actions should global warming not occur and the risks and costs of not taking precautionary action should global warming occur.

3. *Unavoidable injustice.* There will be unavoidable injustice as a consequence of either error. Should the first error occur, all those who provide the resources for protecting others will have suffered an injustice; something will have been taken from them for which they received nothing in return. Should the second error occur, those citizens who suffer the consequences of the loss of *their* resources because of a failure to act will suffer an injustice; something will have been taken from them in order to preserve the resources of others.

Nevertheless some scientists did set out to discover what the effects of global warming would be in Florida if it did occur. How could they bring scientific information to bear on this issue in the most effective way? Modes 1, 2, and 3 are completely infeasible; we cannot carry out physical experiments that will approximate the conditions of global warming. Modes 5 and 6, of course, are highly feasible, but they already have led to dispute. Use of Mode 4A, however, makes it possible to employ more features of analytical cognition than either Mode 5 or 6 allows. But, as we can expect from Figure 9-1, it is far more demanding.

In the present example, considerable scientific knowledge about the sea, the Florida flora, and hydrology would be needed; that knowledge would have to be sufficient to allow scientists to build a model; that means they would need a theory of the changes in sea level to be anticipated in response to a change in global temperature. Fortunately, we do possess sufficient dependable knowledge—we know enough empirical laws—to build models of the changes in climate and plant species that justify prediction of what should occur in response to changes in temperature. And that is precisely the task several ecologists undertook:

> Simulation of the effects of sea level rise due to global warming . . . indicates that southern Florida could lose twenty percent of its wetlands with a one-meter rise in the next century. In peninsular Florida mangroves and salt marshes would migrate at the expense of freshwater marshes and swamps, then the coastal wetlands would gradually decline in area. Some freshwater wetlands would in turn migrate to higher elevations as the water table is raised adjacent to the coast. The Florida Keys initially would experience a shift from roughly equal areas of salt marsh and mangroves to greater dominance by mangroves, followed by a decline in all wetlands with depletion of adjacent lowlands suitable for colonization. Dire consequences are predicted for the many protected natural areas in the region. Large areas of the Everglades and Biscayne National Parks could be lost; the Crocodile Lake, Great White Heron, and Key West National Wildlife Refuges and the National Key Deer Refuge could be severely affected; and some State parks, recreational areas, and preserves could be lost entirely.[3]

The authors' method was to construct the appropriate model of—describe the dynamic relations among—all the variables involving temperature change and sea level, to acquire all the data related to sea level and temperature, and to interface the data with the model. Despite the technical jargon I include the following paragraph that summarizes their method.

> For efficient data processing and modeling on the desktop computer, the simulation model, SLAMM3, was linked with a geographic information system (GIS) and image processing system. The Earth Resources Data Analysis System (ERDAS) was used to process Landsat MSS data to generate class information, and pc-ARC/INFO was used to digitize contour data. A set of interface routines were written in FORTRAN 77 to interface the two systems with the SLAMM3 model. The input data were read into SLAMM3, and the simulation results were written to GIS files for generation of maps.[4]

The theory of judgment presented in Chapters 6 and 7 tells us why the ability to present results in pictorial form is so helpful and so often desired. Pictorial (in contrast to numerical) displays allow cognition to oscillate between the intuitive and the analytical poles of the cognitive continuum. Pattern recognition and comparison are also induced. We should also expect to see alternation between searches for coherent patterns and for the presence of multiple fallible indicators. (The reader should recall remarks about similar alternation in the meteorologists' cognition.) In addition to these intuitive judgments, the model allows us to turn back to analytical cognition, to check, to retrace, for we can now say to ourselves, Is it really true? How credible is the model? How credible are the data that went into it? The policymaker can then ask for the details of the model, ask that it be examined for errors in logic, in its scientific base, and in the sources of the data.

At this point the judgment of other scientists enters the process; their judgments are largely the product of analytical cognition. The object of their scrutiny—the parameters, the equations, the sources of the data, the reliability of the data—are studied in a manner that must stand up to the analytical cognition of persons qualified to apply it in these circumstances. There will be differences in such judgments, but they will be explicit, overt, and thus readily criticized. The model may or may not stand up, but, in all likelihood, all parties will be at their cognitive best; the situation demands it; intuitive judgments will have to be defended; dogmatic arguments will be exposed as such. And when we return to look at the conclusions, we will do so knowing that we are, or are not, justified in accepting or rejecting them. That is the prediction based on the theory expressed in Figure 9-1.

That is not to say that the mere use of a model produces angelic behavior. But the use of a model (and its data) ordinarily rules out behavior seen in Modes 5 and 6. And it may reduce the countless ad hominem disputes so characteristic of Modes 5 and 6 that drag policy formation out into years and years of fruitless, irrelevant argumentation and charges of venality.

I use the word "may" because there is a glaring weakness in the Mode 4A effort just described. The *empirical validity* of the model has yet to be demonstrated; acceptance of the validity of the model (and the data) therefore must depend on scientific consensus. That means that scientists have to exercise their judgment about the validity of the model, and although their judgments are largely overt and analytical in nature, they remain covert to some degree. Moreover, few models satisfy *every* expert. There remains room for suspicion, and, as we have learned, suspicion there will be. For example, do any of the experts whose judgments will determine the acceptability of the results stand to gain or lose if the conclusions are accepted or rejected? Have they been funded by people or governmental agencies that have a vested interest in the results? These questions are now standard, and well they might be.

In addition, we must ask about the cognitive activity of the policymakers. How will they respond to the conclusions indicated by the pictures and the researchers' conclusions? Will their judgments be above reproach? Will they be retraceable, or must we depend on the honesty of their reports of how they arrived at their conclusions? Will all this work be sabotaged by policymakers who have something to gain because of a priori commitments to one form of action or another?

The following column in *The Wall Street Journal* illustrates the kind of criticisms that are brought to bear on Mode 4A experiments:

Computer models are notoriously friendly to their sponsors' interests. A computer model found that if airlines could not hire replacement workers during a strike, fares would rise so high that only the rich could fly; the study was prepared for the Air Transport Association. A computer model showed that if advertising were taxed in Minnesota, the industry as well as the state's entire economy would be damaged; the study was sponsored by the Communications Industry Coalition. Computer models found that if the U.S. adopted a Canadian-style national medical plan, health-care costs would either increase by \$38 billion (people who oppose such a plan) or decrease by \$241 billion (people who favor it).[5]

It is also possible to pick and choose among the results from the same models, to accept those that support your argument and reject those that don't, as this example from Laura Tyson, chairwoman of the President's Council of Economic Advisors, shows.

Economics models have produced estimates of the substantial gains to be had from increased trade resulting from the Uruguay Round. But many of these estimates are too conservative. Economic benefits of trade liberalization in services or of enhanced protection of intellectual property rights. And most of the models miss something even more important: that higher productivity will result in increased investment and innovation.[6]

However legitimate Tyson's complaints may be, they illustrate the point that economic models, like others of Mode 4A, do not *always* drive out intuitive judgments and settle disputes.

Despite the model's advantages over Modes 5 and 6, the fact that questions such as these can be raised shows the weakness of Mode 4A. As a result, scientists try to employ a stronger form of Mode 4A, as the next example shows.

The Importance of Prior Validation

E. O. Box, D. W. Crumpacker, and E. D. Hardin employed a computer model to "predict responses of plant species to various scenarios of climate change."[7]

There is an important difference between the temperature-sea level model described earlier and the temperature-vegetation model used by Box and his colleagues, and that is that the latter model has received *prior validation*; it has been tested on data already available (a step probably impossible with the sea level-temperature model) and its predictive validity established. As the authors explain:

> Site tests were performed by two methods, called verification and validation. . . . Verification involves testing to see how well a model recreates the relationships upon which it is based. This was done by determining how well the model predicts the actual presence/absence of the 125 species at the twenty-one Florida sites used to refine the model through five iterations. Validation of a model involves testing with an independent data set, either collected anew or held back from the data base used to build the model.[8]

This step drives out a great deal—but not all—of the expert judgment that was needed for the use of the unverified, unvalidated temperature-sea level model. In the temperature-sea level case we must rest our faith on scientific consensus. In the case of climate change and flora, the verification and validation steps indicated that the model was indeed a useful model because it was tested against *data* and found to be accurate to a degree sufficient for its policy purposes.

## Can Models Be Validated?

Strong objections have been raised to the use of such terms as "verified," "validated," and "confirmed" in relation to models such as those just described. Indeed, N. Oreskes, K. Shrader-Frechette, and K. Belitz argue that "verification and validation of numerical models of natural systems is impossible."[9] And, they argue, it is precisely because such models are increasingly being used for forming social policy that their limitations must be understood. One of the critical arguments they make is that "the congruence between a numerical and an analytical solution entails nothing about the correspondence of either one to material reality."[10] Readers might well have anticipated that argument; they have encountered it many times before, beginning in Chapter 4 where the "tension" between coherence and correspondence theories was first pointed out. Here the authors are saying that coherence is not enough; they demand "correspondence . . . to material reality."

The first step from active manipulation to hypothetical manipulation in Figure 9-1 rests on internal coherence for justification, and it is a step away from correspondence with "material reality represented by multiple fallible indicators." Is this important? Oreskes and his colleagues certainly think so. They point out that "the U.S. Department of Energy defines validation as the determination 'that the code or model indeed reflects the behavior of the real world'" and that "the International Atomic Energy Agency has defined a validated model as one that provides 'a good representation of the actual processes occurring in a real system.'"[11] But the authors claim that "the establishment that a model accurately represents the 'actual processes occurring in a real system' is not even a theoretical possibility."[12] And they cite the arguments of other analytical philosophers to support their contentions.

J. D. Sterman, a professor of management science at the Massachusetts Institute of Technology, wrote to *Science* in support of the argument by Oreskes and his colleagues: "[T]he principles discussed [by Oreskes et al.] apply to models outside the earth sciences, including economics and the social sciences. . . . Economic models are routinely described as 'being valid' or 'having been validated,' and [yet] the principal (and often only) criterion for 'validity' is the correspondence of simulated and actual data."[13] After describing the discovery by the General Accounting Office of the use of a "fudge factor" by a "leading econometric forecasting firm," Sterman observes that "such practices persist in part through the failure of model consumers (academics, policy-makers, managers, and citizens at large) to look behind the 'tests' of 'validity' offered by the model makers."[14]

Nevertheless, the authors are not blind to the advantages of computer models. After their harsh attack on them they ask: "Then what good are models?" and answer in this way:

> Models can corroborate a hypothesis by offering evidence to strengthen what may be already established through other means. . . . Models can also be used for sensitivity analysis—for exploring "what if" questions—thereby illuminating which aspects of the system are most in need of further study, and where more empirical data are most needed. Thus, the primary value of models is heuristic: Models are *representations* [italics added], useful for guiding further study but not susceptible to proof.[15]

They further note that one should ask, How much of the model is "drawn from real life and how much is artifice[?] . . . How much is based on observation and measurement of acceptable phenomena, how much is based on informed judgment, and how much is convenience?"[16]

This is not the place to develop this argument in detail. The point to be observed is that the logical basis of the hypothetical experiments of Mode 4A will be seriously challenged by those with credentials to do so; despite the appeal of Mode 4A experiments, policymakers who attempt to make use of such procedures will find it necessary to resort to intuitive, cognitive processes to decide among competing claims and arguments beyond their comprehension, and quasirational judgments will follow and dispute will not be far behind.

As Figure 9-1 predicts, there are advantages and disadvantages to using computer models for purposes of policy formation: They make (or should make) explicit the theorizing about the system in question, they make clear the hypothetical manipulations of variables by the researchers, and they make "what if" questions possible; these capacities make them extremely valuable aids to human judgment. But computer models demand credibility from the researchers in much the same way any method does and cannot completely drive out intuition. In many circumstances computer models are less useful, although more feasible, than the quasiexperiments of Mode 3. Mode 4A offers greater scope and complexity but depends greatly on coherence for its justification. That is a negative in the eyes of many researchers and policymakers who demand a greater demonstration of correspondence with "reality," a feature more readily demonstrated by the quasiexperiments of Mode 3, which are grounded in "real" people and "real" conditions. We can anticipate dispute and vacillation among policymakers with regard to Mode 4A, generally to some greater degree than with Mode 3, depending on the quality of each.

## Mode 4B: The Correspondence Approach

The correspondence approach to representation of the circumstances in society is well known; it consists of populational statistics such as means and percentages and their changes over time. This type of information is produced by the *social survey* often considered the social sciences' greatest achievement. The survey is a useful tool for policymakers; it provides simple, straightforward information. Its weakness is that it tells us *that* something is the case; it does not tell us *why* it is the case, and the work of policymakers almost always brings them to the question of *why*. (I describe this distinction between learning *that* and learning *why* in more detail later in this section.)

Correlational statistics goes a step beyond acquiring information about populational statistics. The correlational method offers more information than the reporting of populational statistics such as means and percentages because it measures the relationship between two variables—for example, income and IQ—and thus hints at, although it cannot claim, a causal relationship between the two. It is commonplace to point out that "correlation is not causation"; newspaper reporters now point this out, and statistics textbooks unfailingly give examples of the fallacious use of correlational statistics to imply cause-effect relationships. Nevertheless, policymakers' need to learn *why*, to learn cause-effect relationships in society is so strong, and our methods for ascertaining these are so weak, that correlation is regularly taken for causation, although almost no one will admit to this mistake.

One of the reasons the examples provided in textbooks of the faulty use of correlation as the basis for inferring causation are so convincing is that the example always involves relationships that the reader *already knows* cannot possibly have a cause-effect relationship. A favorite textbook example used to be the known correlation between the viscosity of asphalt roads and sales of ice cream. This example is nice because the reader already knows that a change in neither of these variables could possibly *cause* a change in the other. Indeed, the reader already knows that this relationship is a result of a *third* variable—seasonal changes in temperature.

But now consider a correlation in an area in which our knowledge is not so certain, such as the relationship between income level and IQ. R. J. Herrnstein and C. Murray report this relationship to be of a small but statistically significant size (.33, on a range from −1.00 to +1.00).[17] Can the reader honestly say that, when informed of this relationship, small though it might be, she or he did not infer that higher intelligence causes one to have a higher income? Or, at least, that intelligence probably causes higher incomes? Won't the reader's belief in a causal relation between IQ and performance in life increase? And when Herrnstein and Murray tell the reader that they believe that the third variable that accounts for the small but persistently positive relationship among all intellective tasks is something called "g," why shouldn't the reader believe that to be the case? Something must be causing all these positive relationships. If the reader finds this hypothesis to be plausible, why shouldn't policymakers? And if they do, why shouldn't their social policies reflect their belief? Indeed, why shouldn't social scientists, psychologists in particular (after all, intelligence testing was invented, researched, and developed by psychologists), point with pride to the value of the work and urge policymakers to make use of it? Here is scientific information collected and digested by psychologists for over a century and supported by funds from several nations; why shouldn't it be used?

Psychologists, and other social scientists, have been ambivalent about the use of this information provided by the late Richard Herrnstein, a psychologist, and Charles Murray, largely because the authors took into account ethnic differences (see especially their Chapters 13 and 14). It is easy to take exception to their conclusions because of the weak nature of correlational data. Even Herrnstein and Murray keep reminding their readers that "correlation is not causation."

In short, statistical representation of social phenomena are generally acceptable in the form of demographic data, but statistical relationships that pretend to offer explanations in the form of cause-effect statements, just what the policymaker wants, although just strong enough to gain attention and strong enough to encourage policymakers to use them, are weak enough to make them vulnerable to attack. That is what makes a book such as *The Bell Curve*, which is based almost entirely on correlational data, earn the adjective "controversial." Indeed, all such reports based on correlations readily earn that adjective and therefore provide a dubious basis for policymaking. They engender endless dispute because the inferences drawn from them are legitimately disputable.

## Mode 4C: The Cognitive Activity of Policymakers

The cognitive activity of scientists and artists is treated by psychologists as if it were a tender and precious matter, as indeed it may be.[18] Why shouldn't the cognitive activity of the policymaker receive equal respect, if not awe, and equally careful study? The policymaker's task of integrating scientific information into the fabric of social values is an extraordinarily difficult task, for which there is no textbook, no handbook, no operating manual, no equipment, no set of heuristics, no theory, not even a tradition—unless a record of confusion may be called a tradition. Young scientists learning their trade have all of those advantages, all of those supports for successful cognition. Young artists are accorded at least some appreciation for the difficulties of their creative efforts. But young policymakers learning their trade have none of these supports; each effort to integrate scientific facts and social values starts fresh, as if it had never been attempted before. Is there an ancient Greek philosopher who would be impressed by advances in modern political thought?

Few critics of policymakers acknowledge the difficult nature of the policymaker's task, the necessity for coping with the interdependency of variables or conditions (a difficulty made evident by Hume three centuries ago). But every day we can see policymakers struggling with the interrelations among a city's industrial pollutants, its zoning requirements, its transportation modes, its altitude, climate, and terrain— not to mention the recreational, cultural and ethnic, and political traditions of its inhabitants. Change one of these and who knows what the consequences will be? Which of a variety of interdependent environmental intrusions (e.g., carbon monoxide, noise, visible pollution) most seriously affects a variety of interdependent aspects of human health and performance? And which interdependent social and political circumstances will permit the negative effects of such intrusions to be introduced? Worse still, irreducible uncertainty means that action under these circumstances often results in unintended, or even unimagined, consequences.[19] And inaction may be worse.

The persisting ecological crises illustrate these difficulties. Although it is possible to isolate and thus to analyze various cause-effect relations concerning physical, chemical, physiological, and psychological variables under controlled conditions inside the laboratory, it is far more difficult to isolate, and therefore far more difficult to understand, specific cause-effect relations outside the laboratory, particularly when such relations involve the measurement of functionally interdependent social and physical variables. As social scientists and ecologists have learned to their sorrow, cause-effect analysis in the social environment is very difficult indeed. Some day some serious methodologists may declare it to be logically impossible.

Moreover, interdependency of conditions is a formidable obstacle to separation of fact and value. C. E. Lindblom emphasized this point for decades:

> Inventive as man has been in extending his analytical capacities, he cannot follow through to a conclusive analysis of the merits of alternative policies. Policy problems simply run beyond his *analytical* [italics added] competence. In particular, the merits of many of the goals or values that men contemplate pursuing through public policy cannot be empirically verified as can beliefs about facts, but are instead subject to endless dispute.[20]

Unfortunately, many, if not most, of the problems of technology assessment in particular, and social problems in general, cannot be removed from the physicosocial context in which they occur; their analysis ordinarily falls outside the experimental laboratory. And when problems are removed from their naturally occurring context for study, their results lack credibility, a circumstance noted by U.S. Supreme Court Justice Stephen Breyer (see his remarks later in this chapter). Thus, instead of creating and controlling the circumstances in which the relations between variables are to be studied, social scientists and ecologists must take them as they find them and apply their knowledge to the disentanglement of the relations among variables after, rather than before, the fact of their occurrence. As a result, policymakers frequently find themselves in the methodological quagmire of ex post facto analyses—the consequences of which have yet to become highly visible in discussions involving policy formation.

The theory presented here is intended to offer a guide to the study of the cognitive activity of the policymaker that confronts the conditions just described—irreducible uncertainty, entangled variables and conditions, and strong barriers to learning under conditions of ex post facto analysis. The methods to be used for such studies follow from the theory; they have been applied in a variety of circumstances.

Although this is not the place to describe these efforts in detail,[21] the general procedure can be described as having two steps: (1) analyzing the task—the information environment—and (2) analyzing the policymaker's judgments in relation to such environments. The judgment and decision-making specialist, who could be called a policy consultant, can then ascertain whether the task demands, or is best suited for, coherence or correspondence. If coherence, the appropriate model can be sought; if correspondence, the information environment can be decomposed into the appropriate fallible indicators, as well as the relationships among them. In addition, the policymaker's use of these and his or her dependence on each can be ascertained (and compared with that of other policymakers). The match between the relative importance of each indicator in the task and the relative importance attached to each can also be determined. Much more can be done to externalize the cognitive activity of the policymaker. In those cases where it has been done, the results have been fruitful.[22]

## Why Policymakers Seldom Learn

For about a century psychologists studied learning under conditions in which feedback—the response from the environment—told learners whether they were right or wrong or what the correct answer was. Rats ran into blind alleys or the right alley and found food every time; college sophomores were told "right" or "wrong" and given the correct answer every time. That is, *outcome feedback* was unambiguous and fully informative because the learning environment was fully determined. In virtually all of these studies, learning was taking place under conditions of *certainty*. It was not until the 1950s that the question of learning under conditions of multiple fallible indicators and irreducible uncertainty began to be investigated.[23] Although correspondence theorists have conducted numerous studies, it is a topic that still needs systematic investigation.

What exactly does "feedback" mean? It denotes the response of the environment to some action by the actor. The response may be direct, immediate, and dependent on the learner's action. I press the light switch, and the light comes on every time; it goes off every time I press the switch to "off." That is the kind of feedback we like; we learn quickly and easily. And when engineers get an opportunity to build our information environments, that is the kind they try to build.

In uncontrolled, naturalistic circumstances, the response may be direct and dependent on my action, but it may be delayed; I fertilize my lawn, but the response may not be seen for weeks. It is harder to learn under these conditions for obvious reasons. B. Brehmer has demonstrated that feedback delay is seriously detrimental to learning under uncertainty, particularly in dynamic tasks—that is, when task conditions are changing. Now we must consider a more complex question: Why is learning under uncertainty difficult? Learning is difficult under uncertainty because there is a *distribution* of responses from the environment; that is, a number of *different* responses are fed back to the learner on different occasions, rather than a single one, as in the case of the light switch and the light. In the case of the lawn, sometimes fertilization works very well, sometimes not so well. And that means trouble; where does the problem lie? In the fertilizer? The time of application? The amount? If the lawn responds differently on different occasions, how am I to *learn* from the response of the lawn (the outcome feedback) what to do next time? I may have done everything right, but the indeterministic nature of the lawn system (rain, the absence of rain, variations in humidity levels, changing soil conditions) may mean that, despite my correct behavior, the lawn responds differently on different occasions. The point is this: If the environment is not fully controlled, if there is irreducible uncertainty in the behavior of the environment, then even though I have the correct (lawn-fertilizing) *policy,* the response from the environment, the outcome feedback, may tell me (falsely) that my policy was wrong. Of course, that is a terrible situation for learning, for it means that even if one is correct in his or her judgment policy, the outcome feedback from the environment will often indicate that the policy is wrong! How often this occurs is determined by how irreducibly uncertain the environmental system is. If it is highly uncertain, then it will occur frequently.

Worse is yet to come. Not only can the environment tell me that I was wrong even though I was correct in principle; the opposite can happen as well. I can be right for the wrong reason. That is, I may have an incorrect lawn fertilizing policy (I fertilize too soon) but optimal weather can overcome my incorrect lawn-fertilizing policy so that, lo and behold, I have a beautiful lawn; I must have been right! And when I find next year that my policy doesn't work, where shall I place the blame? How will I know where to place the blame?

Hillel Einhorn provides a nice example of how we can be right for the wrong reason[24] and shows how our actions can falsely lead us to believe that we have validated our ideas. His example is this: A waiter in a restaurant sees two couples sit down at two of his tables. One couple is middle-aged and nicely dressed; the other couple is young and looks scruffy. He decides that the middle-aged couple will tip well if he gives good service, but the young couple lacks the resources; he'll get a small tip from them. So he lavishes care on the middle-aged couple and minimizes services to the young couple. Sure enough! He is well tipped by the middle-aged couple, poorly tipped by the young couple. Although the example is a simple one, it illustrates the difficulty of entertaining and testing a hypothesis that one believes to be false. And that is why it took humankind so long to include the placebo group in its clinical trials; indeed, the idea of a "clinical trial" with a control group is relatively new (see Chapter 9).

The conclusion to be drawn is that if the system for which one is making predictions is one that can be described as irreducibly uncertain, as most social policy situations are, learning from outcome feedback is virtually impossible. The greater the uncertainty in the system, the less the value of outcome feedback.

Political scientists, economists, sociologists, and others who urge us to learn from experience (or history) don't know about learning under uncertainty, however. They know what they were taught, namely, that outcome feedback is essential and that learning won't take place without it. Quite naturally, therefore, they urge us to learn from the outcome of an action. But the learning they studied was learning under conditions of certainty.

Warnings from respected social scientists that the "inability to learn is fatal" are announced frequently, as are sarcastic remarks about one's opponents' failures to learn the "lessons of history," although the possibility that policymakers—or anyone else—may be unable *in principle* to learn from irreducibly uncertain environments is rarely examined. And exhortations to learn *this time*, based on the unjustified but unquestioned assumption that learning can occur, are also commonplace. Thus, for example, C. J. Hitch insists that in order to cope with the "energy dilemma . . . we must have a plan that can . . . be adjusted frequently as we learn."[25] But there is no evidence that Hitch has any plans for making learning possible or, indeed, whether he has ever examined and set forth the conditions that are necessary for making learning possible.

Unfortunately, outcome feedback under uncertainty is what the world ordinarily provides us. We make a judgment and act on it, and sometimes we get feedback, usually long delayed, usually of doubtful validity or reliability, usually open to a variety of interpretations—in short, under conditions of irreducible uncertainty. That is the way the world works, and that is why we have so much difficulty improving matters. And that is why irreducible uncertainty causes the trouble it does; it makes it very difficult to learn to do better.

Note that it is the information environment that is causing the trouble, not our cognitive abilities. If we change the way the world works by taking the uncertainty out of it, our prowess is remarkable indeed. That is exactly what engineers do when they devise, create, and build information systems. And that is why they make life better (except when they are making it worse, a topic I take up in the final chapter).

It will help to consider an analogy. Think of the phrase "the fog of war," so often used to indicate the difficulty of military decision making and to explain the celebrated blunders of generals and admirals. That apt phrase is intended to describe situations in which the generals and admirals must cope with information that is missing, contradictory, changing, unreliable, deceptive, or simply wrong, and the difficulties attendant upon knowing which is which. The policymaker is subject to all of the problems that gave rise to the phrase "the fog of war"; we might well speak of creating the "fog of feedback" for policymakers. Learning under these circumstances is virtually impossible. We deceive ourselves when we think otherwise. The evidence is plentiful, from both inside and outside the laboratory.

## The Role of Instruction in Judgment Under Uncertainty

Learning is indeed possible under conditions of uncertainty in one circumstance, and that is when there is sufficient knowledge about the environment and when *instruc-*

*tion* occurs. It must be *appropriate* instruction, however; most instruction for learning under uncertainty is *not* appropriate. When Mark Twain's teacher told him, "By and by you will just naturally *know* one [wind reef] from the other [bluff reef], but you never will be able to explain why or how you know them apart,"[26] he was admitting to his failure as a teacher; he was also admitting that he could not teach because he didn't know *what* to teach; that is, he was not consciously aware of how to use the information from his information environment, the "face of the river."

A good teacher must first know whether she or he is offering the student an opportunity to learn through coherence or correspondence. Teachers of physics know that they are offering a coherent theory held together by mathematics; the model and its logic are then explained. Teaching and learning are more difficult for the teacher and the student when the model lacks a mathematical base; nevertheless, we know how to communicate knowledge based on coherence more or less effectively. It is not so easy, however, with regard to correspondence. If asked, Twain's teacher probably would have said (in effect) that he was offering a correspondence theory; he had no model of the river's currents, eddies, and other hazards in mind; he was prepared, however, to point out, insofar as he was aware of them, multiple fallible indicators of navigational hazards. But his remarks to Twain made it plain that he was *not* aware of all the fallible indicators that he made use of, nor could he describe their relative importance. Twain would have to acquire the information in some mysterious way, "by and by" just as his teacher had (insofar as he had). It is precisely that process that correspondence researchers have studied in terms of "multiple cue probability learning."

The results of those studies have made it clear that the "instruction" afforded by outcomes (discovery that a presumed harmless "wind reef" turned out to be a harmful "bluff reef") is not only slow but expensive. Fortunately, it is possible in laboratory studies to simulate effectively those information environments that are faced by riverboat pilots, weather forecasters, physicians, and countless other professionals who frequently make judgments under uncertainty on the basis of multiple fallible indicators. These studies show beyond any reasonable doubt that learning under these conditions is very slow and often occurs without awareness. And if there is a lack of awareness, then, of course, teachers don't know what to teach. Twain's teacher was not unique; people often learn to make reasonably accurate judgments without being able to describe how they do it or, worse still, wrongly describe how they do it. Many students of a professional are taught what their teacher *thinks* she or he is doing but is, in fact, *not* doing.

The trouble with these teachers is the manner in which *they* learned. They learned as a result of folklore (recall the surgeon who said that he predicted cardiovascular collapse on the operating table through a prior hand shake with the patient), and they pass along such folklore as if it were true knowledge (sometimes for a long time, sometimes, a short time). Or they learned from (dubious) outcome feedback over a period of time. Because information learned under these conditions is frequently described incorrectly, they are in fact poor teachers. Indeed, it is raw experience itself that is a poor teacher, and, therefore, those who learn from such experience are likely to be poor, even dangerous, teachers. (Think of all those physicians who perpetuated "childbed fever" because they told their students it was unnecessary to wash their hands, or, more recently, those who taught their students that stomach ulcers were caused by "stress.")

The conclusion from judgment research is that it may not be *impossible* to learn under such conditions, but it is slow and difficult and carries the heavy risk of learning the wrong thing and communicating that misinformation to others.

Is there a better way? Yes. It is made possible by cognitive feedback.

Cognitive Feedback

The customary form of feedback is outcome feedback; a judgment is made, action is taken, and the environment responds, sooner or later (sometimes no response ever appears). Earlier I claimed that because of irreducible uncertainty and interrelationships among variables and conditions, learning from outcome feedback was virtually impossible, particularly in connection with social policies. Now I claim that a better form of instruction can come from (1) an empirical analysis of the relation of various fallible indicators to the target or (2) those who have achieved—and can prove that they know why they achieved—empirical accuracy in their judgments in relation to a specific well-defined task. The critical information for accurate judgments is the degree of relationship between each indicator and the target, *not* the relationship between a judgment and the target.

Research has indicated that if learners can be shown which indicators are valid (and to what extent each is valid), they can quickly put that information to use in making their judgments. Thus, learning can take place very quickly; tasks that might take weeks to learn with outcome feedback can in fact be learned in an hour.[27]

The major problem in learning from uncertain environments is that the critical information is generally lacking. The empirical relation between various indicators and the target is unknown; without that information the learner is thrown back to what is virtually an impossible task.

*Learning "That" Versus Learning "Why."*    Learning that certain events have occurred is, of course, far easier than learning why they occurred. (It is not difficult to learn that an airplane has crashed; learning why is usually very difficult, and often impossible.) Researchers in all fields generally have had to reduce naturally occurring events to a simpler form in order to discover answers to "why" (cause-effect) questions. In the social and ecological worlds such reduction is far more difficult and the generalization back to the natural circumstances far more difficult than in the physical world. That is one reason—perhaps the major reason—why physical science and molecular biology have advanced so much further than social science.[28] That situation has serious consequences for social policy formation.

Whenever there are numerous interdependencies among the variables and conditions of interest, disentanglement of those interdependencies and generalization back to the original conditions of interest is a strong barrier to success. That is why politicians wrangle about what should or should not be in a piece of legislation. After discovering *that* one or two empirical relationships support their political views, they pronounce—and perhaps believe—that they have found the cause, the reason why certain good (or bad) effects have occurred. Opponents, of cource, always point out that there are other relationships involved. All may agree *that* a certain good (or bad) event occurred, but the inevitable entanglement of the relationships between multiple causes and effects, which perhaps can never be disentangled, means that learning *why* is impossible.

But social policy and legislation must try to answer the "why" question. If air quality is bad, then someone must decide why so that air quality can be improved. That means ascertaining the cause-effect relationship that interfered with air quality. But as has been evident in so many cities, many pollutants will be found to contribute to poor air quality, and each polluter will point to some other pollutant as the principal cause of the undesirable effects.

Disentanglement of the causes of crime and welfare is a task that has proved daunting to policymakers—and to sociologists—for centuries. Doctors are often seen on television explaining new discoveries about the causes of certain diseases, and physicists and chemists are interviewed about new scientific achievements, but sociologists are not seen explaining proven causes of welfare dependency or crime. Determination and separation of multiple causes of multiple effects that occur in social circumstances outside the laboratory remains virtually impossible. Duality of error is observed as the pendulum swings back and forth between environmental and genetic causes, and social policy vacillates between efforts to reduce each type of error. Our methodological inability to disentangle multiple causes and effects in either biological or social ecology is the source of ineffectual social policy and persistent dispute.

The anguish caused by the failure to cope successfully with these problems can be seen in the remarks by an outspoken policy maker, U.S. Senator Daniel Patrick Moynihan.[29] Moynihan's views and pronouncements deserve our attention because of his long record of interest and achievements in this field.[30] Frustration over our inability to learn from experience, and thus to find a better way, have long been apparent in virtually everyone's reaction to these problems, but Moynihan has been particularly frank in expressing his disappointment. His response to a reporter's hostile question regarding current welfare proposals was illuminating: "Those of us who first spotted . . . [the present problem] are entitled to be heard a generation later when we are saying we still don't understand it."[31]

Crime and welfare for the poor are problems that have existed for as long as records exist, and vast amounts of information have been collected over the centuries. But Moynihan's complaint that "we still don't understand it" provides clear evidence of the difficulty—if not impossibility—of policymakers dealing with the "why" question from experience under uncontrolled circumstances. Franklin Roosevelt was famous for his exhortation to "try something—if it doesn't work, try something else—but try *something*." That exhortation shows strong motivation for the necessity of learning from experience that "something" did or didn't work, despite the lack of understanding "why" that Moynihan mentioned in connection with crime and welfare. In times of desperation, learning "that" is sufficient; learning "why" becomes important as soon as short-term measures begin to fail.

## Mode 5: Expert Judgment

It was the "counterculture" of the 1960s that called into question scientific and technical expertise as well as other forms of authority. And it is now commonplace for citizens without the slightest scientific or technical knowledge to challenge—with enthusiasm—the judgments of engineers, doctors, and other professionals. Indeed, the public hearings that are now mandatory regarding government activities invite citizens to do just that. There seem to be three assumptions that encourage such challenges:

1. The professionals may be dishonest; they may be acting in the interests of those who will gain by virtue of their judgments (and that includes the professionals themselves).
2. The professionals' training may be inadequate; they cannot see the larger picture—which the citizens supposedly can—and therefore their judgments are of limited value.
3. The public will somehow "feel better" if it has "input," even if the final decision goes against its wishes; thus, the dispute will quiet down more rapidly because "having had input" removes at least one cause for complaint—namely, not having had "input."

All of these changes, in addition to the challenging scientific questions regarding the question of how experts think in comparison to novices or laypersons, made the subject of expert judgment an attractive research topic for psychologists by the 1960s. (See Chapter 5 for a description of the beginning of research on clinical judgment.) And they were not alone; researchers in the field of artificial intelligence moved rapidly into this area of inquiry. Their interest was in the development of "expert systems" that would emulate, or somehow reproduce, the cognitive processes of the expert in the form of a computer program or model. The rewards for such an effort were and are obvious; substituting a computer program for an expensive expert was an idea whose time had come. The work continues, and the field of applications increases.

Psychologists may look with envy on the widespread application of expert systems, which has robbed them of their authority with regard to the topic of expertise. They are, however, quick to point out that computerized expert systems do not in fact demonstrate any understanding of how experts think; they merely replicate what experts tell others about how they think. Their success, psychologists are likely to say, is merely an interesting application of computer programming.

In making note in 1987[32] of the disparate paths taken by the developers of expert systems within the artificial intelligence community and the judgment and decision-making community, I used a comment by B. G. Buchanan, a prominent early AI investigator, to indicate the theme of AI goals regarding expert systems:

> The hallmark of expert systems is high performance. Using weak methods to perform any useful task requires expertise. And it requires skill on the part of the designer to shape these programs into "world-class" problem solvers. Thus we see relatively few expert systems, and those we do see include considerable domain-specific knowledge codified over months or years. High performance requires that the programs have not only general facts and principles but the specialized ones that separate human experts from novices. Unfortunately for all of us, specialized expertise includes almost by definition, knowledge that is *not* codified in print. Thus high performance has to be courted with patience.
>
> In addition to utility and performance, I have added transparency, or understandability, as a third characteristic of expert systems. This separates AI programs from

very good numerical algorithms. It is not necessary that expert systems are psychological models of the reasoning of experts. However, they must be understandable to persons familiar with the problem. Statistical pattern recognition programs, for example, perform well on many important problems, but there is little illumination to be gained from rehashing algebraic manipulations of Bayes' Theorem.[33]

In sharp contrast, there is little of this sort of admiration of experts to be seen in the judgment and decision-making literature; indeed, it is quite the opposite, and the best way to illustrate these opposing views of expertise is to repeat the remarks of Lopes and Oden quoted earlier:

> On the one hand, there is a large body of research that documents striking failures of naive humans when confronting relatively simple tasks in probability theory, decision making, and elementary logic. [Here they are referring to the research by Kahneman and Tversky and colleagues.] On the other hand, there is the continuing belief of psychologists and computer scientists that by understanding human problem solving performance we will be better able to build machines that are truly intelligent. One can only wonder at the puzzlement of lay readers who come across articles like one published recently in *Newsweek* that spent several columns describing people's failures at decision making in scathing terms ("sap", "sucker", "woefully muddled") only to conclude that researchers hope to "model human decision makers' rules of thumb so that they can be reduced to computer software" and so speed the progress of artificial intelligence, the aim of which is "not to replace humans but to give them an important tool."[34]

Thus we have the peculiar situation of leaders in one field, judgment and decision making (particularly the coherence theorists), denigrating the very cognitive processes that AI researchers hope to simulate! In addition to this peculiar circumstance, other differences should be pointed out.

## Domain-Dependency vs. Domain-Independency

AI expert systems are *domain-specific*; that is, they include rules pertaining to the use of information in the specific task at hand (e.g., the study of an infectious disease, the exploration of geological strata). A program built for one task thus cannot be used for another, although claims are made for metaprograms. E. A. Feigenbaum, possibly the best known exponent of the AI expert systems approach, made it clear in 1977 that lessons of the past showed that a domain-specific approach was necessary for advancement:

*Lessons—the Past*
   Two insights from previous work are pertinent to this essay.
   The first concerns the quest for generality and power of the inference engine used in the performance of intelligent acts (what Minsky and Papert [see Goldstein and Papert, 1977] have labeled "the power strategy"). We must hypothesize from our experience to date that the problem solving power exhibited in an intelligent agent's performance is primarily a consequence of the specialist's knowledge employed by the agent, and only very secondarily related to the generality and power of the inference method employed. Our agents must be knowledge-rich, even if they are methods-poor. In 1970, reporting the first major summary-of-results of the DENDRAL program (to be discussed later), we addressed this issue as follows:

General problem-solvers are too weak to be used as the basis for building high-performance systems. The behavior of the best general problem-solvers we know, human problem-solvers, is observed to be weak and shallow, except in the areas in which the human problem-solver is a specialist. And it is observed that the transfer of expertise between specialty areas is slight. A chess master is unlikely to be an expert algebraist or an expert mass spectrum analyst, etc. In this view, the expert is the specialist, with a specialist's knowledge of his area and a specialist's methods and heuristics.[35]

In short, because experts are *specialists*, each representation of expert judgment is peculiar to the expert's specialty.

The judgment and decision-making approach, on the other hand, aims at the development of a *domain-independent* representation of various experts. Thus, for example, discussions of expert judgment in the judgment and decision-making community systematically consider variations in such abstract, formal, that is, domain-independent task properties as (1) task uncertainty, (2) redundancy of dimensions, (3) order of presentation of information, and (4) number of task dimensions.

The primary areas of study for the judgment and decision-making research programs have been efficiency of *learning* under uncertainty, the *accuracy* of judgments under uncertainty, the extent to which judgment meets *standards of rationality*, and the nature of the *cognitive mechanisms* (called "cognitive algebra" by N. H. Anderson[36]) by which uncertain information is organized into a judgment. Indeed, expert judgment within a variety of disciplines has been studied in relation to these basic questions. For example, G. J. Gaeth and J. Shanteau demonstrated that soil experts were unwittingly giving undue weight to irrelevant cues in their judgments of soil conditions, thus diminishing their accuracy.[37] For Gaeth and Shanteau the problem thus came to be: How can experts be taught to ignore irrelevant cues? But it was of little consequence to judgment and decision-making researchers what the specific irrelevant cues happened to be. The interesting question was: "Will other experts in other fields be found to be less accurate in their judgments than they should be because of weight given to irrelevant cues?" If so, would Gaeth and Shanteau's training methods generalize to experts other than soil experts?

A similar example is provided by R. M. Poses, R. D. Cebul, R. S. Wigton, and M. Collins. Their study addressed the question of whether *computer-based feedback* regarding appropriate weights for cues in "simulated cases could improve physicians' . . . diagnostic judgments for actual patients."[38] The authors concluded that such feedback "can improve MD's clinical judgment in actual patient care."[39]

The authors use the concept of *cognitive feedback* to enhance the accuracy of experts' judgment in medicine. The same principle can be applied to other experts in other fields because it is an *abstract* principle; it is not intended to be confined to diagnosing sore throats or indeed to any specific task. The success of this approach defies Buchanan's claim that "a separate and simple representation of the domain-specific knowledge was essential for successfully transferring expertise to a program."[40] Note also that Poses and his colleagues sought to *improve* the performance of their experts, which, as they demonstrated, badly needed improvement. Improvement of experts is not a topic for those developing expert systems; the experts are assumed to be the epitome of knowledge.

A further disadvantage of the *domain-specific* approach is that each development of an expert system starts from ground zero for that particular application, except for the not inconsequential tricks of the programming trade or, better, except for the advances in computer sciences. That disadvantage is reflected in the much longer time that is required for the development of an AI-derived expert system relative to that required for a judgment and decision-making analysis of expert judgment. Moreover, the domain-independent approach brings the same general set of principles to each task. But it can hardly be denied that the AI-expert system approach is far richer, far more plausible, and far more interesting to the *experts* than the judgment and decision-making-derived information precisely because it *is* domain-specific; it rests on content, and content is what experts know. The judgment and decision-making-derived information interests psychologists far more than the domain experts, however, because it tests domain-independent psychological theories about cognitive functioning, and that, of course, is what psychologists know, or try to know.

## Rules Versus Probabilities; Analysis Versus Intuition

A second difference between the two approaches is that the AI expert system focuses on discovering or "capturing" the *rules* used seriatim by the expert. Although a probability may be attached to each rule as an indication of the expert's confidence in the truth or applicability of that rule, the basis of the probability judgment is never decomposed or "unfolded"; it remains a mystery. Just the reverse is true for judgment and decision making; the experts' rule is never sought by questioning; it is a product of a research procedure used by the researcher, and great care is taken to "unfold," or determine, the basis of the probability judgment. In the approach taken by Tversky and Kahneman,[41] for example, the source of probability estimates are the entire focus of research; rules linking pieces of information are seldom, if ever, mentioned. On the other hand, within the approach to the study of experts by correspondence judgment and decision-making researchers, probabilities and rules are discovered through the a posteriori analysis of a series of judgments; experts make judgments regarding future states or events based on observable data, and the relative weights employed and rules used are captured a posteriori by analyzing those judgments.[42]

This distinction has another side to it, and that is the premise in the AI approach that all expert cognition is best described in terms of rules. A second premise is that rules must be, or at least should be, definable. Thus, for example, the expert system NEOMYCIN is taken to be an improvement over MYCIN, an earlier expert system, because it defends the rule given to the user; that is, it answers the question "why," should the user choose to ask it. Judgment and decision-making researchers (within the correspondence approach) ignore all step-by-step, rule-based expert cognition; they prefer to examine cue-judgment relations, the differential weights attached to them, and the principle or method by which the weighted information is "integrated" or aggregated over the various cues attended to. The heuristics and biases approach ignores the latter question; examining the heuristic that leads to a biased judgment is the main focus of interest. The AI approach thus emphasizes reflection, consideration, and reconsideration of the defensibility of the rule. This takes time. Judgment and decision-making researchers, on the other hand, by presenting a number of cues, items of information, or vignettes contemporaneously, ask for no rule but simply for a series of judgments.[43] The time involved therefore is brief, perhaps not more than a few seconds per judgment, and thus intuition is induced.

It is in this sense that the AI approach can be characterized as focusing on the more analytical elements of judgment, whereas the judgment and decision-making approach focuses on the more intuitive elements of judgment, those aspects of judgment assumed to be the special attribute of the expert.

### Experts Whose Work Is to Be Emulated and Simulated Versus Experts in Need of Help

A third important difference between the two approaches is the conclusion reached regarding the quality of the performance of experts. AI-derived expert systems take as a premise that experts do very well whatever it is they do and that no one does it better. By virtue of their status as experts, experts are highly competent and deserving of emulation and simulation. Moreover, expert judgment and the problem-solving tactics they employ provide the criteria by which novices and others are to be evaluated. This assumption is so firmly embedded in AI-derived expert systems research that it is rarely, if ever, questioned, made explicit, or criticized.

Studies of experts by judgment and decision-making researchers, however, take an iconoclastic view of experts, and do so with what they believe is good reason. As far back as 1955 I found that experts (clinical psychologists in this case) were, in fact, no better than novices.[44] To the best of my knowledge every study (with perhaps one exception[45]) carried out within the judgment and decision-making framework has shown experts to be highly fallible. Not only do their judgments fail to agree with an empirical criterion; those judgments are highly unreliable; the experts disagree with one another, an observation made early on even by some workers following the problem-solving approach.[46] Here is a recent and typical observation:

> One of the puzzling findings from studies of expert-novice differences in problem-solving behavior has been the fact that differences between experts in the means used to solve a given problem are often as great as the differences between experts and novices (e.g., Chase & Simon, 1973; Elstein, Shulman, & Sprafka, 1978). In the judgment tasks of the present study, experts often reached a common diagnostic judgment that was linked to agreement in the interpretation of a relatively small number of critical data cues. Agreement among experts held, however, only so long as the task information did not appear anomalous. When faced with patient data sets containing potentially discrepant or incongruent combinations of cues, the expert clinicians adopted different interpretations of the critical cues as well as divergent judgments. These findings suggest that at a global level of reasoning where judgment outcomes and critical data cues are at issue, experts tend to agree, while at a more detailed level of reasoning involving the interpretation of individual data cues and specific reasoning steps, they diverge.[47]

Because the testimony of experts provides the basis for much of our legislation, it is clear that expert judgment is something we can hardly do without, yet surely it deserves much more systematic research than it is getting. Certainly, expertise should not be taken for granted.

### Validation Procedures

A fourth major difference between judgment and decision making and the AI approach is in the methods for appraising the value of the expert system each approach produces. Buchanan offers the following defense of MYCIN:

> MYCIN is one program whose performance has been externally validated. There have been different empirical studies of MYCIN's performance, each simpler than the last but all of them time consuming. In the last of these (Yu, Fagan, Wraith, Clancey, Scott, Hannigan, Blum, Buchanan, & Cohen, 1979), we were trying to determine how outside experts compared MYCIN's final conclusions with conclusions of local experts and other physicians. Ten meningitis cases were selected randomly and their descriptions were presented to seven Stanford physicians and one student. We asked them to give their therapy recommendations for each case. Then we collected all recommendations, together with MYCIN's recommendation for each case and the actual therapy, in a 10 X 10 matrix—ten cases each with ten therapy recommendations. We asked a panel of eight experts not at Stanford to give each recommendation a zero if, in his opinion, it was unacceptable for the case and a one if the recommendation was acceptable. They did not know which, if any, recommendation came from a computer. . . . The differences between MYCIN's score and the scores of the infectious disease experts at Stanford are not significant. But we can claim to have shown that MYCIN's recommendations were viewed by outside experts to be as good as the recommendations of the local experts, and all of those better than the recommendations of physicians (and the student) who are not meningitis experts.[48]

The procedure described by Buchanan reflects AI experts systems developers' veneration for the uncontested judgments of experts; validation is produced by asking experts to rate various procedures, but no effort whatever is made to examine the ratings (judgments) of the experts themselves; their validity is taken for granted. This form of validation does not even begin to approach the standards to which psychologists are accustomed. Were such a validation argument submitted to the APA Committee on Tests half a century ago, it would have been rejected outright as incompetent.

The procedure also illustrates the isolation of the two literatures, for any judgment and decision-making researcher would immediately (1) declare the inductive base of ten cases to be too small (and show why), (2) ask for evidence of interobserver and intraobserver agreement, (3) ask for evidence that indicates that each rater was using the same judgment policy (i.e., weighting the same cues in the same way) so that we could be confident that we were not observing a "false agreement," and (4) ask why unexamined expert judgment was being employed in this loose way when so much evidence exists showing how poor expert judgment can be.

Procedures for validating conclusions drawn in the context of judgment and decision-making research on expert judgment are quite different; they rest on empirical evaluation of the actual performance of an expert, aided or unaided, against either an *external* criterion (e.g., correlational measures, hits versus misses), or against *internal* criteria (e.g., performance standards of intersubjective or intrasubjective reliability, congruence between the parameters of the policy the expert intended to execute and the one actually executed, comparison with normative criteria of rationality). The procedures described above by Poses and his colleagues meet both criteria. They show the accuracy of expert judgments before and after the use of a judgment aid, where accuracy is measured in diagnostic hits and misses.

### Experts and Experience

Experience is reputed to be a necessary element of expertise, and the AI approach places great emphasis on this point. Yet in nearly every study of experts carried out within the judgment and decision-making approach, experience has been shown to be unrelated to the empirical accuracy of expert judgments. Indeed, on some occasions studies within the judgment and decision-making approach have shown experience to be negatively related to accuracy.[49] There are good empirical reasons that argue against the value of experience; experts may simply have had a great deal of experience doing the wrong thing. The history of medicine offers numerous examples.

### Time Consumed in Developing the Expert Systems

Researchers within the AI expert systems approach expect to spend considerable time—at least months, and often years—extracting rules from their experts. In startling contrast, judgment and decision-making researchers seldom spend more than a day in this effort. This striking difference strongly indicates that very different cognitive processes are being examined.[50]

Space does not permit a complete review of research on expert judgment within the judgment and decision-making framework.[51] But there can be little doubt about the overall conclusion that such a review would provide: Expert judgment is poor and far from deserving of emulation or simulation.

This odd and perhaps embarrassing situation is rarely brought to light because the two areas rarely if ever meet to discuss these issues. (Together with Gary Bradshaw in 1987 I organized a two-day conference supported by the National Science Foundation that brought representatives of these two fields together to discuss such matters. It was a complete failure. Everyone talked past everyone else, mainly because, with few exceptions, each side was ignorant of the work of the other side.)

Thus we are left with the question of how much credence we should place in Mode 5 as a source of information for policymakers. On the one hand, researchers in the field of artificial intelligence urge the policymaker to listen, learn, and accept the wisdom of the experts. On the other hand, researchers within the field of judgment and decision making are far more cautious, even negative about the value of expert judgment; they cite disagreements, unreliability, irrationality, and lack of empirical accuracy, probably also throwing in examples of gross errors in the judgments of experts.[52]

*Does It Matter?*

These directly contradictory conclusions regarding the competence of expert judgment are disquieting. Expert judgment plays a critical role in policy formation, particularly with regard to the policymakers' efforts to make use of scientific information. Consider, for example, the role of expert judgment in the question of the risk, if any, imposed by radon in drinking water. A report in *Science* states:

> For much of the past year, a group of scientists in the Environmental Protection Agency (EPA) has been at the center of a gathering storm of controversy. Their work on the potential health risks from radon in water, culminating in a report suggesting that strict limits should be imposed, rejected advice from the agency's own science adviser and drew fire from an outside panel of experts. . . .
>
> The issue is what if any, steps should be taken to keep radon out of the nation's drinking water. The answer could involve hundreds of millions of dollars in new purification technology, so it's no surprise passions are aroused. . . . And for another, uncertainties in the science underlying the risk analysis provide room for different interpretations and divergent views on regulation.
>
> To EPA's critics, this case is a prime example of how hard it is for the agency to incorporate science into decision making. . . . "It troubles me the extent to which science is largely treated as an afterthought" in developing regulations, says Richard Sextro, a physicist at Lawrence Berkeley Laboratory who serves on the radiation advisory committee of EPA's Science Advisory Board (SAB). "Policy is arrived at largely for ascientific reasons," he says. . . .
>
> The agency's science adviser, William Raub, was first to sound the alarm after reviewing the documents the water office was using. In February he urged EPA scientists to consider the "enormous uncertainty" that underlies risk estimates of radon. Expressing sentiments shared by outside researchers, Raub said there were "inconclusive epidemiological findings as to whether radon (either ingested or inhaled) actually presents an appreciable risk within the typical American household if none of the occupants smokes tobacco products."[53]

There was really nothing new about discovering "how hard it is for [any] agency to incorporate science into decision making." In 1991 Roberts described how the National Acid Precipitation Project (NAPAP) carried out its research over a ten-year period, at a cost of $500 million and involving "some 2,000 scientists [who] studied everything from lake sediments to atmospheric processes to damage to chain link fences."[54] But "when Congress and the Bush Administration were haggling over the president's acid rain bill . . . NAPAP was nowhere to be found."[55] Why not? According to Roberts, NAPAP's chair explained that "in 1980, there were no models for doing this: NAPAP was the first big effort at marrying science and public policy,"[56] an observation that might have caused earlier politicians some surprise.[57] Which group of researchers—the artificial intelligence group or the judgment and decision-making group—would have been better able to help "marry science and social policy"?

I will let the AI researchers speak for themselves in this regard. But the contemporary view of the progress of artificial intelligence has not been kind. Frederick Allen, managing editor of the quarterly magazine *American Heritage of Invention*

& *Technology*, flatly states that "today traditional artificial intelligence, or AI, is a backwater at best, and the confidence with which it was once pursued seems unimaginable."[58]

I now turn to the question of what the coherence theorists and the correspondence theorists have learned about expert judgment.

## What Judgment and Decision-Making Coherence Theorists Have Learned About Expert Judgment

As the reader will anticipate, coherence theorists discover that experts are incoherent. The researchers demonstrate incoherence by showing that judgments of probability change as the context of the judgment changes. The prototypical example is one in which a majority of subjects choose one course of action in one context, but not the logic, over the opposite course of action in the opposite context, although the formal structure of the situation (the probabilities) remains the same. Tversky and Kahneman, for example, used the effects of "framing" to show how context can shift probability judgments even though the logic of the problem remains the same:

> Imagine that the U.S. is preparing for the outbreak of an unusual Asian disease, which is expected to kill 600 people. Two alternative programs to combat the disease have been proposed. Assume that the exact scientific estimate of the consequences of the programs are as follows:
>
> If Program A is adopted, 200 people will be saved. [72 percent]
>
> If Program B is adopted, there is 1/3 probability that 600 people will be saved, and 2/3 probability that no people will be saved. [28 percent]
>
> Which of the two programs would you favor?[59]

Tversky and Kahneman found that 72 percent of their respondents preferred to save two hundred lives for certain rather than gamble on saving a larger number of lives. But when the problem was framed differently, Tversky and Kahneman found a very different result. The problem given to a second set of respondents was the same problem in principle but it was framed in terms of death, instead of lives saved:

> If Program C is adopted 400 people will die. [22 percent]
>
> If Program D is adopted there is 1/3 probability that nobody will die, and 2/3 probability that 600 people will die. [78 percent][60]

Programs C and D in the "death" frame are numerically equivalent to Programs A and B in the "lives saved" frame. But in the second case, 78 percent of the responders preferred to gamble, rather than accept a sure loss of four hundred lives. This example has been used again and again to illustrate how context induces departures from the logic of probability. It is used also to illustrate a general principle, namely, "a preference to gamble rather than accept a sure loss," by no means a trivial principle.

B. J. McNeil and her colleagues followed up on this example with a study of physicians.[61] The question was whether professionals, in this case medical doctors, would be victims of the "framing" effect. If so, this phenomenon would be shown to be not a product of a mere laboratory experiment but one that exists in the everyday judgments of professionals whose judgments are of undoubted importance. The results clearly showed the framing effect.

The example is instructive in relation to human judgment and social policy, error, and injustice. It places the probability calculus as the standard for coherence; judgments of professionals in relation to that standard constitute the object of interest. If such judgments shift as context shifts, then they are determined not merely by the standard of rationality but by contextual variables of which the subjects are not aware. (If they *were* aware of the effect of the contextual variables, they would presumably reject them, although, surprisingly, this does not always occur.)

The example carries significance for human judgment and social policy formation because it adds the possibility of systematic error—error that tends to occur in one direction rather than the other—to that already present. That is, the expert's systematic error can result from the way the issue is "framed." Although such framing effects were well known to McNeil and her colleagues, the predicted *direction* (uncertainty over a sure loss) was not. The phenomenon also suggests an increase in injustice, insofar as a loss is incurred by some rather than others as a result of the framing of the issue. Equally important is the implication that even expert judgment is vulnerable to such judgmental flaws.

Does all this matter? Yes, indeed. The conclusions about irrationality in human judgment, even that of experts, has not escaped the notice of persons in high places. In his treatise on regulation and risk, Stephen Breyer, later appointed to the U.S. Supreme Court, cited the coherentists' conclusions in his 1991 Holmes lectures, *Breaking the Vicious Circle:*

> Evidence suggests that experts have their own biases in the risk assessment process: they may test and retest until they get positive results; they may not fully understand the low predictive power of small samples; they may become overconfident. . . . Experts may also often be prey to the same cognitive tendencies that dog the lay public. Amos Tversky, a leading cognitive psychologist who studies decision theory, has noted, "Whenever you find an error that statistically naive people make, you can find a more sophisticated version of the same problem that will trip the experts." Kevin McKean, "Decisions, Decisions," *Discover*, June 1985, at 22, 31. See also Paul Slovic, "Perception of Risk," 236 *Science* 280, 281 (April 17, 1987) ("experts' judgments appear to be prone to many of the same biases as those of the general public") (citing sources).[62]

Breyer thus made it clear that his confidence in expert judgment and the judgments of risk had been significantly diminished as a result of judgment and decision-making research. In doing so he implicitly rejected the opposite view, which is the basis of the artificial intelligence and expert systems research. But Justice Breyer may have to think again, particularly if he reads the article by L. L. Lopes in which his conclusions about risk judgments are challenged.

First, Lopes shows that the press has also taken note of the risk perception research. She quotes a writer for the *Saturday Evening Post* (1988) who "recently summed matters up, 'when it comes to risk, we are idiots. . . . The remarkable thing is not that the world is full of hazards but that we are so bad at assessing them',"[63] a view expressed by Breyer as well. But these conclusions are challenged by Lopes. She examines the classic study by S. Lichtenstein and her colleagues[64] and claims that "the experiments tell us little about the layman either psychologically or politically, but tell us much about how certain professionals construe the world and their role in it."[65]

Lopes's summary of the results indicates that the subjects were often "way off" when the "true ratio [of deaths due to two different causes, e.g., tornadoes and asthma] was 2:1 or greater . . . they often misordered events with smaller true ratios."[66] But Lopes notes that "direct ratings of event frequencies were generally related to actual frequencies with linear correlations of .89 or better."[67] (A value of 1.00 indicates a perfect relation; correlations of .89 are considered to be very high in behavioral research.) P. Sedlmeier and G. Gigerenzer also challenge the coherence theorists' conclusions regarding erroneous judgments about small samples and put forward considerable empirical evidence to show that when erroneous judgments occur they do so in the context of coherence judgments but not in the context of correspondence judgments.[68]

## What Correspondence Theorists Have Learned About Expert Judgment

Earlier I described how, from the very start, judgment and decision-making correspondence theorists doubted the value of clinical psychologists' and psychiatrists' expert judgments. That critical analysis has been extended to other professionals. T. R. Stewart and his colleagues found that there was little relationship between the amount and quality of information available to expert meteorologists and the accuracy of their forecasts of an important but uncertain event (severe weather).[69] The researchers had meteorologists make forecasts under a total of four different information conditions, ranging from paper maps showing only storm location and shape to detailed computer displays on an advanced workstation. In general, forecast accuracy was low, and there was only a modest increase in the accuracy of forecasts, coupled with a significant decrease in agreement among forecasters, as the amount and quality of available information increased substantially. Indeed, important components of judgmental skill, particularly the reliability of judgments, deteriorated with additional information. This result is, of course, exactly the opposite of what meteorological experts would expect, and what the proponents of increased spending for technology would expect.

Recently, my colleagues and I examined the judgments of expert meteorologists in their efforts to predict the occurrence of microbursts (the sudden downburst of air that can cause airliners to crash).[70] This topic was chosen because the circumstances for a careful analysis of expert judgment appeared to be excellent. The director of the operation was enthusiastic about the study on the grounds that it might provide useful information that would increase the accuracy of such forecasts (in fact, a life-and-death matter); the five meteorologists were cooperative for the same reason.

The study was of particular significance because it was based on circumstances highly representative of the meteorologists' actual working conditions. Tapes of Doppler radar projections were replayed for the meteorologists who made independent predictions of the probability of the occurrence of a microburst for each of twenty-four displays. As in Stewart's study of hail forecasting,[71] the focus of the work is the correspondence of the forecasts, based on multiple fallible indicators, with events empirically observed (did the microburst occur or didn't it? Did hail occur or didn't it?).

The five meteorologists were indeed experts. They may not have "written the book" on microburst forecasting,[72] but they certainly wrote the definitive articles.[73] Moreover, each expert was studied individually over a series of actual cases, rather than averaging the results derived from large numbers of "experts" of assumed expertise.[74] One of the coauthors of the study, R. J. Potts, is himself a microburst meteorologist whose task it was to see that the researchers met meteorological standards of research.

The results of this research did not lend credence to the views of those who value expert judgment but did support the value of empirical analysis of the judgments of experts—at least in the eyes of the judgment researchers; the meteorologists did not appear to be impressed. However, I present a brief description of the research, together with a diagram (see Figure 10-1) to show how the work was done.

The first study provided the forecasters with specific, unambiguous values for storm indicators; the forecasters were then asked to provide judgments regarding the probability of a microburst. That is, all the forecasters were given the same data (represented by column D in Figure 10-1). Individual differences with respect to subjective observations of the objective radar data (column C) were thus eliminated as a source of forecaster disagreement. Modest agreement was observed among the forecasters' judgments. In addition, the results indicated that the meteorologists' forecasts were adequately predicted by a simple linear model (as is true for clinical psychologists and other experts).

In the second study forecasters viewed radar tapes of storms under dynamic (i.e., changing) conditions representative of their usual operational setting. They made judgments regarding the values (column C) of the storm indicators (forecasters call these "precursors"), as well as of the probability that a microburst would occur. Agreement among the forecasters was found to be lower than in the first study; agreement regarding the (subjectively) most important precursor value was near zero. These results indicate that there are indeed practical advantages to be gained from a separation of the precursor identification phase and the prediction phase of the forecasting process.

What do these results mean? They mean that the forecasters were *given* the numerical value of each fallible indicator ("precursor" or "cue"); instead of asking each meteorologist to evaluate the numerical value of an indicator, the researchers gave the same value to each forecaster. Yet only *modest* agreement was found among the forecasters. That is an indication of trouble among experts that has been found in virtually every correspondence study of expert judgment; it indicates that even when each expert gets exactly the same information, they do not use it in the same way. Also, despite forecasters' beliefs, the forecasts were predicted quite well by a simple model of their organizational processes (they added up the information), much as has been found in more than one hundred studies of clinical decision making as described by R. M. Dawes, D. Faust, and P. E. Meehl).[75] Significantly, however, when the meteorologists were themselves required to provide judgments about the numerical values of the precursors based on their observations of the radar screen—a far

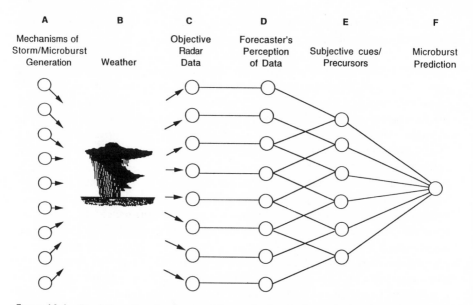

Figure 10-1    Depiction of a microburst and the mechanism for its prediction. *From left to right*:
A—the conditions that produce the thunderstorm; B—the microburst; C—the microburst data
produced on the Doppler radar; D—the forecasters' perception of the microburst data (wind
speeds and direction at various altitudes); E—the objective data transformed into an indicator
or "precursor," for example, "descending column"; F—forecasters' predictions. (*Source: Lusk,
Stewart, Hammond, & Potts, 1990, p. 628.*)

more difficult situation—agreement among the forecasters diminished substantially.
Astonishingly, agreement with respect to the presence or absence of what the forecasters agreed was the single most important precursor was near zero! In addition,
little change in judgments occurred over time; additional information about the storm
resulted in few changes of the initial judgments. On the other hand, confidence in
the initial judgment increased! This is similar to the result obtained by Stewart and
his colleagues (1992) in their analysis of the value of added information given to
forecasters.

The implications of these results are obvious, but the forecasters, by and large,
ignored them, much to the surprise and, of course, disappointment of the researchers. Indeed, subsequent efforts to teach *new* forecasters were based on the *presumed*
expertise of the forecasters whose forecasts had been empirically demonstrated to
be wrong! Expert judgment is indeed an interesting topic, and one to which I will
return in Chapter 11.

## Expert Judgment of Risk

The contributions of judgment and decision-making researchers to the study of the
"perception" of risk have been significant. Led primarily by the energetic and imagi-
native work by Paul Slovic, a substantial literature has been developed[76] that has had
an impact on those who must cope with regulation. Perhaps the best way for the reader

to see this is to examine Stephen Breyer's book, *Breaking the Vicious Cycle*.[77] Breyer's Holmes lectures are doubly interesting because much of the thesis of the first lecture is based on conclusions derived from the work of the judgment and decision-making researchers Paul Slovic and Baruch Fischhoff.[78]

Breyer's lecture interests us here because it is a remarkable commentary on our times—and on the importance of human judgment and social policy—that a nominee to the U.S. Supreme Court at his Holmes lectures would find this topic deserving of his own, and the audience's, attention. The lecture contains many references to topics discussed in this book, including the competence of human judgment, both by the lay public and by experts. Moreover, all three lectures focus on the problems of incorporating scientific information into social policy—in this case, social policy about the regulation and control of various hazards to the public. Of particular interest are Breyer's comments on the adequacy of physical science research methods (Mode 1) and social science research methods (Modes 2 and 3) for policy formation. Breyer emphasizes the irreducible uncertainty that frustrates policymakers, particularly those who must regulate. He also makes note of the difficulties faced by scientists who must confront policy questions: "Predicting risk is a scientifically related enterprise, but it does not involve scientists doing what they do best, namely developing theories about how $x$ responds to $y$, other things being equal. Rather, it asks for predictions of events in a world where the 'other things' include many potentially relevant, rapidly changing circumstances, requiring the expertise of many different disciplines to reach a conclusion."[79] Breyer thus shows his awareness of the difficulties facing scientists of all varieties when they must do what they are not accustomed to doing— namely, applying their judgment regarding results obtained in their laboratories to conditions outside the laboratory involving "many potentially relevant, rapidly changing circumstances." (The reader should consult the contrast between laboratory and field researchers discussed earlier.)

A good example of Breyer's point can be found in an editorial by R. H. Abelson, the editor of *Science*:

It has been known that $SO_2$, $NO_x$, and $O_3$ can have toxic effects on plants. In the early days, experiments tended to be performed "scientifically"; that is, plants were exposed in chambers in which the chemicals were tested one at a time. Under those circumstances, it was noted that concentrations of $SO_2$ and $NO_2$ greater than ambient were required to produce notable pathology. Indeed, low concentrations of $NO_2$ were sometimes beneficial (perhaps a fertilizer effect). However, in the real world, pollutants are present together. When experiments were conducted with ambient midday levels of ozone present (for example, 50 to 100 parts per billion), toxicity was noted. When the ozone was supplemented with $NO_2$, there was usually a substantial additional toxicity attributable to $NO_2$. Similar results were noted when ozone was supplemented with $SO_2$.[80]

Notice how the problem of generalization from the laboratory to the world outside is almost always the same; results obtained when a variable (or substance) is *isolated* (a principal condition in all laboratory work, including psychology) do not hold up when the variable (or substance) is *not* isolated, as in Abelson's example. It is more than curious that the editor of *Science* magazine would in 1955 (!) think that his colleagues so badly needed to be reminded of this matter—hardly a complicated one—that he should write an editorial about it.

There is a certain irony in the way Breyer makes use of the coherence theorists' research, for he fails to see that his sagacious remarks about extrapolating from physical science results also apply to the problem of extrapolating results from judgment and decision-making coherence research. That is, he accepts without question conclusions from coherentist researchers and applies them to empirical judgments about risk, as if the truth of such conclusions were firmly established in the circumstances he is addressing. But such extrapolations are as doubtful and difficult as those facing physical scientists whose prediction from their laboratories must, as he says, face "many potentially relevant, rapidly changing circumstances." (This, incidentally, is what Egon Brunswik meant when he referred to the "causal *texture* of the environment.") Will this apparent commitment to the conclusion that expert judgment is flawed affect Justice Breyer's opinions on the bench? Will he be able to persuade his fellow Justices to adopt a similar commitment? And if he rejects expert judgment, where will he turn?

## Ex Post Facto Analysis

Ex post facto analysis is the term applied to the analysis of a set of events after they have occurred. The topic deserves discussion because expert judgment is often based on ex post facto analyses—descriptions of what has happened in past situations that bear similarities to a present one or one that is expected to occur. When the president of the United States assembled a committee to inquire into the cause of the *Challenger* disaster, he was in effect asking the members to make an ex post facto analysis of the event in order to determine causal factors. When a member of Congress asks a head of an agency why it did not achieve its goals, he asks for an ex post facto analysis. To ask a person for an ex post facto analysis is to ask that person to disentangle and separate artifactual, or merely apparent, relationships from functional or truly causative ones by *thinking* about them. Thinking, or imagining, is necessary because there is usually no way of actually making the factors vary over the ranges necessary for an interpretation. That is, during observation Event A may have covaried with Event B but not with Event C simply because of the special circumstances of time and place. Given a representative set of circumstances of time and place, however, Event A may be related not to Event B but to Event C.

After considering the general problem of such designs in detail, P. E. Meehl observes that "the ex post facto design is in most instances so radically defective in its logical structure that it is in principle incapable of answering the kinds of theoretical questions which typically give rise to its use."[81] Everyone who reexamines events of the past should keep Meehl's admonition in mind, particularly when instructed to learn "lessons" from the past. Meehl is not alone in his doubts about what can be accomplished by after-the-fact analyses. In 1971 H. M. Blalock Jr. published a large collection of sociological and econometric papers that provide a sobering indication of the difficulties encountered by current logical, mathematical, and statistical ex post facto attempts to cope with the causal ambiguity of entangled sociological variables.[82] No easy remedial methods have since appeared.

If it is indeed true that policy formation involves the evaluation of some change in a complex network of functionally interdependent variables, then we must acknowledge that in such "thought experiments" variables of interest ordinarily cannot be made subject to isolation and independent manipulation. Physicists can do "thought experiments" because they can imagine controllable circumstances in the lab; social scientists do not have this luxury. Conclusions produced by after-the-fact analyses are therefore vulnerable to a variety of alternative interpretations. Aside from a few methodologically inclined social scientists, however, policymakers, political scientists, and the scientific community in general have yet to give careful consideration to the question of where the limits of scientific analysis lie with respect to such problems, or how to (or whether to) extend such limits once they are found. Neither have psychologists considered how such limits can be expected to affect the cognitive activity of policymakers. Indeed, it is the "radically defective nature" of ex post facto designs that lend considerable doubt to the proposition that we can learn from experience.

McNamara's "Lessons of Vietnam"

We are constantly being admonished to learn from experience. Nowhere is this admonition delivered with more self-righteous enthusiasm than in the case of lost causes, and, of all lost causes, the case of the Vietnam War stands out above all, at least for Americans. As a result, not only are the lessons of history urged upon all, but the "lessons of Vietnam" are given special, and often emotional, emphasis. There is a difficulty, however; no one can say with a justified certainty just what the lessons are. Many have tried, of course, but one recent effort deserves particular mention, and that is the attempt by Robert McNamara, U.S. secretary of defense during the early and major part of the war. That position earned him credit—it was often called "McNamara's war"—he would rather not have had. His book *In Retrospect: The Tragedy and Lessons of Vietnam* attracted severe criticism and, often, denunciation. It constitutes a remarkable explanation for his wartime judgments under uncertainty, particularly those that were mistaken.

McNamara leaves us in no doubt about his retrospection; he put it in words that will often be quoted: "We were wrong, we were terribly wrong."[83] But he wants us to *learn* from these mistaken judgments; that is the avowed purpose of his book. The title of his book includes the phrase "lessons of Vietnam."

Readers of *this* book, however, should at this point be wiser than McNamara; they should know that it is impossible to learn from the circumstances and events of that war, or of any war. If it is difficult to learn from Mode 2 experiments outside the laboratory and very difficult to learn from Mode 3, both of which impose some controls on circumstances and events, how can it be possible to learn lessons from the chaos in the fields of action or, what may be worse, from the confusing, contradictory, often secret, unrecorded activities of the policymakers who set those actions in motion? How can such events be related to one another when there is so much ambiguity about them? If we are to learn from our observations of the behavior of others (and that is what McNamara asks us to do), we must observe the occurrence of some unambiguous events isolated from others, some unambiguous responses must be observed to have been made in relation to them, and then some unambiguous set of consequences must have been seen to follow, if not immediately, then within some limited time period. That situation was never even approximated in the Vietnam War, and perhaps never in any war. It is seldom the case in the world of behavior outside the laboratory.

But if the policymakers at the time could not learn lessons from their mistakes (and remember they were termed "the best and the brightest")—a badly described set of environmental circumstances (the "fog of war") combined with obscure, misrepresented actions, with deliberate obfuscations and lies, as well as with sheer ineptitude in dispersing and storing information (ineptitude that appears laughable to later generations)—how can those outside the process be expected to link environmental events, responses, and outcomes? Who can say, without challenge, exactly "what led to what"? And whenever anyone attempts to tell us what led to what (as McNamara does), there will be challenges.

McNamara admits on the first page of his chapter on "lessons" that other equally well-informed policymakers of the Vietnam era will disagree with his "lessons." For example, pointing out the more obvious costs of the war, "58,000 men and women, . . . an economy . . . damaged by years of heavy and improperly finance war spending; . . . the political unity of our country . . . shattered, not to be restored for decades," McNamara asks: "Were such high costs justified?" His answer is clearly no. But he acknowledges that "Dean Rusk, Walt Rostow, and Lee Kwan Yew and many other geopoliticians to this day answer yes"; he then goes on to explain why they do. How is one to learn lessons if the teachers cannot agree on the outcome of the action? It is clear that they would also disagree about the specific events that precipitated the actions taken or even about exactly what actions were taken in response to which events (which may or may not have occurred).

To put this in slightly different terms, it is true that we sometimes learn that some sequence of events, responses, and outcomes did occur in relatively unambiguous fashion. But learning that is never enough; we always want more; we want to learn *why* so that we can generalize our knowledge to future circumstances, the next war. We may indeed learn that the United States sent five hundred thousand soldiers to Vietnam, that fifty-eight thousand died, that 3 million Vietnamese died, that the United States withdrew after more than ten years of war. But learning that these events occurred leads us to ask *why*. And the answer is what an ex post facto analysis cannot give us, because, as Meehl stated, it is "so radically defective in its logical structure that it is . . . incapable of answering the kinds of theoretical questions [that is, questions of "why"] which typically give rise to its use."[84]

Does this mean that McNamara's book was an exercise in futility? Yes, because it does not provide generalizable lessons that are derived from the use of a defensible method; no, because it does offer plausible hypotheses (not lessons) about why certain events might have occurred as they did. Such hypotheses may serve as important and useful conjectures to be entertained on future occasions when military judgments under uncertainty are required. But they are no more than that; they become dangerous obstacles to the exercise of good judgment when they are given more credibility than they deserve. It may well be that Santayana's admonition,

"Those who cannot remember the past are condemned to repeat it," is true; much, however, depends on whether unjustified generalizations are included in the memories.

Admonitions to learn "lessons" from experience occasionally are successful—to the detriment of all concerned—for they generalize "lessons" that have dreadful consequences. That happened in the case of the Vietnam War, as McNamara unwittingly reveals to us.

As he notes, one of the most compelling reasons for the decision by the United States to send advisers and then combat troops to Vietnam was to curtail the spread of communism to Southeast Asia. The great fear, expressed early and often, was that if Vietnam fell, then one country after another would also go to the communists. That was the essence of the domino theory. And that theory was ever present—implicitly or explicitly—in the debates about whether to escalate or withdraw. In a meeting between President Dwight D. Eisenhower and John F. Kennedy on Eisenhower's last full day in office, McNamara reports that his notes show that "President Eisenhower stated without qualification, 'if Laos is lost to the free world, in the long run we will lose all of Southeast Asia.' "[85] McNamara followed that report by stating: "The meeting made a deep impression on Kennedy and us all. It heavily influenced our subsequent approach to Southeast Asia."[86] He then describes a second meeting, on 17 February 1965, when Eisenhower was invited to the White House to discuss the question of bombing North Vietnam, and notes that "Ike began by saying LBJ's first duty was to contain communism in Southeast Asia."[87] Thus the domino theory—which turned out to be false—was emphasized and advocated by Eisenhower. Why would a man of Eisenhower's military experience in World War II advocate a theory that turned out to be mistaken? Because he had indeed learned a lesson from his experience in World War II—namely, that if one domino falls then the rest will follow, that containment is essential. His experience in Northwest Europe during the late 1930s and 1940s taught him that lesson. Thus, the difficulty is not that we fail to learn lessons when we should; it is that we misapply the lessons we learn. The difficulty with all such lessons is the same—inappropriate generalization, a consequence generally discovered after the fact.

Jason De Parle put the matter of "learning lessons" succinctly: "One [lesson] is the lesson of Munich: that aggression in the heart of Europe must not be appeased. The other is the lesson of Vietnam: that foreign crusades can easily trap American in blood baths. One lesson says get in; one says stay out."[88]

Had the domino theory been treated as a plausible hypothesis to be critically examined for its generalizability from Northwest Europe to Southeast Asia, it might have been useful to consider why it was inappropriate. But according to McNamara, it was held until the end and, indeed, is held by some today.

Under conditions of irreducible uncertainty, as McNamara, Kennedy, Johnson, and others learned, there is always the risk of taking action when one shouldn't as well as the risk of not taking action when one should and thus imposing injustice on some. In the case of Vietnam, the lesson Eisenhower learned from his experience in Northwest Europe may have been responsible for a great deal of injustice in Southeast Asia. So we should treat McNamara's admonition to learn the "lessons of Vietnam" with great skepticism; the lessons he proposes to teach us may well do more harm than good.

Indeed, that may well be the case with the latest admonition about "lessons" to be learned. This time it is Colin Powell who offers lessons. He advised President Clinton that air strikes against the Bosnian Serbs would not induce them to refrain from shelling Sarajvo; only massive force would intimidate the Serbs—a "lesson" to be learned from the Gulf War. But, in fact, a few air strikes did bring the Bosnian Serbs to the peace table.

Weak as Mode 5 may be, the use of a known, delimited set of data in the form of objective indicators is far better than the use of the weak quasirational cognitive activity of Mode 6, to which we now turn.

## Mode 6: Unrestricted Judgment

In Mode 6 we find what should be the cognitive activity of last resort; unhappily, it is often the cognitive activity of first resort. Only when all else fails, when all recourse to more analytical, more powerful modes of thought have been found to be unfeasible, can the use of the weakest mode of cognition (unaided human judgment based on an unrestricted or even unknown set of data) be justified. Yet anyone who observes policymakers at work will recognize at once that weak quasirational thought (Mode 6) is their typical form of cognitive activity, for the simple reason that it is so easy to employ and is highly feasible. Scientists, whose typical mode of cognition involves the strong or moderate forms of analytical thought present in Modes 1 or 2, are quick to detect the sloppy thinking typical of Mode 6 and are scornful of it. Indeed, anyone who has heard scientists discuss the process of policy formation knows that scientists believe that if only policymakers were exposed to the discipline of the strong form of analytical thought so successfully employed in Mode 1, most of the problems of policy formation would disappear.

Self-satisfying as that belief may be, when scientists serve as advisors to policymakers, their first resort is to the weak cognitive activity of Mode 5; as I will illustrate shortly, they too often resort to Mode 6. We can be no more certain about the boundaries of the data set being employed by scientists in their role as consultants than they can be about the same information being employed by policymakers. Nor can we be any more certain about the cognitive processes that scientists use to organize the fuzzily bound information on which their judgments are based. When scientists offer advice regarding the desirability of various sources of energy or the effects of measures to control crime, improve the economy, or reform the health care system, they are forced to move from the strong analytical modes of cognition (on which their intellectual authority rests) to the weak, quasirational forms of cognition of Mode 5 (at best) and Mode 6 (at worst).

A study by C. Waddell provides rare insights into an effort to include scientific knowledge in the policy-making process through the use of experts.[89] The matter at issue was whether Harvard's establishment of a recombinant DNA research facility would create a hazard to the citizens of Cambridge, Massachusetts. Because of considerable opposition to the project, two public hearings were held in 1976. The hearings proved to be unsatisfactory, and a debate was arranged that allowed cross-examination by peers. The interesting and unusual circumstances here are that distinguished scientists as well as interested citizens participated directly on both sides of the debate and that Waddell's interviews with the experts and others show us how weak the process is.

There was no lack of talent at this debate. Opponents of the project included a professor of biology at Harvard who was also a Nobel laureate, an associate professor in the biology department at Harvard, two professors from the department of microbiology at Harvard, and a local physician. Advocates of the project were equally noteworthy: a professor of microbiology and Nobel laureate at MIT, a professor in the department of biochemistry and microbiology at Harvard, a professor in the department of microbiology at Harvard who received the Nobel Prize in chemistry four years after the debate, a professor in the department of biology at Harvard, a physician specializing in hematology and oncology, and a director of a prominent laboratory specializing in infectious diseases at the Harvard Medical School. I offer these details regarding the scientists who participated in the debate because it is rare that such prominent scientists publicly line up on different sides in a debate of this sort and rarer still that the scientists—and those who listened to them—consent to be interviewed subsequent to the debate.

Waddell draws a distinction between appeals to emotion and appeals to reason and offers example after example of how these experts appealed to emotion when appeals to reason were to be expected. For example, one board member criticized one of the Nobel laureates for holding a position that was formed of "all emotion and all undocumented statements and perceptions."[90] Winning a Nobel Prize is thus not a barrier to operating in Mode 6. But this scientist's opponent *also* offered emotional appeals. As Waddell observes, scientists on each side combined "appeals to reason, emotion, and character,"[91] thus offering typical examples of testimony I have placed in Mode 6. A physician provided the best example of what is to be expected in Mode 6. When speaking for the project, he exclaimed, "I deal with children with cancer and I deal with children with inherited disease. *And I don't share Dr. Wald's love of the germ plasm!* I must tell you that I have had *rough encounters* with germ plasm all my medical career. If I had a lot of mothers in here who have children with difficulty in their germ plasm, I think you'd know why I feel the way I do."[92]

The reader should keep in mind that the debate was to settle the issue of whether the DNA research facility would be a hazard to the health of the citizens of Cambridge, not whether the germ plasm is "good" or "bad." Irrelevant outbursts of this sort are unsurprising at city council meetings or public hearings, but one might have expected better at this high-level "debate" among top-level scientists. Making a passionate speech about a different topic—an uncontroversial one—is a form of persuasion frequently found in Mode 6. Too often the discourse never returns to the issue at hand. This is one of the reasons Mode 6 excites interpersonal conflict.

As might be expected, under these circumstances neither consultant nor policymaker develops high regard for the contribution of the other or for the contributions of colleagues on the same side of the fence; memoirs from both diplomats and scientists abound with strong doubts about the intellectual capabilities of their peers as well as of their opposite numbers. Nor can we expect such mutual disappointment to disappear unless and until stronger modes of inquiry are found that can both decrease the covertness of cognition and increase the availability of conflict-reducing mechanisms to both policymakers and scientists in their effort to form public policy. As the Cambridge debate illustrates so vividly, the constantly reiterated hope that better policy will be forthcoming if the personalities involved in forming policy are changed is a false and misleading hope that should be abandoned. As I have noted elsewhere, airline safety was improved not by changing pilots but by changing their decision-making environment. Virtually perfect navigation was achieved in the same way.

Our best hope for the future lies not in new personalities but in changing the present incompetent mode of inquiry to a more powerful analytical one that produces less conflict. The future is too dangerous, too precarious, to be left to personalities, however colorful or prestigious or however appealing their homely simplicity; imprisonment in Mode 6 makes personality more visible and clouds the fundamentals of the problem at hand. Although incompetence may be more tolerable when combined with rectitude than with villainy, in the end, failure remains failure.

Some readers may find the general categorization of modes of inquiry in Figure 9-1 acceptable yet doubt my assertions about the weakness of the cognitive activity of policymakers and that of scientists in their role as advisors. Fortunately, no one needs to accept my assertions on faith, for both policymakers and scientists have spoken plainly on these matters themselves. Indeed, policymakers who write their memoirs often take pains to point out how whimsical the policy-making process is. Somehow, *after* retirement they appear to feel duty-bound to disabuse us of the false notion that Mode 6 should be put to work in high circles.

## Summary

Although intervention is the strongest mode of inquiry, it remains unsatisfactory as a means of providing information for policymakers; it does not sufficiently reduce uncertainty regarding causal relations in society. There are sharp limits to learning via intervention, a problem that is well known, if not well understood, among policymakers.

They are, therefore, prepared to listen to and even occasionally to accept the results of weaker methods of inquiry. These methods purport to *represent* the circumstances of interest, usually when intervention is not feasible. Computer modeling is more and more frequently used, particularly by economists, to represent social and ecological circumstances and thus to advise policymakers. The primary advantages of computer models are that their coherence can be tested and thus challenged and that their correspondence to reality can be tested and challenged. Most important is their "what if" capability. Various policies can be enacted and their hypothetical consequences examined. The credibility of the results, however, rests on the coherence and correspondence claims of the theoretical model that stands between input and output.

Correlational methods such as those employed by Herrnstein and Murray and countless other researchers do not have the analytical power of computer models, and therefore the results they produce are far more subject to contention and controversy. They induce unjustified beliefs in causal relations, although only inferences about association can be justified.

It is not always possible for policymakers to turn to computer models or statistical methods for purposes of representation; neither may be available. At this point (sometimes *before* this point) policymakers turn to experts for their judgments, not only for representations of social phenomena but for analyses of their causes. This is a weaker mode of inquiry, for, although experts can and do refer to data, it is impossible to ascertain exactly how they are organizing the data underlying their judgments—and, of course, experts invariably disagree on the most important issues. In addition, judgment and decision-making researchers have cast considerable doubt on the value of expert judgment, from both a coherence and a correspondence point of view. Expert judgment remains a topic that is far from perfectly understood by the researchers, however, and, as a result, policymakers will continue to rely on expert judgment in the foreseeable future.

The weakest mode of inquiry is that which does not rely on data but on opinion. It is therefore the mode that is most dependent on intuition and most conflict producing. It is apparent at most hearings and government representations. It claims to rest on common sense, but, as the readers of this book know, common sense requires an analytical component too often missing from this mode of inquiry.

We must find wisdom somewhere, however, and that is the topic of the next chapter: Where, indeed, will it be found? *Can* it be found?

# 11 Possibilities for Wisdom

The whole world's future hangs on proper judgment . . . of what can best be done, on what must be done.

—General George C. Marshall,
announcing what became known
as the Marshall Plan, June 5, 1947

If conventional methods of inquiry do not—cannot—meet the needs of policymakers, where shall the policymakers turn? Psychologists, particularly those who study judgment and decision making, are inclined to believe, naturally enough, that policymakers should turn to them. And so they have, on occasion. In what follows I first offer some examples of psychologists' past efforts to assist with the policymaking process, as well as a suggestion from a new and unexpected source. I then examine the conventional source of wisdom, the wisdom of the elders. Does that source continue to deserve our confidence?

## Hadley Cantril and Friends: Franklin Roosevelt and Dwight Eisenhower

One of the most interesting—and little known—examples of a determined effort to bring the benefits of psychological research to bear on social policy occurred in the 1930s, long before psychologists developed their lobbying organization and long before current federal granting agencies existed. Hadley Cantril, then a psychology professor at Princeton, told his story in a semiautobiographical book, *The Human Dimension: Experiences in Policy Research.* Cantril's experience is significant because he went beyond the usual duty to bring substantive knowledge produced by his discipline to the office of the politician; he attempted to affect the policymaking process itself. As he put it in his preface: "I recount here some of my attempts to inject a way of thinking into policy formulation at the highest levels of Government."[1] Injecting a "way of thinking into policy formulation" is very different from merely informing a government official that recent research has shown that a certain condition affects, say, the growth of the crime rate in certain neighborhoods. Cantril wanted to change the process of forming policy by offering officials "a way of thinking," by which he meant "using all necessary psychological factors in the formulation of any given problem."[2] His aim therefore antedated mine by more than half a century. The difference is that, although Cantril had far less scientific knowledge about human judgment and social policy than I am able to provide, he was far more successful in reaching the primary policymakers of his day; he was able to reach the President of the United States directly on more than one occasion.

Cantril discusses how he was accidentally "propelled into policy research for Franklin D. Roosevelt during World War II" and how he went on to serve "as special consultant to the White House for a while during the Eisenhower Administration and on a few occasions worked with the Kennedy Administration." However, Cantril says, "at no time was I ever a paid member of any Government staff. . . . [And] I am not eager to give the impression that my relationship with occupants of the White House was especially intimate, for many social scientists have worked closer than I ever did, but none, I believe, as a psychologist *with a similar purpose* [italics added]."[3]

Cantril pessimistically notes that as of 1967, "in spite of the millions of dollars spent by Government and private sources for social science research of one kind or another, there actually is still very little such research initiated, or even utilized, by those most responsible for Government policies on either the domestic or foreign fronts." He maintains that this was not "entirely the fault of Government officials," because "all too many social scientists, including psychologists, have been satisfied to spend their lives conducting research that is concerned with theory or technique only, much of which assumes the character of playing games or building models that will impress their peers." As might be expected, Cantril further observes that most research "has very little demonstrated relevance to the decisions which policymakers must reach, and it is little wonder that they become impatient with it."[4]

The situation has surely changed since 1967. The federal government now initiates research in many fields; the military has many research offices (the navy, the air force, and the army have their own research agencies) as do the National Institutes of Health (NIH), the Office of Education, and, of course, the National Academy of Sciences (NAS) and its operational arm, the National Research Council (NRC), with their thousands of staff members and liaison scientists providing information and advice over a vast array of topics. Nevertheless, Cantril's view that "all too many social scientists themselves, including psychologists," do not produce meaningful research is still frequently seconded by social scientists, including psychologists, as well as by the consumers of their research. Neither can we say that Cantril's main goal, "to inject a way [read *new* way] of thinking into policy formulation at the highest levels of Government," has been achieved. It can hardly be claimed that the research on cognitive psychology or social psychology has been reflected in government policymaking.

Cantril had specifics in mind. He thought that there were three ways in which the results of psychological research might affect "policy formulation at the highest levels of Government." These included: (1) providing substantive knowledge (e.g., information on improving child care, a goal that has been achieved), (2) aiding public opinion research and manipulation (e.g., providing surveys that inform policymakers about the number of citizens for and against a piece of legislation, also a goal that has been achieved), and (3) improving the process of policy formulation (a goal that has not been achieved). Each is discussed in turn.

## Providing Substantive Knowledge

Typically, information about psychological research findings reaches policymakers in the form of substantive findings. Research results may come to their attention because Congress or the executive branch has requested the information from the NAS or the NRC and gets it in the form of a report or because a professional society holds a briefing or seminar for government officials (usually congressional staff members), possibly in relation to specific legislation under consideration. The assumption, or hope, is that if the appropriate government officials are apprised of the results of relevant research, better, or at least more informed, legislation will appear. And professional societies are quite willing, if not anxious, to provide information seminars for policymakers. Matters are certainly different—and better—in this regard than they were in the 1940s and 1950s, the time Cantril spoke of, although, no doubt, scientists are far from satisfied that all that could and should be done is being done; all scientists believe that the social utility of their work—if people would only recognize it—means that their discipline deserves a larger share of the federal budget.

## Representing Public Opinion

Cantril saw a second way that psychology could be helpful to those charged with formulating social policy, and that is by providing data on, and manipulating, public opinion. Cantril also foresaw the risks; psychology "could, of course, be misused by those in power or those who aspire to power by pandering in irresponsible ways to public opinion or to the deep aspirations men and women feel and express."[5] His optimism, seen from the vantage of a quarter century later, is touching: "Fortunately, the American people have by now, I think, developed sufficient sensitivity to be able to recognize attempts to exploit their feelings purely for political gain and are quick to discount the glib generalizations of those who overpromise or overpromote." Yet it may well be that Cantril was indeed prescient; the bad temper of the American electorate today may be due to its "sensitivity to . . . attempts to exploit" and its ability to "discount glib generalizations."

Cantril's relationship with President Franklin Roosevelt marks the first time that survey data were used periodically to guide a president in his policymaking. In 1940 Roosevelt had learned about the work Cantril and his colleagues were doing at Princeton and asked, through an intermediary, for some examples of their work. Cantril complied and, within a week, learned that the president wanted more; "one of the questions that particularly intrigued him was: 'Which of these two things do you think is more important for the United States to try to do, to keep out of war ourselves or to help England win, even at the risk of getting into the war?'"[6] (In July 1940, 59 percent thought we should keep out of the war, and 37 percent were willing to risk war to help England.) Roosevelt wanted this question asked periodically. As the Germans appeared to be more and more likely to win the war, Roosevelt's use of Cantril increased.

It is clear that Cantril was a gentleman and a scholar. He sums up his relationship with Roosevelt in this way:

> Roosevelt regarded the reports sent him the way a general would regard information turned in by his intelligence services as he planned the strategy of a campaign. As far as I am aware, Roosevelt never altered his goals because public opinion appeared against him or was uninformed. Rather he utilized such information to try to bring the public around more quickly or more effectively to the course of action he felt was best for the country. I am certain he would have agreed with Churchill's comment that "Nothing is more dangerous than to live in the temperamental atmosphere of a Gallup poll, always taking one's pulse and taking one's temperature. . . . There is only one duty, only one safe course, and that is to try to be right and not to fear to do or say what you believe to be right."
>
> Finally, I want to emphasize that no claim is made here that the data and suggestions Lambert and I provided the President were crucial in his decisions. But actions taken were certainly very often completely consistent with our recommendations.[7]

Cantril continued to serve President Roosevelt throughout the war.

Presidents have continued to use public opinion surveys from those days to the present. Hadley Cantril would surely be impressed to learn that President Clinton spent nearly $2 million on surveys and "focus groups" during 1993—a nonelection year.[8]

## Providing Psychological Knowledge for the Process of Policy Formation

Cantril's third idea for improving policy formulation concerned generalization the results of basic psychological research to aid in the process of policy formation. Cantril was specific about this. He was convinced that the results of perceptual research, specifically the "Ames room" (described in this section) at Princeton, carried direct and obvious meaning for policymakers. By the 1950s his prestige at the White House was so great that he was able to arrange the demonstration of the Ames room in the "Fish-Bowl" Room at the White House. The circumstances in which he made the attempt are so astonishing—indeed, they must be unique in the history of government—that I present them in Cantril's own words:

> The general orientation I had been pursuing since 1932 was reinforced, extended, and elaborated when in 1947 I met and began to work closely with Adelbert Ames, Jr., one of the leading men in the world in the field of physiological optics. Ames had devised a number of ingenious and exciting demonstrations in perception which illustrated the role played by the assumptions a person brings to a situation in determining the nature of the experience he will have in that situation. While I was a consultant to the White House, working with Nelson Rockefeller [later to be vice president], then a special assistant to Eisenhower on psychological problems relating to the cold war, Nelson arranged to have me show the President some of the demonstrations in perception developed by Del Ames. Our thought was that a few of the basic points the demonstrations were designed to illustrate might be useful in the Government's attempt to influence the reactions of people in other nations to the United States and its policies. The demonstrations particularly showed how difficult it is to make people see things dif-

ferently by means of any purely intellectual, argumentative approach. The obvious conclusion then is that any approach should be made in a person's own terms, from the point of view of his experience, his purposes, and his understanding of the proper means to accomplish his ends.

Accordingly, I arranged with Mr. Kimball Whipple of Hanover, New Hampshire, who had constructed all our demonstrations, to meet me in Washington on the evening of July 4, 1955. The demonstrations we had chosen to show the President were taken down from our Princeton laboratory that day. Whipple and I stayed up until early morning assembling the equipment in what is known as the Fish-Bowl Room of the White House, near the President's office. As we went about our job, we could hear the Fourth of July fireworks being set off around the Washington Monument.

I showed the demonstrations to the President the next morning. Also present were James Haggerty, press secretary, Nelson Rockefeller, General Theodore Parker, and Lloyd Free. The session quickly assumed a relaxed and informal atmosphere. I asked the President to take a seat while I first showed him the "revolving trapezoid window." This is a demonstration in which a trapezoidal shape that looks like a window frame is continuously rotated by a small motor. But to the observer, the "window" appears to oscillate back and forth. The illusion is due to the fact that we have become so used to rectangular windows that we assume the two ends of the window are the same length; hence if one edge of the window subtends a slightly larger angle on the retina we interpret it as being closer to us than the other edge. For that is the way we have experienced windows all our lives when we were not looking at them head on and when they formed a trapezoid on our retinas. The trapezoidal window is so designed that the longer edge always subtends a larger angle on the retina; hence when one looks at it, this longer edge, though moving, is never seen to go farther away from us than the shorter edge; and so we see it oscillate instead of revolve. And even after a person is shown how the illusion is created and is told the theory behind it, he still sees it oscillate back and forth when he looks at it again. *His intellectual knowledge does not change his perception* [italics added; this is the point Cantril wanted to get across to President Roosevelt].

When this was finished, the President asked, "Well, doctor, what do you want me to do now?" I then had him sit in front of the "distorted room"—a room which looks quite rectangular when a person sees it from a certain vantage point with one eye, but which in reality is distorted in such a way that it produces the same image on the retina as a normal room. One of the standard procedures in this demonstration is to ask a person to "swat the fly" with a long wand held in the left hand. The "fly" is simply a black mark painted over one of the windows on the right side of the distorted room. But since the room is so constructed that the left wall is twice as long as the right wall and the back wall comes in at a sharp angle to connect the two, no one ever swats the fly but, instead, runs the wand against the back wall. The point of the procedure is to illustrate that even though we know "intellectually" that the room is distorted in the way it is, this knowledge does not correct the action, since the action is based on the way we perceive the room and the way we have learned to act with respect to such a perception. After three trials in which he missed the fly, the President, after initial spontaneous laughter, became somewhat *irritated*, [italics added] put the wand down and said, "Well, doctor, after all I'm not left-handed."

I presented one or two other demonstrations and we discussed their relationship to programs and messages meant to influence people abroad. Eisenhower got all the points quickly. He related that years ago he had almost given up trying to figure out how the other fellow felt. When he was a young officer in Asia, he said, there was a court-martial case in which a man was being tried for cruelty to a woman to whom he was engaged and with whom he was living. One night the man had told the woman he no longer loved her and threw her out of the house. He was acquitted. The President said he had been shocked at this Oriental conception of justice and remarked to himself at the time: "Boy, but you're a whale of a long way from Abilene, Kansas."

This occasion, to my knowledge, marks the first time a psychologist, in his professional role, had directly drawn a President's attention to the possible value of psychological theory in Government policy-making.[9]

Exciting as all this may have been to Cantril, nothing came of it, in sharp contrast to his successful efforts to convince policymakers of the value of public opinion polling. The Ames room is still shown in a few places (e.g., the Exploratorium in San Francisco), but it is doubtful that anyone now believes that the Ames room demonstrates a psychological principle that every president, prime minister, or public policymaker should master in order to appreciate "how difficult it is to make people see things differently by means of any purely intellectual, argumentative approach."[10] Even Eisenhower seemed to believe that this demonstration was unnecessary but was too polite to say so.

Nevertheless, Cantril was on the right track in several ways. First, he was searching hard for substantive results from basic psychological research that would, if applied correctly, "inject a [new] way of thinking into policy formulation at the highest levels of Government." Not only was his goal correct; his efforts were heroic. Second, although it seems miraculous in view of today's political world that Cantril was able to arrange that demonstration in the White House, he was surely right in taking the demonstration to the highest level rather than attempting to persuade a lower-ranking official to make use of his suggestion. No mere staff member would have dared to suggest the use of this "principle" in policy formation. Third, Cantril was essentially right in his effort to show Eisenhower that not all persuasion involves "intellectual, argumentative approach[es]," although that idea was hardly news to Eisenhower, nor would it have been to others. The thought bears repeated demonstration. But the question remains: What is to replace "intellectual, argumentative approaches"?

## The "Romantic" Period

Psychology succeeded in answering this question to an extraordinary degree between 1940 and 1970. The fascinating and seldom-told story of how this was accomplished, the astounding results achieved, and the lasting impact of these results on U.S. society are documented by Ellen Herman in her book, *The Romance of American Psychology: Political Culture in the Age of Experts*. Herman, a historian, describes how psychology developed rapidly from having a minor role in academia, becoming a significant player in psychological warfare during World War II and later acting as a major force in the mental health movement as a result of its role in the treatment of World War II veterans. Psychology continued to be of importance to the State Department and to the military during the Cold War period and further expanded its role largely through the development of social psychology. Its impact on the nation's view of race relations and what should be done to improve them was significant during the 1950s. By 1962 R. C. Tryon[11] noted that psychology had reached a "'real turning point' because psychologists employed outside of universities outnumbered their academic colleagues for the first time."[12] Herman notes that the concept of psychological "adjustment" was so prominent, even in Congress, that the GI Bill "was formally titled the Servicemen's *Readjustment* Act of 1944."[13] She also notes that psychological experts' "impact on public culture in general—on the very definition of 'the political' and on the direction and style of civic participation—offers further evidence of the complexity of psychology's political history."[14] To which I would add, the political history of the nation itself.

In her excellent history of psychology and social policy between the period of World War II and the decade of the 1970s, Herman shows that psychological theories and research had an enormous impact on social policy during that period. It is a curious history, for all of the theories and much of the research were hotly disputed then and are hardly remembered now. What was not disputed then, or at least not disputed much, and what is largely taken for granted now, was the newly found significance of the subjectivity of experience, the raison d'être of psychology. As Herman points out:

> Psychology in our time is a veritable worldview. . . . In the late-twentieth-century United States psychology's face is so familiar that it is tempting, but wrong, to consider it an ahistorical fact of life or an entity so amorphous and all-pervasive that it eludes definition altogether. Psychology my have seeped into virtually every facet of existence, but this does not mean that it has always been there, or that what experts say has always mattered as much as it matters today. . . . Psychological experts shaped the direction and texture of public life deliberately, with results that were striking and unprecedented.[15]

Although this period of enormous change in the influence of psychology on public policy was indeed remarkable (and utterly unforeseen by anyone) and is as yet unappreciated, one topic remained largely untouched—the cognitive process of policy formation itself, the topic raised by Cantril. No one seemed to consider this an appropriate matter for serious discussion, let alone research. Issues of judgment and decision making do not appear in Herman's history; they simply were not yet seen as relevant to social policy making. The work of Irving Janis changed that, however; it increased the visibility of judgment and decision making. I therefore turn now to a description of the nature of his influence.

## Janis's Attempts to Link Psychology and Policy Making

Although many historians and political scientists have written about the policy-making process, during the 1980s it was Irving Janis (1918–1990) who made the most visible effort to bring psychological theory and research on judgment and decision making to bear on policymaking, both public and private. He and his colleagues, notably Leon Mann, produced numerous books and articles on this topic as well as on the effects of stress on judgment and decision making.[16]

Janis's work was noteworthy for its persistence and for its cumulative and coherent character. He incorporated other investigators' findings into his theory; he made frequent contact with policymakers outside academia and thus brought his ideas to bear on their problems, and vice versa. In many ways, his work offers a model for those interested in judgment and decision making, policy making, and the effects of stress.

Cantril, no doubt, would have heartily approved, for Janis's point of departure was the same as Cantril's. He believed that the policy-making process at the highest levels of government is deeply flawed and has led to catastrophic consequences, a conclusion he took pains to document in his final book, *Crucial Decisions: Leadership in Policymaking and Crisis Management*. In the preface to this book he states that

> one of the main goals . . . is to try to answer the following fundamental questions: *When and why do leaders of large organizations make avoidable errors that result in faulty policy decisions? How can such errors be prevented or at least be kept to a minimum?*[17]

He notes that "it is not a very closely guarded secret that . . . when you consult the writings of experts in management, political science, and other social sciences . . . the experts certainly do not agree with one another." Nevertheless, he also believed that "despite all the fuzziness, disagreements and chaotic lack of integration that currently characterize the relevant social science disciplines, we already have at hand substantial pieces of established knowledge on which to build."[18] By 1989 Janis was convinced that "some order had already been created out of the widespread chaos in the policy sciences," and he was optimistic that "many of the diverse strands of existing theory and research might be brought together in the not-very-distant future" so that we would understand better the "social and psychological factors that play a significant causal role in determining whether policymakers will use effective or ineffective procedures to arrive at a policy decision."[19]

Janis comes back to this point again and again. He notes that:

> Political scientists have been particularly vocal in bemoaning the lack of a comprehensive theory about psychological processes that might account for the frequent failures of the leaders of national governments to arrive at sound policy decisions. For example, Richard Ned Lebow, in a pioneering analysis of international crises containing many insights about errors in policymaking, asserts that research on foreign policy decisions is impeded because "there is as yet no integrated statement of psychological principles and processes that could be considered to represent a paradigm of decisionmaking. There are instead several different schools of thought, each of which attempts to explain nonrational processes in terms of different causation."[20]

Unhappily, then, the field of judgment and decision making suffers from the same problems of disagreement as do others. Janis writes:

> The traditional theory of decisionmaking, Lebow points out, is no longer tenable. That theory describes the process of arriving at a policy decision as essentially rational: Policymakers are rational actors who generally deal with policy problems by trying to find the best alternative, the one that emerges from thorough information search and careful deliberation as most likely to succeed in attaining the goals or values they want to maximize. Lebow calls attention to research from several different disciplines indicating that the rational actor model does not stand up very well as a descriptive theory. What has replaced the traditional model is a "variety of models and approaches," which makes us aware of the multiplicity of personal, social, and political factors that shape the process of decisionmaking. But "no one perspective provides a satisfactory explanation of decisionmaking." Each theoretical approach, Lebow concludes, "offers its

own particular insights and is more or less useful depending upon the analytical concerns of the investigator and the nature of the decision involved."[21]

Yet Janis again asserts his optimism: He believes that all these "perspectives" can be drawn together into "a fairly coherent view":

> Despite all the fragmentation and lack of agreement to be found in the research literature, it seems to me that many bits of theorizing and pieces of sound empirical evidence can be fitted together to form a fairly coherent view of decisionmaking processes.[22]

But he was never convincing in his attempts to demonstrate that conclusion (weakened as it is by the use of the modifier "fairly"), and no one else has been, either.

There are no equations in Janis's work; his work was not quantitative. But the vast majority of scientific articles published by members of the Judgment and Decision Making Society are quantitative in nature. For that reason, contact between the two was minimal. To see the difference in approach, consider Janis's chart, reproduced in Table 11-1.

Virtually all the concepts in Table 11-1 are familiar to us whether we are professionals or laypersons; without further explanation they make sense to us. That is, of course, at once their strength and their weakness. Explanations in which we already believe, once they are called to our attention, inspire confidence among the lay public but not among those committed to a hard scientific point of view. As noted previously, scientists are doubtful and mistrustful of common sense. Therefore, although Janis's ideas may indeed be valid and useful at a very general descriptive level they do not satisfy those who have already decided that a more analytical, more mathematical approach is required.

As a result, Janis's work had little direct influence on research in the judgment and decision-making community. His publications draw frequent citations,[23] but few investigators base their work on his. Seldom have his ideas drawn researchers into testing them, if, indeed, they are testable. In the ten-year existence of the Judgment and Decision Making Society, Janis never appeared, either by invitation or otherwise. To what extent his work has influenced policymakers is unknown; there is no documentation of such influence, so far as I know.

A recent book edited by F. Heller illustrates the point.[24] A eulogy of Janis is provided by the editor, but references to Janis by the various authors are limited, and there is no substantive follow-up of his work by any of the chapter authors in that book.

One exception (perhaps there will be others) is the book by P. 't Hart that describes "groupthink" in various governmental policymaking efforts.[25] 't Hart's work makes no contact with the current research and theory in judgment and decision making, however. Even 't Hart recognizes that the concept of "groupthink" (perhaps Janis's most visible contribution) has been vulnerable to considerable criticism from social psychologists interested in group behavior. 't Hart includes, for example, sharp criticisms made by J. Longley and D. G. Pruitt[26] and others.[27] It may well be that Janis's innovative ideas such as "groupthink" receive little attention from judgment and decision-making researchers because the latter rarely examine group decision making. R. Hastie and N. Pennington are among the very few judgment and decision-making researchers who do examine group decision making;[28] they make little, if any contact with Janis's work, however.

Table 11-1   Major Constraints That Can Obstruct Vigilant Problem Solving and Some
Typical Decision Rules Used to Cope with Them.

| Cognitive Constraints | Affiliative Constraints | Egocentric (Self-Serving and Emotive) Constraints |
|---|---|---|
| Limited time | Need to maintain: | Strong personal motive: |
| Perceived limitations of available resources for information search and appraisal | power status compensation social support | e.g., greed, desire for fame |
| | | Arousal of an emotional need: e.g., anger, elation |
| Multiple tasks | Need for acceptability of new policy within the organization | Emotional stress of decisional conflict |
| Perplexing complexity of issue | | |
| Perceived lack of dependable knowledge | | |
| Ideological commitments | | |

| Cognitive Decision Rules | Affiliative Decision Rules | Egocentric (Self-Serving and Emotive) Decision Rules |
|---|---|---|
| Availability | Avoid punishment | Personal aggrandizement: "What's in it for me?" |
| Satisficing | "Rig" acceptance | |
| Analogizing | Exercise one-upmanship in the power struggle | Angry retaliation |
| Nutshell briefing | | Audacity: "Can do!" |
| Operational code | Groupthink: preserve group harmony | Elated choice: "Wow! Grab it" |
| | | Defensive avoidance: procrastinate, pass-the-buck, or bolster |
| | | Hypervigilant escape: "Get the hell out fast" |

Source: Janis. (1989, p. 149).

The concept of "groupthink" was, however, applied to the catastrophic decision-making process at the launch of the *Challenger* by G. Moorhead, R. Ference, and C. P. Neck, who claim that the several defects pointed out by Janis were present: (1) few alternatives, (2) no reexamination of alternatives, (3) rejection of expert opinions, (4) rejection of negative information, and (5) lack of contingency plans.[29] They add: "The leaders had a preferred solution and engaged in behaviors designed to promote it rather than critically appraise alternatives."[30] But even these authors seriously weaken their support for the "groupthink" concept by stating that "the groupthink symptoms result from the group characteristics, as proposed by Janis, but *only* [italics added] in the presence of the moderator variables of time and *certain* [italics added] leadership styles."[31]

To summarize, Janis continued to pursue throughout most of his professional life the goal set by Cantril, although there is no indication that Janis was aware of Cantril's efforts. It is important to observe that for both Cantril and Janis the goal was a *didactic* one. Both Cantril and Janis were academics whose aim was to *instruct* policymakers; they did not propose to *intervene* in any specific decision-making problem, although Janis and Mann later modified their views somewhat.

Nevertheless, Janis's work will have a long life; the word "groupthink" has become a part of everyday language, at least among the intelligentsia, and as a result has achieved dictionary status; it appears in the 1992 edition of the *American Heritage Dictionary of the English Language*, although, astonishingly—and regrettably—none of the negative aspects of this concept, so strongly emphasized by Janis, are included in the definition.

## My Turn at the White House

My attempt to influence the manner in which policy is formed at the highest levels was far more modest than either Cantril's or Janis's.

The opportunity appeared in 1979 when I received a telephone call from the president's office—I initially misunderstood it to be a call from the office of the president of the university—inquiring whether I would be willing to offer a two-day seminar at the White House. To this day I have no idea why I was singled out for this invitation. But I accepted it on the spot. The question then became: What should this seminar be about? What should be presented? I decided almost immediately that I did not want to present the usual academic seminar on judgment and decision making. Even in 1979 that seminar would have consisted of a lot of information about human judgment that policymakers would rather not hear. So I called back and said: "I don't want to offer the usual academic seminar. Give me a problem to solve. Tell me about a policy problem President Carter is working on and send me copies of his remarks that will indicate how he is thinking about the problem." I could tell from the long pause that the person at the other end of the line was uncertain about how to reply, other than to say that she would call back. But she did call back and did give me a problem and did send almost ten pounds of President Carter's remarks on the question of whether he should establish a new cabinet office, a department of education. The president, she said, was uncertain about whether this was a good idea; help with the process would be appreciated. My idea was that I should try to make a positive contribution; I should solve a problem rather than take a lofty, "teachy" approach.

I discussed the problem with a group of graduate students. We came up with the idea of offering a more effective way of conveying the judgments of those staff members or outside consultants to the president. Our premises were these:

1. In ordinary practice, the president sifts through the verbiage (I use the word intentionally) of a number of position papers and memoranda that contain words and phrases with ambiguous referents in order to discover the basis for the judgments offered. This practice is very time-consuming and is generally acknowledged not to be very effective. Yet President Carter seemed to be especially committed to this method.

2. The core features of each adviser's policies could be observed and displayed by the use of numbers and diagrams instead of words, with two consequences: (1) much less time would be consumed, and (2) much less conflict and dispute about the referents, words, and phrases would be created.
3. The judgments offered would be based largely, if not entirely, on multiple fallible indicators of what is, what can be, and what ought to be.
4. The indicators on which each adviser's judgments were based could be readily ascertained and displayed, as well as the relative weights placed on each. Thus, the indicator and the relative weight profile of each adviser could simply be shown to the president in pictorial form; the essentials of each adviser's judgment would be apparent without each adviser's writing a memorandum that the president would then have to read.[32] If the president wished to deepen his inquiry, judgments regarding each indicator could be "unfolded" into the subset of indicators. (All the computer technology for these steps existed even in 1979.)

I have only given the briefest outline of the procedure that two of my then graduate students, Richard Cook and Jeryl Mumpower, and I presented at the Old Executive Office Building to about fifty staff members. The result was hardly a success—no one rushed us into the Oval Office crying, "Just listen to this," but it was not a complete failure, either. We were invited to continue the seminar for a second day (we were told this was an unusual sign of interest), and promises were made about continuing communication, promises that were kept for almost three weeks. The political distance between Washington, D.C., and Colorado was too great for communicating radical ideas. And suggesting that the president's memos regarding policy were to come up to him in essentially nonverbal form was indeed a radical idea. (Jeryl Mumpower and Thomas Stewart at the Policy Research Center at SUNY Albany have continued to develop these ideas.)

It is interesting to note that the practice of presenting the president with heavy binders of memoranda persists. In his description of (chaotic) policy making at the Clinton White House, R. Woodward notes that, on President Clinton's return from a brief trip abroad, "his staff presented him with a two-inch-thick binder of memos."[33] Moreover, the person who wrote the four-page summary, according to Woodward, now "realized that he had become a salesman for a [two-inch-thick] plan that neither he nor Clinton believed in."[34] No doubt the procedure we invented can be improved, but I am convinced that there must be a better way to present the basis for judgments than traditional memoranda that, by the time they are presented, are already obsolete or disproved.

## Suedfeld and Tetlock: Broadening the Perspective

Virtually all attempts to bring the results of psychological research (or research in history or political science) to bear on policy formation are based on the premise that improvement would follow were the proposed change to be accepted. P. Suedfeld and P. E. Tetlock broaden this perspective, but in doing so they may actually negate the premise. Their anthology, *Psychology and Social Policy*, is, with two exceptions that are discussed below, directed toward substantive issues to which psychological research might contribute.[35] These include such topics as international relations and foreign policy and domestic issues, including affirmative action, civil liberties, pornography, and television violence and aggression. But they are very careful to admonish their colleagues about advocacy. They describe ways in which advocacy creeps into the material that a consultant or researcher might provide for a policy-maker, and give examples of past mistakes. These are worth noting.

Suedfeld and Tetlock take pains to define, clarify, and insist on the separation of the roles of policy *advocates* and policy *researchers*:

> Psychologists should be scrupulously careful to differentiate their participation in policy debates as interested citizens or advocates from participation as behavioral scientists. ... The normative guidelines for these two roles differ significantly. Participation as a behavioral scientist calls for making explicit the distinction between facts and values; for stating one's values clearly; and, when discussing the facts, for presenting all of the relevant evidence (including its limits, gaps, and contradictions).[36]

Suedfeld and Tetlock also admonish psychologists interested in psychology and social policy to be cautious when generalizing the results of laboratory studies—what psychologists like to call "basic research"—to circumstances that they like to call the "real world":

> One set of problems in this category concerns all of the familiar issues related to the external or ecological validity of research evidence. Real-world policies involve many more causal variables than researchers can manipulate, randomize, hold constant, or simply be aware of, even in the most rigorous and meticulous research program. At a minimum, great caution is advised. Research experience in a remarkably broad range of the subareas of psychology—cognitive, social, environmental, educational, health, personality, and industrial/organization—indicates that the main effects of today frequently become the first- and higher-order interaction effects of tomorrow (cf. Cronbach & Snow, 1977; Gergen & Davis, 1985; McGuire, 1983; Meehl, 1978). The literature abounds in references to interactions between personality and situational variables, aptitudes and treatments, and contexts and tasks.[37]

Having made clear their cautions and worries about advocacy and generalization, Suedfeld and Tetlock demonstrate in the remainder of their anthology the reasons for such caution and worries. Each topic is discussed by a pair of researchers, each of whom advocates a different policy regarding the topic. In relation to nuclear policy, R. K. White advocates the use of psychological research to reduce the likelihood of nuclear war,[38] but J. G. Blight debunks its value.[39] In relation to affirmative action, H. J. Harrington and N. Miller advocate not only the application of psychological research but affirmative action itself. As they put it, "We . . . wish to establish a continuing case for affirmative action and describe how social psychological theory and research can contribute to strategies for its success in industry."[40] And in compliance with Suedfeld and Tetlock's admonitions they make their values clear: "redressing past injustices, protecting against contemporary prejudice, and enlightening self-interest for the long-term peace and prosperity of society."[41] These authors buttress their views by referring to theory, concept, and social and psychological studies of various forms. In his chapter, however, W. R. Beer disagrees sharply and vigorously:

> There is little empirical research on which the effects of affirmative action can be evaluated. There is no adequate measure of the alleged impact of the past discrimination for which affirmative action is supposed to atone. Public opinion is clearly hostile to affir-

mative action in the established form of preferential treatment. Measures of discrimination show its effects to be extremely modest. None of the underlying concepts used to justify and elaborate the policy is publicly and rationally articulated. In sum, affirmative action is a social policy without a scientific base.

Social scientists have refused to look at its effects for two sets of reasons. First, there is self-interest. Most academic social scientists, being older and tenured, are not affected by affirmative action and are therefore not interested in damages it may inflict. Indeed, they can and often do make exhortations about its moral rightness without suffering its consequences. At the same time, younger and untenured academic social scientists are likely to be female and Black beneficiaries of a policy they are not inclined to examine critically. The few White untenured men are in a precarious enough position to want to avoid taking the contentious stand of questioning the biases of mainstream academia, since their careers are at stake.

Second, biased toward the liberal/left wing of the political spectrum as they are, most social scientists do not choose to examine the effects of one of the most cherished policies of liberalism's "Great Society" for fear of what they might find. Accordingly, affirmative action has become a shibboleth, and opponents of it can be, by definition, identified as racists (Sniderman & Tetlock, 1986, pp. 145–147). Since affirmative action is primarily a way of expiating Whites' guilt about Black suffering, a guilt artfully stimulated by shrewd Black politicians, it is evidently a policy aimed at White atonement, rather than at real Black achievement. The effects of affirmative action therefore are irrelevant—its existence is its own justification. The constant call for more minority hiring and college admissions is an incantation, not a rationally examined policy.[42]

By pairing opposing positions about these important policy problems, Suedfeld and Tetlock demonstrate what is common to so many efforts to base social policy on scientific evidence—disagreement among the scientists that leaves policymakers in doubt, which in turn forces them to rely on judgments that can neither be fully justified on analytical grounds nor accepted on purely intuitive grounds. Quasirational judgments that entangle fact and value are thus inevitable.

The pairing that is most closely related to cognitive competence is that which pits I. L. Janis and L. Mann[43] against Suedfeld and Tetlock.[44] Janis and Mann base their conclusions about ineffective decision making at the highest governmental levels on psychological research. But Suedfeld and Tetlock attack the value of that research in general and the work of D. Kahneman and A. Tversky in particular. Suedfeld and Tetlock are sharply critical of the conclusions drawn by those researchers as well as of the methods used to produce them.

Suedfeld and Tetlock do not hold the laboratory methods of psychologists in high regard; their methodological position is in direct opposition to that of laboratory psychologists such as W. K. Estes.[45] After recapitulating the list of putative cognitive flaws put forward by judgment and decision-making researchers and providing examples of how these have been used in post hoc examinations of governmental decisions, the authors state their conclusions:

> In our judgment, the psychological literature (experimental and extrapolated) does not justify any serious belief that decision making is generally poor, nor that complex decisions (i.e., those not using shortcuts) are necessarily better than simple ones. This is true even for complicated situations and critical issues.[46]

The authors become specific in their analysis of many of the studies carried out by Kahneman and Tversky and their associates and indicate their preference for the conclusions reached by H. A. Simon:

> The need to make many choices in a short period of time, the complexity of the inter-actions that determine outcomes, and the uncertainty surrounding probabilities, all compel human beings to make their choices by bounded rationality: a simplified model of the decision environment. Simon's (1983) behavioral model of decision making is based on this concept, which emphasizes how people actually solve problems by focusing attention, generating solution alternatives, and collecting and interpreting information. The process . . . draws upon intuition and the emotional processes that direct attention.[47]

Thus we meet again the antinomy between those committed to conventional methodology and those who reject it in favor of the ecological approach.

## Fact and Value in the Formation of Social Policy

No discussion of the use of scientific information in the formation of social policy would be complete without a consideration of the relation between facts and values. Although long a matter of debate among philosophers, this topic has received little consideration from those interested in human judgment and social policy, yet it is critical.[48] Many a policy debate has found one person implicitly and unwittingly accusing the other of confusing an "is" with an "ought" and vice versa. For example, "we have always done it this way" implies "that's the way it *is*; *therefore*, that's the way it *ought* to be." Suedfeld and Tetlock devote most of their introductory chapter to the recent volume *Psychology and Social Policy* to the question of separating facts from values, thus giving the topic the prominence it deserves but seldom gets.[49] They observe that the "disaggregating of fact and value is rare in social science research,"[50] as indeed it is. At the risk of self-service, I must mention that the only study Suedfeld and Tetlock found to satisfy the separation criterion is one carried out by Leonard Adelman and myself.[51]

The primary difficulty with the fact-value distinction is that it has been approached in terms of semantics. That is, the language used to express facts and values has been examined in detail—usually by philosophers—and they have not been satisfied with the separation of these concepts; the distinction has been difficult—some argue impossible—to maintain. The steps that Adelman and I took were to separate facts from values in a *behavioral, functional* manner. Scientists were assigned the role of determining the facts; policymakers were assigned the role of expressing values. That behavioral separation was new and different, and it worked. But that step not only challenged conventional wisdom; it required a great deal of work and does not rank high on "feasibility." Adelman and I predicted at the time that it would be under-taken only when the administrators are desperate—when every other mechanism would have been tried without success and a catastrophe was imminent. So far we have been right, which is regrettable, because in my view (possibly dictated by proud parentage) this general procedure is a valuable and practical one.

Many would like to leave fact-value decisions up to lay members of the public and thus encourage them to somehow integrate complex, uncertain factual data with their personal (often changing) values. But that solution passes off the decision from those who should be competent to frame it and solve it—within any individual's value system—to those who cannot do either. Research within the coherence metatheory has demonstrated time and again that although this type of decision problem is susceptible to understanding through the work of a decision analyst, it is not understood by those not trained in statistical reasoning. Statistical reasoning may not provide a complete answer, but the problem cannot be understood without it. Long ago David Eddy demonstrated this point with medical students as subjects.[52] He gave them a problem that required that they estimate the probability of breast cancer in a patient before and after receiving information from an x-ray and with all the data regarding false positives and false negatives. Eddy's results showed that the intuitively produced answers by medical students (and physicians) untrained in decision analysis were far wrong, if the criterion of rationality (i.e., coherence) is applied. It was research of this sort that led to the introduction of courses in judgment and decision making in some medical schools and to physicians' interest in participating in the Society for Medical Decision Making. The goal was to improve the rationality of such decisions. Should everyone take these courses before reaching a decision about surgery?

In Chapter 2 I explained how values determine one error preference. Each error entails values that attract constituencies, each of which pleads for accepting the error that will do the least harm to their values and thus afford the least injustice to them. The bombing of Hiroshima—the never-to-be-forgotten event of the twentieth century—offers an example of all of this, in quite an unexpected way. Some fifty years later, the bombing remains controversial because it continues to be discussed in terms of morality: The differential risks of error are largely ignored. The Japanese regard the bombing as a terrible error that ought not to have been made—an immoral act that left one hundred thousand dead. The Americans believe that the bomb ought to have been dropped, that failure to do so would have been an immoral act; if it had not been used tens, if not hundreds, of thousands of American troops would have been killed in an invasion of Japan. There has been no reconciliation of these views, nor is the dispute diminishing in importance. The persistence of this impasse illustrates the consequences of the failure to acknowledge that irreducible uncertainty and the presence of differential error make injustice unavoidable.

In his review of I. Buruma's 1994 book, *The Wages of Guilt: Memories of War in Germany and Japan*, the historian Gordon Craig observed.

> The sacralizing of Hiroshima naturally prevents any attempt to give an objective account of the war preceding the bombing. Buruma tells us that in 1992, during a United Nations conference on disarmament in Hiroshima, a Harvard professor urged that the dropping of the bomb had shortened the war and thus saved a million *Japanese lives* [italics added]; he went on to say that millions more were living because the horror of what had happened to Hiroshima and Nagasaki had helped prevent the use of nuclear weapons ever since. The Japanese were outraged, and a leading newspaper expressed its disgust and warned that the United States would experience much opposition from non-nuclear countries unless it "disentangled itself from this kind of view."[53]

It is instructive to think of this matter in terms of the four-cell diagram described in Chapter 1 (see Table 1-1). The Japanese and the Americans held exactly opposite views with regard to cells 1 and 3, which indicate "success" (bomb kills one hundred thousand) and "failure" (bomb kills no one). In terms of errors (cells 2 and 4), successfully dropping the bomb was a terrible moral error from the Japanese viewpoint; not dropping the bomb when it would "succeed" would have been a moral error from the American viewpoint but correct from the Japanese viewpoint. The moral error for the American was obvious (enormous casualties would have been suffered in the attack on the Japanese islands). Not dropping the bomb when it would "succeed" would have indeed been a serious error. Thus, for the Japanese, there was no question as to what should have been done; the bomb simply should not have been dropped under any circumstances. From the American viewpoint, however, there was a choice to be made, albeit under uncertainty; that meant the possibility of error and injustice.

At least this was the situation until the Harvard professor mentioned by Craig agreed that the dropping of the bomb "had shortened the war and thus saved a million *Japanese* (italics added) lives." This suggestion meant that *not* dropping the bomb would have been an error from the Japanese viewpoint as well. In short, because of the introduction of new factual considerations (a million Japanese casualties), the Japanese must now ponder values like those considered by the Americans; this means weighing the error of not dropping the bomb when (from *their* point of view, as well as from the Americans') it should have been dropped. That error—not dropping the bomb—would, the professor argued, have cost the Japanese ten times as many lives as were lost at Hiroshima. But a "leading newspaper expressed its disgust" at this suggestion, thus refusing to consider one of the four possibilities in Table 1-1 because it was morally revolting.

The reader might now ask: Was the Harvard professor justified in raising this factual possibility? Was the leading newspaper justified in rejecting it out of moral disgust? Should the reader express disgust—or despair or sorrow—at the newspaper's refusal to consider the matter in a rational, analytical way? Perhaps there is no room, no place for analysis in such circumstances. Indeed, that may have been the source of the disgust. Perhaps one's value system permits only intuitive reactions to the suggestion that one should treat such problems in the light of cold analytical reasoning. Or perhaps disgust was directed toward the suggestion that one should kill, maim, and burn one hundred thousand men, women, and children—even if 1 million are thereby saved from similar killing, maiming, and burning. What would the nine hundred thousand who putatively were saved by the bomb at Hiroshima say to this? Doesn't justice argue that they should have a voice? Here is unavoidable injustice writ large; surely the one hundred thousand who were killed at Hiroshima would claim that a mistake was made; many have made the claim for them. But the nine hundred thousand who (probably) would have been killed, maimed, and burned had that action not been taken would approve of that action over the inaction that could have cost *their* lives. Would they side with the Americans in choosing this (lesser?) form of injustice? Would they not justify their choice analytically? Perhaps morally?

There have been suggestions that this is too narrow a point of view, that alternatives to dropping or not dropping the bomb existed. Policymakers have claimed that they evaluated these and found them wanting, for reasons that do not concern us here.

I raise this issue to demonstrate how an act of this magnitude is discussed fifty years later in terms that still evoke disgust, an emotion apparently shared by many Japanese (and some Americans). Will the Harvard professor's arguments about differential error (for that is what it comes down to) in relation to shared values persuade any Japanese? Or anybody else?

In short, by 1992 Suedfeld and Tetlock had suggested a change in the direction of research on psychology and public policy.[54] They took a much broader perspective than either Cantril or Janis (or myself) in their attempt to bring psychological research to bear on social policy formation. The emphasis on the flawed nature of human judgment that is apparent in Cantril and Janis, and that dominates the thinking of so many current researchers in the field of judgment and decision making, is flatly rejected by Suedfeld and Tetlock. To what extent this change in direction will be followed remains to be seen. Their approach will surely find support among political scientists, but, in all likelihood, judgment and decision-making researchers will continue the relentless pursuit of flawed judgment. (I will have more to say about the future in Chapter 12.) The advice that policymakers are now receiving—from an unexpected source—is just the opposite of that offered by the researchers, although it much resembles that offered by Suedfeld and Tetlock, and to that advice I now turn.

## The Reappearance of Common Sense: Philip Howard and His Friends—President Clinton, Senator Dole, and Company

So far as I know, no key policymaker—those Cantril, Janis, Suedfeld, Tetlock, and I tried to reach—ever turned to researchers in the judgment and decision-making field for advice regarding the policy-making process. But, surprisingly, they *did* turn to a lawyer, and did so with enthusiasm. This happened because the lawyer, Philip Howard, knew just what was wrong with the way human judgment was being applied to social policy formation; it lacked common sense. Oddly enough, it never occurred to any of the judgment researchers to suggest that policymakers make greater use of common sense—quite the reverse! Many coherence researchers have concluded that common sense is the enemy of good judgment.

When his book, titled *The Death of Common Sense: How Law Is Suffocating America*, appeared, it immediately caught the attention of policymakers as well as the public and appeared on the *New York Times* best-seller list for several months. The impact of Howard's book on policymakers can only be described as phenomenal, especially when compared with the previous efforts of psychologists. *The Wall Street Journal*'s review of the book noted that "for weeks, politicians of both parties have been falling over each other to declare that they are Howardites, too. Like him, they see that paperwork, litigation and rulemaking have gone beyond all bounds of common sense."[55] In the same edition of that newspaper, an article reported that "both President Clinton and Senator Dole have praised Mr. Howard's ideas."[56] What new ideas does Mr. Howard have that are drawing such interest and praise from the public as well as from politicians?

Howard's ideas are centered on the use of common sense and its omission from the laws, rules, and regulations that he claims are "suffocating America," a proposition widely and enthusiastically embraced. His book is replete with horror stories of analytical cognition gone awry. The examples generally illustrate gross errors that follow from the bureaucratic application of carefully detailed, analytically derived regulations that impede, delay, or derail projects or activities that are otherwise imminently desirable. His examples are fetching and have already become widely quoted. Here is one: "Fixing a $50 lock in a New York public school takes ten steps over a six-month period, including review by someone called a 'supervising supervisor.'"[57] One example achieved instant notoriety. He describes an effort by Mother Theresa, the Nobel laureate, to remodel an abandoned building in New York City so that her order of nuns could provide a refuge for the homeless. All the bureaucratic formalities had been satisfied—except one. It seems that Mother Theresa's order, Missionaries Charity, does not permit the use of modern conveniences. After several years had elapsed—and after remodeling had begun—Mother Theresa was told that the building code required that her building have an elevator; otherwise, no remodeling would be allowed. Neither side would give ground. The nuns could not because of their religious beliefs; the city could not because, well, the law is the law. (Both sides were trapped by coherent belief systems.) The result? No building for the homeless.

Howard uses numerous examples like these, coupled with such appealing assertions as "people constantly making judgments is the breeze that drives out dank air and invigorates us."[58] His enthusiasm for human judgment seems unbounded: "By exiling human judgment in the last few decades [is there a thirty-year cycle here?], modern law changed its role from useful tool to brainless tyrant."[59] And "judgment is to law as water is to crops."[60] Howard ends his treatise with a plea: "Let judgment and personal conviction be important again. . . . Relying on ourselves is not, after all, a new ideology. It's just common sense."[61] His thesis is that analytical cognition, particularly as it is experienced in law, should be replaced with common sense, although no explanation of what is meant by common sense will be found other than in such breezy generalizations indicated above.

I do not disagree with Howard's principal thesis, that the drive toward the analytical pole of the cognitive continuum (described in Chapter 6) has gone so far as to create blunders—even catastrophes—and thus to exhibit the fragility of this form of cognition. Nor do I think Holmes and Cardozo and other great justices of the U.S. Supreme Court would disagree with Howard's thesis. They too, cautioned against the dangers of logic. And I cannot imagine a politician declaring that he or she is against common sense or that he or she is opposed to the use of good judgment.

The trouble with Howard's treatise is that his analysis stops there; it is a treatise supported only by assertion and anecdote. Thus, it is, at best, a good idea presented in shallow form.

But if it is a good idea, why not leave well enough alone? Because Howard's enthusiasm for common sense, unencumbered by acknowledgments of the deficiencies of that process, serve his—and my—cause badly. For as soon as the deficiencies of common sense are made apparent, as indeed they will be, the general thesis will be mocked, as indeed it already has.[62]

The topic deserves better, because common sense, or quasirationality, is a form of cognition that *does* have valuable attributes. In the next section, therefore, I criticize Howard's superficial treatment of this important topic.

## Negative Features of Howard's
## The Death of Common Sense

I use the term "superficial" advisedly. Here is an example of the treatment of rationalism. After an anecdote regarding the numerous forms the mayor of Chicago must sign, he declares: "Rationalism rears its head again. Process is a kind of rule. It tells us not what to do, but how to do it."[63] Howard overlooks the fact that he, too, is telling us *what process* to apply, or "how to do it." For he tells us again and again that rationalism should not be allowed to raise its head, that the cognitive activity he calls "common sense" is all that is necessary; indeed, it is exactly what we should employ in the making of policy. He apparently does not realize that common sense is a cognitive process, too; nor does he realize that, because it is a cognitive process, it is also subject to decomposition or analytical and empirical scrutiny just as intuition and analysis are. Howard not only fails to acknowledge that common sense is a form of cognition that can be compared with others in its processes and outcomes, he ignores the necessity of defining or explaining what he means by "judgment," other than by using dubious metaphors, as in "people making judgments is the breeze that drives out dank air and invigorates us."[64] Expressions of that sort certainly have their appeal, but they don't help us to understand how judgment produces social policy or how common sense—however described—improves social policy judgments.

Howard uses the practice of mandatory sentencing as one of his examples of analytical cognition gone awry. But his treatment of this difficult topic is as misleading as it is shallow. First, his history of mandatory sentencing is faulty (see my excerpts in Chapter 6 from Supreme Court Justice Breyer's description of this history). Second, his description of the process is so skimpy that it is little more than a caricature. (For an example of the process, see my excerpts in Chapter 12 from Judge Davies's sentencing memorandum regarding the police officers who beat Rodney King.) Third, although he acknowledges that a "sentencing commission" was established, he ignores what members of the commission said when they justified the use of mandatory sentencing. Howard simply says that the "idea developed momentum, and a 'sentencing commission' was established."[65] But that commission examined both sides of the issue in commendable detail and showed that it was reliance on judges' discretion—that is, judgment—that had created an intolerable situation in the first place. Howard does not engage or even acknowledge the commission's thoughtful treatment of this difficult problem; instead, he makes a mockery of the process and follows with atrocity stories, examples of what seem to be egregious sentencing errors. For example:

> The commission ultimately created a 258-box matrix from which federal courts had to calculate all jail sentences. Judges are now permitted only minimal leeway.
>
> All the components of the sentencing grid—whether it was first offense, whether a weapon was used, how many drugs were sold—are the best that our smartest legal minds could come up with. All the judges would have to do is calculate the points. At last, many believed, we had created a fair and uniform way of treating criminal defendants. It all sounded perfect.
>
> Most who use it—judges, lawyers, prosecutors—consider it a disaster.[66]

In order to reinforce his point, Howard repeats that description and adds that "policeman and prosecutors now huddle over the complex 258-box grid in their offices, figuring out how to make arrests so that they can maximize sentences and gain more leverage."[67] He then makes the incorrect assertion that "judges' hands are tied by the sentencing grid" (a statement confounded by Judge Davies's sentencing memorandum), followed by what can only be described as a ridiculous assertion ("judges, at least are impartial").[68] In fact, it was the *lack* of impartiality on the part of judges that gave rise to the need for mandatory sentencing; previous "common sense" judgments were the source of the problem. Judges prejudiced against minorities gave them harsher sentence; therefore, rules were introduced to punish the crime, not the offender. Therein lies their advantages, as well as their disadvantages.

A *thirty-year cycle*? As we saw in Chapter 2, whenever there is irreducible uncertainty, duality of error, and unavoidable injustice, we are likely to find a cycle, movement of tolerance for one type of error to tolerance for the other and back again. That may well be the case with mandatory sentencing (as well as other social policies). Certainly African-Americans and other minorities received harsh and unfair sentences from judges who were allowed to rely on their judgment and to exercise their intuitions and their prejudices prior to the civil rights movement in the 1960s. Certainly the mandatory sentencing procedures as now employed result in obvious errors and injustices (see Judge Jack Weinstein's criticisms in Chapter 3). Perhaps the one result of Howard's success in persuading policymakers of the value of common sense will be a strong push toward the opposite error, overreliance on judges' discretions, and the situation will revert to what it was thirty or so years ago.

Nearly fifty years ago, Stephen Pepper, a philosopher at the University of California at Berkeley, described cycling from common sense to analysis in a passage I find unforgettable:

> This tension between common sense and expert knowledge, between cognitive security without responsibility and cognitive responsibility without full security, is the interior dynamics of the knowledge situation. The indefiniteness of much detail in common sense, its contradictions, its lack of established grounds, drive thought to seek definiteness, consistency, and reasons. Thought finds these in the criticized and refined knowledge of mathematics, science, and philosophy, only to discover that these tend to thin out into arbitrary definitions, pointer readings, and tentative hypotheses. Astounded at the thinness and hollowness of these culminating achievements of conscientiously responsible cognition, thought seeks matter for its definitions, significance for its pointer readings, and support for its wobbling hypotheses. Responsible cognition finds itself insecure as a result of the very earnestness of its virtues. But where shall it turn? It does, in fact, turn back to common sense, that indefinite and irresponsible source which it so lately scorned. But it does so, generally, with a bad grace. After filling its empty definitions and pointer readings and hypotheses with meanings out of the rich confusion of common sense, it generally turns its head away, shuts its eyes to what it has been doing, and affirms dogmatically the self-evidence and certainty of the common-sense significance it has drawn into its concepts. Then it pretends to be securely based on self-evident principles or indubitable facts. If our recent criticism of dogmatism is correct, however, this security in self-evidence and indubitability has proved questionable. And critical knowledge hangs over a vacuum unless it acknowledges

openly the actual, though strange, source of its significance and security in the uncriticized material of common sense. Thus the circle is completed. Common sense continually demands the responsible criticism of refined knowledge, and refined knowledge sooner or later requires the security of common-sense support.[69]

Pepper didn't mention specific time periods for the swing of this pendulum, nor do I think it matters much. The important lesson to draw from Pepper is that the deficiencies of each mode of cognition lead us to adopt the other in turn. The person who has learned that has learned to anticipate the future with some degree of accuracy. Cycling (described as oscillation in Chapter 7) also can be seen in the movement in Figure 9-1 from modes of inquiry near Mode 1 to Mode 6 and back.

Policymakers are not helpless, however. They have a favorite strategy for coping with uncertainty, and that is the subject of the next section.

## The Conventional Road to Wisdom: Dependence on the Elders

One of the most persistent and prominent of the traditional methods used by policymakers in arriving at decisions is the creation of a "commission" to which a policy problem is assigned. Matters of crime, health care, education, and the nation's budget deficit regularly wind up in the hands of such commissions. That is because of a general belief that wisdom, or, as General George C. Marshall put it, "proper judgment," resides, or has a better chance of residing, in such commissions. It is at this point that elitism meets democracy.

One absolute criterion that each member of such commissions must meet is that she or he must be untainted both politically and financially. Thus free of motivation for political or personal gain, the members of the special commission are expected to be at their cognitive best. That is why it is important for us to look at the quality of their work; the possibility that their cognitive activity will be distorted by personal motives is markedly lower than, say, that for a congressional committee, whose collective urge for reelection makes its judgment suspect. Traditionally, such commissions are made up of elder statesmen, of persons of unblemished reputation who also have gained a record for good judgment, or who at least have avoided blame for gross errors.

A new element has been introduced that threatens to challenge faith in this tradition. That new element is the increased visibility of research findings in the field of judgment and decision making that weaken our faith in the judgments rendered by such commissions. The visibility of judgment and decision-making research that casts doubt on expert judgment was increased substantially when Justice Breyer cited it in his efforts to change social policies regarding the regulation of risk. Justice Breyer clearly preferred to accept the results and conclusions of the judgment and decision-making researchers than the positive views of expertise that are the basis of the development of artificial intelligence and expert systems.[70]

The negative view of the wisdom of human judgment, experts included, was succinctly expressed by P. Slovic, S. Lichtenstein, and B. Fischhoff, who recently announced that "the world does not work in a way that helps us recognize our deficiencies in probabilistic judgment. As a result, we maintain an exaggerated sense of our judgmental prowess."[71] This profound conclusion, based as it is on a recent review of the research on judgment and decision making by three of its most distinguished researchers, must be taken very seriously. Suppose that it is true. How does that conclusion speak to George Marshall's 1947 declaration that "the whole world's future hangs on proper judgment"? It speaks directly. For if the "world does not work in a way that helps us recognize our deficiencies in probabilistic judgment," then the whole world's future was—and is—dependent on a process of human judgment that prominent researchers steadfastly claim to be deficient. The researchers' conclusion must also mean that General Marshall's statement was simply a product of "an exaggerated sense of our [that is, General Marshall's, as well as the reader's] judgmental prowess." If the researchers are correct, then the great success of the Marshall Plan simply led to a further exaggeration of our false belief in our "judgmental prowess." That's because the world works the way it does; success often follows mistaken judgments, and failure often follows correct ones. That's what the research tells us.

Will the reader believe the researchers? Or will the reader think it is the researchers who have an "exaggerated sense" of their prowess?

General Marshall's 1947 statement is not the only one to be made by a reputedly wise and certainly respected citizen. There are literally thousands of such expressions from antiquity to the present; the reader need not be reminded of them. And expressions of our dependence on the wisdom of human judgment for policy questions continue to be made by our most respected citizens. George Kennan, unquestionably one of our highly distinguished citizens, as well as the outstanding scholar of the diplomatic corps, grounds his "personal and political philosophy" in a belief in wisdom generated by experience. That belief can be seen in his recent book in which he criticizes the U.S. governmental system because it lacks a place for "flexible judgment."[72] In the closing chapter, "What Is To Be Done?," of perhaps his final memoir he suggests the establishment of a "Council of State," a council, resembling a Council of Elders,[73] composed of men and women of wisdom. No doubt, were it possible, Marshall would be a member of this council. (I will suggest others below.) What task would be assigned to council members? Kennan suggests that—as the reader might now anticipate—this body would offer "judgment" as to "what is to be done" (a phrase made famous by Lenin).

At this point I hope I have brought the reader face to face with a situation of importance. On the one hand, the negative appraisal of the competence of human judgment by researchers[74] sharply weakens our confidence in it. And surely, any student who takes seriously the recent textbook on judgment and decision making by S. Plous[75] will laugh, if not sneer, at Marshall's and Kennan's expressions of their confidence in judgment in the wisdom of elders. On the other hand, those among us—the Marshalls, the Kennans—who have earned the admiration of millions indicate that they place their faith, and urge us to place our faith, in precisely that process. Should we believe the judgment and decision-making researchers or those whose judgments have earned our trust? Readers may wish to pause at this point and answer that question for themselves before proceeding to find my answer in what follows.

## Tension Between the Wisdom of the Elders
## and the Wisdom of the Researchers

Were those on Kennan's Council of State shown the conclusions of the researchers, they might well say, "If we are to believe the researchers, then our council should disband; there is not much to be gained by our efforts, for little confidence can be and should be placed in the judgments we reach. If the coherence theorists are correct, we are vulnerable to a variety of cognitive errors and biases that produce irrationality. If true, that could have serious consequences, although we can't be sure. And although the correspondence theorists do not think we are necessarily irrational, they think we are faced with an impossible task. They think we can hardly be expected to cope with irreducible uncertainty by making use of a wide variety of fallible indicators, most of which are providing us with unreliable data and all of which are so inextricably entangled with one another that we cannot discern cause and effect, in the past, present, or future. In any case, although we might reach a consensus, it is doubtful that we will be able to retrace it or defend it in rational or empirical grounds, based as it must be, if the researchers are to be believed, on a very shaky foundation. They are telling us, in short, that whatever it is we have learned from history, or experience, whatever 'lessons' we have drawn, are probably wrong, or at least indefensible, partly because of our cognitive limitations and partly because of unreliable information and ineffectual feedback due to the way the world works. Indeed, even resorting to the traditional modes of intervening and representing in order to acquire information would serve us poorly; we could not rely on them to eliminate errors. If that is the case, our contribution may do more harm than good."

Some researchers would go further. If they were to be asked, "Does Kennan's suggestion for a Council of State resembling a Council of Elders have value?" their answer would be no; it merely beguiles, for Kennan has assigned his councilors an impossible task. The public is beguiled because setting up the council, or any special commission, leads them to believe that a constructive step has been taken, when in fact nearly all researchers would say that this solution moves us in exactly the wrong direction. Metaphorically speaking, Kennan would have us improve our maritime navigation by seeking older, more experienced pilots rather than by improving navigational aids. He would have us improve our social navigation by the same means. But there isn't the slightest evidence for the efficacy of that solution, and much against it.

For example, suppose Kennan's Council of State included Albert Einstein, and suppose Einstein was asked in 1932, well after he had established himself as one of the most brilliant men in the world, about the future of nuclear energy. Here's what he said when he *was* asked that question: "There is not the slightest indication that [nuclear] energy will ever be obtainable. It would mean that the atom would have to be shattered at will."[76] And if Lord Ernest Rutherford, who was the first to split the atom, was also on the Council, he would have supported Einstein by saying (as he did), "Anyone who expects a source of power from the transformation of these atoms is talking moonshine."[77] So too would Admiral William Daniel Leaky who said, "This is the biggest damn fool thing we have ever done. . . . The bomb will never go off, and I speak as an expert in explosives."[78] Or suppose that prior to World War I the Council had been asked for advice about the future role of aircraft in warfare, and suppose one of the members was one of the most respected military men in France, Marshal Ferdinand Foch, professor of strategy at and commandant of the École Supérieure de Guerre. He would have replied, as he did in 1911, that airplanes "are interesting toys but of no military value."[79] And we know what Robert Hutchins, the distinguished president of the University of Chicago, would have said about participation in World War II, had he been a member of the Council; his advice on May 22, 1941, was that it "is fairly certain that capitalism will not survive American participation in this war. . . . If we enter this war, we shall lose what we have of the four freedoms. . . . War for this country, is a counsel of despair. It is a confession of failure. It is a national suicide."[80] There certainly should be a respected economist on the Council. John Maynard Keynes thought very highly of Irving Fisher, a professor of economics at Yale and a very prominent economist during the 1920s, and he would have nominated Professor Fisher. It would be natural to ask Fisher about the stock market crash and how long it would last. He *was* asked, and he knew what would happen: "The end of the decline of the stock market will . . . probably not be long, only a few more days at most."[81] (It lasted for a decade.)

In case readers think that I have selected a few bizarre exceptions from the wisdom expressed by esteemed personalities, I encourage them to look at a three-hundred-page catalog of wild misjudgments and woefully wrong forecasts that can be found in *The Experts Speak: The Definitive Compendium of Authoritative Misinformation*, from which my examples were taken. A few minutes with this book will make it hard to retain one's faith in the wisdom of persons likely to be nominated for a seat on Kennan's Council of Elders.[82]

Of course, there have been many wise and perceptive statements and forecasts made by men and women in high places, and it is perhaps unfair to point out egregious mistakes. My point in doing so is simply to illustrate the risks entailed in turning over difficult and generally unsolvable problems to a group of elders in the hope that age, experience, or reputation will solve a policy problem. It might be well to remind ourselves that one of the most successful commissions of all time—the fifty-five-member Constitutional Convention of 1787 in Philadelphia—was not composed of elders. As C. D. Bowen points out: "It was a young gathering. Charles Pinckney was twenty-nine; Alexander Hamilton, thirty. Rufus King was thirty-two, Jonathan Dayton of New Jersey, twenty-six. . . . Benjamin Franklin's eighty-one years raised the average considerably, but it never went beyond forty-three."[83] Whether the participants were old or young, however, Bowen recognized the role of chance in that undertaking. She labeled this success a "miracle."

Nevertheless, the persistent reference to "our founding fathers" supports the myth that the United States was created by a Council of Elders.

Contradictions: Stephen Breyer and George Kennan
Regarding Wisdom from Commissions

Stephen Breyer, now a U.S. Supreme Court justice, demonstrated in his Holmes lectures that he understands the difficulty of learning under uncertainty. As he put it, "it is difficult or impossible for predictors to obtain empirical feedback, which is necessary (for themselves as for all of us) to confirm or correct their theories."[84] Justice Breyer can thus be seen to have advanced beyond those social scientists and others who, without examining the processes by which we are supposed to learn, warn us that a "failure to learn is fatal." Justice Breyer points out that failure to learn is to be expected. It is not anyone's fault; it is simply that the "world does not work in a way" that allows us—that's all of us—to learn—most of the time.[85]

If that assertion is troublesome, think of what we are asking of these men and women who are to sit on our special commissions and seek wisdom. Since the problem presented to them will surely involve multiple fallible indicators, entangled to unknown and uncertain degrees, we ask that they be skilled in coping with circumstances of this kind. How did these members of our commission learn to do that? They would have had to learn this skill under conditions of uncertainty from a world that is not organized to provide the unambiguous kind of feedback that permits anyone to learn. Is success likely under these conditions? Look at the record.

In fact, Justice Breyer didn't go as far as he might have in describing the difficulty of learning under uncertainty. He mentioned the problem of lack of feedback, but he could have also mentioned the problem of getting feedback that misleads. Correspondence theorists have shown that irreducible uncertainty also means getting the "right" answer from the environment when, in fact, your judgment was wrong, and vice versa. Irreducible uncertainty also means the possibility that feedback from the environment will tell you that you made the wrong judgment, when in fact you were right; learning under conditions of irreducible uncertainty is far more difficult than Justice Breyer made it out to be.[86] But, as I noted, Justice Breyer expressed great misgivings about the value of expertise, derived from his study of the judgment and decision-making literature. So we may assume from these remarks (and others[87]) that Justice Breyer does not support the notion that wisdom resides in a council of experts.

That assumption, however, turns out to be wrong. For he too succumbs to that very notion. When he offers his "solutions" to the problems of regulating environmental risk, he proposes that the problems of such regulation be resolved by "creation of a small, centralized administrative group, charged with a rationalizing mission."[88] Breyer also is prepared to avoid the problems created by the quasirational judgments of individuals who attempt to achieve coherence or correspondence by turning the problem over to a commission.

According to Breyer, the commission must have five features: (1) a "specified risk-related mission" (i.e., "building an improved *coherent* [italics added] risk-regulatory system, . . . helping to create priorities . . . and comparing programs to determine how better to allocate resources to reduce risks"); (2) "interagency jurisdiction"; (3) "a degree of political insulation"; (4) "prestige"; and (5) "authority."[89] These features bear a close resemblance to those of Kennan's Council of State and to those required of all such commissions.

What is not required by Justice Breyer, or by George Kennan, or by others who create such committees is evidence that, once the bureaucratic criteria are met, the judgments exercised by the committee members will be, or can be, any better than those that have already been shown to be inadequate. The members of the commission may be less susceptible to political or monetary bribes, but will they be better able to achieve the coherence in their judgments that Justice Breyer found missing in the past? Will the coherence errors cancel out? There is no evidence for that. And if Janis is allowed to speak, little is likely to be forthcoming; he would anticipate that "groupthink" will result in failure to consider enough alternatives, failure to reexamine alternatives already chosen or omitted, rejection of information incongruent with present beliefs, and omission of contingency plans. In what ways will the committee members be better able to achieve a greater degree of correspondence in their judgments by virtue of constituting a committee? Will they be more skilled, somehow, in extrapolating findings from the physics laboratory to the messy and uncertain world of industrial pollution and danger than the individual experts whose expertise has been called into question by Breyer? Although Justice Breyer may well have found a satisfactory set of bureaucratic criteria that the commission must meet, he is silent with regard to the cognitive criteria the people on the committee must meet.

Curiously, Kennan also is inconsistent, for he too lacked unrestricted faith in the wisdom of high-level committees, despite his enthusiasm for a Council of Elders. Consider this unexpected—and inexplicable—description of the planning process in the State Department that he provides as he attempts to explain to students at the National War College "what the task of a governmental planner in the field of foreign affairs was like." He offered the following "parallel":

> I have a largish farm in Pennsylvania. . . . The farm includes two hundred thirty-five acres, and a number of buildings. On every one of those acres, I have discovered, things are constantly happening. Weeds are growing. Gullies are forming. Fences are falling down. Paint is fading. Wood is rotting. Insects are burrowing. Nothing seems to be standing still. The days . . . pass in a . . . succession of alarms and excursions. Here a bridge is collapsing. No sooner do you start to repair it than a neighbor comes to complain about a hedgerow which you haven't kept up—a half-mile away on the other side of the farm. At that very moment your daughter arrives to tell you that someone left the gate to the hog pasture open and the hogs are out. On the way to the hog pasture you discover that the beagle hound is happily liquidating one of the children's pet kittens. In burying the kitten you look up and notice that a whole section of the barn roof has been blown off, and needs instant repair. Somebody shouts pitifully from the bathroom window that the pump must have busted—there's no water in the house. At that moment a truck arrives with five tons of stone for the lane. And as you stand helplessly there, wondering which of these crises to attend to first, you notice the farmer's little boy standing silently before you with that maddening smile that is halfway a leer, and when you ask him what's up, he says triumphantly, "The bull's busted out and he's eating the strawberry bed."[90]

This metaphor will seem strange coming from a man who, in later years, would urge that we rely on the wisdom of elder statesmen. Nor was this message from Kennan an accident of the moment. Kennan drove his point home by describing a hypothetical conference in the State Department:

> Assume, for example, that you were examining the plight of a friendly European country which had not been able to revive its economic life by its own resources in the wake of

the war. You are confronted immediately with a babble of tongues and conflicting opinions:

You say: "This shouldn't be so difficult. Why don't we tell these people to draw up a plan for the reconstruction of their economic life and submit it to us and we'll see whether we can support it or not?"

That starts it off. Someone says: "That's no good. They are too tired to draw up a plan. We have to do it for them."

Someone else says: "Even if they do draw up a plan, they wouldn't have the internal economic discipline to carry it out. The Communists would spike it."

Someone else says: "Oh, it isn't the Communists who would spike it—it is the local business circles."

Then someone says: "Maybe what we need isn't a plan at all. Maybe we just haven't given them enough in the past. If we just give them more, things will work out all right."

Another then says: "That's probably true, but we've got to figure out how the money is going to be spent. Congress just won't pour money down any more ratholes."

Then somebody says: "That's right; we need a program. We've got to figure out just what's to be done with the money and make sure that it does the whole job this time."

To that someone else replies: "Ah, yes, but it would be a mistake for us to try to draw this program up all by ourselves. The Commies would just take potshots at it and the European government would shrug off the responsibility."

Then someone says: "That's absolutely right. The thing for us to do is to tell these Europeans to draw up a plan and submit it to us and we'll see whether we can support it or not."

And then you ask: "Didn't somebody say that before?" And we're off again.[91]

Curiously, then, the very people who advocate the use of high councils repudiate them: Kennan first urges us to place our faith in a Council of State and then ridicules the performance of such councils; Justice Breyer proceeds the other way round, first casting doubts on the ability of experts to overcome the cognitive limitations he attributes to them and then ignoring his own admonitions and asking us to place our faith in a "small, centralized group" with "a rationalizing mission." The use of a council or commission as a solution seems as inescapable as it is mythical.

If Kennan's hypothetical mishmash really describes the formulation of the Marshall Plan, then one must ask, How could the Marshall Plan have been such a success? His are not the words of a carping outsider. These come from an insider, a participant in one of the greatest and most successful planning efforts ever made by any government. So we should give credence to his views. Whatever else might be said, surely Kennan wants us to know that, even if the committees' actions turn out to be brilliant, rational, analytical cognitive activity is not likely to be found in high-level committees. And if *that* is true, why then did Kennan, some twenty-five years later, recommend that we place our faith in such committees? My answer: He did not know where else to turn. (Indeed, where would the reader turn?)

That description of chaos in diplomatic circles may lead scientists to say, "Just as I thought." But the memoirs of George Kistiakowsky,[92] Eisenhower's science adviser and a man of high repute in both scientific and governmental circles, have been reviewed by H. Scoville Jr., who was assistant director for science and technology for the CIA during Kistiakowsky's tenure as science adviser. Scoville, who worked very closely with Kistiakowsky, had this to say about scientists' use of analytical cognition in relation to policy matters:

> Kistiakowsky's book will quickly disillusion anyone who has assumed that scientific decisions related to national policy are carefully developed on the basis of rigorous scientific principles and procedures to produce an incontrovertible solution to the problem at hand. Policy-making by scientists is no more precise than policy-making by politicians, economists, or diplomats.[93]

Regrettably, we do not have the actual minutes of the "intragovernmental debates that preceded the formulation of the Marshall Plan," but we do have the minutes of another equally powerful committee, the Federal Open Market Committee, and it is to these we now turn.

### The Federal Open Market Committee at Work

The minutes of the Federal Open Market Committee, a part of the Federal Reserve Banking System, which focuses on foreign exchange rates, were opened for the first time in 1994.

Examination of the minutes of the committee for August 16, 1988, shows clearly (1) the presence of irreducible uncertainty facing the committee members, (2) the role of quasirational judgments on the part of the committee members, and (3) the fact that the members' judgments are based on multiple fallible indicators, exactly as so many other crucial judgments are (when not constrained by rules, such as those on mandatory sentencing). Although the committee members often refer to results produced by econometric models, these, too, are simply used as indicators. And the end result of the deliberations is produced by voting, not by a model. There is considerable reference to how members "feel" as well as to their "comfort level" regarding various positions. Some examples of comments prior to a vote follow. (Italics have been added to comments that refer to the three features [1, 2, and 3] already mentioned.)

> [CHAIRMAN GREENSPAN.] And what that tells me is that *the odds* are obviously strong that we will be having to tighten again in the future. As a consequence, I think there's *no doubt* that we should be continuing with asymmetrical language. At the moment I myself am content to sit tight, at least for the short run, largely because I think we shocked the market with the discount rate more than I thought we would. I was, I would say, *uncomfortable* with the Japanese markets and a little *uncomfortable* with our own. I think they're stabilizing now, but I do think that they still have adjustments coming from the discount rate for a while. I don't know whether or not it's several weeks, or longer, but I'd feel quite *comfortable* at this stage staying with the $600 million of borrowing requirement, but maintaining asymmetrical language, as a consequence of acute awareness that any forms of evident problems get met with tightening.[94]

> MR. JOHNSON. I think the Chairman said it; his statement is clearly consistent with mine. As I said before, I think that the *risks* are still on the upside. I think we need time to see how the market *digests* this discount rate change, but I think we should be prepared to move [on the basis of] the economy's performance—I think at this stage, the appropriate action is to support asymmetry in the language and maintain the $600 million borrowing with the discount rate where it is. *Let's see how those winds blow.*[95]

MR. HELLER.  You've got to make it easy. I'm happy to support alternative "B." And I think the Ms are right in the middle of the target range; that's very good. I think we should avoid adopting a stop-go policy so we are not overdoing it on the right side and see that danger would be there. I think I'd go along with Governor Angell on giving the monetary aggregates a bit more prominence. *I'm not sure* I want to move it to the first spot, but somewhere in the middle is fine. I think that that would be very good in front of foreign exchange and domestic financial markets. Overall, I support $600 million borrowing and I'd prefer symmetric language but be *happy to go along with* [italics added] asymmetric.[96]

MR. LAWARE.  I'm completely in agreement with the analysis of the strength of the economy. *I feel a little bit* like I was in a vehicle that was accelerating down the road and I have an *instinctive* desire to hit the brakes a little bit and snub it down. But the thing that worries me is that I think the road's *a little slipperier than it looks* in the sense that there's some fragility in the infrastructure of the economy. . . .

Another one that *I guess tends to slip out of our minds occasionally* is the real estate situation. It has been getting better, not only in the banks—which have increased their capital in order to sustain the possible losses in this area—but also in the country generally. The country has been benefiting from lower interest rates and the ability to restructure some of that. It seems to me that a lot of that ground that has been gained could be lost if the cost of servicing that debt goes up significantly, as it would because much of it is denominated in variable rates. Finally this thrift situation—an aspect of which we intend to discuss at the luncheon today—has not gone away. It's getting worse. And a significant increase in the cost of money to these troubled thrifts is just going to accelerate the rate of loss in that industry. [Note that at this point Mr. Laware has aggregated the information from numerous fallible indicators.]

When you take all of those in the aggregate, it seems to me if *we snub the brakes too hard and too fast, or oversteer this vehicle, we have a risk of going into the ditch.*[97]

Is this the way in which we want our Council of Elders to talk about problems of such imposing significance? Do these remarks represent wisdom? Would the reader wish these elders to be more analytical? What dangers would that impose?

## Why the Wisdom of the Elders Is Diminishing in Importance

Why do we have confidence in the wisdom of the elders? Why is such confidence virtually universal, and why so prominent among Western European, as well as primitive, societies? Is it entirely unjustified?

Think for a moment about our early ancestors and their environment. I have asserted that they were completely dependent on multiple fallible indicators for their judgments about the world around them. I have also asserted that we have learned from numerous laboratory experiments[98] that we *Homo sapiens* still learn very slowly from multiple fallible indicators under conditions of uncertainty, and I explained in Chapter 10 why it is so hard to learn from experience in an uncertain world.

If these assertions are true, then it follows that in the earliest days of *Homo sapiens* it would have been the older members of the community—those who had been exposed to the environment for the longest time and had slowly learned—who would perform best. Older persons would have developed reputations for good judgment and knowing *best*, that is, knowing better than anyone else, because they had greater opportunities to learn, having had the greatest number of trials. And because knowledge gained from learning of this type is very hard to pass on to others—because so much of it does not reach the level of awareness—the skills of the elders would remain covert and thus somewhat mysterious. (Recall Mark Twain's difficulties in learning about multiple fallible indicators from his pilot/teacher.) Without a World 3, a world of books and libraries, early *Homo sapiens* could learn only by observation of others—the older ones. Thus, our present confidence in the wisdom of the elders has a long and justifiable history. Evolution must have played a role here; fitness would be enhanced if one *did* learn from elders, and those who did learn would be selected to pass on their genes by an environment offering multiple fallible indicators.

But, of course, a World 3 has now been constructed. And although multiple fallible indicators are still an important part of our social, political, and economic information environment, the modern World 3 contains much that is analytical and coherent and thus demands analytical skills and coherence from those who would profit from it. We learn from books and computer files, so learning not only goes much more rapidly, it does not require mimicry or otherwise learning from an elder. The need for and the practice of learning from elders has thus been reduced markedly.

But the entire structure of World 3, the world of learning, is changing. Next time you are near a university's computer laboratory, look at the age of the teachers. It will be hard to distinguish between the teacher and the students; both will be about the same age (and tend to dress alike). The tweedy gray beards within whom wisdom was assumed to reside by virtue of age and experience, and who were unmistakably different from students, are being replaced by those whose knowledge is tested by its coherence. There are few old men (and no old women) to be seen in the workplaces of the high-tech companies. The need for skill in the use of multiple fallible indicators is disappearing as the environment that offers this type of information disappears and is replaced by an environment that offers, and demands, coherence. That division will be at the root of all the other divisions that follow from economic disparity.

Herrnstein and Murray emphasize the importance of that division when they point out its benefits: "Life has been increasingly good for the cognitive elite. . . . The steep rise in high-IQ jobs over the course of the century was to some important extent a picture of people moving from unsatisfying jobs to lucrative and interesting ones."[99] I pursue the implications of this change in the organization and structure of knowledge in the next chapter.

### A Commission Committed to Analytical Cognition—and Its Defeat

No better example of change from trust in the elders to reliance on the analytical power of a (young) blue-ribbon committee devoted to coherence can be found than in the Clinton administration's attempt in 1993–1994 to form a national health policy. The result was, in Gulf War vernacular, the "mother of all commissions." More than five hundred experts from a variety of disciplines worked for many months to produce a thirteen-hundred-page, carefully reasoned document, a perfect testimony to faith in a fully analytical, coherent process. No one who watched Hillary Rodham Clinton, the president's wife and the designated head of the commission, defend the reasoning in that plan before a hostile Congress could doubt her full commitment to analytical cognition; no one did. She had anticipated every question and prepared every answer. Every assertion in the plan was retraceable; logic ruled supreme, as even her sometimes harsh opponents acknowledged. In short, Hillary Clinton set out to do her work in Mode 4 of Figure 9-1. She could not set up an experiment of the sort depicted in Modes 1, 2, or even 3. She could not intervene in a fashion that would allow her to claim the analytical power of an experiment, but she could and did make use of computer models as well as statistical analyses. Within the constraints of "representing" without the benefits of "intervention," her commission's work relied on analytical cognition insofar as it could. But without the strengths afforded by intervention, the result was vulnerable to attacks, not only from within Mode 4 (other computer models, other statistics) but from within Mode 5 (other experts) and Mode 6 (confusion and obfuscation) as well. And those attacks occurred; the efforts by the insurance companies and other organized interests to defeat the plan were prodigious. Her plan was given little attention by Congress, and it was not long before it became common knowledge that no effort of that kind would be attempted again—at least by the Clinton administration.

The attacks drove the discussion from Mode 4 to Modes 5 and 6, as is so often the case when politicians must react to a product of analytical cognition. This change in mode can also be observed when scientists attempt to present scientific information to politicians. Intellectually derived information that requires World 3 competence demands analytical work over a sustained period of time. Policymakers who are politicians, that is, persons with a careful eye on the judgments of their constituents, are likely to make their judgments on the basis of multiple fallible indicators, rather than of the intricate dynamics of the plan in question. As a result, they turn the discussion to multiple fallible indicators, a mode of cognition present in Modes 5 and 6 that (literally) comes naturally to the nonexpert; Mode 4 gives way to Modes 5 and 6, regrettable processes understandable to researchers, elders, and politicians alike.

Earlier I posed a question to the reader: Should we believe in the judgment and decision-making researchers (who deny the coherence competence of the elders), or should we believe in those whose judgments have earned our trust? I now propose an answer. It explains *why* we have faith in the wisdom of the elders and explains *when* we should and should not maintain that faith. My answer thus rests *also* on faith in the wisdom of the researchers.

Our faith in the wisdom of commissions derives from our long-standing faith in the judgments of our elders, a faith that continues today. It is a faith that is understandable from the correspondence theorists' point of view. Faith in the judgments of elders was justified as long as those judgments were based on experience with the only type of information the natural environment offered—multiple fallible indicators. But that faith is now misplaced; neither age nor experience is any longer necessary for acquiring the coherence competence that is so much in demand in contemporary society. This situation is far removed from the one that faced our distant ancestors. As a result, the criteria for wisdom have shifted from the content of the judgments, uttered by those deemed wise, to the examination of the cognitive process by which the judgment was produced. That change is exactly what Hadley Cantril was hoping to achieve more than half a century ago when he said he wanted to "inject a way of thinking into policy formulation at the highest levels of Government."[100] In the next chapter I pursue the implications of this change.

# 12 The Possible Future of Cognitive Competence

> But hope of continuing improvement, if it survives at all now, is now largely without evidence. . . . Making rational calculation of consequences the sole foundation of public policies [has] so far favored, and [is] still favoring, a new callousness in policy, a dullness of sensibility, and sometimes moral despair, at least in respect of public affairs.
>
> —*Stuart Hampshire*, philosopher

The search for wisdom has led us to an examination of our faith in the wisdom of our elders. That examination has in turn brought us to a recognition of *change* in the nature of cognitive competence. In the past, wisdom was based on the use of multiple fallible indicators and the correspondence theory of truth. However useful in the past this form of cognitive competence was, it is diminishing in value. This change parallels the change in the relative importance of the natural and the artificial environments. Because of it, there has been a sharp increase in the demand for analytical, coherent cognition. Will that continue? With what consequences? In this chapter I briefly reexamine the past and present, then make predictions of the future.

## Past

If we *Homo sapiens* have not been competent in our efforts to survive, we certainly have been lucky; despite all the inhumanity, the horrors we have inflicted upon ourselves, the attacks by all our other predators, large and infinitesimally small, that have on occasion decimated huge numbers of us, the natural disasters that have repeatedly demolished our attempts to provide for ourselves, we seem to be thriving, indeed, reproducing ourselves at an impressive rate. And we *have* been lucky; natural selection saw to it that, somehow, early hominids and *Homo sapiens* developed a cognitive system that could effectively decode the multiple fallible indicators to survival that the natural environment offered. Steven Pinker put it nicely:

> The mind is a product of the brain, and the brain is a product of evolution's organizing force, natural selection. This simple Darwinian truth has illuminated vast stretches of our mental life. [Would that were so! Generations of psychologists ignored simple

327

Darwinian truths with enthusiasm.] Why do we see in depth and enjoy sweets? Not because minds have to be that way. Most mammals lack stereo vision, and dung flies surely find dung delicious. No, our experiences are adaptations of a brain that allowed our ancestors to survive in an environment where a fall from a tree could mean death, and ripe fruit contained precious glucose.[1]

Pinker doesn't say so, but the examples he gives all involve the effective use of multiple fallible indicators; all involve a species guided by a correspondence theory of truth that enabled its members to make empirically accurate judgments. Will that branch hold? The indicators say yes. Then grab it! Does that fruit contain glucose? The indicators say no. Then don't waste energy on it. Our past, our deep past, was surely ruled by a mind, a cognitive system, that used the uncertain information provided by the more or less valid indicators of World 1 so effectively that we are here today, still making use of the multiple fallible indicators nature has always provided—and creating them when we wanted them. Correspondence competence, in short, was in demand then and is in demand today. Coherence competence, on the other hand, was unnecessary then; there was little to be coherent about.

Along the way, however, our environment changed, because we changed it. Not only did we create multiple fallible indicators (as, for example, when, much later, we created "leading economic indicators"); language appeared, and we invented tools and discovered *causal relations*. Once that happened, we began to seek and then to rely on the coherence of our knowledge, as well as its correspondence with the reality of objects and events. I don't know exactly when that happened, of course (neither does anyone else), but surely by the time Pythagoras showed that the square of the hypotenuse equaled the sum of the squares of the other two sides of a triangle, we were committed to seeking, demanding, and making use of coherence as a criterion for truth.

With two theories of truth came two different sets of criteria to be satisfied, and two methods for seeking truth. That duality created tension between them that has never gone away. Indeed, tension may be seen in the disparate ways in which we study human judgment and decision making. Some researchers have focused on the coherence of our judgments, and have found incompetence; some have focused on correspondence and found competence when circumstances permit.

## Present

If our past can be characterized by the dominance of our reliance on the use of multiple fallible indicators, our present can be characterized in terms of the tension created by the decreasing importance of correspondence in relation to coherence. Where the correspondence of a judgment was necessary and sufficient, understanding was unnecessary. But the creative engineering of coherence in the environment removed the uncertainty inherent in fallible indicators, and that, in turn, removed the *sufficiency* of expertise in the use of fallible indicators; it is continuing to be removed, not slowly, but surely. If you wish to climb a tree, seek out fruit, infer the meaning of a facial expression, use the information in the leading economic or social indicators, or try to forecast the behavior of nations, reliance on multiple fallible indicators will be necessary; there is no reliable coherence in any of these systems. But skill in the use of multiple fallible indicators, which we all share, will not be sufficient when coping with the rapidly increasing number of information environments that demand coherent, analytical cognition, as many youthful seekers of a secure place in modern society have found. Björkman used Popper's terms to point out that skill in coherent, analytical cognition cannot be acquired through raw experience in World 1; it can be acquired only through immersion in World 3, the world of knowledge stored in books and libraries, and, yes, computer programs described in those awful manuals.

## Future

In his intellectual autobiography, Jerome Bruner, one of the fathers of the cognitive revolution, wrote in 1983:

> My "generation" created and nurtured the Cognitive Revolution—a revolution whose limits we still cannot fathom, for it lies at the center of a postindustrial society that is still in roaring growth. The central premise of this emerging society is that it is the generation and management of knowledge, rather than the mere brute conversion of power and material into goods for distribution, which is the key to the industrial and social process. The new capital is know-how, forecast, intelligence. As the revolution progresses, it is evident that "wisdom" gets added to its list of assets as well—harder to define, harder to achieve. In any case, the epistemic sciences and their metaphors have replaced the engineering of power and materials as the pragmatic base of the management of human affairs. The result has been not simply a renewal of interest in how "mind" works, but rather a new search for mind and for how mindfulness is cultivated.[2]

As the twentieth century ends, it is apparent that Bruner was prescient; the "cognitive revolution" made itself felt not only in academic circles but in the corporate and industrial world and has led to a division between classes of persons outside the academy.[3] Those whose only cognitive resource is reliance on multiple fallible indicators and commerce within World 1 are now developing class interests that drive them apart from those who have gained analytical competence from immersion in World 3. The tension is growing to the point where some are frightened by it, some have been plunged into despair, and some take desperate steps to deny that it matters, or should matter.

Fright is painfully evident in the writings of the well-known historian Paul Kennedy and his colleagues. They depict a future in which the prosperous North, especially northern Europe, that is well acquainted with World 3 and the attendant demands for coherence competence builds immigration walls to keep from being overrun by hordes from the poverty-stricken South. These immigrants are the people who know only the correspondence theory of truth and are equipped only with skill in the use of multiple fallible indicators. The future predicted by Kennedy has already shown signs of its appearance in Europe. (The same fears are expressed in the United States regarding the porous border between the United States and Mexico.) For example, M. Connelly and P. Kennedy state:

France's tough new Conservative government began this year by announcing a series of crackdowns on illegal immigrants including mass deportation. "When we have sent home several planeloads, even boatloads and trainloads, the world will get the message," claimed Charles Pasqua, the hardline [French] Cabinet Minister in charge of security and immigration affairs. "We will close our frontier." Last year he announced that France would become a "zero immigration" country, a stunning reversal of its 200-year old policy of offering asylum to those in need. That Pasqua believed it was in fact possible to halt immigration was called into doubt when he later remarked, "The problems of immigration are ahead of us and not behind us." By the year 2000, he asserted, there will be 60 million people in Algeria, Morocco, and Tunisia under the age of twenty and "without a future." Where else to go but France, whose television programs they can view every evening, much as Albanians goggle at Italian cat-food commercials?[4]

Deep concern, if not despair, can also be seen in warnings from the management expert Peter Drucker, who sees the future bringing a shift in demand from correspondence competence to coherence competence. He asserts that the "free-market countries—which contain less than a fifth of the earth's population but are a model for the rest . . . are all, in the last decade of this century, *qualitatively* and *quantitatively* different not only from what they were in the first years of this century but also from what has existed at any other time in history."[5] The reason for the change is that "before the First World War, farmers composed the largest single group in every country."[6] Farmers, it will be remembered, rely primarily on the correspondence theory of truth and multiple fallible indicators of what is important to them— the weather, the conditions of the soil, their livestock. But "they no longer . . . [make] up the population everywhere, as they . . . [have] from the dawn of history to the end of the Napoleonic Wars," for in these free market countries "farmers today are at most five percent of the population and work force—that is, one tenth of the proportion of eighty years ago. . . . *Productive* farmers [are] no more than two percent of the work force."[7] Domestic servants and the blue-collar workforce have diminished sharply in number, to be replaced *in importance*, but not in numbers, by the emerging "knowledge workers [who] will give the emerging knowledge society its character, its leadership, its social profile."[8] Drucker sees that it is "formal education," that is, participation in World 3, with its access to the understanding of how to reach judgments and decisions on the basis of coherent knowledge and analytical cognition, that gives the "knowledge workers" "access to jobs and social position."

Drucker makes frequent reference to the "knowledge society," as do many others with an eye to the future. He makes note of the "shift to knowledge-based work"; the knowledge society will be the first society, he says, in which "ordinary people— and that means most people—do not earn their daily bread by the sweat of their brow. It . . . [will be] the first society in which honest work does not mean a callused hand."[9] Although Drucker has many useful things to say about how the nature and content of knowledge will change and about how education will change as a result, he does not inquire into the consequent change in *cognitive processes* that will occur. Richard Herrnstein and Charles Murray, however, do.

Herrnstein and Murray emphasize the relation between cognition and work in their controversial book, *The Bell Curve: Intelligence and Class Structure in American*

*Life*, which begins with a section titled "The Emergence of the Cognitive Elite" (a phrase in increasing use). According to Herrnstein and Murray, the twentieth century began at the time "the ancient lines of separation based on heredity rank were being erased"[10] and were being replaced by distinctions based on differences in cognitive ability, so much so that "the twenty-first [century] will open on a world in which cognitive ability is the decisive dividing force."[11] They also say, "The shift is more subtle than the previous one but more momentous. Social class remains the vehicle of social life, but *intelligence* [Italics added] now pulls the train."[12] For Herrnstein and Murray, the concept of intelligence exhausts, for all practical purposes, the concept of cognitive competence. Although they acknowledge what virtually all psychologists acknowledge, that there is a variety of cognitive functions that contributes to cognitive competence, they are far more convinced that a (putative) general intellective factor (Spearman's "g") is sufficiently well measured by modern intelligence tests to be useful. Indeed, they relate intelligence test scores to an impressive variety of social facts and conditions, including success in schools and in the workplace. Although their conclusions are sharply contested by others,[13] they make a strong case for the costs inflicted on society by its failure to take these relationships into account in the formation of social policy regarding welfare, crime, and the operation of various government agencies.

The compendium of empirical facts presented in *The Bell Curve* is not likely to be successfully contested (if one accepts the authors' commitment to the general concept of intelligence). But the authors' interpretations have been, and will be, contested (and denounced) for some time.[14] Because differences in intelligence were related by Herrnstein and Murray to ethnic differences, their conclusions immediately brought the authors' motivations into question, and the book became a matter of political controversy. I present my views of this matter later in this chapter, but first it is important to learn what Robert Reich, secretary of labor in the Clinton administration, has to say about cognitive competence.

In his book titled *The Work of Nations: Preparing Ourselves for 21st-Century Capitalism*, Reich finds that the "three jobs of the future" will consist of "routine production services," "in-person services," and "symbolic-analytic services." We are all familiar with the first two: routine production services "entail the kinds of repetitive tasks performed by the old foot soldiers of American capitalism in the high-volume enterprise. They are done over and over—one step in a sequence of steps."[15] And, although they are often thought of as blue-collar jobs,

> contrary to the prophets of the "information age" who buoyantly predicted an abundance of high-paying jobs even for people with the most basic of skills, the sobering truth is that many information-processing jobs fit easily into this category. . . . The "information revolution" . . . has . . . produced huge piles of raw data which must be processed in much the same monotonous way that assembly-line workers and . . . textile workers processed piles of other raw materials.[16]

Reich makes an important observation here; it is what you do with your mind that counts. It doesn't matter whether that raw pile of stuff to be processed is a pile of metal, cloth, numbers, or words; the work is done in a mindless, repetitive, monotonous way. It all comes down to the same thing: low status, low pay, low cognitive

activity, low job satisfaction. The information environment for the routine production worker has been engineered to remove all opportunities for judgment. That is
done by removing all fallible indicators in the production line to the greatest extent
possible, because the presence of fallible indicators would mean that workers would
have to make judgments. That would inevitably mean error, and production lines,
being analytically derived, cannot tolerate error. The workers are therefore presented
with the simplest possible information environment, namely, *infallible indicators that
appear in sequence*, to be used again and again in the same way. Ironically, our
ancestors in the distant past could cope with the contemporaneous appearance of multiple fallible indicators very effectively, choosing the branch that would hold or the
fruit that contained sugar. The mindless tasks of the modern routine production
worker are far beneath the cognitive competence of our ancestors, often described
as "primitive."[17]

The second type of job described by Reich involves "in-person services." These
"also entail simple and repetitive tasks," and they do not require much education ("at
most, a high school diploma"[18]). The services are "provided person-to-person."

> In-person servers are in direct contact with the ultimate beneficiaries of their work;
> their immediate objects are specific customers rather than streams of metal, fabric, or
> data. In-person servers work alone or in small teams. Included in this category are retail
> sales workers, waiters and waitresses, hotel workers, janitors, cashiers, hospital atten-
> dants and orderlies, nursing-home aides, child-care workers, house cleaners, home
> health-care aides, taxi drivers, secretaries, hairdressers, auto mechanics, sellers of resi-
> dential real estate, flight attendants, physical therapists, and—among the fastest-growing
> of all—security guards.[19]

Reich does not specify the kind of cognitive activity demanded of persons in this
job category, and it is here that I believe he has made a mistake. Most "in-person
servers" are not carrying out "simple, repetitive tasks." When considered from a
cognitive point of view, their tasks are far more complex than the tasks involved in
"routine production services" that are built on simple repetitions in response to
infallible indicators. The information environment of an in-person server is far from
the highly engineered, fully determined environment that requires only simple cognitive work of this-then-that, over and over. The in-person server must *differentiate*
among various customers and clients, or there will be no sales, no tips, and no return
business. It is a highly uncertain environment, indeed. Nevertheless, the in-person
server will have multiple fallible indicators to rely on and, fortunately, will need little
training in the effective use of them.

Reich is aware of this. He points out that in-person servers must not only be "punc-
tual, reliable, and tractable" but also "have a pleasant demeanor. They must smile
and exude confidence and good cheer, even when they feel morose. . . . they must
make others feel happy and at ease."[20] In order to be successful, then, in-person
servers must rely on the multiple fallible indicators on which accurate social perception depends—the facial expressions, the postures, the tone of voice that expresses
irritation or satisfaction for the in-person service rendered. Curiously, accuracy is
the very aspect of social perception that most psychologists have found uninterest-
ing (as I mentioned earlier). Fortunately, Funder,[21] and F. J. Bernieri, J. S. Gillis,

and J. M. Davis[22] have pursued it, however, and they have found that the ordinary college student can make reasonably accurate social judgments. (Interestingly, Gillis and Bernieri found in direct empirical assessments of this ability that it is unrelated to conventional measures of intelligence.)

Moreover, much as we all dread carrying out those "simple, repetitive tasks" hour after deadly hour, we like to engage in tasks that offer us multiple fallible indicators and challenge us to make a good judgment. That activity is part of what E. O. Wilson called "biophilia" (see Chapter 6).

The words of Mark Twain explain this point best. Here he is again, this time being exuberant about piloting on the Mississippi:

> The face of the water, in time, became a wonderful book—a book that was a dead language to the uneducated passenger, but which told its mind to me without reserve, delivering its most cherished secrets as if it uttered them with a voice. And it was not a book to be read once and thrown aside, for it had a new story to tell every day. Throughout the long twelve hundred miles there was never a page that was void of interest, never one that you could leave unread without loss, never one that you would want to skip, thinking you could find higher enjoyment in some other thing. There never was so wonderful a book written by man; never one whose interest was so absorbing so unflagging, so sparklingly renewed with every reperusal.[23]

No better description of the joy of learning perceptual skills is likely to be found. But Twain followed his observations about learning to read the face of the river with a truly remarkable and unexpected conclusion:

> Now when I had mastered the language of this water, and had come to know every trifling feature that bordered the great river as familiarly as I knew the letters of the alphabet, I had made a valuable acquisition. But I had lost something too. I had lost something which could never be restored to me while I lived. All the grace, the beauty, the poetry, had gone out of the majestic river![24]

Here is something new! Many readers will recognize the process of "learning without awareness" (that is how psychologists would describe it), but who has considered the possibility that costs might be attached to this benefit? Twain describes it in a way that, for me, is unforgettable:

> A day came when I began to cease from noting the glories and the charms which the moon and the sun and the twilight wrought upon the river's face; another day came when I ceased altogether to note them. Then, if that sunset scene had been repeated, I should have looked upon it without rapture, and should have commented upon it, inwardly, after this fashion: "This sun means that we are going to have wind to-morrow; that floating log means that the river is rising, small thanks to it; that slanting mark on the water refers to a bluff reef which is going to kill somebody's steamboat one of these nights, if it keeps on stretching out like that; those tumbling 'boils' show a dissolving bar and a changing channel there; the lines and circles in the slick water over yonder are a warning that troublesome place is shoaling up dangerously; that silver streak in the shadow of the forest is the 'break' from a new snag, and he has located himself in the very best place he could have found to fish for steamboats; that tall dead tree, with a single living branch, is not going to last long, and then how is a body ever going to get through this blind place at night without the friendly old landmark?"[25]

Twain had become *consciously aware* of what his teacher had described as an "instinct." Contrary to his teacher's assertion, now he could indeed "explain why or how" he discriminated between danger and safety (as he explained to us). He had learned which cues indicated the weather, which indicated danger, and so on: "This sun means that we are going to have wind to-morrow; that floating log means that the river is rising."[26] Twain had, in short, moved a significant step from intuition toward analysis. Whereas early in his training he had learning without awareness, he had now reached the point where he was keenly aware of the cues he was using to guide him down the river. But he found that he had paid an emotive price for the advances in his perceptual skills: "No, the romance and beauty were all gone from the river. All the value any feature of it had for me now was the amount of usefulness it could furnish toward compassing the safe piloting of a steamboat."[27]

There are two important points here that should be kept in mind regarding the cognitive features of the in-person server's job. One is that Twain has not only learned (we know that from his correspondence competence—he did not sink his river boats); he also became *aware* of what he learned. And what he learned was the *content* of the multiple fallible indicators that he relied upon—"the sun means," "the "floating log means," "that slanting mark on the water refers to." That is the way we learn from all good teachers (Twain's teacher was not a good teacher because he didn't give him this), and the way *Homo sapiens* has learned from time immemorial: either by trying to figure out how a more experienced elder makes his or her judgments (a long, slow, mistake-ridden process) or by having the benefit of a Mark Twain as a teacher, a teacher who points out and names the (fallible) indicators available in a specific information environment and that must be used if the job is to be done.[28] These two ways of learning can be observed in any professional school.

The second point is that Twain describes what is now called burnout. Once he became consciously aware of what the information environment (the "face of the water") offered, learned how to make use of it and knew that he knew how to do it, then "the romance and the beauty were all gone from the river." All that mattered was its use for "the safe piloting of the steamboat." "Burnout" is certainly important (especially to those who have experienced it), but there is a more important point to be observed here. Note Twain's expression of love for piloting while he was *learning* "to read the face of the water." He is referring to a certain sense of ecstasy that is induced in us when we respond to nature's multiple fallible indicators. It is at the core of our love for the ocean, forest, flowers, ski run, birds, horses, dogs. When we are deprived of these indicators (as in routine production jobs) or whenever the process becomes routinized through conscious awareness, we lose something important —a part of our intuitive cognitive capacities, a link to our millions of years of using them.

Before that "burn-out" occurs, however, in-person servers will rely on their heritage of skill in the use of multiple fallible indicators. That skill enables them to make reasonably accurate judgments about the people they serve and the generally uncertain information environment in which they must work. This skill is one we need to understand and cultivate more than we have so far, particularly since it is one generally overlooked. Although in-person servers clearly make judgments under conditions of uncertainty, no one thinks it necessary to teach them about the probability calculus; correspondence competence, not coherence competence, is what counts. Reliance on and skill in the use of multiple fallible indicators was—and is—a critical aspect of all work involving interpersonal relations, the core of the in-person server's duties.

The situation is different for those in the third category of Reich's job classification—the *symbolic analyst*. According to Reich, *"symbolic-analytic services . . .* include all the problem-solving, problem-identifying, and . . . brokering of many people who call themselves research scientists, design engineers, software engineers, civil engineers, biotechnology engineers, sound engineers, public relations executives, investment bankers, lawyers, real estate developers, and even a few creative accountants."[29] Reich includes also many consultants in this category.

> Symbolic analysts solve, identify, and broker problems by manipulating symbols. They simplify reality into abstract images that can be rearranged, juggled, experimented with, communicated to other specialists, and then, eventually, transformed back into reality. The manipulations are done with analytic tools, sharpened by experience. The tools may be mathematical algorithms, legal arguments, financial gimmicks, scientific principles, psychological insights about how to persuade or to amuse, systems of induction or deduction, or any other set of techniques for doing conceptual puzzles. . . .
>
> [Symbolic analysts epitomizing analytical cognizers] sit before computer terminals— examining words and numbers, moving them, altering them, trying out new words and numbers, formulating and testing hypotheses, designing or strategizing. They also spend long hours in meetings or on the telephone, and even longer hours in jet planes and hotels—advising, making presentations, giving briefings, doing deals. Periodically, they issue reports, plans, designs, drafts, memoranda, layouts, renderings, scripts, or projections—which, in turn, precipitate more meetings to clarify what has been proposed and to get agreement on how it will be implemented, by whom, and for how much money. Final production is often the easiest part. The bulk of the time and cost (and, thus real value) comes in conceptualizing the problem, devising a solution, and planning its execution.[30]

These behaviors depend on cognitive activity that must be retraceable and defensible. The world of the symbolic analyst is a world that demands coherence, just as the world of the in-person server demands correspondence. One might say that Reich's symbolic analyst lives in, and is evaluated by others who live in, Popper's World 3 (the world of ideas), whereas the in-person server lives in, and is evaluated by others who live in, Popper's World 1 (the world of objects and events).

Reich, like Herrnstein and Murray and others, emphasizes that it has become harder and harder to enter World 3; it requires not only higher education but early immersion. As Herrnstein and Murray put it:

> Another force for cognitive partitioning is the increasing physical segregation of the cognitive elite from the rest of society. Members of the cognitive elite work in jobs that usually keep them off the shop floor, away from the construction site, and close to others who also tend to be smart. Computers and electronic communication make it increasingly likely that people who work mainly with their minds collaborate only with other such people. The isolation of the cognitive elite is compounded by its choices of where to live, shop, play, worship, and send its children to school.[31]

But the invisible migration of the twentieth century has done much more than let the most intellectually able succeed more easily. It has also segregated them and socialized them. The members of the cognitive elite are likely to have gone to the same kinds of schools, live in similar neighborhoods, go to the same kinds of theaters and restaurants, read the same magazines and newspapers, watch the same television programs, even drive the same makes of cars.[32]

Herrnstein and Murray's description of the isolation of the cognitive elite, as well as Reich's identification and treatment of the symbolic analyst, help us to see the homogeneity of the cognitive activity of the elite, and the importance of early immersion of their young into a world that demands, and offers support for, coherence competence. They fail to note, however, that those who are not among the cognitive elite also share early—and continued—immersion in a different world that demands an identifiable form of cognitive competence, namely correspondence competence. Physical and social perceptual skills, accuracy in the judgments of the objects, events, and people with which they must cope are the skills that are prized by those who will not become "symbolic analysts." More diverse, perhaps, in skin color, religion, and ethnic origin, they are, nevertheless, homogeneous to a large extent in their cognitive training. Indeed, it is their lack of training in coherence competence and strong training in correspondence competence that more than anything else separates them from the cognitive elite, and thus separates them from the rewards the elite obtain. It is the training in correspondence competence that prepares the way for participation in Reich's category of "in-person server."

In brief, Reich's different job categories make very different cognitive demands on those who occupy them. Routine production services require mindless attention to an environment that makes no demand whatsoever on a person's judgment; indeed, virtually all cognitive activity—particularly judgment—must be suppressed. Attention and tolerance for repetition are what is critical. Those who supply in-person services must not only be attentive to those they serve but must exercise their judgment; social judgment, in particular, is everything. But the case is different for Reich's symbolic analyst. "Mastery of old domains of knowledge"—as the judgment of interpersonal behavior surely is—"isn't nearly enough to guarantee a good income. . . . What is much more valuable is the capacity to effectively and creatively *use* the knowledge."[33] Rational, accountable cognition is the work of the symbolic analyst. And one must prepare for that early on.

Researchers in the field of psychology and education offer support for these conclusions. In the preface to their book, *Informal Reasoning and Education*, J. F. Voss, D. N. Perkins, and J. W. Segal point to the increased emphasis on reasoning in various occupations: "The workplace is . . . changing in ways that place greater demands on reasoning. Recent trend data suggest that, in the economy of the future, a substantially larger segment of the workforce can expect to encounter challenging reasoning."[34] But our schools have not prepared students for this change. The authors state: "We have never seriously accepted the challenge of teaching all members of . . . [a] diverse population how to become competent thinkers and reasoners."[35] Moreover, current studies "indicate that large numbers of students complete their years of secondary schooling without having acquired sufficient proficiency in reasoning to cope with citizenship and work responsibilities."[36] Although efforts have been made to remedy the situation, they have been judged to be unsuccessful.

When the authors review past efforts, they note that "until recently, the phenomenon of contextualized reasoning, as opposed to abstract mathematical or logical reasoning, has received very little theoretical attention from psychologists. . . . [And] studies undertaken to date have been limited to a narrow range of reasoning situations."[37] Voss, Perkins, and Segal consider this restriction to be unfortunate and wish to call readers' attention to "informal reasoning," which, they claim, is the stuff of life. It is found everywhere: "Deciding which car to buy, which political candidate to vote for, . . . [it] involves inferences, justifications of beliefs . . . [and] is found in virtually all professional, business, and other working contexts, in medical diagnoses, in legal arguments, in foreign policies, in management decision making, and in repairing cars. . . . Informal reasoning pervades all facets of life."[38] The reader should discern a similarity between these pronouncements and the general theory of judgment in the present volume, for these are convergent points of view. The "informal reasoning" of which Voss, Perkins, and Segal speak is the "quasirational cognition" of which I speak and for which I offer a theoretical structure in Part III. Although a parallel theoretical structure does not appear in Voss, Perkins, and Segal, they agree that the coherence theory (which encompasses only logic and mathematics) should not dominate our interest in reasoning to the exclusion of interest in informal reasoning (or quasirational cognition).

The utility of informal reasoning or quasirational cognition, has also been demonstrated by R. Sternberg and his colleagues in their studies of "practical intelligence."[39] They take a psychometric approach to this topic and develop measures of practical intelligence which they compare with measures of "academic intelligence" (conventional measures of IQ). In line with the theory developed here, as well as with the work by Voss and his colleagues, Sternberg suggests that measures of practical intelligence should be better predictors of job performance, whereas conventional IQ tests should be better predictors of academic performance. This seems to be the case. In a recent article, R. Sternberg, R. Wagner, W. Williams, and J. Horvath have assembled an impressive amount of evidence to support their claims for the importance of practical intelligence in the world outside academia.[40]

Much, but not all, of what they put forward as practical intelligence falls readily within what I have described as the effective use of multiple fallible indicators. And much of what is measured by conventional IQ tests is what has been acquired by academic experience. Sternberg is impressed (as am I) that research shows that there is no correlation between these two putative forms of intelligence. That is what would be expected if (as the theory put forward here suggests) cognitive competence described as coherence competence is developed by, and restricted to, immersion in World 3, whereas correspondence competence is essentially shared by all *Homo sapiens* through their experience in World 1.

Nevertheless, focusing on theories of cognition without a parallel theory of *cognitive tasks* (like that offered in Chapter 6) will not help us greatly. Consider, for example, the cognitive tasks faced by the chief justice of the U.S. Supreme Court, William Rehnquist, as described by A. J. McClurg.[41] The problems faced by Rehnquist were, as McClurg shows, deductive problems, easily cast in the form of a syllogism. Informal logic should not be applied to such problems when they are of such importance, for when it is applied, unacceptable errors follow.

McClurg found fallacious reasoning by Rehnquist in several categories: (1) formal fallacies (as in the case of the undistributed middle term); (2) fallacies deriving from false, omitted, or insufficient premises; (3) fallacies of proof and authority; (4) fallacies of definition, classification, and qualification; and (5) fallacies of irrelevance and diversion. The reader will recognize that McClurg's criticisms are not trivial.

The easiest fallacy to demonstrate is that of the "undistributed middle term," well known to students of elementary logic.[42] McClurg provides this example of Rehnquist's use of the *undistributed middle* fallacy in syllogistic reasoning:

> Murder is a felony;
> burglary is a felony;
> therefore, murder is burglary.

> The fallacy results because, absent a complete distribution of the class of felonies, no valid inference as to the relationship between murder and burglary can be drawn from showing that they both belong to the class. A simple notation establishes this more clearly:

> $p$ is $q$; $s$ is $q$; therefore $p$ is $s$.

> The syllogism can be made valid (though not true) by altering it to read:

> All felonies are murder;
> burglary is a felony;
> therefore, burglary is murder.

> This syllogism is valid because the middle term—felonies—is distributed in the major premise.[43]

McClurg then shows that Rehnquist commits the logical fallacy of drawing conclusions on the basis of an undistributed middle term:

> The . . . fallacy was evident in *Ybarra v. Illinois*, where the Court invalidated a search of patrons of a tavern who were present at the time a search warrant for the tavern was executed. While other officers were searching the tavern, one officer patted down each of the customers. The officer frisked Ybarra and moved on to other customers, but then returned to Ybarra and removed a cigarette pack from his pocket which was found to contain heroin. The majority, relying upon *Terry v. Ohio*, held there was no probable cause to justify an evidentiary search of the customers and that they could be frisked for weapons only if an individualized reasonable suspicion existed that they were armed and dangerous.

> In dissent, Justice Rehnquist argued that the searches were reasonable because of the possibility that the patrons were drug users or traffickers who presented a danger to police. As in *Bertine*, however, the argument was flawed for failing to distribute the relevant class (persons who are patrons of taverns where narcotics are sold). It can be expressed as:

> *First premise:* Some people who are patrons of taverns where narcotics are sold are involved in drug trafficking.
> *Second premise:* These people were patrons of a tavern where narcotics were sold.
> *Conclusion:* Therefore, these people were involved in drug trafficking.

The major premise failed to render the conclusion even probably true. The mere "possibility" that customers of a tavern where drugs are sold may be involved with drugs was not enough to justify searches in a situation that would otherwise require some individualized showing of a probability of criminal activity. The danger of the fallacy of the undistributed middle term is that it permits extravagant extrapolations of principles based upon the most minimal kind of empirical support. For instance, though Justice Burger, in a separate dissent, commented sarcastically that the tavern in *Ybarra* was not the Waldorf ballroom, there is nothing in the reasoning of Justice Rehnquist's dissent that would preclude its extension to patrons of any establishment suspected of being a drug distribution point. Rules or exceptions to rules cannot be fashioned upon such narrow premises, certainly not where the premises involve only naked possibilities.[44]

McClurg then shows that in *New York* v. *Quarles* and other cases Rehnquist demonstrated a second type of fallacy, that of *drawing positive conclusions from negative premises.*

It should be emphasized that the errors McClurg charges to Chief Justice Rehnquist were made not in response to syllogisms presented in symbolic form (e.g., all $s$ is $m$; all $p$ is $m$; therefore all $s$ is $p$), but in the context of natural language, in rather rigorously formed sentences. We may assume that his reasoning was scrutinized by his law clerks and by other justices and their clerks. Thus, it seems fair to say that in the one place in the United States where one would hope that coherence is achieved, informal logic or quasirationality in fact prevail, at least on some occasions, in relation to tasks of logical structure precisely where it should *not* appear. Later in this chapter I show how two other Supreme Court Justices employ quasirational cognition in a different form. First, however, I describe a fourth class of occupation—one omitted from Reich's list—that makes use of multiple fallible indicators exclusively, and that is the occupation of the criminal.

## A Fourth Occupation: Crime

Although Reich omitted crime from his tripartite classification of occupations, it is one occupation that many analysts anticipate will grow substantially; some believe it will grow because of the tensions between classes. The criminal that we fear most commits assault, rape, robbery, and burglary. (White-collar criminals who tend to be symbolic analysts may steal more, but we do not have the same fierce emotional reaction to them; their crimes are impersonal.) The economic, social, and psychological motivations for entering into criminal activity have often been examined and explained, but none of these explanations has been judged to be satisfactory.

A good example of the coherence-based approach to criminal behavior can be seen in the book *The Reasoning Criminal: Rational Choice Perspectives on Offending*, edited by D. B. Cornish and R. V. Clarke.[45] As the title suggests, the rational calculations of the person intent on committing a crime such as robbery or burglary can be carefully analyzed, and departures from coherence evaluated. A chapter by the psychologists J. Carroll and F. Weaver does show an interest in the criminals' use of the correspondence approach, however, and therefore they take note of the use of multiple fallible indicators.[46] The authors interviewed a number of shoplifters and identified a number of indicators that shoplifters apparently used in deciding whether to steal an item from a store. They found striking differences between novices and expert shoplifters in their evaluations of "crime opportunities"; the experts made many more explicit references to shoplifting strategies than the novices. These "experts" exhibit the same phenomenon that we saw in Mark Twain, who after he became an expert pilot, could define the nature of his judgments and detail the information he used. What are often called "street smarts" is simply another example of the use of multiple fallible indicators to make judgments about the street behavior of others (e.g., are they dangerous? vulnerable?).

Judgments of "crime opportunities" can easily be described in terms of multiple fallible indicators. Muggers must rely on several fallible indicators to judge whether the risk of attacking someone will pay off: Are there signs indicating that the intended victim is carrying enough money to make it worthwhile, won't fight back, and are there no police nearby? Those who rob stores and gas stations, as well as those who burglarize homes, also use multiple fallible indicators to judge whether a specific place can be robbed or burglarized successfully.

Many years ago, one of my students studied such judgments (in terms of the lens model described in Chapter 6) with the aid of a career robber who identified for him convenience stores that he would and would not attempt to rob. My student was able to discover the indicators used by convenience store robbers, information eagerly used by the owners to restructure their stores so as to make them unattractive targets.[47]

The security guards and police officers mentioned by Reich also use multiple fallible indicators, but they use them to select persons they suspect to be lawbreakers. A special unit of New Jersey state troopers patrols the highways in New Jersey searching for drug smugglers. How do they decide which cars to stop? The multiple fallible indicators they use are ethnicity (denied, but observed in practice), make of car, speed, nervousness of the driver, and the driver's inconsistent explanations of his activities.[48] But, just as store owners change the characteristics of their stores (once they discover what the indicators robbers look for in order to make them unattractive to robbers, criminals change their patterns of operation once they know what the police are looking for. Drug smugglers, for example, are now making more use of women and children as carriers to deceive the law enforcement officials.[49]

R. Wright, R. H. Logie, and S. H. Decker studied forty-seven active residential burglars who were very experienced (their average number of breakins was 147).[50] The authors were interested in discovering the differences between these experienced burglars and a group of nonoffenders in the use of indicators in planning a successful burglary. They showed pictures of houses that varied in several indicators (e.g., occupancy, an alarm, special locks, a dog) to both groups and found that there were some important differences between the two groups. Indications that the house was occupied, for example, was of prime importance. Moreover, the indicators used by these American burglars were similar to those used by a sample of British burglars. The authors concluded that experienced burglars were "drawing on cognitive skills directly related to their experience of residential burglar."[51] They also state that "the implications for crime prevention are clear: Attempts to manipulate criminal activities are unlikely to succeed in reducing offending unless these efforts are based on a firm understanding of the way in which offenders actually view and interpret such opportunities."[52]

Those who are willing to risk punishment can, and do, rise above the "routine production" job category—with its monotonous, poorly paid, dead-end cognitive life that probably would not challenge or interest a Neanderthal—by moving to the cognitive challenges afforded by multiple fallible indicators in criminal occupations such as robbery and burglary. They will meet these challenges with modest success, inasmuch as criminals, like all the rest of us, can "read" the appropriate indicators with a certain skill. They can also enjoy the creation of misleading displays. Absent a moral sense, they will find crime a meaningful and satisfying occupation, at least for a while. And if they go to prison, as some will, they can find satisfaction in instructing and being instructed by others in the proper use of multiple fallible indicators for successful criminal activity. There will be little or no incentive to pursue analytical cognition, an unfamiliar kind of cognitive activity, when doing what comes naturally offers the satisfaction of success, excitement, and cash payoffs.

Can the correspondence competence that comes naturally to all of us be shifted from criminal to noncriminal activities? Only if legitimate opportunities for correspondence competence are available. Street life suggests the sort of job training that unemployed or poorly educated youth might find interesting enough to move them from a life, or at least a youth, of crime. Job training should require the skillful use of multiple fallible indicators rather than offer dull, routine activities, on the one hand, or activities that demand coherent cognitive work for which they have not been prepared, or for which they have no interest, on the other. Youths who, for one reason or another, do not acquire analytical skills should be given the opportunity to apply their correspondence competence in occupations that require it. An emphasis on the correspondence approach and the use of multiple fallible indicators in such occupations, together with a deemphasis on the coherence-based approach, should make training for such occupations more palatable and success more likely for the reason that it is based on doing what comes naturally, for *all* of us.

## Social Class and Cognitive Competence

Participation in each of Reich's job categories depends on different kinds of cognitive functioning, the roots of which run deep. Skill in the use of multiple fallible indicators is suppressed in jobs that involve routine production services and demanded from those who offer in-person services (including criminal "services"). The symbolic analyst, in contrast, must acquire competence in coherence-based knowledge, an achievement that requires *education*; one does not become expert in logic or the probability calculus or achieve computer literacy through raw experience in World 1. One acquires coherence competence through education, and, to an increasing degree, that education requires early immersion and participation in a social class that includes the cognitive elite. Without such education, without immersion in World 3, in the world of books, libraries, and abstract ideas, one is unlikely to join that class. And if Connelly and Kennedy, Reich, Herrnstein and Murray, and Drucker are right, the sooner that immersion begins, the better. With it, one can become a symbolic analyst and enjoy the benefits thereof; without it, one's chances of enjoying these benefits are slim.

That said, it is important to note that these analysts have overlooked a skill that makes us all a part of a *second* knowledge society. Our ability to use multiple fallible indicators to make accurate inferences is an important one. Many of our natural and artificial job-related environments are still amenable to that skill, and many more that have been downgraded to mindless, single-indicator sequential operations could be upgraded to induce the use of this natural, widely shared talent. It appears that industries that move in this direction can be successful in raising morale and increasing efficiency. A determined effort should be made to take advantage of the natural talent that exists in the *second* knowledge society, rather than to eliminate it from job-related environments, as we now do. If it is true that differences in cognitive competence have materialized in a new way—in tension between social classes, between the two knowledge societies—we have considerable reason to consider this possibility. Otherwise, this tension may well stretch as far forward in our future as its academic form goes back in our past.

# 13 Rivalry, Tension—Forever?

> The *first* indeterminacy lies in the *indeterminate content* of scientific knowledge. . . . a *second* indeterminacy [is] that *coherence* . . . can be only *vaguely defined*, and a third indeterminacy [is] that the *data . . . are not fully identifiable*.
>
> —*Michael Polanyi*

The rivalry between intuition and analysis, and the tension between coherence and correspondence, developed in the course of coping with irreducible uncertainty, duality of error, and injustice. These circumstances are as old as humankind, are they not? Why should we not expect them to continue? There are no signs of their disappearance. Nor is there any indication that the system that responds to all this—the brain of *Homo sapiens*—has changed since we first appeared.

Fortunately, there is no indication that our competence in the use of multiple fallible indicators has decreased. What has changed is the competitive strength of analytical cognition due to our increasingly engineered environment and the growth of World 3 in relation to the (static?) level of intuitive cognition. That means that the rivalry between intuition and analysis that barely existed in our beginning is now very sharp and growing sharper. Nevertheless, this rivalry is seldom recognized for what it is. But it can be seen in the conflicting opinions of two supreme court justices over the most serious questions this court faces—the constitutionality of the death penalty.

## The Persistence of Rivalry Between Intuition and Analysis at the Supreme Court

The question of the moral and constitutional legitimacy of the death penalty received considerable publicity in 1994 when a justice of the U.S. Supreme Court, Harry A. Blackmun, said that "the death penalty experiment has failed" and that "from this day forward I no longer shall tinker with the machinery of death."[1] Justice Blackmun's dissent illustrates the principal thesis of this book. When he said, "The problem is that the inevitability of factual, legal, and moral error gives us a system

343

that we know must wrongly kill some defendants,"[2] Blackmun acknowledged error to be inevitable and injustice to be unavoidable. In the effort to cope with these ubiquitous consequences of irreducible uncertainty, he encountered the rivalry between intuition and analysis; each competed for his judgment. He confronted the fact that "the death penalty must be imposed 'fairly, and with reasonable consistency, or not at all' [quotation from a famous case, *Eddings v. Oklahoma*, 1982]."[3] But it is very difficult to explain our intuitions about fairness, easy to treat consistency analytically. Here is Blackmun's attempt:

> To be fair, a capital sentencing scheme must treat each person convicted of a capital offense with that "degree of respect due the uniqueness of the individual. . . ." That means affording the sentencer the power and discretion to grant mercy in a particular case, and providing avenues for the consideration of any and all relevant mitigating evidence that would justify a sentence less than death.[4]

Justice Blackmun then made clear the role of intuitive cognition: "It seems that the decision whether a human being should live or die is so inherently subjective, rife with all of life's understandings, experiences, prejudices, and passions, that it inevitably *defies* [italics added] the rationality and consistency required by the Constitution,"[5] a startling pronouncement.

Had Justice Blackmun recently been reading Justice Holmes's paragraph explaining why "the life of the law has not been logic: it has been experience"? It is reasonable to wonder, for here is what Holmes offered to replace logic: "The felt necessities of the time, the prevalent moral and political theories, intuitions of public policy, avowed or unconscious, even the prejudices which judges share with their fellowmen."[6] Holmes further said, in a sentence often quoted: "General propositions do not decide concrete cases." Seldom quoted is his next sentence—which explains what does decide concrete cases: "The decision will depend upon a judgment or *intuition* [italics added] more subtle than any articulate major premise."[7] These statements are very close to Blackmun's references to decisions based on cognitive activity that "defies the rationality and consistency required by the Constitution."

But the rivalry persisted in Justice Blackmun's mind; he didn't leave the matter there, for after acknowledging the role of intuitive cognition, he returned to the demands of analytical cognition: "Reasonable consistency, on the other hand, requires that the death penalty be inflicted evenhandedly, in accordance with reason and objective standards [note the contrast with his earlier statement that the decision is "inherently subjective"], rather than by whim, caprice, or prejudice."[8]

Finding that he cannot meet these demands, Justice Blackmun departs from complete dependence on analysis, and concludes that: "It surely is beyond dispute that if the death penalty cannot be administered consistently and rationally, it may not be administered at all."[9] Thus, he believes (as did Holmes) that intuitive cognition cannot be driven out, but since the absolute consistency and rationality demanded by the Constitution cannot be achieved, the death penalty, therefore, cannot be imposed.

Did Justice Blackmun's colleagues congratulate him on his wisdom? Speak highly of his willingness to acknowledge the rivalry between intuition and analysis and to abandon the use of the death penalty because he could not meet the demands of analytical cognition in this circumstance? No. Justice Scalia was the only justice to respond, and he rejected Justice Blackmun's views outright, and with enthusiasm.

Scalia begins his argument against Blackmun exactly as the reader of this book would expect; he attacked Blackmun's failure to stay with the analytical interpretation of the Constitution as well as Blackmun's capitulation to his intuitions about fairness. For Scalia, analysis should drive out intuition, not the reverse. Although Scalia agrees with Blackmun's statement about the incompatibility of the demands for fairness and consistency, at least at the Supreme Court, he rejects fairness and demands that rationality and consistency be applied to the death penalty—the reverse of Blackmun's position: "He [Blackmun] unfortunately draws the wrong conclusion from the acknowledgment"[10] of the rivalry between intuition and analysis. Scalia establishes his allegiance to analytical cognition in his opening paragraph:

> Justice Blackmun dissents from the denial of certiorari in this case with a statement explaining why the death penalty "as currently administered," . . . is contrary to the Constitution of the United States. That explanation often refers to "intellectual, moral and personal" perceptions, but never to the text and tradition of the Constitution. It is the latter rather than the former that ought to control.[11]

He could hardly have been more plain. Scalia then quotes that part of the Constitution that he believes permits the death penalty:

> The Fifth Amendment provides that "[n]o person shall be held to answer for a capital . . . crime, unless on a presentment or indictment of a Grand Jury, . . . nor be deprived of life . . . without due process of law." This clearly permits the death penalty to be imposed, and establishes beyond doubt that the death penalty is not one of the "cruel and unusual punishments" prohibited by the Eighth Amendment.[12]

But then something very curious—and unexpected—occurs. One would have thought that different views between two experts about the constitutionality of an issue as significant as the imposition of the death sentence would be expressed in terms of rational analysis, cool logic. If a justice should succumb to his or her intuitions (as both Blackmun and Holmes indicated was likely), others would calmly bring them back to the analytical pole. But that was not the case here; both justices chose to inflame the argument by references to grotesque circumstances. Scalia, for example, scathingly refers to Blackmun's description of "the death of a convicted murderer by lethal injection":

> He [Blackmun] chooses, as the case in which to make that statement, one of the less brutal of the murders that regularly come before us—the murder of a man ripped by a bullet suddenly and unexpectedly, with no opportunity to prepare himself and his affairs, and left to bleed to death on the floor of a tavern. The death-by-injection which Justice Blackmun describes looks pretty desirable next to that.
>
>   It looks even better next to some of the other cases currently before us which Justice Blackmun did not select as the vehicle for his announcement that the death penalty is always unconstitutional—for example, the case of the 11-year-old girl raped by four men and then killed by stuffing her panties down her throat. . . . How enviable a quiet death by lethal injection compared with that![13]

For Justice Scalia to introduce this strong, unnecessary appeal to our intuitions and emotions about morality in relation to those brutal, offensive actions is startling.

It is startling because it follows his demand for the persistent, unflinching application of analytical cognition, for consistency, and for rationality. If we are to have a government of laws, not men, as Scalia argued, then we should ignore such appeals to our intuitions about morality and simply follow the law as the Constitution proclaims it. But he doesn't do this. Although scornful of Blackmun's appeal to our emotions regarding lethal injection, Scalia simply raises the ante with his own appeal to our intuitions by calling our attention to a child "killed by stuffing her panties down her throat," thus completing *his* cycle from analysis to intuition.

Justice Blackmun's appeal to our intuitions was more than Justice Scalia's commitment to analysis could stand. He relaxed his commitment to analytical cognition, his commitment to the consistency he had just praised, and demanded, from Justice Blackmun. Thus, Justice Scalia capitulated to the intuition-inducing properties of Justice Blackmun's statement and in response offered his own intuitions, albeit of a more vivid character.

## The Persistence of Tension Between Correspondence and Coherence in Sentencing

To the best of my knowledge, neither of these metatheories has been heretofore explicitly applied to judicial reasoning. I am convinced, however, on the basis of the work of N. Pennington and R. Hastie, who stressed the importance of the narrative,[14] that these are appropriate concepts to be used to increase our understanding of the cognitive processes of judges, jurors, and attorneys. Because coherence is the key element of a narrative, it is often the condition upon which a story or explanation is believed and, therefore, a condition upon which guilt or innocence is decided.

A prime example of the critical role of coherence in deciding responsibility for a crime appeared in an article by Norman Mailer that examines the question of whether Jack Ruby's murder of Lee Harvey Oswald was premeditated. In fact, Mailer's question is more specific: Was Ruby a hit man hired by the Mafia in order to cover up its role in the assassination of President Kennedy? Based on his knowledge of Ruby's behavior immediately prior to the shooting, Mailer concludes that this act could not have been premeditated. The reason? There is incontestable evidence that Ruby visited a Western Union office and stood in line to send money to a friend at 11:17 A.M., *four minutes* before he shot Oswald in the police station "less than two hundred steps away."[15] Mailer argues that it is incomprehensible that someone planning to kill Oswald while the police were transferring him from one place to another—an act that would require exquisite timing—would take his chances on being served at the Western Union counter only a few minutes before carrying out his plan. A single fact thus destroys the required coherence of such a plan, and Mailer therefore concludes that Ruby "was not planning to kill Oswald on Sunday at 11:21 A.M."[16] Destroying the coherence of a witness's story is one of the opposing attorney's primary goals; such destruction may require only the establishment of a single fact, because coherence demands completeness. In the example I offer next, I concentrate on the cognitive activity of a judge whose sentencing memorandum will show the tension between coherence and correspondence theories in his reasoning processes.

The case of Rodney King, the black California motorist whose ferocious beating by white police officers was video recorded and displayed countless times on television, became widely known. Four of the police officers were tried twice, once in a local court, where they were declared innocent, and then, in 1993, in a federal court, where two were found guilty of certain charges and were sentenced by Judge John G. Davies to "the low end of the prescribed Guideline range [mandatory sentence] to a term of 30 months."[17] The judge's departure from the guidelines and his clearly stated rationale for doing so offer an excellent illustration of what Holmes meant when he emphasized the importance of experience over logic. Indeed, Judge Davies's sentencing memorandum is remarkable for its detailed documentation of why he departed from the guidelines, and for his recognition of what Holmes called "the felt necessities of the time."

Judge Davies first takes note of the content of the guidelines which specify how he must calculate the "offense level" applicable to the defendants' behavior. He then notes:

> For purposes of calculating Mr. Powell's base offense level, the Court considers his relevant conduct to be the blows he administered after 1:07:28. Mr. Koon, on the other hand, was convicted of an offense of omission, and is liable for failing to stop Powell's and Wind's excessive use of force when he could have and should have. The excessive force used by Powell and Wind with Koon's permission constitutes "relevant conduct" for purposes of calculating Koon's base offense level.[18]

To follow the guidelines, Judge Davies must now *calculate*. He explains that "to calculate the defendants' base offense level under Section 2H1.4, the Court must first determine the appropriate underlying offense and its corresponding offense level. The sum of the corresponding offense level and 6 represents the proper base level offense, if it exceeds 10."[19] Judge Davies reasoned that "because Powell's side handle baton was 'otherwise used,' and because Koon permitted such use, the aggravated assault base offense is increased by 4 levels for both defendants Koon and Powell."[20]

The reader should observe the analytical, rule-based logical nature of the judge's reasoning; it is perfectly rational and retraceable; there are no appeals, up to this point, to the "felt necessities of the time." Indeed, Judge Davies supplied a table of calculations for the "total offense level," as follows:

C. Applicable Guideline Range
 The offense level calculations for both defendants Koon and Powell are summarized as follows:

| | |
|---|---|
| Aggravated Assault Base Offense Level (§ 2A2.2): | +15 |
| Dangerous weapon "otherwise used" (§ 2A2.2(b) (2) (B)): | + 4 |
| Bodily injury (§ 2A2.2(b) (3) (A)): | + 2 |
| Violation of 18 U.S.C. § 242 (§ 2H1.4(a) (2)): | + 6 |
| TOTAL OFFENSE LEVEL | 27[21] |

Judge Davies then notes that "under the Guidelines Sentencing Table, an offense level of 27 with Criminal History Category I results in a prescribed range of 70 to 87 months."

This procedure is, of course, exactly the procedure that R. M. Dawes, D. Faust, and P. E. Meehl[22] (and I) want clinical psychologists to employ. Recall our discussion of the competence of clinical judgment, and Meehl's urging clinical psychologists to take note of the cashier at the supermarket: "When you check out at a supermarket, you don't eyeball the heap of purchases and say to the clerk, 'Well it looks to me as if it's about $17.00 worth; what do you think?' *The clerk adds it up* [italics added]."[23] The situation facing the clinician and the judge are fundamentally alike; both must make a probabilistic inference about an impalpable aspect of a person's character—the clinician about, say, a personality disorder, the judge about the degree of punishment a person deserves, based on multiple fallible indicators.

Legislative bodies have forced the analytical, rule-based procedure on judges in order to advance the cause of justice—that is, punishment of the crime, not the person. Justice is better served by the rule-based procedure because (almost) every judge will reach the same conclusion regarding the sentence; uncertainty about punishment will thus be reduced; matters that ought not to be considered (race, sex, national origin, creed, religion, and socioeconomic status) will not be introduced; fairness and equality will be achieved.

But Judge Davies wasn't finished.

Having laid out his rationale for the "Total Offense Level" that would determine the sentence to be imposed, Judge Davies then turned his attention to mitigating factors under the subhead of "Downward Departure."[24] He noted that "the Sentencing Commission expressly recognized the inherent difficulties in prescribing 'a single set of guidelines that encompasses the vast range of human conduct relevant to a sentencing decision.'"[25] Yet, as he noted, "sentencing outside the prescribed range is unusual." Furthermore, such factors as "race, sex, national origin, creed, religion, and socio-economic status, may never be considered as 'aggravating or mitigating circumstances' warranting a departure."[26] Nevertheless, he said, "[t]he Commission did not intend to limit the kinds of factors which may constitute grounds for departure in an atypical case."[27] Judge Davies was cognizant of the Commission's intent to leave the door open for Holmes's "felt necessities of the time" and for intuitive judgments in the sentencing process. After documenting the atypicality of the case, the judge cited the conclusions of the Ninth Circuit Court of Appeals, which asks for wisdom in sentencing and finds it in the *coherence* theory of truth:

> Of these four factors, only Mr. King's wrongful conduct independently warrants a sentence reduction. See Guideline § 5K2.10. *Standing alone* [italics added], none of the other enumerated factors clearly justifies a departure from the Guidelines. However, the Court's decision whether to depart "require[s] the evaluation of a complex of factors." *Cook*, 938 F2d at 151. As the Ninth Circuit observed in *Cook*:
>
> > No single factor may be enough to point to the wise course of decision. But a wise person will not look on each particular factor abstractly and alone. Rather, it will be how the particular pieces fit together, converge, and influence each other that will lead to the correct decision.[28]

Judge Davies found that reasoning appealing and stated that "the Court finds that the second, third and fourth factors *taken together* [italics added] justify a reduced sentence."[29]

Thus, when proceeding to justify the "Total Offense Level," Judge Davies looked at three violations of the law and *added them up* because that's what the Sentencing Commission orders him to do (and as researchers within the correspondence framework would urge him to do). Nothing was said about any disadvantages that might accrue from looking at "each particular factor abstractly and alone." Indeed, that was exactly one of the *advantages* of the scoring system; it guaranteed rigor and retraceability (just as it does at the supermarket). But the judge then found justification for opening the door to mitigating circumstances in the coherence theory; he believed that noticing how "the particular pieces fit together, converge, and influence each other . . . will lead to a correct decision." (That *wouldn't* count for much at the supermarket.)

Judge Davies thus appealed to a correspondence theory of truth in adducing what the sentence would be for the defendants *before* considering mitigating factors (in accordance with his instructions from the Sentencing Commission) and then appealed to a coherence theory of truth in reducing these sentences *after* considering mitigating factors (when he was free to use his discretion to do so).

But Judge Davies's mitigation of the federally mandated sentence for Koon and Powell had a short life. Only three months later, in an opinion written by Judge Betty Fletcher of the Ninth Circuit Court of Appeals Judge Davies's coherence-based reasoning, which supported his "downward departure" to thirty months from the federally mandated sentence, was rejected; the full sentence of eighty-seven months was restored. (Ironically, this is the same court that provided the opinion Judge Davies relied on for his "downward departure.")

Can the reader anticipate the nature of Judge Fletcher's attack on Judge Davies's reasoning? Did she offer a competitive, somehow more compelling, coherence-based argument? Or did she employ a correspondence-based argument that attacked the empirical truth of each point in the coherence-based argument? (This question was introduced in a dramatic way to scientists by Thomas Kuhn in 1962.[30])

Although I am uncertain, I believe that in law it is far more difficult to replace a coherence-based argument with a coherence-based competitor. Advantages of one coherence-based theory over another are very hard to establish; it is difficult to argue that Story A is more coherent than Story B. On the other hand, a correspondence-based attack can demolish a coherence-based argument by simply showing that one or two crucial facts that form part of the coherent story are false or unjustified (as I indicated in my description of Maier's rejection of Ruby's plan to kill Oswald). And that is what Judge Fletcher did when she rejected Judge Davies's argument for a "downward departure"; she simply ignored Judge Davies's appeal to the manner in which "the particular pieces fit together, converge, and influence one another." (Never mind that that is just what Judge Cook of the Ninth Circuit had previously suggested might form the basis for departure.) Instead, she used the same correspondence-based form of reasoning that Judge Davies used when he produced his original sentence of eighty-seven months. As any good correspondence theorist would, she noted each point of Judge Davies's argument separately and then denied the validity of each one of them in turn (ten major arguments and numerous sub-arguments). No coherent set of facts "taken together" was offered as a counter-argument; none was needed. In her conclusion she simply stated:

> We affirm appellants' convictions. After a careful review of the record and the relevant authorities, we are convinced that the district judge correctly resolved each of the legal issues raised by appellants as to the *guilt* [italics added] phase of the proceedings. He conducted the trial with impeccable fairness and careful and thoughtful attention to its every aspect. We appreciate the magnitude of the task, given the unusual number and complexity of the issues involved, and the difficult circumstances caused by the extraordinary publicity surrounding every phase of the proceedings. However, we are also convinced that the sentences imposed by the district court are inconsistent with the structure and policies of the Sentencing Guidelines and the federal sentencing statutes, and we therefore vacate the sentences and remand for resentencing consistent with this opinion.[31]

But Judge Davies had already acknowledged that "[o]f . . . [the] four factors, only Mr. King's wrongful conduct *independently* [italics added] warrants a sentence reduction." And he showed that he *knew* that "none of the other enumerated factors clearly justifies a departure from the Guidelines." He justified his downward departure solely on the basis of Judge Cook's admonition that "a wise person will not look on each particular factor abstractly and alone."[32] But isn't looking on "each particular factor abstractly and alone" exactly what Judge Fletcher did? Is she therefore unwise? Doesn't this indicate that the tension between coherence and correspondence persists in the justice system? And doesn't this example suggest that it will be forever thus, that there will always be tension and alternation between coherence and correspondence? Should we be surprised when we learn that in September 1995 the U.S. Supreme Court decided that it should review these two incommensurable arguments? Will the court come down on the side of coherence or correspondence?

# Conclusion

This book is based on two major ideas about human judgment: (1) Persistent rivalry exists between intuition and analysis, and (2) persistent tension exists between our use of coherence and correspondence theories of truth. Both ideas have been well known to scientists and philosophers for centuries, and that is why there are references to the history of thought in this book. That is also why I included references to evolution and evolutionary psychology. I wanted to show that the rivalry between intuition and analysis and the tension between coherence and correspondence are products of the interaction between our biological nature and our natural and artificial environments; this rivalry and this tension are rooted in our nature just as language and tool-building are rooted in our nature.

## Some Conjectures About Competence

Correspondence competence of judgment is closely linked to the structure and function of the brain; that is because cognitive processes are a product of natural selection. Our brain has led to our natural ecological fitness and to reproductive success, and vice versa. In short, correspondence competence is a product of evolution. We should therefore expect such competence among all *Homo sapiens* in circumstances affording multiple fallible indicators and not expect it when these are absent. Although we are obviously capable of achieving coherence competence, whether we do or not is largely dependent on instruction that teaches us how to code and organize information from various sources—teachers, the printed page, a computer terminal. We do not share these sources of information with other species. Whereas correspondence competence is phylogenetic (it benefits from perhaps millions of years of evolution), coherence competence is ontogenetic (it benefits only from each person's opportunity and ability to acquire the appropriate concepts from education and training). We cannot expect coherence competence when these are lacking. Therefore, we achieve vastly different levels of coherence competence, depending on our education.

Early *Homo sapiens* were endowed not only with a capacity for language but with a capacity for making effective use of multiple fallible indicators. These indicators were first offered by the natural environment, then created by us to accommodate our natural talent. Our natural cognitive skill was such that we could make use of information from multiple fallible indicators in both intuitive and analytical forms. It is not clear whether the use of multiple fallible indicators came before or after language, but since we share the former—but not the latter—with numerous other species, it seems likely language appeared later. A rivalry between intuitive and analytical forms of cognition ensued, together with our remarkable capacity for quasirational cognition—*not* shared with other species—that we have for centuries labeled "common sense." So "common" is it that even twentieth-century writers advising political leaders can urge them to rely upon it without ever defining or explaining it. Error ridden as it may be, quasirationality emerges as a valuable form of cognition because it tries to avoid the irresponsibility of intuition as well as the fragility of analysis. Quasirationality is a superior form of cognition that has been the mainstay of our survival, all the while offering us all the negative consequences of an imperfect form of reasoning.

Correspondence competence was with us from the start; coherence competence may well have made its appearance together with language and tool making. Once these three factors—coherence competence, language, and tool making—were joined, cognition based on coherence began to play a larger and larger role in human judgment; it has begun to dominate Western civilization and has made large inroads in the rest of the world. There seems to be no end in sight.

Yet a demand for coherence in social policy has been shown to be a dangerous demand, indeed; the appeal of coherent cognition must be treated with great caution. When the coherence of the ideologies of the twentieth century captured the hearts and minds of hundreds of millions (content seemed to matter little), it not only led them to misery and death but encouraged them to carry out the worst sort of atrocities in the belief that they were right to inflict misery and death on others. If ever there was a lesson from history, this may be the best example.

No doubt we will always be urged to learn lessons from experience, as Robert McNamara has poignantly admonished us to do with such embarrassing enthusiasm. But examination of our methods of learning—intervention and representation— shows us that these are very weak methods for informing policymakers. As a result, quasirationality is seldom driven out by analytical competence—that is, fully defensible, retraceable cognition—even at the Supreme Court. Nor can we expect that wisdom can be simply found by turning to a council of elders. Useful as they may once have been, in a world now dominated by coherence competence our elders can no longer provide the competence once provided by long experience with multiple fallible indicators.

Analytical cognition is now to be found successfully driving out intuition and quasirationality in governmental bureaucracies and corporate management, as the importance of the symbolic analyst ever increases. Concomitantly, however, those who fail to acquire the education necessary to achieve competence in symbolic analysis will have to rely on the correspondence competence that is part of their natural endowment. If Reich (and many others) are correct, skill in the use of multiple fallible indicators will continue to be useful only for those who become "in-person servers"—those who must skillfully appraise the attitudes, mood, and personas of the persons they serve in their capacity of retail sales workers, cashiers, child-care workers, flight attendants, and the like.

Social analysts who emphasize the emergence of the knowledge society—particularly Connelly and Kennedy, Drucker, Herrnstein and Murray, and Reich—point out that social classes are being constructed (and divided) in terms of these cognitive functions. By assigning the term "elite" to those with coherence competence, they point to the current invidious nature of the distinction; they do not acknowledge that those who possess correspondence competence but not coherence competence form a *second* "knowledge society," not a "no-knowledge society." Correspondence competence is not currently worthless, as is shown by the existence of Reich's in-person servers, and as the persistent occupation of criminal also shows. Greater development of a place for the application of correspondence competence in the workplace, together with reduction of routine production operations, might serve to reduce the numbers of young males who prefer to use their correspondence competence, even if criminally, rather than be numbed by the mindless duties of routine production.

Finally, quasirationality will continue to serve as the basis of human judgment applied to the formation of social policy—now and forever. Cognition may oscillate from intuition to analysis and back, but in the end it will settle on quasirationality or, as we have known it for so long, common sense. The consequences will also be the ones we have long known: imperfect reasoning, inconsistency, conflict, and, inevitably, error, with its attendant injustices, sometimes to society, sometimes to individuals.

Tension will persist between coherence and correspondence, and that tension will be exacerbated as these two forms of cognition become identified with social classes that represent the "haves" and the "have-nots." And that tension will be reflected in the cognitive activity of the policy makers who must cope with the troubles that will arise from these circumstances.

Is there an advantage in recognizing this state of affairs? Indeed there is. We no longer need be confined to choosing between defining those who oppose us, or who have made errors of judgment in the past, as either stupid or evil. We now have a better alternative. If I have correctly described the nature of human judgment and the circumstances to which it is applied, we can now examine opposition or error in terms of our cognitive activity. Am I and my opponent employing incommensurable modes of cognition (much as Judge Davies and Judge Fletcher appear to be doing)? Are we making use of different fallible indicators in different ways (much as forecasters do)? Is one of us a trained analyst, expert in the use of analytical techniques, while the other is restricted to intuitive judgments? Or could it be that our indicators are so error ridden that argumentation is futile? The pursuit of the nature of human judgment, and the examination of when it fails us, may very well enable us to shift our understanding of our troubles in a new direction—and perhaps improve matters.

Even though human judgment has come under scientific investigation only within the last fifty years, we have considerable knowledge now. That knowledge should become common knowledge. Naturally, I hope this book is a step toward achieving that goal.

# Epilogue

In the introduction I raised several questions about the competence of human judgment and promised to answer them. Here I repeat the questions and offer brief answers:

1. *How good is human judgment?* The reader now knows that the answer to that question requires that we differentiate between coherence and correspondence judgments. *Coherence* judgments tend to be poor unless one is trained in the discipline of statistics. When these calculated judgments are made by experts, they are precisely correct or wildly incorrect. *Correspondence* judgments are very accurate in the realm of physical perception but become less so as the conceptual context of the task increases and as the uncertainty in the task system increases. They are robust and imprecise.

2. *How does one acquire competence in judgment? Coherence:* Persons must be educated with respect to the principles of probability; they can be (more should be). Raw experience is a poor teacher with respect to these principles. *Correspondence:* Correspondence accuracy in relation to physical perception is part of our biological endowment; competence that depends on the use of multiple fallible indicators is generally slowly (and often painfully) acquired through experience with outcomes. It is doubtful that high competence and accuracy in social perception, in any absolute sense, can be achieved, because of the high uncertainty in the targets—the behavior of the people perceived. Modest success is the best to be hoped for.

3. *What about differences among us? Coherence:* Education matters, a great deal! Experience matters little. *Correspondence:* Experience matters, but much depends on the nature of the experience.

4. *How do you find out who has good judgment and who doesn't? Coherence:* That is easy; test the person's knowledge of probability and statistics. (Recall Richard Feynman's question to the *Challenger* officials: "Don't you understand the principles of probability?") *Correspondence:* Ascertaining correspondence competence is difficult because field tests are apparently the only answer (see, e.g., the research on clinical psychologists, and weather forecasters).

354

*5. Why does one person have better judgment than another? What is the source of good judgment? Coherence:* There is only one source: education. Those who have studied and have become proficient in the field of probability are better at calculating probabilities than those not so fortunate. No doubt the ability to acquire this form of education requires high intelligence and motivation. *Correspondence:* There is no simple answer to this question. Some of us are endowed with better vision or other perceptual skills; some have better conceptual skills; some have greater cognitive capacities not yet specified by intellective measures; and some perhaps have emotive characteristics that assist them in acquiring and organizing information more efficiently under less than ideal conditions. There is much to be learned here; we know only a fraction of what we need to know. Nevertheless, we should expect correspondence competence to be generally high among all *Homo sapiens* under naturalistic conditions involving multiple fallible indicators. Group or ethnic differences should be virtually nonexistent.

# Notes

*Acknowledgments*

1. K. R. Hammond. (1995). Expansion of Egon Brunswik's psychology (1955–1995). In *Wahrnehmung und gegenstandswelt: Egon Brunswik*. Wien: Hölder-Pichler-Tempsky.
2. K. R. Hammond. (Ed.). (1966). *The psychology of Egon Brunswik* (2nd ed.). New York: Holt, Rinehart, and Winston.
3. K. R. Hammond. (1968). Brunswik, Egon. In *International encyclopedia of the social sciences* (pp. 156–158). New York: Macmillan.

*Introduction*

1. W. Edwards. (1954). The theory of decision making. *Psychological Bulletin, 41,* 380–417.
2. K. R. Hammond. (1955). Probabilistic functioning and the clinical method. *Psychological Review, 62,* 255–262.
3. A somewhat different version of this history can be found in G. Gigerenzer, Z. Swijtink, T. Porter, L. Daston, J. Beatty, & L. Krueger. (1989). *The empire of chance: How probability changed science and everyday life.* New York: Cambridge University Press. It will be a corrective to my (possibly) egocentric version.
4. See Gigerenzer, Swijtink, Porter, Daston, Beatty, & Krueger; I. Hacking. (1975). *The emergence of probability: A philosophical study of early ideas about probability, induction and statistical inference.* London: Cambridge University Press.
5. For his latest work, see D. von Winterfeldt, & W. Edwards. (1986). *Decision analysis and behavioral research.* Cambridge, UK: Cambridge University Press.
6. P. Slovic, & S. Lichtenstein. (1971). Comparison of Bayesian and regression approaches to the study of information processing in judgment. *Organizational Behavior and Human Performance, 6,* 649–744.
7. B. Mazlish. (1993). *The fourth discontinuity: The co-evolution of humans and machines.* New Haven: Yale University Press, p. 3.
8. Quoted by G. T. Allison. (1971). *Essence of decision: Explaining the Cuban missile crisis.* Boston: Little, Brown, p. vi.
9. R. W. Southern. (1953). *The making of the middle ages.* London: Hutchinson, p. 176.
10. Southern, p. 176.

## 1. Irreducible Uncertainty and the Need for Judgment

1. Thucydides. (1972). *History of the Peloponnesian War* (R. Warner, Trans.). Harmondsworth, UK: Penguin Books, p. 85.

2. D. Brooks. (September 28, 1992). It's a bird, it's a plane, it's multilateral man! *The Wall Street Journal,* p. A14.

3. R. Heilbroner. (March 3, 1994). Acts of an apostle [Review of *John Maynard Keynes: Vol. 2. The economist as saviour 1920–1937*]. *The New York Review of Books,* p. 8.

4. Laplace, *Oeuvres, Vol. VII, Théorie Analytique des Probabilités* [1812–1820], introduction; quoted in J. Bartlett. (1968). *Familiar quotations: A collection of passages, phrases and proverbs traced to their sources in ancient and modern literature* (14th ed.). Boston: Little, Brown, p. 479.

5. For a history of this term, see I. Hacking. (1990). *The taming of chance.* Cambridge, UK: Cambridge University Press, pp. 151–154.

6. R. M. Hogarth. (1987). *Judgement and choice: The psychology of decision* (2nd ed.). Chichester, UK: Wiley, p. 30.

7. L. Lusted. (1991). The clearing "haze": A view from my window. *Medical Decision Making, 11,* p. 79.

8. G. Gigerenzer. (1993). The superego, the ego, and the id in statistical reasoning. In G. Keren & C. Lewis (Eds.), *A handbook for data analysis in the behavioral sciences: Methodological issues* (pp. 311–339). Hillsdale, NJ: Erlbaum, p. 312.

9. J. Gleick. (1987). *Chaos: Making a new science.* New York: Viking, p. 311.

10. J. Gross. (January 3, 1993). Conversations/Allan G. Lindh: Is 1993 the year of the big one? Rumblings from a California prophet. *New York Times,* p. E7.

11. L. H. Gelb. (January 3, 1993). Surprise, surprise, surprise. *New York Times,* p. E11.

12. A. Schlesinger, Jr. (April 11, 1993). A Clinton report card, so far. *New York Times,* sec. 4, p. 13.

13. R. J. Herrnstein, & C. Murray. (1994). *The bell curve: Intelligence and class structure in American Life.* New York: Free Press, p. 509.

14. A. Lewis. (1991). *Make no law: The Sullivan case and the First Amendment.* New York: Random House.

15. For an exposition of this view, see especially J. Rasmussen. (1983). Skills, rules, and knowledge: Signals, signs, and symbols, and other distinctions in human performance models. *IEEE Transactions on Systems Man and Cybernetics, SMC-13*(3), 257–266.

16. I. Hacking. (1975). *The emergence of probability: A philosophical study of early ideas about probability, induction and statistical inference.* London: Cambridge University Press.

17. I. Hacking. (1990). *The taming of chance.* Cambridge, UK: Cambridge University Press.

18. G. Gigerenzer, Z. Swijtink, T. Porter, L. Daston, J. Beatty, & L. Krueger. (1989). *The empire of chance: How probability changed science and everyday life.* New York: Cambridge University Press.

19. S. K. Duran. (November 18, 1995). Residents decry police policy. *Daily Camera,* pp. A1, A2.

20. B. J. Shapiro. (1986). "To a moral certainty": Theories of knowledge and Anglo-American juries 1600–1850. *Hastings Law Journal, 38,* pp. 174–175.

21. Coffin v. United States, 156 U.S. 432, 455 (1895).

22. Coffin v. United States, 156 U.S. 432, 456 (1895).

23. Blackstone, quoted in *The Oxford dictionary of quotations* (3rd ed.). (1979). Oxford: Oxford University Press, p. 85.

24. Furman v. Georgia, 408 U.S. 238, 367 (1972).

25. Harper's index. (September, 1995). *Harper's Magazine*, p. 9.

26. D. K. Kagehiro. (1990). Defining the standard of proof in jury instructions. *Psychological Science, 1*, p. 194.

27. U.S. v. Fatico, 458 F. Supp. 388, 410 (1978).

28. N. L. Rabinovitch. (1973). *Probability and statistical inference in ancient and medieval Jewish literature*. Toronto: University of Toronto Press, p. 77.

29. Rabinovitch, p. 65.

30. Justinian in *The civil law: Including the Twelve tables, the Institutes of Gaius, the Rules of Ulpian, the Opinions of Paulus, the Enactments of Justinian, and the Constitutions of Leo* (translated from the original Latin, edited and compared with all accessible systems of jurisprudence ancient and modern by S. P. Scott). (1932). Cincinnati: Central Trust Co., Vol. 11, p. 110.

31. E. Gibbon. (1776/1960). *The decline and fall of the Roman Empire*. New York: Harcourt, Brace, p. 207.

32. Gibbon, p. 207.

33. Genesis Rabbah 29:6 indicates that *both* errors were considered but this interpretation should perhaps be attributed to enthusiasm for the wisdom of the Almighty rather than documentation. For a discussion of Abraham's plea for mercy for the innocent in Gomorrah, see A. Laytner. (1990). *Arguing with God: A Jewish tradition*. Northvale, NJ: Jason Aronson.

34. *In re* Winship, 397 U.S. 358, 367 (1970).

35. *In re* Winship, p. 364.

36. *In re* Winship, p. 370.

37. *In re* Winship, pp. 370–371.

38. *In re* Winship, p. 372.

39. *In re* Winship, p. 378.

40. Callins v. Collins, No. 93–7054, 1994 S. Ct. LEXIS 1327 (Feb. 22, 1994), p. 1130.

41. Callins v. Collins, p. 1130.

42. Callins v. Collins, p. 1127.

43. *In re* Winship, p. 378.

44. W. Ningkun. (1993). *A family's persecution, love, and endurance in communist China*. New York: Atlantic Monthly Press.

45. Quoted by J. Shapiro. (February 28, 1993). 22 years as a class enemy. *New York Times*, sec. 17, p. 12.

46. T. Connolly. (1987). Decision theory, reasonable doubt, and the utility of erroneous acquittals. *Law and Human Behavior, 11*, 101–112.

47. Connolly, p. 105.

48. See also M. DeKay. (in press). The difference between Blackstone-like error ratios and probabilistic standards of proof. *Law & Social Inquiry*.

49. H. S. Cumming, H. H. Hazen., A. H. Sanford, F. E. Senear, W. M. Simpson, & R. A. Vonderlehr. (1935). *The evaluation of serodiagnostic tests for syphilis in the United States: Report of results*. Washington, DC: Government Printing Office.

50. J. Yerushalmy. (1947). Evaluating roentgenographic techniques. *Public Health Reports, 62*, 1431–1456.

51. J. Berkson. (1947). "Cost-utility" as a measure of the efficiency of a test. *Journal of the American Statistical Association, 42*, 246–255.

52. S. Greenhouse, & N. Mantel. (1950). The evaluation of diagnostic tests. *Biometrics, 6*, 399–412.

53. W. J. Youden. (1950). Index for rating diagnostic tests. *Cancer, 3,* 32–35.

54. J. Neyman, & E. S. Pearson. (1933). On the problem of the most efficient tests of statistical hypotheses. *Philosophical Transactions of the Royal Society of London. Series A, 231,* 289–337.

55. R. S. Ledley, & L. B. Lusted. (1959). Reasoning foundations of medical diagnosis. *Science, 130,* 9–21.

56. L. B. Lusted. (1968). *Introduction to medical decision making.* Springfield, IL: Charles C. Thomas.

57. Lusted, The clearing "haze," p. 77.

58. For a similar argument and some empirical studies of medical teaching, see K. R. Hammond, E. Frederick, N. Robillard, & D. Victor. (1989). Application of cognitive theory to the student-teacher dialogue. In D. A. Evans & V. L. Patel (Eds.), *Cognitive science in medicine* (pp. 173–210). Cambridge, MA: MIT Press.

59. Lusted, The clearing "haze," p. 80.

60. J. C. Bailar, III, & F. Mosteller. (1992). *Medical uses of statistics* (2nd ed.). Boston: NEJM Books.

61. J. A. Freiman, T. C. Chalmers, H. Smith, Jr., & R. R. Kuebler. (1992). The importance of beta, the type II error, and sample size in the design and interpretation of the randomized controlled trial: Survey of two sets of "negative" trials. In J. C. Bailar, III & F. Mosteller (Eds.), *Medical uses of statistics* (pp. 357–373). Boston: NEJM Books, p. 357.

62. Freiman, Chalmers, Smith, & Kuebler, p. 357.

63. Freiman, Chalmers, Smith, & Kuebler, p. 372.

64. L. S. Cooper, T. C. Chalmers, M. McCally, J. Berrier, & H. S. Sacks. (1988). The poor quality of early evaluations of magnetic resonance imaging. *Journal of the American Medical Association, 259,* p. 3277.

65. B. H. Lerner. (1991). Scientific evidence versus therapeutic demand: The introduction of the sulfonamides revisited. *Annals of Internal Medicine, 115,* p. 319.

66. Lerner, p. 319. For a history of the use of antibiotics against tuberculosis see F. Ryan. (1993). *The forgotten plague: How the battle against tuberculosis was won—and lost.* Boston: Little, Brown.

67. Lerner, p. 319.

68. J. E. Brody. (September 20, 1992). Nationwide tests set for prostate cancer, but doubts surface. *New York Times,* p. 18. Note how Dr. Mettlin's preference offers an example of Connolly's argument about the differential weighting of the four possibilities described above.

69. T. M. Burton. (1993, February 16). Blood test for prostate cancer is raising issue of reliability, drug-industry role. *The Wall Street Journal,* p. B1.

## 2. Duality of Error and Policy Formation

1. R. J. Herrnstein, & C. Murray. (1994). *The bell curve: Intelligence and class structure in American life.* New York: Free Press. For a cogent and comprehensive critique of *The Bell Curve,* see R. J. Sternberg. (1995). For whom the bell curve tolls: A review of *The bell curve. Psychological Science, 6,* 257–261.

2. For interesting and informative histories, see I. Hacking. (1975). *The emergence of probability: A philosophical study of early ideas about probability, induction and statistical inference.* London: Cambridge University Press; I. Hacking. (1990). *The taming of chance.* Cambridge, UK: Cambridge University Press; S. M. Stigler. (1986). *The history of statistics: The measurement of uncertainty before 1900.* Cambridge, MA: Belknap Press of Harvard University Press.

3. See J. Gleick. (1992). *Genius: The life and science of Richard Feynman*. New York: Pantheon Books.

4. E. Marshall. (1986). Feynman issues his own shuttle report, attacking NASA's risk estimates. *Science, 232,* 1596.

5. Marshall, p. 1596.

6. Marshall, p. 1596.

7. Marshall, p. 1596.

8. For example, see Presidential Commission on the Space Shuttle Challenger Accident (1986). *Report of the Presidential Commission on the Space Shuttle Challenger Accident.* Washington, DC: Author.

9. S. R. Dalal, E. B. Fowlkes, & B. Hoadley. (1989). Risk analysis of the space shuttle: Pre-Challenger prediction of failure. *Journal of the American Statistical Association, 84,* 945–957.

10. Dalal, Fowlkes, & Hoadley, p. 945.

11. J. Neyman, & E. S. Pearson. (1933). On the problem of the most efficient tests of statistical hypotheses. *Philosophical Transactions of the Royal Society of London. Series A, 231,* 289–337.

12. Neyman & Pearson, p. 296.

13. Neyman & Pearson, p. 296.

14. H. C. Taylor, & J. T. Russell. (1939). The relationship of validity coefficients to the practical applications of tests in selection. *Journal of Applied Psychology, 23,* 565–578.

15. Q. McNemar. (1949). *Psychological statistics.* New York: Wiley.

16. W. P. Tanner, Jr., & J. A. Swets. (1954). A decision-making theory of visual detection. *Psychological Review, 61,* 401–409.

17. C. M. Judd, & G. H. McClelland. (1989). *Data analysis: A model comparison approach.* New York: Harcourt Brace Jovanovich (see especially pp. 89–99); see also C. M. Judd, & G. H. McClelland. (1995). Data analysis: Continuing issues in the everyday analysis of psychological data. *Annual Review of Psychology, 46,* 433–465 (see especially pp. 445–446).

18. Tanner & Swets. For an interesting description of the origins of the approach, see D. M. Green, & J. A. Swets. (1974). *Signal detection theory and psychophysics.* Huntington, NY: Krieger.

19. J. A. Swets. (1992). The science of choosing the right decision threshold in high stakes diagnostics. *American Psychologist, 47,* p. 523.

20. Swets, p. 522. For applications to policy formation, see K. R. Hammond, L. O. Harvey, Jr., & R. Hastie. (1992). Making better use of scientific knowledge: Separating truth from justice. *Psychological Science, 3,* 80–87.

21. R. S. Ledley, & L. B. Lusted. (1959). Reasoning foundations of medical diagnosis. *Science, 130,* 9–21.

22. B. D. Underwood. (1977). The thumb on the scales of justice: Burdens of persuasion in criminal cases. *Yale Law Journal, 86,* p. 1331.

23. Swets, p. 523.

24. Swets, p. 522.

25. I. B. Mason. (1982). A model for assessment of weather forecasts. *Australian Meteorological Magazine, 30,* 291–303.

26. Swets; R. S. Wigton, V. L. Hoellerich, J. P. Ornato, V. Leu, L. A. Mazzotta, & I.-H. C. Cheng. (1985). Use of clinical findings in the diagnosis of urinary tract infection in women. *Archives of Internal Medicine, 145,* 2222–2227; R. S. Wigton, J. L. Connor, & R. M. Centor. (1986). Transportability of a decision rule for the diagnosis of streptococcal pharyngitis. *Archives of Internal Medicine, 146,* 81–83.

27. Herrnstein & Murray, p. 68.

28. Herrnstein & Murray, p. 88.

29. For a broad discussion of numerical guidance in judicial decision making, see A. Lovegrove. (1989). *Judicial decision making, sentencing policy, and numerical guidance.* New York: Springer-Verlag.

30. B. Meier. (February 27, 1995). 'Sexual predators' finding sentence may last past jail. *New York Times,* p. A8.

31. For examples, see K. R. Hammond, & L. Adelman. (1976). Science, values, and human judgment. *Science, 194,* 389–396; K. R. Hammond, L. O. Harvey, Jr., & R. Hastie. (1992). Making better use of scientific knowledge: Separating truth from justice. *Psychological Science, 3,* 80–87.

32. See especially R. Dworkin. (1993). *Life's Dominion: An argument about abortion, euthanasia, and individual freedom.* New York: Knopf.

33. R. Dworkin. (January 13, 1994). Will Clinton's plan be fair? [Review of Health Security Act]. *The New York Review of Books,* pp. 20–25.

34. Dworkin, Will Clinton's plan be fair, p. 20.

35. Dworkin, Will Clinton's plan be fair, p. 21.

36. Dworkin, Will Clinton's plan be fair, p. 21.

37. Dworkin, Will Clinton's plan be fair, p. 21.

38. Dworkin, Will Clinton's plan be fair, p. 21.

39. Dworkin, Will Clinton's plan be fair, pp. 21–22.

40. Dworkin, Will Clinton's plan be fair, p. 22.

41. Dworkin, Will Clinton's plan be fair, p. 22.

42. Dworkin, Will Clinton's plan be fair, p. 22.

43. Dworkin, Will Clinton's plan be fair, p. 22.

44. G. Kolata. (December 27, 1993). Mammogram debate moving from test's merits to its cost. *New York Times,* p. A1.

45. Kolata, p. A9.

46. Kolata, p. A9.

47. Kolata, p. A9.

48. Kolata, p. A9.

49. Kolata, p. A9.

50. Kolata, p. A9.

51. Kolata, p. A1.

52. Kolata, p. A1.

53. J. Pernick. (January 16, 1994). The mammogram controversy: It confuses women, raises unfounded fears [Editorial]. *The New York Times,* p. 16.

54. A. M. Schlesinger, Jr. (1986). *The cycles of American history.* Boston: Houghlin Mifflin.

55. A. M. Schlesinger, Jr. (1965). *A thousand days: John F. Kennedy in the White House.* Boston: Houghton Mifflin.

56. Schlesinger, *The cycles of American history,* p. 27.

57. Schlesinger, *The cycles of American history,* p. 6.

58. H. Petroski. (1994). *Design paradigms: Case histories of error and judgment in engineering.* Cambridge, UK: Cambridge University Press, p. 166.

59. P. G. Sibly, & A. C. Walker. (1977). Structural accidents and their causes. *Proceedings of the Institution of Civil Engineers, 62,* 191–208.

60. Petroski, p. 168.

61. S. Lipin. (January 4, 1995). 'Portfolio management' catches on for bank loans. *The Wall Street Journal,* p. C1.

62. For a recent study of banker judgments in relation to less developed countries, see R. A. Somerville, & R. J. Taffler. (1995). Banker judgment versus formal forecasting models: The case of country risk assessment. *Journal of Banking and Finance, 19*, 281–297.

63. R. M. Cooper. (Ed.). (1991). *Food and drug law.* Washington, DC: Food and Drug Law Institute, pp. 16–17

64. L. McGinley. (December 12, 1994). GOP takes aim at FDA, seeking to ease way for approval of new drugs, medical products. *The Wall Street Journal,* p. A16. The struggle goes on and on. For a recent description of the current bitter battle between constituencies of each error preference see A. Lawler, & R. Stone. (1995). FDA: Congress mixes harsh medicine. *Science, 269,* 1038–1041.

65. J. Dewey. (1929). *The quest for certainty: A study of the relation of knowledge and action.* New York: Minton, Balch and Company.

3. *Coping with Uncertainty: The Rivalry Between Intuition and Analysis*

1. I. Berlin. (1978). *Russian thinkers.* New York: Viking Press, pp. 78–79.

2. B. Pascal. (1966). *Pensées* (translated with an introduction by A. J. Krailsheimer). Harmondsworth, UK: Penguin Books, pp. 210–212.

3. H. Gruber. (1981). *Darwin on man: A psychological study of scientific creativity* (2nd ed.). Chicago: University of Chicago Press.

4. C. M. Abernathy, & R. M. Hamm. (1994). *Surgical intuition: What it is and how to get it.* Philadelphia: Hanley & Belfus, p. 17.

5. H. Reichenbach. (1938). *Experience and prediction: An analysis of the foundations and the structure of knowledge.* Chicago: University of Chicago Press, p. 6.

6. D. J. Kevles. (August 2, 1993). Cold facts [Review of *Bad science: The short life and weird times of cold fusion*]. *The New Yorker,* p. 82.

7. J. Wechsler. (Ed.). (1978). *On aesthetics in science.* Cambridge, MA: MIT Press, p. 72.

8. F. Dyson. (1979). *Disturbing the universe.* New York: Harper and Row, pp. 55–56.

9. Dyson, p. 56.

10. J. Gleick. (1992). *Genius: The life and science of Richard Feynman.* New York: Pantheon Books, p. 244.

11. Gleick, p. 245.

12. Gleick, p. 245.

13. H. A. Simon. (1991). *Models of my life.* New York: Basic Books, p. 106.

14. Simon, p. 375.

15. See A. R. Damasio. (1994). *Descartes' error: Emotion, reason, and the human brain.* New York: G. P. Putnam.

16. E. S. Ferguson. (1992). *Engineering and the mind's eye.* Cambridge, MA: MIT Press, p. 37.

17. Ferguson, p. 37.

18. Ferguson, p. 170.

19. Ferguson, p. 194.

20. Ferguson, p. xii.

21. Ferguson, p. 41.

22. H. Petroski. (1994). *Design paradigms: Case histories of error and judgment in engineering.* Cambridge, UK: Cambridge University Press, p. 11.

23. Petroski, p. 11.

24. Petroski, p. 11.

25. Petroski, pp. 21–22.

26. M. J. Horwitz. (1992). *The transformation of American law 1870–1960: The crisis of legal orthodoxy.* New York: Oxford University Press, p. 109.

27. B. N. Cardozo. (1931). Mr. Justice Holmes. *Harvard Law Review, 44,* p. 684. For a recent definitive biography of Holmes, see G. E. White. (1993). *Justice Oliver Wendell Holmes: Law and the inner self.* New York: Oxford University Press. For a fascinating description of the "rise and fall" of Justice Holmes, see G. E. White. (1978). *Patterns of American legal thought.* Indianapolis: Bobbs-Merrill.

28. See P. P. Wiener. (1949/1969). *Evolution and the founders of pragmatism.* Gloucester, MA: Peter Smith.

29. O. W. Holmes. (1881/1923). *The common law.* Boston: Little, Brown, p. 1.

30. Lerner in O. W. Holmes. (1943). *The mind and faith of Justice Holmes: His speeches, essays, letters, and judicial opinions* (selected and edited with introduction and commentary by Max Lerner). Boston: Little, Brown, p. 46.

31. Lerner, p. 46.

32. O. W. Holmes. (1897). The path of the law. *Harvard Law Review, 10,* pp. 465–466.

33. Holmes, The path of the law, p. 466.

34. Lerner, p. 47.

35. S. J. Burton. (1985). *An introduction to law and legal reasoning.* Boston, MA: Little, Brown, p. 95.

36. R. Pound. (1921). *The spirit of the common law.* Boston: Marshall Jones.

37. R. Pound. (1923). The theory of judicial decision: A theory of judicial decision for today. *Harvard Law Review, 36,* p. 951.

38. Pound, The theory, p. 951.

39. R. Pound. (1908). Mechanical jurisprudence. *Columbia Law Review, 8,* 605–623.

40. Quoted in J. Elliot. (1941). *The debates in the several state conventions on the adoption of the federal Constitution as recommended by the general convention in Philadelphia, in 1787* (2nd ed.). Michie Co., Vol. 2, p. 293.

41. J. B. Treaster. (1992, March 11). Colombian gets 6 years for giving false name. *New York Times,* p. A19.

42. Treaster, p. A19.

43. A. Quindlen. (March 11, 1992). Marking time. *New York Times,* p. A21.

44. J. B. Weinstein. (1993, July). [Speech] The war on drugs: A judge goes AWOL. *Harper's Magazine,* p. 13.

45. D. L. Sackett. (1989). Inference and decision at the bedside. *Journal of Clinical Epidemiology, 42*(4), pp. 309–310.

46. Sackett, p. 315.

47. Sackett, p. 315.

48. Sackett, p. 315.

49. Sackett, p. 315.

50. I. Berlin. (1980). *Against the current: Essays in the history of ideas.* New York: Viking Press, pp. 264–265.

51. Berlin, *Against the current,* p. 276.

52. I. Berlin. (1981). *Personal Impressions.* New York: Viking Press, p. 27.

53. Berlin, *Personal impressions,* pp. 27–28.

54. V. Havel. (March 1, 1992). The end of the modern era. *New York Times,* sec. 4, p. 15.

55. H. L. Meltzer. (March 17, 1992). With apologies to Havel, let reason rule [Letter to the editor]. *New York Times,* p. A14.

56. D. E. Rosenbaum. (December 1, 1995). A budget debate not about dollars, but about whose plan makes sense. *New York Times,* p. A10.

57. G. Steiner. (1992, March 2). Books: Bad Friday. *The New Yorker*, p. 86.

58. M. Twain. (1896/1985). *Life on the Mississippi*. Toronto: Bantam Books, p. 47.

59. J. S. Bruner. (1986). *Actual minds, possible worlds*. Cambridge, MA: Harvard University Press.

60. Bruner, *Actual minds*, p. 11.

61. Bruner, *Actual minds*, p. 11.

62. N. Pennington, & R. Hastie. (1993a). The story model for juror decision making. In R. Hastie (Ed.), *Inside the juror: The psychology of juror decision making* (pp. 192–221). Cambridge, UK: Cambridge University Press, p. 193.

63. Pennington & Hastie, p. 205.

64. S. Epstein. (1994). Integration of the cognitive and the psychodynamic unconscious. *American Psychologist, 49*, p. 712.

65. Epstein, p. 709.

66. Epstein, p. 712; J. R. Anderson. (1976). *Language, memory, and thought*. Hillsdale, NJ: Erlbaum; J. R. Anderson. (1982). Acquisition of cognitive skill. *Psychological Review, 89*, 369–406; P. N. Johnson-Laird. (1983). *Mental models*. Cambridge, MA: Harvard University Press; E. Rosch. (1983). Prototype classification and logical classification: The two systems. In E. Scholnick (Ed.), *New trends in conceptual representation: Challenges to Piaget's theory* (pp. 73–86). Hillsdale, NJ: Erlbaum; T. Winograd. (1975). Frame representations and the declarative-procedural controversy. In D. G. Bobrow & A. M. Collins (Eds.), *Representation and understanding: Studies in cognitive science* (pp. 185–210). New York: Academic Press.

67. J. Piaget. (1973). The affective unconscious and the cognitive unconscious. *Journal of the American Psychoanalytic Association, 21*, 249–261.

68. A. Tversky, & D. Kahneman. (1974). Judgment under uncertainty: Heuristics and biases. *Science, 185*, 1124–1131; A. Tversky, & D. Kahneman. (1983). Extensional versus intuitive reasoning: The conjunction fallacy in probability judgment. *Psychological Review, 90*, 293–315.

69. Epstein, p. 713.

70. M. B. Brewer. (1988). A dual process model of impression formation. In T. K. Srull & R. S. Wyer (Eds.), *Advances in social cognition* (Vol. 1, pp. 1–36). Hillsdale, NJ: Erlbaum.

71. Epstein, p. 713.

72. P. Slovic, B. Fischhoff, & S. Lichtenstein. (1977). Behavioral decision theory. *Annual Review of Psychology, 28*, 1–39.

73. J. Bruner. (1961). *The process of education*. Cambridge: Harvard University Press, p. 13.

74. H. A. Simon. (1991). *Models of my life*. New York: Basic Books, pp. 104–105.

75. J. Bruner. (1992). Another look at New Look 1. *American Psychologist, 47*, 780–783, p. 782.

76. Plato. (1937). *Dialogues* (B. Jowett, Trans.). New York: Random House, Vol. 1, p. 777.

77. T. Powers. (1993). *Heisenberg's war: The secret history of the German bomb*. New York: Alfred A. Knopf, pp. 398–399.

78. Quoted in M. R. Westcott. (1968). *Toward a contemporary psychology of intuition: A historical, theoretical, and empirical inquiry*. New York: Holt, Rinehart, & Winston, p. 39.

79. Michael Polanyi, a well-known philosopher, described this form of cognition as "tacit knowing." See M. Polanyi. (1966). *The tacit dimension*. Garden City, NY: Doubleday. For a summary of Polanyi's point of view, see R. Gelwick. (1977). *The way of discovery: An introduction to the thought of Michael Polanyi*. New York: Oxford University Press.

80. Readers who prefer mathematical or statistical descriptions of the application of the lens model can read an excellent account in R. Cooksey. (1996). *Judgment analysis: Theory, methods, and applications.* San Diego: Academic Press.

81. D. Kahneman, P. Slovic, & A Tversky. (Eds.). (1982). *Judgment under uncertainty: Heuristics and biases.* Cambridge, UK: Cambridge University Press; J. W. Payne, J. R. Bettman, & E. J. Johnson. (1992). Behavioral decision research: A constructive processing perspective. *Annual Review of Psychology, 43,* 87–131; G. F. Pitz, & N. J. Sachs. (1984). Judgment and decision: Theory and application. *Annual Review of Psychology, 35,* 139–163; Slovic, Fischhoff, & Lichtenstein.

82. P. Slovic. (1976). Towards understanding and improving decisions. In I. Salkovitz (Ed.), *Science technology, and the modern Navy: Thirtieth anniversary 1946–1976.* Arlington, VA: Department of the Navy, Office of Naval Research.

83. R. M. Dawes. (1988). *Rational choice in an uncertain world.* San Diego: Harcourt, Brace, Jovanovich, p. 7.

84. For similar conclusions see R. M. Hogarth. (1987). *Judgement and choice: The psychology of decision* (2nd ed.). Chichester, UK: Wiley; Kahneman, Slovic, & Tversky; R. L. Keeney. (1992). *Value-focused thinking: A path to creative decisionmaking.* Cambridge, MA: Harvard University Press; P. E. Meehl. (1954). *Clinical vs. statistical prediction: A theoretical analysis and a review of the evidence.* Minneapolis, MN: University of Minnesota Press; and J. F. Yates. (1990). *Judgment and decision making.* Englewood Cliffs, NJ: Prentice-Hall.

85. E. Brunswik. (1956). *Perception and the representative design of psychological experiments* (2nd ed.). Berkeley, CA: University of California Press, p. 93.

86. J. March. (1978). Bounded rationality, ambiguity, and the engineering of choice. *Bell Journal of Economics, 9,* p. 588.

87. See also C. E. Lindblom, & D. K. Cohen. (1979). *Usable knowledge: Social science and social problem solving.* New Haven: Yale University Press.

88. L. L. Lopes, & G. C. Oden. (1991). The rationality of intelligence. In E. Eells & T. Maruszewski (Eds.), *Probability and rationality: Studies on L. Jonathan Cohen's philosophy of science* (pp. 199–223). Amsterdam: Rodopi.

89. P. K. Howard. (1994). *The death of common sense: How law is suffocating America.* New York: Random House.

90. Brunswik, pp. 91–92.

91. See Lopes & Oden.

92. Brunswik, p. 92.

93. Brunswik, pp. 92–93.

94. Brunswik, p. 93.

95. V. Denes-Raj, & S. Epstein. (1994). Conflict between experiential and rational processing: When people behave against their better judgment. *Journal of Personality and Social Psychology, 66,* 819–827; S. Epstein, A. Lipson, C. Holstein, & E. Huh. (1992). Irrational reactions to negative outcomes: Evidence for two conceptual systems. *Journal of Personality and Social Psychology, 62,* 328–339; L. A. Kirkpatrick, & S. Epstein. (1992). Cognitive-experiential self-theory and subjective probability: Further evidence for two conceptual systems. *Journal of Personality and Social Psychology, 63,* 534–544.

96. Epstein, p. 714.

97. Epstein, p. 714.

98. Epstein, p. 714.

99. Epstein, p. 715.

100. Epstein, p. 715. Cf. the final sentence to Brunswik's remark quoted earlier.

101. Brunswik, p. 93.

102. Berlin, *Russian thinkers,* p. 78.

103. B. Berger, N. Glazer, & C. Stimpson. (1991). The idea of the university. *Partisan Review, 58*, 315–349. p. 322.

104. G. Holton. (1993). *Science and anti-science*. Cambridge, MA: Harvard University Press, pp. 152–153.

105. Holton, p. 153.

106. Holton, p. 153.

107. Havel.

## 4. Tension Between Coherence and Correspondence Theories of Competence

1. N. Adler. (1994). *Adolescent sexual behavior looks traditional—But looks are deceiving*. Washington, DC: Federation of Behavioral, Psychological, and Cognitive Sciences, p. 6.

2. Adler, p. 7.

3. Adler, p. 7.

4. G. Lowenstein, & F. Furstenberg. (1991). Is teenage sexual behavior rational? *Journal of Applied Social Psychology, 21*, p. 983.

5. Although coherence and correspondence theories of truth are well known among philosophers, there are few comprehensive, comparative treatments of them. The reason for this appears in the first sentence of a philosopher's recent book: "You are holding in your hand the only book-length introduction to theories of truth" (R. L. Kirkham. [1992]. *Theories of truth: A critical introduction*. Cambridge, MA: MIT Press, p. ix). The author notes that "this is a surprising state of affairs in view of the importance [of] theories of truth" (p. ix). Kirkham describes these theories, among others, in considerable detail, but his description will be intelligible only to those competent in analytical philosophy and fluent in symbolic logic. Despite my limited description of these theories—and the agonies these limitations will inflict on philosophers—I remain convinced that the basic ideas of these theories will enable readers to understand much in the field of human judgment and social policy that would otherwise be confusing. The reader who wishes to learn more will find more in J. Searle. (1995). *The construction of social reality*. New York: Free Press; more complex treatments can be found in N. Rescher. (1982). *The coherence theory of truth*. Washington, DC: University Press of America, and in D. Davidson. (1984). *Inquiries into truth and interpretation*. Oxford, UK: Oxford University Press.

6. R. P. Feynman. (1988, February). An outsider's inside view of the Challenger inquiry. *Physics Today*, pp. 26–37.

7. Feynman, p. 33.

8. Feynman, p. 34.

9. S. R. Dalal, E. B. Fowlkes, & B. Hoadley. (1989). Risk analysis of the space shuttle: Pre-Challenger prediction of failure. *Journal of the American Statistical Association, 84*, p. 945.

10. D. M. Eddy. (1982). Probabilistic reasoning in clinical medicine: Problems and opportunities. In D. Kahneman, P. Slovic, & A. Tversky (Eds.), *Judgment under uncertainty: Heuristics and biases* (pp. 249–267). Cambridge, UK: Cambridge University Press.

11. Eddy, p. 252.

12. Eddy, p. 252.

13. Eddy, p. 253.

14. See J. Dowie, & A. Elstein. (Eds.). (1988). *Professional judgment: A reader in clinical decision making*. New York: Cambridge University Press.

15. M. Moser. (1994). Can the cost of care be contained and quality of care maintained in the management of hypertension? *Archives of Internal Medicine, 134*, p. 1671.

16. P. Newbold, & T. Bos. (1990). *Introductory business forecasting.* Cincinnati, OH: South-Western, p. 347.

17. W. A. McEachern. (1991). *Economics: A contemporary introduction* (2nd ed.). Cincinnati: South-Western, p. 13.

18. McEachern, p. 10.

19. Newbold & Bos, p. 410.

20. Newbold & Bos, p. 410.

21. Quoted in C. D. Bowen. (1966). *Miracle at Philadelphia: The story of the Constitutional Convention, May to September, 1787.* Boston: Little, Brown, p. 44.

22. L. Laudan. (1981). A problem-solving approach to scientific progress. In I. Hacking (Ed.), *Scientific revolutions* (pp. 144–155). Oxford: Oxford University Press, p. 146. See also the *Encyclopedia of Philosophy:* Prior, A. N. (1967). Correspondence theory of truth. In P. Edwards (Ed.), *Encyclopedia of Philosophy* (Vol. 2, pp. 223–232). New York: Macmillan and Free Press; A. R. White. (1967). Coherence theory of truth. In P. Edwards (Ed.), *Encyclopedia of Philosophy* (Vol. 2, pp. 130–133). New York: Macmillan and Free Press. For technical discussions see R. G. Millikan. (1984). *Language, thought, and other biological categories: New foundations for realism.* Cambridge, MA: MIT Press; N. Rescher. (1982). *The coherence theory of truth.* Washington, DC: University Press of America.

23. ORAU Panel on Health Effects of Low-Frequency Electric and Magnetic Fields. (1993). EMF and cancer [Letter to the editor]. *Science, 260,* p. 14.

24. K. J. Vicente. (1990). Coherence- and correspondence-driven work domains: Implications for systems design. *Behaviour & Information Technology, 9,* p. 493.

25. W. Edwards. (1954). The theory of decision making. *Psychological Bulletin, 41,* 380–417.

26. K. R. Hammond. (1955). Probabilistic functioning and the clinical method. *Psychological Review, 62,* 255–262.

27. P. Slovic, & S. Lichtenstein. (1971). Comparison of Bayesian and regression approaches to the study of information processing in judgment. *Organizational Behavior and Human Performance, 6,* 649–744; P. Slovic, & S. Lichtenstein. (1973). Comparison of Bayesian and regression approaches to the study of information processing in judgment. In L. Rappoport & D. A. Summers (Eds.), *Human judgment and social interaction* (pp. 16–108). New York: Holt, Rinehart, & Winston.

28. D. von Winterfeldt, & W. Edwards. (1986). *Decision analysis and behavioral research.* Cambridge, UK: Cambridge University Press.

29. R. Hastie, & K. A. Rasinski. (1988). The concept of accuracy in social judgment. In D. Bar-Tal & A. W. Kruglanski (Eds.), *The social psychology of knowledge* (pp. 193–208). Cambridge, UK: Cambridge University Press.

30. J. F. Yates. (1990). *Judgment and decision making.* Englewood Cliffs, NJ: Prentice-Hall.

31. Yates, pp. 137–139.

32. K. R. Hammond. (1990). Functionalism and illusionism: Can integration by usefully achieved? In R. M. Hogarth (Ed.), *Insights in decision making: A tribute to Hillel J. Einhorn* (pp. 227–261). Chicago: University of Chicago Press, p. 256.

33. L. J. Savage. (1954). *The foundations of statistics.* New York: Wiley, p. 308.

34. D. Frisch, & R. T. Clemen. (1994). Beyond expected utility: Rethinking behavioral decision research. *Psychological Bulletin, 116,* p. 48.

35. Frisch & Clemen, p. 49.

36. Frisch & Clemen, p. 52.

37. H. A. Simon. (1983). *Reason in human affairs.* Stanford, CA: Stanford University Press, pp. 13–14.

38. Simon, pp. 16–17. Despite the sharply worded argument by Simon, it is doubtful that the SEU theory is headed for extinction. In 1991, for example, Baron and Brown, two prominent researchers in the field of judgment and decision making, reprinted an article published in the *Washington Post* in 1988 in which they used SEU theory to demonstrate the value of teaching decision making to adolescents; see J. Baron, & R. Brown. (1991). Prologue. In J. Baron & R. Brown (Eds.), *Teaching decision making to adolescents* (pp. 1–6). Hillsdale, NJ: Erlbaum.

39. Vilayanur Ramachandran quoted by S. Blakeslee. (1996, January 23). Figuring out the brain from its acts of denial. *New York Times*, p. B7.

40. Blakeslee, p. B7.

41. Blakeslee, p. B7.

42. See A. Tversky, & D. Kahneman. (1974). Judgment under uncertainty: Heuristics and biases. *Science, 185*, 1124–1131; et seq.

43. For example, see R. M. Dawes. (1988). *Rational choice in an uncertain world*. San Diego: Harcourt, Brace, Jovanovich.

44. See D. Kahneman, P. Slovic, & A. Tversky. (Eds.). (1982). *Judgment under uncertainty: Heuristics and biases*. Cambridge, UK: Cambridge University Press; et seq.

45. A. Tversky, & D. Kahneman. (1983). Extensional versus intuitive reasoning: The conjunction fallacy in probability judgment. *Psychological Review, 90*, p. 313.

46. For example, see W. Edwards. (1992). Discussion: Of human skills. *Organizational Behavior and Human Decision Processes, 53*, 267–277; D. Funder. (1987). Errors and mistakes: Evaluating the accuracy of social judgment. *Psychological Bulletin, 101*, 75–90; G. Gigerenzer. (1991a). From tools to theories: A heuristic of discovery in cognitive psychology. *Psychological Review, 98*, 254–267; G. Gigerenzer. (1991b). How to make cognitive illusions disappear: Beyond "heuristics and biases." *European Review of Social Psychology, 2*, 83–115; G. Gigerenzer. (1991c). On cognitive illusions and rationality. In E. Eells & T. Maruszewski (Eds.), *Probability and rationality: Studies on L. Jonathan Cohen's philosophy of science* (pp. 225–249). Amsterdam: Rodopi; G. Gigerenzer, U. Hoffrage, & H. Kleinbölting. (1991). Probabilistic mental models: A Brunswikian theory of confidence. *Psychological Review, 98*, 506–528.

47. R. L. Klatzky, J. Geiwitz, & S. C. Fischer. (1994). Using statistics in clinical practice: A gap between training and application. In M. S. Bogner (Ed.), *Human error in medicine* (pp. 123–140). Hillsdale, NJ: Erlbaum.

48. D. N. Kleinmuntz, & D. A. Schkade. (1993). Information displays and decision processes. *Psychological Science, 4*, p. 221.

49. D. Kahneman, & A. Tversky. (1984). Choices, values, and frames. *American Psychologist, 39*, p. 343.

50. Kahneman & Tversky, p. 343.

51. Kahneman & Tversky, p. 343.

52. For examples, see H. R. Arkes, & K. R. Hammond. (Eds.). (1986). *Judgment and decision making: An interdisciplinary reader*. Cambridge, UK: Cambridge University Press; Kahneman, Slovic, & Tversky. For a textbook completely devoted to this point of view, see especially S. Plous. (1993). *The psychology of judgment and decision making*. Philadelphia: Temple University Press.

53. For example, see Edwards, Discussion.

54. J. R. Anderson. (1990). *The adaptive character of thought*. Hillsdale, NJ: Erlbaum.

55. B. Brehmer. (1994). The psychology of linear judgement models. *Acta Psychologica, 87*, 137–154; E. Brunswik. (1952). The conceptual framework of psychology. In *International encyclopedia of unified science* (Vol. 1, no. 10, pp. 4–102). Chicago: University of Chicago Press; E. Brunswik. (1956). *Perception and the representative design of psychological*

*experiments* (2nd ed.). Berkeley, CA: University of California Press; S. Epstein. (1994). Integration of the cognitive and the psychodynamic unconscious. *American Psychologist, 49,* 709–724; K. R. Hammond. (Ed.). (1966). *The psychology of Egon Brunswik* (2nd ed.). New York: Holt, Rinehart, and Winston; K. R. Hammond, R. M. Hamm, J. Grassia, & T. Pearson. (1986). Direct comparison of the efficacy of intuitive and analytical cognition in expert judgment. *IEEE Transactions on Systems, Man, and Cybernetics, 17,* 753–770.

   56. Brunswik, The conceptual framework; *Perception and the representative design.*

   57. Hammond, Probabilistic functioning.

   58. For an anthology of studies, see B. Brehmer, & C. R. B. Joyce. (Eds.). (1988). *Human judgment: The SJT view.* Amsterdam: Elsevier. For a detailed application of the theory, see R. Cooksey. (1996). *Judgment analysis: Theory, methods, and applications.* San Diego: Academic Press. Bruner, Goodnow, & Austin's classic *The Study of Thinking* was dedicated to Brunswik: J. S. Bruner, J. Goodnow, & G. A. Austin. (1956). *A study of thinking.* New York: Wiley.

## 5. The Evolutionary Roots of Correspondence Competence

   1. T. von Schantz, G. Göransson, G. Andersson, I. Fröberg, M. Grahn, & A. Helgée, & Witzell, H. (1989). Female choice selects for a viability-based male trait in pheasants. *Nature, 337,* p. 166.

   2. von Schantz et al., p. 166.

   3. von Schantz et al., p. 166.

   4. G. Göransson, T. von Schantz, I. Fröberg, A. Helgée, & H. Wittzell. (1990). Male characteristics, viability and harem size in the pheasant, *Phasianus colchicus. Animal Behaviour, 40,* p. 89.

   5. E. Brunswik. (1943). Organismic achievement and environmental probability. *Psychological Review, 50,* 255–272; E. Brunswik. (1952). The conceptual framework of psychology. In *International encyclopedia of unified science* (Vol. 1, no. 10, pp. 4–102). Chicago: University of Chicago Press; E. Brunswik. (1956). *Perception and the representative design of psychological experiments* (2nd ed.). Berkeley, CA: University of California Press; see also K. R. Hammond. (Ed.). (1966). *The psychology of Egon Brunswik* (2nd ed.). New York: Holt, Rinehart, and Winston.

   6. von Schantz et al., p. 166.

   7. C. Darwin. (1874). *The descent of man and selection in relation to sex* (2nd ed.). New York: A. L. Fowle, p. vi.

   8. D. M. Buss. (1992). Mate preference mechanisms: Consequences for partner choice and intrasexual competition. In J. H. Barkow, L. Cosmides, & J. Tooby (Eds.), *The adapted mind: Evolutionary psychology and the generation of culture* (pp. 249–266). New York: Oxford University Press.

   9. Buss, p. 251.

   10. Buss, p. 249.

   11. Buss, p. 250.

   12. Buss, p. 250.

   13. Buss, p. 251. Buss has brought his research results together in a book that affords fascinating evidence for the correspondence view of judgment: D. M. Buss. (1994). *The evolution of desire: Strategies of human mating.* New York: Basic Books.

   14. F. J. Bernieri, J. S. Gillis, & J. M. Davis. (1993). *The judgment of rapport: A lens model analysis.* Corvallis: Oregon State University; J. S. Gillis, F. J. Bernieri, & E. Wooten. (1995). The effects of stimulus medium and feedback on the judgment of rapport. *Organizational Behavior and Human Decision Processes, 63,* 33–45.

15. F. Bernieri, & J. Gillis. (1995). The judgment of rapport: A cross-cultural comparison between American and Greeks. *Journal of Nonverbal Behavior, 19*, 115–130.

16. For an excellent review of bird migration, see P. Berthold. (1993). *Bird migration: A general survey* (H-G Bauer & T. Tomlinson, Trans.). Oxford, UK: Oxford University Press; see also R. Ranvaud, K. Schmidt-Koenig, J. U. Ganzhorn, J. Kiepenheuer, O. C. Gasparotto, & L. R. G. Britto. (1991). The initial orientation of homing pigeons at the magnetic equator: Compass mechanisms and the effect of applied magnets. *Journal of Experimental Biology, 161*, 299–314.

17. H. G. Wallraff. (1990). Navigation by homing pigeons. *Ethology Ecology & Evolution, 2*, p. 83.

18. L. Seachrist. (1994). Sea turtles master migration with magnetic memories. *Science, 264*, p. 661, referring to work by Kenneth Lohmann.

19. D. Singer. (June 19, 1994). Surprise! Kim Il Sung smiles for the camera. *New York Times*, sec. 4, p. 5.

20. See Gillis for studies of "narrow focus" and "wide focus" tasks in his laboratory studies of schizophrenic patients.

21. R. Byrne. (1995). *The thinking ape: Evolutionary origins of intelligence*. Oxford, UK: Oxford University Press, p. 177.

22. Byrne, p. 178.

23. Byrne, p. 182. The term "cognitive map" was introduced by Edward Tolman, the eminent psychologist at the University of California at Berkeley in 1948 in an article titled "Cognitive Maps in Rats and Man" (E. C. Tolman. [1948]. Cognitive maps in rats and men. *Psychological Review, 55*[4], 189–208). It was regarded with great suspicion by the positivist psychologists of the time and has been used far more often outside than within the field of psychology.

24. G. Hausfater, (1975). *Dominance and reproduction in baboons (Papio cynocephalus)*. Basel: S. Karger.

25. Byrne, p. 199.

26. Byrne, pp. 205–206.

27. Byrne, p. 207.

28. Bernieri & Gillis.

29. Byrne, p. 232.

30. Byrne, p. 232.

31. Byrne, p. 233.

32. Byrne, p. 234.

33. For a discussion of the genetics of courtship behavior in Drosophila, see J. C. Hall. (1994). The mating of a fly. *Science, 264*, 1702–1714.

34. For a detailed treatment of these questions, particularly the origin of language in relation to the developing architecture of the brain, see M. Donald. (1991). *Origins of the modern mind: Three stages in the evolution of culture and cognition*. Cambridge, MA: Harvard University Press.

35. C. Darwin. (1872/1965). *The expression of the emotions in man and animals*. Chicago: University of Chicago Press.

36. K. D. Schick, & N. Toth. (1993). *Making silent stones speak: Human evolution and the dawn of technology*. New York: Simon & Schuster, p. 77.

37. S. J. Mithen. (1990). *Thoughtful foragers: A study of prehistoric decision making*. Cambridge, UK: Cambridge University Press, p. 1.

38. Mithen, p. 59.

39. Mithen, p. 70.

40. For a review, see B. Brehmer, & C. R. B. Joyce. (Eds.). (1988). *Human judgment: The SJT view*. Amsterdam: Elsevier.

41. D. Funder. (1987). Errors and mistakes: Evaluating the accuracy of social judgment. *Psychological Bulletin, 101*, 75–90.

42. For detailed descriptions of Quetelet's innovative work, see I. Hacking. (1990). *The taming of chance*. Cambridge, UK: Cambridge University Press, pp. 105–114; S. M. Stigler. (1986). *The history of statistics: The measurement of uncertainty before 1900*. Cambridge, MA: Belknap Press of Harvard University Press, pp. 162–182. *Social Indicators Research* issued its first volume 100 years after Quetelet's death in 1874.

43. P. Thevanayagam. (1993, June 3). Index of leading indicators rises an anemic 0.1%. *The Wall Street Journal*, p. A2.

44. R. J. A. Skidelsky. (1992). *John Maynard Keynes: The economist as savior (1920– 1937)*. New York: Penguin Press, p. 106.

45. Skidelsky, p. 106.

46. H. F. Myers. (1993, June 14). The outlook: Economy may benefit from Clinton's woes. *The Wall Street Journal*, p. A1.

47. A. Raghavan. (August 16, 1993). Bear market isn't in sight, some think, noting tempered optimism of investors. *The Wall Street Journal*, p. C1.

48. L. Harper. (May 11, 1994). Commerce department now measures economy's impact on the environment. *The Wall Street Journal*, p. A2.

49. Greenspan takes the gold. (February 28, 1994). *The Wall Street Journal*, p. A14.

50. R. Woodward. (1994). *The agenda*. New York: Simon & Schuster, pp. 103–131.

51. W. J. Bennett. (1993). *The index of leading cultural indicators: Vol. 1*. Washington, DC: Heritage Foundation, p. i.

52. Bennett, p. i.

53. Bennett, p. i.

54. Bennett, p. i.

55. Bennett, p. i.

56. Bennett, p. 1.

57. A. Etzioni. (1993). Individual rights and community responsibilities. *The Futurist, 27*(6), p. 64.

58. S. H. Schneider. (1994). Detecting climatic change signals: Are there any "fingerprints"? *Science, 263*, p. 341.

59. An excellent treatment of the topic of the measurement and use of social indicators in social policy formation can be found in J. E. Innes. (1990). *Knowledge and public policy: The search for meaningful indicators*. New Brunswick: Transaction.

60. J. A. Del Regato. (1970). Diagnosis, treatment and prognosis. In L. V. Ackerman (Ed.), *Cancer*. St. Louis: Mosby, pp. 860–861; quoted by D. M. Eddy. (1982). Probabilistic reasoning in clinical medicine: Problems and opportunities. In D. Kahneman, P. Slovic, & A. Tversky (Eds.), *Judgment under uncertainty: Heuristics and biases* (pp. 249–267). Cambridge, UK: Cambridge University Press, p. 250.

61. Eddy, p. 250.

62. D. G. Burnside, & E. Faithfull. (1993). Judging range trend: Interpretation of rangeland monitoring data drawn from sites in the western Australian shrublands. *Rangeland Journal, 15*, 247–269.

63. Burnside & Faithfull, p. 247.

64. L. I. Dalgleish. (1988). Decision making in child abuse cases: Applications of social judgment theory and signal detection theory. In B. Brehmer & C. R. B. Joyce (Eds.), *Human judgment: The SJT view* (pp. 317–360). Amsterdam: Elsevier; L. I. Dalgleish. (1991, April). *Assessment of perceived risk in child protection: A model, some data and implications for practice*. Address to Child Maltreatment Conference, Prince of Wales Children's Hospital, Randwick, Sydney, Australia; L. I. Dalgleish & E. C. Drew. (1989). The relationship of child

abuse indicators to the assessment of perceived risk and to the court's decision to separate. *Child Abuse and Neglect, 13*, 491–506.

65. C. Cobb, T. Halstead, & J. Rowe. (1995). If the GDP is up, why is America down? *Atlantic Monthly, 276*(4), 59–60, 62–68, 70, 72–73, 76, 78.

66. Cobb et al., p. 65.

67. Cobb et al., p. 65.

68. Cobb et al., p. 66.

69. Cobb et al., p. 66.

70. C. W. J. Granger. (1989). *Forecasting in business and economics* (2nd ed.). New York: Academic Press, p. 169.

71. N. Lemann. (1995a). The great sorting. *The Atlantic Monthly, 276*(3), 84–88, 90–92, 94, 96–98, 100; N. Lemann. (1995b). The structure of success in America. *The Atlantic Monthly, 276*(2), 41–43, 56, 48, 50–53, 56, 58–60.

72. For a good description of Fechner's place in history, see G. Gigerenzer, Z. Swijtink, T. Porter, L. Daston, J. Beatty, & L. Krueger. (1989). *The empire of chance: How probability changed science and everyday life.* New York: Cambridge University Press. See also E. G. Boring. (1942). *Sensation and perception in the history of psychology.* New York: Appleton-Century.

73. For a detailed history, see Boring.

74. J. J. Gibson. (1950). *The perception of the visual world.* Boston: Houghton Mifflin, p. 14. The results of Gibson's life work can be seen in J. J. Gibson. (1979). *The ecological approach to visual perception.* Boston: Houghton Mifflin. He would be dismayed to see the extent to which optical illusions continue to dominate in the textbooks of today.

75. E. Brunswik. (1944). Distal focussing of perception: Size constancy in a representative sample of situations. *Psychological Monographs*, No. 254; Brunswik, *Perception and the representative design.*

76. Brunswik, *Perception and the representative design,* p. 47.

77. For an attempt to demonstrate this point, see K. R. Hammond. (1990). Functionalism and illusionism: Can integration by usefully achieved? In R. M. Hogarth (Ed.), *Insights in decision making: A tribute to Hillel J. Einhorn* (pp. 227–261). Chicago, IL: University of Chicago Press.

78. T. R. Sarbin. (1941). Clinical psychology: Art or science? *Psychometrika, 6*, 391–401; T. R. Sarbin. (1942). A contribution to the study of actuarial and individual methods of prediction. *American Journal of Sociology, 48*, 593–602; T. R. Sarbin. (1944). The logic of prediction in psychology. *Psychological Review, 51*, 210–228.

79. A. S. Elstein, G. B. Holzman, M. M. Ravitch, W. A. Metheny, M. M. Holmes, R. B. Hoppe, M. L. Rothert, & D. R. Rovner. (1986). Comparison of physicians' decisions regarding estrogen replacement therapy for menopausal women and decisions derived from a decision analytic model. *American Journal of Medicine, 80*, 246–258.

80. P. E. Meehl. (1954). *Clinical vs. statistical prediction: A theoretical analysis and a review of the evidence.* Minneapolis, MN: University of Minnesota Press, p. 6.

81. Meehl, p. 137.

82. Meehl, p. 136.

83. Meehl, p. 132.

84. K. R. Hammond. (1955). Probabilistic functioning and the clinical method. *Psychological Review, 62*, 255–262.

85. H. A. Wallace. (1923). What is in the corn judge's mind? *Journal of the American Society of Agronomy, 15*, 300–304.

86. T. R. Sarbin. (1986). Prediction and clinical inference: Forty years later. *Journal of Personality Assessment, 50*, p. 362.

87. R. M. Dawes, D. Faust, & P. E. Meehl. (1989). Clinical versus actuarial judgment. *Science, 243,* 1668–1673.

88. Sarbin, Prediction and clinical inference, p. 368.

89. J. Dewey. (1922). *Human nature and conduct.* New York: Henry Holt, pp. 155–156; quoted in Sarbin, Prediction and clinical inference, p. 366.

90. Sarbin, Prediction and clinical inference, p. 368.

91. Sarbin, Prediction and clinical inference, p. 368.

92. P. E. Meehl. (1986). Causes and effects of my disturbing little book. *Journal of Personality Assessment, 50,* 370–375.

93. Meehl, Causes and effects, p. 370.

94. Meehl, Causes and effects, p. 372.

95. Meehl, *Clinical vs. statistical prediction,* p. 119.

96. Meehl, Causes and effects, p. 372.

97. See Brehmer & Joyce.

98. Meehl, Causes and effects, p. 372.

99. See Brehmer & Joyce.

100. Meehl, Causes and effects, p. 372.

101. Brehmer & Joyce; K. R. Hammond, & D. A. Summers. (1972). Cognitive control. *Psychological Review, 79,* 58–67.

102. Dawes, Faust, & Meehl, p. 1672.

103. Dawes, Faust, & Meehl, p. 1672.

104. C. McCauley. (1991). Selection of National Science Foundation graduate fellows: A case study of psychologists failing to apply what they know about decision making. *American Psychologist, 46,* p. 1287.

105. McCauley, p. 1287.

106. McCauley, p. 1291.

107. E. L. Thorndike. (1918). Fundamental theorems in judging men. *Journal of Applied Psychology, 2,* 67–76.

108. E. L. Thorndike. (1920). A constant error in psychological ratings. *Journal of Applied Psychology, 4,* 25–29.

109. Cf. Brunswik, *Perception and the representative design,* p. 40.

110. R. Pintner. (1918). Intelligence as estimated from photographs. *Psychological Review, 25,* 286–296.

111. P. C. Gaskill, N. Fenton, & J. P. Porter. (1927). Judging the intelligence of boys from their photographs. *Journal of Applied Psychology, 11,* 394–403.

112. S. G. Estes. (1938). Judging personality from expressive behavior. *Journal of Abnormal and Social Psychology, 33,* 216–236.

113. M. S. Viteles, & K. R. Smith. (1932). The prediction of vocational aptitude and success from photographs. *Journal of Experimental Psychology, 15,* 615–629.

114. P. Ekman, & M. O'Sullivan. (1991). Who can catch a liar? *American Psychologist, 46,* 913–920.

115. L. D. Anderson. (1921). Estimating intelligence by means of printed photographs. *Journal of Applied Psychology, 5,* 152–155.

116. G. U. Cleeton, & F. B. Knight. (1924). Validity of character judgments based on external criteria. *Journal of Applied Psychology, 8,* p. 215.

117. Cleeton & Knight, p. 215.

118. Cleeton & Knight, p. 215.

119. Cleeton & Knight, p. 216.

120. See, for example, p. 25 of the review by Jones, who uses the results of such a study

to support an important conclusion without recognizing this flaw in the study: E. E. Jones. (1990). *Interpersonal perception*. New York: Freeman.

121. For the same exorbitant imbalance, see also S. Plous. (1993). *The psychology of judgment and decision making*. Philadelphia: Temple University Press.

122. L. J. Cronbach. (1955). Processes affecting scores on "understanding of others" and "assumed similarity." *Psychological Bulletin, 52,* 177–193.

123. Jones, p. 25.

124. For example, see Brunswik, *Perception and the representative design;* Hammond, *The psychology of Egon Brunswik.*

125. Jones, p. 25.

126. Funder, Errors and mistakes; D. C. Funder, & C. D. Sneed. (1993). Behavioral manifestations of personality: An ecological approach to judgmental accuracy. *Journal of Personality and Social Psychology, 64,* 479–490.

127. Funder, Errors and mistakes, p. 75.

128. Funder, Errors and mistakes, p. 76.

129. Jones, p. 25.

130. Jones, p. 33.

131. Jones, p. 33.

132. Funder, Errors and mistakes, p. 76.

133. Funder, Errors and mistakes, p. 76.

134. Funder, Errors and mistakes, p. 84.

135. Funder & Sneed, p. 479.

136. Funder & Sneed, p. 489.

137. L. Ross, & R. E. Nisbett. (1991). *The person and the situation: Perspectives of social psychology*. New York: McGraw-Hill.

138. D. C. Funder. (1992). Everything you know is wrong [Review of *The person and the situation: Perspectives of social psychology*]. *Contemporary Psychology, 37,* p. 319.

139. Funder, Everything you know is wrong, p. 319.

*Part III. Compromise and Reconciliation*

1. K. Popper. (1963). *Conjectures and refutations: The growth of scientific knowledge*. New York: Harper & Row, p. 241.

2. J. Bronowski. (1977). *A sense of the future*. Cambridge, MA: MIT Press, p. 101.

*6. Reducing Rivalry Through Compromise*

1. See S. Epstein. (1994). Integration of the cognitive and the psychodynamic unconscious. *American Psychologist, 49,* 709–724.

2. J. S. Bruner. (1986). *Actual minds, possible worlds*. Cambridge, MA: Harvard University Press; J. S. Bruner, J. Goodnow, & G. A. Austin. (1956). *A study of thinking*. New York: Wiley.

3. See especially J. Bruner. (1962). *On knowing: Essays for the left hand*. New York: Atheneum. For an informative history of the development of interest in intuitive cognition, see Chapter 1 in Bruner, *Actual minds.*

4. Bruner, *Actual minds,* p. 11.

5. Bruner, *Actual minds,* p. 11.

6. Thomas Reid has been described as one of the early exponents of common sense; see Chapter 2 ["Of Common Sense"], Essay VI ["Of Judgment"] in T. Reid. (1785). *Essays*

*on the intellectual powers of man*. Edinburgh, Scotland: John Bell. For further discussion of the topic, see K. R. Popper., Sir (1972). *Objective knowledge: An evolutionary approach*. Oxford, UK: Clarendon Press.

7. B. Russell. (1945). *A history of western philosophy and its connection with political and social circumstances from the earliest times to the present day*. New York: Simon & Schuster, p. 161.

8. Russell, p. 162.

9. Russell, p. 165.

10. Russell, p. 180.

11. E. O. Wilson. (1992). *The diversity of life*. Cambridge, MA: Harvard University Press, pp. 85–86.

12. Wilson, p. 86.

13. See, for example, the *American Heritage Dictionary*, 1992.

14. S. Mydans. (April 9, 1993). Prosecutor in officers' case ends with focus on beating. *New York Times*, p. A8.

15. D. G. McCullough. (1992). *Truman*. New York: Simon & Schuster.

16. W. Clinton. (February 16, 1993). Transcript of president's address on the economy. *New York Times*, p. A14.

17. G. F. Kennan. (1993). *Around the cragged hill: A personal and political philosophy*. New York: Norton, p. 145.

18. P. K. Howard. (1994). *The death of common sense: How law is suffocating America*. New York: Random House.

19. F. Heider. (1958). *The psychology of interpersonal relations*. New York: Wiley, p. 5.

20. Heider, pp. 5–6.

21. A. N. Whitehead. (1929). *The aims of education and other essays*. New York: New American Library, p. 110; quoted in Heider, p. 6.

22. H. A. Simon. (1991). *Models of my life*. New York: Basic Books, p. 360.

23. Simon, p. 361.

24. R. E. Nisbett, & L. Ross. (1980). *Human inference: Strategies and shortcomings of social judgment*. Englewood Cliffs, NJ: Prentice-Hall.

25. P. Slovic, B. Fischhoff, & S. Lichtenstein. (1977). Behavioral decision theory. *Annual Review of Psychology*, *28*, 1–39.

26. H. J. Einhorn, & R. M. Hogarth. (1981). Behavioral decision theory: Processes of judgment and choice. *Annual Review of Psychology*, *32*, 53–88.

27. A. Tversky, & D. Kahneman. (1983). Extensional versus intuitive reasoning: The conjunction fallacy in probability judgment. *Psychological Review*, *90*, 293–315; L. Ross, & R. E. Nisbett. (1991). *The person and the situation: Perspectives of social psychology*. New York: McGraw-Hill.

28. Einhorn & Hogarth, pp. 55–56.

29. P. Newbold, & T. Bos. (1990). *Introductory business forecasting*. Cincinnati, OH: South-Western, p. 409.

30. J. Mumpower, S. Livingston, & T. J. Lee. (1987). Expert judgments on political riskiness. *Journal of Forecasting*, *6*, 51–65.

31. Newbold & Bos, p. 409.

32. See especially D. Kahneman, P. Slovic, & A. Tversky. (Eds.). (1982). *Judgment under uncertainty: Heuristics and biases*. Cambridge, UK: Cambridge University Press.

33. J. Q. Wilson. (1993). *The moral sense*. New York: Free Press.

34. K. R. Foster, D. E. Bernstein, & P. W. Huber. (1993). *Phantom risk: Scientific inference and the law*. Cambridge, MA: MIT Press, p. 346.

35. D. M. Berwick. (1991). Controlling variation in health care: A consultation from Walter Shewhart. *Medical Care, 29*, pp. 1212–1213.

36. W. Schivelbusch. (1986). *The railway journey: The industrialization of time and space in the 19th century.* Berkeley, CA: University of California Press, p. 133.

37. Schivelbusch, p. 133. For a thorough treatment of the topic of human error in relation to modern technology, see J. Reason. (1990). *Human error.* Cambridge, UK: Cambridge University Press.

38. Howard, p. 50.

39. Howard, p. 49.

40. Howard, p. 23.

41. Howard, p. 23.

42. Howard, p. 18.

43. J. Bruner. (1961). *The process of education.* Cambridge, MA: Harvard University Press, p. 13.

44. K. R. Hammond, R. M. Hamm, J. Grassia, & T. Pearson. (1986). Direct comparison of the efficacy of intuitive and analytical cognition in expert judgment. *IEEE Transactions on Systems, Man, and Cybernetics, 17*, 753–770.

45. E. Brunswik. (1956). *Perception and the representative design of psychological experiments* (2nd ed.). Berkeley, CA: University of California Press.

46. E. Brunswik. (1952). The conceptual framework of psychology. In *International encyclopedia of unified science* (Vol. 1, no. 10, pp. 4–102). Chicago: University of Chicago Press, p. 24.

47. Quoted in K. R. Hammond. (Ed.). (1966). *The psychology of Egon Brunswik* (2nd ed.). New York: Holt, Rinehart, and Winston, p. 491.

48. C. Darwin. (1874). *The descent of man and selection in relation to sex* (2nd ed.). New York: A. L. Fowle.

49. T. von Schantz, G. Göransson, G. Andersson, I. Fröberg, M. Grahn, A. Helgée, & Witzell, H. (1989). Female choice selects for a viability-based male trait in pheasants. *Nature, 337*, 166–169.

50. D. M. Buss. (1992). Mate preference mechanisms: Consequences for partner choice and intrasexual competition. In J. H. Barkow, L. Cosmides, & J. Tooby (Eds.), *The adapted mind: Evolutionary psychology and the generation of culture* (pp. 249–266). New York: Oxford University Press; D. M. Buss. (1994). *The evolution of desire: Strategies of human mating.* New York: Basic Books.

51. M. Twain. (1896/1985). *Life on the Mississippi.* Toronto: Bantam Books, p. 47.

52. Shackle the Sick? [Editorial]. (1993, January 18). *New York Times,* p. A14.

53. H. A. Simon. (1979). Rational decision making in business organizations. *American Economic Review, 69*, p. 501.

54. H. A. Simon. (1981). *The sciences of the artificial* (2nd ed.). Cambridge, MA: MIT Press; H. A. Simon, & C. A. Kaplan. (1989). Foundations of cognitive science. In M. I. Posner (Ed.), *Foundations of cognitive science* (pp. 1–47). Cambridge, MA: MIT Press; J. Larkin, J. McDermott, D. P. Simon, & H. A. Simon. (1980). Expert and novice performance in solving physics problems. *Science, 208*, 1335–1342.

55. H. A. Simon. (1980). The behavioral and social sciences. *Science, 209*, 71–77.

56. J. March. (1978). Bounded rationality, ambiguity, and the engineering of choice. *Bell Journal of Economics, 9*, p. 591.

57. March, p. 598.

58. March, p. 593; see also L. L. Lopes, & G. C. Oden. (1991). The rationality of intelligence. In E. Eells & T. Maruszewski (Eds.), *Probability and rationality: Studies on L. Jonathan Cohen's philosophy of science* (pp. 199–223). Amsterdam: Rodopi.

59. March, p. 594.

60. H. A. Simon. (1957). *Models of man: Social and rational; mathematical essays on rational human behavior in society setting.* New York: Wiley, p. 200.

61. Simon, *Models of man,* p. 200.

62. H. A. Simon. (1992). What is an "explanation" of behavior? *Psychological Science, 3,* p. 155.

63. Simon, What is an "explanation," p. 155.

64. For an example of "creative people at work," see D. B. Wallace, & H. E. Gruber. (Eds.). (1989). *Creative people at work: Twelve cognitive case studies.* New York: Oxford University Press.

65. R. Cooksey. (1996). *Judgment analysis: Theory, methods, and applications.* San Diego: Academic Press.

66. See K. R. Hammond, C. J. Hursch, & F. J. Todd. (1964). Analyzing the components of clinical inference. *Psychological Review, 71,* 438–456; C. J. Hursch, K. R. Hammond, & J. L. Hursch. (1964). Some methodological considerations in multiple-cue probability studies. *Psychological Review, 71,* 42–60.

67. L. R. Tucker. (1964). A suggested alternative formulation in the developments by Hursch, Hammond, and Hursch, and by Hammond, Hursch, and Todd. *Psychological Review, 71,* 528–530. For recent mathematical or statistical advances, see N. J. Castellan, Jr. (1992). Relations between linear models: Implications for the lens model. *Organizational Behavior and Human Decision Processes, 51,* 364–381; J.-W. Lee, & J. F. Yates. (1992). How quantity judgment changes as the number of cues increases: An analytical framework and review. *Psychological Bulletin, 112,* 363–377; T. R. Stewart, & C. M. Lusk. (1994). Seven components of judgmental forecasting skill: Implications for research and the improvement of forecasts. *Journal of Forecasting, 13,* 579–599.

68. For a collection of recent studies, see B. Brehmer, & C. R. B. Joyce. (Eds.). (1988). *Human judgment: The SJT view.* Amsterdam: Elsevier; for reviews of this anthology, see R. Hastie. (1990). Social judgment theory and its accomplishments [Review of *Human judgment: The SJT view*]. *Contemporary Psychology, 35,* 959–960; C. R. B. Joyce, & T. R. Stewart. (1994). Applied research in judgment: What should happen. *Acta Psychologica, 87,* 217–227.

69. D. R. Sease. (1992, June 1). What could go wrong? Here are some market "nightmares." *The Wall Street Journal,* pp. C1–2.

70. Increasing the number of observations with the same instrument will increase ecological reliability (we can be more certain of the correct reading) but will not increase the ecological validity of an indicator. If it is a good (or poor) indicator it will remain so regardless of the number of readings taken. The term "ecological validity" has been sadly abused by psychologists. Introduced in 1952 by Brunswik specifically to denote the degree of relationship between a perceptual cue and an object, many psychologists, ignorant of this, have extended the term to refer to the generalizability of the results of a laboratory experiment to conditions outside the laboratory. I have tried to return the meaning of this term to its original purpose, but the abuse has spread and this is now a lost cause. See K. R. Hammond. (1978). *Psychology's scientific revolution: Is it in danger?* (Tech. Rep. No. 211). Boulder: University of Colorado, Center for Research on Judgment and Policy, which was rejected for publication by the *American Psychologist.*

71. Buss, Mate preference mechanisms.

72. R. M. Dawes, & B. Corrigan. (1974). Linear models in decision making. *Psychological Bulletin, 81,* 95–106.

73. E. O. Wilson. (1994). *Naturalist.* Washington, DC: Island Press, p. 360.

74. G. Chasseigne. (1995, November). *Aging and multiple cue probability learning: The case of inverse relationships; cognitive feedback versus outcome feedback.* Paper presented at the 11th International Meeting of the Brunswik Society, Los Angeles.

75. For more information about function forms, see Cooksey.

76. R. G. Nelson, & D. A. Bessler. (1992). Quasi-rational expectations: Experimental evidence. *Journal of Forecasting, 11,* 141–156.

77. M. Nerlove, D. M. Grether, & J. L. Carvalho. (1979). *Analysis of economic time series: A synthesis.* New York: Academic Press.

78. Nelson & Bessler p. 141.

79. R. H. Thaler. (Ed.). (1991). *Quasi rational economics.* New York: Russell Sage Foundation.

80. T. Russell, & R. H. Thaler. (1991). The relevance of quasi rationality in competitive markets. In R. H. Thaler (Ed.), *Quasi rational economics* (pp. 239–257). New York: Russell Sage, p. 239.

81. Russell & Thaler, p. 241.

82. See I. H. Nagel, S. Breyer, & T. MacCarthy. (1989). Panel V: Equality versus discretion in sentencing (Introduction by the Honorable Frank H. Easterbrook). *The American Criminal Law Review, 26,* 1813–1838.

83. Nagel, Breyer, & MacCarthy, p. 1813.

84. Nagel, Breyer, & MacCarthy, p. 1816.

85. Nagel, Breyer, & MacCarthy, p. 1816.

86. Nagel, Breyer, & MacCarthy, p. 1820.

87. Nagel, Breyer, & MacCarthy, pp. 1816–1817.

88. Nagel, Breyer, & MacCarthy, p. 1819.

89. Howard, p. 44.

80. See the March 30, 1995, issue of *The Wall Street Journal.*

91. Nagel, Breyer, & MacCarthy, p. 1826.

92. Nagel, Breyer, & MacCarthy, p. 1829. Dawes, Faust, & Meehl would have cheered!

93. J. Handler. (1992). Discretion: power, quiescence, and trust. In K. Hawkins (Ed.), *The uses of discretion* (pp. 331–360). Oxford, UK: Oxford University Press; K. Hawkins. (Ed.). (1992). *The uses of discretion.* Oxford, UK: Oxford University Press.

94. O. W. Holmes. (1881/1923). *The common law.* Boston: Little, Brown, p. 1.

95. Holmes, p. 1.

## 7. Task Structure and Cognitive Structure

1. For a discussion of the use of scientific metaphors by the makers of the U.S. Constitution, see I. B. Cohen. (1995). *Science and the founding fathers: Science in the political thought of Jefferson, Franklin, Adams and Madison.* New York: Norton.

2. K. R. Hammond, R. M. Hamm, J. Grassia, & T. Pearson. (1986). Direct comparison of the efficacy of intuitive and analytical cognition in expert judgment. *IEEE Transactions on Systems, Man, and Cybernetics, 17,* 753–770.

3. V. Havel. (March 1, 1992). The end of the modern era. *New York Times,* sec. 14, p. 15.

4. H. A. Simon. (1981). *The sciences of the artificial* (2nd ed.). Cambridge, MA: MIT Press, pp. 126–127.

5. See Hammond, Hamm, Grassia, & Pearson.

6. See E. S. Ferguson. (1992). *Engineering and the mind's eye.* Cambridge, MA: MIT Press.

7. G. F. Kennan. (1993). *Around the cragged hill: A personal and political philosophy.* New York: Norton, p. 150.

8. D. J. Boorstin. (1983). *The discoverers.* New York: Random House, p. 53. See also D. Sobel. (1995). *Longitude: The true story of a lone genius who solved the greatest scientific problem of his time.* New York: Walker.

9. R. M. Dawes. (1988). *Rational choice in an uncertain world.* San Diego: Harcourt, Brace, Jovanovich, p. 227.

10. N. Postman. (1992). *Technopoly: The surrender of culture to technology.* New York: Alfred A. Knopf, p. 118.

11. F. W. Taylor. (1911). *The principles of scientific management.* New York: Harper & Brothers.

12. Postman, p. 51.

13. V. Havel. (July 26, 1992). In his own words/Vaclav Havel: In accord with a vision of civility [From speech at World Economic Forum, Davos, Switzerland, February 4, 1992]. *New York Times,* p. E7.

14. Havel, In his own words.

15. D. P. Moynihan. (1993). *Pandaemonium: Ethnicity in international politics.* Oxford, UK: Oxford University Press, p. 146.

16. Compare J. E. Innes. (1990). *Knowledge and public policy: The search for meaningful indicators.* New Brunswick, NJ: Transaction.

17. For impressive scholarship regarding the development of navigation skills over a 2000-year span, see E. G. R. Taylor. (1957). *The haven-finding art: A history of navigation from Odysseus to Captain Cook* (with a foreword by K. St. B. Collins). New York: Abelard-Schuman. For the specifics of the development of the means for determining longitude, see E. G. Forbes. (1974). *The birth of scientific navigation: The solving in the 18th century of the problem of finding longitude at sea.* Greenwich, CT: National Maritime Museum; Bowditch, N. (1802/1984). *American practical navigator: An epitome of navigation.* Washington, DC: Defense Mapping Agency Hydrographic/Topographic Center. For a less technical account, see Boorstin.

18. Moynihan, pp. 48–49.

19. Compare Dawes.

20. N. Glazer. (1988). *The limits of social policy.* Cambridge, MA: Harvard University Press, pp. 1–2.

21. Glazer, pp. 142–143.

22. P. L. Berger, & R. J. Neuhaus. (1977). *To empower people: The role of mediating structures in public policy.* Washington, DC: American Enterprise Institute.

23. Glazer, p. 145.

24. Quoted in Glazer, pp. 145–146.

25. Glazer, p. 146.

26. H. E. Gruber. (1978). Darwin's "tree of nature" and other images of wide scope. In J. Wechsler (Ed.), *On aesthetics in science* (pp. 121–140). Cambridge, MA: MIT Press, p. 127.

27. R. D. Tweney, M. E. Doherty, & C. R. Mynatt. (Eds.). (1981). *On scientific thinking.* New York: Columbia University Press.

28. For an attempt to redress this shortcoming, see Hammond, Hamm, Grassia, & Pearson.

29. M. Polanyi. (1958). *Personal knowledge: Towards a post-critical philosophy.* Chicago, IL: University of Chicago Press, pp. 130–131.

30. Polanyi, p. 131.

31. N. R. Hanson. (1958). *Patterns of discovery.* New York: Cambridge University Press, p. 25.

32. K. R. Hammond, E. Frederick, N. Robillard, & D. Victor. (1989). Application of cognitive theory to the student-teacher dialogue. In D. A. Evans & V. L. Patel (Eds.), *Cognitive science in medicine* (pp. 173–210). Cambridge, MA: MIT Press.

33. H. Margolis. (1987). *Patterns, thinking, and cognition: A theory of judgment.* Chicago, IL: University of Chicago Press.

34. H. R. Arkes, & K. R. Hammond. (Eds.). (1986). *Judgment and decision making: An interdisciplinary reader.* Cambridge, UK: Cambridge University Press; B. Brehmer, & C. R. B. Joyce. (Eds.). (1988). *Human judgment: The SJT view.* Amsterdam: Elsevier; R. M. Hogarth. (Ed.). (1990). *Insights in decision making: A tribute to Hillel J. Einhorn.* Chicago: University of Chicago Press; D. Kahneman, P. Slovic, & A. Tversky. (Eds.). (1982). *Judgment under uncertainty: Heuristics and biases.* Cambridge, UK: Cambridge University Press; M. F. Kaplan, & S. Schwartz. (Eds.). (1975). *Human judgment and decision processes.* New York: Academic Press.

35. J. Baron. (1988). *Thinking and deciding.* Cambridge, UK: Cambridge University Press; Dawes; R. M. Hogarth. (1987). *Judgement and choice: The psychology of decision* (2nd ed.). Chichester: Wiley; S. R. Watson, & D. M. Buede. (1987). *Decision synthesis: The principles and practice of decision analysis.* Cambridge, UK: Cambridge University Press.

36. K. R. Hammond, G. H. McClelland, & J. Mumpower. (1980). *Human judgment and decision making: Theories, methods, and procedures.* New York: Hemisphere/Praeger; P. Slovic, & S. Lichtenstein. (1971). Comparison of Bayesian and regression approaches to the study of information processing in judgment. *Organizational Behavior and Human Performance, 6,* 649–744.

37. B. F. Anderson, D. H. Deane, K. R. Hammond, G. H. McClelland, & J. C. Shanteau. (1981). *Concepts in judgment and decision research: Definitions, sources, interrelations, comments.* New York: Praeger.

38. D. von Winterfeldt, & W. Edwards. (1986). *Decision analysis and behavioral research.* Cambridge, UK: Cambridge University Press.

39. D. E. Broadbent. (1971). *Decision and stress.* London: Academic Press, p. 270.

40. W. R. Garner. (1970). Good patterns have few alternatives. *American Scientist, 58,* p. 34.

41. Garner, p. 34.

42. W. B. Rouse. (1983). Models of human problem solving: Detection, diagnosis, and compensation for system failures. *Automatica, 19,* pp. 620–621.

43. N. Moray. (1994). Error reduction as a systems problem. In M. S. Bogner (Ed.), *Human error in medicine* (pp. 67–91). Hillsdale, NJ: Erlbaum, p. 74.

44. For example, see G. Klein, J. Orasanu, R. Calderwood, & C. E. Zsambok. (Eds.). (1993). *Decision making in action: Models and methods.* Norwood, NJ: Ablex.

45. J. Kittler. (Ed.). (1988). *Pattern recognition: Proceedings of the 4th international conference, Cambridge, U.K., March 28–30, 1988.* Berlin: Springer-Verlag.

46. Hogarth, *Judgement and choice,* p. 30.

47. A. R. Feinstein. (1967). *Clinical judgment.* Huntington, NY: Krieger, p. 323.

48. Feinstein, p. 323.

49. Feinstein, p. 323.

50. An article by Massaro (D. W. Massaro. [1994]. A pattern recognition account of decision making. *Memory and Cognition, 22,* 616–627) claims to be a pattern recognition account of decision making but does not, in my view, meet the traditional criterion for the presence of a "pattern." The article does, however, offer an interesting challenge to Tversky and Kahneman's interpretation of decision making as inherently flawed (A. Tversky, & D. Kahneman. [1983]. Extensional versus intuitive reasoning: The conjunction fallacy in probability judgment. *Psychological Review, 90,* 293–315).

51. See Kahneman, Slovic, & Tversky.

52. R. Hastie. (Ed.). (1993a). *Inside the juror: The psychology of juror decision making.* New York: Cambridge University Press; N. Pennington, & R. Hastie. (1991). A cognitive theory of juror decision making: The story model. *Cardozo Law Review, 13*, 519–557; N. Pennington, & R. Hastie. (1993b). A theory of explanation-based decision making. In G. Klein, J. Orasanu, R. Calderwood, & C. E. Zsambok (Eds.), *Decision making in action: Models and methods* (pp. 188–201). Norwood, NJ: Ablex.

53. R. Hastie. (1993b). Introduction. In R. Hastie (Ed.), *Inside the juror: The psychology of juror decision making* (pp. 3–41). New York: Cambridge University Press, p. 24.

54. Hastie, Introduction, p. 24.

55. J. S. Bruner. (1986). *Actual minds, possible worlds.* Cambridge, MA: Harvard University Press.

56. H. Petroski. (1994). *Design paradigms: Case histories of error and judgment in engineering.* Cambridge, UK: Cambridge University Press. p. 33–34.

57. Petroski, p. 34.

## 8. Reducing Tension Through Complementarity

1. S. Epstein. (1994). Integration of the cognitive and the psychodynamic unconscious. *American Psychologist, 49*, p. 719.

2. R. E. Nisbett. (1993). Reasoning, abstraction, and the prejudices of 20th century psychology. In R. E. Nisbett (Ed.), *Rules for reasoning* (pp. 1–12). Hillsdale, NJ: Erlbaum.

3. G. Gigerenzer. (1991c). On cognitive illusions and rationality. In E. Eells & T. Maruszewski (Eds.), *Probability and rationality: Studies on L. Jonathan Cohen's philosophy of science* (pp. 225–249). Amsterdam: Rodopi.

4. L. L. Lopes, & G. C. Oden. (1991). The rationality of intelligence. In E. Eells & T. Maruszewski (Eds.), *Probability and rationality: Studies on L. Jonathan Cohen's philosophy of science* (pp. 199–223). Amsterdam: Rodopi.

5. P. Suedfeld, & P. E. Tetlock. (1992b). Psychologists as policy advocates: The roots of controversy. In P. Suedfeld & P. E. Tetlock (Eds.), *Psychology and social policy* (pp. 1–30). New York: Hemisphere.

6. J. M. Fraser, P. J. Smith, & J. W. Smith, Jr. (1992). A catalog of errors. *International Journal of Man-Machine Studies, 37*, 265–307.

7. For example, see D. Kahneman, P. Slovic, & A. Tversky. (Eds.). (1982). *Judgment under uncertainty: Heuristics and biases.* Cambridge, UK: Cambridge University Press; A. Tversky, & D. Kahneman. (1983). Extensional versus intuitive reasoning: The conjunction fallacy in probability judgment. *Psychological Review, 90*, 293–315; A. Tversky, & D. Kahneman. (1986). Rational choice and the framing of decisions. *Journal of Business, 59*, S251–S278; A. Tversky, S. Sattath, & P. Slovic. (1988). Contingent weighting in judgment and choice. *Psychological Review, 93*, 371–384. See also H. R. Arkes. (1991). Costs and benefits of judgment errors: Implications for debiasing. *Psychological Bulletin, 110*, 486–498; J. W. Payne, J. R. Bettman, & E. J. Johnson. (1992). Behavioral decision research: A constructive processing perspective. *Annual Review of Psychology, 43*, 87–131; P. Slovic, B. Fischhoff, & S. Lichtenstein. (1977). Behavioral decision theory. *Annual Review of Psychology, 28*, 1–39; P. Slovic, S. Lichtenstein, & B. Fischhoff. (1988). Decision making. In R. C. Atkinson, R. J. Herrnstein, G. Lindzey, & R. D. Luce (Eds.), *Handbook of experimental psychology: Vol 2. Learning and cognition* (pp. 673–738). New York: Wiley. For a new approach, see J. Klayman. (1993). Debias the environment instead of the judge: An alternative approach to reducing error in diagnostic (and other) judgement. *Cognition, 49*, 97–122.

8. See S. Plous. (1993). *The psychology of judgment and decision making*. Philadelphia: Temple University Press.

9. R. E. Nisbett, G. T. Fong, D. R. Lehman, & P. W. Cheng. (1987). Teaching reasoning. *Science, 238*, p. 625.

10. D. R. Lehman, R. O. Lempert, & R. E. Nisbett. (1988). The effects of graduate training on reasoning: Formal discipline and thinking about everyday-life events. *American Psychologist, 43*, 431–442.

11. D. R. Lehman, & R. E. Nisbett. (1990). A longitudinal study of the effects of undergraduate training on reasoning. *Developmental Psychology, 26*, p. 962.

12. Nisbett, Reasoning, pp. 3–4.

13. Nisbett, Reasoning, p. 4.

14. J. A. Paulos. (1988). *Innumeracy: Mathematical illiteracy and its consequences*. New York: Hill and Wang, p. 133.

15. Paulos, p. 134.

16. Paulos, p. 33.

17. A. Baddeley. (1993). Working memory or working attention? In A. Baddeley & L. Weiskrantz (Eds.), *Attention: Selection, awareness, and control* (pp. 152–170). Oxford, UK: Clarendon Press.

18. D. Kahneman, & A. Tversky. (1982). On the study of statistical intuitions. In D. Kahneman, P. Slovic, & A. Tversky (Eds.), *Judgment under uncertainty: Heuristics and biases* (pp. 493–508). Cambridge, UK: Cambridge University Press, p. 493.

19. For example, see G. Gigerenzer. (1987). Probabilistic thinking and the fight against subjectivity. In L. Krüger, G. Gigerenzer, & M. S. Morgan (Eds.), *The probabilistic revolution: Vol. 2. Ideas in the sciences* (pp. 11–33). Cambridge, MA: MIT Press; G. Gigerenzer, W. Hell, & H. Blank. (1988). Presentation and content: The use of base rates as a continuous variable. *Journal of Experimental Psychology: Human Perception and Performance, 14*, 513–525; G. Gigerenzer, U. Hoffrage, & H. Kleinbölting. (1991). Probabilistic mental models: A Brunswikian theory of confidence. *Psychological Review, 98*, 506–528; G. Gigerenzer, & D. J. Murray. (1987). *Cognition as intuitive statistics*. Hillsdale, NJ: Erlbaum; G. Gigerenzer, Z. Swijtink, T. Porter, L. Daston, J. Beatty, & L. Krueger. (1989). *The empire of chance: How probability changed science and everyday life*. New York: Cambridge University Press. See also M. H. Birnbaum. (1983). Base rates in Bayesian inference: Signal detection analysis of the cab problem. *American Journal of Psychology, 96*, 85–94.

20. G. Gigerenzer. (1991b). How to make cognitive illusions disappear: Beyond "heuristics and biases." *European Review of Social Psychology, 2*, p. 83.

21. Gigerenzer, Hoffrage, & Kleinbölting, p. 506.

22. Gigerenzer, On cognitive illusions, p. 229.

23. Gigerenzer, On cognitive illusions, p. 241.

24. See Gigerenzer, Hell, & Blank.

25. Lopes & Oden, pp. 200–201.

26. See especially pp. 238–252 in D. Crevier. (1993). *The tumultuous history of the search for artificial intelligence*. New York: Basic Books.

27. See especially R. M. Dawes. (1988). *Rational choice in an uncertain world*. San Diego: Harcourt, Brace, Jovanovich.

28. Lopes & Oden, p. 201.

29. Lopes & Oden, pp. 205–209.

30. Lopes & Oden, p. 205.

31. Lopes & Oden, p. 205.

32. Lopes & Oden, p. 203. Taken from D. Kahneman, & A. Tversky. (1972). Subjective probability: A judgment of representativeness. *Cognitive Psychology, 3*, p. 432.

33. Lopes & Oden, p. 206.

34. D. Kahneman, & A. Tversky. (1984). Choices, values, and frames. *American Psychologist, 39*, p. 433.

35. Lopes & Oden, p. 201.

36. Lopes & Oden, p. 219.

37. Lopes & Oden, p. 220.

38. A. S. Elstein, G. B. Holzman, M. M. Ravitch, W. A. Metheny, M. M. Holmes, R. B. Hoppe, M. L. Rothert, & D. R. Rovner. (1986). Comparison of physicians' decisions regarding estrogen replacement therapy for menopausal women and decisions derived from a decision analytic model. *American Journal of Medicine, 80*, p. 255.

39. Elstein et al., p. 255; see also J. F. Smith, & T. Kida. (1991). Heuristics and biases: Expertise and task realism in auditing. *Psychological Bulletin, 109*, 472–489.

40. L. L. Lopes. (1991). The rhetoric of irrationality. *Theory & Psychology, 1*(1), pp. 65–67.

41. J. R. Platt. (1964). Strong inference. *Science, 164*, 347–353.

42. A. Tversky, & D. Kahneman. (1973). Availability: A heuristic for judging frequency and probability. *Cognitive Psychology, 5*, p. 211.

43. Lopes, p. 73.

44. Lopes, p. 75.

45. Lopes, p. 75.

46. A. Tversky, & D. Kahneman. (1971). Belief in the law of small numbers. *Psychological Bulletin, 76*, p. 110.

47. Tversky & Kahneman, Belief in the law of small numbers, p. 109.

48. Tversky & Kahneman, Belief in the law of small numbers, p. 108.

49. Tversky & Kahneman, Belief in the law of small numbers, p. 107.

50. Lopes, p. 80.

51. P. Suedfeld, & P. E. Tetlock. (1992a). Psychological advice about political decision making: Heuristics, biases, and cognitive defects. In P. Suedfeld & P. E. Tetlock (Eds.), *Psychology and social policy* (pp. 51–70). New York: Hemisphere.

52. Suedfeld & Tetlock, Psychological advice, p. 55.

53. Suedfeld & Tetlock, Psychological advice, p. 58.

54. Suedfeld & Tetlock, Psychological advice, p. 59. The reader should compare this view with that of William Estes, an experimental psychologist who holds exactly the opposite view: W. K. Estes. (1994). *Classification and cognition*. New York: Oxford University Press.

55. Suedfeld & Tetlock, Psychological advice, p. 67.

56. S. Zabell. (1993). A mathematician comments on models of juror decision making. In R. Hastie (Ed.), *Inside the juror: The psychology of juror decision making* (pp. 263–269). Cambridge: Cambridge University Press, p. 264.

57. Zabell, p. 264.

58. J. W. Payne, J. R. Bettman, & E. J. Johnson. (1993). *The adaptive decision maker*. New York: Cambridge University Press. p. xi.

59. Payne, Bettman, & Johnson, *The adaptive decision maker,* p. xi.

60. Payne, Bettman, & Johnson, *The adaptive decision maker,* p. xi. This is an argument that correspondence theorists had been making for some time; see K. R. Hammond, G. H. McClelland, & J. Mumpower. (1980). *Human judgment and decision making: Theories, methods, and procedures*. New York: Hemisphere/Praeger.

61. J. Feldman, & M. K. Lindell. (1990). On rationality. In I. Horowitz (Ed.), *Organization and decision theory* (pp. 83–164). Boston: Kluwer.

62. Payne, Bettman, & Johnson, *The adaptive decision maker,* p. xii.

63. Payne, Bettman, & Johnson, *The adaptive decision maker,* p. 249.

64. Payne, Bettman, & Johnson, *The adaptive decision maker,* p. 249.

65. Payne, Bettman, & Johnson, *The adaptive decision maker,* p. 89.

66. Payne, Bettman, & Johnson, *The adaptive decision maker,* p. 89.

67. For a discussion and empirical study related to this question, see R. P. Larrick, R. E. Nisbett, & J. N. Morgan. (1993). Who uses the cost-benefits rules of choice? Implications for the normative status of microeconomic theory. *Organizational Behavior and Human Decision Processes, 56,* 331–347.

68. Payne, Bettman, & Johnson, *The adaptive decision maker,* p. 90.

69. K. R. Hammond, R. M. Hamm, J. Grassia, & T. Pearson. (1986). Direct comparison of the efficacy of intuitive and analytical cognition in expert judgment. *IEEE Transactions on Systems, Man, and Cybernetics, 17,* 753–770.

70. W. Edwards. (1954). The theory of decision making. *Psychological Bulletin, 41,* 380–417.

71. T. S. Purdum. (1994, August 7). The newest Moynihan. *New York Times Magazine,* p. 52.

72. M. Björkman. (1984). From dualism to pluralism: The third world in judgment under uncertainty. In K. M. J. Lagerspetz & P. Niemi (Eds.), *Psychology in the 1990s* (p. 399). Amsterdam: Elsevier. Note Popper did not capitalize "world"; I do so for ease of reading.

73. Sir K. R. Popper. (1972). *Objective knowledge: An evolutionary approach.* Oxford, UK: Clarendon Press, p. 106.

74. R. E. Nisbett. (Ed.). (1993). *Rules for reasoning.* Hillsdale, NJ: Erlbaum.

75. See Björkman; Hammond, Hamm, Grassia, & Pearson.

76. Kahneman & Tversky, On the study of statistical intuitions.

77. Kahneman & Tversky, On the study of statistical intuitions, p. 493.

78. M. Bar-Hillel. (1980). The base-rate fallacy in probability judgments. *Acta Psychologica, 44,* p. 232.

79. D. Lyon, & P. Slovic. (1976). Dominance of accuracy information and neglect of base rates in probability estimation. *Acta Psychologica, 40,* pp. 296–297.

80. Björkman, p. 409.

81. A. Tversky, & D. Kahneman. (1974). Judgment under uncertainty: Heuristics and biases. *Science, 185,* p. 1130.

82. Björkman, p. 412.

83. The role of theory in the observation of events was emphasized by N. R. Hanson, when he said, "seeing is a theory-laden undertaking." (N. R. Hanson. (1958). *Patterns of discovery.* New York: Cambridge University Press, p. 19); see also T. Kuhn. (1962). *The structure of scientific revolutions.* Chicago: University of Chicago Press.

84. For example, see J. F. Yates. (1990). *Judgment and decision making.* Englewood Cliffs, NJ: Prentice-Hall, pp. 112–146.

85. Kahneman & Tversky, Subjective probability, p. 443.

86. See B. Brehmer, & C. R. B. Joyce. (Eds.). (1988). *Human judgment: The SJT view.* Amsterdam: Elsevier.

87. D. C. Geary. (1995). Reflections of evolution and culture in children's cognition: Implications for mathematical development and instruction. *American Psychologist, 50,* p. 26.

88. Popper's creation of the idea of an autonomous World 3 was prescient. Now that our libraries are employing radically new methods of storing information—the memory of society—in digital, electronic forms rather than on paper, a new form of World 3 is coming into existence. In the past, libraries took advantage of our natural propensity to use indicators (e.g., key words) to search for information (title, authors, subject matter) and set up catalogs for our convenience. Thus, libraries capitalized on our correspondence competence. The new

capacity to store enormous amounts of electronically based, digitalized knowledge in one place (rather than duplicating paper copies in many places, as we do at present) demands better organization, however. As the librarian Nina Matheson points out in a farsighted article for the medical profession, "The knowledge generated in our university health science centers needs to be brought together into *coherent* [italics added] systems. Ultimately . . . these systems will be the World Brain that [H. G.] Wells envisioned" (N. Matheson. (1995). Things to come: Postmodern digital knowledge management and information. *Journal of the American Medical Informatics Association*, 2, p. 77). The organization of knowledge in World 3 changes from one in which correspondence competence was sufficient, to one in which coherence competence will be required, both on the part of those who must organize knowledge, and those who seek it. Thus the changing organization of knowledge in World 3 recapitulates the changing of the organization of knowledge in World 2.

89. E. Brunswik. (1943). Organismic achievement and environmental probability. *Psychological Review*, 50, 255–272; E. Brunswik. (1956). *Perception and the representative design of psychological experiments* (2nd ed.). Berkeley, CA: University of California Press; for explications, see also K. R. Hammond. (Ed.). (1966). *The psychology of Egon Brunswik* (2nd ed.). New York: Holt, Rinehart, and Winston; Hammond, Hamm, Grassia, & Pearson.

90. Estes, p. 9.

91. Estes, p. 9.

92. Estes, p. 9. As an example of how thin that hope has become, consider this conversation reported by William Howell, the American Psychological Association's executive director for science, in the January 1995 *Monitor*, an APA house organ. The conversation with Alan Kraut, executive director of the American Psychological Society, went like this: "'What,' [Kraut] asked, 'do X (a prominent cognitive neuroscientist) and Y (a prominent private practitioner) have in common?' . . . I [Howell] considered it a fair question, and had to admit, probably very little." I have argued that this situation is due to psychologists' regrettable commitment to a methodology that will not permit generalization.

93. For an example of the first attempts to study the judgments of predictions of weather forecasters by means of simulations of their information environment, see C. M. Lusk, & K. R. Hammond. (1991). Judgment in a dynamic task: Microburst forecasting. *Journal of Behavioral Decision Making*, 4, 55–73; C. M. Lusk, T. R. Stewart, K. R. Hammond, & R. J. Potts. (1990). Judgment and decision making in dynamic tasks: The case of forecasting the microburst. *Weather and Forecasting*, 5, 627–639; T. R. Stewart, W. R. Moninger, J. Grassia, R. H. Brady, & F. H. Merrem. (1989). Analysis of expert judgment in a hail forecasting experiment. *Weather and Forecasting*, 4, 24–34; T. R. Stewart, W. R. Moninger, K. F. Heideman, & P. Reagan-Cirincione. (1992). Effects of improved information on the components of skill in weather forecasting. *Organizational Behavior and Human Decision Processes*, 53, 107–134. Hammond and Kern made use of simulation (sound motion pictures to simulate a doctor interviewing a patient) as a means of testing medical students abilities (K. R. Hammond, F. Kern, Jr., W. J. Crow, J. H. Githens, B. Groesbeck, & J. W. Gyr. [1959]. *Teaching comprehensive medical care: A psychological study of a change in medical education.* Cambridge, MA: Harvard University Press). Wigton and his associates have used modern techniques of simulation in studies of physicians' diagnostic judgments. For a simulation study of audiologists' judgments of the need for a hearing aid, see J. Doyle, & S. A. Thomas. (1995). Capturing policy in hearing-aid decisions by audiologists. *Medical Decision Making*, 15, 58–64.

94. For a review, see Brehmer & Joyce.

95. Hammond, Hamm, Grassia, & Pearson.

96. A. Newell, & H. A. Simon. (1972). *Human problem solving*. Englewood Cliffs, NJ: Prentice-Hall, p. 10.

97. Newell and Simon, p. 874.

98. E. O. Wilson, quoted in J. Diamond. (January 12, 1995). Portrait of the biologist as a young man. *The New York Review of Books*, p. 18.

99. Diamond, p. 18.

100. Diamond, p. 18.

101. Diamond, p. 18.

102. R. M. Poses, R. D. Cebul, & R. S. Wigton. (1995). You can lead a horse to water—Improving physicians' knowledge of probabilities may not affect their decisions. *Medical Decision Making, 15*, p. 65.

103. Poses, Cebul, & Wigton, p. 70.

### 9. Is It Possible to Learn by Intervening?

1. C. W. Churchman. (1971). *The design of inquiring systems: Basic concepts of systems and organization*. New York: Basic Books.

2. Churchman, p. 17.

3. I. Hacking. (1983). *Representing and intervening: Introductory topics in the philosophy of natural science*. Cambridge, UK: Cambridge University Press. The psychologist Lee Cronbach made a similar distinction in a famous article in which he referred to the "two disciplines of psychology": L. J. Cronbach. (1975). Beyond the two disciplines of scientific psychology. *American Psychologist, 30*, 116–127.

4. For an early example, see M. D. Mesarovic, & E. Pestel. (1974). *Mankind at the turning point: The second report to the Club of Rome*. New York: Dutton.

5. See various judgment and decision making textbooks—for example, J. F. Yates. (1990). *Judgment and decision making*. Englewood Cliffs, NJ: Prentice-Hall. See also L. Adelman. (1992). *Evaluating decision support and expert systems*. New York: Wiley-Interscience; K. R. Hammond, & L. Adelman. (1976). Science, values, and human judgment. *Science, 194*, 389–396.

6. E. I. Schwartz. (1993, March 6). Health care: The video game. *New York Times,* sec. 3, p. 7.

7. T. D. Cook, & D. T. Campbell. (1979). *Quasi-experimentation: Design and analysis issues for field settings*. Boston: Hougton-Mifflin.

8. For example, see H.-U. Fisch, K. R. Hammond, C. R. B. Joyce, & M. O'Reilly. (1981). An experimental study of the clinical judgment of general physicians in evaluating and prescribing for depression. *British Journal of Psychiatry, 138*, 100–109; T. R. Stewart, & C. R. B. Joyce. (1988). Increasing the power of clinical trials through judgment analysis. *Medical Decision Making, 8*, 33–38.

9. For an example, see T. R. Stewart, C. R. B. Joyce, & M. K. Lindell. (1975). New analyses: Application of judgment theory to physicians' judgments of drug effects. In K. R. Hammond & C. R. B. Joyce (Eds.), *Psychoactive drugs and social judgment: Theory and research* (pp. 249–262). New York: Wiley.

10. D. T. Campbell. (1969). Reforms as experiments. *American Psychologist, 24*, 409–429.

11. On behalf of science: Violence research produces controversy. (1992). *Psychological Science Agenda American Psychological Association, 5*(6), p. 9.

12. K. R. Hammond, L. O. Harvey, Jr., & R. Hastie. (1992). Making better use of scientific knowledge: Separating truth from justice. *Psychological Science, 3*, 80–87.

13. J. A. Hausman, & D. A. Wise. (1985). Introduction. In J. A. Hausman & D. A. Wise (Eds.), *Social experimentation* (pp. 1–10). Chicago: University of Chicago Press, p. 1.

14. Hausman & Wise, p. 1.

15. Hausman & Wise, p. 1.

16. Hausman & Wise, p. 1.

17. Hausman & Wise, p. 1.

18. Hausman & Wise, p. 1.

19. Hausman & Wise, p. 2.

20. See Campbell.

21. D. J. Aigner. (1985). The residential electricity time-of-use pricing experiments: What have we learned? In J. A. Hausman & D. A. Wise (Eds.), *Social Experimentation* (pp. 11–41). Chicago: University of Chicago Press.

22. L. D. Taylor. (1985). Comment. In J. A. Hausman & D. A. Wise (Eds.), *Social Experimentation* (pp. 49–50). Chicago: University of Chicago Press, p. 50.

23. G. K. Ingram. (1985). Comment. In J. A. Hausman & D. A. Wise (Eds.), *Social Experimentation* (pp. 87–94). Chicago: University of Chicago Press, p. 93.

24. S. Rosen. (1985). Comment. In J. A. Hausman & D. A. Wise (Eds.), *Social Experimentation* (pp. 134–137). Chicago: University of Chicago Press, p. 137.

25. Z. Griliches. (1985). Comment. In J. A. Hausman & D. A. Wise (Eds.), *Social Experimentation* (pp. 137–138). Chicago: University of Chicago Press, p. 137.

26. L. L. Orr. (1985). Comment: Choosing between macroexperiments and micro-experiments. In J. A. Hausman & D. A. Wise (Eds.), *Social experimentation* (pp. 172–181). Chicago: University of Chicago Press, p. 180.

27. D. L. McFadden. (1985). Comment. In J. A. Hausman & D. A. Wise (Eds.), *Social experimentation* (pp. 214–218). Chicago: University of Chicago Press, p. 217.

28. H. Aaron. (1985). Comment. In J. A. Hausman & D. A. Wise (Eds.), *Social experimentation* (pp. 272–277). Chicago: University of Chicago Press, p. 275.

29. F. Mosteller, & M. C. Weinstein. (1985). Toward evaluating the cost-effectiveness of medical and social experiments. In J. A. Hausman & D. A. Wise (Eds.), *Social experimentation* (pp. 221–246). Chicago: University of Chicago Press, p. 244.

30. B. Healy. (1993, December 26). Mammograms—Your breasts, your choice. *The Wall Street Journal,* p. A10.

31. J. A. McCulloch. (January 19, 1994). The mammography controversy [Letters to the editor]. *The Wall Street Journal,* p. A15; L. N. Newcomer. (January 19, 1994). The mammography controversy [Letters to the editor]. *The Wall Street Journal,* p. A15.

32. J. E. Innes. (1990). *Knowledge and public policy: The search for meaningful indicators.* New Brunswick, NJ: Transaction, p. 112.

33. See R. F. Boruch, & H. W. Riecken. (1975). *Experimental testing of public policy: The Proceedings of the 1974 Social Science Research Council Conference on Social Experiments.* Boulder: Westview Press; Cook & Campbell; M. Goldberg. (1990). A quasi-experiment assessing the effectiveness of TV advertising directed to children. *Journal of Marketing Research, 27,* 445–454.

34. D. T. Campbell, & J. C. Stanley. (1966). *Experimental and quasi-experimental designs for research.* Chicago: Rand McNally.

35. Sir R. A. Fisher. (1925). *Statistical methods for research workers.* Edinburgh, Scotland: Oliver & Boyd.

36. J. Neyman, & E. S. Pearson. (1933). On the problem of the most efficient tests of statistical hypotheses. *Philosophical Transactions of the Royal Society of London. Series A, 231,* 289–337.

37. Campbell & Stanley, p. 3.

38. Campbell & Stanley, p. 3.

39. Campbell & Stanley, p. 3.

40. Campbell & Stanley, p. 3.

41. Campbell & Stanley, p. 5.
42. Campbell & Stanley, pp. 5–6.
43. Campbell & Stanley, p. 17.
44. Campbell, Reforms as experiments; Cook & Campbell; K. R. Hammond. (1986). Generalization in operational contexts: What does it mean? Can it be done? *IEEE Transactions on Systems, Man, and Cybernetics, 16*, 428–433; K. R. Hammond, R. M. Hamm, & J. Grassia. (1986). Generalizing over conditions by combining the multitrait-multimethod matrix and the representative design of experiments. *Psychological Bulletin, 100*, 257–269; K. R. Hammond, J. Mumpower, R. L. Dennis, S. Fitch, & W. Crumpacker. (1983). Fundamental obstacles to the use of scientific information in public policy making. *Technological Forecasting and Social Change, 24*, 287–297.
45. Goldberg, p. 447.
46. Goldberg, p. 447.
47. Goldberg, p. 447.
48. Goldberg, p. 453.
49. Goldberg, p. 453.
50. Goldberg, p. 453.
51. Goldberg, p. 453.
52. E. Brunswik. (1943). Organismic achievement and environmental probability. *Psychological Review, 50*, 255–272.
53. For example, see K. R. Hammond. (Ed.). (1966). *The psychology of Egon Brunswik* (2nd ed.). New York: Holt, Rinehart, and Winston; Hammond, Generalization in operational contexts; Hammond, Hamm, & Grassia.
54. P. Suedfeld, & P. E. Tetlock. (1992a). Psychological advice about political decision making: Heuristics, biases, and cognitive defects. In P. Suedfeld & P. E. Tetlock (Eds.), *Psychology and social policy* (pp. 51–70). New York: Hemisphere, p. 59.
55. W. K.. Estes. (1994). *Classification and cognition*. New York: Oxford University Press, p. 9.
56. Hammond, *The psychology of Egon Brunswik;* Hammond, Generalization in operational contexts; Hammond, Hamm, & Grassia.
57. B. Brehmer, & C. R. B. Joyce. (Eds.). (1988). *Human judgment: The SJT view.* Amsterdam: Elsevier; R. Cooksey. (1996). *Judgment analysis: Theory, methods, and applications.* San Diego: Academic Press.
58. For further reading, see Hammond, *The psychology of Egon Brunswik.*
59. C. Anderson. (1994). Measuring what works in health care. *Science, 263*, 1080–1082.
60. Anderson, p. 1080.
61. Anderson, p. 1080.
62. Anderson, p. 1080.
63. Anderson, p. 1080.
64, Anderson, p. 1080.
65. Anderson, p. 1080.
66. Anderson, p. 1082.
67. Anderson, p. 1082.
68. Anderson, p. 1082.
69. J. Q. Wilson. (1995, Winter). Welfare reform and character development. *City Journal*, p. 56.
70. Wilson, p. 56.
71. G. Gigerenzer, Z. Swijtink, T. Porter, L. Daston, J. Beatty, & L. Krueger. (1989). *The empire of chance: How probability changed science and everyday life*. New York: Cambridge University Press, p. 108.

### 10. Is It Possible to Learn from Representing?

1. Sir R. A. Fisher. (1925). *Statistical methods for research workers.* Edinburgh, Scotland: Oliver & Boyd; J. Neyman, & E. S. Pearson. (1933). On the problem of the most efficient tests of statistical hypotheses. *Philosophical Transactions of the Royal Society of London. Series A, 231,* 289–337.

2. A comprehensive treatment of judgment and decision making in relation to systems engineering can be found in A. Sage. (1992). *Systems engineering.* New York: Wiley.

3. R. A. Park, & J. K. Lee. (1993). *Potential impacts of sea level rise on south Florida natural areas* (Tech. Rep.). Bloomington: Indiana University, School of Public & Environmental Affairs, p. 1.

4. Park & Lee, p. 4.

5. C. Crossen. (May 17, 1994). How "tactical research" muddied diaper debate. *The Wall Street Journal,* p. B1.

6. L. Tyson. (May 27, 1994). U.S. triumphant in trade policy. *The Wall Street Journal,* p. A8.

7. E. O. Box, D. W. Crumpacker, & E. D. Hardin. (1993). A climatic model for location of plant species in Florida, U.S.A. *Journal of Biogeography, 20,* p. 629.

8. Box, Crumpacker, & Hardin, pp. 633–634.

9. N. Oreskes, K. Shrader-Frechette, & K. Belitz. (1994). Verification, validation, and confirmation of numerical models in the earth sciences. *Science, 263,* p. 641.

10. Oreskes, Shrader-Frechette, & Belitz, p. 642.

11. Oreskes, Shrader-Frechette, & Belitz, p. 642.

12. Oreskes, Shrader-Frechette, & Belitz, p. 642.

13. J. D. Sterman. (1994). The meaning of models [Letter to the editor]. *Science, 264,* p. 330.

14. Sterman, p. 330.

15. Oreskes, Shrader-Frechette, & Belitz, p. 644.

16. Oreskes, Shrader-Frechette, & Belitz, p. 644.

17. R. J. Herrnstein, & C. Murray. (1994). *The bell curve: Intelligence and class structure in American life.* New York: Free Press.

18. For an interesting set of vignettes, see D. B. Wallace, & H. E. Gruber. (Eds.). (1989). *Creative people at work: Twelve cognitive case studies.* New York: Oxford University Press.

19. For examples, see K. R. Hammond, J. Mumpower, R. L. Dennis, S. Fitch, & W. Crumpacker. (1983). Fundamental obstacles to the use of scientific information in public policy making. *Technological Forecasting and Social Change, 24,* 287–297.

20. C. E. Lindblom. (1968). *The policy-making process.* Englewood Cliffs, NJ: Prentice-Hall, p. 116.

21. R. Cooksey. (1996). *Judgment analysis: Theory, methods, and applications.* San Diego: Academic Press. For an example still relevant see K. R. Hammond, & L. Adelman. (1976). Science, values, and human judgment. *Science, 194,* 389–396.

22. For a review, see B. Brehmer, & C. R. B. Joyce. (Eds.). (1988). *Human judgment: The SJT view.* Amsterdam: Elsevier.

23. It was introduced as "multiple cue probability learning" by Egon Brunswik. For a brief history, see E. Brunswik. (1956). *Perception and the representative design of psychological experiments* (2nd ed.). Berkeley, CA: University of California Press; K. R. Hammond. (Ed.). (1966). *The psychology of Egon Brunswik* (2nd ed.). New York: Holt, Rinehart, and Winston; for reviews, see Brehmer & Joyce; Cooksey.

24. H. J. Einhorn. (1980). Learning from experience and suboptimal rules in decision making. In T. S. Wallsten (Ed.), *Cognitive processes in choice and decision behavior* (pp. 1–20). Hillsdale, NJ: Erlbaum.

25. C. J. Hitch. (1977). Unfreezing the future. *Science, 195,* 825.

26. M. Twain. (1896/1985). *Life on the Mississippi.* Toronto: Bantam Books, p. 47.

27. W. K. Balzer, M. E. Doherty, & R. O'Connor, Jr. (1989). Effects of cognitive feedback on performance. *Psychological Bulletin, 106,* 410–433; K. R. Hammond. (1971). Computer graphics as an aid to learning. *Science, 172,* 903–908; R. M. Poses, R. D. Cebul, R. S. Wigton, & M. Collins. (1986). Feedback on simulated cases to improve clinical judgment [meeting abstract]. *Medical Decision Making, 6,* 274.

28. Parsons has drawn this distinction succinctly: "Seeing that something is the case is quite different from seeing an event or process on which the seeing-that is based." (T. Parsons. [1985]. Underlying events in the logical analysis of English. In E. LePore & B. P. McLaughlin [Eds.], *Actions and events: Perspectives on the philosophy of Donald Davidson.* Oxford, UK: Basil Blackwell, p. 247; see also chapter 1 of N. R. Hanson [1958]. *Patterns of discovery.* New York: Cambridge University Press.)

29. R. Toner. (June 18, 1995). Moynihan battles view he gave up on welfare fight. *New York Times,* sec. 1, pp. 1, 11.

30. No other record approaches his; for a description of his early studies, the antagonistic reaction to them, and their impact on social policy, see E. Herman. (1995). *The romance of American psychology: Political culture in the age of experts.* Berkeley: University of California Press.

31. Toner, sec. 1, p. 11

32. F. Bolger, & G. Wright. (1994). Assessing the quality of expert judgment: Issues and analysis. *Decision Support Systems, 11,* 1–24; K. R. Hammond. (1987). *Reducing disputes among experts* (Tech. Rep. No. 268). Boulder: University of Colorado, Center for Research on Judgment and Policy; K. R. Hammond. (1987). Toward a unified approach to the study of expert judgment. In J. L. Mumpower, L. D. Phillips, O. Renn, & V. R. R. Uppuluri (Eds.), *NATO ASI Series F: Computer and systems sciences: Vol. 35. Expert judgment and expert systems* (pp. 1–16). Berlin: Springer-Verlag.

33. B. G. Buchanan. (1982). New research on expert systems. In J. E. Hayes, D. Michie, & Y.-H. Pao (Eds.), *Machine Intelligence 10* (pp. 269–299). Chichester, UK: Ellis Horwood, pp. 269–270.

34. L. L. Lopes, & G. C. Oden. (1991). The rationality of intelligence. In E. Eells & T. Maruszewski (Eds.), *Probability and rationality: Studies on L. Jonathan Cohen's philosophy of science* (pp. 199–223). Amsterdam: Rodopi, pp. 200–201.

35. E. A. Feigenbaum. (1977). The art of artificial intelligence: I. Themes and case studies of knowledge engineering. In L. Erman (Ed.), *Proceedings of the International Joint Conference on Artificial Intelligence* (Vol. 2, pp. 1014–1029). Pittsburgh, PA: International Joint Conference on Artificial Intelligence, pp. 1016–1017.

36. N. H. Anderson. (1981). *Foundations of Information Integration Theory.* New York: Academic Press.

37. G. J. Gaeth, & J. Shanteau, J. (1984). Reducing the influence of irrelevant information on experienced decisionmakers. *Organizational Behavior and Human Performance, 33,* 263–282.

38. Poses, Cebul, Wigton, & Collins, p. 274. See also Einhorn, Learning from experience.

39. Poses, Cebul, Wigton, & Collins, p. 274.

40. Buchanan, p. 270.

41. D. Kahneman, P. Slovic, & A. Tversky. (Eds.). (1982). *Judgment under uncertainty: Heuristics and biases.* Cambridge, UK: Cambridge University Press.

42. For examples, see H. R. Arkes, & K. R. Hammond. (Eds.). (1986). *Judgment and decision making: An interdisciplinary reader.* Cambridge, UK: Cambridge University Press; K. R. Hammond, G. H. McClelland, & J. Mumpower. (1980). *Human judgment and decision making: Theories, methods, and procedures.* New York: Hemisphere/Praeger; J. F. Yates. (1990). *Judgment and decision making.* Englewood Cliffs, NJ: Prentice-Hall.

43. See Brehmer & Joyce; Cooksey.

44. K. R. Hammond. (1955). Probabilistic functioning and the clinical method. *Psychological Review, 62,* 255–262. For preceding work casting doubt on the competence of experts, see E. Frenkel-Brunswik. (1942). Motivation and behavior. *Genetic Psychology Monographs, 26,* 121–265; E. L. Kelly, & D. W. Fiske. (1951). *The prediction of performance in clinical psychology.* Ann Arbor: University of Michigan Press; E. L. Thorndike. (1918). Fundamental theorems in judging men. *Journal of Applied Psychology, 2,* 67–76; H. A. Wallace. (1923). What is in the corn judge's mind? *Journal of the American Society of Agronomy, 15,* 300–304. For contemporary views on experts' prediction of violence, see J. Monahan, & H. Steadman. (Eds.). (1994). *Violence and mental disorder: Developments in risk assessment.* Chicago, IL: University of Chicago Press.

45. R. H. Phelps, & J. Shanteau. (1978). Livestock judges: How much information can an expert use? *Organizational Behavior and Human Performance, 21,* 209–219; J. Shanteau, & R. Phelps. (1977). Judgment and swine: Approaches and issues in applied judgment analysis. In M. Kaplan & S. Schwartz (Eds.), *Human judgment and decision processes in applied settings* (pp. 255–272). New York: Academic Press.

46. W. Chase, & H. Simon. (1973). Perception in chess. *Cognitive Psychology, 4,* 55–81.

47. P. E. Johnson, F. Hassebrock, A. S. Duran, & J. H. Moller. (1982). Multimethod study of clinical judgment. *Organizational Behavior and Human Performance, 30,* p. 226. For some examples, see H.-U. Fisch, K. R. Hammond, & C. R. B. Joyce. (1982). On evaluating the severity of depression: An experimental study of psychiatrists. *British Journal of Psychiatry, 140,* 378–383; H.-U. Fisch, K. R. Hammond, C. R. B. Joyce, & M. O'Reilly. (1981). An experimental study of the clinical judgment of general physicians in evaluating and prescribing for depression. *British Journal of Psychiatry, 138,* 100–109; Poses, Cebul, Wigton, & Collins. See also D. M. Frederick, & R. Libby. (1986). Expertise and auditors' judgments of conjunctive events. *Journal of Accounting Research, 24,* 270–290; Gaeth & Shanteau. For a bibliography on research on the use of irrelevant facts on judgments, see G. J. Gaeth, & J. Shanteau. (1981). *A bibliography of research on the effects of irrelevance in psychology* (Rep. No. 81-13). Manhattan: Kansas State University, Department of Psychology.

48. Buchanan, pp. 280–281.

49. For a recent example, see K. R. Hammond, R. M. Hamm, J. Grassia, & T. Pearson. (1986). Direct comparison of the efficacy of intuitive and analytical cognition in expert judgment. *IEEE Transactions on Systems, Man, and Cybernetics, 17,* 753–770.

50. Brehmer & Joyce; Cooksey; C. M. Lusk, T. R. Stewart, K. R. Hammond, & R. J. Potts. (1990). Judgment and decision making in dynamic tasks: The case of forecasting the microburst. *Weather and Forecasting, 5,* 627–639; T. R. Stewart, W. R. Moninger, J. Grassia, R. H. Brady, & F. H. Merrem. (1989). Analysis of expert judgment in a hail forecasting experiment. *Weather and Forecasting, 4,* 24–34.

51. For a recent collection of articles on "decision aiding," see P. C. Humphreys, O. Svenson, & A. Vari. (Eds.). (1983). *Analysing and aiding decision processes.* Amsterdam: North Holland; see also L. Adelman. (1992). *Evaluating decision support and expert systems.* New York: Wiley-Interscience; see also Bolger & Wright.

52. J. Reason. (1990). *Human error.* Cambridge, UK: Cambridge University Press.

53. R. Stone. (1993). EPA analysis of radon in water is hard to swallow. *Science, 261,* p. 1514.

54. L. Roberts. (1991). Learning from an acid rain program. *Science, 251,* p. 1302.

55. Roberts, p. 1302.

56. Roberts, p. 1302.

57. K. R. Hammond, L. O. Harvey, Jr., & R. Hastie. (1992). Making better use of scientific knowledge: Separating truth from justice. *Psychological Science, 3,* 80–87.

58. F. Allen. (1994). Unreasonable facsimile: Do we really want computers to be more like us? *Atlantic Monthly, 274*(2), p. 20.

59. A. Tversky, & D. Kahneman. (1981). The framing of decisions and the psychology of choice. *Science, 211,* p. 453.

60. Tversky & Kahneman, p. 453.

61. B. J. McNeil, S. G. Pauker, H. C. Sox, & A. Tversky. (1982). On the elicitation of preferences for alternative therapies. *New England Journal of Medicine, 306,* 1259–1262.

62. S. Breyer. (1993). *Breaking the vicious circle: Toward effective risk regulation.* Cambridge, MA: Harvard University Press, p. 108.

63. L. L. Lopes. (1992). Risk perception and the perceived public. In D. W. Bromley & K. Segerson (Eds.), *The social response to environmental risk: Policy formulation in an age of uncertainty* (pp. 57–74). Boston: Kluwer, p. 57.

64. S. Lichtenstein, P. Slovic, B. Fischhoff, M. Layman, & B. Combs. (1978). Judged frequency of lethal events. *Journal of Experimental Psychology: Human Learning and Memory, 4,* 551–578.

65. Lopes, p. 59.

66. Lopes, p. 60.

67. Lopes, p. 60.

68. P. Sedlmeier, & G. Gigerenzer. (1994). *Intuitions about sample size: The empirical law of large numbers.* In press, *Journal of Behavioral Decision Making.*

69. T. R. Stewart, W. R. Moninger, K. F. Heideman, & P. Reagan-Cirincione. (1992). Effects of improved information on the components of skill in weather forecasting. *Organizational Behavior and Human Decision Processes, 53,* 107–134.

70. C. M. Lusk. (1993). Assessing components of judgments in an operational setting: The effects of time pressure on aviation weather forecasting. In O. Svenson & A. J. Maule (Eds.), *Time pressure and stress in human judgment and decision making* (pp. 309–321). New York: Plenum; C. M. Lusk, & K. R. Hammond. (1991). Judgment in a dynamic task: Microburst forecasting. *Journal of Behavioral Decision Making, 4,* 55–73; Lusk, Stewart, Hammond, & Potts.

71. See Stewart, Moninger, Grassia, Brady, & Merrem.

72. There is no textbook; but see T. T. Fujita. (1985). *The downburst, microburst and macroburst.* Chicago: University of Chicago, Department of Geophysical Sciences.

73. For example, see R. D. Roberts, & J. W. Wilson. (1989). A proposed microburst nowcasting procedure using single-Doppler radar. *Journal of Applied Meteorology, 28,* 285–303.

74. Compare S. Plous. (1993). *The psychology of judgment and decision making.* Philadelphia: Temple University Press.

75. R. M. Dawes, D. Faust, & P. E. Meehl. (1989). Clinical versus actuarial judgment. *Science, 243,* 1668–1673.

76. For example, see P. Slovic. (1987). Perception of risk. *Science, 236,* 280–285.

77. See the review: S. Kazman. (November 5, 1993). Risk regulation run amok. *The Wall Street Journal,* p. A7; and the comment by John Graham, Director of the Center for Risk Analysis at the Harvard School of Public Health: J. Graham. (May 18, 1994). Regulation: A risky business. *The Wall Street Journal,* p. A14.

78. See especially Breyer, pp. 17, 34, and 37.

79. Breyer, pp. 42–43.

80. P. H. Abelson. (1985). Air pollution and acid rain. *Science, 230*, 617.

81. P. E. Meehl. (1970). Nuisance variables and the ex post facto design. In M. Radner & S. Winokur (Eds.), *Minnesota studies in the philosophy of science: Vol. 4. Analyses of theories and methods of physics and psychology* (pp. 373–402). Minneapolis: University of Minnesota Free Press, p. 402.

82. H. M. Blalock, Jr. (1971). *Causal models in the social sciences*. Chicago: Aldine Atherton.

83. R. McNamara. (1995). *In retrospect: The tragedy and lessons of Vietnam*. New York: Times Books, p. xvi.

84. Meehl, p. 402.

85. McNamara, p. 36.

86. McNamara, p. 37.

87. McNamara, p. 172.

88. J. De Parle. (August 20, 1995). The man inside Bill Clinton's foreign policy. *New York Times Magazine*, p. 34.

89. C. Waddell. (1989). Reasonableness versus rationality in the construction and justification of science policy decisions: The case of the Cambridge Experimentation Review Board. *Science, Technology, & Human Values, 14*(1), 7–25; C. Waddell. (1990). The role of *pathos* in the decision-making process: A study in the rhetoric of science policy. *Quarterly Journal of Speech, 76*, 381–400.

90. Waddell, The role of *pathos*, p. 385.

91. Waddell, The role of *pathos*, p. 385.

92. Waddell, The role of *pathos*, p. 387.

*11. Possibilities for Wisdom*

1. H. Cantril. (1967). *The human dimension: Experiences in policy research*. New Brunswick, NJ: Rutgers University Press, p. vii.

2. Cantril, p. vii.

3. Cantril, p. vii.

4. Cantril, p. viii.

5. Cantril, p. ix.

6. Cantril, p. 35.

7. Cantril, p. 42.

8. J. M. Perry. (March 23, 1993). Clinton relies heavily on White House pollster to take words right out of the public's mouth. *The Wall Street Journal*, p. A14.

9. Cantril, pp. 17–20.

10. Cantril, p. 17.

11. My thesis adviser at the University of California, Berkeley.

12. E. Herman. (1995). *The romance of American psychology: Political culture in the age of experts*. Berkeley: University of California Press, p. 244.

13. Herman, p. 232.

14. Herman, p. 237.

15. Herman, pp. 4–5.

16. For an obituary that includes references to Janis's written work as well as his many other accomplishments, see M. B. Smith, & L. Mann. (1992). Irving L. Janis (1918–1990). *American Psychologist, 47*, 812–813; see, for example, I. L. Janis. (1982). *Groupthink: Psychological studies of policy decisions and fiascoes* (2nd ed.). Boston: Houghton Mifflin;

I. L. Janis. (1989). *Crucial decisions: Leadership in policymaking and crisis management.* New York: Free Press; I. L. Janis, & L. Mann. (1977). *Decision making: A psychological analysis of conflict, choice, and commitment.* New York: Free Press.

17. Janis, *Crucial decisions,* p. ix.

18. Janis, *Crucial decisions,* p. 12.

19. Janis, *Crucial decisions,* p. 12.

20. Janis, *Crucial decisions,* p. 13.

21. Janis, *Crucial decisions,* p. 13.

22. Janis, *Crucial decisions,* pp. 13–14.

23. See particularly Janis & Mann.

24. F. Heller. (Ed.). (1992). *Decision-making and leadership.* London: Cambridge University Press.

25. P. 't Hart. (1990). *Groupthink in government: A study of small groups and policy failure.* Amsterdam: Swets & Zeitlinger.

26. J. Longley, & D. G. Pruitt. (1980). Groupthink: A critique of Janis' theory. *Review of Personality and Social Psychology, 1,* 74–93.

27. Hart, pp. 15–27.

28. R. Hastie, & N. Pennington. (1991). Cognitive and social processes in decision making. In L. B. Resnick, J. M. Levine, & S. D. Teasley (Eds.), *Perspectives on socially shared cognition* (pp. 308–330). Washington, DC: American Psychological Association; see also R. Hastie, S. D. Penrod, & N. Pennington. (1983). *Inside the jury.* Cambridge, MA: Harvard University Press.

29. G. Moorhead, R. Ference, & C. P. Neck. (1991). Group decision fiascoes continue: Space shuttle Challenger and a revised groupthink framework. *Human Relations, 44,* p. 545.

30. Moorhead, Ference, & Neck, p. 546.

31. Moorhead, Ference, & Neck, p. 547.

32. See K. R. Hammond. (1977). Facilitation of interpersonal learning and conflict reduction by on-line communication. In J. D. White (Ed.), *The general systems paradigm: Science of change and change of science* (pp. 170–179). Washington, DC: Society for General Systems Research; for examples, see also K. R. Hammond, & L. Adelman. (1976). Science, values, and human judgment. *Science, 194,* 389–396.

33. R. Woodward. (1994). *The agenda.* New York: Simon & Schuster, p. 261.

34. Woodward, p. 261.

35. P. Suedfeld, & P. E. Tetlock. (Eds.). (1992c). *Psychology and social policy.* New York: Hemisphere.

36. P. Suedfeld, & P. E. Tetlock. (1992b). Psychologists as policy advocates: The roots of controversy. In P. Suedfeld & P. E. Tetlock (Eds.), *Psychology and social policy* (pp. 1–30). New York: Hemisphere, p. 25.

37. Suedfeld & Tetlock, Psychologists as policy advocates, p. 13.

38. R. K. White. (1992). Nuclear policies: Deterrence and reassurance. In P. Suedfeld & P. E. Tetlock (Eds.), *Psychology and social policy* (pp. 71–82). New York: Hemisphere.

39. J. G. Blight. (1992). Nuclear crisis psychologies: Still "crazy" (and still irrelevant) after all these years. In P. Suedfeld & P. E. Tetlock (Eds.), *Psychology and social policy* (pp. 83–93). New York: Hemisphere.

40. H. J. Harrington, & N. Miller. (1992). Overcoming resistance to affirmative action in industry: A social psychological perspective. In P. Suedfeld & P. E. Tetlock (Eds.), *Psychology and social policy* (pp. 121–135). New York: Hemisphere, p. 121.

41. Harrington & Miller, p. 121.

42. W. R. Beer. (1992). Affirmative action: Social policy as shibboleth. In P. Suedfeld & P. E. Tetlock (Eds.), *Psychology and social policy* (pp. 137–147). New York: Hemisphere, p. 146.

43. I. L. Janis, & L. Mann. (1992). Cognitive complexity in international decision making. In P. Suedfeld & P. E. Tetlock (Eds.), *Psychology and social policy* (pp. 33–49). New York: Hemisphere.

44. P. Suedfeld, & P. E. Tetlock. (1992a). Psychological advice about political decision making: Heuristics, biases, and cognitive defects. In P. Suedfeld & P. E. Tetlock (Eds.), *Psychology and social policy* (pp. 51–70). New York: Hemisphere.

45. W. K. Estes. (1994). *Classification and cognition.* New York: Oxford University Press.

46. Suedfeld & Tetlock, Psychological advice, p. 55.

47. Suedfeld & Tetlock, Psychological advice, p. 67.

48. R. L. Keeney. (1992). *Value-focused thinking: A path to creative decisionmaking.* Cambridge, MA: Harvard University Press.

49. See also H. H. Kendler. (1993). Psychology and the ethics of social policy. *American Psychologist, 48,* 1046–1053.

50. P. Suedfeld, & P. E. Tetlock. (1992b). Psychologists as policy advocates: The roots of controversy. In P. Suedfeld & P. E. Tetlock (Eds.), *Psychology and social policy* (pp. 1–30). New York: Hemisphere, p. 14.

51. Several others were carried out at our research center subsequently.

52. D. M. Eddy. (1982). Probabilistic reasoning in clinical medicine: Problems and opportunities. In D. Kahneman, P. Slovic, & A. Tversky (Eds.), *Judgment under uncertainty: Heuristics and biases* (pp. 249–267). Cambridge, UK: Cambridge University Press.

53. G. A. Craig. (July 14, 1994). An inability to mourn (Review of *The wages of guilt: Memories of war in Germany and Japan*). *The New York Review of Books*, p. 44.

54. Suedfeld & Tetlock, *Psychology and social policy.*

55. W. Olson. (March 30, 1995). The bard of bureaucracy. *The Wall Street Journal*, p. A14.

56. T. Noah. (March 30, 1995). Best-selling author urges both political parties to find common ground on regulatory reform. *The Wall Street Journal*, p. A18.

57. P. K. Howard. (1994). *The death of common sense: How law is suffocating America.* New York: Random House, p. 74.

58. Howard, p. 184.

59. Howard, p. 174.

60. Howard, p. 175.

61. Howard, p. 187.

62. See R. Lacayo. (April 10, 1995). Anecdotes not antidotes. *Time*, pp. 40–41.

63. Howard, p. 75.

64. Howard, p. 184.

65. Howard, p. 35.

66. Howard, p. 35.

67. Howard, p. 44.

68. Howard, p. 44.

69. S. C. Pepper. (1942). *World hypothesis: A study in evidence.* Berkeley: University of California Press, pp. 44–46.

70. S. Breyer. (1993). *Breaking the vicious circle: Toward effective risk regulation.* Cambridge, MA: Harvard University Press; see especially Chapter 1.

71. P. Slovic, S. Lichtenstein, & B. Fischhoff. (1988). Decision making. In R. C. Atkinson, R. J. Herrnstein, G. Lindzey, & R. D. Luce (Eds.), *Handbook of experimental psychology: Vol 2. Learning and cognition* (pp. 673–738). New York: Wiley, p. 689.

72. G. F. Kennan. (1993). *Around the cragged hill: A personal and political philosophy.* New York: Norton, p. 145.

73. Kennan, p. 239.

74. See Slovic, Lichtenstein, & Fischhoff.

75. S. Plous. (1993). *The psychology of judgment and decision making.* Philadelphia: Temple University Press.

76. C. Cerf, & V. Navasky. (1984). *The experts speak: The definitive compendium of authoritative misinformation.* New York: Pantheon Books, p. 215.

77. Cerf & Navasky, p. 215.

78. Cerf & Navasky, p. 252.

79. Cerf & Navasky, p. 243.

80. Cerf & Navasky, p. 113.

81. Cerf & Navasky, p. 47.

82. A compilation of 100-year forecasts (1893–1993) can be found in D. Walter. (1992). *Today then: America's best minds look 100 years into the future on the occasion of the 1893 World's Columbian Exposition.* Helena, MT: American and World Geographic Publishing. See also J. F. Coates. (1994). From my perspective: A chrestomathy of flawed forecasts. *Technological Forecasting and Social Change, 45,* 307–311.

83. C. D. Bowen. (1966). *Miracle at Philadelphia: The story of the Constitutional Convention, May to September, 1787.* Boston: Little, Brown, p. 4.

84. Breyer, p. 43.

85. For a detailed description of the research base, see W. K. Balzer, M. E. Doherty, & R. O'Connor, Jr. (1989). Effects of cognitive feedback on performance. *Psychological Bulletin, 106,* 410–433; see also R. Cooksey. (1996). *Judgment analysis: Theory, methods, and applications.* San Diego: Academic Press.

86. For further reading, see H. R. Arkes, & K. R. Hammond. (Eds.). (1986). *Judgment and decision making: An interdisciplinary reader.* Cambridge, UK: Cambridge University Press; Balzer, Doherty, & O'Connor; Cooksey; K. R. Hammond. (1971). Computer graphics as an aid to learning. *Science, 172,* 903–908; K. R. Hammond, G. H. McClelland, & J. Mumpower. (1980). *Human judgment and decision making: Theories, methods, and procedures.* New York: Hemisphere/Praeger; K. R. Hammond, D. A. Summers, & D. H. Deane. (1973). Negative effects of outcome feedback in multiple-cue probability learning. *Organizational Behavior and Human Performance, 9,* 30–34.

87. See Breyer, Chapter 1.

88. Breyer, p. 60.

89. Breyer, pp. 60–61.

90. G. F. Kennan. (1967). *Memoirs: 1925–1950.* Boston: Little, Brown, p. 348.

91. Kennan, *Memoirs,* pp. 349–350.

92. G. B. Kistiakowsky. (1976). *A scientist at the White House: The private diary of President Eisenhower's Special Assistant for Science and Technology* (with an introduction by Charles S. Maier). Cambridge, MA: Harvard University Press.

93. H. Scoville, Jr. (1977). An inside view [Review of *A scientist at the White House*]. *Science, 195,* p. 168.

94. Federal Open Market Committee (1988). *Transcript: Federal Open Market Committee Meeting, August 16, 1988,* p. 43.

95. Federal Open Market Committee, p. 44.

96. Federal Open Market Committee, p. 44.

97. Federal Open Market Committee, pp. 45–46.

98. See B. Brehmer, & C. R. B. Joyce. (Eds.). (1988). *Human judgment: The SJT view.* Amsterdam: Elsevier.

99. R. J. Herrnstein, & C. Murray. (1994). *The bell curve: Intelligence and class structure in American life.* New York: Free Press, p. 511. See the graph on p. 56.

100. Cantril, p. vii.

*12. The Possible Future of Cognitive Competence*

1. S. Pinker. (September 25, 1994). Is there a gene for compassion? (Review of the book *The moral animal: The new science of evolutionary psychology*). *New York Times Book Review*, p. 3.

2. J. Bruner. (1983). *In search of mind: Essays in autobiography*. New York: Harper and Row, pp. 274–275.

3. For other predictions of the future from cognitive psychologists, see K. J. Arrow. (1995). Viewpoint: The future. *Science, 267*, 1617–1618; S. M. Kosslyn. (1995). Viewpoint: The future. *Science, 267*, 1615; N. J. Smelser. (1995). Viewpoint: The future. *Science, 267*, 1618.

4. M. Connelly, & P. Kennedy. (1994, December). Must it be the rest against the west? *The Atlantic Monthly*, p. 69.

5. P. F. Drucker. (1994, November). The age of social transformation. *The Atlantic Monthly*, p. 53.

6. Drucker, p. 54.

7. Drucker, p. 54.

8. Drucker, p. 64.

9. Drucker, p. 64.

10. R. J. Herrnstein, & C. Murray. (1994). *The bell curve: Intelligence and class structure in American life*. New York: Free Press, p. 25.

11. Herrnstein & Murray, p. 25.

12. Herrnstein & Murray, p. 25.

13. See S. Fraser. (1995). *The bell curve wars*. New York: Basic Books.

14. See Fraser; R. J. Sternberg. (1995). For whom the bell curve tolls: A review of *The bell curve*. *Psychological Science, 6*, 257–261.

15. R. B. Reich. (1992). *The work of nations: Preparing ourselves for 21st-century capitalism*. New York: Vintage Books, p. 174.

16. Reich, p. 175.

17. The period of sharpest cognitive change apparently came in the eighteenth and nineteenth centuries when the agricultural worker moved into the harsh workplaces of industrial routine; the change must have been shocking to the workers. Zuboff quotes Josiah Tucker's 1757 pamphlet that describes the reaction of domestic weavers who went to work in the factory: The workers' "only happiness is to get drunk and make life pass away with as little *thought* [italics added] as possible." (Zuboff, S. [1988]. *In the age of the smart machines: The future of work and power*. New York: Basic Books, p. 35). Deprived of the opportunity to apply their cognitive skills as correspondence experts, they would hardly have wanted to think, to engage in coherent, analytical cognition; they were slaves to that in their work, simple-minded and repetitive as it might have been. For a detailed history of the Luddite revolt see K. Sale. (1995). *Rebels against the future*. New York: Addison-Wesley.

18. Reich, p. 176.

19. Reich, p. 176.

20. Reich, p. 176.

21. D. Funder. (1987). Errors and mistakes: Evaluating the accuracy of social judgment. *Psychological Bulletin, 101*, 75–90.

22. F. J. Bernieri, J. S. Gillis, & J. M. Davis. (1992, September). *The judgment of rapport*. Paper presented at the Research on Individual Judgment Processes International Workshop, Amsterdam, The Netherlands.

23. M. Twain. (1896/1985). *Life on the Mississippi*. Toronto: Bantam Books, p. 47.

24. Twain, p. 48.

25. Twain, pp. 48–49.

26. Twain, p. 48.

27. Twain, p. 49.

28. Professional job analysts may find Twain's descriptions to be overly romanticized, and thus distorted, job descriptions. But I find them to be precisely focused and more informative than the professionals' efforts to describe cognitive activity at work. See, for example, Zuboff, pp. 36–58; F. W. Taylor. (1911). *The principles of scientific management*. New York: Harper & Brothers.

29. Reich, p. 177.

30. Reich, pp. 178–179.

31. Herrnstein & Murray, p. 91.

32. Herrnstein & Murray, p. 513. Michael Lind, a senior editor of *Harper's Magazine*, made a similar observation of the homogeneity of the lifestyle of the cognitive elite (M. Lind. [1995, June]. To have and have not: Notes on the progress of the American class war. *Harper's Magazine*, pp. 35–39, 42–47).

33. Reich, p. 182.

34. J. F. Voss, D. N. Perkins, & J. W. Segal. (Eds.). (1991). *Informal reasoning and education*. Hillsdale, NJ: Erlbaum, p. vii.

35. Voss, Perkins, & Segal, p. viiii.

36. Voss, Perkins, & Segal, p. xi.

37. Voss, Perkins, & Segal, p. xi.

38. Voss, Perkins, & Segal, p. xiii.

39. Their work is derived at least in part from Michael Polanyi (M. Polanyi. [1966]. *The tacit dimension*. Garden City, NY: Doubleday; M. Polanyi. [1969]. *Knowing and being: Essays by Michael Polanyi*. Chicago: University of Chicago Press; see especially Part III).

40. R. J. Sternberg, R. K. Wagner, W. M. Williams, & J. A. Horvath. (1995). Testing Common Sense. *American Psychologist, 50*, 912–927.

41. A. J. McClurg. (1988). Logical fallacies and the Supreme Court: A critical examination of Justice Rehnquist's decisions in criminal procedure cases. *University of Colorado Law Review, 59*, 741–844.

42. For example, see R. Jeffrey. (1981). *Formal logic: Its scope and limits* (2nd ed.). New York: McGraw-Hill.

43. McClurg, p. 767.

44. McClurg, p. 769.

45. D. B. Cornish, & R. V. Clarke. (Eds.). (1986). *The reasoning criminal: Rational choice perspectives on offending*. New York: Springer-Verlag.

46. J. Carroll, & F. Weaver. (1986). Shoplifters' perceptions of crime opportunities: A process tracing study. In D. B. Cornish & R. V. Clarke (Eds.), *The reasoning criminal: Rational choice perspectives on offending* (pp. 19–38). New York: Springer-Verlag.

47. This study by Wayman Crow never made its way into the scientific literature, but I was able to make use of it in understanding a part of my environment. There is a shopping center near where I live that I visit occasionally and which has a medium-size meat shop. When I first saw it, I thought "Oh no! This place will be robbed in short order." Why? Among the high-priority indicators used by robbers are the location and the street visibility of the cash register. If it is close to the door—good! If it is not visible from the street—good! Both these conditions were present in this store in, one might say, pristine form. But the store was not robbed. Why not? Because the third indicator of success is missing: Quick getaway is almost impossible. No store in this shopping center has ever been robbed in the thirty or so years since the center was built.

48. M. Janofsky. (March 5, 1995). In drug fight, police now take to the highway. *New York Times,* sec. 1, p. 12.

49. The same game of reciprocal description can be seen at the insect level; see any entomological text.

50. R. Wright, R. H. Logie, & S. H. Decker. (1995). Criminal expertise and offender decision making: An experimental study of the target selection process in residential burglary. *Journal of Research in Crime and Delinquency, 32,* 39–53.

51. Wright, Logie, & Decker, p. 52.

52. Wright, Logie, & Decker, p. 52.

### 13. Rivalry, Tension—Forever?

1. Callins v. Collins, No. 93–7054, 1994 S. Ct. LEXIS 1327 (Feb. 22, 1994), p. 1130.

2. Callins v. Collins, p. 1130.

3. Callins v. Collins, p. 1129.

4. Callins v. Collins, p. 1129.

5. L. Greenhouse. (February 23, 1994). Death penalty is renounced by Blackmun. *New York Times,* p. A10.

6. O. W. Holmes. (1881/1923). *The common law.* Boston: Little, Brown, p. 1.

7. Lochner v. New York, 198 U.S. 45 (1905), p. 75.

8. Callins v. Collins, p. 1129.

9. Callins v. Collins, p. 1131.

10. Callins v. Collins, p. 1128.

11. Callins v. Collins, p. 1127.

12. Callins v. Collins, p. 1127. Stuart Hampshire, a well-respected British philosopher, offers an excellent treatment of the basis of morality in S. Hampshire. (Ed.). (1978). *Public and private morality.* Cambridge, UK: Cambridge University Press.

13. Callins v. Collins, p. 1128.

14. N. Pennington, & R. Hastie. (1993a). The story model for juror decision making. In R. Hastie (Ed.), *Inside the juror: The psychology of juror decision making* (pp. 192–221). Cambridge, UK: Cambridge University Press.

15. N. Mailer. (1995, May). The amateur hit man. *The New York Review of Books,* p. 58.

16. Mailer, p. 59.

17. U.S. v. Koon, No. 92–686 (C.D. Cal. Aug. 4, 1993) (Sentencing Memorandum), p. 51.

18. U.S. vs. Koon, p. 20.

19. U.S. vs. Koon, p. 20.

20. U.S. vs. Koon, p. 25.

21. U.S. vs. Koon, p. 31.

22. R. M. Dawes, D. Faust, & P. E. Meehl. (1989). Clinical versus actuarial judgment. *Science, 243,* 1668–1673.

23. P. E. Meehl. (1986). Causes and effects of my disturbing little book. *Journal of Personality Assessment, 50,* p. 372.

24. U.S. vs. Koon, p. 31.

25. U.S. vs. Koon, p. 32.

26. U.S. vs. Koon, p. 32.

27. U.S. vs. Koon, p. 32.

28. U.S. vs. Koon, p. 34.

29. U.S. vs. Koon, p. 34.

30. See T. Kuhn. (1962). *The structure of scientific revolutions*. Chicago: University of Chicago Press, in which he argued that no coherence-based argument was overthrown until a more compelling one was established; failures in correspondence were tolerated.

31. U.S. v. Koon, No. 93–50561, 1994 U.S. App. LEXIS 22588 (9th Cir. Cal. Aug. 19, 1994), p. *140.

32. U.S. vs. Koon, 1993, p. 34.

# References

Aaron, H. (1985). Comment. In J. A. Hausman & D. A. Wise (Eds.), *Social experimentation.* Chicago: University of Chicago Press.

Abelson, P. H. (1985). Air pollution and acid rain. *Science, 230,* 617.

Abernathy, C. M., & Hamm, R. M. (1994). *Surgical intuition: What it is and how to get it.* Philadelphia: Hanley & Belfus.

Adelman, L. (1992). *Evaluating decision support and expert systems.* New York: Wiley-Interscience.

Adler, N. (1994). *Adolescent sexual behavior looks irrational—But looks are deceiving.* Washington, DC: Federation of Behavioral, Psychological, and Cognitive Sciences.

Aigner, D. J. (1985). The residential electricity time-of-use pricing experiments: What have we learned? In J. A. Hausman & D. A. Wise (Eds.), *Social Experimentation.* Chicago: University of Chicago Press.

Allen, F. (1994). Unreasonable facsimile: Do we really want computers to be more like us? *Atlantic Monthly, 274*(2), 20–23.

Allison, G. T. (1971). *Essence of decision: Explaining the Cuban missile crisis.* Boston, MA: Little, Brown.

Anderson, B. F., Deane, D. H., Hammond, K. R., McClelland, G. H., & Shanteau, J. C. (1981). *Concepts in judgment and decision research: Definitions, sources, interrelations, comments.* New York: Praeger.

Anderson, C. (1994). Measuring what works in health care. *Science, 263,* 1080–1082.

Anderson, J. R. (1976). *Language, memory, and thought.* Hillsdale, NJ: Erlbaum.

Anderson, J. R. (1982). Acquisition of cognitive skill. *Psychological Review, 89,* 369–406.

Anderson, J. R. (1990). *The adaptive character of thought.* Hillsdale, NJ: Erlbaum.

Anderson, L. D. (1921). Estimating intelligence by means of printed photographs. *Journal of Applied Psychology, 5,* 152–155.

Anderson, N. H. (1981). *Foundations of Information Integration Theory.* New York: Academic Press.

Anderson, R. (1972). Hunt and deceive: Information management in Newfoundland deep-sea trawler fishing. In R. Anderson & C. Wadel (Eds.), *North Atlantic fishermen: Anthropological essays on modern fishing. Newfoundland social and economic papers No. 5.* Toronto: University of Toronto Press.

Arkes, H. R. (1991). Costs and benefits of judgment errors: Implications for debiasing. *Psychological Bulletin, 110,* 486–498.

Arkes, H. R., & Hammond, K. R. (Eds.). (1986). *Judgment and decision making: An interdisciplinary reader.* Cambridge, UK: Cambridge University Press.

Arrow, K. J. (1995). Viewpoint: The future. *Science, 267,* 1617–1618.

Ashworth, A. (1992). *Sentencing and criminal justice.* London: Weidenfeld & Nicolson, Ltd.

Baddeley, A. (1993). Working memory or working attention? In A. Baddeley & L. Weiskrantz (Eds.), *Attention: Selection, awareness, and control.* Oxford, UK: Clarendon Press.

Bailar, J. C., III, & Mosteller, F. (1992). *Medical uses of statistics* (2nd ed.). Boston, MA: NEJM Books.

Balzer, W. K., Doherty, M. E., & O'Connor, R., Jr. (1989). Effects of cognitive feedback on performance. *Psychological Bulletin, 106,* 410–433.

Bar-Hillel, M. (1980). The base-rate fallacy in probability judgments. *Acta Psychologica, 44,* 211–233.

Baron, J. (1988). *Thinking and deciding.* Cambridge, UK: Cambridge University Press.

Baron, J., & Brown, R. (1991). Prologue. In J. Baron & R. Brown (Eds.), *Teaching decision making to adolescents.* Hillsdale, NJ: Erlbaum.

Bartlett, J. (1968). *Familiar quotations: A collection of passages, phrases and proverbs traced to their sources in ancient and modern literature* (14th ed.). Boston: Little, Brown.

Beer, W. R. (1992). Affirmative action: Social policy as shibboleth. In P. Suedfeld & P. E. Tetlock (Eds.), *Psychology and social policy.* New York: Hemisphere.

Bennett, W. J. (1993). *The index of leading cultural indicators: Vol. 1.* Washington, DC: Heritage Foundation.

Berger, B., Glazer, N., & Stimpson, C. (1991). The idea of the university. *Partisan Review, 58,* 315–349.

Berger, P. L., & Neuhaus, R. J. (1977). *To empower people: The role of mediating structures in public policy.* Washington, DC: American Enterprise Institute.

Berkson, J. (1947). "Cost-utility" as a measure of the efficiency of a test. *Journal of the American Statistical Association, 42,* 246–255.

Berlin, I. (1978). *Russian thinkers.* New York: Viking Press.

Berlin, I. (1980). *Against the current: Essays in the history of ideas.* New York: Viking Press.

Berlin, I. (1981). *Personal Impressions.* New York: Viking Press.

Bernieri, F., & Gillis, J. (1995). The judgment of rapport: A cross-cultural comparison between American and Greeks. *Journal of Nonverbal Behavior, 19,* 115–130.

Bernieri, F. J., Gillis, J. S., & Davis, J. M. (1992, September). *The judgment of rapport.* Paper presented at the Research on Individual Judgment Processes International Workshop, Amsterdam, The Netherlands.

Bernieri, F. J., Gillis, J. S., & Davis, J. M. (1993). *The judgment of rapport: A lens model analysis.* Corvallis: Oregon State University.

Berthold, P. (1993). *Bird migration: A general survey* (H-G Bauer & T. Tomlinson, Trans.). Oxford, UK: Oxford University Press.

Berwick, D. M. (1991). Controlling variation in health care: A consultation from Walter Shewhart. *Medical Care, 29,* 1212–1225.

Birnbaum, M. H. (1983). Base rates in Bayesian inference: Signal detection analysis of the cab problem. *American Journal of Psychology, 96,* 85–94.

Björkman, M. (1984). From dualism to pluralism: The third world in judgment under uncertainty. In K. M. J. Lagerspetz & P. Niemi (Eds.), *Psychology in the 1990s.* Amsterdam: Elsevier.

Blakeslee, S. (1996, Janury 23). Figuring out the brain from its acts of denial. *New York Times,* pp. B5, B7.

Blalock, H. M., Jr. (1971). *Causal models in the social sciences.* Chicago: Aldine Atherton.

Blight, J. G. (1992). Nuclear crisis psychologies: Still "crazy" (and still irrelevant) after all these years. In P. Suedfeld & P. E. Tetlock (Eds.), *Psychology and social policy.* New York: Hemisphere.

Blurton-Jones, N., & Konner, M. J. (1976). !Kung knowledge of animal behaviour. In R. Lee & I. DeVore (Eds.), *Kalahari hunter-gatherers*. Cambridge, MA: Harvard University Press.

Bolger, F., & Wright, G. (1994). Assessing the quality of expert judgment: Issues and analysis. *Decision Support Systems, 11*, 1–24.

Boorstin, D. J. (1983). *The discoverers*. New York: Random House.

Boring, E. G. (1942). *Sensation and perception in the history of psychology*. New York: Appleton-Century.

Boruch, R. F., & Riecken, H. W. (1975). *Experimental testing of public policy: The Proceedings of the 1974 Social Science Research Council Conference on Social Experiments*. Boulder: Westview Press.

Bowditch, N. (1984). *American practical navigator: An epitome of navigation*. Washington, DC: Defense Mapping Agency Hydrographic/Topographic Center. (Original work published 1802)

Bowen, C. D. (1966). *Miracle at Philadelphia: The story of the Constitutional Convention, May to September, 1787*. Boston: Little, Brown.

Box, E. O., Crumpacker, D. W., & Hardin, E. D. (1993). A climatic model for location of plant species in Florida, U.S.A. *Journal of Biogeography, 20*, 629–644.

Brehmer, B. (1994). The psychology of linear judgement models. *Acta Psychologica, 87*, 137–154.

Brehmer, B., & Joyce, C. R. B. (Eds.). (1988). *Human judgment: The SJT view*. Amsterdam: Elsevier.

Brewer, M. B. (1988). A dual process model of impression formation. In T. K. Srull & R. S. Wyer (Eds.), *Advances in social cognition* (Vol. 1, pp. 1–36). Hillsdale, NJ: Erlbaum.

Breyer, S. (1993). *Breaking the vicious circle: Toward effective risk regulation*. Cambridge, MA: Harvard University Press.

Broadbent, D. E. (1971). *Decision and stress*. London: Academic Press.

Brody, J. E. (1992, September 20). Nationwide tests set for prostate cancer, but doubts surface. *New York Times*, pp. 1, 18.

Bronowski, J. (1977). *A sense of the future*. Cambridge, MA: MIT Press.

Brooks, D. (1992, September 28). It's a bird, it's a plane, it's multilateral man! *The Wall Street Journal*, p. A14.

Bruner, J. (1961). *The process of education*. Cambridge: Harvard University Press.

Bruner, J. (1962). *On knowing: Essays for the left hand*. New York: Atheneum.

Bruner, J. (1983). *In search of mind: Essays in autobiography*. New York: Harper and Row.

Bruner, J. S. (1986). *Actual minds, possible worlds*. Cambridge, MA: Harvard University Press.

Bruner, J. S., Goodnow, J., & Austin, G. A. (1956). *A study of thinking*. New York: Wiley.

Brunswik, E. (1943). Organismic achievement and environmental probability. *Psychological Review, 50*, 255–272.

Brunswik, E. (1944). Distal focussing of perception: Size constancy in a representative sample of situations. *Psychological Monographs*, No. 254.

Brunswik, E. (1952). The conceptual framework of psychology. In *International encyclopedia of unified science* (Vol. 1, no. 10, pp. 4–102). Chicago: University of Chicago Press.

Brunswik, E. (1956). *Perception and the representative design of psychological experiments* (2nd ed.). Berkeley, CA: University of California Press.

Buchanan, B. G. (1982). New research on expert systems. In J. E. Hayes, D. Michie, & Y.-H. Pao (Eds.), *Machine Intelligence 10*. Chichester, UK: Ellis Horwood.

Burnside, D. G., & Faithfull, E. (1993). Judging range trend: Interpretation of rangeland monitoring data drawn from sites in the western Australian shrublands. *Rangeland Journal, 15*, 247–269.

Burton, S. J. (1985). *An introduction to law and legal reasoning*. Boston, MA: Little, Brown.

Burton, T. M. (1993, February 16). Blood test for prostate cancer is raising issue of reliability, drug-industry role. *The Wall Street Journal*, p. B1.

Buss, D. M. (1992). Mate preference mechanisms: Consequences for partner choice and intrasexual competition. In J. H. Barkow, L. Cosmides, & J. Tooby (Eds.), *The adapted mind: Evolutionary psychology and the generation of culture*. New York: Oxford University Press.

Buss, D. M. (1994). *The evolution of desire: Strategies of human mating*. New York: Basic Books.

Byrne, R. (1995). *The thinking ape: Evolutionary origins of intelligence*. Oxford, UK: Oxford University Press.

Callins v. Collins, No. 93–7054, 1994 S. Ct. LEXIS 1327 (Feb. 22, 1994).

Campbell, D. T. (1969). Reforms as experiments. *American Psychologist, 24*, 409–429.

Campbell, D. T., & Stanley, J. C. (1966). *Experimental and quasi-experimental designs for research*. Chicago: Rand McNally.

Cantril, H. (1967). *The human dimension: Experiences in policy research*. New Brunswick, NJ: Rutgers University Press.

Cardozo, B. N. (1931). Mr. Justice Holmes. *Harvard Law Review, 44*, 682–692.

Carroll, J., & Weaver, F. (1986). Shoplifters' perceptions of crime opportunities: A process tracing study. In D. B. Cornish & R. V. Clarke (Eds.), *The reasoning criminal: Rational choice perspectives on offending*. New York: Springer-Verlag.

Castellan, N. J., Jr. (1992). Relations between linear models: Implications for the lens model. *Organizational Behavior and Human Decision Processes, 51*, 364–381.

Cerf, C., & Navasky, V. (1984). *The experts speak: The definitive compendium of authoritative misinformation*. New York: Pantheon Books.

Chase, W., & Simon, H. (1973). Perception in chess. *Cognitive Psychology, 4*, 55–81.

Chasseigne, G. (1995, November). *Aging and multiple cue probability learning: The case of inverse relationships; cognitive feedback versus outcome feedback*. Paper presented at the 11th International Meeting of the Brunswik Society, Los Angeles.

Christensen-Szalanski, J. J. J., & Beach, L. R. (1984). The citation bias: Fad and fashion in the judgment and decision literature. *American Psychologist, 39*, 75–78.

Churchman, C. W. (1971). *The design of inquiring systems: Basic concepts of systems and organization*. New York: Basic Books.

*The civil law: Including the Twelve tables, the Institutes of Gaius, the Rules of Ulpian, the Opinions of Paulus, the Enactments of Justinian, and the Constitutions of Leo* (translated from the original Latin, edited and compared with all accessible systems of jurisprudence ancient and modern by S. P. Scott). (1932). Cincinnati: Central Trust Co.

Cleeton, G. U., & Knight, F. B. (1924). Validity of character judgments based on external criteria. *Journal of Applied Psychology, 8*, 215–231.

Clinton, W. (1993, February 16). Transcript of president's address on the economy. *New York Times*, p. A14.

Coates, J. F. (1994). From my perspective: a chrestomathy of flawed forecasts. *Technological Forecasting and Social Change, 45*, 307–311.

Cobb, C., Halstead, T., & Rowe, J. (1995). If the GDP is up, why is America down? *Atlantic Monthly, 276*(4), 59–60, 62–68, 70, 72–73, 76, 78.

Coffin v. United States, 156 U.S. 432 (1895).

Cohen, I. B. (1995). *Science and the founding fathers: Science in the political thought of Jefferson, Franklin, Adams, and Madison*. New York: Norton.

Cohn, H. E. (1972). Mammography in its proper perspective. *Surgery, Gynecology and Obstetrics, 134*, 97–98.

Commonwealth v. Webster, 59 Mass. (5 Cush.) 320 (1850).

Connelly, M., & Kennedy, P. (1994, December). Must it be the rest against the west? *The Atlantic Monthly*, pp. 61–63, 66, 68–70, 72, 76, 79, 82, 84–86, 88, 91.

Connolly, T. (1987). Decision theory, reasonable doubt, and the utility of erroneous acquittals. *Law and Human Behavior, 11*, 101–112.

Cook, M. (1984). *Issues in person perception*. London: Methuen.

Cook, T. D., & Campbell, D. T. (1979). *Quasi-experimentation: Design and analysis issues for field settings*. Boston: Houghton-Mifflin.

Cooksey, R. (1996). *Judgment analysis: Theory, methods, and applications*. San Diego: Academic Press.

Cooper, L. S., Chalmers, T. C., McCally, M., Berrier, J., & Sacks, H. S. (1988). The poor quality of early evaluations of magnetic resonance imaging. *Journal of the American Medical Association, 259*, 3277–3280.

Cooper, R. M. (Ed.). (1991). *Food and drug law*. Washington, DC: Food and Drug Law Institute.

Cornish, D. B., & Clarke, R. V. (Eds.). (1986). *The reasoning criminal: Rational choice perspectives on offending*. New York: Springer-Verlag.

Craig, G. A. (1994, July 14). An inability to mourn [Review of *The wages of guilt: Memories of war in Germany and Japan*]. *The New York Review of Books*, pp. 43–45.

Crandall, C. S. (1984). The overcitation of examples of poor performance: Fad, fashion, or fun [Comment]? *American Psychologist, 39*, 1499–1500.

Crevier, D. (1993). *The tumultuous history of the search for artificial intelligence*. New York: Basic Books.

Cronbach, L. J. (1955). Processes affecting scores on "understanding of others" and "assumed similarity." *Psychological Bulletin, 52*, 177–193.

Cronbach, L. J. (1975). Beyond the two disciplines of scientific psychology. *American Psychologist, 30*, 116–127.

Cronbach, L. J., & Snow, R. E. (1977). *Aptitudes and instructional methods: A handbook for research on interactions*. New York: Irvington.

Crossen, C. (1994, May 17). How "tactical research" muddied diaper debate. *The Wall Street Journal*, p. B1.

Cumming, H. S., Hazen, H. H., Sanford, A. H., Senear, F. E., Simpson, W. M., & Vonderlehr, R. A. (1935). *The evaluation of serodiagnostic tests for syphilis in the United States: Report of results*. Washington, DC: Government Printing Office.

Dalal, S. R., Fowlkes, E. B., & Hoadley, B. (1989). Risk analysis of the space shuttle: Pre-Challenger prediction of failure. *Journal of the American Statistical Association, 84*, 945–957.

Dalgleish, L. I. (1988). Decision making in child abuse cases: Applications of social judgment theory and signal detection theory. In B. Brehmer & C. R. B. Joyce (Eds.), *Human judgment: The SJT view* (pp. 317–360). Amsterdam: Elsevier.

Dalgleish, L. I. (1991, April). *Assessment of perceived risk in child protection: A model, some data and implications for practice*. Address to Child Maltreatment Conference, Prince of Wales Children's Hospital, Randwick, Sydney, Australia.

Dalgleish, L. I., & Drew, E. C. (1989). The relationship of child abuse indicators to the assessment of perceived risk and to the court's decision to separate. *Child Abuse and Neglect, 13*, 491–506.

Damasio, A. R. (1994). *Descartes' error: Emotion, reason, and the human brain*. New York: G. P. Putnam.

Darwin, C. (1874). *The descent of man and selection in relation to sex* (2nd ed.). New York: A. L. Fowle.

Darwin, C. (1965). *The expression of the emotions in man and animals.* Chicago: University of Chicago Press. (Original work published 1872)

Davidson, D. (1984). *Inquiries into truth and interpretation.* Oxford, UK: Oxford University Press.

Dawes, R. M. (1988). *Rational choice in an uncertain world.* San Diego: Harcourt, Brace, Jovanovich.

Dawes, R. M., & Corrigan, B. (1974). Linear models in decision making. *Psychological Bulletin, 81,* 95–106.

Dawes, R. M., Faust, D., & Meehl, P. E. (1989). Clinical versus actuarial judgment. *Science, 243,* 1668–1673.

DeKay, M. (in press). The difference between Blackstone-like error ratios and probabilistic standards of proof. *Law & Social Inquiry.*

Del Regato, J. A. (1970). Diagnosis, treatment and prognosis. In L. V. Ackerman (Ed.), *Cancer.* St. Louis: Mosby.

Denes-Raj, V., & Epstein, S. (1994). Conflict between experiential and rational processing: When people behave against their better judgment. *Journal of Personality and Social Psychology, 66,* 819–827.

De Parle, J. (1995, August 20). The man inside Bill Clinton's foreign policy. *New York Times Magazine,* pp. 33–39, 46, 55, 57.

Dewey, J. (1922). *Human nature and conduct.* New York: Henry Holt.

Dewey, J. (1929). *The quest for certainty: A study of the relation of knowledge and action.* New York: Minton, Balch.

Diamond, J. (1995, January 12). Portrait of the biologist as a young man. *The New York Review of Books,* pp. 16–19.

Donald, M. (1991). *Origins of the modern mind: Three stages in the evolution of culture and cognition.* Cambridge, MA: Harvard University Press.

Dowie, J., & Elstein, A. (Eds.). (1988). *Professional judgment: A reader in clinical decision making.* New York: Cambridge University Press.

Doyle, J., & Thomas, S. A. (1995). Capturing policy in hearing-aid decisions by audiologists. *Medical Decision Making, 15,* 58–64.

Drucker, P. F. (1994, November). The age of social transformation. *The Atlantic Monthly,* pp. 53–56, 59, 62, 64, 66–68, 71–72, 74–78, 80.

Duran, S. K. (1995, November 18). Residents decry police policy. *Daily Camera,* pp. A1, A2.

Dworkin, R. (1993). *Life's Dominion: An argument about abortion, euthanasia, and individual freedom.* New York: Knopf.

Dworkin, R. (1994, January 13). Will Clinton's plan be fair? [Review of Health Security Act]. *The New York Review of Books,* pp. 20–25.

Dyson, F. (1979). *Disturbing the universe.* New York: Harper and Row.

Eddy, D. M. (1982). Probabilistic reasoning in clinical medicine: Problems and opportunities. In D. Kahneman, P. Slovic, & A. Tversky (Eds.), *Judgment under uncertainty: Heuristics and biases* (pp. 249–267). Cambridge, UK: Cambridge University Press.

Edwards, W. (1954). The theory of decision making. *Psychological Bulletin, 41,* 380–417.

Edwards, W. (1992). Discussion: Of human skills. *Organizational Behavior and Human Decision Processes, 53,* 267–277.

Einhorn, H. J. (1980). Learning from experience and suboptimal rules in decision making. In T. S. Wallsten (Ed.), *Cognitive processes in choice and decision behavior.* Hillsdale, NJ: Erlbaum.

Einhorn, H. J., & Hogarth, R. M. (1981). Behavioral decision theory: Processes of judgment and choice. *Annual Review of Psychology, 32,* 53–88.

Ekman, P., & O'Sullivan, M. (1991). Who can catch a liar? *American Psychologist, 46,* 913–920.

Elliot, J. (1941). *The debates in the several state conventions on the adoption of the federal Constitution as recommended by the general convention in Philadelphia, in 1787* (2nd ed.). Charlottesville, VA: Michie.

Elstein, A. S., Holzman, G. B., Ravitch, M. M., Metheny, W. A., Holmes, M. M., Hoppe, R. B., Rothert, M. L., & Rovner, D. R. (1986). Comparison of physicians' decisions regarding estrogen replacement therapy for menopausal women and decisions derived from a decision analytic model. *American Journal of Medicine, 80,* 246–258.

Elstein, A. S., Shulman, L. S., & Sprafka, S. A. (1978). *Medical problem solving: An analysis of clinical reasoning.* Cambridge, MA: Harvard University Press.

Epstein, S. (1994). Integration of the cognitive and the psychodynamic unconscious. *American Psychologist, 49,* 709–724.

Epstein, S., Lipson, A., Holstein, C., & Huh, E. (1992). Irrational reactions to negative outcomes: Evidence for two conceptual systems. *Journal of Personality and Social Psychology, 62,* 328–339.

Estes, S. G. (1938). Judging personality from expressive behavior. *Journal of Abnormal and Social Psychology, 33,* 216–236.

Estes, W. K. (1994). *Classification and cognition.* New York: Oxford University Press.

Etzioni, A. (1993). Individual rights and community responsibilities. *The Futurist, 27*(6), 64.

Evans, J. St. B. T. (1984). In defense of the citation bias in the judgment literature. *American Psychologist, 39,* 1500–1501.

Federal Open Market Committee (1988). *Transcript: Federal Open Market Committee Meeting, August 16, 1988.*

Feigenbaum, E. A. (1977). The art of artificial intelligence: I. Themes and case studies of knowledge engineering. In L. Erman (Ed.), *Proceedings of the International Joint Conference on Artificial Intelligence* (Vol. 2, pp. 1014–1029). Pittsburgh, PA: International Joint Conference on Artificial Intelligence.

Feinstein, A. R. (1967). *Clinical judgment.* Huntington, NY: Krieger.

Feldman, J., & Lindell, M. K. (1990). On rationality. In I. Horowitz (Ed.), *Organization and decision theory* (pp. 83–164). Boston: Kluwer.

Ferguson, E. S. (1992). *Engineering and the mind's eye.* Cambridge, MA: MIT Press.

Feynman, R. P. (1988, February). An outsider's inside view of the Challenger inquiry. *Physics Today,* pp. 26–37.

Fisch, H.-U., Hammond, K. R., & Joyce, C. R. B. (1982). On evaluating the severity of depression: An experimental study of psychiatrists. *British Journal of Psychiatry, 140,* 378–383.

Fisch, H.-U., Hammond, K. R., Joyce, C. R. B., & O'Reilly, M. (1981). An experimental study of the clinical judgment of general physicians in evaluating and prescribing for depression. *British Journal of Psychiatry, 138,* 100–109.

Fisher, R. A., Sir. (1925). *Statistical methods for research workers.* Edinburgh, Scotland: Oliver & Boyd.

Forbes, E. G. (1974). *The birth of scientific navigation: The solving in the 18th century of the problem of finding longitude at sea.* Greenwich, CT: National Maritime Museum.

Foster, K. R., Bernstein, D. E., & Huber, P. W. (1993). *Phantom risk: Scientific inference and the law.* Cambridge, MA: MIT Press.

Fraser, J. M., Smith, P. J., & Smith, J. W., Jr. (1992). A catalog of errors. *International Journal of Man-Machine Studies, 37,* 265–307.

Fraser, S. (1995). *The bell curve wars.* New York: Basic Books.

Frederick, D. M., & Libby, R. (1986). Expertise and auditors' judgments of conjunctive events. *Journal of Accounting Research, 24,* 270–290.

Freiman, J. A., Chalmers, T. C., Smith, H., Jr., & Kuebler, R. R. (1992). The importance of beta, the type II error, and sample size in the design and interpretation of the randomized controlled trial: Survey of two sets of "negative" trials. In J. C. Bailar, III & F. Mosteller (Eds.), *Medical uses of statistics.* Boston, MA: NEJM Books.

Frenkel-Brunswik, E. (1942). Motivation and behavior. *Genetic Psychology Monographs, 26,* 121–265.

Frisch, D., & Clemen, R. T. (1994). Beyond expected utility: Rethinking behavioral decision research. *Psychological Bulletin, 116,* 46–54.

Fujita, T. T. (1985). *The downburst, microburst and macroburst.* Chicago: University of Chicago, Department of Geophysical Sciences.

Funder, D. C. (1987). Errors and mistakes: Evaluating the accuracy of social judgment. *Psychological Bulletin, 101,* 75–90.

Funder, D. C. (1992). Everything you know is wrong [Review of *The person and the situation: Perspectives of social psychology*]. *Contemporary Psychology, 37,* 319–320.

Funder, D. C., & Sneed, C. D. (1993). Behavioral manifestations of personality: An ecological approach to judgmental accuracy. *Journal of Personality and Social Psychology, 64,* 479–490.

Furman v. Georgia, 408 U.S. 238 (1972).

Gaeth, G. J., & Shanteau, J. (1981). *A bibliography of research on the effects of irrelevance in psychology* (Rep. No. 81–13). Manhattan: Kansas State University, Department of Psychology.

Gaeth, G. J., & Shanteau, J. (1984). Reducing the influence of irrelevant information on experienced decisionmakers. *Organizational Behavior and Human Performance, 33,* 263–282.

Garner, W. R. (1970). Good patterns have few alternatives. *American Scientist, 58,* 34–42.

Gaskill, P. C., Fenton, N., & Porter, J. P. (1927). Judging the intelligence of boys from their photographs. *Journal of Applied Psychology, 11,* 394–403.

Geary, D. C. (1995). Reflections of evolution and culture in children's cognition: Implications for mathematical development and instruction. *American Psychologist, 50,* 24–37.

Gelb, L. H. (1993, January 3). Surprise, surprise, surprise. *New York Times,* p. E11.

Gelwick, R. (1977). *The way of discovery: An introduction to the thought of Michael Polanyi.* New York: Oxford University Press.

Gergen, K., & Davis, K. E. (1985). *The social construction of the person.* New York: Springer-Verlag.

Gibbon, E. (1960). *The decline and fall of the Roman Empire.* New York: Harcourt, Brace. (Original work published 1776)

Gibson, J. J. (1950). *The perception of the visual world.* Boston: Houghton Mifflin.

Gibson, J. J. (1979). *The ecological approach to visual perception.* Boston: Houghton Mifflin.

Gigerenzer, G. (1987). Probabilistic thinking and the fight against subjectivity. In L. Krüger, G. Gigerenzer, & M. S. Morgan (Eds.), *The probabilistic revolution: Vol. 2. Ideas in the sciences.* Cambridge, MA: MIT Press.

Gigerenzer, G. (1991a). From tools to theories: A heuristic of discovery in cognitive psychology. *Psychological Review, 98,* 254–267.

Gigerenzer, G. (1991b). How to make cognitive illusions disappear: Beyond "heuristics and biases." *European Review of Social Psychology, 2,* 83–115.

Gigerenzer, G. (1991c). On cognitive illusions and rationality. In E. Eells & T. Maruszewski (Eds.), *Probability and rationality: Studies on L. Jonathan Cohen's philosophy of science.* Amsterdam: Rodopi.

Gigerenzer, G. (1993). The superego, the ego, and the id in statistical reasoning. In G. Keren & C. Lewis (Eds.), *A handbook for data analysis in the behavioral sciences: Methodological issues.* Hillsdale, NJ: Erlbaum.

Gigerenzer, G., Hell, W., & Blank, H. (1988). Presentation and content: The use of base rates as a continuous variable. *Journal of Experimental Psychology: Human Perception and Performance, 14,* 513–525.

Gigerenzer, G., Hoffrage, U., & Kleinbölting, H. (1991). Probabilistic mental models: A Brunswikian theory of confidence. *Psychological Review, 98,* 506–528.

Gigerenzer, G., & Murray, D. J. (1987). *Cognition as intuitive statistics.* Hillsdale, NJ: Erlbaum.

Gigerenzer, G., Swijtink, Z., Porter, T., Daston, L., Beatty, J., & Krueger, L. (1989). *The empire of chance: How probability changed science and everyday life.* New York: Cambridge University Press.

Gillis, J., Bernieri, F., & Wooten, E. (1995). The effects of stimulus medium and feedback on the judgment of rapport. *Organizational Behavior and Human Decision Processes, 63,* 33–45.

Glazer, N. (1988). *The limits of social policy.* Cambridge, MA: Harvard University Press.

Gleick, J. (1987). *Chaos: Making a new science.* New York: Viking.

Gleick, J. (1992). *Genius: The life and science of Richard Feynman.* New York: Pantheon Books.

Goldberg, M. (1990). A quasi-experiment assessing the effectiveness of TV advertising directed to children. *Journal of Marketing Research, 27,* 445–454.

Graham, J. (1994, May 18). Regulation: A risky business. *The Wall Street Journal,* p. A14.

Granger, C. W. J. (1989). *Forecasting in business and economics* (2nd ed.). New York: Academic Press.

Green, D. M., & Swets, J. A. (1974). *Signal detection theory and psychophysics.* Huntington, NY: Krieger.

Greenhouse, L. (1994, February 23). Death penalty is renounced by Blackmun. *New York Times,* pp. A1, A10.

Greenhouse, S., & Mantel, N. (1950). The evaluation of diagnostic tests. *Biometrics, 6,* 399–412.

Greenspan takes the gold. (1994, February 28). *The Wall Street Journal,* p. A14.

Griliches, Z. (1985). Comment. In J. A. Hausman & D. A. Wise (Eds.), *Social Experimentation.* Chicago: University of Chicago Press.

Gross, J. (1993, January 3). Conversations/Allan G. Lindh: Is 1993 the year of the big one? Rumblings from a California prophet. *New York Times,* p. E7.

Gruber, H. E. (1978). Darwin's "tree of nature" and other images of wide scope. In J. Wechsler (Ed.), *On aesthetics in science.* Cambridge, MA: MIT Press.

Gruber, H. E. (1981). *Darwin on man: A psychological study of scientific creativity* (2nd ed.). Chicago: University of Chicago Press.

Gubser, N. J. (1965). *The Nunamiut Eskimos: Hunters of caribou.* New Haven: Yale University Press.

Hacking, I. (1975). *The emergence of probability: A philosophical study of early ideas about probability, induction and statistical inference.* London: Cambridge University Press.

Hacking, I. (1983). *Representing and intervening: Introductory topics in the philosophy of natural science.* Cambridge, UK: Cambridge University Press.

Hacking, I. (1990). *The taming of chance.* Cambridge, UK: Cambridge University Press.

Hall, J. C. (1994). The mating of a fly. *Science, 264,* 1702–1714.

Hammond, K. R. (1955). Probabilistic functioning and the clinical method. *Psychological Review, 62*, 255–262.

Hammond, K. R. (Ed.). (1966). *The psychology of Egon Brunswik* (2nd ed.). New York: Holt, Rinehart, and Winston.

Hammond, K. R. (1968). Brunswik, Egon. In *International encyclopedia of the social sciences* (pp. 156–158). New York: Macmillan.

Hammond, K. R. (1971). Computer graphics as an aid to learning. *Science, 172*, 903–908.

Hammond, K. R. (1977). Facilitation of interpersonal learning and conflict reduction by on-line communication. In J. D. White (Ed.), *The general systems paradigm: Science of change and change of science*. Washington, DC: Society for General Systems Research.

Hammond, K. R. (1978). *Psychology's scientific revolution: Is it in danger?* (Tech. Rep. No. 211). Boulder: University of Colorado, Center for Research on Judgment and Policy.

Hammond, K. R. (1986). Generalization in operational contexts: What does it mean? Can it be done? *IEEE Transactions on Systems, Man, and Cybernetics, 16*, 428–433.

Hammond, K. R. (1987a). *Reducing disputes among experts* (Tech. Rep. No. 268). Boulder: University of Colorado, Center for Research on Judgment and Policy.

Hammond, K. R. (1987b). Toward a unified approach to the study of expert judgment. In J. L. Mumpower, L. D. Phillips, O. Renn, & V. R. R. Uppuluri (Eds.), *NATO ASI Series F: Computer and systems sciences: Vol. 35. Expert judgment and expert systems*. Berlin: Springer-Verlag.

Hammond, K. R. (1990). Functionalism and illusionism: Can integration be usefully achieved? In R. M. Hogarth (Ed.), *Insights in decision making: A tribute to Hillel J. Einhorn*. Chicago: University of Chicago Press.

Hammond, K. R. (1996). Expansion of Egon Brunswik's psychology (1955–1996). In *Wahrnehmung und gegenstandswelt: Egon Brunswik*. Vienna: Hölder-Pichler-Tempsky.

Hammond, K. R., & Adelman, L. (1976). Science, values, and human judgment. *Science, 194*, 389–396.

Hammond, K. R., Frederick, E., Robillard, N., & Victor, D. (1989). Application of cognitive theory to the student-teacher dialogue. In D. A. Evans & V. L. Patel (Eds.), *Cognitive science in medicine*. Cambridge, MA: MIT Press.

Hammond, K. R., Hamm, R. M., & Grassia, J. (1986). Generalizing over conditions by combining the multitrait-multimethod matrix and the representative design of experiments. *Psychological Bulletin, 100*, 257–269.

Hammond, K. R., Hamm, R. M., Grassia, J., & Pearson, T. (1986). Direct comparison of the efficacy of intuitive and analytical cognition in expert judgment. *IEEE Transactions on Systems, Man, and Cybernetics, 17*, 753–770.

Hammond, K. R., Harvey, L. O., Jr., & Hastie, R. (1992). Making better use of scientific knowledge: Separating truth from justice. *Psychological Science, 3*, 80–87.

Hammond, K. R., Hursch, C. J., & Todd, F. J. (1964). Analyzing the components of clinical inference. *Psychological Review, 71*, 438–456.

Hammond, K. R., Kern, F., Jr., Crow, W. J., Githens, J. H., Groesbeck, B., Gyr, J. W., & Saunders, L. H. (1959). *Teaching comprehensive medical care: A psychological study of a change in medical education*. Cambridge, MA: Harvard University Press.

Hammond, K. R., McClelland, G. H., & Mumpower, J. (1980). *Human judgment and decision making: Theories, methods, and procedures*. New York: Hemisphere/Praeger.

Hammond, K. R., Mumpower, J., Dennis, R. L., Fitch, S., & Crumpacker, W. (1983). Fundamental obstacles to the use of scientific information in public policy making. *Technological Forecasting and Social Change, 24*, 287–297.

Hammond, K. R., & Summers, D. A. (1972). Cognitive control. *Psychological Review, 79*, 58–67.

Hammond, K. R., Summers, D. A., & Deane, D. H. (1973). Negative effects of outcome feedback in multiple-cue probability learning. *Organizational Behavior and Human Performance, 9*, 30–34.

Hampshire, S. (Ed.). (1978). *Public and private morality*. Cambridge, UK: Cambridge University Press.

Handler, J. (1992). Discretion: power, quiescence, and trust. In K. Hawkins (Ed.), *The uses of discretion*. Oxford, UK: Oxford University Press.

Hanson, N. R. (1958). *Patterns of discovery*. New York: Cambridge University Press.

Harper, L. (1994, May 11). Commerce department now measures economy's impact on the environment. *The Wall Street Journal*, p. A2.

Harper's index. (1995, September). *Harper's Magazine*, p. 9.

Harrington, H. J., & Miller, N. (1992). Overcoming resistance to affirmative action in industry: A social psychological perspective. In P. Suedfeld & P. E. Tetlock (Eds.), *Psychology and social policy*. New York: Hemisphere.

Hart, P. 't. (1990). *Groupthink in government: A study of small groups and policy failure*. Amsterdam: Swets & Zeitlinger.

Hastie, R. (1990). Social judgment theory and its accomplishments [Review of *Human judgment: The SJT view*]. *Contemporary Psychology, 35*, 959–960.

Hastie, R. (Ed.). (1993a). *Inside the juror: The psychology of juror decision making*. New York: Cambridge University Press.

Hastie, R. (1993b). Introduction. In R. Hastie (Ed.), *Inside the juror: The psychology of juror decision making*. New York: Cambridge University Press.

Hastie, R., & Pennington, N. (1991). Cognitive and social processes in decision making. In L. B. Resnick, J. M. Levine, & S. D. Teasley (Eds.), *Perspectives on socially shared cognition* (pp. 308–330). Washington, DC: American Psychological Association.

Hastie, R., Penrod, S. D., & Pennington, N. (1983). *Inside the jury*. Cambridge, MA: Harvard University Press. (Translated into Spanish and published in 1986; into Chinese and published in 1987)

Hastie, R., & Rasinski, K. A. (1988). The concept of accuracy in social judgment. In D. Bar-Tal & A. W. Kruglanski (Eds.), *The social psychology of knowledge*. Cambridge, UK: Cambridge University Press.

Hastorf, A. H., & Bender, I. E. (1952). A caution respecting the measurement of empathic ability. *Journal of Abnormal and Social Psychology, 47*, 574–576.

Hausfater, G. (1975). *Dominance and reproduction in baboons (Papio cynocephalus)*. Basel: S. Karger.

Hausman, J. A., & Wise, D. A. (1985). Introduction. In J. A. Hausman & D. A. Wise (Eds.), *Social experimentation*. Chicago: University of Chicago Press.

Havel, V. (1992a, March 1). The end of the modern era. *New York Times*, sec. 14, p. 15.

Havel, V. (1992b, July 26). In his own words/Vaclav Havel: In accord with a vision of civility [From speech at World Economic Forum, Davos, Switzerland, February 4, 1992]. *New York Times*, p. E7.

Hawkins, K. (Ed.). (1992). *The uses of discretion*. Oxford, UK: Oxford University Press.

Heider, F. (1958). *The psychology of interpersonal relations*. New York: Wiley.

Heilbroner, R. (1994, March 3). Acts of an apostle [Review of *John Maynard Keynes: Vol. 2. The economist as saviour 1920–1937*]. *The New York Review of Books*, pp. 6, 8–9.

Heller, F. (Ed.). (1992). *Decision-making and leadership*. London: Cambridge University Press.

Herman, E. (1995). *The romance of American psychology: Political culture in the age of experts*. Berkeley: University of California Press.

Herrnstein, R. J., & Murray, C. (1994). *The bell curve: Intelligence and class structure in American life*. New York: Free Press.

Hitch, C. J. (1977). Unfreezing the future. *Science, 195*, 825.

Hogarth, R. M. (1987). *Judgement and choice: The psychology of decision* (2nd ed.). Chichester, UK: Wiley.

Hogarth, R. M. (Ed.). (1990). *Insights in decision making: A tribute to Hillel J. Einhorn*. Chicago: University of Chicago Press.

Holmes, O. W. (1897). The path of the law. *Harvard Law Review, 10*, 457–478.

Holmes, O. W. (1923). *The common law*. Boston: Little, Brown. (Original work published 1881)

Holmes, O. W. (1943). *The mind and faith of Justice Holmes: His speeches, essays, letters, and judicial opinions* (selected and edited with introduction and commentary by Max Lerner). Boston: Little, Brown.

Horwitz, M. J. (1992). *The transformation of American law 1870–1960: The crisis of legal orthodoxy*. New York: Oxford University Press.

Howard, P. K. (1994). *The death of common sense: How law is suffocating America*. New York: Random House.

Humphreys, P. C., Svenson, O., & Vari, A. (Eds.). (1983). *Analysing and aiding decision processes*. Amsterdam: North Holland.

Hursch, C. J., Hammond, K. R., & Hursch, J. L. (1964). Some methodological considerations in multiple-cue probability studies. *Psychological Review, 71*, 42–60.

In re Winship, 397 U.S. 358 (1970).

Ingram, G. K. (1985). Comment. In J. A. Hausman & D. A. Wise (Eds.), *Social Experimentation*. Chicago: University of Chicago Press.

Innes, J. E. (1990). *Knowledge and public policy: The search for meaningful indicators*. New Brunswick, NJ: Transaction.

Janis, I. L. (1982). *Groupthink: Psychological studies of policy decisions and fiascoes* (2nd ed.). Boston: Houghton Mifflin.

Janis, I. L. (1989). *Crucial decisions: Leadership in policymaking and crisis management*. New York: Free Press.

Janis, I. L., & Mann, L. (1977). *Decision making: A psychological analysis of conflict, choice, and commitment*. New York: Free Press.

Janis, I. L., & Mann, L. (1992). Cognitive complexity in international decision making. In P. Suedfeld & P. E. Tetlock (Eds.), *Psychology and social policy*. New York: Hemisphere.

Janofsky, M. (1995, March 5). In drug fight, police now take to the highway. *New York Times*, sec. 11, p. 12.

Jeffrey, R. (1981). *Formal logic: Its scope and limits* (2nd ed.). New York: McGraw-Hill.

Johnson, P. E., Hassebrock, F., Duran, A. S., & Moller, J. H. (1982). Multimethod study of clinical judgment. *Organizational Behavior and Human Performance, 30*, 201–230.

Jones, E. E. (1990). *Interpersonal perception*. New York: Freeman.

Joyce, C. R. B., & Stewart, T. R. (1994). Applied research in judgment: What should happen. *Acta Psychologica, 87*, 217–227.

Judd, C. M., & McClelland, G. H. (1989). *Data analysis: A model comparison approach*. New York: Harcourt Brace Jovanovich.

Judd, C. M., & McClelland, G. H. (1995). Data analysis: Continuing issues in the everyday analysis of psychological data. *Annual Review of Psychology, 46*, 433–465.

Kagehiro, D. K. (1990). Defining the standard of proof in jury instructions. *Psychological Science, 1*, 194–200.

Kahneman, D., Slovic, P., & Tversky, A. (Eds.). (1982). *Judgment under uncertainty: Heuristics and biases*. Cambridge, UK: Cambridge University Press.

Kahneman, D., & Tversky, A. (1972). Subjective probability: A judgment of representativeness. *Cognitive Psychology, 3*, 430–454.

Kahneman, D., & Tversky, A. (1973). On the psychology of prediction. *Psychological Review, 80*, 237–251.

Kahneman, D., & Tversky, A. (1982). On the study of statistical intuitions. In D. Kahneman, P. Slovic, & A. Tversky (Eds.), *Judgment under uncertainty: Heuristics and biases.* Cambridge, UK: Cambridge University Press.

Kahneman, D., & Tversky, A. (1984). Choices, values, and frames. *American Psychologist, 39*, 341–350.

Kaplan, M. F., & Schwartz, S. (Eds.). (1975). *Human judgment and decision processes.* New York: Academic Press.

Kazman, S. (1993, November 5). Risk regulation run amok. *The Wall Street Journal*, p. A7.

Keeney, R. L. (1992). *Value-focused thinking: A path to creative decisionmaking.* Cambridge, MA: Harvard University Press.

Kelly, E. L., & Fiske, D. W. (1951). *The prediction of performance in clinical psychology.* Ann Arbor: University of Michigan Press.

Kendler, H. H. (1993). Psychology and the ethics of social policy. *American Psychologist, 48*, 1046–1053.

Kennan, G. F. (1967). *Memoirs: 1925–1950.* Boston: Little, Brown.

Kennan, G. F. (1993). *Around the cragged hill: A personal and political philosophy.* New York: Norton.

Kevles, D. J. (1993, August 2). Cold facts [Review of *Bad science: The short life and weird times of cold fusion*]. *The New Yorker*, pp. 79–82.

Kirkham, R. L. (1992). *Theories of truth: A critical introduction.* Cambridge, MA: MIT Press.

Kirkpatrick, L. A., & Epstein, S. (1992). Cognitive-experiential self-theory and subjective probability: Further evidence for two conceptual systems. *Journal of Personality and Social Psychology, 63*, 534–544.

Kistiakowsky, G. B. (1976). *A scientist at the White House: The private diary of President Eisenhower's Special Assistant for Science and Technology* (with an introduction by Charles S. Maier). Cambridge, MA: Harvard University Press.

Kittler, J. (Ed.). (1988). *Pattern recognition: Proceedings of the 4th international conference, Cambridge, U.K., March 28–30, 1988.* Berlin: Springer-Verlag.

Klatzky, R. L., Geiwitz, J., & Fischer, S. C. (1994). Using statistics in clinical practice: A gap between training and application. In M. S. Bogner (Ed.), *Human error in medicine.* Hillsdale, NJ: Erlbaum.

Klayman, J. (1993). Debias the environment instead of the judge: An alternative approach to reducing error in diagnostic (and other) judgement. *Cognition, 49*, 97–122.

Klein, G., Orasanu, J., Calderwood, R., & Zsambok, C. E. (Eds.). (1993). *Decision making in action: Models and methods.* Norwood, NJ: Ablex.

Kleinmuntz, D. N., & Schkade, D. A. (1993). Information displays and decision processes. *Psychological Science, 4*, 221–228.

Kolata, G. (1993, December 27). Mammogram debate moving from test's merits to its cost. *New York Times*, pp. A1, A9.

Kosslyn, S. M. (1995). Viewpoint: The future. *Science, 267*, 1615.

Kuhn, T. (1962). *The structure of scientific revolutions.* Chicago: University of Chicago Press.

Kurland, J. A., & Beckerman, S. J. (1985). Optimal foraging and hominid evolution: Labour and reciprocity. *American Anthropologist, 87*(1), 73–93.

Lacayo, R. (1995, April 10). Anecdotes not antidotes. *Time*, pp. 40–41.

Laird, N. M., Weinstein, M. C., & Stason, W. B. (1979). Sample-size estimation: A sensitivity analysis in the context of a clinical trial for treatment of mild hypertension. *American Journal of Epidemiology, 109,* 408–419.

Larkin, J., McDermott, J., Simon, D. P., & Simon, H. A. (1980). Expert and novice performance in solving physics problems. *Science, 208,* 1335–1342.

Larrick, R. P., Nisbett, R. E., & Morgan, J. N. (1993). Who uses the cost-benefits rules of choice? Implications for the normative status of microeconomic theory. *Organizational Behavior and Human Decision Processes, 56,* 331–347.

Laudan, L. (1981). A problem-solving approach to scientific progress. In I. Hacking (Ed.), *Scientific revolutions.* Oxford: Oxford University Press.

Lawler, A., & Stone, R. (1995). FDA: Congress mixes harsh medicine. *Science, 269,* 1038–1041.

Ledley, R. S., & Lusted, L. B. (1959). Reasoning foundations of medical diagnosis. *Science, 130,* 9–21.

Lee, J.-W., & Yates, J. F. (1992). How quantity judgment changes as the number of cues increases: An analytical framework and review. *Psychological Bulletin, 112,* 363–377.

Lehman, D. R., & Nisbett, R. E. (1990). A longitudinal study of the effects of undergraduate training on reasoning. *Developmental Psychology, 26,* 952–960.

Lemann, N. (1995a). The great sorting. *The Atlantic Monthly, 276*(3), 84–88, 90–92, 96–98, 100.

Lemann, N. (1995b). The structure of success in America. *The Atlantic Monthly, 276*(2), 41–43, 46, 48, 50–53, 56, 58–60.

Lerner, B. H. (1991). Scientific evidence versus therapeutic demand: The introduction of the sulfonamides revisited. *Annals of Internal Medicine, 115,* 315–320.

Lewis, A. (1991). *Make no law: The Sullivan case and the First Amendment.* New York: Random House.

Lichtenstein, S., Slovic, P., Fischhoff, B., Layman, M., & Combs, B. (1978). Judged frequency of lethal events. *Journal of Experimental Psychology: Human Learning and Memory, 4,* 551–578.

Lind, M. (1995, June). To have and have not: Notes on the progress of the American class war. *Harper's Magazine,* pp. 35–39, 42–47.

Lindblom, C. E. (1968). *The policy-making process.* Englewood Cliffs, NJ: Prentice-Hall.

Lindblom, C. E., & Cohen, D. K. (1979). *Usable knowledge: Social science and social problem solving.* New Haven: Yale University Press.

Lipin, S. (1995, January 4). 'Portfolio management' catches on for bank loans. *The Wall Street Journal,* p. C1.

Lochner v. New York, 198 U.S. 45 (1905).

Loewenstein, G., & Furstenberg, F. (1991). Is teenage sexual behavior rational? *Journal of Applied Social Psychology, 21,* 957–986.

Longley, J., & Pruitt, D. G. (1980). Groupthink: A critique of Janis' theory. *Review of Personality and Social Psychology, 1,* 74–93.

Lopes, L. L. (1991). The rhetoric of irrationality. *Theory & Psychology, 1*(1), 65–82.

Lopes, L. L. (1992). Risk perception and the perceived public. In D. W. Bromley & K. Segerson (Eds.), *The social response to environmental risk: Policy formulation in an age of uncertainty.* Boston: Kluwer.

Lopes, L. L., & Oden, G. C. (1991). The rationality of intelligence. In E. Eells & T. Maruszewski (Eds.), *Probability and rationality: Studies on L. Jonathan Cohen's philosophy of science.* Amsterdam: Rodopi.

Lovegrove, A. (1989). *Judicial decision making, sentencing policy, and numerical guidance.* New York: Springer-Verlag.

Lusk, C. M. (1993). Assessing components of judgments in an operational setting: The effects of time pressure on aviation weather forecasting. In O. Svenson & A. J. Maule (Eds.), *Time pressure and stress in human judgment and decision making*. New York: Plenum.

Lusk, C. M., & Hammond, K. R. (1991). Judgment in a dynamic task: Microburst forecasting. *Journal of Behavioral Decision Making, 4*, 55–73.

Lusk, C. M., Stewart, T. R., Hammond, K. R., & Potts, R. J. (1990). Judgment and decision making in dynamic tasks: The case of forecasting the microburst. *Weather and Forecasting, 5*, 627–639.

Lusted, L. B. (1968). *Introduction to medical decision making*. Springfield, IL: Charles C. Thomas.

Lusted, L. B. (1991). The clearing "haze": A view from my window. *Medical Decision Making, 11*, 76–87.

Lyon, D., & Slovic, P. (1976). Dominance of accuracy information and neglect of base rates in probability estimation. *Acta Psychologica, 40*, 287–298.

Mailer, N. (1995, May). The amateur hit man. *The New York Review of Books*, pp. 52–59.

March, J. (1978). Bounded rationality, ambiguity, and the engineering of choice. *Bell Journal of Economics, 9*, 587–608.

Margolis, H. (1987). *Patterns, thinking, and cognition: A theory of judgment*. Chicago: University of Chicago Press.

Marshall, E. (1986). Feynman issues his own shuttle report, attacking NASA's risk estimates. *Science, 232*, 1596.

Mason, I. B. (1982). A model for assessment of weather forecasts. *Australian Meteorological Magazine, 30*, 291–303.

Massaro, D. W. (1994). A pattern recognition account of decision making. *Memory and Cognition, 22*, 616–627.

Matheson, N. (1995). Things to come: Postmodern digital knowledge management and information. *Journal of the American Medical Informatics Association, 2*, 73–78.

Mazlish, B. (1993). *The fourth discontinuity: The co-evolution of humans and machines*. New Haven: Yale University Press.

McCauley, C. (1991). Selection of National Science Foundation graduate fellows: A case study of psychologists failing to apply what they know about decision making. *American Psychologist, 46*, 1287–1291.

McClurg, A. J. (1988). Logical fallacies and the Supreme Court: A critical examination of Justice Rehnquist's decisions in criminal procedure cases. *University of Colorado Law Review, 59*, 741–844.

McCulloch, J. A. (1994, January 19). The mammography controversy [Letters to the editor]. *The Wall Street Journal*, p. A15.

McCullough, D. G. (1992). *Truman*. New York: Simon & Schuster.

McEachern, W. A. (1991). *Economics: A contemporary introduction* (2nd ed.). Cincinnati: South-Western.

McFadden, D. L. (1985). Comment. In J. A. Hausman & D. A. Wise (Eds.), *Social experimentation*. Chicago: University of Chicago Press.

McGinley, L. (1994, December 12). GOP takes aim at FDA, seeking to ease way for approval of new drugs, medical products. *The Wall Street Journal*, p. A16.

McGuire, W. J. (1983). A contextualist theory of knowledge: Its implications for innovation and reform in psychological research. In L. Berkowitz (Ed.), *Advances in experimental social psychology*. New York: Academic Press.

McNamara, R. (1995). *In retrospect: The tragedy and lessons of Vietnam*. New York: Times Books.

McNeil, B. J., Pauker, S. G., Sox, H. C., & Tversky, A. (1982). On the elicitation of preferences for alternative therapies. *New England Journal of Medicine, 306,* 1259–1262.

McNemar, Q. (1949). *Psychological statistics.* New York: Wiley.

Meehl, P. E. (1954). *Clinical vs. statistical prediction: A theoretical analysis and a review of the evidence.* Minneapolis: University of Minnesota Press.

Meehl, P. E. (1970). Nuisance variables and the ex post facto design. In M. Radner & S. Winokur (Eds.), *Minnesota studies in the philosophy of science: Vol. 4. Analyses of theories and methods of physics and psychology.* Minneapolis: University of Minnesota Free Press.

Meehl, P. E. (1978). Theoretic risks and tabular asterisks: Sir Karl, Sir Ronald, and the slow progress of soft psychology. *Journal of Consulting and Clinical Psychology, 46,* 806–834.

Meehl, P. E. (1986). Causes and effects of my disturbing little book. *Journal of Personality Assessment, 50,* 370–375.

Meier, B. (1995, February 27). 'Sexual predators' finding sentence may last past jail. *New York Times,* pp. A1, A8.

Meltzer, H. L. (1992, March 17). With apologies to Havel, let reason rule [Letter to the editor]. *New York Times,* p. A14.

Mesarovic, M. D., & Pestel, E. (1974). *Mankind at the turning point: The second report to the Club of Rome.* New York: Dutton.

Millikan, R. G. (1984). *Language, thought, and other biological categories: New foundations for realism.* Cambridge, MA: MIT Press.

Mithen, S. J. (1990). *Thoughtful foragers: A study of prehistoric decision making.* Cambridge, UK: Cambridge University Press.

Monahan, J., & Steadman, H. (Eds.). (1994). *Violence and mental disorder: Developments in risk assessment.* Chicago: University of Chicago Press.

Moorhead, G., Ference, R., & Neck, C. P. (1991). Group decision fiascoes continue: Space shuttle Challenger and a revised groupthink framework. *Human Relations, 44,* 539–550.

Moray, N. (1994). Error reduction as a systems problem. In M. S. Bogner (Ed.), *Human error in medicine.* Hillsdale, NJ: Erlbaum.

Moser, M. (1994). Can the cost of care be contained and quality of care maintained in the management of hypertension? *Archives of Internal Medicine, 134,* 1665–1672.

Mosteller, F., & Weinstein, M. C. (1985). Toward evaluating the cost-effectiveness of medical and social experiments. In J. A. Hausman & D. A. Wise (Eds.), *Social experimentation.* Chicago: University of Chicago Press.

Moynihan, D. P. (1993). *Pandaemonium: Ethnicity in international politics.* Oxford, UK: Oxford University Press.

Mumpower, J., Livingston, S., & Lee, T. J. (1987). Expert judgments on political riskiness. *Journal of Forecasting, 6,* 51–65.

Mydans, S. (1993, April 9). Prosecutor in officers' case ends with focus on beating. *New York Times,* p. A8.

Myers, H. F. (1993, June 14). The outlook: Economy may benefit from Clinton's woes. *The Wall Street Journal,* p. A1.

Nagel, I. H., Breyer, S., & MacCarthy, T. (1989). Panel V: Equality versus discretion in sentencing (Introduction by the Honorable Frank H. Easterbrook). *The American Criminal Law Review, 26,* 1813–1838.

Nelson, R. G., & Bessler, D. A. (1992). Quasi-rational expectations: Experimental evidence. *Journal of Forecasting, 11,* 141–156.

Nerlove, M., Grether, D. M., & Carvalho, J. L. (1979). *Analysis of economic time series: A synthesis.* New York: Academic Press.

Newbold, P., & Bos, T. (1990). *Introductory business forecasting*. Cincinnati: South-Western.

Newcomer, L. N. (1994, January 19). The mammography controversy [Letters to the editor]. *The Wall Street Journal*, p. A15.

Newell, A., & Simon, H. A. (1972). *Human problem solving*. Englewood Cliffs, NJ: Prentice-Hall.

Neyman, J., & Pearson, E. S. (1933). On the problem of the most efficient tests of statistical hypotheses. *Philosophical Transactions of the Royal Society of London. Series A, 231*, 289–337.

Ningkun, W. (1993). *A family's persecution, love, and endurance in communist China*. New York: Atlantic Monthly Press.

Nisbett, R. E. (Ed.). (1993). *Rules for reasoning*. Hillsdale, NJ: Erlbaum.

Nisbett, R. E., Fong, G. T., Lehman, D. R., & Cheng, P. W. (1987). Teaching reasoning. *Science, 238*, 625–631.

Nisbett, R. E., & Ross, L. (1980). *Human inference: Strategies and shortcomings of social judgment*. Englewood Cliffs, NJ: Prentice-Hall.

Noah, T. (1995, March 30). Best-selling author urges both political parties to find common ground on regulatory reform. *The Wall Street Journal*, p. A18.

Olson, W. (1995, March 30). The bard of bureaucracy. *The Wall Street Journal*, p. A14.

On behalf of science: Violence research produces controversy. (1992). *Psychological Science Agenda American Psychological Association, 5*(6), pp. 1, 9.

ORAU Panel on Health Effects of Low-Frequency Electric and Magnetic Fields. (1993). EMF and cancer [Letter to the editor]. *Science, 260*, 13–14.

Oreskes, N., Shrader-Frechette, K., & Belitz, K. (1994). Verification, validation, and confirmation of numerical models in the earth sciences. *Science, 263*, 641–646.

Orr, L. L. (1985). Comment: Choosing between macroexperiments and microexperiments. In J. A. Hausman & D. A. Wise (Eds.), *Social experimentation*. Chicago: University of Chicago Press.

*The Oxford dictionary of quotations* (3rd ed.). (1979). Oxford: Oxford University Press.

Park, R. A., & Lee, J. K. (1993). *Potential impacts of sea level rise on south Florida natural areas* (Tech. Rep.). Bloomington: Indiana University, School of Public & Environmental Affairs.

Parsons, T. (1985). Underlying events in the logical analysis of English. In E. LePore & B. P. McLaughlin (Eds.), *Actions and events: Perspectives on the philosophy of Donald Davidson* (pp. 235–267). Oxford, UK: Basil Blackwell.

Pascal, B. (1966). *Pensées* (translated with an introduction by A. J. Krailsheimer). Harmondsworth, UK: Penguin Books.

Paulos, J. A. (1988). *Innumeracy: Mathematical illiteracy and its consequences*. New York: Hill and Wang.

Payne, J. W., Bettman, J. R., & Johnson, E. J. (1992). Behavioral decision research: A constructive processing perspective. *Annual Review of Psychology, 43*, 87–131.

Payne, J. W., Bettman, J. R., & Johnson, E. J. (1993). *The adaptive decision maker*. New York: Cambridge University Press.

Pennington, N., & Hastie, R. (1991). A cognitive theory of juror decision making: The story model. *Cardozo Law Review, 13*, 519–557.

Pennington, N., & Hastie, R. (1993a). The story model for juror decision making. In R. Hastie (Ed.), *Inside the juror: The psychology of juror decision making*. Cambridge, UK: Cambridge University Press.

Pennington, N., & Hastie, R. (1993b). A theory of explanation-based decision making. In G. Klein, J. Orasanu, R. Calderwood, & C. E. Zsambok (Eds.), *Decision making in action: Models and methods*. Norwood, NJ: Ablex.

Pepper, S. C. (1942). *World hypothesis: A study in evidence.* Berkeley: University of California Press.

Pernick, J. (1994, January 16). The mammogram controversy: It confuses women, raises unfounded fears [Editorial]. *New York Times,* p. 16.

Perry, J. M. (1993, March 23). Clinton relies heavily on White House pollster to take words right out of the public's mouth. *The Wall Street Journal,* p. A14.

Petroski, H. (1994). *Design paradigms: Case histories of error and judgment in engineering.* Cambridge, UK: Cambridge University Press.

Phelps, R. H., & Shanteau, J. (1978). Livestock judges: How much information can an expert use? *Organizational Behavior and Human Performance, 21,* 209–219.

Pinker, S. (1994, September 25). Is there a gene for compassion? [Review of the book *The moral animal: The new science of evolutionary psychology*]. *New York Times Book Review,* pp. 3, 34–35.

Pintner, R. (1918). Intelligence as estimated from photographs. *Psychological Review, 25,* 286–296.

Pitz, G. F., & Sachs, N. J. (1984). Judgment and decision: Theory and application. *Annual Review of Psychology, 35,* 139–163.

Platt, J. R. (1964). Strong inference. *Science, 164,* 347–353.

Plous, S. (1993). *The psychology of judgment and decision making.* Philadelphia: Temple University Press.

Polanyi, M. (1958). *Personal knowledge: Towards a post-critical philosophy.* Chicago: University of Chicago Press.

Polanyi, M. (1966). *The tacit dimension.* Garden City, NY: Doubleday.

Polanyi, M. (1969). *Knowing and being: Essays by Michael Polanyi.* Chicago: University of Chicago Press.

Popper, K. (1963). *Conjectures and refutations: The growth of scientific knowledge.* New York: Harper & Row.

Popper, K. R., Sir (1972). *Objective knowledge: An evolutionary approach.* Oxford, UK: Clarendon Press.

Poses, R. M., Cebul, R. D., & Wigton, R. S. (1995). You can lead a horse to water—Improving physicians' knowledge of probabilities may not affect their decisions. *Medical Decision Making, 15,* 65–75.

Poses, R. M., Cebul, R. D., Wigton, R. S., & Collins, M. (1986). Feedback on simulated cases to improve clinical judgment [meeting abstract]. *Medical Decision Making, 6,* 274.

Postman, N. (1992). *Technopoly: The surrender of culture to technology.* New York: Alfred A. Knopf.

Pound, R. (1908). Mechanical jurisprudence. *Columbia Law Review, 8,* 605–623.

Pound, R. (1921). *The spirit of the common law.* Boston: Marshall Jones.

Pound, R. (1923). The theory of judicial decision: A theory of judicial decision for today. *Harvard Law Review, 36,* 940–959.

Presidential Commission on the Space Shuttle Challenger Accident (1986). *Report of the Presidential Commission on the Space Shuttle Challenger Accident.* Washington, DC: Author.

Prior, A. N. (1967). Correspondence theory of truth. In P. Edwards (Ed.), *Encyclopedia of Philosophy* (Vol. 2). New York: Macmillan and Free Press.

Purdum, T. S. (1994, August 7). The newest Moynihan. *New York Times Magazine,* pp. 25–29, 37, 48, 52.

Quindlen, A. (1992, March 11). Marking time. *New York Times,* p. A21.

Rabinovitch, N. L. (1973). *Probability and statistical inference in ancient and medieval Jewish literature.* Toronto: University of Toronto Press.

Raghavan, A. (1993, August 16). Bear market isn't in sight, some think, noting tempered optimism of investors. *The Wall Street Journal*, p. C1.

Ranvaud, R., Schmidt-Koenig, K., Ganzhorn, J. U., Kiepenheuer, J., Gasparotto, O. C., & Britto, L. R. G. (1991). The initial orientation of homing pigeons at the magnetic equator: Compass mechanisms and the effect of applied magnets. *Journal of Experimental Biology, 161*, 299–314.

Rasmussen, J. (1983). Skills, rules, and knowledge: Signals, signs, and symbols, and other distinctions in human performance models. *IEEE Transactions on Systems Man and Cybernetics, SMC-13*(3), 257–266.

Reason, J. (1990). *Human error*. Cambridge, UK: Cambridge University Press.

Reich, R. B. (1992). *The work of nations: Preparing ourselves for 21st-century capitalism*. New York: Vintage Books.

Reichenbach, H. (1938). *Experience and prediction: An analysis of the foundations and the structure of knowledge*. Chicago: University of Chicago Press.

Reid, T. (1785). *Essays on the intellectual powers of man*. Edinburgh, Scotland: John Bell.

Rescher, N. (1982). *The coherence theory of truth*. Washington, DC: University Press of America.

Roberts, L. (1991). Learning from an acid rain program. *Science, 251*, 1302–1305.

Roberts, R. D., & Wilson, J. W. (1989). A proposed microburst nowcasting procedure using single-Doppler radar. *Journal of Applied Meteorology, 28*, 285–303.

Rosato, F., Thomas, J., & Rosato, E. (1973). Operative management of nonpalpable lesions detected by Mammography. *Surgery, Gynecology, and Obstetrics, 137*, 491–493.

Rosen, S. (1985). Comment. In J. A. Hausman & D. A. Wise (Eds.), *Social Experimentation*. Chicago: University of Chicago Press.

Rosenbaum, D. E. (1995, December 1). A budget debate not about dollars, but about whose plan makes sense. *New York Times*, p. A10.

Ross, L., & Nisbett, R. E. (1991). *The person and the situation: Perspectives of social psychology*. New York: McGraw-Hill.

Rouse, W. B. (1983). Models of human problem solving: Detection, diagnosis, and compensation for system failures. *Automatica, 19*, 613–625.

Russell, B. (1945). *A history of western philosophy and its connection with political and social circumstances from the earliest times to the present day*. New York: Simon & Schuster.

Russell, T., & Thaler, R. H. (1991). The relevance of quasi rationality in competitive markets. In R. H. Thaler (Ed.), *Quasi rational economics*. New York: Russell Sage.

Ryan, F. (1993). *The forgotten plague: How the battle against tuberculosis was won—and lost*. Boston: Little, Brown.

Sackett, D. L. (1989). Inference and decision at the bedside. *Journal of Clinical Epidemiology, 42*(4), 309–316.

Sage, A. (1992). *Systems engineering*. New York: Wiley.

Sale, K. (1995). *Rebels against the future*. New York: Addison-Wesley.

Sarbin, T. R. (1942). A contribution to the study of actuarial and individual methods of prediction. *American Journal of Sociology, 48*, 593–602.

Sarbin, T. R. (1944). The logic of prediction in psychology. *Psychological Review, 51*, 210–228.

Sarbin, T. R. (1986). Prediction and clinical inference: Forty years later. *Journal of Personality Assessment, 50*, 362–369.

Savage, L. J. (1954). *The foundations of statistics*. New York: Wiley.

Schick, K. D., & Toth, N. (1993). *Making silent stones speak: Human evolution and the dawn of technology*. New York: Simon & Schuster.

Schivelbusch, W. (1986). *The railway journey: The industrialization of time and space in the 19th century.* Berkeley, CA: University of California Press.

Schlesinger, A. M., Jr. (1965). *A thousand days: John F. Kennedy in the White House.* Boston: Houghton Mifflin.

Schlesinger, A. M., Jr. (1986). *The cycles of American history.* Boston: Houghlin Mifflin.

Schlesinger, A., Jr. (1993, April 11). A Clinton report card, so far. *New York Times*, p. E13.

Schneider, D. J., Hastorf, A. H., & Ellsworth, P. C. (1979). *Person perception* (2nd ed.). Reading, MA: Addison-Wesley.

Schneider, S. H. (1994). Detecting climatic change signals: Are there any "fingerprints"? *Science, 263*, 341–347.

Schwartz, E. I. (1993, March 6). Health care: The video game. *New York Times*, sec. 3, p. 7.

Scoville, H., Jr. (1977). An inside view [Review of *A scientist at the White House*]. *Science, 195*, 168–169.

Seachrist, L. (1994). Sea turtles master migration with magnetic memories. *Science, 264*, 661–662.

Searle, J. (1995). *The construction of social reality.* New York: Free Press.

Sease, D. R. (1992, June 1). What could go wrong? Here are some market "nightmares." *The Wall Street Journal*, pp. C1–2.

Sedlmeier, P., & Gigerenzer, G. (1994). *Intuitions about sample size: Law of large numbers or law of averages?* Manuscript submitted for publication.

Shackle the Sick? [Editorial]. (1993, January 18). *New York Times*, p. A14.

Shanteau, J., & Phelps, R. (1977). Judgment and swine: Approaches and issues in applied judgment analysis. In M. Kaplan & S. Schwartz (Eds.), *Human judgment and decision processes in applied settings.* New York: Academic Press.

Shapiro, B. J. (1986). "To a moral certainty": Theories of knowledge and Anglo-American juries 1600–1850. *Hastings Law Journal, 38*, 153–193.

Shapiro, J. (1993, February 28). 22 years as a class enemy. *New York Times*, sec. 7, p. 12.

Sibly, P. G., & Walker, A. C. (1977). Structural accidents and their causes. *Proceedings of the Institution of Civil Engineers, 62*, 191–208.

Simon, H. A. (1957). *Models of man: Social and rational; mathematical essays on rational human behavior in society setting.* New York: Wiley.

Simon, H. A. (1979). Rational decision making in business organizations. *American Economic Review, 69*, 493–513.

Simon, H. A. (1980). The behavioral and social sciences. *Science, 209*, 71–77.

Simon, H. A. (1981). *The sciences of the artificial* (2nd ed.). Cambridge, MA: MIT Press.

Simon, H. A. (1983). *Reason in human affairs.* Stanford, CA: Stanford University Press.

Simon, H. A. (1991). *Models of my life.* New York: Basic Books.

Simon, H. A. (1992). What is an "explanation" of behavior? *Psychological Science, 3*, 150–161.

Simon, H. A., & Kaplan, C. A. (1989). Foundations of cognitive science. In M. I. Posner (Ed.), *Foundations of cognitive science.* Cambridge, MA: MIT Press.

Singer, D. (1994, June 19). Surprise! Kim Il sung smiles for the camera. *New York Times*, sec. 4, p. 5.

Skidelsky, R. J. A. (1992). *John Maynard Keynes: The economist as savior (1920–1937).* New York: Penguin Press.

Slovic, P. (1976). Towards understanding and improving decisions. In I. Salkovitz (Ed.), *Science technology, and the modern Navy: Thirtieth anniversary 1946–1976.* Arlington, VA: Department of the Navy, Office of Naval Research.

Slovic, P. (1987). Perception of risk. *Science, 236*, 280–285.

Slovic, P., Fischhoff, B., & Lichtenstein, S. (1977). Behavioral decision theory. *Annual Review of Psychology, 28*, 1–39.

Slovic, P., & Lichtenstein, S. (1971). Comparison of Bayesian and regression approaches to the study of information processing in judgment. *Organizational Behavior and Human Performance, 6,* 649–744.

Slovic, P., & Lichtenstein, S. (1973). Comparison of Bayesian and regression approaches to the study of information processing in judgment. In L. Rappoport & D. A. Summers (Eds.), *Human judgment and social interaction.* New York: Holt, Rinehart, & Winston.

Slovic, P., Lichtenstein, S., & Fischhoff, B. (1988). Decision making. In R. C. Atkinson, R. J. Herrnstein, G. Lindzey, & R. D. Luce (Eds.), *Handbook of experimental psychology: Vol 2. Learning and cognition.* New York: Wiley.

Smelser, N. J. (1995). Viewpoint: The future. *Science, 267,* 1618.

Smith, J. F., & Kida, T. (1991). Heuristics and biases: Expertise and task realism in auditing. *Psychological Bulletin, 109,* 472–489.

Smith, M. B., & Mann, L. (1992). Irving L. Janis (1918–1990). *American Psychologist, 47,* 812–813.

Sniderman, P., & Tetlock, P. (1986). Symbolic racism: Problems of motive attribution in political analysis. *Journal of Social Issues, 42,* 129–150.

Snyder, R. E. (1966). Mammography: Contributions and limitations in the management of cancer of the breast. *Clinical Obstetrics and Gynecology, 9,* 207–220.

Sobel, D. (1995). *Longitude: The true story of a lone genius who solved the greatest scientific problem of his time.* New York: Walker.

Somerville, R. A., & Taffler, R. J. (1995). Banker judgment versus formal forecasting models: The case of country risk assessment. *Journal of Banking and Finance, 19,* 281–297.

Southern, R. W. (1953). *The making of the middle ages.* London: Hutchinson.

Steiner, G. (1992, March 2). Books: Bad Friday. *The New Yorker,* pp. 86–91.

Sterman, J. D. (1994). The meaning of models [Letter to the editor]. *Science, 264,* 329–330.

Sternberg, R. J. (1995). For whom the bell curve tolls: A review of *The bell curve. Psychological Science, 6,* 257–261.

Sternberg, R. J., Wagner, R. K., Williams, W. M., & Horvath, J. A. (1995). Testing Common Sense. *American Psychologist, 50,* 912–927.

Stewart, T. R., & Joyce, C. R. B. (1988). Increasing the power of clinical trials through judgment analysis. *Medical Decision Making, 8,* 33–38.

Stewart, T. R., Joyce, C. R. B., & Lindell, M. K. (1975). New analyses: Application of judgment theory to physicians' judgments of drug effects. In K. R. Hammond & C. R. B. Joyce (Eds.), *Psychoactive drugs and social judgment: Theory and research.* New York: Wiley.

Stewart, T. R., & Lusk, C. M. (1994). Seven components of judgmental forecasting skill: Implications for research and the improvement of forecasts. *Journal of Forecasting, 13,* 579–599.

Stewart, T. R., Moninger, W. R., Grassia, J., Brady, R. H., & Merrem, F. H. (1989). Analysis of expert judgment in a hail forecasting experiment. *Weather and Forecasting, 4,* 24–34.

Stewart, T. R., Moninger, W. R., Heideman, K. F., & Reagan-Cirincione, P. (1992). Effects of improved information on the components of skill in weather forecasting. *Organizational Behavior and Human Decision Processes, 53,* 107–134.

Stigler, S. M. (1986). *The history of statistics: The measurement of uncertainty before 1900.* Cambridge, MA: Belknap Press of Harvard University Press.

Stone, R. (1993). EPA analysis of radon in water is hard to swallow. *Science, 261,* 1514–1516.

Suedfeld, P., & Tetlock, P. E. (1992a). Psychological advice about political decision making: Heuristics, biases, and cognitive defects. In P. Suedfeld & P. E. Tetlock (Eds.), *Psychology and social policy.* New York: Hemisphere.

Suedfeld, P., & Tetlock, P. E. (1992b). Psychologists as policy advocates: The roots of controversy. In P. Suedfeld & P. E. Tetlock (Eds.), *Psychology and social policy*. New York: Hemisphere.

Suedfeld, P., & Tetlock, P. E. (Eds.). (1992c). *Psychology and social policy*. New York: Hemisphere.

Swets, J. A. (1992). The science of choosing the right decision threshold in high stakes diagnostics. *American Psychologist, 47*, 522–532.

Taft, R. (1955). The ability to judge people. *Psychological Bulletin, 52*, 1–23.

Tanner, W. P., Jr., & Swets, J. A. (1954). A decision-making theory of visual detection. *Psychological Review, 61*, 401–409.

Taylor, E. G. R. (1957). *The haven-finding art: A history of navigation from Odysseus to Captain Cook* (with a foreword by K. St. B. Collins). New York: Abelard-Schuman.

Taylor, F. W. (1911). *The principles of scientific management*. New York: Harper & Brothers.

Taylor, H. C., & Russell, J. T. (1939). The relationship of validity coefficients to the practical applications of tests in selection. *Journal of Applied Psychology, 23*, 565–578.

Taylor, L. D. (1985). Comment. In J. A. Hausman & D. A. Wise (Eds.), *Social Experimentation*. Chicago: University of Chicago Press.

Thaler, R. H. (Ed.). (1991). *Quasi rational economics*. New York: Russell Sage Foundation.

Thevanayagam, P. (1993, June 3). Index of leading indicators rises an anemic 0.1%. *The Wall Street Journal*, p. A2.

Thorndike, E. L. (1918). Fundamental theorems in judging men. *Journal of Applied Psychology, 2*, 67–76.

Thucydides (1972). *History of the Peloponnesian War* (R. Warner, Trans.). Harmondsworth, UK: Penguin Books.

Tolman, E. C. (1948). Cognitive maps in rats and men. *Psychological Review, 55*(4), 189–208.

Toner, R. (1995, June 18). Moynihan battles view he gave up on welfare fight. *New York Times*, sec. 1, pp. 1, 11.

Treaster, J. B. (1992, March 11). Colombian gets 6 years for giving false name. *New York Times*, p. A19.

Tucker, L. R. (1964). A suggested alternative formulation in the developments by Hursch, Hammond, and Hursch, and by Hammond, Hursch, and Todd. *Psychological Review, 71*, 528–530.

Tversky, A., & Kahneman, D. (1971). Belief in the law of small numbers. *Psychological Bulletin, 76*, 105–110.

Tversky, A., & Kahneman, D. (1973). Availability: A heuristic for judging frequency and probability. *Cognitive Psychology, 5*, 207–232.

Tversky, A., & Kahneman, D. (1974). Judgment under uncertainty: Heuristics and biases. *Science, 185*, 1124–1131.

Tversky, A., & Kahneman, D. (1981). The framing of decisions and the psychology of choice. *Science, 211*, 453–458.

Tversky, A., & Kahneman, D. (1983). Extensional versus intuitive reasoning: The conjunction fallacy in probability judgment. *Psychological Review, 90*, 293–315.

Tversky, A., & Kahneman, D. (1986). Rational choice and the framing of decisions. *Journal of Business, 59*, S251–S278.

Tversky, A., Sattath, S., & Slovic, P. (1988). Contingent weighting in judgment and choice. *Psychological Review, 93*, 371–384.

Twain, M. (1985). *Life on the Mississippi*. Toronto: Bantam Books. (Original work published 1896)

Tweney, R. D., Doherty, M. E., & Mynatt, C. R. (Eds.). (1981). *On scientific thinking*. New York: Columbia University Press.

Tyson, L. (1994, May 27). U.S. triumphant in trade policy. *The Wall Street Journal*, p. A8.

U.S. v. Fatico, 458 F. Supp. 388 (1978).

U.S. v. Koon, No. 92–686 (C.D. Cal. Aug. 4, 1993) (Sentencing Memorandum).

U.S. v. Koon, No. 93–50561, 1994 U.S. App. LEXIS 22588 (9th Cir. Cal. Aug. 19, 1994).

Underwood, B. D. (1977). The thumb on the scales of justice: Burdens of persuasion in criminal cases. *Yale Law Journal, 86*, 1299–1348.

Vernon, P. E. (1933). Some characteristics of the good judge of personality. *Journal of Social Psychology, 4*, 42–58.

Vicente, K. J. (1990). Coherence- and correspondence-driven work domains: Implications for systems design. *Behaviour & Information Technology, 9*, 493–502.

Viteles, M. S., & Smith, K. R. (1932). The prediction of vocational aptitude and success from photographs. *Journal of Experimental Psychology, 15*, 615–629.

von Schantz, T., Göransson, G., Andersson, G., Fröberg, I., Grahn, M., Helgée, A., & Witzell, H. (1989). Female choice selects for a viability-based male trait in pheasants. *Nature, 337*, 166–169.

von Winterfeldt, D., & Edwards, W. (1986). *Decision analysis and behavioral research*. Cambridge, UK: Cambridge University Press.

Waddell, C. (1989). Reasonableness versus rationality in the construction and justification of science policy decisions: The case of the Cambridge Experimentation Review Board. *Science, Technology, & Human Values, 14*(1), 7–25.

Waddell, C. (1990). The role of *pathos* in the decision-making process: A study in the rhetoric of science policy. *Quarterly Journal of Speech, 76*, 381–400.

Wallace, D. B., & Gruber, H. E. (Eds.). (1989). *Creative people at work: Twelve cognitive case studies*. New York: Oxford University Press.

Wallace, H. A. (1923). What is in the corn judge's mind? *Journal of the American Society of Agronomy, 15*, 300–304.

Wallraff, H. G. (1990). Navigation by homing pigeons. *Ethology Ecology & Evolution, 2*, 81–115.

Walter, D. (1992). *Today then: America's best minds look 100 years into the future on the occasion of the 1893 World's Columbian Exposition*. Helena, MT: American and World Geographic Publishing.

Watson, S. R., & Buede, D. M. (1987). *Decision synthesis: The principles and practice of decision analysis*. Cambridge, UK: Cambridge University Press.

Wechsler, J. (Ed.). (1978). *On aesthetics in science*. Cambridge, MA: MIT Press.

Weinstein, J. B. (1993, July). [Speech] The war on drugs: A judge goes AWOL. *Harper's Magazine*, pp. 13–14.

White, A. R. (1967). Coherence theory of truth. In P. Edwards (Ed.), *Encyclopedia of Philosophy* (Vol. 2). New York: Macmillan and Free Press.

White, G. E. (1978). *Patterns of American legal thought*. Indianapolis: Bobbs-Merrill.

White, G. E. (1993). *Justice Oliver Wendell Holmes: Law and the inner self*. New York: Oxford University Press.

White, R. K. (1992). Nuclear policies: Deterrence and reassurance. In P. Suedfeld & P. E. Tetlock (Eds.), *Psychology and social policy*. New York: Hemisphere.

Whitehead, A. N. (1929). *The aims of education and other essays*. New York: New American Library.

Wiener, P. P. (1969). *Evolution and the founders of pragmatism*. Gloucester, MA: Peter Smith. (Original work published 1949)

Wigton, R. S., Connor, J. L., & Centor, R. M. (1986). Transportability of a decision rule for the diagnosis of streptococcal pharyngitis. *Archives of Internal Medicine, 146,* 81–83.

Wigton, R. S., Hoellerich, V. L., Ornato, J. P., Leu, V., Mazzotta, L. A., & Cheng, I.-H. C. (1985). Use of clinical findings in the diagnosis of urinary tract infection in women. *Archives of Internal Medicine, 145,* 2222–2227.

Wilson, E. O. (1992). *The diversity of life.* Cambridge, MA: Harvard University Press.

Wilson, E. O. (1994). *Naturalist.* Washington, DC: Island Press.

Wilson, J. Q. (1993). *The moral sense.* New York: Free Press.

Wilson, J. Q. (1995, Winter). Welfare reform and character development. *City Journal,* pp. 56–64.

Wimsatt, W. C. (1980). Reductionist research strategies and their biases in the units of selection controversy. In T. Nickles (Ed.), *Scientific discovery: Case studies.* Dordrecht, Holland: D. Reidel.

Wolfe, J. N. (1966). Mammography: Errors in diagnosis. *Radiology, 87,* 214–219.

Woodward, R. (1994). *The agenda.* New York: Simon & Schuster.

Wright, R., Logie, R. H., & Decker, S. H. (1995). Criminal expertise and offender decision making: An experimental study of the target selection process in residential burglary. *Journal of Research in Crime and Delinquency, 32,* 39–53.

Yates, J. F. (1990). *Judgment and decision making.* Englewood Cliffs, NJ: Prentice-Hall.

Yerushalmy, J. (1947). Evaluating roentgenographic techniques. *Public Health Reports, 62,* 1431–1456.

Youden, W. J. (1950). Index for rating diagnostic tests. *Cancer, 3,* 32–35.

Yu, V. L., Fagan, L. M., Wraith, S. M., Clancey, W. J., Scott, A. C., Hannigan, J., Blum, R. L., Buchanan, B. G., & Cohen, S. N. (1979). Antimicrobial selection by a computer— A blinded evaluation by infectious disease experts. *Journal of the American Medical Association, 242,* 1279–1282.

Zabell, S. (1993). A mathematician comments on models of juror decision making. In R. Hastie (Ed.), *Inside the juror: The psychology of juror decision making.* Cambridge: Cambridge University Press.

Zuboff, S. (1988). *In the age of the smart machines: The future of work and power.* New York: Basic Books.

# Author Index

# Subject Index

Abraham, 25–26
academics vs. lay persons, 5, 10
accuracy. *See also* perception: physical, social
  correspondence theory and, 9, 95, 103–4, 106
  empirical, 46, 95, 103–4, 106–7, 216, 270, 278
  of experts, 216, 274, 278, 282–84
  of indicators (cues), 128, 170, 274
  in interpersonal perception, 138–40; *see also* rapport
  of intuition, 86, 158
  of judgments under uncertainty, 274
  origins in psychology of, 130
  oscillation and, 195
  Payne, John on, 214–16
  of prediction, 42, 45–46, 48, 55
administrators
  desperate, 241
  experimenting, 241–42
  trapped, 239–41
admissions, university, 46–48
  SAT and, 129
alternation
  between coherence and correspondence, 201, 350
  between indicators and patterns, 198–200
  between intuition and computation, 194
  oscillation vs., 201–2
analysis. *See also* common sense; law; task structure
  defined, 60
  in history of thought, 60–63
  negative views of, 89–90
  obstacles to, 154–57
  positive views of, 89–90
  rivalry between intuition and, 60–93
  as continuum, 147–50
  as dichotomy, 147–50
artificial intelligence. *See also* systems: expert
  anomaly in, 208
  common sense and, 151

criticisms of, 151, 279–80
  science, social policy, and, 279
attributes, intangible, 87, 112–14, 139, 168, 171, 173
averaging, 18–19, 119, 142, 171

Bayes' theorem, 4, 174, 193, 221, 273
Bayesian approach, 4
Blackstone's ratio, 23, 28–30
bounded rationality
  common sense and, 153
  irrationality vs., 166
  Simon, Herbert and, 153, 155–56, 165–67, 308
bridges, thirty-year cycles of failure in, 57–58
British tradition, 23–24
Bruner, Jerome
  as innovator in cognitive revolution, 149, 329
  and narrative, 83–84, 200
  on two modes of cognitive functioning, 83, 149

certainty, 157, 160, 287, 314. *See also* Holmes, Oliver Wendell; intuition
  learning under conditions of, 266, 268
  longing for, 70
  quest for, 59
*Challenger*
  launch of
    assessment of risks in, 37–39, 99
    duality of error and, 39
    Feynman, Richard, role in, 37–39, 97–99
    principles of probability of failure in, 97–99
    statisticians review of, 39–40, 99
    subjective probabilities vs. relative frequencies in, 36–39
chaos, 13–14, 225
  in diplomatic circles, 321
  in physical systems, 16
  in policy sciences, 301, 321
  in war, 287

431